Handbook of Foster Youth

Currently, there are over 400,000 youth living in foster care in the United States, with over 20,000 aging out of the child welfare system each year. Foster youth are more prone to experience short- and long-term adverse developmental outcomes including diminished academic achievement and career opportunities, poor mental and overall health, financial struggles, homelessness, early sexual intercourse, and substance abuse; many of these outcomes are risk factors for involvement in the juvenile justice system. Despite their challenges, foster youth have numerous strengths and positive assets that carry them through their journeys, helping them to overcome obstacles and build resilience. The *Handbook of Foster Youth* brings together a prominent group of multidisciplinary experts to provide nuanced insights on the complex dynamics of the foster care system, its impact on youth's lives, and the roles of institutions and policies in the foster care system. It discusses current gaps and future directions as well as recommendations to advance the field. This book provides an opportunity to reflect on the many challenges and strengths of foster youth and the child welfare system, and the combined efforts of caregivers, community volunteers, policy makers, and the professionals and researchers who work with them.

Elizabeth Trejos-Castillo is the C.R. Hutcheson Endowed Associate Professor of Human Development & Family Studies at Texas Tech University. Her research interests include individual/contextual factors, deviance and risk-taking behaviors in youth using a cross-cultural comparative mixed-method lens.

Nancy Trevino-Schafer, MS, ABD, is a Doctoral Candidate in Human Development & Family Studies at Texas Tech University. Her research interests include program evaluation, adolescent development, prevention science (specifically teen pregnancy prevention), minority studies, and social justice.

Handbook of Foster Youth

Edited by
Elizabeth Trejos-Castillo and
Nancy Trevino-Schafer

NEW YORK AND LONDON

First published 2018
by Routledge
711 Third Avenue, New York, NY 10017

and by Routledge
2 Park Square, Milton Park, Abingdon, Oxon, OX14 4RN

Routledge is an imprint of the Taylor & Francis Group, an informa business

© 2018 Taylor & Francis

The right of Elizabeth Trejos-Castillo and Nancy Trevino-Schafer to be identified as the authors of the editorial material, and of the authors for their individual chapters, has been asserted in accordance with sections 77 and 78 of the Copyright, Designs and Patents Act 1988.

All rights reserved. No part of this book may be reprinted or reproduced or utilized in any form or by any electronic, mechanical, or other means, now known or hereafter invented, including photocopying and recording, or in any information storage or retrieval system, without permission in writing from the publishers.

Trademark notice: Product or corporate names may be trademarks or registered trademarks, and are used only for identification and explanation without intent to infringe.

Library of Congress Cataloging-in-Publication Data
Names: Trejos-Castillo, Elizabeth, editor. | Trevino-Schafer, Nancy, editor.
Title: Handbook of foster youth / edited by Elizabeth Trejos-Castillo and Nancy Trevino-Schafer.
Description: New York, NY : Routledge, 2018. | Includes bibliographical references and index.
Identifiers: LCCN 2017048312| ISBN 9781138670785 (hbk : alk. paper) | ISBN 9781138670792 (pbk : alk. paper) | ISBN 9781351168243 (ebk : alk. paper)
Subjects: LCSH: Foster children—United States—Social conditions. | Youth—United States—Social conditions.
Classification: LCC HV881. H36 2018 | DDC 362.73/30973—dc23
LC record available at https://lccn.loc.gov/2017048312

ISBN: 978-1-138-67078-5 (hbk)
ISBN: 978-1-138-67079-2 (pbk)
ISBN: 978-1-351-16824-3 (ebk)

Typeset in Bembo
by Keystroke, Neville Lodge, Tettenhall, Wolverhampton

To all foster youth,
for whom we strive to become better professionals and advocates

In Memoriam of my Grandmother "Mariquita"
who raised me above troubled waters and gave me wings
— Elizabeth Trejos-Castillo

For my children, Dante and Emma, who mean the world to me
— Mom (Nancy Trevino-Schafer)

Contents

Contributors	*xi*
Preface	*xvii*
Elizabeth Trejos-Castillo and Nancy Trevino-Schafer	

SECTION I   1

PART I
Understanding the Child Welfare/Foster Care System:
History and Structure   1

1 History of Foster Care: Policy, Practice, and Reformation   3
    John R. Seita

2 Foster Care Placement Process and Settings   20
    Donna M. Aguiniga and Elissa E. Madden

PART II
Foster Youth Individual Development   39

3 Neurobiological Development in Foster Youth: Outcomes and Intervention   41
    Kristin Bernard, Allison Frost, and Sierra Kuzava

4 Trauma and Socioemotional Development in Foster Youth: Lessons Learned from LONGSCAN   57
    Alan J. Litrownik, Laura J. Proctor, and May Yeh

5 Foster Youth Voices: An Exploratory Study on their Challenges and Strengths   77
    Nancy Trevino-Schafer and Elizabeth Trejos-Castillo

PART III
Impact of Foster Care on Youth's Overall Health   99

6 Assessment of Youth in Foster Care   101
    Jeffrey N. Wherry

Contents

7   Physical Health and Foster Youth   117
    Yo Jackson and Lindsay Huffhines

8   The Sexual and Reproductive Health of Youth in Foster Care   133
    Amy Dworsky

9   Substance Use and Addiction Problems in Foster Youth   155
    Jordan M. Braciszewski

PART IV
Foster Youth Development in Context   171

10 Natural Mentoring to Support the Establishment of Permanency for Youth in Foster Care   173
    John Paul Horn and Renée Spencer

11 Youth in Foster Care Relationships with Biological, Foster, and Adoptive Families   190
    Armeda Stevenson Wojciak and Nathan A. Hough

12 Factors Affecting the Educational Trajectories and Outcomes of Youth in Foster Care   208
    Katherine C. Pears, Hyoun K. Kim, and Kimbree L. Brown

SECTION II   223

PART V
Aging Out of Foster Care into Independent Living: Challenges and Opportunities   223

13 Self-Sufficiency: Employment, Earnings, and Receipt of Public Benefits by Former Foster Youth   225
    Loring P. Jones

14 Supportive Housing Contexts and Educational Opportunities for Foster Youth Transitioning Out of Care   258
    Harriett D. Romo and Sophia M. Ortiz

15 Human Capital Accumulation: A Proposed Measure and Theoretical Framework for Foster Youth Job Placement Intervention Strategies   282
    Toni Naccarato, Emily J. Bruce, Derek J. Stafford, and Nathaniel Hawkes

16 Access and Continuity of Transitional Living Services for Foster Youth   301
    Mary Elizabeth Collins and Michelle Banks

PART VI
Areas of Special Consideration in Foster Youth   317

17 Youth with Disabilities in Foster Care   319
    Katharine Hill and Elizabeth Lightfoot

18 Racial and Ethnic Disproportionality in Foster Care   335
    Samuel L. Myers, Jr., William J. Sabol, Man Xu, and Diana Vega Vega

19 Commercial Sexual Exploitation and Sex Trafficking of Foster Children
    and Youth   362
    Nadine M. Finigan-Carr and Amelia Rubenstein

20 Undocumented Immigrant Latin@ Youth and the U.S. Child
    Welfare System   376
    Frank Anthony Rodriguez, Vivian J. Dorsett and John Jacob Rodriguez

21 Sexual and Gender Expansive Youth in Foster Care   401
    Nicholas Forge and Robin Hartinger-Saunders

PART VII
Social Policy and Institutional Support   425

22 Fostering "Belonging-ness": The Role of Private Foster Care Agencies
    with Foster Parents and Youth   427
    Marlo A. Perry and Mary E. Rauktis

23 Continuous Quality Improvement (CQI) in Child Welfare Agencies   444
    Jane Burstain, Brock Boudreau, and Jesse Booher

24 Foster Care and Juvenile Justice Systems: Crossover and Integration
    of Services   456
    Melissa Jonson-Reid, Allison Dunnigan, and Joseph Ryan

25 Permanent and Formal Connections: Mentors, Community Services, and
    Connectedness   473
    Preston A. Britner and Ciara M. Collins

Index   *488*

Contributors

Donna M. Aguiniga is Associate Professor with the University of Alaska Anchorage School of Social Work. Dr. Aguiniga's research interests include child welfare permanency outcomes, poverty and family functioning, and young adult homelessness. Her practice background is in child protective services and community mental health.

Michelle Banks is a Licensed Certified Social Worker in Massachusetts. She has worked with youth/young adults in child welfare, juvenile justice, and healthcare systems for 20 years. Michelle is currently the Massachusetts ETV State Coordinator, Adolescent Program Supervisor at the Massachusetts Department of Children and Families, and Lecturer and curriculum developer at Boston University School of Social Work.

Kristin Bernard is Assistant Professor at Stony Brook University, New York. She earned her Doctorate in Clinical Psychology at the University of Delaware in 2013. Dr. Bernard takes a translational approach to her research on childhood maltreatment by integrating methods across fields of developmental psychology, neuroscience, and prevention science.

Jesse Booher is the Division Administrator for Texas Child Protective Services' (CPS) Regional Systems Improvement Division. Using experience from the field and in systems improvement, Jesse leads a team that embeds Continuous Quality Improvement (CQI) principles into CPS's regional operations. His Division firmly believes that strong and stable regional systems protect the children whom CPS serves.

Brock Boudreau leads the Texas Child Protective Services' (CPS) Analytics and Evaluation team. He oversees the development of predictive models to prevent problems before they occur and CQI applications to make course corrections in near real time. His focus is on helping leadership find solutions, measure progress, and communicate results.

Jordan M. Braciszewski is a Licensed Clinical Psychologist and Assistant Scientist at the Center for Health Policy & Health Services Research, part of the Henry Ford Health System, Detroit. He is broadly interested in expanding access to quality behavioral healthcare services for underserved populations, often through the use of new technologies.

Preston A. Britner is Professor of Human Development and Family Studies at the University of Connecticut. A Fellow of the American Psychological Association (APA) and Editor Emeritus of *The Journal of Primary Prevention*, he has researched mentoring, college preparation, and family interventions for youth in foster care.

Contributors

Kimbree L. Brown is the Clinical Director for the Kids in Transition to School (KITS) Program at the Oregon Social Learning Center. She studies family-focused interventions to improve psychosocial outcomes for at-risk youth and increase parental engagement in schools. Her recent work focuses on coaching teachers to support effective instruction.

Emily J. Bruce is Associate Professor at San José State University, School of Social Work. She became a full-time member of the faculty in 2002 after completing her PhD. She teaches social welfare policy in the undergraduate program, and child welfare policy and research methods in the graduate program.

Jane Burstain is Director of Systems Improvement for Texas Child Protective Services (CPS). Her team leads the agency's quality improvement efforts by supporting leadership in continuously and proactively identifying systemic issues and understanding and resolving root causes before they become crises.

Ciara M. Collins, MA, received her Master's in Human Development and Family Studies (HDFS) with an emphasis in Marriage and Family Therapy at the University of Connecticut. Now a Doctoral student with an emphasis in Prevention and Early Intervention, her research focuses on all aspects of the foster care experience.

Mary Elizabeth Collins is Associate Dean for Academic Affairs and Professor at Boston University School of Social Work. Her research includes: child welfare, adolescent-focused policy, and community-based interventions for youth. She is the author of *Macro Perspectives on Youth Aging Out of Foster Care* (2015, NASW Press) and numerous research articles.

Vivian J. Dorsett is Assistant Professor at the Texas A&M University–Commerce. Her research interests include delinquency prevention, restorative justice, juvenile justice, and the public welfare system.

Allison Dunnigan is a Doctoral Candidate at Washington University, St. Louis, in the Brown School of Social Work. Ms. Dunnigan has an MSW and 10 years of practice experience with youth in foster care and in the juvenile justice system. Ms. Dunnigan's research focuses on youth with multi-system involvement.

Amy Dworsky is a Research Fellow at Chapin Hall at the University of Chicago. Her research has focused on vulnerable youth populations. Her research interests include youth aging out of foster care, pregnant and parenting foster youth, and youth experiencing homelessness. Dr. Dworsky received her PhD from the University of Wisconsin–Madison in 2002.

Nadine M. Finigan-Carr is Assistant Director of the Ruth H. Young Center for Children and Families at the University of Maryland's School of Social Work. As a prevention scientist focused on the application of behavioral and social science perspectives, her primary research initiatives involve the prevention of adolescent risk behaviors.

Nicholas Forge is Clinical Assistant Professor in the School of Social Work at the Andrew Young School of Policy Studies, Georgia State University. His research and practice focus is homelessness among sexual and gender expansive identified youth, particularly in the area of child welfare involvement, service provision, and evidence-based practices.

Contributors

Allison Frost, MA, is a Clinical Psychology graduate student at Stony Brook University, New York. She is interested in how early adversity can impact neurobiology and socioemotional functioning in children, and how these effects may confer risk for later psychopathology. Allison is the recipient of a competitive National Science Foundation (NSF) Graduate Research Fellowship.

Robin Hartinger-Saunders is Associate Professor in the School of Social Work at Georgia State University. She has more than 25 years of experience in the field of child welfare. Research interests include multilevel factors that contribute to child welfare issues and predict outcomes for children and families.

Nathaniel Hawkes is a Clinical Social Worker at Citywide Case Management in San Francisco. He currently works to support mentally ill offenders, and previously spent more than 10 years as an employment specialist for at-risk youth. He holds a Master of Social Work degree from California State University, East Bay (CSUEB).

Katharine Hill is Associate Professor at St. Catherine University–University of St. Thomas School of Social Work, Minnesota. Her areas of research include child welfare and disability policy, and the intersections between special education and child welfare services.

John Paul Horn, a Doctoral student at Boston University School of Social Work, specializes in studying higher education as a social and economic mobility mechanism for former foster youth, examining innovative approaches that bolster social capital development. He is a former foster youth of the California child welfare system.

Nathan A. Hough is a PhD student in the Couple and Family Therapy program at the University of Iowa. Nathan's research has focused on the effects of sibling relationship on development as well as sibling attachment during childhood. Nathan was also a foster parent for several years and is now an adoptive parent.

Lindsay Huffhines is a Doctoral Candidate in the Clinical Child Psychology Program at the University of Kansas. She is a Doris Duke Fellow, and has received funding from the National Institute of Child Health and Human Development for her work on adversity, systemic inflammation, and physical health in foster youth.

Yo Jackson is Professor in the Clinical Child Psychology Program at the University of Kansas. She is the Principal Investigator in several research programs funded by grants from the National Institutes of Health on the mechanisms for resilience in youth exposed to trauma and child maltreatment.

Loring P. Jones is Professor of Social Work at San Diego State University where he has taught since 1989. His research and teaching areas are in child and family policy. His most recent research has focused on alternative policies for improving outcomes for "aging out" foster youth.

Melissa Jonson-Reid is Ralph and Muriel Pumphrey Professor in Social Work and Director, Center for Violence and Injury Prevention at Washington University, St. Louis. Her work focuses on improving outcomes for low-income and maltreated populations, with a focus on cross-sector children's services trajectories and children's services policy. She directed two Foster Youth Services programs in California prior to academia.

Contributors

Hyoun K. Kim is a Senior Scientist at Oregon Social Learning Center and Associate Professor in the Department of Child and Family Studies at Yonsei University, South Korea. Her research interests center on identifying developmental pathways leading to psychosocial adjustment among youth with at-risk backgrounds, including those in foster care.

Sierra Kuzava, MA, is a Clinical Psychology graduate student at Stony Brook University, New York. She is interested in the mechanisms through which early life stress may impact children's development, as well as the psychobiology of responsive parenting. Sierra is the recipient of a competitive NSF Graduate Research Fellowship.

Elizabeth Lightfoot is Professor and Director of the Doctoral Program at the University of Minnesota's School of Social Work. She has published extensively on the intersection of social work and disability.

Alan J. Litrownik is Professor Emeritus of Psychology at San Diego State University, former Chair, and co-founder of the SDSU's Joint Doctoral Program in Clinical Psychology with the University of California, San Diego. His primary research interests as Principal Investigator of the San Diego LONGSCAN site focus on at-risk children and factors that determine adaptive and maladaptive outcomes.

Elissa E. Madden is Assistant Professor with the Garland School of Social Work at Baylor University, Waco, Texas. Her research interest is in child welfare, with a focus on adoption and ways to promote permanency for children in care. Dr. Madden is a Licensed Social Worker and a former CPS worker.

Samuel L. Myers, Jr., is Roy Wilkins Professor of Human Relations and Social Justice, Humphrey School of Public Affairs, University of Minnesota. He is an expert on public procurement and contracting, discrimination in credit markets, racial and ethnic disproportionality in child welfare systems, and faculty under-representation in science, technology, engineering, and mathematics (STEM) fields.

Toni Naccarato is Associate Professor at California State University, East Bay (CSUEB). Her research focuses on human capital accumulation of at-risk adolescents in the areas of employment, education, positive youth development, and health and mental health with a special focus on youth transitioning out of foster care.

Sophia M. Ortiz obtained her BS and MS in Sociology from the University of Texas at San Antonio (UTSA). She is Assistant Director of the UTSA Child and Adolescent Policy Research Institute. She has coordinated grants from the U.S. Department of Housing and Urban Development, the U.S. Office of Education, and local agencies.

Katherine C. Pears is a Senior Scientist and Director of the Kids in Transition to School (KITS) Program at the Oregon Social Learning Center. She studies school readiness and achievement in high-risk youth, including youth in foster care, youth with developmental disabilities, and youth from impoverished environments.

Marlo A. Perry is Assistant Research Professor with the Child Welfare Education and Research Programs in the University of Pittsburgh's School of Social Work. Her work focuses on curriculum evaluation for child welfare workers and supervisors, transfer of learning, and family engagement with child- and family-serving systems.

Contributors

Laura J. Proctor is Research Assistant Professor of Psychology at San Diego State University and Research Scientist at the Child and Adolescent Services Research Center. She received a PhD in Clinical Psychology from the University of Southern California, and studies adversity and adjustment among current and former foster youth.

Mary E. Rauktis is Assistant Research Professor with the Child Welfare Education and Research Programs in the University of Pittsburgh's School of Social Work. Her work focuses on evaluating alternative strategies to out-of-home care, as well as the quality of residential group home care for children involved in the child welfare system.

Frank Anthony Rodriguez is Assistant Professor at North Carolina Central University in Durham, NC. His research interests include U.S. immigration policy, law enforcement, juvenile justice, multiculturalism in criminal justice, and race, ethnicity, and justice.

John Jacob Rodriguez, PhD, is an Associate Professor with the Department of Criminology and Criminal Justice at the University of Texas at Arlington. He received his PhD in juvenile justice from Prairie View A & M University in 2007. John's research interests include gangs, transnationalism, immigration, police issues and Latinos in the criminal justice system.

Harriett D. Romo is Professor of Sociology at the University of Texas at San Antonio (UTSA) and Director of the UTSA Mexico Center and the UTSA Child and Adolescent Policy Research Institute. She holds a PhD in Sociology from the University of California, San Diego.

Amelia Rubenstein, MSW, Licensed Certified Social Worker-Clinical, is Clinical Research Specialist for the Child Sex Trafficking Victims Initiative at the University of Maryland's School of Social Work. Drawing on her clinical work with trafficked youth, she now builds capacity among child-serving agencies to comprehensively respond to sex trafficking of children and adolescents. Ms. Rubenstein previously co-founded the Anti-Trafficking Program at TurnAround, Inc., a victim services non-profit organization in Baltimore, where she provided clinical services to survivors of human trafficking.

Joseph Ryan is Associate Professor and Co-Director of the Child and Adolescent Data lab at the University of Michigan. Ryan worked in a variety of residential and community-based programs serving adolescents involved with the child welfare and juvenile justice systems.

William J. Sabol, Professor in the Department of Criminal Justice and Criminology at the Andrew Young School of Policy Studies, Georgia State University, has held academic, government, and private sector research positions over the past 30 years, focusing on corrections and sentencing policy, the impacts of incarceration in communities, crime and victimization statistics, and racial disparities.

John R. Seita is a former youth at risk who was removed from his home at the age of eight and spent his childhood in foster care. Today he is on the faculty of the School of Social Work at Michigan State University. He also has appointments with MSU Extension and the Michigan Agricultural Experimental Station.

Renée Spencer, Professor of Human Behavior at Boston University School of Social Work, specializes in the study of youth mentoring and innovative approaches for special populations of young people, including those in foster care and military-connected youth. She is widely known for her qualitative analysis of both long-term and early-ending mentoring relationships.

Derek J. Stafford is a 1989 graduate of Hastings College of the Law, University of California, and has been advising clients and practicing law in the San Francisco Bay Area for more than 25 years. He is a Court Appointed Special Advocate (CASA) for abused and neglected children in San Mateo County, California.

Diana Vega Vega, Research Assistant, Roy Wilkins Center for Human Relations and Social Justice, Humphrey School of Public Affairs, holds a Bachelor of Science degree in Economics from the University of Minnesota. Her work centers on projects that promote racial and social justice through policy analysis.

Jeffrey N. Wherry, PhD, ABPP, After completing his Doctorate, Jeff earned the Diploma (clinical) from the American Board of Professional Psychology. He has worked with residential, foster, and outpatient clients; has been funded by the National Child Traumatic Stress Network (NCTSN); and has been tenured at four universities. Jeff has provided consultation related to assessment to the National Children's Alliance and the NCTSN.

Armeda Stevenson Wojciak is Assistant Professor in Couple and Family Therapy at the University of Iowa. Armeda's research has focused on improving outcomes for children and families involved with the child welfare system by examining sibling relationships, parent–child relationships, and foster caregiver–child relationships.

Man Xu, Doctoral student at the Humphrey School of Public Affairs, University of Minnesota, holds a Master of Public Policy (MPP) degree and is Research Assistant at the Roy Wilkins Center for Human Relations and Social Justice. Her research interests are the intersections of public policy, labor economics, and racial inequality.

May Yeh is Associate Professor of Psychology at San Diego State University, Research Scientist at the Child and Adolescent Services Research Center, and Associate Adjunct Professor of Psychiatry at the University of California, San Diego. Her interests include factors (e.g., socio-cultural) associated with mental health outcomes for at-risk youth.

Preface

Elizabeth Trejos-Castillo and Nancy Trevino-Schafer

It is easier to build strong children than to repair broken men.

(Frederick Douglass, 1817–1895)

Coming a Long Way . . .

As we reflect back on how this book came about, we realize that fate and passion have been crucial elements. We met our editor at a conference publishers' booth while sipping coffee, looking for a textbook . . . a heartfelt conversation, a random afternoon, the "best partner in crime" and a long-term visualization of a dream.

During the planning stages of this edited volume, I (Elizabeth) unexpectedly lost my father. Being disoriented for several months, I deeply appreciated the persevering calls from our editor at Routledge and her encouragement to resume the project whenever I was ready. After the book was approved and almost a year after our initial planning time, we were preparing to reach out to potential contributors when my grandmother suddenly passed away. Her loss left me adrift. When I was just a baby, she elevated me above all dangers, and throughout my life she showed me a world of compassion, forgiveness, devotion, love, appreciation, and dreams. Months later, one afternoon, after hours of mesmerized staring at a hummingbird in my backyard—who had kept me company during my distress—and a deep contemplation on the fragility and the miracle of life, I regained the courage to continue this project. Though losing both of my parents has deeply shaken my world during the completion of this book, it made me realize how privileged I was to have had them for 42 years in my life. In the midst of that grief, pondering on how children and youth coming from fragmented families rise above their difficulties and thrive has been a very humbling experience.

Also during this time, I (Nancy) was engaged in a lengthy health battle. My body had begun to fight itself, triggered by the plentiful stress of making the transition to a blended family, the illness and death of my own grandmother, and the impending doom that I felt about launching my professional career. The prescription that was supposed to help me instead left me with severe toxicity, difficulty with daily functioning, and an unsettling uncertainty about the future that looked so dark. It was a long road of advocating for myself and finding what I needed to recover and function more normally again. It was during this time, seeing the pain in my daughter's eyes, that I began to develop a deeper understanding of the heartbreak that children who become involved with child welfare services feel, when they are left without the loving involvement of their parents, through absolutely no fault of their own.

Why the *Handbook of Foster Youth*?

In the course of our work with foster youth, we have continuously felt that puzzling questions regarding foster youth were half-answered and investigated with limited regard for the youth's own voices. We came back home with more queries after every field visit, every interview, every focus group. Somehow, through the small opportunities available to meet and talk with these youth and to listen to their personal experiences, the idea of this edited volume materialized. As educators and researchers, we serve the profession and society at large in many capacities; however, we believe we have been placed in one of the most perplexing but gratifying roles in our lives through our work with the foster youth. We thought that all these years, we were serving as "Door Openers"; little did we know, doors were being opened in our hearts and minds with hope that our work would support better opportunities for the youth in care.

This book aims to honor the voices and stories of the youth in care, many that we have yet to hear and to bring out to the light. We wanted to call this edited volume the *Handbook of Foster Youth*, because this book is about them and for them, not just about the child welfare system. We hope that this book provides an opportunity to reflect on the many challenges and strengths of the foster youth and the child welfare system, and the combined efforts of caregivers (e.g., foster parents, kin, case workers, etc.), community volunteers, policy makers, and all the professionals and researchers working with them.

What Is the Book About?

This book is organized in two sections: Section I comprises 12 chapters and Section II consists of 13 chapters, for a total of 25 chapters. The chapters are organized in seven parts:

Section I

  I. Understanding the Child Welfare/Foster Care System: History and Structure (two chapters)
 II. Foster Youth Individual Development (three chapters)
III. Impact of Foster Care on Youth's Overall Health (four chapters)
IV. Foster Youth Development in Context (three chapters)

Section II

  V. Aging Out of Foster Care into Independent Living: Challenges and Opportunities (four chapters)
 VI. Areas of Special Consideration in Foster Youth (five chapters)
VII. Social Policy and Institutional Support (four chapters)

A brief description of the book parts and the chapters is provided below.

Section I

Understanding the Child Welfare/Foster Care System: History and Structure

Part I provides a general background of the history and structure of the child welfare system in the United States and the services it provides. In Chapter 1, "History of Foster Care: Policy, Practice and Reformation", **Seita** provides a historical review of the child welfare system, including laws and policies that have shaped the system over time; discusses foster youth's insights on the system and their recommendations for foster care reform; and reflects on the current impact, progress, leadership, and change moving forward. In Chapter 2, entitled "Foster Care Placement Process and

Settings," **Aguiniga and Madden** examine key considerations in the foster care placement process with an emphasis on the role of race and ethnicity, provide a comprehensive review of current foster care placements, and discuss the importance of permanency planning and concurrent planning.

Foster Youth Individual Development

In Part II, the book goes on to focus on individual development of foster youth, including neurobiological and socioemotional development and their experiences in and out of the child welfare system. Chapter 3 by **Bernard, Frost, and Kuzava**, entitled "Neurobiological Development in Foster Youth: Outcomes and Intervention," examines the neurobiological consequences of maltreatment and foster care placement in regulation of the hypothalamus pituitary adrenal (HPA) axis, brain development, and immune system and its association to mental and physical health problems; the authors discuss interventions aiming to enhance functioning of key neurobiological systems. Chapter 4, "Trauma and Socioemotional Development in Foster Youth: Lessons Learned from LONGSCAN," by **Litrownik, Proctor, and Yeh**, reviews the 27-year multisite Longitudinal Studies of Child Abuse and Neglect (LONGSCAN) Consortium and the unique features of the San Diego LONGSCAN Foster Care Study site. Based on both quantitative and qualitative findings, the authors also discuss lessons learned over the years about maltreatment, experiences of adversities by youth in and out of the foster care system, and child welfare system practices related to youth developmental outcomes. In Chapter 5, entitled "Foster Youth Voices: An Exploratory Study on their Challenges and Strengths", **Trevino-Schafer and Trejos-Castillo** use a qualitative approach to examine the strengths and challenges identified by foster youth in their individual experiences in the child welfare system and their transitioning out of care into adults living independently.

Impact of Foster Care on Youth's Overall Health

Part III provides insights into the impact of the child welfare system on youth's mental, physical, and reproductive health and related outcomes. In Chapter 6, "Assessment of Youth in Foster Care", **Wherry** reviews abuse and trauma-related symptoms that are commonly experienced by foster youth, assessment measurements and diagnosis/misdiagnosis issues, and conceptualizations and formulations of symptoms. He discusses best practices for assessing youth in foster care as well as practical guidelines for administration of measures and feedback. In Chapter 7, entitled "Physical Health and Foster Youth", **Jackson and Huffhines** examine the prevalence, nature, and state of physical health among youth in foster care, review potential contributors to the trajectory of physical health of youth and barriers to care, and discuss the challenges associated with providing consistent and effective medical services to youth in foster care. In Chapter 8, "The Sexual and Reproductive Health of Youth in Foster Care", **Dworsky** provides an overview of existing knowledge on sexual behavior, pregnancy, and parenting among foster youth, discusses their sexual and reproductive healthcare needs as well as the federal and state policies responding to those needs, and examines evidence on interventions aimed at preventing pregnancy and promoting sexual health among foster youth. Chapter 9 by **Braciszewski**, entitled "Substance Use and Addiction Problems in Foster Youth," discusses current literature and a theoretical framework for understanding substance use among foster youth, describes an intervention designed by former foster youth to address substance misuse, and provides recommendations for bridging the gap between knowledge and service.

Foster Youth Development in Context

Part IV focuses on contextual issues affecting youth development including mentoring and permanency, relationships with biological and foster families, education, and associated outcomes.

Chapter 10 by **Horn and Spencer**, entitled "Natural Mentoring to Support the Establishment of Permanency for Youth in Foster Care," focuses on adult outcomes of former foster youth. The authors review existing legislation attempting to address youth's challenges aging out of the child welfare system, with an emphasis on connecting youth with mentors; they also review permanency needs using a theoretical framework. In Chapter 11, "Youth in Foster Care Relationships with Biological, Foster, and Adoptive Families", **Stevenson Wojciak and Hough** review current scholarship on foster youth's relationships with biological, foster, and adoptive families, using a strength lens focused on youth's individual perspectives; they also discuss implications for practice and policy. In Chapter 12, entitled "Factors Affecting the Educational Trajectories and Outcomes of Youth in Foster Care," **Pears, Kim, and Brown** present a longitudinal model of potential factors affecting the educational trajectories of youth in foster care and discuss multiple approaches aiming to promote improved educational outcomes across different developmental stages.

Section II

Aging Out of Foster Care into Independent Living: Challenges and Opportunities

Part V of this edited volume addresses key challenges that foster youth face when aging out of the foster system; namely, financial self-sufficiency, housing, education opportunities, human capital, and accessing out-of-care services. In Chapter 13, "Self-Sufficiency: Employment, Earnings, and Receipt of Public Benefits by Former Foster Youth", **Jones** discusses the challenges experienced by emancipated and aging-out foster youth, which include becoming financially independent and stable, securing additional education opportunities, receiving public benefits, and asset accumulation; Jones also discusses strategies for improving employment outcomes in this population. Chapter 14 by **Romo and Ortiz**, "Supportive Housing Contexts and Educational Opportunities for Foster Youth Transitioning Out of Care", presents a 2-year mixed methods study on the housing needs of foster youth transitioning to adulthood. The authors discuss different strategies, informed by a theoretical framework, to alleviate housing instability and prevent homelessness among aging-out foster youth, and provide policy recommendations for improving current services. In Chapter 15, "Human Capital Accumulation: A Proposed Measure and Theoretical Framework for Foster Youth Job Placement Intervention Strategies", **Naccarato, Bruce, Stafford, and Hawkes** discuss human capital accumulation in foster youth and propose a measure and a theoretical framework for evaluating interventions to support their successful transitioning out of the child welfare system. Chapter 16, entitled "Access and Continuity of Transitional Living Services for Foster Youth," by **Collins and Banks**, reviews key theoretical perspectives on transitioning out of foster care and discusses access and continuity of services available for foster youth, with a particular emphasis on policies and practices in housing, education, and employment.

Areas of Special Consideration in Foster Youth

Part VI brings attention to areas of special consideration pertaining to foster youth in and out of the system; more specifically, disabilities, racial and ethnic disproportionalities, sexual exploitation and human trafficking, undocumented immigration and unaccompanied minors, and sexual and gender expansive youth. Chapter 17 by **Hill and Lightfoot**, "Youth with Disabilities in Foster Care", discusses key challenges experienced by foster youth with disabilities, including employment, education attainment, mental and physical health, placement disruptions and permanency, and access to multiple disability services across different service systems. The authors provide recommendations for improving services for youth with disabilities involved in the child welfare system. In Chapter 18, entitled "Racial and Ethnic Disproportionality in Foster Care", **Myers, Sabol, Xu, and Vega** measure disparities, disproportionality, and discrimination to differentiate between causes of disparities and observed outcomes in the child welfare system, using national data on child maltreatment cases, substantiations, and foster care placements. They also discuss practical implications for professionals working in the child welfare system. Chapter 19, "Commercial Sexual Exploitation and Sex Trafficking of Foster Children and Youth," by **Finigan-Carr and Rubenstein**, examines the disproportionate involvement of foster youth in sex trafficking, identifies the needs and problems of victims of sexual abuse and human trafficking, reviews and critiques child welfare's current response and treatment practices, and provides practice and policy recommendations. In Chapter 20, entitled "Undocumented Immigrant Latin@ Youth and the U.S. Child Welfare System", **Rodriguez, Dorsett and Rodriguez** address the challenges faced by unaccompanied undocumented immigrant youth and U.S.-born children with undocumented parents (detained/deported) in their journey through the United States' child welfare system. They discuss the child welfare system policies and practices through historico-contemporary, sociological, legal, and ethical lenses. Chapter 21 by **Forge and Hartinger-Saunders**, "Sexual and Gender Expansive Youth in Foster Care", discusses the unique trajectories, needs, experiences, and outcomes of sexual and gender expansive youth in the foster care system; outlines best practices for working with this vulnerable population; and describes educational, supportive, and networking resources available for sexual and gender expansive youth, professionals, foster and adoptive parents, and scholars.

Social Policy and Institutional Support

Finally, Part VII addresses issues related to social policy, legislation, and the role of multiple institutional systems and services, including private foster agencies, adoption agencies, child welfare agencies, the juvenile justice system, and community services. Chapter 22, "Fostering 'Belonging-ness': The Role of Private Foster Care Agencies with Foster Parents and Youth," by **Perry and Rauktis**, reviews the role of private foster care agencies in recruiting, hiring, training, and monitoring foster parents. The authors identify the characteristics and behaviors of foster parents that support a successful transitioning into adulthood, using a qualitative approach focused on foster youth and informed by the theoretical frameworks of emerging adulthood, therapeutic alliance, and capital development. In Chapter 23, "Continuous Quality Improvement (CQI) in Child Welfare Agencies," **Burstain, Boudreau, and Booher** discuss the theoretical framework and conceptual model for Continuous Quality Improvement (CQI) in the context of public child welfare agencies, and describe lessons learned and recommendations for child welfare agencies making the transition from a traditional quality assurance (QA) system to CQI. Chapter 24 by **Jonson-Reid, Dunnigan, and Ryan**, entitled "Foster Care and Juvenile Justice Systems: Crossover and Integration of Services," reviews current scholarship on foster youth pathways from foster care to juvenile justice involvement, as well as the path from juvenile justice to foster care, and the ongoing relationship between the two. The authors also discuss potential policy solutions and means of evaluation including the increasing use of big data. Finally, in Chapter 25, entitled "Permanent and Formal Connections: Mentors, Community Services, and Connectedness," **Britner and Collins** describe several theoretical models used to explain the development of permanent and formal connections for youth in or aging out of foster care, and discuss existing research on permanent relationships and mentoring, and community-based and educational-vocational programs.

Not Far Enough Yet . . .

We humbly present this book as a stepping stone in the growing literature on foster youth. When we started dreaming of this project and after digging deeper in the extant literature, our wish list of topics grew exponentially every week. Certainly, not every single topic made the cut, but we are confident that this book addresses timely and salient issues affecting youth in care, and that it will support opportunities for dialogues across researchers, policy makers, care providers, and professionals in general working with foster youth. It is our hope that this book will serve as a strong educational tool for current and future professionals, and that additional similar efforts will be developed in the near future to support the advancement of the field and the well-being of foster youth.

Beyond Thankful!

At the culmination of this project, we find ourselves without enough words to deeply thank our contributing authors for their support and commitment, but more importantly for passionately dreaming with us to make this book possible. Words cannot summarize how grateful we are for our colleagues' encouraging and honest emails, their precise inquiries, their trust and their continued enthusiasm to participate in this edited volume. We have embarked together on this joint effort to advance the current knowledge on foster youth that will—it is hoped—propel the improvement of the child welfare system to better support their overall well-being and resiliency. Thank you for all your dedication to improve the lives of foster youth! You are a true inspiration to us to continue building a better future for all children and youth involved in the child welfare system! Thank you! ¡Muchas Gracias!

SECTION I

Part I

Understanding the Child Welfare/Foster Care System

History and Structure

1

History of Foster Care

Policy, Practice, and Reformation

John R. Seita

The foster care system is broadly considered to be necessary on one hand, and a failure on the other hand. On the one hand, there is a need to find safe shelter for vulnerable and dependent minors when, for whatever reason, their parents are incapable of caring for them. On the other hand, the shocking outcomes of many who have been in foster care clearly indicate an inadequate and failing system, with many damaged lives as a result (Levesque, 1995; Pecora, Whittaker, Maluccio, & Barth, 2012; Roman & Wolfe, 1995). "Emotional pain, the kind that says you are unworthy, that you are less than, that you do not belong, that if you died nobody would weep for you, is common in foster homes" (Folman, 2009, p. 147).

Beyond the scholarship of identifying the numbing and startling numbers are the individual voices and perspectives of those who have endured foster care. My own foster care experience found me living with strangers in 15 different foster homes. Like many, I was in foster care due to abuse and neglect by a biological parent. My own encounter was as sad and emotionally disturbing as Folman's.

Still, regardless of documented outcomes of trauma, pain, loss, and adult onset health problems (Jee et al., 2010; Zlotnick, Tam, & Soman, 2012), foster care continues to be a core component of out-of-home care for abused and neglected young people. According to the Children's Bureau, a U.S. government agency (Child Welfare Information Gateway, 2017), as of 2015, there were 427,910 children living in foster care in the United States. Forty-six percent of them lived in non-relative foster homes, while 29% lived in foster homes with relatives, also called "kinship care" situations. The remainder lived in other settings, such as institutions, group homes, trial home visits, pre-adoptive homes, and supervised independent living. Those who live in foster care are much more than mere numbers; the real story of foster care is that of young people who have been placed out of their homes into the homes of strangers, through no fault of their own. Their journey into, and sometimes during, foster care, is a series of loss, neglect, abuse, and trauma. More significantly, it can, for some, be a journey of courage and resilience. Lives both shattered and saved are the real story of foster care. Their shared insights are an untapped resource toward creating an improved foster care experience. To better understand foster care, and provide context for their stories, their lives, and their shared ideas, it is worth briefly exploring the history of foster care and modern child welfare legislation.

It is probable that some form of out-of-home placements or alternative homes for children, known today as foster care, is as old as humankind itself. There have always been children in need of homes that were not their birth homes for various reasons. A series of historical events, both human-made and natural, have contributed to absent parents whose children needed to be placed out of their birth homes (Downs & Sherraden, 1983). Wars and internal civil conflicts, genocide, the Holocaust, great epidemics such as AIDS and influenza, and periodic economic despair created by recessions and the Great Depression all have contributed to creating the current and historical populations of homeless, abused, and neglected children in need of foster care (Croke, 2003; Dauge-Roth, 2012; Michaels & Levine, 1992).

In ancient texts, examples of children in need of homes are cited as far back as the books of the Old Testament of the Bible and the Qur'an. Exodus states, "you shall not mistreat any widow or fatherless child" (Exodus 22:22, English Standard Version), while the Qur'an includes the statement, "They ask you about orphans. Say, 'Promotion of their welfare is an act of great goodness'" (2:21, Quran: A Simple English Translation [Khan & Hilaali, 1997]).

More recently, the American foster care movement would probably trace its roots back roughly a century and a half to evangelical minister Charles Loring Brace, who was also the founding director of the New York Children's Aid Society (Brace, C. L., 1880; Brace, E., 1894; Brown & Seita, 2014; O'Connor, 2004). Brace witnessed great multitudes of needy children, estimated at somewhere between 150,000 and 400,000, wandering the streets of New York City. They were often immigrants, lacking food, housing, and safety, and typically sleeping outside on the streets (Brown & Seita, 2014; Cook, 1995; O'Connor, 2004; Warren, 1998). Led by Brace, social reformers devised a program to find homes for homeless and drifting children (Brace, C. L., 1880, 1894; Holt, 2006; Marten, 2005; O'Connor, 2004).

Beginning in 1854, a Brace-led initiative, which came to be known as the Orphan Train Movement, helped to jumpstart an early form of foster care. Trains transported homeless young people from New York City to non-relative homes in various locations across the country. The first "orphan train" transported 45 young people to Dowagiac, Michigan, into area homes (Caravantes, 2013; Smith, 2012). Between 1854 and 1929, Brace's orphan trains were used to transport more than 200,000 orphaned, abandoned, homeless, and poor children who were placed with families across the United States, and in parts of Mexico and Canada (Cook, 1995; Warren, 1998).

As might be expected, given the lack of structure with respect to child welfare and children's protective polices in this era, this seemingly generous initiative had some unexpected, negative outcomes. For example, there is no evidence of polices, regulations, or oversight regarding the process of young people being dumped into these faraway placements (Courtney, 2005; Holt, 2006; O'Connor, 2004). Consequently, the moment these needy children departed the East Coast for other parts of the country, Brace and his reformers dropped contact, either seemingly confident that un-screened caregivers would provide nurturing homes, or maybe unconcerned with what might happen to the disconnected and pitiful orphans (Brown & Seita, 2009). The orphans found themselves at risk as a result of the caprices of untrained and uncertified substitute caregivers, many of whom took in the orphans for less than honorable reasons. According to Trammell (2009, p. 5), "Criticisms of the orphan train movement focused on concerns that placements were made hastily, and, that there was insufficient follow up on placements."

Some might argue that these children were not unlike indentured domestics who received less than minimal food and housing as compensation for countless hours of back-breaking work (Cook, 1995). Many families simply took in these children as laborers for their farms and ranches. Without a system to monitor their living conditions and with few laws to safeguard them, these early foster children likely experienced severe physical and emotional pain due to the lack of affection, safety, and protection offered by their caregivers.

The Development of Laws and Policies

Prior to 1875, there were few, if any, laws specifically designed for and focused on the protection of children (Myers, 2008; Shelman & Lazoritz, 2005). Of course, the lack of explicit child protection laws especially impacted children without homes, who, as noted earlier, were dumped into unlicensed, unmonitored homes during the Orphan Train Movement. Oddly, though, it was not the widespread movement of homeless children into orphan trains to be shipped westward that spurred the evolution toward a policy framework focused on child protection. Rather, the impetus for widespread consciousness and subsequent child protection laws and policies was the well-publicized child abuse case in New York City of 10-year-old Mary Ellen Wilson while in foster care (Lazoritz, 1990; Watkins, 1990).

Mary Ellen was born in March 1864 into the loving embrace of her biological parents, Tom and Fanny Wilson. Tom was a Union soldier during the American Civil War and engaged in brutal hand-to-hand combat with soldiers of the Confederate Army. Meanwhile, Fanny toiled as a seamstress in a factory sweatshop weaving stockings to support Mary Ellen and herself (Mallon, 2013; Shelman & Lazoritz, 2005). While Mary Ellen was still an infant, Fanny received a letter informing her of Tom's death from battle wounds. Tom's death was one of an estimated 850,000 deaths during the war, and these deaths resulted in a great many fatherless children (Cashin & Wood, 2015).

Following the death of her beloved Tom, Fanny fell into despair and turned to alcohol for solace. Soon thereafter, feeling unable to care for Mary Ellen, she gave her to a caregiver, thus starting Mary Ellen's descent into the looming darkness of foster care and horrific caregiver abuse.

> "Mamma has been in the habit of whipping and beating me almost every day," the little girl testified. "She used to whip me with a twisted whip — a rawhide. I have now on my head two black-and-blue marks which were made by Mamma with the whip, and a cut on the left side of my forehead which was made by a pair of scissors in Mamma's hand; she struck me with the scissors and cut me.... I never dared speak to anybody, because if I did I would get whipped."
> (Mignon, 2016, p.25)

Mary Ellen eventually came to the attention of Etta Wheeler, considered to be a friendly visitor, or more likely a religious missionary. Deeply concerned about the safety and well-being of Mary Ellen, Wheeler contacted the police who failed to investigate. Lacking child protection laws or a juvenile court, Wheeler turned to existing children's charities; however, they had no authority to act. Wheeler next turned to a friend, Henry Bergh. Bergh was the founder of the American Society for the Prevention of Cruelty to Animals. Bergh enlisted his lawyer, Elbridge Gerry, who reportedly used a legal strategy known as a writ of habeas corpus in order to remove Mary Ellen from her abusive foster home (Jalongo, 2006; Shelman & Lazoritz, 2005; Thomas, 1971).

Soon after, Mary Ellen went to live with one of Wheeler's sisters, who raised Mary Ellen as her own. Mary Ellen married when she was 24 years old and raised two daughters, both of whom went to college and became teachers; she died at the age of 92 (Mallon, 2013; Myers, 2008). Mary Ellen became an unwitting icon of child welfare reformers (Mallon, 2013; Shelman & Lazoritz, 2005).

The attention generated by Mary Ellen's well-documented abuse became a powerful force in the founding of the world's first child protection agency, the New York Society for the Prevention of Cruelty to Children, in 1874, about 20 years after the Orphan Train Movement (Myers, 2008). The intervention on behalf of Mary Ellen by her advocates and the subsequent founding of the Society may have been the antecedents for the emergence of modern child welfare laws.

The Federal Legislation that Shaped Child Welfare Services

The child welfare reform legislation discussed below is confined to federal legislation since 1974 that has been classified as major federal legislation by the Children's Bureau (Child Welfare Information Gateway, 2016) and does not include state or local legislation. According to the Child Welfare Information Gateway (2016), a total of 31 major pieces of child protection legislation have been passed since 1974. This chapter is intended to provide a brief history of child welfare, enhanced by the actual voices of alumni of the foster care system; it is not a comprehensive treatment. Thus, while all child welfare legislation is important, and intended to improve the lives of young people needing the care and safety that was not provided by their families, only selected laws that might be considered milestones in the history of child welfare are included in the discussion. Those selected laws are as follows:

1. The Child Abuse Prevention and Treatment Act (CAPTA)

The CAPTA was passed in 1974 with the aim of providing funding in order to improve states' response for the prevention, identification, and treatment of child abuse and neglect. The CAPTA also provided funds for the training of professional child welfare workers and to improve the reporting of abuse and neglect (Myers, 2008; Stoltzfus, 2017). This Act was amended several times, with the most recent amendment in 2010. "CAPTA provides Federal funding to States in support of prevention, assessment, investigation, prosecution, and treatment activities and also provides grants to public agencies and nonprofit organizations, including Indian Tribes and Tribal organizations, for demonstration programs and projects" (Child Welfare Information Gateway, 2011, p. 1). The CAPTA is the only federal legislation exclusively dedicated to the prevention, assessment, identification, and treatment of child abuse and neglect.

2. The Indian Child Welfare Act (ICWA)

The ICWA is another major law enacted during the same era as CAPTA. Passed by Congress in 1978, it seeks to keep American Indian children with American Indian families in order to protect and preserve Native culture on behalf of Native children. A related intent of the Act was to reduce the disproportionate number of Indian children being removed from their homes of origin and placed in non-native homes (MacEachron, Gustavsson, Cross, & Lewis, 1996).

3. The Foster Care Independence Act of 1999 (the "Chafee Legislation")

This Act was enacted into law in December 1999. It is also known as the Chafee legislation, as it was sponsored by the late Rhode Island Senator John H. Chafee. The intent of the Chafee legislation is to support the transition process for young people aging out of foster care. The legislation provides amplified funds to states to help young people make the transition from dependent care to community-based living. The Act allows states the freedom to choose creative methods in devising independent living programs. The Act embeds accountability expectations for states in executing programs. States must create outcome measures to evaluate the quality of life for young people who age out of care. Outcome measures include educational attainment, employment, avoidance of dependency, homelessness, non-marital childbirth, high-risk behaviors, and incarceration (Courtney & Dworsky, 2006; Dworsky, 2005; Guinn, 2000; Hill, 2009; Lopez & Allen, 2007; Reilly, 2003).

> The Chafee Program has five purposes: (1) identify children who are expected to be in foster care to age 18 and help them make a transition to self-sufficiency; (2) help these children receive the education, training, and services necessary to obtain employment; (3) help them prepare for and enter post-secondary training and education institutions; (4) provide personal and emotional support for children aging out of foster care; (5) provide a range of services and support for former foster care recipients between ages 18 and 21 to complement their own efforts to achieve self-sufficiency and to assure that the program participants recognize and accept their personal responsibility for adulthood.
>
> (Collins, 2004, p. 1053)

With regard to "personal responsibility," please understand that this concept is dripping with a failure by policymakers to understand individual context such as family privilege (McCall, 2003; Pike, Millspaugh, & DeSalvatore, 2005; Seita & Brendtro, 2004; Unrau, 2011; Unrau, Seita, & Putney, 2008). Family privilege is a form of social capital demonstrated by a variety of tools, both visible and invisible, that are typically available to young people with live in, or are the unearned beneficiaries, of a healthy well-functioning family. Family privilege resources express themselves in the form of intangible supports such as unconditional love, family values and traditions, experienced guidance into the next phase of life; or in more tangible resources such as money, helping to pay for tuition, or furniture for that first apartment or dorm room.

Drawing upon personal experiences when I transitioned from foster care into the community, and upon related research, the phrase "personal responsibility" needs to be considered cautiously and augmented with the reality of personal resources, personal support, and the impact of the tolls of a personal history that is often traumatic. Sandra Bloom (2013) suggests that the trauma perspective changes the fundamental perspective of caregivers from seeking flaws to seeking critical traumatic events in the lives of young people in order to reclaim them. Leaving foster care was miserable for me when making the transition to so-called independent adulthood: I endured homelessness, unemployment, incarceration, and abandonment (Brown & Seita, 2014; Seita & Brendtro, 2004; Seita, Mitchell, & Tobin, 1996).

4. The Adoption Assistance and Child Welfare Act (AACWA)

This Act was passed in 1980, and was intended to support family preservation approaches in order to maintain families and to reduce the frequency with which children were being moved into out-of-home placements such as foster care. The Act also focuses on family reunification or adoption if a child is removed from the home. An adoption subsidy reimbursed by the federal government is also provided through this law for children with special needs. The Act also sought to make progress in the areas of child welfare and social services.

5. The Adoption and Safe Families Act of 1997

This may be one of the most important pieces of child welfare legislation in the past 25 years, as it focused on shortening the time to find permanent homes for children and adolescents who are placed out of their biological home. The Act was signed into law by President Clinton on November 19, 1997. The law, which amends the 1980 Adoption Assistance and Child Welfare Act, clarifies that the health and safety of children served by child welfare agencies must be their paramount concern, and aims to move children from foster care more quickly into permanent homes. Among the provisions, the law shortens the time-frame for a child's first permanency hearing, offers states financial incentives for increasing the number of adoptions, sets new requirements for states to petition for termination of parental rights, and reauthorizes the Family Preservation and Support Program, which was established in 1993 by the federal government in order to strengthen families by providing community-based support services such as home visits, parental counseling and skill development, and child care (Ahsan, 1996).

6. The Multiethnic Placement Act of 1994 (MEPA)

The MEPA, enacted in late 1994, requires states to find foster and adoptive families that mirror the ethnic and racial composition of children in the state for whom foster and adoptive homes are needed. Concerns emerged among advocates and other stakeholders that children of color were being removed from their biological homes at a higher rate than white children, and were being placed in white homes; this act was an attempt to rectify that situation (Murray & Gesiriech, 2005).

In the end, each of these laws was intended to improve the quality of life for young people needing the support of child protection and foster care. The degree to which these aggregate policies have been effective is debatable, but the voices of those who have experienced foster care are not debatable.

Who Are these Young People?

Statistics maintained by the federal government show that 38% of young people in foster care are African American, 37% are white, and 17% are of Hispanic origin. The remainder are of mixed or unknown race. Overall, 52% are male and 48% female. The average age of young people entering care is almost 9 years, and the average length of stay is around 3 years (U.S. Department of Health & Human Services, 2015).

Infants, toddlers, adolescents, and teenagers enter foster care primarily due to abuse and/or neglect by a parent or caregiver (Anderson & Seita, 2005; Palmer, Brown, Rae-Grant, & Loughlin, 1999; Pfohl, 1977; Tyler, 2006). Consequently, most children who enter foster care are traumatized and have behavior disorders and emotional problems (Bath & Seita, 2018; Greeson et al., 2011; Seita & Brendtro, 2004). They often are mistrustful of caregivers, even those who attempt to help. After all, in their own private logic (Adler & Brett, 1998; Seita & Brendtro, 2004), adults produced the suffering that punctuates their lives (Brendtro, Mitchell, Freado, & du Toit, 2012; Seita, 2010; Seita & Brendtro, 2004, 2007).

Young people who enter foster care eventually leave it; some return home, while others are adopted, put into independent living programs, or age out of the system. Some die in foster care, with a reported 700 deaths in the system in California over a 7-year period from 1988 to1994 (Barth & Blackwell, 1998).

However, anyone who has lived in foster care has endured pain, dislocation, trauma, and fear; they are more than statistics. They are individuals who, like all of us, have dreams, hopes, goals, and the desire to be happy and to contribute to society. Unfortunately, this population is also more likely to experience mental health challenges. "The prevalence of lifetime PTSD was significantly higher among alumni (30.0%) than among the general population (7.6%). This lifetime PTSD rate was comparable to Vietnam War veterans (30.9% for male and 26.9% for female veterans)" (Kulka et al. 1990, p. 139). "The 12-month rate of PTSD among alumni was nearly five times that of the general population and, at 21.5%, exceeded the rates for American war veterans for recent campaigns (Afghanistan, 6%; and the first USA–Iraq conflict, 12–13%)" (Pecora, White, Jackson, & Wiggins, 2009).

What happens to many young people who enter foster care is unconscionable. What are their lives like? What recommendations and insights can they share about foster care? Do all of the statistics and stories of woe, and occasional success, contain lessons that might inform future child welfare policy and practice?

Voices of Alumni: Reflecting on the Foster Care System

We now turn to the voices of foster care alumni for authentic insight regarding their experiences in foster care and, further, their opinions and recommendations for foster care reform. In their voices, you may feel and experience their pain, despair, and loss, but you will also witness reflection, wisdom, redemption, and ultimately, hope. Each perspective presented is from a foster care survivor, someone who endured abuse, neglect, abandonment, pain, and loss before being placed into foster care, often with poor results.

> After all, I was a foster child and therefore had no sense of entitlement. "I know, but what kind of chance would I have of winning? I'm a foster kid, an orphan, Miss Nobody," I rationalized.

> Maybe I could finally escape my past and start a new life, a normal life, not the life of an unwanted foster child.
>
> (Sutherland, 2009, p. 112)

> Being a foster child was, for me, hell on earth. My transition from living with a dysfunctional mother and stepfather to residing in a foster care placement with a witch of a guardian truly deprived me of knowing genuine happiness in my youth. Recalling the dire series of events that led to the division of my family never completely leaves my mind, almost as if they took place yesterday. In fact, I am still healing.
>
> (Barney, 2009, p. 97)

> My final foster home was located thirty miles outside the city of Detroit. My foster parents had a daughter four years older than I was. She hated me on sight and I had made up my mind to hate them. I refused to speak to anyone in the household and my form of communication was grunts, nodding yes and no or hunching my shoulders.
>
> (Watson, 2009, p. 92)

> Perhaps most of all, I never had the opportunity to reconnect emotionally with my younger brother Sandy. Foster care killed him a little bit at a time, tormenting his soul and robbing him of an identity, reducing him to an addict who escaped the reality of his loveless, transient life through drug-induced stupor. I still grieve for him daily. My foster care experiences affected me in numerous ways
>
> (Watson, 2009, p. 94)

Relationships continued to change and in many ways to be a mystery for these young people.

> By the end of my first year of college, my relationship with Ms. Jones came to an abrupt and eye-opening end. When my social worker quit sending funds to Ms. Jones for my support, diverting them to me at college, I learned the sad truth about our relationship. In front of my independent living worker, she stated I could "no longer live with her if the State would not pay for my bed." I had mistakenly believed that she loved me as a mother loves her son, rather than as a foster parent paid to care for a foster child. The fact that she concerned herself more about the money than she did about me nearly broke my heart."
>
> (Webb, 2009, p. 80)

> The family had some religious issues that included praying over us and then waiting for the demons to come out. They even dropped us off for several days with an old blind woman who had a rodent problem. She sprinkled rat poison on everything in the house, including the candy she kept out. Like most kids, when we saw the candy lying about, we ate it. Even though she knew we were sick from eating the candy, she did not call a doctor or have us taken to the hospital. Instead, she prayed over us, until the family finally came to pick us up. Although I do not know this as fact, it seemed that the foster parents were trying to hide us until they received payment from Catholic Social Services.
>
> (Echols, 2009, p. 59)

Webb admits being broken-hearted upon discovering that his longtime foster mother was more concerned about the money she received from the state than about him. Watson deplores her foster care experience for being hated "on sight" and for, in her mind, killing the soul of her brother.

Sutherland recalls foster care as being "hell on earth" in a riveting chapter that laments her lack of belonging and safety. Echols echoes Sutherland's feelings of not feeling safe, sharing how the blind lady put rat poison in the candy.

Note that there are exceptions. There are also stories of hope, joy, and lives well lived in foster care.

> Shortly thereafter, Cathy and I entered our first foster home placement. I was four at the time. My memories of this placement are few, but pleasant. I remember being clean, fed and cared for, but most of all, I have fond memories of going to work with the foster mother, Mrs. Padget. She was a big woman with a big smile and an even bigger heart who worked in a hospital laundry, where Cathy and I frolicked in a sea of white bed sheets and pillowcases. After we graduated high school, Cathy and I made a return visit to thank Mrs. Padget for taking such good care of us. The foster parents and the boarders treated us with kindness, fed us well and made us attend church with them.
> (Braxton, 2009, p. 130)

> In foster care, we enjoyed three meals a day, even on weekends. My foster mother was a wonderful cook. Occasionally, she and her husband even took us to a restaurant, a treat that never happened when we lived with my mother.
> (Day, 2009, p. 47)

A sunnier view of life in foster care is shared by both Day and Braxton, who recall being the beneficiaries of tangible resources like food, which was scarce prior to foster care, and intangible nurturing; in the words of Braxton, "being clean, fed and cared for and treated . . . with kindness" (2009, p. 128). For a few in the foster care system, there is hope, support, love, kindness, and success, but for many, such luxuries are not among their memories of foster care.

> The last move I didn't really want to move but I left foster care shortly after that. My time in foster care was pretty positive I guess. I didn't have to experience the bad things I saw other kids experience. I had good foster parents. At one point my biological mom said you seem to like your foster parents better than your real parents, and at the time she probably was right.
> (Unrau et al. 2008, p. 1259)

Improving Foster Care

An examination of shared thoughts and feelings from foster care alumni reveals emergent and consistent themes that include a lack of belonging (Brendtro & Brokenleg, 2012), feeling unloved or unwanted, and even feeling hated by foster care providers and their families. What is noteworthy about the voices profiled here is that, in spite of their common experiences of rejection, abuse, neglect, trauma, and pain, this group is diverse in terms of race and gender, including whites and African Americans, females and males. It would seem that race and gender are not predictors or correlates of foster care satisfaction. Embedded in their lived experiences are lessons learned for improving practice, policy, and resource allocation.

As previously stated, most children enter foster care already traumatized. Folman (2009) notes that foster youth view the world as an unstable and uncaring place where adults cannot be trusted and they tend to regard themselves in negative terms, including being bad, worthless, undeserving, and unlovable. They also often lack the emotional resources that are necessary to develop healthy relationships, such as the ability to trust, to care, and to empathize. Folman's painfully astute observation, and those of others who have lived in foster care, are often overlooked by policymakers, funders, and practitioners in their seemingly misguided and feckless attempts to improve the foster care system. Her voice, like that of most alumni of foster care, has been largely unnoticed or disregarded.

A survey of 108 child welfare agencies by Seita (2005) found that none of the agencies had foster care alumni in any kind of leadership positions. This small survey needs to be replicated; it might be indicative of a lack of voices from inside foster care shaping policy and practice. Further research would be valuable, not only to explore the numbers of foster care alumni in child welfare leadership roles, but also to examine attitudes regarding the inclusion or exclusion of such alumni in various roles within foster care policy development and governance.

Therefore, scholars, practitioners, and other stakeholders must seek the guidance of foster care alumni and pose key questions respecting their views of foster care. Alumni, in turn, might ask those in charge how it is they claim to know what they know without alumni guidance and leadership.

Pathways to Progress

Beyond critical legislation and policy considerations, important questions about foster care must be asked relating to impact, change, leadership, and progress going forward. What progress has been made in 30 years? How well have policies worked, and do we need new policies? How do we involve those who have lived in foster care in shaping and leading child welfare going forward? What innovations and new partnerships can be formed in order to reform foster care and foster care transition, and to improve outcomes for young people who have been in care?

There are multiple ways to address the flaws in the child welfare system. Community-based support groups and foster care alumni involvement in foster care policy, practice, and leadership are two examples. Other novel approaches would be legislation requiring child welfare agency boards to include foster care alumni, new agency accreditation standards for alumni involvement, and funder insistence on alumni involvement.

Leadership

One of the many challenges facing the foster care system is that very few of those managing and leading the system have experienced foster care. Despite this, they don't seem to seek the experiential wisdom of those who have been in the foster care system. "You're an orphan, right? Do you think I'd know the first thing about how hard your life has been, how you feel, who you are because I read Oliver Twist? Does that encapsulate you?" (Damon & Affleck, 1997, p. 27).

The above quote from the published script for the movie *Good Will Hunting* (1997) was part of a conversation between a roguish counselor and a hostile foster care alumnus. This give-and-take portrays the difference between the lived experience of being an orphan and merely studying it. Since the outcomes for many foster care alumni are disturbing and there are few, if any, foster care alumni in agency leadership roles, perhaps it is time to explore their integration into such roles. The dismal outcomes demonstrated by the child welfare system could only be improved by building the capacity of foster care alumni to participate effectively in the system.

Making the case for building the capacity of foster care alumni to assume leadership in child welfare agencies recognizes the reality that a white person does not lead the NAACP (National Association for the Advancement of Colored People) or the National Urban League. A man does not lead the National Organization of Women (NOW), heterosexuals do not lead the Gay and Lesbian Alliance (GLAAD), and a young, 20-something whiz-kid does not lead the American Association of Retired Persons (AARP). The Bureau of Indian Affairs reports that most of its employees are American Indian or Alaska Native, representing a number larger than at any time in its history (U.S. Bureau of Indian Affairs, n.d.).

Can anyone deny that a person of color has a better understanding of the experience of being a person of color in America than a white person? Can anyone deny that a woman more clearly understands the experience of being a woman in America than a man? Can anyone deny that a person with disabilities better understands the challenges of being disabled than someone who is not? Can anyone deny that a gay man or lesbian is not better equipped to understand the challenges of being gay? Who besides alumni of the foster care system has a better understanding of what it is like to leave home with no family? Who else better understands what it is like to be embarrassed to talk about your family, which you do not really have, with friends? Who other than alumni of the foster care system understand more clearly what it is like to not be able to rely upon a mother, father, aunt, uncle, brother, or sister for a small loan during a time of need, the use of a car, ideas about what to do with one's life, or simply a place to crash during times of transition? Who else is better prepared to inform, implement, and propose policy changes and agency leadership than those who have lived in the foster care system?

A recent example of constituency-led activism for constituent leadership occurred when students at Gallaudet University, a university for the hearing impaired in Washington, DC, demanded that one of their own, someone who was hearing impaired, Dr. I. King Jordan, would become the next president of the university. The Gallaudet Board of Directors' original choice was a hearing person (Gallaudet University, n.d.). A 4-day protest involving students, faculty, and staff shut down the university; the Gallaudet Board of Directors reconsidered and hired the first hearing-impaired president in university history (Gannon, Beatty, & Louie, 1989).

Leadership Capacity Building

There are multiple ways to build the capacity of foster care alumni to be leaders in foster care and to include them in the formation of policy and practice. One strategy might involve a university-based curriculum and support program to prepare such alumni to be leaders in the system. The program might include a course of study focusing on leadership in child welfare, recruitment of those formerly in care, retention services while in college, placement services, and partnership development with child welfare agencies and advocacy groups from across the United States. Other strategies might include a community college program, a leadership institute, or a fellowship program.

Legislation

Legislation could be modeled after existing efforts to redress the wrongs suffered by mainstream minority groups. Examples include set-asides for economic development, dedicated scholarship programs for those who attend college, and linking the funding of foster care programming to alumni participation levels. A legislative change might be modeled after Title IX, which is the portion of the Education Amendments of 1972 that prohibits sex discrimination in educational institutions that receive federal funds. In brief, Title IX states: "No person in the United States shall, on the basis of sex, be excluded from participation in, be denied the benefits of, or be subjected to discrimination under any education program or activity receiving Federal financial assistance" (Office for Civil Rights, U.S. Department of Education, 2015). Title IX applies to any educational program in an institution that receives federal funds, which includes the majority of schools in the United States, from elementary schools through to colleges. Almost all private colleges, for example, are covered because they receive federal funding through financial aid programs like the Pell grants.

If educational institutions are found to violate Title IX, their federal funding can be withdrawn. In all cases to date, however, institutions found to violate Title IX have agreed to specific plans to comply with the law rather than lose funding. It's hard to exaggerate the far-reaching effect of Title IX on American society. For example, it is credited with an increase in female participation in intercollegiate athletics. The year before Title IX was enacted, there were about 310,000 girls and women in America playing high school and college sports; today, there are more than 3.4 million (Barra, 2012).

Legislative relief would serve two purposes: a) it will likely improve the capacity of foster care alumni to be more successful in society, and b) it may also improve their capacity to be prepared for leadership roles in foster care agencies in the future.

Leverage by Funders of Foster Care

Funders of foster care agencies, including the government, private philanthropic foundations, and other funding bodies, can promote full participation by foster care alumni in the foster care system in much the same way that universities receiving federal funding must comply with federal regulations such as Title IX in order to receive funding.

Accreditation Changes

Accrediting bodies can play a role in encouraging an increased role for foster care alumni in the leadership of foster care agencies. Standards by accreditation bodies may include language that supports diversity to promote the participation of alumni in leadership roles in foster care agencies. Moreover, membership bodies such as the Children's Defense Fund, the Child Welfare League of America, and the Michigan Federation for Families and Children can encourage their members to recruit foster care alumni for leadership roles.

Board Leadership

Including service consumers on boards, commissions, and panels is not unusual; in fact, this practice might be pretty common. For example, the Michigan Mental Health Code requires local agency mental health boards to include consumers:

> The composition of a community mental health services board shall be representative of providers of mental health services, recipients or primary consumers of mental health services, agencies and occupations having a working involvement with mental health services, and the general public. At least 1/3 of the membership shall be primary consumers or family members, and of that 1/3 at least 1/2 of those members shall be primary consumers.
> (Michigan Mental Health Code of 1974, Act 258, Section 330.1222, Sec. 222. (1), n.p.)

Another example from Michigan is the Michigan Council on Developmental Disabilities. This is a group of citizens from across the state; its membership is made up of people with developmental disabilities, people who have family members with developmental disabilities, and professionals from state and local agencies charged with assisting people with developmental disabilities. The Michigan Developmental Disabilities Council, a constituent-led leadership group which is appointed by the governor, is made up of 21 people with disabilities, and their parents, guardians, or other relatives (Michigan Department of Health & Human Services, 2017).

Quality of Foster Care

Only those who have been in foster care can fully understand the fear and terror of being removed from your biological home and placed in the company of strangers. Moreover, recognition of the anxiety caused by multiple foster home placements, changing schools, and leaving behind friends and known routines ought to be a powerful force in shaping foster care policy and practice. This insider experience, unique to those who have been in foster care, might be likened to honoring the wisdom of indigenous people (Kunnie & Goduka, 2006; Semali & Kincheloe, 2002).

Similarly, the concept of cultural humility, which is to acknowledge that one's own cultural practices, traditions, language, and history are unique, and do not reflect or assume superiority over the importance or value of another culture to a group of individuals or a single individual, fits here, as it can be argued that the foster care experience could be likened to a culture (Cruess, S. R., Cruess, R. L., & Steinert, 2010; Hook, Davis, Owen, Worthington, & Utsey, 2013; Ortega & Faller, 2011).

All of this begs the question, how do you examine the quality of foster care and incorporate the voices of its alumni in order to assess the quality and impact of the foster care system? The voices of foster care alumni and youth currently in care must be cultivated, valued, listened to, acted upon, and disseminated in order to accurately assess the quality of the foster care system. Their perspectives can inform stakeholders with respect to important developmental issues being provided for, or not, in foster care. Safety, feelings of belonging, and family privilege (Seita & Brendtro, 2004), emotional and academic support, a sense of purpose, career pathways, and what Seita et al. (1996) call connections, continuity, opportunity, and dignity might be more important barometers of quality than aggregate outcomes.

Observations

There comes a time in every industry where a paradigm shift occurs (Kuhn, 2012). Such shifts emerge due to the recognition that existing practices are not effective. For example, paradigm shifts have arisen in manufacturing where just-in-time distribution has replaced overstocked warehouses and delayed delivery of products. With just-in-time distribution, the product is delivered almost immediately. Other examples of paradigm shifts include the consumer switch to buying goods online as opposed to in brick-and-mortar stores. Consumers tend to find comparison shopping online to be more convenient, less expensive, and offering greater selection than in a brick-and-mortar store. Moreover, shopping online is more convenient. For the first time, consumers say they bought more of their purchases on the web than in stores, according to an annual survey of more than 5,000 online shoppers by United Parcel Service Inc. (Stevens, 2016).

A similar paradigm shift must occur in foster care. As evidenced by numerous lawsuits against those leading foster care, the time has come to rely more on the voices and expertise provided by its alumni to advise, guide, and lead the foster care system. Between 1995 and 2005 alone, there were 35 reported major lawsuits.

> Over the past ten years alone, there has been child welfare class action litigation in 32 states, with consent decrees or settlement agreements in 30 of these 35. These lawsuits have often resulted in settlement agreements that become "consent decrees" upon approval by the court.
> (Kosanovich, Joseph, & Hasbargen, 2005, p. 2)

This paradigm shift must happen on multiple levels to include administration and leadership, policy formation, research and evaluation, and resource allocation. A logical place to start is by funding research and evaluation based on the authentic and qualitative experiences of foster care alumni.

The question remains, what are the qualities of a good foster care home? There appears to be scant scholarship on the characteristics of quality foster care. Cohen (1986) explored elements like the qualifications of child welfare staff, treatment goals for residents, and a perceived normal environment. Quality of care assessments and standards might be elusive. Quality of kinship foster care is extraordinarily difficult to assess. Some studies point to the lack of supervision that many kinship foster homes receive from county social workers. A review of the kinship foster care system in Maryland indicated that fully one-third of kinship foster parents in their sample had not had any contact with their county caseworker in the previous year (Dubowitz, 1990). However, a more consistent approach might be to combine the recommendations put forward by the foster care alumni into one coherent theory of change.

Putting Words into Action

In the end, though, the voices of foster care alumni should inform recommendations for foster care quality improvement. After all, we have lived in and studied foster care. The following are key recommendations from foster care alumni, which we have learned from their own words (Brown & Seita, 2009).

1. "Constantly monitor those in-service delivery roles with the intent to minimize the trauma of intervention and its consequences for the lives of children" (Quinn, 2009, p. 38).
2. "Avoid punishing children for being normal. Anger, for example, is the second recognized stage of grief. This natural stage of the grieving process is too often misunderstood and punished, forcing children to suppress, deny, delay, or avoid this most important step in the healing process" (Quinn, 2009, p. 40).
3. "Screen foster families carefully, monitor them closely, and train them well" (Watson, 2009, p. 95).
4. "Keeping siblings together must be a priority" (Watson, 2009, p. 95).
5. "Foster care must become a preventive measure that is not just an intervention to alleviate immediate crises, but one geared toward preventing lifelong disastrous outcomes" (Folman, 2009, p. 155).
6. "Foster care professionals must learn to listen to the voices of foster children, both present and past. We know what is in our best interests and what is not. We know what policies and procedures work for our betterment and which do not." (Folman, 2009, p. 156).

Perhaps the paradigm shift is here and the time has come to formally include the voices of foster care alumni in the shaping of policy and practice. Their recommendations shared here are not comprehensive, and are only a sample of the thoughts of those who have lived in foster care. Given the relatively limited pool of contributors offering suggestions in this chapter, caution must be used when deliberating and implementing changes in the foster care system.

On the other hand, it is hard, perhaps impossible, to ignore or to delegitimize any thoughts shared by the alumni of foster care toward systemic improvement of such a demonstratively unhelpful way to treat traumatized children as is foster care. At a minimum, increased alumni participation in shaping foster care, along with more emphasis on scholarship in the area of alumni leadership, is warranted.

Acknowledgments

I would like to thank the Michigan State University School of Social Work, the Michigan Agricultural Experiment Station, and Extension/4H at Michigan State University for creating an environment conducive to scholarship and community engagement.

References

Adler, A., & Brett, C. (1998). *Understanding life*. Center City, MN: Hazelden Publishing.
Adoption and Safe Families Act of 1997, Pub. L. 105-89. (1997).
Adoption Assistance and Child Welfare Act of 1980, H.R.3434. (1980).
Ahsan, A. (1996). The Family Preservation and Support Services Program. *The Future of Children*, 6(3), 157–160
Anderson, G., & Seita, J. (2005). Family and social factors affecting youth in the child welfare system. In N. B. Webb (Ed.), *Working with traumatized youth in child welfare (Clinical practice with children, adolescents, and families)* (pp. 67–92). New York: The Guilford Press.
Barney, M. (2009). Upward bound in foster care: What worked for me & what remains to be done. In W. K. Brown & J. Seita (Eds.), *Growing up in the care of strangers: The experiences, insights, and recommendations of eleven former foster kids* (pp. 97–110). Tallahassee, FL: William Gladden Foundation Press.

Barra, A. (2012, June 16). Before and after Title IX: Women in sports. *The New York Times, Sunday Review: The Opinion Pages.* Retrieved from www.nytimes.com/interactive/2012/06/17/opinion/sunday/sundayreview-titleix-timeline.html

Bath, H., & Seita, J. (2018). *The three pillars of trauma.* Winnipeg: University of Winnipeg Publications.

Barth, R. P., & Blackwell, D. L. (1998). Death rates among California's foster care and former foster care populations. *Children and Youth Services Review, 20*(7), 577–604.

Bloom, Sandra L. (2013). *Creating sanctuary: Toward the evolution of sane societies.* London: Routledge,

Brace, C. L. (1880). *The dangerous classes of New York, and twenty years' work among them.* New York: Wynkoop & Hallenbeck.

Brace, E. (Ed.). (1894). *The life of Charles Loring Brace: Chiefly told in his own letters.* New York: C. Scribner's Sons.

Braxton. C. (2009). Pay me now or pay me later. In W. K. Brown & J. Seita (Eds.), *Growing up in the care of strangers: The experiences, insights, and recommendations of eleven former foster kids* (pp. 127–139). Tallahassee, FL: William Gladden Foundation Press.

Brendtro, L., & Brokenleg, M. (2012). *Reclaiming youth at risk: Our hope for the future.* Bloomington, IN: Solution Tree Press.

Brendtro, L. K., Mitchell, M. L., Freado, M. D., & du Toit, L. (2012). The developments audit: From deficits to strengths. *Reclaiming Children and Youth, 21*(1), 7–13.

Brown, W. K., & Seita, J. (Eds.). (2009). *Growing up in the care of strangers: The experiences, insights and recommendations of eleven former foster kids.* Tallahassee, FL: William Gladden Foundation Press.

Brown, W. K., & Seita, J. (2014). *A foster care manifesto: Defining the alumni movement.* Tallahassee, FL: William Gladden Foundation Press.

Caravantes, P. (2013). *The orphan trains: A history perspectives book.* Ann Arbor, MI: Cherry Lake.

Cashin, J. E., & Wood, K. E. (2015). Widows Union. *The world of the Civil War: A daily life encyclopedia.* Santa Barbara, CA: ABC-CLIO.

Child Abuse Prevention and Treatment Act [CAPTA] of 1974, Pub. L. 93-247. (1974).

Child Welfare Information Gateway. (2011, July). About CAPTA: A legislative history. Retrieved from www.childwelfare.gov/pubPDFs/about.pdf#page=2&view=Summary%20of%20Legislative%20History

Child Welfare Information Gateway. (2016). *Major federal legislation concerned with child protection, child welfare, and adoption.* Retrieved from www.childwelfare.gov/pubpdfs/majorfedlegis.pdf

Child Welfare Information Gateway. (2017). *Foster care statistics 2015.* Retrieved from www.childwelfare.gov/pubPDFs/foster.pdf

Cohen, N. A. (1986). Quality of care for youths in group homes. *Child Welfare, 65*(5), 481–494.

Collins, M. E. (2004). Enhancing services to youths leaving foster care: Analysis of recent legislation and its potential impact. *Children and Youth Services Review, 26*(11), 1051–1065.

Cook, J. F. (1995). A history of placing-out: The orphan trains. *Child Welfare, 74*(1), 181–193.

Courtney, M. E. (2005). Book review: Stephen O'Connor, *Orphan trains: The story of Charles Loring Brace and the children he saved and failed. Social Service Review, 79*(4), 742–744.

Courtney, M. E., & Dworsky, A. (2006). Early outcomes for young adults transitioning from out-of-home care in the USA. *Child & Family Social Work, 11*(3), 209–219.

Croke, R. G. (2003). *Situating the HIV/AIDS epidemic in a historical context: A case study of orphans in Nguludi Mission Community, Malawi* (Unpublished doctoral dissertation). University of Cape Town.

Cruess, S. R., Cruess, R. L., & Steinert, Y. (2010). Linking the teaching of professionalism to the social contract: A call for cultural humility. *Medical Teacher, 32*(5), 357–359.

Damon, M., & Affleck, B. (1997). *Good Will Hunting: A screenplay.* New York: Miramax.

Dauge-Roth, A. (2012). Fostering a listening community through testimony: Learning with orphans of the genocide in Rwanda. *Journal of Community Engagement and Scholarship, 5*(2), 61–71.

Day, A. (2009). Coming full circle: From child victim to childcare professional. In W. K. Brown & J. Seita (Eds.), *Growing up in the care of strangers: The experiences, insights, and recommendations of eleven former foster kids* (pp. 41–52). Tallahassee, FL: William Gladden Foundation Press.

Downs, S. W., & Sherraden, M. W. (1983). The orphan asylum in the nineteenth century. *Social Service Review, 57*(2), 272–290.

Dubowitz, H. (1990). Pediatrician's role in preventing child maltreatment. *Pediatric Clinics of North America, 37*(4), 989–1002.

Dworsky, A. (2005). The economic self-sufficiency of Wisconsin's former foster youth. *Children and Youth Services Review, 27*(10), 1085–1118.

Echols, D. (2009). The degree of caring. In W. K. Brown & J. Seita (Eds.), *Growing up in the care of strangers: The experiences, insights, and recommendations of eleven former foster kids* (pp. 53–68). Tallahassee, FL: William Gladden Foundation Press.

Folman, R. D. (2009). It is how children live that matters, not where children live. In W. K. Brown & J. Seita (Eds.), *Growing up in the care of strangers: The experiences, insights, and recommendations of eleven former foster kids* (pp. 140–158). Tallahassee, FL: William Gladden Foundation Press.

Foster Care Independence Act of 1999, Pub. L. 106-169, 113 Stat. 1882, enacted December 14. (1999).

Gallaudet University. (n.d.). *History behind DPN: What happened . . .* Retrieved from www.gallaudet.edu/about/history-and-traditions/deaf-president-now/the-issues/history-behind-dpn

Gannon, J. R., Beatty, J., & Louie, C. (1989). *The week the world heard Gallaudet.* Washington, DC: Gallaudet University Press.

Greeson, J. K., Briggs, E. C., Kisiel, C. L., Layne, C. M., Ake, G. S. III, Ko, S. J., . . . Fairbank, J. A. (2011). Complex trauma and mental health in children and adolescents placed in foster care: Findings from the National Child Traumatic Stress Network. *Child Welfare, 90*(6), 91–108.

Guinn, R. P. (2000). Passage of the Foster Care Independence Act of 1999: A pivotal step on behalf of youth aging out of foster care and into a life of poverty. *Georgetown Journal on Poverty Law and Policy, 7,* 403–411.

Hill, K. (2009). Individuals with Disabilities Act of 2004 and the John H. Chafee Foster Care Independence Act of 1999: What are the policy implications for youth with disabilities transitioning from foster care? *Child Welfare, 88*(2), 5–23.

Holt, M. I. (2006). Adoption reform, orphan trains, and child-saving, 1851–1929. In L. Askeland (Ed.), *Children and youth in adoption, orphanages, and foster care: A historical handbook and guide* (pp. 17–29). Westport, CT: Greenwood.

Hook, J. N., Davis, D. E., Owen, J., Worthington, E. L. Jr., & Utsey, S. O. (2013). Cultural humility: Measuring openness to culturally diverse clients. *Journal of Counseling Psychology, 60*(3), 353–366.

Indian Child Welfare Act [ICWA] of 1978, Pub. L. 95-608, 92 Stat. 3069, enacted November 8. (1978).

Jee, S. H., Conn, A. M., Szilagyi, P. G., Blumkin, A., Baldwin, C. D., & Szilagyi, M. A. (2010). Identification of social-emotional problems among young children in foster care. *Journal of Child Psychology and Psychiatry, 51*(12), 1351–1358.

Jalongo, M. R. (2006). The story of Mary Ellen Wilson: Tracing the origins of child protection in America. *Early Childhood Education Journal, 34*(1), 1–4.

Khan, M. & Hilaali, T. (1997). *Translation of the meanings of the Noble Qur'an in the English language.* Medina, Saudi Arabia: King Fahd Complex for Printing the Holy Qur'an.

Kosanovich, A., Joseph, R. M., & Hasbargen, K. (2005). *Child welfare consent decrees: Analysis of thirty-five court actions from 1995 to 2005.* Washington, DC: Child Welfare League of America.

Kuhn, T. S. (2012). *The structure of scientific revolutions.* Chicago: University of Chicago Press.

Kulka, R. A., Schlenger, W. E., Fairbank, J. A., Hough, R. L., Jordan, B. K., Marmar, C. R., & Weiss, D. S. (1990). *Trauma and the Vietnam war generation: Report of findings from the National Vietnam Veterans Readjustment Study.* New York: Brunner/Mazel.

Kunnie, J., & Goduka, N. I. (Eds.). (2006). *Indigenous peoples' wisdom and power: Affirming our knowledge through narratives.* Farnham, UK: Ashgate Publishing.

Lazoritz, S. (1990). Whatever happened to Mary Ellen? *Child Abuse & Neglect, 14*(2), 143–149.

Levesque, R. J. (1995). The failure of foster care reform: Revolutionizing the most radical blueprint. *Maryland Journal of Contemporary Legal Issues, 6*(1), 1–35.

Lopez, P., & Allen, P. J. (2007). Addressing the health needs of adolescents transitioning out of foster care. *Pediatric Nursing, 33*(4), 345–355.

MacEachron, A. E., Gustavsson, N. S., Cross, S., & Lewis, A. (1996). The effectiveness of the Indian Child Welfare Act of 1978. *Social Service Review, 70*(3), 451–463.

Mallon, G. P. (2013). From the editor: The legend of Mary Ellen Wilson and Etta Wheeler: Child maltreatment and protection today. *Child Welfare, 92*(2), 9–11.

Marten, J. A. (2005). *Childhood and child welfare in the progressive era: A brief history with documents.* Boston, MA: Bedford/St. Martins.

McCall, H. J. (2003). When successful alternative students "disengage" from regular school. *Reclaiming Children and Youth, 12*(2), 113–117.

Michaels, D., & Levine, C. (1992). Estimates of the number of motherless youth orphaned by AIDS in the United States. *Journal of the American Medical Association, 268*(24), 3456–3461.

Michigan Department of Health & Human Services. (2017). Retrieved from www.michigan.gov/mdhhs/0,5885,7-339-71550_2941_4868_4897---,00.html

Michigan Mental Health Code of 1974, Act 258, Section 330.1222, Sec. 222. (1). Retrieved from www.legislature.mi.gov/(S(jxv1fgpskltimazzwd5xiypw))/mileg.aspx?page=GetObject&objectname=mcl-Act-258-of-1974

Multiethnic Placement Act [MEPA] of 1994, Pub. L. 103-82, enacted October 20. (1994).

Mignon, S. (2016). *Child welfare in the United States: Challenges, policy, and practice*. New York: Springer Publishing Company.

Murray, K. O., & Gesiriech, S. (2005). *A brief legislative history of the child welfare system*. Retrieved from www.pewtrusts.org/en/research-and-analysis/reports/2004/11/01/a-brief-legislative-history-of-the-child-welfare-system

Myers, J. (2008). A short history of child protection in America. *Family Law Quarterly, 42*(3), 449–463.

O'Connor, S. (2004). *Orphan trains: The story of Charles Loring Brace and the children he saved and failed*. Chicago: University of Chicago Press.

Office for Civil Rights, U.S. Department of Education. (2015). *Title IX and sex discrimination*. Retrieved from www2.ed.gov/about/offices/list/ocr/docs/tix_dis.html

Ortega, R. M., & Faller, K. C. (2011). Training child welfare workers from an intersectional cultural humility perspective: A paradigm shift. *Child Welfare, 90*(5), 27–49.

Palmer, S. E., Brown, R. A., Rae-Grant, N. I., & Loughlin, M. J. (1999). Responding to children's disclosure of familial abuse: What survivors tell us. *Child Welfare, 78*(2), 259–282.

Pecora, P. J., Kessler, R. C., O'Brien, K., White, C. R., Williams, J., Hiripi, E., . . . Herrick, M. A. (2006). Educational and employment outcomes of adults formerly placed in foster care: Results from the Northwest Foster Care Alumni Study. *Children and Youth Services Review, 28*(12), 1459–1481.

Pecora, P. J., White, C. R., Jackson, L. J., & Wiggins, T. (2009). Mental health of current and former recipients of foster care: A review of recent studies in the USA. *Child & Family Social Work, 14*(2), 132–146.

Pecora, P. J., Whittaker, J. K., Maluccio, A. N., & Barth, R. P. (2012). *The child welfare challenge: Policy, practice, and research*. New Brunswick, CT: Aldine Transaction.

Pfohl, S. J. (1977). The "discovery" of child abuse. *Social Problems, 24*(3), 310–323.

Pike, D. R., Millspaugh, C. M., & DeSalvatore, G. (2005). Controlling behavior or reclaiming youth? *Reclaiming Children and Youth, 13*(4), 213–217.

Quinn, P. (2009). Peter's story. In W. K. Brown & J. Seita (Eds.), *Growing up in the care of strangers: The experiences, insights, and recommendations of eleven former foster kids* (pp. 25–40). Tallahassee, FL: William Gladden Foundation Press.

Reilly, T. (2003). Transition from care: Status and outcomes of youth who age out of foster care. *Child Welfare, 82*(6), 727–746.

Roman, N. P., & Wolfe, P. (1995). *Web of failure: The relationship between foster care and homelessness*. Washington, DC: National Alliance to End Homelessness.

Smith, S. (2012). *In the child's best interest?* (Doctoral dissertation).

Seita, J. (2010). Missing data: Discovering the private logic of adult wary youth. *Reclaiming Youth: The Journal of Strength Based Interventions, 19*(2), 51–54.

Seita, J., & Brendtro, L. (2004). *Kids who outwit adults* (revised ed.). Bloomington, IN: Solution Tree.

Seita, J., Mitchell, M., & Tobin, C. L. (1996). *In whose best interest? One child's odyssey, a nation's responsibility*. Yorktown, PA: Continental Press.

Seita, J. R. (2005). Kids without family privilege: Mobilizing youth development. *Reclaiming Children & Youth: The Journal of Strength Based Interventions, 14*(2), 80–84.

Seita, J. R., & Brendtro, L. K. (2007). Attachment and transformation: A positive bias. *Reclaiming Children and Youth: The Journal of Strength Based Interventions, 16*(3).

Semali, L. M., & Kincheloe, J. L. (2002). *What is indigenous knowledge? Voices from the academy*. London: Routledge.

Shelman, E. A., & Lazoritz, S. (2005). *The Mary Ellen Wilson child abuse case and the beginning of children's rights in 19th century America*. Jefferson, NC: McFarland.

Stevens, L. (2016, June 8). Survey shows rapid growth in online shopping. *The Wall Street Journal*. Retrieved from www.wsj.com/articles/survey-shows-rapid-growth-in-online-shopping-1465358582

Stoltzfus, E. (2017). *Child welfare: An overview of federal programs and their current funding*. Congressional Research Service Report. Retrieved from https://fas.org/sgp/crs/misc/R43458.pdf

Sutherland, E. (2009). Who am I? In W. K. Brown & J. Seita (Eds.), *Growing up in the care of strangers: The experiences, insights, and recommendations of eleven former foster kids* (pp. 111–126). Tallahassee, FL: William Gladden Foundation Press.

Thomas, M. P. Jr. (1971). Child abuse and neglect part I: Historical overview, legal matrix, and social perspectives. *NCL Review, 50*, 293–321.

Trammell, R. (2009). Orphan train myths and legal reality. *Modern American, 5*(2), 3–13.

Tyler, K. A. (2006). A qualitative study of early family histories and transitions of homeless youth. *Journal of Interpersonal Violence, 21*(10), 1385–1393.

Unrau, Y. (2011). From foster care to college: The Seita scholars program at Western Michigan University. *Reclaiming Children and Youth, 20*(2), 17–20.

Unrau, Y. A., Seita, J. R., & Putney, K. S. (2008). Former foster youth remember multiple placement moves: A journey of loss and hope. *Children and Youth Services Review, 30*(11), 1256–1266.

U.S. Bureau of Indian Affairs. (n.d.). Retrieved from https://www.bia.gov/bia

U.S. Department of Health & Human Services (Administration for Children and Families, Administration on Children, Youth & Families, Children's Bureau). (2015). *The AFCARS report. Preliminary FY 2014 estimates as of July 2015. No. 22*. Retrieved from www.acf.hhs.gov/sites/default/files/cb/afcarsreport22.pdf

Warren, A. (1998). *Orphan train rider: One boy's true story*. Boston, MA: Houghton Mifflin Harcourt.

Watkins, S. A. (1990). The Mary Ellen myth: Correcting child welfare history. *Social Work, 35*(6), 500–503.

Watson, D. (2009). Surviving the storm inside me: Growing past foster care. In W. K. Brown & J. Seita (Eds.), *Growing up in the care of strangers: The experiences, insights, and recommendations of eleven former foster kids* (pp. 83–96). Tallahassee, FL: William Gladden Foundation Press.

Webb, M. (2009). Dark past, bright future: Growing past family violence, neglect & abandonment. In W. K. Brown & J. Seita (Eds.), *Growing up in the care of strangers: The experiences, insights, and recommendations of eleven former foster kids* (pp. 69–81). Tallahassee, FL: William Gladden Foundation Press.

Zlotnick, C., Tam, T. W., & Soman, L. A. (2012). Life course outcomes on mental and physical health: The impact of foster care on adulthood. *American Journal of Public Health, 102*(3), 534–540.

2

Foster Care Placement Process and Settings

Donna M. Aguiniga and Elissa E. Madden

There is a consensus within the field of child welfare that youth deserve a safe, stable home environment that supports their achievement of developmental milestones and promotes positive social, emotional, behavioral, and cognitive outcomes. For youth who have come to the attention of child welfare authorities, out-of-home placement in a foster care setting, also referred to as substitute care in some states, is often seen as the best way to ensure that they will experience a safe and caring environment. Youth are most often referred to the child welfare system due to maltreatment, abandonment, incarceration, incapacitation (e.g., mental health issues, substance abuse), and parental death that leaves them without a caregiver. Foster care is defined as "24-hour substitute care for youth placed away from their parents or guardians, and for whom the State agency has placement and care responsibility" (U.S. Government Publishing Office, 2011, p. 267).

While foster care is an inclusive term that encompasses a wide array of settings, the term foster care most commonly refers to the temporary placement of youth who have been removed from their parents' care into foster family homes, homes of relatives, or group homes, as well as more specialized settings such as emergency shelters, residential facilities, and independent or transitional living situations (Child Welfare Information Gateway [henceforth cited as CWIG], 2016a). Regardless, the Social Security Act of 1935 mandates that youth be placed in the least restrictive environment that can adequately meet the youth's needs. The term "least restrictive" is a child welfare concept that refers to the most family-like setting. Some research suggests that the type of placement selected can help to reduce or mitigate some of the trauma that youth experience as a result of being removed from their primary caregivers and entering the foster care system (Chapman, Wall, Barth, & NSCAW Research Group, 2004; Ehrle & Geen, 2002; James, 2004; UC Davis Center for Human Services, 2008). This is an important consideration for child welfare professionals who work with youth in the foster care system, as the type of placement selected has the potential to assist youth in the development of healthy secure relationships.

Attachment Theory

John Bowlby's and Mary Salter Ainsworth's conceptualization and expansion of attachment theory provide a theoretical basis for understanding the importance of stable caregivers in the lives of youth (e.g., Dozier, Stovall, Albus, & Bates, 2001; Goldsmith, Oppenheim, & Wanlass, 2004). Attachment refers to an emotional bond between two people in which there is an expectation of care and protection (Goldberg, 2000). Attachment theory suggests that children's early attachment experiences with caregivers influence their personality development, and their ability to form supportive relationships, as well as their capacity to overcome adversity (Bowlby, 1958; Golding, 2008). The theory posits that youth learn about themselves, and what they can expect from the world and others, through these early relationships.

Therefore, the quality of care that youth receive can have a profound impact on their social functioning and how they perceive themselves and others (Schuerger, 2002). For example, youth who experience responsive, nurturing, and consistent caregiving are more likely to view the world as a safe place and believe that people generally have their best interests in mind. They are also more likely to develop a positive self-image and secure attachments with others. In contrast, youth who are cared for in a harsh, inconsistent, or unresponsive manner learn to view the world as an untrustworthy and unpredictable place to live. Youth who have been cared for in this manner may develop insecure attachments with others and perceive themselves as inadequate or unlovable (Berk, 2000; Rolfe, 2004). Youth who have a consistent caregiver develop a sense of trust and confidence that impacts their future relationships, as attachment has been found to be related to multiple dimensions, including social, psychological, and behavioral ones (Alhusen, Hayat, & Gross, 2013; Bowlby, 1988; Sroufe, Egeland, Carlson, & Collins, 2005).

Child welfare advocates and professionals have long recognized the significance of attachment theory to the child welfare system and have advocated for foster placements that allow youth the opportunity to form attachments to their caregivers. Quiroga and Hamilton-Giachritsis' (2016) systematic review of the literature concluded that youth in family foster home placements demonstrate higher levels of secure attachment than those in institutional settings.

Foster Care Licensure

States license foster homes and facilities to provide care to youth in the foster care system. While the requirements to become a licensed foster home vary, state licensing authorities are responsible for establishing and maintaining standards for foster placements (CWIG, 2014). The purpose of these standards is to minimize risk and to ensure the overall health, safety, and well-being of youth in the foster care system (CWIG, 2014, 2015). Federal law 42 U.S.C. § 671 (a)(20) requires that all states conduct an abuse and neglect background check on prospective foster parents and all adult members of their household. In addition to a registry check within the current state of residence, the law requires that states check the child abuse or neglect registries of any states in which the prospective foster parents may have lived during the preceding 5 years to ensure that no prior instances of maltreatment occurred. The Adam Walsh Child Protection and Safety Act of 2006 strengthened existing laws, by mandating federal criminal background checks for all prospective foster and adoptive parents, including relative caregivers. In addition, the Act stipulated specific crimes that serve as a 5-year or permanent barrier to licensure (e.g., felony child abuse or neglect; domestic violence; or a crime against children, such as child pornography). Additionally, most states require out-of-home caregivers to complete additional in-service training on a yearly basis on topics related to child development, home and child safety, behavior management and discipline, cultural sensitivity, trauma, attachment, separation, and loss. This annual training ensures that out-of-home caregivers will remain up to date on the latest standards and research related to caring for youth in the foster care system.

In addition to extensive background checks, prospective foster families must pass what child welfare officials refer to most commonly as a home study. Home studies are used to assess the safety of the home and the readiness of the prospective caregivers to care for youth who have experienced prior maltreatment and trauma (Chanmugam et al., 2017). Among other things, home studies allow child welfare agencies to assess the family's marital and individual family relationships, their motivation for becoming foster parents, their expectations of youth in foster care, their opinions about discipline, their ability to care for youth who have experienced abuse and/or neglect, as well as their ability to work with youth who exhibit specific kinds of emotional, behavioral, and health needs (CWIG, 2014; Crea, Barth, & Chintapalli, 2007). Home studies provide important insight to child welfare agencies to help them determine if the prospective foster parents' home meets the minimum physical requirements, and if they will be able to provide a safe, appropriate, and nurturing placement for the youth in their care (CWIG, 2014).

While licensing standards often differ greatly from state to state, minimum housing requirements most often include a telephone, utilities (e.g., heat, electricity, water), and adequate space for living, including space that allows youth privacy and their own bed (CWIG, 2014). It is important to note that terms such as "adequate" and "sufficient" are defined by each state. States may provide *variances* for homes that can meet a standard in an equivalent way. For example, a kinship placement without safe drinking water (e.g., water is from a tainted well, or the community water supply does not meet minimum state guidelines for safe drinking water) can be given a variance if the placement purchases bottled water for use (CLASP, 2012; U.S. Department of Health & Human Services, 2011). Additionally, legislation passed in 2008 gave states the ability to grant kinship care providers non-safety-related *waivers* in order to better facilitate the placement of youth with relatives (U.S. Department of Health & Human Services, 2011). Beltran and Epstein (2012) note that states' varying standards surrounding licensure "raise the question about which is the best standard or how standards can be combined to create a model standard" (p. 10). Examples of varying standards include: 1) pre-license training requirements; 2) home study/assessment criteria; 3) capacity standards for the number of foster youth the home can accommodate; and 4) square footage requirements for the home and individual bedrooms. Without national standards to guide the licensure process, it is difficult to argue that all states take equal care in licensing foster care placements that provide an optimal environment for children in care.

Recruitment Barriers

Between 2006 and 2012, the annual number of youth in foster care experienced a downward trend from approximately 505,000 in 2006 to 397,000 in 2012, with national estimates indicating more than a 20% decline during this period; however, more recently, the total number of youth in care has increased, with reported increases in 2013, 2014, and 2015 (U.S. Department of Health & Human Services, 2015, 2016). The recent influx in the number of youth into the foster care system has highlighted both the need for licensed foster homes and the challenges that child welfare agencies have faced in recent years regarding the recruitment and retention of foster families (Chipungu & Bent-Goodley, 2004; Koh, 2010). The extent of the foster home shortage is difficult to ascertain as foster care systems differ by state in their administration (e.g., county-wide versus state-wide). Additionally, a centralized list of out-of-home placements is not maintained by federal or state authorities.

Beltran and Epstein's (2012) evaluation of foster care licensing policies for all 50 states and the District of Columbia found a number of well-intended standards that inadvertently prohibit licensure of otherwise qualified prospective foster parents. These "problematic standards" included upper-age caps on caregivers, citizenship or residency documentation requirements, as well as standards regarding education, language, literacy, income, and employment (p. 63). Beltran and Epstein also note that age and documentation requirements may disproportionately affect potential relative caregivers seeking to foster their kin. Older relatives, such as grandparents, or relatives without residency or citizenship documentation may be willing to take in youth in their family, but will be unable to do so because of stringent licensing requirements. Given the unique nature of kinship care arrangements, kinship care placements will be addressed in greater depth later in the chapter.

The complexity of emotional, behavioral, developmental, and health needs of youth who enter the foster care system is well documented and serves as an additional barrier to the recruitment of foster placements (e.g., Casey Family Services, 2003; Deutsch et al., 2015; Smith & Howard, 1999). Other barriers to becoming a licensed foster home that are identified in the literature include inadequate, poor, or incomplete information provided by the licensing agency, unsupportive workers, challenges with completing the training, and the presence of a difficult or confusing licensure process (Cain, 2015; Riley-Behringer & Cage, 2014).

Retention Barriers

The shortage of foster homes is also due to challenges in retaining licensed foster parents. Some foster parents only commit to provide care for a specific youth (e.g., kinship homes), so attrition of these placements is expected. In 2015, it was estimated that 30% of youth in care are placed with kinship caregivers (Annie E. Casey Foundation, 2017). However, there is evidence that foster parents quit foster care at a greater rate than can be explained by the loss of child-specific licensed homes. For example, Gibbs and Wildfire's (2007) analysis of foster parenting in three states found that foster parents' median length of service was 8 to 14 months, and that, "47% to 62% of foster parents exit foster parenting within a year of the first placement in their home" (p. 597).

A common barrier to retention of foster homes is the poor communication and relationships foster parents report having with child welfare professionals (Geiger, Hayes, & Lietz, 2013; MacGregor, Rodger, Cummings, & Leschied, 2006; Rodger, Cummings, & Leschied, 2006). Research suggests that foster parents receive limited information about the youth in their care and often feel overlooked or disrespected as a member of a youth's care team. High caseloads and caseworker turnover further exacerbate the communication problems between caseworkers and foster parents (Geiger et al., 2013). Inadequate financial support and difficulties meeting the needs of youth in care are also common factors that influence a foster parent's decision to stop fostering (Chipungu & Bent-Goodley, 2004; Geiger et al., 2013; MacGregor et al., 2006). In these circumstances, many foster parents find themselves overwhelmed and under-prepared to foster, without adequate communication with and limited access to caseworkers who can help mitigate their problems and concerns. In addition, some foster parents stop fostering because they are under-utilized as caregivers; it is estimated that one-third of licensed foster homes will not have a placement in any given year (Cox, Orme, & Rhodes, 2002; Marcenko, Brennan, & Lyons, 2009). Foster parents may lose their enthusiasm or motivation for fostering when their perception may be that they are not needed. Additionally, foster parents may not see the need to continue annual training and licensing requirements when their homes are not being utilized.

Permanency and Concurrent Planning

During the 1980s and 1990s, state and federal officials introduced a number of initiatives designed to promote permanency and reduce the number of youth in foster care. Permanency can be defined as "a legal, permanent *family* living arrangement, that is, reunification with the birth family, living with relatives, guardianship, or adoption" (U.S. Department of Health & Human Services, 2005, p. 2). The Adoption Assistance and Child Welfare Act of 1980 (AACWA) was the first piece of legislation specifically intended to address "foster care drift"—youth who remained in foster care indefinitely and experienced multiple placements, without returning to their families or having their parents' parental rights terminated so that they might become available for adoption (Thoennes, 2001; Wilhelm, 2002). The AACWA increased the role of the courts in child protection matters and stipulated that states must consider all placement options, including family reunification, placement with relatives, adoption, as well as long-term foster care (Edwards, 2004). The AACWA also required states to make "reasonable efforts" to prevent the need for placement of youth in foster care and to ensure that youth could return to their birth families after removal (CWIG, 2016b, p. 23). However, critics of the legislation observed that the AACWA provided little guidance regarding what constituted reasonable efforts (Crosson-Tower, 2012; Wilhelm, 2002).

Adoption and Safe Families Act of 1997

In 1997, Congress enacted the Adoption and Safe Families Act (ASFA) with the intention of refocusing efforts to promote safety, permanency, and well-being for youth in the foster care system. In an effort to expedite permanency for youth languishing in the foster care system, the ASFA established strict time frames for states to initiate proceedings to terminate parental rights for youth unable to return to their family's care (CWIG, 2016b; U.S. General Accounting Office, 2004). For example, under the ASFA, states are required to file a petition to terminate parental rights in cases where a youth had been in care for 15 out of the most recent 22 months. The Act also outlined specific circumstances under which states could forgo efforts to reunify families. Circumstances under which efforts could be discontinued include: 1) cases in which a parent's rights to a sibling have been involuntarily terminated; 2) when a parent has killed or assaulted another child; or 3) instances in which the youth has been subjected to aggravated circumstances (e.g., abandonment, torture), as defined in state law. Additionally, the ASFA authorized the provision of financial incentives to states to increase the number of adoptions.

The ASFA also stipulated that long-term care would no longer be a viable permanency option for youth in care. Historically, the term long-term care was used to refer to the indefinite placement of youth in foster care without another permanency plan until the youth exited the foster care system at the age of emancipation (i.e., usually 18 or another pre-determined age stipulated by each state) (Lowry, 2004; Mallon, n.d.). However, the legislation included an alternative permanency category intended for older youth in care, termed "another planned permanent living arrangement" (APPLA). Fiermonte and Renne (2002) note that APPLA is typically utilized when more desirable permanency options such as reunification, relative placement, or adoption have been ruled out. The authors outline three situations in which APPLA is most appropriate: 1) older youth who request emancipation; 2) those who have a significant bond with a parent or caregiver who is not able to care for the youth due to a disability; or 3) when a Native American tribe requests APPLA as the permanency plan for the youth. The enactment of the ASFA represented a fundamental shift in thought within the field of child welfare, as it placed increased emphasis on child safety, permanency, and well-being over family preservation and reunification efforts.

The ASFA also permitted that permanency efforts be made concurrently, allowing child welfare professionals to both work toward reunification with family, but also develop an alternate permanent placement plan for youth while in care. This concurrent planning works in conjunction with the strict reunification guidelines, allowing a state to more easily transition youth whose parents have had their rights terminated into a permanent placement. D'Andrade, Frame, and Berrick (2006) found that child welfare professionals support the philosophical tenets of concurrent planning and believe it leads to faster and more stable permanent homes for youth. However, professionals also recognized that concurrent planning provided foster parents with a clearer picture of their role and "made fostering a more emotionally difficult job" (D'Andrade et al., 2006, p. 88).

Placement Considerations

Preference for Relatives

Enacted as part of the Personal Responsibility and Work Opportunity Reconciliation Act of 1996, federal law "provides that the State shall consider giving preference to an adult relative over a non-related caregiver when determining a placement for a youth, provided that the relative caregiver meets all relevant State child protection standards" (42 U.S.C. § 471). This preference for kinship care was reinforced with the passage of the Fostering Connections to Success and Increasing Adoptions Act of 2008 (Fostering Connections Act), which helped to ensure that youth in foster care maintain family ties. Specifically, the Fostering Connections Act requires that within 30 days of a youth's removal from the home, child welfare agencies make reasonable efforts to identify and notify grandparents and other relatives who might be available to care for the youth. As part of the notification process, states must also provide relatives with information about how to become a licensed foster parent, as well as information on the various services and supports that are available in the state for youth in such placements (CLASP & American Bar Association Center on Children and the Law, 2010). In order to facilitate placement of youth with relatives in safe, licensed placements, the legislation also stipulates that on a case-by-case basis, child welfare agencies may waive non-safety-related licensing standards for relative foster family homes (U.S. Department of Health & Human Services, 2011).

While federal policy supports a preference for relative placement, CLASP (2012) found that perceptions of licensed kinship care impact options presented to prospective kinship providers. Child welfare agencies that support family connections were more likely to review foster care licensing, as compared to those who felt that kin were likely to share negative characteristics with the youth's parents. Even when kin receive information about becoming a licensed foster home, they may still not receive a full picture of placement and permanency options for the youth. Riley-Behringer and Cage (2014) noted that prospective kinship caregivers reported receiving insufficient information about the benefits of legal guardianship versus becoming a licensed foster care placement for their kin.

Consideration of the Youth's Age and Preferences

Another consideration for child welfare agencies in placement decisions is the age of the youth. The permanency designation, "another planned permanent living arrangement" (APPLA) identified in the Adoption and Safe Families Act of 1997 offers a permanency option for youth who are older (i.e., 14 or older in most states), who cannot return home to their families and who do not wish to be adopted or placed with relatives (Fiermonte & Renne, 2002; Renne & Mallon, 2014). While some critics argue that APPLA is overused by child welfare agencies, this permanency designation is intended to provide agencies with flexibility to honor a youth's wishes by pursuing living situations that are positive for the youth, but will not be made legally permanent through adoption or guardianship (Renne & Mallon, 2014). For example, APPLA is an ideal permanency plan for a youth aged 16 and over who does not wish to be adopted, but who has a positive and supportive placement with his or her foster parents. Under APPLA, the youth is allowed to remain in the foster placement until the age of emancipation, provided the caregiver is agreeable to providing long-term care, without fear that they will be moved to another placement in pursuit of another more preferred permanency goal.

Siblings

Placement with siblings supports maintenance of family ties, the continuity of important attachments, and can help to mitigate the trauma and loss associated with foster care placement (CWIG, 2013; Herrick & Piccus, 2005; McCormick, 2010). Additionally, placement with siblings provides much-needed emotional and social connections into adulthood (CWIG, 2013). Federal policy supports sibling placements by encouraging efforts to place siblings together or, if not possible or in the best interests of the youth, to ensure that siblings have an opportunity to maintain their connections with each other (CWIG, 2013). Furthermore, the Fostering Connections to Success and Increasing Adoptions Act provides the possibility that "siblings placed in the same home as a youth eligible for ongoing Title IV-E federal guardianship payments may also receive support even if they are not otherwise eligible" (Beltran, 2014, p. 59); thus ensuring that the eligibility of one sibling for federal guardianship payments does not cancel out the status of another. For example, one federal stipulation is that a youth must have been residing with his or her guardian for at least 6 months to be eligible for the Title IV-E guardianship payment. However, a sibling may have been placed more recently in the same kinship placement. With the Fostering Connections to Success and Increasing Adoptions Act, siblings are now eligible for the guardianship payment as well. This provision is intended to promote child well-being by allowing siblings to remain together in kinship placements regardless of their individual financial status (Children's Defense Fund, 2010). Yet, despite this legislative progress, it is important to note that there is no federal mandate which stipulates that siblings must be placed together.

A key barrier to sibling placement is the lack of foster care homes willing to accept siblings, particularly large sibling groups. Leathers (2005) found that one of the most common reasons for child welfare professionals to separate siblings was "lack of placement resources" (p. 807). However, for those youth who were able to be placed together, there was an increased likelihood of adoption when consistently placed with siblings rather than when placed separately (Leathers, 2005). Therefore, siblings placed together may have a greater likelihood of obtaining a permanent home, but insufficient foster placements that can keep siblings together are available to child welfare agencies.

Race and Culture

Race and culture can influence the likelihood of a child or youth to need a foster care placement. Disproportionality of youth of color is seen at multiple points in child protective services decision-making (e.g., Church, Gross, & Baldwin, 2005; Courtney et al., 1996; CWIG, 2011; Fluke, Yuan, Hedderson, & Curtis, 2003; Garland, Landsverk, & Lau, 2003; Mumpower & McClelland, 2014). Specific to out-of-home placement, Black and American Indian youth are more likely to be placed in care and less likely to be reunited with their families than their White counterparts (CWIG, 2011; Miller, 2008). Russell and Macgill's (2015) analysis of foster care entry rates found that youth of color were more likely to enter care in states with low minority populations. It may be that in these states, racism, unfamiliarity with populations of color, and/or a lack of advocates and professionals of color cultivate a child protective system that contributes to disproportionate rates of youth of color in care.

Two distinct federal protocols around race and ethnicity exist in the child welfare system for youth entering foster care. One is specific to American Indian and Alaska Native youth; the other is for youth from all other cultural, racial, and ethnic groups. These divergent protocols, and their subsequent impact on foster care placement, bring to light both the unique relationship between Native Americans and the United States government and the disproportionate number of youth of color in care.

Indian Child Welfare Act

The Indian Child Welfare Act (ICWA) supports the high value placed on kinship care among American Indian and Alaska Native (AI/AN) communities. Enacted as federal law in 1978, the ICWA was a response to the overrepresentation of AI/AN youth placed in out-of-home care (Crofoot & Harris, 2012). Prior to the ICWA, an estimated 25%–35% of AI/AN youth were removed from their parents for alleged child maltreatment and, typically, placed in non-American Indian and Alaska Native foster placements (Myers, 2008). The ICWA recognized the sovereignty of tribes in the identification and placement of their youth and established minimum requirements to ensure that tribes had jurisdiction over their youth. ICWA requirements include an ordered preference for foster care placement that supports a youth's family, tribal, and cultural connections and mandate expert witness testimony

Multiethnic Placement Act of 1994 and Interethnic Placement Act of 1996

The Multiethnic Placement Act as Amended by the Interethnic Provisions (MEPA-IEP) sought to remove barriers to permanency for youth in the child welfare system related to race and ethnicity (Mitchell et al., 2005). Prior to the passing of this legislation, selection of foster and adoption placements for youth in foster care were predominantly determined by the youth's race or ethnicity (Popple & Vecchiolla, 2007). The MEPA, passed in 1994, addressed this by stipulating that child-placing agencies receiving funds from the federal government could no longer use race or ethnicity as a basis for decision-making in foster care or adoptive placements. The legislation also mandated that states must make diligent efforts to recruit foster and adoptive families that reflected the ethnic diversity of the youth in their care (Pecora, Whittaker, Maluccio, Barth, & DePanfilis, 2012).

The Interethnic Placement Act (IEPA) later amended the MEPA in 1996. The legislation strengthened provisions in the MEPA related to states' diligent recruitment of foster and adoptive homes that mirror the ethnic and racial backgrounds of children in care. Additionally, other key provisions of the legislation stipulated that states and other child welfare placement entities receiving federal funding could not delay or deny: 1) qualified individuals the opportunity to become a foster or adoptive parent based on the race, color, or national origin of the parent; or 2) a youth's foster care or adoptive placement based upon the race, color, or national origin of the parent or the youth (CWIG, 2016b). While the MEPA and IEPA were passed with the intention of increasing the number of foster and adoptive placements of color available to youth in care, a core criticism of the legislation was that it did not provide additional federal funding for targeted recruitment efforts to communities of color (Mitchell et al., 2005).

Placement Decision-Making

While federal legislation provides broad guidelines about placements for youth in care, the actual placement decision-making process is primarily a matter of individual caseworker decision-making and placement availability. Lee and Thompson (2008) note that while policy and conventional wisdom suggest that youth experiencing fewer problems should be placed in less restrictive settings, there is very little evidence or direction available to help child welfare practitioners determine which youth are best served in which environments. The complexity of variables entailed in placement decisions, the limited predictive power of available models, and the influence of individual caseworkers on placement decisions inhibit the usefulness of available research to guide placement decision-making (Bhatti-Sinclair & Sutcliffe, 2013). Currently, there are no protocols used nationwide to help agencies determine the specific types of placements where youth should be placed.

Foster Care Placements

This section reviews a variety of foster care placement types, from home-based settings to institutional facilities. While the placement types vary, each serves to provide youth in care with a safe and stable environment that provides them the emotional support, developmentally-appropriate experiences, and, if necessary, therapeutic treatment they need. To facilitate the ability of youth to participate in age-appropriate events, Congress passed the Preventing Sex Trafficking and Strengthening Families Act in 2014, which permits a designated foster caregiver, whether in a home or institution, the ability to determine a foster youth's participation in "extracurricular, enrichment, cultural, and social activities" (Public Law 113-183, § 111). This new policy both recognizes the decision-making authority of foster caregivers, and promotes child and youth well-being and a sense of normalcy for foster youth by promoting their timely participation in developmentally-appropriate activities (Children's Defense Fund, 2015; Pokempner, Mordecai, Rosado, & Subrahmanyam, 2015).

Home-Based Settings

Home-based settings are preferred to other placement options for children in the child welfare system. Most child welfare advocates agree that home-based settings provide youth in care with increased stability, as well as opportunities for youth to develop positive attachments to their caregivers (Dozier et al., 2014; Roy, Rutter, & Pickles, 2000). While the names of some settings vary from state to state, the following section reviews the most common forms of home-based settings.

Family Foster Care

Family foster care placements refer to placements in the community that are designed to provide a family setting for youth in care. While licensing standards for foster homes vary from state to state, family foster homes provide care for a small number of youth who have limited medical, behavioral, or emotional needs. Foster parents must go through a rigorous vetting and licensing process to be eligible to provide care for foster youth (Berrick, 1998). Unlike other placement settings, the sole focus of this placement setting is providing a child with a safe and nurturing place to live while their parents work with child welfare agency officials and the court system to address safety issues that led to the youth's removal from the home. Family foster placements are appropriate for youth of all ages who can participate in the family life and reside in the community without posing a danger to themselves or others. Typical services that are provided to youth in these settings include: supervised visitation with the youth's birth family; counseling to address issues related to prior trauma; coordination of all medical needs, including medication monitoring and routine annual physical and dental check-ups; and discharge planning when the youth is ready to move to a different placement (e.g., return to parental care, move to a kinship placement, or move to a more restrictive setting).

Many of these family foster homes can be referred to as foster-adopt homes, referencing the foster parents' desire to adopt a youth who has been placed in their care. It was not until the 1980s that foster parents began receiving support as prospective adoptive families. A shift toward viewing them as "valuable resources for waiting children" took more than three decades to materialize (CWIG, 2013, p. 2). Today, in many states, foster-adopt homes are the preferred placement for youth in care who cannot return home or be placed with relatives, as they promote attachment and help to ensure that the youth has a family (CWIG, 2013, 2014). According to the most current statistics (Fiscal Year [FY] 2015), more than half (52%) of the youth in care placed for adoption were adopted by their foster parents (U.S. Department of Health & Human Services, 2016).

Therapeutic Foster Care

The term "therapeutic foster care placements," also called treatment foster care placements, refers to highly structured family-based settings in the community that provide individualized support and therapeutic services for youth in foster care who have more complex medical, behavioral, or emotional needs (Boyd, 2013). Therapeutic foster care placements are most appropriate for youth with emotional, behavioral, or health problems who require increased structured and supportive care. These homes provide a community-based alternative to more restrictive and intensive placements (e.g., residential treatment centers) and, thus, are one of the most common types of placement for youth in care with complex needs (Popple & Vecchiolla, 2007). Therapeutic foster care placements coordinate with child welfare agencies to provide an intensive range of therapeutic services to youth which include services offered in the traditional foster home setting, as well as more specialized services targeted to address their behavioral, emotional, and/or health needs.

Research comparing outcomes between youth in therapeutic foster care placements and outcomes in group settings that are not family-based suggest that youth in therapeutic care experience more favorable outcomes related to time in locked settings, criminal referrals, and delinquent peers at follow-up (Chamberlain & Reid, 1998; Leve & Chamberlain, 2005; Leve, Chamberlain, & Reid, 2005). Furthermore, Chamberlain and Reid (1998) found that compared to males in more intensive settings, male youth in therapeutic foster care settings were more likely to complete treatment and return home to their family.

Kinship Care

Kinship care refers to the placement of youth with relatives or individuals with whom the youth has had a previous relationship (e.g., teacher, coach, friend of the family), rather than placement in a traditional foster home or more restrictive out-of-home setting. The Fostering Connections to Success and Increasing Adoptions Act of 2008 requires child welfare agencies to make reasonable efforts, within 30 days of a child's removal from the home, to identify and notify grandparents and other relatives who might be available to care for the youth. As such, the number of kinship placements has experienced a dramatic increase in recent years. This shift has occurred for other reasons, including state and federal preferences for kinship care and an increased understanding of the emotional and psychological benefits of a youth's placement with family. While kinship placements are not always possible, there is some evidence that kinship placements are more likely than traditional foster care placements to reduce the stigma and trauma of separation from parents and family (Crosson-Tower, 2012). Furthermore, the literature suggests that youth in kinship placements experience fewer behavioral and mental health problems as compared to youth in family foster homes (Sakai, Lin, & Flores, 2011; Winokur, Holtan, & Valentine, 2009). As states and agencies move toward a family-centered approach to permanency placement, some advocates believe that kinship care has the potential to reduce the strain on child welfare agencies that are facing a critical shortage of qualified placements, as this is typically the most ready and available source of placements for youth in care (CWIG, 2010).

Specialized Settings

Specialized settings are most commonly used at different points of transition during a youth's time in foster care; for example, when a youth makes the transition into care, moves to a new placement, or when he or she is preparing to exit the foster care system. A discussion of specialized settings is provided below.

Emergency Shelter

Emergency shelters refer to placements that provide short-term care (i.e., typically less than 90 days) to youth in foster care while a more permanent placement is being planned (Leon, Bai, Fuller, & Busching, 2016). Shelters provide a temporary placement for youth until a more long-term placement can be located by the child welfare agency. Youth may be placed in an emergency shelter at a variety of junctures, including when a child is in immediate danger and subsequently taken into emergency protective care, by court order, voluntary placement, or by juvenile warrant (Oakes & Freundlich, 2005; Wattenberg, Luke, & Cornelius, 2004). Additionally, emergency shelters are often utilized when a youth's out-of-home placement is disrupted and an immediate placement is required.

Currently, few studies have examined the use of emergency shelters (e.g., DeSena et al., 2005; Leon et al., 2016; Oakes & Freundlich, 2005). One factor that may contribute to the dearth of information is the lack of consistent definition. Some states recognize group settings or foster homes as temporary emergency shelters, while other states have more stringent requirements about what constitutes an emergency shelter. DeSena and colleagues (2005) note that while there have been few studies, available research that has examined outcomes associated with youth in emergency shelters suggests that use of shelters should be minimized and frequently monitored to ensure the safety and well-being of youth placed in this temporary setting.

Oakes and Freundlich (2005) conducted a qualitative study of emergency shelter policy and use, and found that older youth, youth of color, and youth with emotional and behavioral disorders spent longer in emergency shelters than other youth. The study noted conflicting reports about why youth with these characteristics spent longer in care (i.e., delay in planning, insufficient placement alternatives). The authors also noted that due to the short-term nature of emergency placements, shelters failed to adequately meet the emotional, social, health, and educational needs of youth.

Respite Care

Respite care refers to temporary, short-term care (i.e., a few days to a few weeks) for youth who are in foster care to allow for temporary relief to the youth's primary caregivers (Owens-Kane, 2007; U.S Department of Health & Human Services, 2002). Respite is typically a paid service, regulated and funded by the state child welfare agency, that is provided by other foster parents, local foster and adoption agencies, or local community support groups (Madden et al., 2016; Owens-Kane, 2007; Smith & Pertman, 2010). While laws vary by state regarding training requirements, respite care is often provided by licensed childcare providers who have received training through the state or local child placement agencies, preparing them for this role (Owens-Kane, 2007). There is growing recognition by many professionals that the experience of providing daily care for youth with extensive behavioral and mental health needs can take an emotional toll on families, and that respite care can provide families with the necessary support and help to reduce caregiver fatigue (Chan & Sigafoos, 2001; Cowen & Reed, 2002). Research on the impact of respite care on youth in care is exceptionally limited. However, studies examining the post-placement needs of families caring for youth involved with the child welfare system have identified respite care as an essential component of the support service continuum that is necessary to help foster caregivers ensure the success and longevity of placements (Reilly & Platz, 2004; Smith & Pertman, 2010).

Transitional Foster Placements

For youth who are expected to age out of care, transitional foster or supportive placements are becoming increasingly available. The Fostering Connections Act allows states to receive federal funds to support extended foster care to age 21. Research has shown that providing foster care through to age 21 can help to reduce some of the negative outcomes associated with aging out of foster care (Dworsky & Courtney, 2010; National Conference of State Legislatures, 2016). Youth who participate in a transitional placement program have access to supportive services that help to ensure stable housing and attainment of basic living skills. Transitional placement options may include family and kinship foster homes, transitional housing, and supervised independent living settings. While program specifics vary by jurisdiction, transitional housing is typically clustered or shared residences for youth that offer more frequent access to a caseworker, as compared to supervised independent living settings that tend to be scattered throughout a community. Transitional housing and supervised independent living settings will have a minimum age requirement that varies by state, and youth who participate in these programs must be able to function independently and without daily adult supervision. A California evaluation of youth participating in extended foster care found that youth viewed the program as a way to help them achieve success as an adult, but reported variable living conditions that impacted their feelings of safety, comfort, and easy accessibility to jobs (Napolitano & Courtney, 2014).

Group and Institutional Care

Though family-type placement settings are preferred, group and institutional settings are also placement options for youth in out-of-home care. For youth who cannot be placed in less restrictive settings, group homes and residential treatment facilities are, at times, the most appropriate and therapeutic option available to help address the needs of youth with more complex mental or behavioral health issues. The following sections discuss these settings in greater depth.

Group Homes

Child welfare group homes are congregate care facilities for foster youth that are more restrictive than traditional and kinship care homes, but less restrictive than residential treatment centers. Group home sizes and treatment modalities vary, but group homes provide 24-hour care to multiple youth with social, behavioral, and/or psychological needs that require more care than may be provided in a home-based foster setting. Chow, Mettrick, Stephan, and Von Waldner's (2014) analysis of 180 youth files in 29 group homes in a mid-Atlantic state found that 76% of the youth had a mental health diagnosis upon placement, but there were no marked improvements in mental health needs or risk behaviors. Furthermore, their analysis found that females were more likely to experience negative long-term psychosocial functioning after placement in a group home than males, while youth placed at a younger age were more likely to experience later mental health needs as compared to older youth. In contrast, Lee and Thompson (2008) found that youth residing in family-style group homes, as compared to those in therapeutic foster homes, were less likely to return to an out-of-home placement upon their return home. Conflicting evidence about the efficacy of group homes highlights the need for thoughtful placement decisions about which youth may best be served by placement in a group home, and evaluation of the type of services the facilities provide. Furthermore, while it would be expected that these facilities are to serve youth with increased needs (e.g., mental health, behavioral), evidence suggests that other criteria may play into the placement decision (James, Roesch, & Zhang, 2012) and that youth with the highest needs may not have access to the most promising placement options (Farmer, Wagner, Burns, & Murray, 2016).

Residential Treatment Centers

Residential treatment centers (RTCs) refer to highly structured, intensive, institutional settings for youth in out-of-home care who have complex emotional, psychiatric, and behavioral needs (Trout et al., 2008). It is not uncommon for youth in residential settings to have experienced other types of placement (e.g., family foster care, therapeutic foster care) prior to their admission into the RTC. This occurs as a result of agency workers' attempt to satisfy federal requirements [i.e., 42 U.S.C. § 675(5)] which mandate that agencies care for youth in the least restrictive environment possible, while systematically working to identify the type of setting that will provide an appropriate and safe level of care for the youth.

The structure and restrictiveness (i.e., locked or unlocked facilities) of RTCs vary greatly. While the particulars of individual RTCs differ, in general, they provide residential, educational, and clinical services for youth in their care. Evidence of the effectiveness of residential care has been mixed. Some findings suggest that youth in foster care who are placed in residential treatment centers experience worse outcomes (Annie E. Casey Foundation, 2010; Barth, 2002; Lee, Bright, Svoboda, Fakunmoju, & Barth, 2011; Magellan Health Services Children's Services Task Force, 2008). Conversely, in a

3-year outcomes follow-up of youth who received either residential treatment or intensive home-based treatment, Preyde and colleagues (2011) found that both groups experienced significant improvements in their psychosocial functioning upon discharge, as measured by the Child and Adolescent Functional Assessment Scale. Similarly, the Brief Child and Family Phone Interview was used to assess mental health symptom severity. Both groups were reported to have fewer youth who scored above the clinical cut-off 3 years post-discharge as compared to youth at time of admission to treatment. Preyde et al. (2011) argue that because youth who receive residential treatment tend to come from a different population (e.g., lack of a stable caregiver and more problematic psychosocial functioning) than those who receive in-home treatment, the merits of residential treatment facilities still need further investigation.

Conclusion

The emergency nature of many placements, the instability of placements, and the myriad types of settings available result in a foster care placement system that often fails to meet the needs of youth. Additional efforts must be made to ensure that recruitment and retention efforts are sufficient to ensure a diverse pool of available foster placements ready to house youth experiencing a wide range of needs. These efforts must include readily available support by licensing and placement specialists, accessible training for foster families, respite care opportunities, and quick responsiveness to inquiries by foster parents and other caregivers. Furthermore, research that adds the perspectives of foster care youth about the placement process and youths' needs could have a positive impact on placement decision-making and reduce the number of transitions that youth experience while in care.

It is hard to separate placement settings and outcomes for youth from the larger child protective services agencies that are making placement decisions. Improving placement settings and outcomes requires additional investment and support for these agencies. Increased investment will result in a lower number of caseloads per child welfare worker, which will help foster worker retention and improve organizational culture and climate. Child welfare workers who have been trained, attained a level of expertise within the field, and are not overburdened by an excessively high caseload will be better able to make thoughtful placement decisions that suit the particular needs of youth in their care.

References

Adam Walsh Child Protection and Safety Act of 2006, Public Law 109-248.
Adoption and Safe Families Act of 1997, Public Law 105-89.
Adoption Assistance and Child Welfare Act of 1980, Public Law 96-172.
Alhusen, J. L., Hayat, M. J., & Gross, D. (2013). A longitudinal study of maternal attachment and infant developmental outcomes. *Archives of Women's Mental Health, 16*, 521–529.
Annie E. Casey Foundation. (2010). *Rightsizing congregate care: A powerful first step in transforming child welfare systems*. Baltimore, MD: Annie E. Casey Foundation.
Annie E. Casey Foundation. (2017). *Children in foster care by placement type*. Retrieved from http://datacenter.kidscount.org/data/tables/6247-children-in-foster-care-by-placement-type?loc=1&loct=1#detailed/1/any/false/573,869,36,868,867/2622,2621,2623,2620,2625,2624,2626/12994,12995
Barth, R. P. (2002). *Institutions vs. foster homes: The empirical base for the second century of debate*. Chapel Hill: University of North Carolina, School of Social Work, Jordan Institute for Families.
Beltran, A. (2014). Policy update: Federal and state legislation to support grandfamilies. *Grandfamilies: The Contemporary Journal of Research, Practice and Policy, 1*, 56–73.
Beltran, A., & Epstein, H. R. (2012). *Improving foster care licensing standards around the United States: Using research findings to effect change*. Retrieved from www.americanbar.org/content/dam/aba/administrative/child_law/FC_Licensing_Standards.authcheckdam.pdf
Berk, L. E. (2000). *Child development* (5th ed.). Boston, MA: Allyn & Bacon.
Berrick, J. (1998). When children cannot remain home: Foster family care and kinship care. *The Future of Children, 8*(1), 72–87.

Bhatti-Sinclair, K., & Sutcliffe, C. (2013). Challenges in identifying factors which determine the placement of children in care? An international review. *Child and Adolescent Social Work Journal, 30*, 345–363. doi: 10.1007/s10560-012-0293-x

Bowlby, J. (1958). The nature of the child's tie to his mother. *International Journal of Psycho-Analysis, 39*, 350–373.

Bowlby, J. (1988). *A secure base: Clinical applications of attachment theory*. London: Routledge.

Boyd, L. W. (2013). *Therapeutic foster care: Exceptional care for complex, trauma-impacted youth in foster care*. State Policy Advocacy and Reform Center. Retrieved from https://childwelfaresparc.files.wordpress.com/2013/07/therapeutic-foster-care-exceptional-care-for-complex-trauma-impacted-youth-in-foster-care.pdf

Cain, J. (2015). *Foster parent perspectives on recruitment and retention in Del Norte County* (Master's thesis). Humboldt State University, Arcata, CA.

Casey Family Services. (2003). *Promising practices for adoption-competent mental health services*. New Haven, CT: Casey Center for Effective Child Welfare Practice. Retrieved from www.aecf.org/resources/promising-practices-in-adoption-competent-mental-health-services/

Chamberlain, P., & Reid, J. B. (1998). Comparison of two community alternatives to incarceration of chronic juvenile offenders. *Journal of Consulting and Clinical Psychology, 66*, 624–633.

Chan, J. B., & Sigafoos. J. (2001). Does respite care reduce parental stress in families with developmentally disabled children? *Child and Youth Care Forum, 30*, 253–263. doi: 10.1023/A:1014467226528

Chanmugam, A., Madden, E. E., Hanna, M., Cody, P., Ayers-Lopez, S., McRoy, R. G., & Ladesma, K. (2017). Agency-related barriers experienced by families seeking to adopt from foster care. *Adoption Quarterly, 17*, 25–43. doi: 10.1080/10926755.2015.1121187

Chapman, M. V., Wall, A. E., Barth, R. P., & NSCAW Research Group. (2004). Children's voices: The perceptions of children in foster care. *The American Journal of Orthopsychiatry, 74*, 293–304.

Child Welfare Information Gateway. (2010). *Placement of children with relatives*. Washington, DC: U.S. Department of Health & Human Services, Children's Bureau.

Child Welfare Information Gateway. (2011). *Addressing racial disproportionality in child welfare*. Washington, DC: U.S. Department of Health & Human Services, Children's Bureau.

Child Welfare Information Gateway. (2013). *Sibling issues in foster care and adoption*. Washington, DC: U.S. Department of Health & Human Services, Children's Bureau.

Child Welfare Information Gateway. (2014). *Home study requirements for prospective foster parents*. Washington, DC: U.S. Department of Health & Human Services, Children's Bureau.

Child Welfare Information Gateway. (2015). *Background checks for prospective foster, adoptive, and kinship caregivers*. Washington, DC: U.S. Department of Health & Human Services, Children's Bureau.

Child Welfare Information Gateway. (2016a). *Foster care statistics: 2014*. Washington, DC: U.S. Department of Health & Human Services, Children's Bureau.

Child Welfare Information Gateway. (2016b). *Major federal legislation concerned with child protection, child welfare, and adoption*. Washington, DC: U.S. Department of Health & Human Services, Children's Bureau.

Children's Defense Fund. (2010). *Fostering Connections to Success and Increasing Adoptions Act summary*. Retrieved from www.childrensdefense.org/library/data/FCSIAA-detailed-summary.pdf

Children's Defense Fund. (2015). *Preventing Sex Trafficking and Strengthening Families Act (P.L. 113-183) to benefit children and youth*. Retrieved from www.childrensdefense.org/library/data/implementing-the-preventing.pdf

Chipungu, S. S., & Bent-Goodley, T. B. (2004). Meeting the challenges of contemporary foster care. *Future of Children, 14*, 75–93.

Chow W. Y., Mettrick, J. E., Stephan, S. H., & Von Waldner, C. A. (2014). Youth in group home care: Youth characteristics and predictors of later functioning. *Journal of Behavioral Health Services & Research, 14*, 503–519. doi: 10.1007/s11414-012-9282-2

Church, W. T., Gross, E. R., & Baldwin, J. (2005). Maybe ignorance is not always bliss: The disparate treatment of Hispanics within the child welfare system. *Children and Youth Services Review, 27*, 1279–1292.

CLASP. (2012). *Possibilities and pitfalls: The role of licensing in supporting relatives in caring for children in foster care*. Retrieved from www.clasp.org/sites/default/files/public/resources-and-publications/files/Licensing-paper-FINAL-11-25-12.pdf

CLASP, & American Bar Association Center on Children and the Law. (2010). *Relative foster care licensing waivers in the states: Policies and procedures*. Retrieved from www.childrensdefense.org/library/misc/relative-foster-care-licensing-waivers-in-the-states-policies-and-possibilities2.pdf

Courtney, M. E., Barth, R., Berrick, J., Brooks, D., Needell, B., & Park, L. (1996). Race and child welfare services: Past research and future directions. *Child Welfare, 75*, 99–137.

Cowen, P. S., & Reed, D. A. (2002). Effects of respite care for children with developmental disabilities: Evaluation of an intervention for at risk families. *Public Health Nursing, 19*, 272–283.

Cox, M. E., Orme, J. G., & Rhodes, K. W. (2002). Willingness to foster special needs children and foster family utilization. *Children and Youth Services Review, 24*, 293–317. doi: 10.1016/S0190-7409(02)00179-2

Crea, T. M., Barth, R. P., & Chintapalli, L. K. (2007). Home study methods for evaluating prospective resource families: History, current challenges, and promising approaches. *Child Welfare, 86*, 141–159.

Crofoot, T. L., & Harris, M. S. (2012). An Indian Child Welfare perspective on disproportionality in child welfare. *Children and Youth Services Review, 34*, 1667–1674. doi: 10.1016/j.childyouth.2012.04.028

Crosson-Tower, C. (2012). *Exploring child welfare: A practice perspective* (6th ed.). Boston, MA: Pearson.

D'Andrade, A., Frame, L., & Berrick, J. D. (2006). Concurrent planning in public child welfare agencies: Oxymoron or work in progress? *Children and Youth Services Review, 28*, 78–95. doi: 10.1016/j.childyouth.2005.02.008

DeSena, A. D., Murphy, R. A., Douglas-Palumberi, H., Blau, G., Kelly, B., Horwitz, S. M., & Kaufman, J. (2005). SAFE Homes: Is it worth the cost? An evaluation of a group home permanency planning program for children who first enter out-of-home care. *Child Abuse & Neglect, 29*, 627–643. doi: 10.1016/j.chiabu.2004.05.007

Deutsch, S. A., Lynch, A., Zlotnik, S., Matone, M., Kreider, A., & Noonan, K. (2015). Mental health, behavioral and developmental issues for youth in foster care. *Current Problems in Pediatric and Adolescent Health Care, 45*(10), 292–297. doi: 10.1016/j.cppeds.2015.08.003

Dozier, M., Kaufman, J., Kobak, R., O'Connor, T. G., Sagi-Schwartz, A., Scott, S., . . . Zeanah, C. H. (2014). Consensus statement on group care for children and adolescents: A statement of policy of the American Orthopsychiatric Association. *American Journal of Orthopsychiatry, 84*, 219–225.

Dozier, M., Stoval, K. C., Albus, K. E., & Bates, B. (2001). Attachment for infants in foster care: The role of caregiver state of mind. *Child Development, 72*, 1467–1477.

Dworsky, A., & Courtney, M. (2010). *Does extending foster care beyond age 18 promote postsecondary educational attainment?* Chicago: Chapin Hall at the University of Chicago.

Edwards, L. (2004). Mediation in child protection cases. *Journal of the Center for Families, Children, and the Courts, 5*, 57–69.

Ehrle, J., & Geen, R. (2002). Kin and non-kin foster care: Findings from a national survey. *Children and Youth Services Review, 24*, 15–35. doi: 10.1016/S0190-7409(01)00166-9

Farmer, E. M., Wagner, H. R., Burns, B. J., & Murray, M. (2016). Who goes where? Exploring factors related to placement among group homes. *Journal of Emotional and Behavioral Disorders, 24*(1), 54–63. doi: 10.1177/1063426615585082

Fiermonte, C., & Renne, J. L. (2002). *Making it permanent: Reasonable efforts to finalize permanency plans for foster children*. Washington, DC: American Bar Association, Center on Children and the Law/National Resource Center on Legal and Judicial Issues.

Fluke, J. D., Yuan, Y. Y. T., Hedderson, J., & Curtis, P. A. (2003). Disproportionate representation of race and ethnicity in child maltreatment: Investigation and victimization. *Children and Youth Services Review, 25*, 359–373. doi: 10.1016/S0190-7409(03)00026-4

Fostering Connections to Success and Increasing Adoptions Act of 2008, Public Law 110-351.

Garland, A., Landsverk, J., & Lau, A. (2003). Racial/ethnic disparities in mental health service use among children in foster care. *Children and Youth Services Review, 25*, 491–507. doi: 10.1016/S0190-7409(03)00032-X

Geiger, J. M., Hayes, M. J., & Lietz, C. A. (2013). Should I stay or should I go? A mixed methods study examining the factors influencing foster parents' decisions to continue or discontinue providing foster care. *Children and Youth Services Review, 35*, 1356–1365. doi: 10.1016/j.childyouth.2013.05.003

Gibbs, D., & Wildfire, J. (2007). Length of service for foster parents: Using administrative data to understand retention. *Children and Youth Services Review, 29*, 588–599. doi: 10.1016/j.childyouth.2006.11.002

Goldberg, S. (2000). *Attachment and development*. London: Hodder Arnold.

Golding, K. (2008). *Nurturing attachments: Supporting children who are fostered or adopted*. London: Athenaeum Press.

Goldsmith, D. F., Oppenheim, D., & Wanlass, J. (2004). Separation and reunification: Using attachment theory and research to inform decisions affecting the placements of children in foster care. *Juvenile & Family Court Journal, 55*, 1–13.

Herrick, M. A., & Piccus, W. (2005). Sibling connections: The importance of nurturing sibling bonds in the foster care system. *Children and Youth Services Review, 27*, 845–861. doi:10.1016/j.childyouth.2004.12.013

Indian Child Welfare Act of 1978, Public Law 95-608.

Interethnic Placement Act of 1996, Public Law 104-188.

James, S. (2004). Why do foster care placements disrupt? An investigation of reasons for placement change in foster care. *Social Service Review, 78*, 601–627. doi: 10.1086/424546

James, S., Roesch, S., & Zhang, J. J. (2012). Characteristics and behavioral outcomes for youth in group care and family-based care: A propensity score matching approach using national data. *Journal of Emotional and Behavioral Disorders, 20*, 144–156. doi: 10.1177/1063426611409041

Koh, E. (2010). Permanency outcomes of children in kinship and non-kinship foster care: Testing the external validity of kinship effects. *Children and Youth Services Review, 32,* 389–398. doi: 10.1016/j.childyouth.2009.10.010

Leathers, S. J. (2005). Separation from siblings: Associations with placement adaptation and outcomes among adolescents in long-term foster care. *Children and Youth Services Review, 27,* 793–819. doi: 10.1016/j.childyouth.2004.12.015

Lee, B., & Thompson, R. (2008). Comparing outcomes for youth in treatment foster care and family-style group care. *Children and Youth Services Review, 30,* 746–757. doi: 10.1016/j.childyouth.2007.12.002

Lee, B. R., Bright, C. L., Svoboda, D. V., Fakunmoju, S., & Barth, R. P. (2011). Outcomes of group care for youth: A review of comparative studies. *Research on Social Work Practice, 21,* 177–189. doi: 10.1177/1049731510386243

Leon, S. C., Bai, G. J., Fuller, A. K., & Busching, M. (2016). Emergency shelter care utilization in child welfare: Who goes to shelter care? How long do they stay? *American Journal of Orthopsychiatry, 86,* 49–60. doi: 10.1037/ort0000102

Leve, L. D., & Chamberlain, P. (2005). Association with delinquent peers: Intervention effects for youth in the juvenile justice system. *Journal of Abnormal Child Psychology, 33,* 339–347.

Leve, L. D., Chamberlain, P., & Reid, J. B. (2005). Intervention outcomes for girls referred from juvenile justice: Effects on delinquency. *Journal of Consulting and Clinical Psychology, 73,* 1181–1185. doi: 10.1037/0022-006X.73.6.1181

Lowry, M. R. (2004). Putting teeth into ASFA: The need for statutory minimum standards. *Children and Youth Services Review, 26,* 1021–1031. doi: 10.1016/j.childyouth.2004.08.003

MacGregor, T. E., Rodger, S., Cummings, A. L., & Leschied, A. W. (2006). The needs of foster parents: A qualitative study of motivation, support, and retention. *Qualitative Social Work, 5,* 351–368. doi: 10.1177/1473325006067365

Madden, E. E., Chanmugam, A., McRoy, R. G., Kaufman, L., Ledesma, K., & Martin-Hushman, D. (2016). The impact of formal and informal respite care on foster and adoptive parents caring for children involved in the child welfare system. *Journal of Child and Adolescent Social Work, 33,* 523–534. doi: 10.1007/s10560-016-0447-3

Magellan Health Services Children's Services Task Force. (2008). *Perspectives on residential and community-based treatment for youth and families.* Puyallup, WA: Magellan Health Services, Inc.

Mallon, G. (n.d.). *National perspectives on long term foster care as a permanency option.* Retrieved from www.hunter.cuny.edu/socwork/nrcfcpp/downloads/ppt/ltfc.ppt

Marcenko, M. O., Brennan, K. D., & Lyons, S. J. (2009). *Foster parent recruitment and retention: Developing resource families for Washington State's children in care.* Seattle, WA: Partners for Our Children.

McCormick, A. (2010). Siblings in foster care: An overview of research, policy, and practice. *Journal of Public Child Welfare, 4,* 198–218. doi: 10.1080/15548731003799662

Miller, M. G. (2008). *Racial disproportionality in Washington State's child welfare system* (Document No. 08-06-3901). Olympia, WA: Washington State Institute for Public Policy.

Mitchell, L. B., Barth, R. P., Green, R., Wall, A., Biemer, P., Berrick, J. D., . . . the National Survey of Child and Adolescent Well-Being Research Group. (2005). Child welfare reform in the United States: Findings from a local agency survey. *Child Welfare, 84,* 5–24.

Mumpower, J. L., & McClelland, G. H. (2014). A signal detection theory analysis of racial and ethnic disproportionality in the referral and substantiation processes of the U.S. child welfare services system. *Judgment and Decision Making, 9,* 114–128.

Myers, J. E. B. (2008). A short history of child protection in America. *Family Law Quarterly, 42,* 449–463.

Napolitano, L., & Courtney, M. E. (2014). *Residential settings of young adults in extended foster care: A preliminary investigation.* Chicago: Chapin Hall at the University of Chicago.

National Conference of State Legislatures. (2016). *Extending foster care beyond 18.* Retrieved from www.ncsl.org/research/human-services/extending-foster-care-to-18.aspx

Oakes, E. J., & Freundlich, M. (2005). *The role of emergency care as a child welfare service.* Washington, DC: CWLA Press.

Owens-Kane, S. (2007). Respite care: Outcomes for kinship and non-kinship caregivers. *Journal of Health & Social Policy, 22*(3–4), 85–99. doi: 10.1300/J045v22n03_06

Pecora, P., Whittaker, J., Maluccio, A., Barth, R., & DePanfilis, D. (2012). *The child welfare challenge.* New Brunswick, NJ: Aldine Transaction.

Personal Responsibility and Work Opportunity Reconciliation Act of 1996, Public Law 104-193.

Pokempner, J., Mordecai, K., Rosado, L., & Subrahmanyam, D. (2015). *Promoting normalcy for children and youth in foster care.* Philadelphia, PA: Juvenile Law Center.

Popple, P., & Vecchiolla, F. (2007). *Child welfare social work: An introduction.* Boston, MA: Pearson Education.

Preventing Sex Trafficking and Strengthening Families Act of 2014, Public Law 113-183.

Preyde, M., Frensch, K., Cameron, G., White, S., Penny, R., & Lazure, K. (2011). Long-term outcomes of children and youth accessing residential or intensive home-based treatment: Three year follow up. *Journal of Child and Family Studies, 20,* 660–668. doi:10.1007/s10826-010-9442-z

Quiroga, M. G., & Hamilton-Giachritsis, C. (2016). Attachment styles in children living in alternative care: A systematic review of the literature. *Child & Youth Care Forum, 45,* 625–653. doi: 10.1007/s10566-015-9342-x

Reilly, T., & Platz, L. (2004). Post-adoption service needs of families with special needs children. *Journal of Social Service Research, 30*(4), 51–67. doi: 10.1300/J079v30n04_03

Renne, J., & Mallon, G. (2014). Unpacking the no of permanency for youth: Overuse and misuse of APPLA. In G. P. Mallon & P. Hess (Eds.), *The handbook of child welfare: Practices, policies and programs* (pp. 455–466). New York, NY: Columbia University Press.

Riley-Behringer, M., & Cage, J. (2014). Barriers experienced by kinship and non-relative caregivers during the foster and adoptive parent licensure and home study process. *Journal of Public Child Welfare, 8,* 212–238. doi: 10.1080/15548732.2014.893223

Rodger, S., Cummings, A., & Leschied, A. W. (2006). Who is caring for our most vulnerable children? The motivation to foster in child welfare. *Child Abuse & Neglect, 30,* 1129–1142. doi: 10.1016/j.chiabu.2006.04.005

Rolfe, S. (2004). *Rethinking attachment for early childhood practice: Promoting security, autonomy and resilience in young children.* Crows Nest, NSW: Allen & Unwin.

Roy, P., Rutter, M., & Pickles, A. (2000). Institutional care: Risk from family background or pattern of rearing? *Journal of Child Psychology and Psychiatry, 41,* 139–149.

Russell, J., & Macgill, S. (2015). Demographics, policy, and foster care rates: A predictive analytics approach. *Children and Youth Services Review, 58,* 118–126. doi: 10.1016/j.childyouth.2015.09.009

Sakai, C., Lin, H., & Flores, G. (2011). Health outcomes and family services in kinship care: Analysis of a national sample of children in the child welfare system. *Archives of Pediatrics & Adolescent Medicine, 165,* 159–165.

Schuerger, K. (2002). *Placement stability.* New York: National Resource Center for Foster Care and Permanency.

Smith, S., & Howard, J. (1999). *Promoting successful adoptions: Practice with troubled families.* Thousand Oaks, CA: Sage.

Smith, S. L., & Pertman, A. (Eds.). (2010). *Keeping the promise: The critical need for post-adoption services to enable children and families to succeed.* Maryville, TN & New York: Harmony Adoption Services & Evan B. Donaldson Adoption Institute.

Social Security Act of 1935, Public Law 74-271.

Sroufe, L. A., Egeland, B., Carlson, E., & Collins, W. A. (2005). Placing early attachment experiences in developmental context. In K. E. Grossmann, K. Grossmann, & E. Waters (Eds.), *The power of longitudinal attachment research: From infancy and childhood to adulthood* (pp. 48–70). New York, NY: Guilford.

Thoennes, N. (2001). *Permanent custody mediation.* Denver, CO: Lucas County Court of Common Pleas Juvenile Division.

Trout, A. L., Hagaman, J. L., Beth Chmelka, M., Gehringer, R., Epstein, M. H., & Reid, R. (2008). The academic, behavioral, and mental health status of children and youth at entry to residential care. *Residential Treatment for Children & Youth, 25,* 359–374. doi: 10.1080/08865710802533654

UC Davis Center for Human Services. (2008). *A literature review of placement stability in child welfare service: Issues, concerns, outcomes and future directions.* Retrieved from www.childsworld.ca.gov/res/pdf/PlacementStability.pdf

U.S. Department of Health & Human Services. (2002). *Respite care services for families who adopt children with special needs.* Child Welfare Information Gateway, Washington, DC.

U.S. Department of Health & Human Services. (2005). *A report to Congress on adoption and other permanency outcomes for children in foster care: Focus on older children.* Washington, DC: Children's Bureau.

U.S. Department of Health & Human Services. (2011). *Report to Congress on states' use of waivers of non-safety licensing standards for relative foster family homes.* Washington, DC: Children's Bureau.

U.S. Department of Health & Human Services. (2015). *Numbers of children in foster care on September 30th, by state FY 2005–FY 2014.* Washington, DC: U.S. Department of Health & Human Services, Children's Bureau.

U.S. Department of Health & Human Services. (2016). *The AFCARS report: Preliminary FY 2015 estimates as of June 2016. No. 23.* Washington, DC: U.S. Department of Health & Human Services, Children's Bureau.

U.S. General Accounting Office. (2004). *Report to Congressional Committees. Child welfare: Improved federal oversight could assist states in overcoming key challenges.* Retrieved from: www.gao.gov/new.items/d04418t.pdf

U.S. Government Publishing Office. (2011). *Subchapter G—The administration on children, youth and families, foster care maintenance payments, adoption assistance, and child and family services.* Retrieved from www.gpo.gov/fdsys/pkg/CFR-2011-title45-vol4/pdf/CFR-2011-title45-vol4-sec1355-20.pdf

Wattenberg, E., Luke, K., & Cornelius, M. (2004). Brief encounters: Children in shelter for 7 days or less. *Child and Youth Services Review, 26,* 591–607. doi: 10.1016/j.childyouth.2004.02.027

Wilhelm, P. A. (2002). Permanency at what cost? Five years of imprudence under the Adoption and Safe Families Act of 1997. *Notre Dame Journal of Law, Ethics, & Public Policy, 16,* 617–623.

Winokur, M., Holtan, A., & Valentine, D. (2009). *Kinship care for the safety, permanency, and well-being of children removed from the home for maltreatment.* Oslo, Norway: Campbell Collaboration.

Part II
Foster Youth Individual Development

3

Neurobiological Development in Foster Youth

Outcomes and Intervention

Kristin Bernard, Allison Frost, and Sierra Kuzava

Foster youth are exposed to various types of adversity, such as maltreatment and disruptions in relationships, which can significantly undermine healthy neurobiological development. Early in life, caregivers serve a key role in co-regulating children's emotions, behaviors, and even physiology (Hofer, 1994). Developing neurobiological systems in a child depend on responsive and sensitive caregiving (Shonkoff, 2010). When there are threats to the caregiving system—such as parental substance abuse that leaves a parent disengaged and unresponsive to his or her infant's cues, extreme poverty that prevents a parent from meeting his or her child's basic needs for food, or domestic violence that interferes with a parent's ability to keep his or her child safe—healthy neurobiological development is undermined in ways that have lasting consequences for the affected child (Gunnar & Fisher, 2006; Sullivan, 2012; Teicher & Samson, 2016). In addition to being exposed to such adversities with their biological parents, foster youth experience the added threat of separation.

Neurobiological consequences of maltreatment and foster care placement can be seen in regulation of the hypothalamus pituitary adrenal (HPA) axis, brain development, and immune system functioning. Disruptions to the neurobiology of foster youth may mediate pathways toward later mental and physical health problems, suggesting that these systems are important targets of interventions for foster youth. Indeed, a number of interventions for foster youth have been found to improve functioning of key neurobiological systems. In this chapter, we first present several theoretical perspectives on the ways that stress may undermine healthy neurobiological development. We then describe research regarding the neurobiological consequences of maltreatment and foster care placement on (1) HPA axis functioning, (2) brain development, and (3) immune system functioning. For each system, we consider typical and atypical neurobiological development, the behavioral outcomes associated with atypical development, and interventions that target each system in vulnerable youth. Finally, we discuss implications and considerations for future research.

Theoretical Perspectives on Neurobiological Consequences of Early Adversity

Several theories and frameworks have been proposed to help guide our understanding of how stressful experiences in a child's environment may become biologically embedded. Here, we consider some of these theories as well as general considerations that are critical to informing how foster care and associated experiences may affect children on a neurobiological level.

When broadly considering the neurobiology of stress, "allostasis" and "allostatic load" are useful terms that help us to understand how overwhelming stress leads to physiological wear and tear on the body (McEwen, 2000). Allostasis refers to the process of maintaining stability (i.e., homeostasis) through adaptation and change. Allostatic load, then, refers to the physiological costs of repeatedly adapting to adverse environmental conditions. Allostatic load has been quantified by summing physiological indicators, such as atypical cortisol levels, high blood pressure, and elevated body mass index (Miller, Chen, & Parker, 2011). This has been a useful approach for examining the cumulative effects of stress, with studies showing evidence of allostatic load among samples exposed to neighborhood poverty (e.g., Brody, Lei, Chen, & Miller, 2014), family poverty (e.g., Chen, Miller, Kobor, & Cole, 2011), and child maltreatment (e.g., Danese et al., 2009). Allostatic load predicts age-related diseases and mortality, and thus can be considered an indicator of general physical health risk (Karlamangla, Singer, & Seeman, 2006).

Although much of this chapter will focus on the main effects of adversity on neurobiological outcomes, foster youth facing similar circumstances may show vastly different outcomes. Some theories have posed frameworks for understanding this phenomenon of individual differences. Boyce and Ellis (2005) proposed the *biological sensitivity to context* model, an evolutionary-developmental theory about stress responsiveness to the environment. This model suggests that physiological mechanisms (e.g., autonomic nervous system reactivity, cortisol regulation, immune reactivity) moderate the effects of environmental stress on outcomes. Thus, individual differences in the magnitude of stress responses modulate how susceptible a child is to environmental influences. Similarly, the *differential susceptibility model* suggests that some children are more susceptible to their caregiving environments than others—including both the negative effects of low-quality caregiving and the positive effects of high-quality caregiving (Belsky, Bakermans-Kranenburg, & van IJzendoorn, 2007). Both temperamental and genetic factors have been considered in explaining children's differential susceptibility to environmental influences. This model has implications for intervention effectiveness, as some children may be more or less responsive to parenting-focused interventions (Bakermans-Kranenburg, van IJzendoorn, Mesman, Alink, & Juffer, 2008).

Finally, in understanding how adverse childhood experiences influence neurobiological development, it is critical to consider developmental timing. There may be sensitive periods (e.g., infancy and preadolescence), during which neurobiological systems are most open to environmental influences. The Bucharest Early Intervention Project used an experimental design to examine the effects of early institutional care on young children's development. Findings suggested that timing is of the essence for remediating effects of early deprivation on children's development across domains of cognitive development (Almas, Degnan, Nelson, Zeanah, & Fox, 2016), cellular aging (Drury et al., 2012), and brain function (Vanderwert, Marshall, Nelson, Zeanah, & Fox, 2010). Across these outcomes, children placed sooner into family foster care (usually under 24 months) tend to show better catch-up developmentally than children who experienced prolonged institutional care.

With these theoretical perspectives and other considerations in mind, we now turn to a discussion of how development is threatened by exposure to adversities commonly faced by foster youth. We describe the typical development of key neurobiological systems, how development may go awry in the context of maltreatment and foster care, and interventions that target issues at the level of neurobiological functioning.

HPA Axis and Stress Response Systems

Typical Development: Stress Reactivity and Diurnal Rhythm

The hypothalamic pituitary adrenal (HPA) axis serves as one of the body's main stress response systems. When an individual encounters a stressor, the HPA axis initiates a cascade of hormonal reactions, resulting in the output of cortisol, a steroid hormone. This release of cortisol leads to increased availability of glucose and directs resources away from processes less critical for survival (e.g., digestion, reproduction), which support an adaptive response to the stressor. As soon as children are born, they show increased cortisol when faced with stressors, such as physical examinations or heel lancets (Gunnar & Fisher, 2006). However, there is a developmentally normative shift in cortisol reactivity throughout the first year of life, such that stressors no longer cause an increase in cortisol. In typically-developing children, this hyporesponsive period (i.e., period of dampened reactivity) persists for much of childhood, with cortisol reactivity being reliably established again during adolescence (Gunnar & Donzella, 2002). It has been suggested that this prolonged period of hyporesponsivity may reflect an evolutionary adaptation that serves to protect the developing brain from high levels of glucocorticoids (Gunnar & Fisher, 2006).

In addition to its role in responding to a stressor (i.e., cortisol reactivity), the HPA axis also maintains a circadian pattern of cortisol production (i.e., cortisol diurnal rhythm). Typically, individuals show a distinct diurnal rhythm of cortisol secretion, in which levels are high when the individual wakes up, peak about 30 minutes after wake-up, and decrease steadily throughout the day, reaching a nadir around bedtime. This pattern develops around 3 months of age (Price, Close, & Fielding, 1983) and becomes fully established by preschool age (Gunnar & Donzella, 2002). This diurnal rhythm of cortisol supports regulatory functions in the body, such as metabolism, temperature regulation, and maintaining circadian sleep/wake patterns (Baum & Contrada, 2010).

HPA Axis Functioning of Foster Youth

Children in foster care often show atypical patterns of cortisol reactivity and diurnal cortisol rhythms. There are more studies characterizing diurnal cortisol activity among children in foster care than studies characterizing cortisol reactivity, so we will begin by describing the former. As described above, typical diurnal cortisol rhythms are characterized by high levels of cortisol in the morning, followed by a steep decline in cortisol throughout the day, and low levels of cortisol at bedtime. Research has shown that children who experience foster care are more likely to show a *blunted* diurnal rhythm of cortisol, characterized by low morning levels and less of a decline throughout the day (Bernard, Butzin-Dozier, Rittenhouse, & Dozier, 2010; Bruce, Fisher, Pears, & Levine, 2009; Dozier et al., 2006; Gunnar & Vazquez, 2001). This blunted pattern of cortisol dysregulation is also found among children who experience early maltreatment (i.e., abuse or neglect), but remain in the care of their biological families (Bernard, Zwerling, & Dozier, 2015; Doom, Cicchetti, & Rogosch, 2014). In fact, some research shows that children who remain with their birth parents after investigation by child protective services show more dysregulated cortisol production than children who are removed from their parents' care and placed in foster care (i.e., Bernard et al., 2010), suggesting that foster care may reflect an effective intervention for vulnerable children. Daily patterns of cortisol may vary based on the type of maltreatment the child experienced prior to being placed in foster care (Bruce, Fisher, et al., 2009; Cicchetti, Rogosch, Gunnar, & Toth, 2010). For instance, Bruce, Fisher, and colleagues (2009) found that foster children who experienced severe physical neglect (e.g., failure to provide adequate food or medical care) had low morning cortisol, whereas foster children who experienced severe emotional maltreatment (e.g., parental rejection, failure to protect from traumatic events) had high morning cortisol.

This pattern of low cortisol among children in foster care shows longitudinal stability in childhood (Laurent, Gilliam, Bruce, & Fisher, 2014), but it is unclear if the pattern persists into adulthood. Some studies suggest that adults with a history of foster care or early maltreatment show increased cortisol output (Gonzalez, Jenkins, Steiner, & Fleming, 2012; Johnson & Tottenham, 2015; Nicolson, Davis, Kruszewski, & Zautra, 2010), whereas other studies suggest blunted cortisol patterns in adult samples (Monteleone et al., 2015; Shea et al., 2007; Weissbecker, Floyd, Dedert, Salmon, & Sephton, 2006).

Given that dysregulated cortisol rhythms have been linked to behavioral and health problems, as described next, it is important to understand how cortisol outcomes are affected longitudinally; future research in this area is needed.

Disruption of the HPA axis can have implications for children's socioemotional and physical development. Numerous studies have shown that cortisol patterns are related to children's risk for developing psychological disorders. Low levels of basal cortisol (McBurnett, Lahey, Rathouz, & Loeber, 2000; Shirtcliff, Granger, Booth, & Johnson, 2005) and blunted cortisol reactivity (Snoek, van Goozen, Matthys, Buitelaar, & van Engeland, 2004; van Goozen et al., 1998) have been associated with externalizing behavior problems (e.g., aggression, oppositional/defiant behavior). In contrast, patterns of high cortisol and hyper-reactivity have been linked to internalizing problems, such as depression (Burke, Davis, Otte, & Mohr, 2005; Lopez-Duran, Kovacs, & George, 2009). These associations may differ based on the age of the child. For instance, Alink and colleagues (2008) found that high basal cortisol was associated with externalizing problems in preschool children, but low basal cortisol was associated with these problems in elementary school children. Dysregulation of the HPA axis can also have implications for physical health. Some studies suggest that increased cortisol secretion contributes to increased risk for obesity (e.g., Warne, 2009) and mediates the relationship between psychosocial stress and cardiovascular disease (Chandola et al., 2008). In addition, low secretion of cortisol places children at risk for autoimmune and inflammatory disorders, including asthma (e.g., Wright, 2011).

Interventions that Enhance HPA Axis Regulation

Several interventions have been shown to impact HPA axis functioning among children who experience early adversity or are placed in foster care (Slopen, McLaughlin, & Shonkoff, 2010). Two such interventions, Multidimensional Treatment Foster Care for Preschoolers (MTFC-P; Fisher, Stoolmiller, Gunnar, & Burraston, 2007) and Attachment and Biobehavioral Catch-Up (ABC; Dozier, Meade, & Bernard, 2014), have integrated HPA regulation into their theories of change and specifically target cortisol as a marker of treatment efficacy.

Multidimensional Treatment Foster Care for Preschoolers (Fisher & Chamberlain, 2000) is a team-based therapeutic intervention delivered to foster children, foster parents, and permanent placement resources (e.g., birth parents, adoptive relatives). The intervention consists of intensive caregiver training in which parents are taught to cultivate a warm, responsive, and consistent environment at home. In addition, children take part in individualized behavioral treatment focusing on prosocial skills and problem-solving. Families typically receive services for 6 to 9 months, and children are followed across placements to promote consistency through each transition (Fisher & Chamberlain, 2000). In a longitudinal randomized control trial comparing MTFC-P participants to those in regular foster care and a community comparison group, Fisher and colleagues (2007) demonstrated that MTFC-P can impact diurnal rhythms of cortisol. Children receiving MTFC-P showed blunted diurnal cortisol at baseline, but their cortisol patterns became more typical over time such that they were comparable to the community sample by the end of 1 year. In contrast, children in regular foster care showed increasingly flattened diurnal cortisol rhythms over the course of the year (Fisher et al., 2007). In addition to these neurobiological outcomes, MTFC-P has been found to enhance placement stability and attachment-related behaviors, which may further support healthy HPA axis functioning (Fisher & Kim, 2007; Fisher, Kim, & Pears, 2009).

Attachment and Biobehavioral Catch-Up (Dozier et al., 2014) is a 10-week home-based intervention for parents and infants who are involved with foster care or at high risk for neglect. The ABC intervention aims to improve parent–child attachment by coaching parents to respond in nurturing ways to their child's cues of distress, follow their child's lead, and reduce their frightening or harsh behavior. In addition to showing effects on parent sensitivity (Bick & Dozier, 2013) and child attachment (Bernard et al., 2012), a randomized control trial demonstrated that infants who receive this intervention show higher morning cortisol levels and a steeper decline in cortisol across the day than children who receive an educational intervention (Bernard, Dozier, Bick, & Gordon, 2015). At a preschool follow-up (approximately 3 years post-intervention), children who received ABC as infants still had more normalized cortisol than children who received the control intervention (Bernard, Hostinar, & Dozier, 2015), indicating that this intervention has lasting effects on children's HPA axis functioning. These interventions illustrate the malleable nature of the HPA axis: the system is vulnerable to the damaging effects of early life stress, but also amenable to change in the context of well-timed interventions.

Brain Structure and Function

Typical Development: Prefrontal Cortex and Amygdala

Next, we turn to research suggesting that adverse experiences commonly faced by foster youth can alter the developing brain. Here, we focus specifically on the prefrontal cortex and the amygdala.

The prefrontal cortex is responsible for a number of executive functions, such as inhibitory control, cognitive flexibility, and problem-solving. Given its connections with other brain regions, it also has a role in many other aspects of behavioral and emotional regulation. With its development extending from birth through to adulthood (Rubia et al., 2006), the prefrontal cortex is susceptible to environmental experiences across development. However, there may be particular developmental windows when the prefrontal cortex has heightened sensitivity to environmental stress. During infancy and then again during adolescence, the density of glucocorticoid receptors in the prefrontal cortex peaks; thus, prolonged or frequent exposure to stressors may impact the developing brain during these times (Teicher & Samson, 2016).

Along with other structures in fronto-limbic networks, the amygdala plays an important role in perceiving emotions, evaluating threat, processing emotional information, and regulating emotion. Similar to the prefrontal cortex, the amygdala has a high density of glucocorticoid receptors. During the first several years of life, the amygdala goes through rapid development, making early childhood a possible sensitive period during which environmental stress may affect structural development; preadolescence may represent another sensitive period, as amygdala growth peaks at this time, followed by synaptic pruning, the selective elimination of neural connections (Uematsu et al., 2012).

Brain Structure and Function of Foster Youth

Although research on brain structure and function of foster youth is quite limited, research about the impact of maltreatment and early life stress on the brain provides relevant insights. For both the prefrontal cortex and amygdala, we describe structural and functional changes that may result from experiences common among foster youth, such as exposure to maltreatment, deprivation, and disruptions in care.

A number of studies have shown decreased volume in areas of the prefrontal cortex in children following experiences of maltreatment, such as physical abuse (e.g., Hanson et al., 2010), as well as in children with interpersonal trauma and symptoms of post-traumatic stress disorder (PTSD; e.g., Carrion, Garrett, Menon, Weems, & Reiss, 2008). Similar findings of reduced grey matter volume in areas of the prefrontal cortex have been found in adults who were exposed to childhood sexual abuse (Andersen et al., 2008) and physical abuse (Tomoda et al., 2009).

Given that the prefrontal cortex is primarily involved in executive functioning, functional magnetic resonance imaging (fMRI; i.e., a neuroimaging approach that measures brain activity by detecting changes in blood flow) studies have examined impairment of the prefrontal cortex by using response inhibition tasks. For example, Mueller et al. (2010) examined cognitive control using a task that required adolescents to inhibit a dominant "go" response (i.e., pressing a button in response to seeing a letter) and switch to an alternative response (i.e., pressing a different button in response to that letter, when they were shown a signal to change the response). Adolescents (approximately 13 years old) in the "early life stress" group had been adopted following foster care or institutional care; on average, the sample spent approximately 28 months in out-of-home care, with several having experienced multiple placements. The adolescents in the early life stress group showed greater activation in regions involved in inhibitory control, such as the inferior prefrontal cortex, among other areas, relative to a control group. Additionally, behavioral evidence suggested impairment in switching from the dominant response to the alternative response when prompted to do so. Taken together, these deficits have implications for their behavioral functioning in areas of attention, inhibitory control, and learning.

Children in foster care show elevated rates of attention deficit hyperactivity disorder (ADHD), difficulty with learning, and behavioral problems (Lewis, Dozier, Ackerman, & Sepulveda-Kozakowski, 2007; Pears & Fisher, 2005), which all reflect deficits in processes largely mediated by the prefrontal cortex (Booth et al., 2005). These deficits, in turn, have implications for children's school readiness and academic success. Indeed, children in foster care tend to show poorer academic competence and poorer math and reading achievement than peers (Berger, Cancian, Han, Noyes, & Rios-Salas, 2015; Pears, Fisher, Bruce, Kim, & Yoerger, 2010).

In general, studies have not found evidence that the structure of the amygdala is affected by abuse and neglect in the context of biological families (Tottenham & Sheridan, 2009). However, institutional care, which reflects a more extreme form of deprivation, has been associated with increased amygdala volume. Tottenham et al. (2010) found that children adopted from institutional care showed enlarged amygdala volume years after adoption, with the length of time spent in institutional care positively correlated with amygdala volume; further, amygdala volume was associated with greater child anxiety (Tottenham et al., 2010).

Maheu et al. (2010) examined amygdala functioning in children in foster care and adopted from institutional care. Children with histories of foster or institutional care showed greater amygdala activation to fearful and angry faces than to neutral faces, relative to comparison children (Maheu et al., 2010). Further, more changes of placement and less time with the adoptive family were associated with greater magnitude of the angry versus neutral contrast in amygdala activation, suggesting that out-of-home placement history has an influence on amygdala function. Similar findings have been seen among institutionalized children, with heightened amygdala activation to fearful versus neutral faces (Tottenham et al., 2011). In addition to fMRI studies, studies using electroencephalogram (EEG) methodology have also shown functional differences in how the brain processes emotion following experiences of early adversity. Event-related potentials (ERPs) can be extracted from ongoing EEG recorded from the scalp, and reflect changes in electrical activity in the brain that occur in response to a specific event, such as seeing a face on a computer screen. In studies of physically abused children, Pollak and colleagues found that abused children showed larger ERP responses to angry target faces than to neutral faces (Pollak, Klorman, Thatcher, & Cicchetti, 2001). Behaviorally, physically abused children also show enhanced attention to and processing of threatening information, such as angry faces (Pollak, 2008).

Children in foster care show elevated rates of internalizing problems, such as anxiety, difficulty regulating emotions, and poorer socioemotional competence (Kaplow & Widom, 2007; Slopen et al., 2010), which probably, at least in part, reflect altered functioning of the amygdala. Indeed, greater amygdala activation to threatening stimuli has been associated with poorer social competence and less eye contact (Tottenham et al., 2011). Further, heightened electrophysiological responses of maltreated children to cues of anger may contribute to maladaptive threat detection, leading to hostile attribution biases, elevated aggressive behavior, and difficulty perceiving, expressing, and regulating emotions.

Taken together, findings across studies highlight structural and functional impairment in brain regions of the prefrontal cortex and amygdala following experiences of deprivation, maltreatment, and foster care. Other brain regions not reviewed here, such as the hippocampus, also show impairments following early adversity (for a review, see Teicher & Samson, 2016).

Interventions that Enhance Brain Structure and Function

Few interventions for foster children, or even more generally for children exposed to early adversity, have examined effects on the brain. There are a couple of notable exceptions. In the Bucharest Early Intervention Project (Zeanah et al., 2003), institutionalized children were randomly assigned to care as usual (i.e., initially staying in the institution) or high-quality family foster care. At baseline, when examining resting state EEG activity, institutionalized children showed greater EEG power in the theta band and reduced power in the alpha and beta bands (Marshall, Fox, & BEIP Core Group, 2004), a pattern similar to children diagnosed with ADHD. Activity in higher frequency bands (i.e., alpha and beta) is associated with better attention and cognitive performance; thus, low power in these bands may reflect impaired or delayed development. At 8 years old, however, children placed into family foster care had greater high frequency (i.e., alpha) EEG power than children in the care-as-usual (i.e., institutional care) group (Vanderwert et al., 2010). Further, placement into family foster care before the age of 2 was associated with the most pronounced effects. These findings suggest that the brain is responsive to improvements in the social environment, but may be less responsive to such recovery as children get older. Along with other findings from the Bucharest Early Intervention Project which show that earlier removal from institutional care is associated with better cognitive, social, and biological outcomes (e.g., Almas et al., 2016; Drury et al., 2012), these findings suggest that timing is of the essence when finding stable and responsive family placements for children.

As described above, MTFC-P is an intervention for preschoolers in foster care that aims to provide a consistent and responsive interpersonal environment in order to reduce behavior problems and improve self-regulation. Foster children who received MTFC-P and foster children who received services as usual were compared on their behavioral and electrophysiological performance on a flanker task requiring cognitive control and response monitoring (Bruce, McDermott, Fisher, & Fox, 2009). The flanker task required children to identify the color of a middle circle in a row of circles, which was either the same color as the other circles (i.e., congruent trials) or a different color (i.e., incongruent trials). Following their response, children received feedback: a smiling face for a correct response, or a frowning face for an incorrect response. Foster children that received MTFC-P showed differences in feedback-locked ERP components (i.e., brain responses to receiving feedback following correct and incorrect trials) compared to foster children who received services as usual. Specifically, MTFC-P foster children showed different neural responses to negative versus positive feedback, similar to non-maltreated children; whereas comparison foster children did not show differences in brain activity between positive versus negative feedback. These results suggest that MTFC-P enhanced children's responsiveness to external feedback, suggesting potential intervention effects on a key aspect of behavioral regulation. Given that a key aspect of behavioral regulation in early childhood is shifting behavior and attention in response to external feedback (e.g., rules, reinforcement, consequences), these changes in brain activity may affect social and academic functioning.

Immune System Functioning

Typical Development: Immune System

Finally, we turn to the immune system, which is also found to be highly susceptible to environmental input. The basic role of the immune system is to protect the individual from injury or illness by mounting a response to pathogens. Host defense, or the role of the immune system in protecting the individual from illness and injury, works largely through dispatching both specific and all-purpose cells to protect against pathogens. Host defense can either take the form of natural immunity, in which broad, all-purpose immune cells respond to the antigen, or specific immunity, in which cells with antigen-specific receptor sites mount a full, specialized defense (Cooper et al., 2009; Litman, Cannon, & Dishaw, 2005). In both cases, natural or specific immune cells rely on communication molecules called cytokines to amplify and facilitate immune response, either by promoting inflammation at the site of injury or illness or through directing the production of antibodies to neutralize pathogens (Cannon, 2000).

Although it was previously thought that the immune system's primary role was to defend against pathogens, current evidence suggests that the immune system may also fill important regulatory or homeostatic functions (Schmitz & Chew, 2008). More specifically, it has been found that inflammatory cytokines are expressed in healthy adult brains without the presence of injury or illness, and experimental evidence suggests that these cytokines may regulate metabolism and sleep behavior (Schmitz & Chew, 2008; Vitkovic, Bockaert, & Jacque, 2001). From a developmental perspective, immune cells are believed to play an important role in normal development of the nervous system, and are crucial in a number of neurodevelopmental processes, such as cell migration and differentiation, synapse formation, and synaptic pruning (Meyer, Feldon, Schedlowski, & Yee, 2006; Nawa & Takei, 2006). At the other end of the developmental spectrum, the immune system also plays a role in supporting healthy aging, particularly through its role in recognizing and eliminating aging, or senescent, cells (Sagiv et al., 2016). Cellular aging typically results from the shortening of caps at the end of each strand of DNA, called telomeres, which function to protect chromosomes.

Immune Functioning of Foster Youth

It has been well documented that the developing immune system is vulnerable to a number of environmental and psychological influences, and that early immune activity may have significant consequences for later health (Bilbo & Schwarz, 2009; Miller et al., 2009; Nusslock & Miller, 2016; Segerstrom & Miller, 2004). Although research on immune system functioning specifically among youth in foster care is lacking, many studies on prenatal adversity and chronic stress offer insights into outcomes we might expect to see for foster youth.

Prenatal infection, particularly during key fetal brain development periods, has been linked to abnormal fetal brain development and increased risk for a number of neurodevelopmental and autoimmune disorders, such as autism, Alzheimer's, and Parkinson's (Bilbo & Schwarz, 2009; Brown, 2012; Meyer et al., 2006; Owen, O'Donovan, Thapar, & Craddock, 2011). These associations between early infection and later disorder are consistent with research indicating that immune cells are crucial in neurodevelopment. Many children in foster care have been exposed to poor maternal prenatal health, including infection, illness, and substance use (Simms, Dubowitz, & Szilagyi, 2000). Thus, the inflammatory correlates of poor maternal prenatal health, especially infection, have the potential to significantly alter brain development, placing children at risk for neurodevelopmental and immune-linked disorders over the course of life.

A growing body of research has indicated that chronic psychological stress, such as maltreatment and disruptions in care, may also lead to immune dysfunction in a similar way to infection or illness. Children who experience chronic stress have greater levels of pro-inflammatory cytokines in adulthood (Danese et al., 2009; Danese, Pariante, Caspi, Taylor, & Poulton, 2007; Miller & Cole, 2012), indicating that inflammation may be a major mechanism through which adversity confers later risk for mental and physical health problems. Further, prior to foster care placement, foster children may have experienced homes characterized by limited financial resources, food insecurity, and chaotic and unpredictable schedules (Ehrle, Geen, & Geen, 2002), all of which have the potential to contribute to immune dysfunction. Additionally, telomeres, the protective caps on the end of chromosomes, have been found to shorten faster in children exposed to maltreatment and other adversities than in non-exposed children (for a meta-analysis, see Ridout et al., 2017). In sum, there is reason to believe that children and adolescents in foster care are at a substantially increased risk for experiencing immune dysfunction secondary to childhood adversity.

Immune dysfunction may exacerbate risk for a number of immune-linked disorders later in life, including metabolic syndrome, obesity, autoimmune disease, and some cancers, as well as psychiatric disorders such as depression and substance abuse, which are thought to have immune correlates (Danese et al., 2009; Nusslock & Miller, 2016; Shonkoff, Boyce, & McEwen, 2009). Bidirectional crosstalk between brain and body suggests that chronic medical conditions may affect threat- and reward-linked brain circuitry, increasing the likelihood of risky health behaviors that perpetuate inflammation and place individuals at risk for a host of negative outcomes.

Interventions Aimed at Enhancing Immune System Functioning

There is much that is yet to be discovered about immune system functioning and early adversity, particularly when considering special populations such as children and adolescents in foster care. However, the growing body of research examining immune correlates of early adversity offers several avenues for interventions that may enhance immune functioning among foster care youth. From a large-scale perspective, interventions providing access to quality prenatal care for at-risk families stand to have significant downstream benefits for children entering foster care. Homeless women, for example, are both more likely to have prenatal infections and be less likely to receive prenatal care (Rimawi, Mirdamadi, & John, 2014). Organizations that support provision of housing services to pregnant homeless women—particularly those that facilitate access to healthcare—may mitigate potentially detrimental effects of prenatal infection on children's later neurodevelopment and risk for immune dysfunction, even if children are later placed in foster care.

Increasing the quality of medical attention and general care provided in foster care settings may also help to reduce some of the consequences of immune dysfunction resulting from adversity. Some researchers have suggested that pediatricians could play a critical role in ensuring consistent care for children who change placements frequently, perhaps by taking part in a larger team of healthcare workers who track the child's whereabouts and monitor health conditions over time (Szilagyi, Rosen, Rubin, & Zlotnik, 2015). Relatedly, there is some evidence to suggest that, compared to non-relative foster care, children who are placed with extended family members experience greater placement stability and are healthier (Dubowitz et al., 1992; Rubin et al., 2008). Efforts to prioritize placement of children with extended family may result in more consistent healthcare, thereby curbing some of the immunological consequences of chronic medical conditions.

Finally, sensitive caregiving may mitigate the neurobiological consequences of stress and early adversity (referred to as "social buffering"), including pro-inflammatory signaling and stress responsiveness (Chen et al., 2011; Gunnar & Hostinar, 2015). Indeed, evidence suggests that alterations to caregiving sensitivity may have neurobiological payoffs. For example, Asok, Bernard, Roth, Rosen, & Dozier (2013) found that high-risk children involved with child protective services showed shorter telomeres than low-risk peers, which is considered an important indicator of physical health risk as it is associated with a number of age-related diseases (Epel et al., 2006). However, this effect was moderated by maternal sensitivity; that is, telomere length among high-risk children with highly responsive parents was comparable to that of low-risk children. Given these findings along with previous research that has established a link between maternal warmth and inflammation (e.g., Chen et al., 2011), there is good reason to believe that interventions aimed at enhancing caregiving may be similarly effective in addressing immune dysfunction. The ABC and MTFC-P interventions, described above, have been shown to enhance cortisol regulation, which may have implications for immune system functioning. Taken together, there are a number of promising intervention avenues that may curb some of the immunological consequences of adversity in foster children and youth.

Future Directions

There is much to be discovered about how foster youth are affected on a neurobiological level by their adverse experiences, offering many important directions for future research. First, much of the research reviewed here focused broadly on samples of children or adults who experienced environmental stressors such as maltreatment and poverty. Although such approaches offer strong evidence that adversity leads to maladaptive development, we lack a more nuanced understanding of how the type, severity, chronicity, and developmental timing of such adverse exposures contribute differentially to negative outcomes. Further, and important for understanding the unique experience of foster youth, few studies have examined the specific effects of separations, multiple placement disruptions, and caregiving context (e.g., kinship versus non-relative care) on children's neurobiological development.

Second, few studies have examined the neurobiological effects of interventions, and even fewer have done so for children in foster care. Given that intervention studies often employ an experimental design (i.e., randomly assigning children to different conditions), they offer key insights into causal mechanisms implicated in positive and negative developmental pathways. By understanding how children's neurobiology is influenced by changing the environment (e.g., enhancing sensitive parenting) or changing the child's capacities (e.g., improving self-regulation), researchers can also identify potential targets for intervention.

Finally, it will be important to continue to examine individual differences in neurobiological outcomes. As suggested by theoretical perspectives like the differential susceptibility model, some foster children seem remarkably resilient in the face of challenges, whereas others quickly follow risky trajectories. It will be important to examine how outcomes of youth in foster care vary based on gender, race and ethnicity, and socioeconomic status. Further, understanding temperamental, genetic, or environmental factors that contribute to risk and resilience may help with identifying the children most in need of intervention and tailoring intervention approaches to maximize effects for different children.

Although there are clear benefits to understanding the neurobiological consequences of foster care, there are a number of challenges relating to this work. In addition to the high cost of neuroscience research, it can be difficult for researchers to access vulnerable populations, such as youth in foster care. Thus, collaborative efforts between researchers, care providers, and child welfare agencies are critical for advancing knowledge in this area. Further, researchers should aim to engage families as active scientific partners, rather than passive participants; such efforts to connect through community-based outreach efforts may improve retention in longitudinal studies and enrich the quality and accuracy of data obtained from families. Finally, research on foster youth would benefit from the use of multi-method designs, combining physiological/neurobiological, observational, and self-report assessments from multiple individuals (e.g., foster youth, birth parents, and foster parents) across multiple time-points. Collectively, such methodologically rigorous and community-informed research efforts have the potential to significantly advance theoretical perspectives and bridge science-to-practice/practice-to-science gaps in our knowledge.

Conclusion

Foster youth experience a number of threats, such as maltreatment, deprivation, and separation, which interfere with their healthy socioemotional, behavioral, and physical development. Examining neurobiological changes that result from such threats can highlight mechanisms that lead to psychopathology and physical health conditions. In particular, changes to stress response systems (e.g., HPA axis and cortisol regulation), brain development (e.g., structural and functional changes to the prefrontal cortex and amygdala), and immune system functioning (e.g., inflammatory processes) may offer targets for interventions that aim to prevent long-term consequences among foster youth. Much more research is needed to understand how foster youth, in particular, are affected on a neurobiological level.

References

Alink, L. R., van IJzendoorn, M. H., Bakermans-Kranenburg, M. J., Mesman, J., Juffer, F., & Koot, H. M. (2008). Cortisol and externalizing behavior in children and adolescents: Mixed meta-analytic evidence for the inverse relation of basal cortisol and cortisol reactivity with externalizing behavior. *Developmental Psychobiology, 50*, 427–450. https://doi.org/10.1002/dev.20300

Almas, A. N., Degnan, K. A., Nelson, C. A., Zeanah, C. H., & Fox, N. A. (2016). IQ at age 12 following a history of institutional care: Findings from the Bucharest Early Intervention Project. *Developmental Psychology, 52*(11), 1858–1866. https://doi.org/10.1037/dev0000167

Andersen, S. L., Tomada, A., Vincow, E. S., Valente, E., Polcari, A., & Teicher, M. H. (2008). Preliminary evidence for sensitive periods in the effect of childhood sexual abuse on regional brain development. *Journal of Neuropsychiatry, 20*(3), 292–301. https://doi.org/10.1176/appi.neuropsych.20.3.292

Asok, A., Bernard, K., Roth, T. L., Rosen, J. B., & Dozier, M. (2013). Parental responsiveness moderates the association between early-life stress and reduced telomere length. *Development and Psychopathology, 25*(3), 577–585. https://doi.org/10.1017/S0954579413000011

Bakermans-Kranenburg, M. J., van IJzendoorn, M. H., Mesman, J., Alink, L. R. A., & Juffer, F. (2008). Effects of an attachment-based intervention on daily cortisol moderated by dopamine receptor D4: A randomized control trial on 1- to 3-year-olds screened for externalizing behavior. *Development and Psychopathology, 20*(3), 805–820. https://doi.org/10.1017/S0954579408000382

Baum, A., & Contrada, R. (2010). *The handbook of stress science: Biology, psychology, and health*. New York: Springer.

Belsky, J., Bakermans-Kranenburg, M. J., & van IJzendoorn, M. H. (2007). For better and for worse: Differential susceptibility to environmental influences. *Current Directions in Psychological Science, 16*(6), 300–304. https://doi.org/10.1111/j.1467-8721.2007.00525.x

Berger, L. M., Cancian, M., Han, E., Noyes, J., & Rios-Salas, V. (2015). Children's academic achievement and foster care. *Pediatrics, 135*(1), e109–e116. https://doi.org/10.1542/peds.2014-2448

Bernard, K., Butzin-Dozier, Z., Rittenhouse, J., & Dozier, M. (2010). Cortisol production patterns in young children living with birth parents vs children placed in foster care following involvement of Child Protective Services. *Archives of Pediatrics & Adolescent Medicine, 164*(5), 438–443. https://doi.org/10.1001/archpediatrics.2010.54

Bernard, K., Dozier, M., Bick, J., & Gordon, M. K. (2015). Intervening to enhance cortisol regulation among children at risk for neglect: Results of a randomized clinical trial. *Development and Psychopathology, 27*(3), 829–841. https://doi.org/10.1017/S095457941400073X

Bernard, K., Dozier, M., Bick, J., Lewis-Morrarty, E., Lindhiem, O., & Carlson, E. (2012). Enhancing attachment organization among maltreated children: Results of a randomized clinical trial. *Child Development, 83*(2), 623–636. https://doi.org/10.1111/j.1467-8624.2011.01712.x

Bernard, K., Hostinar, C., & Dozier, M. (2015). Intervention effects on diurnal cortisol rhythms of child protective services-referred infants in early childhood: Preschool follow-up results of a randomized clinical trial. *JAMA Pediatrics, 169*(2), 112–119. https://doi.org/10.1001/jamapediatrics.2014.2369

Bernard, K., Zwerling, J., & Dozier, M. (2015). Effects of early adversity on young children's diurnal cortisol rhythms and externalizing behavior. *Developmental Psychobiology, 57*(8), 935–947. https://doi.org/10.1002/dev.21324

Bick, J., & Dozier, M. (2013). The effectiveness of an attachment-based intervention in promoting foster mothers' sensitivity toward foster infants. *Infant Mental Health Journal, 34*(2), 95–103. https://doi.org/10.1002/imhj.21373

Bilbo, S. D., & Schwarz, J. M. (2009). Early-life programming of later-life brain and behavior: A critical role for the immune system. *Frontiers in Behavioral Neuroscience, 3*, 14. https://doi.org/10.3389/neuro.08.014.2009

Booth, J. R., Burman, D. D., Meyer, J. R., Lei, Z., Trommer, B. L., Davenport, N. D., . . . Mesulam, M. M. (2005). Larger deficits in brain networks for response inhibition than for visual selective attention in attention deficit hyperactivity disorder (ADHD). *Journal of Child Psychology and Psychiatry, and Allied Disciplines*, *46*(1), 94–111. https://doi.org/10.1111/j.1469-7610.2004.00337.x

Boyce, W. T., & Ellis, B. J. (2005). Biological sensitivity to context: I. An evolutionary-developmental theory of the origins and functions of stress reactivity. *Development and Psychopathology*, *17*(2), 271–301. https://doi.org/10.1017/S0954579405050145

Brody, G. H., Lei, M.-K., Chen, E., & Miller, G. E. (2014). Neighborhood poverty and allostatic load in African American youth. *Pediatrics*, *134*(5), e1362–e1368. https://doi.org/10.1542/peds.2014-1395

Brown, A. S. (2012). Epidemiologic studies of exposure to prenatal infection and risk of schizophrenia and autism. *Developmental Neurobiology*, *72*(10), 1272–1276. https://doi.org/10.1002/dneu.22024

Bruce, J., Fisher, P. A., Pears, K. C., & Levine, S. (2009). Morning cortisol levels in preschool-aged foster children: Differential effects of maltreatment type. *Developmental Psychobiology*, *51*(1), 14–23. https://doi.org/10.1002/dev.20333

Bruce, J., McDermott, J. M., Fisher, P. A., & Fox, N. A. (2009). Using behavioral and electrophysiological measures to assess the effects of a preventive intervention: A preliminary study with preschool-aged foster children. *Prevention Science*, *10*(2), 129–140. https://doi.org/10.1007/s11121-008-0115-8

Burke, H., Davis, M., Otte, C., & Mohr, D. (2005). Depression and cortisol responses to psychological stress: A meta-analysis. *Psychoneuroendocrinology*, *30*(9), 846–856. http://dx.doi.org/10.1016/j.psyneuen.2005.02.010

Cannon, J. G. (2000). Inflammatory cytokines in nonpathological states. *Physiology*, *15*(6), 298–303.

Carrion, V. G., Garrett, A., Menon, V., Weems, C. F., & Reiss, A. L. (2008). Posttraumatic stress symptoms and brain function during a response-inhibition task: An fMRI study in youth. *Depression and Anxiety*, *25*(6), 514–526. https://doi.org/10.1002/da.20346

Chandola, T., Britton, A., Brunner, E., Hemingway, H., Malik, M., Kumari, M., . . . Marmot, M. (2008). Work stress and coronary heart disease: What are the mechanisms? *European Heart Journal*, *29*(5), 640–648. https://doi.org/10.1093/eurheartj/ehm584

Chen, E., Miller, G. E., Kobor, M. S., & Cole, S. W. (2011). Maternal warmth buffers the effects of low early-life socioeconomic status on pro-inflammatory signaling in adulthood. *Molecular Psychiatry*, *16*(7), 729–737. https://doi.org/10.1038/mp.2010.53

Cicchetti, D., Rogosch, F. A., Gunnar, M. R., & Toth, S. L. (2010). The differential impacts of early physical and sexual abuse and internalizing problems on daytime cortisol rhythm in school-aged children. *Child Development*, *81*(1), 252–269. https://doi.org/10.1111/j.1467-8624.2009.01393.x

Cooper, M. A., Elliott, J. M., Keyel, P. A., Yang, L., Carrero, J. A., & Yokoyama, W. M. (2009). Cytokine-induced memory-like natural killer cells. *Proceedings of the National Academy of Sciences of the United States of America*, *106*(6), 1915–1919. https://doi.org/10.1073/pnas.0813192106

Danese, A., Moffitt, T. E., Harrington, H., Milne, B. J., Polanczyk, G., Pariante, C. M., . . . Caspi, A. (2009). Adverse childhood experiences and adult risk factors for age-related disease. *Archives of Pediatrics & Adolescent Medicine*, *163*(12), 716–719. https://doi.org/10.1001/archpediatrics.2009.214

Danese, A., Pariante, C. M., Caspi, A., Taylor, A., & Poulton, R. (2007). Childhood maltreatment predicts adult inflammation in a life-course study. *Proceedings of the National Academy of Sciences of the United States of America*, *104*(4), 1319–1324. https://doi.org/10.1073/pnas.0610362104

Doom, J. R., Cicchetti, D., & Rogosch, F. A. (2014). Longitudinal patterns of cortisol regulation differ in maltreated and nonmaltreated children. *Journal of the American Academy of Child & Adolescent Psychiatry*, *53*(11), 1206–1215. https://doi.org/10.1016/j.jaac.2014.08.006

Dozier, M., Manni, M., Gordon, M. K., Peloso, E., Gunnar, M. R., Stovall-McClough, K. C., . . . Levine, S. (2006). Foster children's diurnal production of cortisol: An exploratory study. *Child Maltreatment*, *11*(2), 189–197. https://doi.org/10.1177/1077559505285779

Dozier, M., Meade, E., & Bernard, K. (2014). Attachment and Biobehavioral Catch-Up: An intervention for parents at risk of maltreating their infants and toddlers. In S. Timmer & A. Urquiza (Eds.), *Evidence-based approaches for the treatment of maltreated children* (pp. 43–59). New York: Springer. https://doi.org/10.1007/978-94-007-7404-9_4

Drury, S. S., Theall, K., Gleason, M. M., Smyke, A. T., De Vivo, I., Wong, J. Y. Y., . . . Nelson, C. A. (2012). Telomere length and early severe social deprivation: Linking early adversity and cellular aging. *Molecular Psychiatry*, *17*(7), 719–727. https://doi.org/10.1038/mp.2011.53

Dubowitz, H., Feigelman, S., Zuravin, S., Tepper, V., Davidson, N., & Lichenstein, R. (1992). The physical health of children in kinship care. *American Journal of Diseases of Children*, *146*(5), 603–610.

Ehrle, J., Geen, R., & Geen, R. (2002). Kin and non-kin foster care: Findings from a national survey. *Children and Youth Services Review*, *24*, 15–35.

Epel, E. S., Lin, J., Wilhelm, F. H., Wolkowitz, O. M., Cawthon, R., Adler, N. E., . . . Blackburn, E. H. (2006). Cell aging in relation to stress arousal and cardiovascular disease risk factors. *Psychoneuroendocrinology*, *31*(3), 277–287. doi: 10.1016/j.psyneuen.2005.08.011

Fisher, P. A., & Chamberlain, P. (2000). Multidimensional Treatment Foster Care: A program for intensive parenting, family support, and skill building. *Journal of Emotional and Behavioral Disorders, 8*(3), 155–164.

Fisher, P. A., & Kim, H. K. (2007). Intervention effects on foster preschoolers' attachment-related behaviors from a randomized trial. *Prevention Science, 8*(2), 161–170. https://doi.org/10.1007/s11121-007-0066-5

Fisher, P. A., Kim, H. K., & Pears, K. C. (2009). Effects of Multidimensional Treatment Foster Care for Preschoolers (MTFC-P) on reducing permanent placement failures among children with placement instability. *Children and Youth Services Review, 31*(5), 541–546. https://doi.org/10.1016/j.childyouth.2008.10.012

Fisher, P. A., Stoolmiller, M., Gunnar, M. R., & Burraston, B. O. (2007). Effects of a therapeutic intervention for foster preschoolers on diurnal cortisol activity. *Psychoneuroendocrinology, 32*(8–10), 892–905. https://doi.org/10.1016/j.psyneuen.2007.06.008

Gonzalez, A., Jenkins, J. M., Steiner, M., & Fleming, A. S. (2012). Maternal early life experiences and parenting: The mediating role of cortisol and executive function. *Journal of the American Academy of Child and Adolescent Psychiatry, 51*(7), 673–682. https://doi.org/10.1016/j.jaac.2012.04.003

Gunnar, M., & Donzella, B. (2002). Social regulation of the cortisol levels in early human development. *Psychoneuroendocrinology, 27*(1–2), 199–220. https://doi.org/10.1016/S0306-4530(01)00045-2

Gunnar, M. R., & Fisher, P. A. (2006). Bringing basic research on early experience and stress neurobiology to bear on preventive interventions for neglected and maltreated children. *Development and Psychopathology, 18*(3), 651–677. https://doi.org/10.1017/S0954579406060330

Gunnar, M. R., & Hostinar, C. E. (2015). The social buffering of the hypothalamic–pituitary–adrenocortical axis in humans: Developmental and experiential determinants. *Social Neuroscience, 10*(5), 479–488. https://doi.org/10.1080/17470919.2015.1070747

Gunnar, M. R., & Vazquez, D. M. (2001). Low cortisol and a flattening of expected daytime rhythm: Potential indices of risk in human development. *Development and Psychopathology, 13*(3), 515–538.

Hanson, J. L., Chung, M. K., Avants, B. B., Shirtcliff, E. A., Gee, J. C., Davidson, R. J., & Pollak, S. D. (2010). Early stress is associated with alterations in the orbitofrontal cortex: A tensor-based morphometry investigation of brain structure and behavioral risk. *The Journal of Neuroscience, 30*(22), 7466–7472. https://doi.org/10.1523/JNEUROSCI.0859-10.2010

Hofer, M. (1994). Hidden regulators in attachment, separation, and loss. *Monographs of the Society for Research in Child Development, 59*, 192–207.

Johnson, A. J., & Tottenham, N. (2015). Regulatory skill as a resilience factor for adults with a history of foster care: A pilot study. *Developmental Psychobiology, 57*(1), 1–16. https://doi.org/10.1002/dev.21227

Kaplow, J. B., & Widom, C. S. (2007). Age of onset of child maltreatment predicts long-term mental health outcomes. *Journal of Abnormal Psychology, 116*(1), 176–187. https://doi.org/10.1037/0021-843X.116.1.176

Karlamangla, A. S., Singer, B. H., & Seeman, T. E. (2006). Reduction in allostatic load in older adults is associated with lower all-cause mortality risk: MacArthur studies of successful aging. *Psychosomatic Medicine, 68*, 500–507. doi: 10.1097/01.psy.0000221270.93985.82

Laurent, H. K., Gilliam, K. S., Bruce, J., & Fisher, P. A. (2014). HPA stability for children in foster care: Mental health implications and moderation by early intervention. *Developmental Psychobiology, 56*(6), 1406–1415. https://doi.org/10.1002/dev.21226

Lewis, E. E., Dozier, M., Ackerman, J., & Sepulveda-Kozakowski, S. (2007). The effect of placement instability on adopted children's inhibitory control abilities and oppositional behavior. *Developmental Psychology, 43*(6), 1415–1427. https://doi.org/10.1037/0012-1649.43.6.1415

Litman, G. W., Cannon, J. P., & Dishaw, L. J. (2005). Reconstructing immune phylogeny: New perspectives. *Nature Reviews. Immunology, 5*(11), 866–879. https://doi.org/10.1038/nri1712

Lopez-Duran, N. L., Kovacs, M., & George, C. J. (2009). Hypothalamic-pituitary-adrenal axis dysregulation in depressed children and adolescents: A meta-analysis. *Psychoneuroendocrinology, 34*(9), 1272–1283. https://doi.org/10.1016/j.psyneuen.2009.03.016

Maheu, F. S., Dozier, M., Guyer, A. E., Mandell, D., Peloso, E., Poeth, K., . . . Ernst, M. (2010). A preliminary study of medial temporal lobe function in youths with a history of caregiver deprivation and emotional neglect. *Cognitive, Affective & Behavioral Neuroscience, 10*(1), 34–49. https://doi.org/10.3758/CABN.10.1.34

Marshall, P. J., Fox, N. A., & BEIP Core Group. (2004). A comparison of the electroencephalogram between institutionalized and community children in Romania. *Journal of Cognitive Neuroscience, 16*(8), 1327–1338. https://doi.org/10.1162/0898929042304723

McBurnett, K., Lahey, B., Rathouz, P., & Loeber, R. (2000). Low salivary cortisol and persistent aggression in boys referred for disruptive behavior. *Archives of General Psychiatry, 57*(1), 38–43. https://doi.org/10.1001/archpsyc.57.1.38

McEwen, B. S. (2000). The neurobiology of stress: From serendipity to clinical relevance. *Brain Research, 886*(1–2), 172–189.

Meyer, U., Feldon, J., Schedlowski, M., & Yee, B. K. (2006). Immunological stress at the maternal–foetal interface: A link between neurodevelopment and adult psychopathology. *Brain, Behavior, and Immunity, 20*(4), 378–388. https://doi.org/10.1016/j.bbi.2005.11.003

Miller, G. E., Chen, E., Fok, A. K., Walker, H., Lim, A., Nicholls, E. F., . . . Kobor, M. S. (2009). Low early-life social class leaves a biological residue manifested by decreased glucocorticoid and increased proinflammatory signaling. *Proceedings of the National Academy of Sciences of the United States of America, 106*(34), 14716–14721. https://doi.org/10.1073/pnas.0902971106

Miller, G. E., Chen, E., & Parker, K. J. (2011). Psychological stress in childhood and susceptibility to the chronic diseases of aging: Moving toward a model of behavioral and biological mechanisms. *Psychological Bulletin, 137*(6), 959–997. https://doi.org/10.1037/a0024768

Miller, G. E., & Cole, S. W. (2012). Clustering of depression and inflammation in adolescents previously exposed to childhood adversity. *Biological Psychiatry, 72*(1), 34–40. https://doi.org/10.1016/j.biopsych.2012.02.034

Monteleone, A. M., Monteleone, P., Serino, I., Scognamiglio, P., Di Genio, M., & Maj, M. (2015). Childhood trauma and cortisol awakening response in symptomatic patients with anorexia nervosa and bulimia nervosa. *International Journal of Eating Disorders, 48*(6), 615–621. https://doi.org/10.1002/eat.22375

Mueller, S. C., Maheu, F. S., Dozier, M., Peloso, E., Mandell, D., Leibenluft, E., . . . Ernst, M. (2010). Early-life stress is associated with impairment in cognitive control in adolescence: An fMRI study. *Neuropsychologia, 48*, 3037–3044. https://doi.org/10.1016/j.neuropsychologia.2010.06.013

Nawa, H., & Takei, N. (2006). Recent progress in animal modeling of immune inflammatory processes in schizophrenia: Implication of specific cytokines. *Neuroscience Research, 56*(1), 2–13. https://doi.org/10.1016/j.neures.2006.06.002

Nicolson, N. A., Davis, M. C., Kruszewski, D., & Zautra, A. J. (2010). Childhood maltreatment and diurnal cortisol patterns in women with chronic pain. *Psychosomatic Medicine, 72*(5), 471–480. https://doi.org/10.1097/PSY.0b013e3181d9a104

Nusslock, R., & Miller, G. E. (2016). Early-life adversity and physical and emotional health across the lifespan: A neuroimmune network hypothesis. *Biological Psychiatry, 80*(1), 23–32. https://doi.org/10.1016/j.biopsych.2015.05.017

Owen, M. J., O'Donovan, M. C., Thapar, A., & Craddock, N. (2011). Neurodevelopmental hypothesis of schizophrenia. *The British Journal of Psychiatry, 198*(3), 173–175. https://doi.org/10.1192/bjp.bp.110.084384

Pears, K., & Fisher, P. A. (2005). Developmental, cognitive, and neuropsychological functioning in preschool-aged foster children: Associations with prior maltreatment and placement history. *Journal of Developmental and Behavioral Pediatrics, 26*(2), 112–122.

Pears, K. C., Fisher, P. A., Bruce, J., Kim, H. K., & Yoerger, K. (2010). Early elementary school adjustment of maltreated children in foster care: The roles of inhibitory control and caregiver involvement. *Child Development, 81*(5), 1550–1564. https://doi.org/10.1111/j.1467-8624.2010.01491.x

Pollak, S. D. (2008). Mechanisms linking early experience and the emergence of emotions: Illustrations from the study of maltreated children. *Current Directions in Psychological Science, 17*(6), 370–375. https://doi.org/10.1111/j.1467-8721.2008.00608.x

Pollak, S. D., Klorman, R., Thatcher, J. E., & Cicchetti, D. (2001). P3b reflects maltreated children's reactions to facial displays of emotion. *Psychophysiology, 38*(2), 267–274.

Price, D., Close, G., & Fielding, B. (1983). Age of appearance of circadian rhythm in salivary cortisol values in infancy. *Archives of Disease in Childhood, 58*(6), 454–456.

Ridout, K. K., Levandowski, M., Ridout, S. J., Gantz, L., Goonan, K., Palermo, D., . . .Tyrka, A. R. (2017). Early life adversity and telomere length: A meta-analysis. *Molecular Psychiatry*. https://doi.org/10.1038/mp.2017.26

Rimawi, B. H., Mirdamadi, M., & John, J. F. (2014). Infections and homelessness: Risks of increased infectious diseases in displaced women. *World Medical & Health Policy, 6*(2), 118–132. https://doi.org/10.1002/wmh3.95

Rubia, K., Smith, A. B., Woolley, J., Nosarti, C., Heyman, I., Taylor, E., & Brammer, M. (2006). Progressive increase of frontostriatal brain activation from childhood to adulthood during event-related tasks of cognitive control. *Human Brain Mapping, 27*(12), 973–993. https://doi.org/10.1002/hbm.20237

Rubin, D. M., Downes, K. J., O'Reilly, A. L. R., Mekonnen, R., Luan, X., & Localio, R. (2008). Impact of kinship care on behavioral well-being for children in out-of-home care. *Archives of Pediatrics & Adolescent Medicine, 162*(6), 550. https://doi.org/10.1001/archpedi.162.6.550

Sagiv, A., Burton, D. G. A., Moshayev, Z., Vadai, E., Wensveen, F., Ben-Dor, S., . . . Krizhanovsky, V. (2016). NKG2D ligands mediate immunosurveillance of senescent cells. *Aging, 8*(2), 328–344. https://doi.org/10.18632/aging.100897

Schmitz, T., & Chew, L.-J. (2008). Cytokines and myelination in the central nervous system. *The Scientific World Journal, 8*, 1119–1147. https://doi.org/10.1100/tsw.2008.140

Segerstrom, S. C., & Miller, G. E. (2004). Psychological stress and the human immune system: A meta-analytic study of 30 years of inquiry. *Psychological Bulletin, 130*(4), 601–630. https://doi.org/10.1037/0033-2909.130.4.601

Shea, A. K., Streiner, D. L., Fleming, A., Kamath, M. V., Broad, K., & Steiner, M. (2007). The effect of depression, anxiety and early life trauma on the cortisol awakening response during pregnancy: Preliminary results. *Psychoneuroendocrinology, 32*(8), 1013–1020. https://doi.org/10.1016/j.psyneuen.2007.07.006

Shirtcliff, E. A., Granger, D. A., Booth, A., & Johnson, D. (2005). Low salivary cortisol levels and externalizing behavior problems in youth. *Development and Psychopathology, 17*(1), 167–184. https://doi.org/10.1017/S0954579405050091

Shonkoff, J. P. (2010). Building a new biodevelopmental framework to guide the future of early childhood policy. *Child Development, 81*(1), 357–367. https://doi.org/10.1111/j.1467-8624.2009.01399.x

Shonkoff, J. P., Boyce, W. T., & McEwen, B. S. (2009). Neuroscience, molecular biology, and the childhood roots of health disparities. *JAMA, 301*(21), 2252–2259. https://doi.org/10.1001/jama.2009.754

Simms, M. D., Dubowitz, H., & Szilagyi, M. A. (2000). Health care needs of children in the foster care system. *Pediatrics, 106*, 909–918.

Slopen, N., McLaughlin, K. A., & Shonkoff, J. P. (2010). Interventions to improve cortisol regulation in children: A systematic review. *Pediatrics, 133*(2), 312–326. https://doi.org/10.1542/peds.2013-1632

Snoek, H., van Goozen, S. H. M., Matthys, W., Buitelaar, J. K., & van Engeland, H. (2004). Stress responsivity in children with externalizing behavior disorders. *Development and Psychopathology, 16*, 389–406. https://doi.org/10.1017/S0954579404044578

Sullivan, R. M. (2012). The neurobiology of attachment to nurturing and abusive caregivers. *Hastings Law Journal, 63*, 1553–1570.

Szilagyi, M. A., Rosen, D. S., Rubin, D., & Zlotnik, S. (2015). Health care issues for children and adolescents in foster care and kinship care. *Pediatrics, 136*(4), e1131–e1140. https://doi.org/10.1542/peds.2015-2655

Teicher, M. H., & Samson, J. A. (2016). Annual research review: Enduring neurobiological effects of childhood abuse and neglect. *Journal of Child Psychology and Psychiatry, and Allied Disciplines, 57*(3), 241–266. https://doi.org/10.1111/jcpp.12507

Tomoda, A., Suzuki, H., Rabi, K., Sheu, Y.-S., Polcari, A., & Teicher, M. H. (2009). Reduced prefrontal cortical gray matter volume in young adults exposed to harsh corporal punishment. *NeuroImage, 47*, T66–71. https://doi.org/10.1016/j.neuroimage.2009.03.005

Tottenham, N., Hare, T. A., Millner, A., Gilhooly, T., Zevin, J. D., & Casey, B. J. (2011). Elevated amygdala response to faces following early deprivation. *Developmental Science, 14*(2), 190–204. https://doi.org/10.1111/j.1467-7687.2010.00971.x

Tottenham, N., Hare, T. A., Quinn, B. T., McCarry, T. W., Nurse, M., Gilhooly, T., . . . Casey, B. J. (2010). Prolonged institutional rearing is associated with atypically large amygdala volume and difficulties in emotion regulation. *Developmental Science, 13*(1), 46–61. https://doi.org/10.1111/j.1467-7687.2009.00852.x

Tottenham, N., & Sheridan, M. A. (2009). A review of adversity, the amygdala and the hippocampus: A consideration of developmental timing. *Frontiers in Human Neuroscience, 3*, 68. https://doi.org/10.3389/neuro.09.068.2009

Uematsu, A., Matsui, M., Tanaka, C., Takahashi, T., Noguchi, K., Suzuki, M., & Nishijo, H. (2012). Developmental trajectories of amygdala and hippocampus from infancy to early adulthood in healthy individuals. *PloS One, 7*(10), e46970. https://doi.org/10.1371/journal.pone.0046970

Vanderwert, R. E., Marshall, P. J., Nelson, C. A., Zeanah, C. H., & Fox, N. A. (2010). Timing of intervention affects brain electrical activity in children exposed to severe psychosocial neglect. *PloS One, 5*(7), e11415. https://doi.org/10.1371/journal.pone.0011415

van Goozen, S. H. M., Matthys, W., Cohen-Kettenis, P. T., Gispen-de Wied, C., Wiegant, V. M., & van Engeland, H. (1998). Salivary cortisol and cardiovascular activity during stress in oppositional-defiant disorder boys and normal controls. *Biological Psychiatry, 43*(7), 531–539. https://doi.org/10.1016/S0006-3223(97)00253-9

Vitkovic, L., Bockaert, J., & Jacque, C. (2001). "Inflammatory" cytokines. *Journal of Neurochemistry, 74*(2), 457–471. https://doi.org/10.1046/j.1471-4159.2000.740457.x

Warne, J. P. (2009). Shaping the stress response: Interplay of palatable food choices, glucocorticoids, insulin and abdominal obesity. *Molecular and Cellular Endocrinology, 300*(1–2), 137–146. https://doi.org/10.1016/j.mce.2008.09.036

Weissbecker, I., Floyd, A., Dedert, E., Salmon, P., & Sephton, S. (2006). Childhood trauma and diurnal cortisol disruption in fibromyalgia syndrome. *Psychoneuroendocrinology, 31*(3), 312–324. https://doi.org/10.1016/j.psyneuen.2005.08.009

Wright, R. J. (2011). Epidemiology of stress and asthma: From constricting communities and fragile families to epigenetics. *Immunology and Allergy Clinics of North America, 31*(1), 19–39. https://doi.org/10.1016/j.iac.2010.09.011

Zeanah, C. H., Nelson, C. A., Fox, N. A., Smyke, A. T., Marshall, P., Parker, S. W., & Koga, S. (2003). Designing research to study the effects of institutionalization on brain and behavioral development: The Bucharest Early Intervention Project. *Development and Psychopathology, 15*(4), 885–907. https://doi.org/10.1017/S0954579403000452

4

Trauma and Socioemotional Development in Foster Youth

Lessons Learned from LONGSCAN

Alan J. Litrownik, Laura J. Proctor, and May Yeh

U.S. Child Welfare System (i.e., government) interventions have evolved from an initial focus on first protecting children and youth who were at risk for experiencing maltreatment, and then finding them a safe and stable living environment, to concerns about promoting healthy development or well-being (Samuels, 2012). With this relatively new focus on well-being, the importance of understanding the risks that foster children and youth face (e.g., abuse, neglect, caregiver instability) at various times (e.g., prior to, during, and after Child Welfare involvement), and how this impacts their socioemotional development is critical to informing those responsible for children and youth in need of care. Before moving forward in an effort to set the agenda for research, policy, and practice that emphasizes well-being in foster youth, we move back in time to set the context for the creation of the multi-site Longitudinal Studies of Child Abuse and Neglect (LONGSCAN) Consortium, and discuss what we now know, and how it informs future efforts.

Looking back three decades, there was much hope. It appeared that as a nation, the United States was beginning to recognize the dangers of maltreatment and the need for action to protect our most vulnerable populations. The Child Abuse Prevention and Treatment Act (CAPTA) of 1974 had been passed, establishing the National Center on Child Abuse and Neglect (NCCAN), which was charged with monitoring child maltreatment, guiding the nation's response to it, and supporting research to inform that response (see Institute of Medicine & National Research Council, 2014). As the nation increased its attention to the problem of abuse and neglect, official reports began to rise at an alarming rate, from 669,000 in 1976 to almost 2.2 million by 1987 (Knudsen, 1989; U.S. Department of Health & Human Services, 1992). Nearly half a million children and youth were in foster care at any point in time during this period, with many youth remaining in care for extended periods of time (Myers, 2008). The Adoption Assistance and Child Welfare Act of 1980 soon followed, emphasizing the need to protect children and youth who had been exposed to maltreatment, and to make every effort to maintain them at home, if at all possible, and if not, to return them to their families following placement in substitute care. The effect of this law was to make family preservation a guiding principle in child welfare decisions (see Institute of Medicine & National Research Council, 2014).

At the same time, NCCAN recognized that no one discipline had a monopoly on understanding and combating maltreatment, and that only through working together could we hope to begin making a difference. As a recipient of one of the ten interdisciplinary training grants funded by NCCAN in 1986, the San Diego LONGSCAN site was in the forefront of preparing students from a variety of disciplines to address the issues resulting from abuse and neglect. At one of the first annual meetings for the training sites sponsored by NCCAN in 1987, one of the authors (AJL) had the opportunity to celebrate the promise of this new commitment, and at the same time hear from professionals at other government agencies who questioned the research base for the field. They pointed out that the main variable of interest—that is, maltreatment—was poorly defined. The vast majority of studies collected data at a single point in time, and lacked a strong theoretical foundation that would allow for links across studies.

As the 1980s came to a close, we learned that this sentiment was much more broadly shared, both outside and inside the maltreatment research arena. Specifically, the Institute of Medicine (IOM) initiated its seminal review of the field, *Understanding Child Abuse and Neglect* (National Research Council, 1993), NCCAN put out its first call for proposals to conduct a longitudinal study in 1988, and David Fanshel and colleagues published a volume evaluating youth who had exited care from the Casey Family Programs (Fanshel, Finch, & Grundy, 1990). All three pointed out that there was an absence of theory-based prospective studies in the field. The National Research Council (NRC) and NCCAN noted that such studies were needed to facilitate our definitions of abuse and neglect and identification of their antecedents and consequences. Fanshel et al. (1990) called for "true" prospective studies of foster children and youth to gain a better understanding of their development from a life course perspective.

LONGSCAN Multi-Site Study

It was in this context that NCCAN announced in 1990 that it would support the 20-year multi-site LONGSCAN Consortium's efforts to identify the antecedents and consequences of maltreatment. Two important factors required attention when the Consortium began in 1990: selection of the samples, and identification of a salient theoretical framework.

Multi-Site Samples

To reduce potential time and cost limitations inherent in a longitudinal design, the architects of LONGSCAN identified ongoing studies of samples from five sites (Baltimore, North Carolina, Chicago, Seattle, and San Diego) that represented varying levels and types of risk and exposure to maltreatment. These samples were then recruited into LONGSCAN at ages 4 and 6.

The Baltimore sample ($n=282$) was comprised of low-income, inner-city children recruited into an earlier study from primary health care clinics (e.g., at risk due to low birth-weight, drug exposure) independent of their involvement with Child Protective Services (CPS).

The North Carolina sample was originally recruited for a statewide "High Priority Infant Tracking Program" which identified "at-risk" infants (e.g., with teenage mothers, low socioeconomic status [SES]) who then participated in a program to ensure that the children received adequate follow-up in the health care system. For LONGSCAN, a subsample ($n=243$) was identified and recruited from the original "at-risk" sample by matching CPS non-reported to reported children on a 2:1 ratio.

In the Chicago site ($n=245$), two-thirds of the sample of 1 to 2 year olds were recruited from families reported to CPS, with half of the families receiving comprehensive services and half receiving the typical CPS intervention. The other third of the sample included families with 1 to 2 year olds from the same neighborhood who had not been reported to CPS.

All children in the Seattle site ($n=254$) had been reported to CPS, participated in a risk assessment study, and those who were found to be at moderate risk for subsequent maltreatment and remained at home were recruited into LONGSCAN.

At the most extreme level, the San Diego Foster Care Study grew out of two earlier studies originally funded by NCCAN and the National Institute of Mental Health. These two companion studies, referred to jointly as the Foster Care Mental Health (FCMH) Study, identified children and youth (birth to 16) who entered foster care in San Diego between May 1990 and October 1991. Those youth ($n=1221$) who were determined to be dependents of the court, and were placed and remained in substitute care for at least 5 months, were then followed for an 18-month period during the FCMH study. The 532 children from the initial FCMH study who were younger than 3.5 years of age when they entered foster care comprised the group from which participants were subsequently recruited for the San Diego LONGSCAN study. A total of 330 children who represented the larger cohort of 532 eligible children were successfully recruited and completed LONGSCAN baseline assessments.

Overall, these five cohorts provided the LONGSCAN Consortium with samples of children who were at risk for maladaptive development due to varying exposure to maltreatment, family dysfunction, and low socioeconomic status. The use of common measures and procedures to acquire information about each sample has provided an opportunity to conduct cross-site analyses addressing specific research questions about how best to define maltreatment and understand its consequences. In addition, we are able to focus specifically on the San Diego LONGSCAN Foster Care Study in the present chapter to address issues about the socioemotional development of foster youth.

Theoretical Framework and Design

At the time when LONGSCAN began, past research in child maltreatment had generally been goal-driven, rather than theory-based, with maltreatment generally identified retrospectively as either occurring or not occurring (see National Research Council, 1993). In response, the LONGSCAN investigative team initially identified Ecological-Developmental Theory to guide the design of the multi-site studies; for example, age-specific research questions, measurement, and analyses. According to Ecological-Developmental Theory, a child develops within a series of multiple, nested social systems beginning with direct interaction with the primary caregiver and family and extending through indirect influence from cultural traditions (Bronfenbrenner, 1993). In the evolution of LONGSCAN, we recognized Social-Development Theory as a complementary theoretical framework in understanding the impact of child maltreatment and integrated it into our theoretical paradigm. The social development model (Catalano & Hawkins, 1996) hypothesizes that characteristics of interactions with others (e.g., social skills, perceived rewards, attachment and commitment, and belief in the values of others) mediate the influences of individual constitutional and social-structural factors on outcomes. This model incorporates biological, psychological, and social factors within multiple social domains, from the family to the community in an effort to predict child outcomes (Catalano & Hawkins, 1996). Both theories recognize that the link between risk factors and behavior is often indirect and influenced by social-psychological factors.

Measurement

With this theoretical framework, the LONGSCAN Consortium was ready to identify and develop common measurement protocols and data collection methods. Specifically, LONGSCAN was designed as a longitudinal follow-through study that began with children at 4 years of age or younger and continued to follow them at regularly scheduled intervals (ages 6, 8, 12, 14, 16, and 18) using extensive face-to-face (FTF) interviews with the primary caregiver and the child. During each intervening year, there were annual telephone interviews designed to enhance sample retention and track service utilization, life events, and child behavior problems.

Based on Ecological-Developmental Theory, age-specific risk and protective factors at the child, parent or caregiver, family, neighborhood, and cultural level were assessed. The longitudinal design of the project reflects the developmental changes in risk and protective factors and child outcomes that occur as children develop from preschool to young adulthood. Data collection was designed to measure outcome variables as well as intervening variables that may influence the link between risk status and outcome.

The specific domains assessed and examples of information obtained across FTF interviews included:

1. Child Characteristics (e.g., demographics, health, cognitive functioning, adaptive behavior, behavior problems, and peer relationships);
2. Caregiver Characteristics (e.g., demographics, physical and mental health, parenting attitudes, and substance use);
3. Microsystems (e.g., family demographics, family functioning, child–parent relationship, parental monitoring, conflict tactics with partner and child, father involvement, daily stressors, life events);
4. Exosystems (e.g., neighborhood and social environment, mental health service use, and Child Welfare involvement).

Starting at age 12, youth were asked to self-report experiences of abuse and neglect, and at ages 14 and 18, youth completed the Diagnostic Interview Schedule for Children and Young Adults (DISC), respectively (Shaffer et al., 1996). Interviews during the adolescent years (i.e., 12, 14, 16, and 18) focused primarily on age-specific outcomes known or hypothesized to be impacted by maltreatment, including: academic achievement, employment, health and health risk behaviors, pregnancy and parenting, mental health status, delinquent and violent behavior, involvement with the criminal justice and penal systems, independent living skills, peer relationships, and community or extracurricular involvement. The developmental focus of these interviews was on issues related to: 1) increasing autonomy and separation from caregivers; 2) social relations; and 3) future orientation and preparation for adulthood. We also continued to assess age-specific risk and protective factors at each level of the ecological model, along with youth outcomes (see the LONGSCAN website for a complete listing of the measures administered at each interview, and summary descriptive statistics: www.iprc.unc.edu/longscan/).

Throughout the LONGSCAN study period, CPS case records were reviewed to identify reported allegations of maltreatment. Any identified reports were then coded using a modified version of Barnett, Manly, and Cicchetti's (1993) Maltreatment Classification System (see the LONGSCAN website). Data obtained included maltreatment type and severity, substantiation status, and case disposition.

Subsequent funding by the Doris Duke Charitable Foundation (DDCF) allowed us to focus on dissemination of our findings, culminating in a Congressional Hearing in 2013. Finally, a current National Institute of Drug Abuse (NIDA) funded project has resulted in the recent collection of online survey responses focusing on the transition to adulthood and adult functioning among more than 480 multi-site LONGSCAN participants in their mid-20s.

Specific to the San Diego LONGSCAN Foster Care Study, several sources of qualitative data have been collected over the life of the study. First, we developed a procedure for writing descriptive "life event narratives" (birth to age 18) for 200 participants that included anecdotal information obtained from all contacts, including FTF and phone interviews. Second, five biological parents whose children were still in substitute care at the time were interviewed approximately 7 to 10 years after their children had been removed. These interviews focused on the removal experience, their parenting fitness, and expectations for the future. Third, seven individuals between the ages of 21 and 24 participated in a focus group funded by the DDCF to share their views on participating in LONGSCAN and their experiences in foster care. And most recently, another NIDA grant supported semi-structured interviews with 40 LONGSCAN participants who were stratified based on data collected during adolescence on substance use history and stability of living situation. These interviews focused on the themes of changes, adversities, supports, services, and their life course effects.

The Changing Context of LONGSCAN

As with any longitudinal study, there are likely to be a number of intervening events that may impact the participants and ultimately the research methods of the study. A number of such events deserve mention here. First, a little more than 6 years into the intended 20-year study, the 1997 CAPTA amendments eliminated NCCAN, downgrading it to the Office on Child Abuse and Neglect (OCAN). Questions were raised about OCAN's research funding for LONGSCAN, and efforts to educate policy makers about the need for such a study of vulnerable children were made. Continued funding for LONGSCAN was secured, and a new initiative emerged which led to funding of the National Survey of Child and Adolescent Well-Being (NSCAW; see Institute of Medicine & National Research Council, 2014), a shorter prospective study of children and youth referred to CPS across the nation that was informed by much of LONGSCAN's early work.

Following the Adoption Assistance and Child Welfare Act of 1980, a number of other laws that specifically targeted the Child Welfare System were passed; for example, the Adoption and Safe Families Act of 1997, the Promoting Safe and Stable Families Amendments of 2001, and the Fostering Connections to Success and Increasing Adoptions Act of 2008 (see Institute of Medicine & National Research Council, 2014). These Acts, in combination with specific initiatives within the U.S. Department of Health & Human Services and many subsequently published studies, focused on taking less time to find a permanent placement, reducing the number of children and youth in foster care, and promoting what were identified as positive exits from foster care (i.e., reunification, adoption, and kinship guardianship; see Courtney, 2009; Institute of Medicine & National Research Council, 2014). Though there has been some indication that these initiatives have been successful, their impact on child well-being has not been examined (e.g., Samuels, 2012). Finally, while greater attention (i.e., laws, research) has been given to youth who "age out" of foster care or exit care when they emancipate (i.e., reach 18), the importance of continuing to follow up and monitor the well-being of children and youth who exit care at earlier ages is still underestimated.

In the follow-up volume to the National Research Council (1993) report, the Institute of Medicine and National Research Council (2014) concluded that "a new science of child abuse and neglect had been launched," (p. 1), though much remained to be done. In terms of Child Welfare practice, the authors of the follow-up volume noted that relative foster care had become the option of choice over the last 15 years when placing a child in out-of-home care, as it has been associated with better behavior outcomes and a more stable placement. Though identifying placement instability as a critical factor in negative outcomes, the authors (Institute of Medicine & National Research Council, 2014) pointed out that little research had been conducted on this relationship to date. Similarly, the report noted that well-being of foster children and youth had become an increasing concern since 2009. Nevertheless, we would highlight the fact that the focus of assessments, evaluations, and mandated reports to Congress (e.g., *The AFCARS Report*; U.S. Department of Health & Human Services, 2015) continues to be on numbers in substitute care, stability of placements, and types of exit rather than well-being. Finally, the complexity of the Child Welfare System is identified, given the differences in legislation across States and in practice across various jurisdictions. Thus, we recognize that what we find in the San Diego LONGSCAN Foster Care Study may not be simply generalized to other regions. Indeed, our goal is not to establish what works best, but rather to identify what key factors need to be considered in order to determine what works best for a given individual.

What we Have Learned from LONGSCAN

Since 1991, LONGSCAN has generated more than 130 peer-reviewed studies of child maltreatment and related adversities. Below, we summarize the most salient LONGSCAN research findings with regard to foster youth. First, we examine what LONGSCAN's multi-site findings have taught us about defining and measuring the multiple dimensions of maltreatment and their socioemotional consequences. We then present findings from the San Diego Foster Care Study site that focus on three key issues: prior trauma and socioemotional problems in early care; continuing trauma in care and permanent placements; and long-term socioemotional development for youth who have been in foster care.

Trauma and Socioemotional Development in At-Risk Youth: Multi-Site Findings

Definitions

After identifying the theoretical framework to be used by LONGSCAN, the next task was to begin developing a better understanding of the maltreatment experience, how to measure it, and what its consequences were. Initial work by the LONGSCAN investigators utilized official CPS reports in an effort to determine how best to characterize maltreatment. Based on coding these reports (see the LONGSCAN website), we published a series of papers in a Special Issue of the journal *Child Abuse & Neglect*. Results from these papers suggest that: 1) LONGSCAN's modification of the Maltreatment Classification System (MCS) was better at predicting subsequent outcomes (behavior problems, adaptive functioning, and trauma symptoms) than official CPS designations (Dubowitz et al., 2005; Runyan et al., 2005); 2) unsubstantiated reports do not differ from substantiated reports when predicting outcomes (Hussey et al., 2005); and 3) characterizations of maltreatment based on type (Lau et al., 2005), severity (Litrownik et al., 2005), and chronicity (English, Graham, et al., 2005) add to our understanding of maltreatment effects (English, Upadhyaya, et al., 2005).

Subsequent efforts to characterize maltreatment by LONGSCAN investigators have benefited from two relatively unique developments. The first is the development of self-report measures of maltreatment that were administered to LONGSCAN subjects at the age 12 interview (and at subsequent interviews). The second was the application of a latent modeling, person-centered analytic strategy, leading to the classification of individuals based on their pattern of experiences (see Roesch, Villodas, M.T., & Villodas, F., 2010). These two developments resulted in a series of studies that have examined the utility of self-reports, as well as patterns of self-reports and CPS reports individually, over time, and in combination.

Specifically, self-reports of abuse and neglect were found to be useful in not only characterizing the abuse (Nooner et al., 2010) and neglect (Dubowitz et al., 2011) experiences of youth, but were also more likely to be associated with outcomes (e.g., behavior problems, trauma symptoms, and adaptive functioning) than official CPS reports (see Everson et al., 2008). Though self-reports were found to be most useful, it was also the case that each report (i.e., self and official CPS) contributed uniquely to the assessment of abuse. That is, the self-report interview elicited prevalence rates of physical and sexual abuse four to six times higher than those found in CPS records. At the same time, 20 of the 45 adolescents with CPS determinations of sexual abuse failed to self-report sexual abuse when interviewed (see Everson et al., 2008). Thus, the findings not only provided evidence for the *predictive* validity of self-reported abuse, but also suggested that the most accurate characterizations of abuse may require multiple informants or sources of information.

Utilizing a latent variable modeling approach, Villodas et al. (2012) were able to identify individuals with common patterns of maltreatment exposure based on CPS reports during three different periods (ages 0–4, 5–8, and 9–12). Classes or groups of individuals included those with no maltreatment allegations, those tending to have neglect and emotional maltreatment reports, and those having allegations for all maltreatment types. These findings confirmed that children are likely to experience multiple forms of maltreatment. Further, it was found that children in the maltreatment groups were more likely to experience subsequent victimization.

Building on what we had learned in these studies, we applied a latent modeling approach in an effort to identify groups or classes of individuals, based on both official CPS reports of the severity of each type of maltreatment from birth to age 12, as well as self-reports on that type of maltreatment at age 12. The resulting three class solutions for sexual and physical abuse each included 1) low or no abuse, 2) early abuse, and 3) late abuse groups. Three neglect groups were identified: 1) no or low neglect, 2) early neglect only, and 3) high early and high late neglect. Finally, two emotional abuse classes were identified: 1) early, and 2) early plus late.

The power of these empirically identified classes of maltreatment (i.e., physical, sexual, and emotional abuse; and neglect) to predict trajectories of problem behaviors over time (ages 6, 8, 10, and 12) was then examined. Multilevel regression modeling (Raudenbush & Bryk, 2002) was used to examine these relationships within the context of exposure to other adversities (e.g., family dysfunction, instability, and harm to self or others) assessed at each of the four ages (see Lau, Litrownik, Newton, & Landsverk, 2003). In addition, gender and site were considered in the final analytic models. Variable patterns emerged based upon type of behavior, gender, data collection site, sexual abuse group, family dysfunction scores, harm to self or others, and a number of significant Maltreatment by Life Events interactions. Specifically, aggressive problem behaviors decreased as the children aged, with males tending to be more aggressive than females, while no temporal pattern or gender difference was observed for anxious/depressed problem behaviors. The overall decreasing pattern of aggressive problem behaviors was not apparent in the two exclusive Child Welfare sites (i.e., San Diego and Seattle) in that they showed a flat slope (i.e., did not evidence a decrease in aggressive behavior over time), and had significantly higher intercepts (i.e., aggressive behavior at age 12) than the other three sites. The findings not only suggest that specific maltreatment experiences and life events (e.g., early sexual abuse, family dysfunction, harm to self/others) are related to subsequent behavior problems at age 12, but also indicate that maltreatment and life events can moderate the impact that the other has on its relationship to problem behaviors. Thus, relationships between the different life events (family dysfunction, harm to self/others, and instability) and problem behaviors are stronger when children are neglected early, sexually abused in mid to late childhood, and exposed to physical abuse later in childhood.

These findings are critical in the development of LONGSCAN's approach to characterizing maltreatment and determining its effect. First, maltreatment is defined by both officially coded CPS reports and youth self-reports. The timing of the CPS reports is considered as well as the severity of the alleged maltreatment for each type. Second, the prospective nature of the study is utilized to not only characterize maltreatment, but also to define the outcomes of interest. Finally, the relationship between maltreatment and the problem behaviors are considered in the context of other time-varying adverse life events, and all these relationships take into account the gender of the participants as well as the site that they came from. The approach taken demonstrates one method for considering the complexity of maltreatment, the context in which it occurs, and how it, along with other adversities, can impact individuals over time.

Another approach taken by the LONGSCAN investigators has been to examine a count of early childhood adversities (see Flaherty et al., 2009; Thompson et al., 2012). Though finding a relationship between health outcomes and a count of adversities, the Flaherty et al. (2009) study did not differentiate between adversities or consider interactive or moderating effects (see McLaughlin & Sheridan [2016] for a critique of this approach). On the other hand, Thompson et al. (2012) did begin to break down timing and types of adversities in predicting suicidal ideation at age 16. First, a distinction was made between childhood (before the age of 12) and adolescent (between age 12 and 16) adversities, and then the strength of association between individual adversities and suicidal ideation was considered. As expected, there was a significant link between cumulative lifetime adversities and suicidal ideation. Similar to the prior described latent modeling findings, this study found that the timing and nature of adversities are important in understanding youth suicidal ideation. For example, childhood adversities were found to moderate the effects of adolescent adversities on suicidal ideation such that the effects of adolescent adversities were strongest at low levels of childhood adversities.

Socioemotional Consequences

LONGSCAN investigators have not only made substantial contributions to how we characterize maltreatment, but also to how we understand the socioemotional consequences of maltreatment and other adversities.

In addition to the studies described in the previous section, other multi-site studies have further demonstrated the negative impact of maltreatment and other adversities on child and adolescent externalizing/disruptive behavior problems (Kotch et al., 2008; Litrownik et al., 2003; Merrick et al., 2015; Thompson et al., 2011; Villodas et al., 2015), trauma symptoms (Lewis et al., 2012), youth parenting attitudes (Thompson et al., 2014), sexual activity or sexual acting out (Black et al., 2009; Jones et al., 2013; Thompson et al., 2017), and substance use (Lewis et al., 2011; Proctor et al., 2017). These studies used a prospective design that followed participants over time, thus providing strong support for the causal pathways between maltreatment and the various short- and long-term consequences. Additionally, maltreatment has been characterized along a number of dimensions, allowing for the identification of specific aspects of the maltreatment experience (e.g., timing, type, severity) assessed via multiple informants (CPS reports, self-reports), that are linked to these outcomes. Finally, the longitudinal design provides an opportunity to utilize the temporal ordering of observed variables to begin identifying factors that mediate the relationship between maltreatment and outcomes (e.g., the work of Lewis et al. [2011] on emotional distress; the work of Merrick et al. [2015] on sexualized behaviors; the work of Proctor et al. [2017] on externalizing problems; the work of Thompson et al. [2017] on trauma symptoms), and to examine the impact of childhood trauma on trajectories or transitions of problematic socioemotional behavior (e.g., Villodas et al., 2015). Such studies hold the promise of identifying mechanisms that may inform us about how maltreatment leads to the many specific negative outcomes that have been observed.

Trauma and Socioemotional Development in Foster Youth: San Diego Foster Care Study

Data from the San Diego Foster Care Study suggest that young children who are removed from their homes due to maltreatment are exposed to multiple adversities prior to, during, and after involvement with the Child Welfare System, and that these exposures are directly linked to their long-term socioemotional development.

Prior Trauma and Socioemotional Problems in Early Care

Multiple maltreatment reports per child, details culled from resulting investigative reports, and qualitative data from life narratives all attest to the trauma that these youngsters were facing early in their lives. For example, 79% of the children and youth who participated in the FCMH study had an adult caregiver in their home at the time of removal who had a substance use problem (Besinger, Garland, Litrownik, & Landsverk, 1999). All five of the parents whom we interviewed approximately 7 to 10 years later admitted that they had an alcohol or drug problem at the time of removal, could not provide for their child, and that CPS and the courts did the right thing when placing their children in foster care. One particularly surprising finding was that the parents continued to believe they would get their children back, even though it had been more than 7 years since they had been removed from the home.

It is not surprising that children and youth enter foster care with more socioemotional problems than would be expected in the general population, given their exposure to maltreatment and a dysfunctional caregiving environment prior to out-of-home placement, as well as the trauma of removal. For example, we found relatively high numbers (35%–66%) of foster care youth from three

California counties (Monterey, Santa Cruz, and San Diego) to evidence Total or Externalizing Behavior Problems in the borderline or clinical range on the Child Behavior Checklist (CBCL; Achenbach, 1991) soon after entering care (Clausen, Landsverk, Ganger, Chadwick, & Litrownik, 1998). Additionally, San Diego LONGSCAN site caregivers reported that nearly half of the 4 year olds that they cared for evidenced an emotional, communication, cognitive, or physical disability with a quarter having two or more disabilities (Romney, Litrownik, Newton, & Lau, 2006). Thus, foster children and youth typically begin their journey in out-of-home care following multiple trauma exposure (e.g., maltreatment, removal) evidencing significant socioemotional problems.

Continuing Trauma in Care and Permanent Placements

At the time we initiated the LONGSCAN study, there was much concern about the potential iatrogenic effects of foster care, specifically youth becoming further traumatized by not only remaining in substitute care (i.e., being stuck), but also being passed from one caregiver to another. There was also concern about how difficult it was for substitute caregivers to handle children and youth with socioemotional problems, especially those who were acting out.

In a seminal study, we attempted to disentangle the relationship between early (i.e., first 18 months) experiences in foster care and youth behavior problems (Newton, Litrownik, & Landsverk, 2000). Using data from the FCMH study, we found that the foster care population in San Diego experienced multiple moves in an 18-month period following their removal (range=1–16; mean=4.43), that the number of moves was both predicted by initial behavior problems of the children and youth (especially externalizing), and that the number of moves predicted subsequent behavior problems, especially for those who did not evidence problems initially. A number of subsequent prospective studies examining other samples (e.g., NSCAW) similarly found that multiple placements during the first 12 to 36 months have a negative impact on foster youth (e.g., Aarons et al., 2010).

These findings support legislation that emphasizes the importance of securing a stable living situation, or permanent placement, preferably with the biological parent or adoptive parent, and if neither is available, then with a relative in a guardian relationship. Unfortunately, this policy emphasis has led to research and practice which assumes that the desired outcome is a permanent placement. Though the Child Welfare System (see Samuels, 2012) has expanded its task to go beyond safety, permanence, and providing a stable family-like setting to include the well-being of foster care children and youth, the latter is neither assessed nor ensured, but rather assumed once a child in foster care is reunified, adopted, or placed with a relative guardian.

The San Diego LONGSCAN foster care cohort provided us with the opportunity to follow those children and youth who exit care, to determine the relative benefits of the specific exits in terms of safety, stability, and well-being. Two early studies of children who had been reunified by age 4 or 6 provided mixed findings. In the first (Litrownik, Newton, Mitchell, & Richardson, 2003), we report that those children who were reunified by age 6 were more likely to be exposed to violence, both directed at them and witnessed, than those who were not reunified. The second study (Lau et al., 2003) found that children who had been reunified by age 4, compared to children who were not reunified, were more likely to report higher levels of social connectedness, but evidenced more internalizing behavior problems, which were mediated by higher levels of family dysfunction, instability, and harm.

Similarly, mixed findings resulted when examining other placement types (see Litrownik et al., 2003). For example, adopted caregivers reported using more physical methods to remedy parent–child conflicts than foster caregivers, but adopted youth reported seeing less violence in their home than foster youth. Finally, relative foster caregivers reported that they were more likely to use harsh punishment than non-relative foster caregivers. This latter finding was replicated in a subsequent study using data from the 8-year-old interview (Tripp De Robertis & Litrownik, 2004) which found relative caregivers reporting that they would use harsher discipline procedures to resolve hypothetical situations where a child was disobedient than non-relative foster caregivers. Additionally, it was found that 8 year olds whose relative caregivers indicated they would rely on more harsh disciplinary procedures were more likely to report using aggressive means to resolve their social problems.

Longer-term prospective quantitative analyses examining continuing trauma exposure, examination of life narratives, and qualitative interviews with the cohort suggested that their early dysfunctional, chaotic lives continue during and after exit from care, regardless of their permanent placement. For example, Proctor et al. (2012) found that more than two-thirds of the children from the San Diego and Seattle sites who had been reported to CPS by age 4 had a subsequent report between the ages of 4 and 12. Two concerning trajectory classes emerged from the analyses, one with continuous reports throughout the 8-year follow-up period, and the other with intermittent reports throughout this period. Factors predicting membership in these two re-report groups included: initial reports for physical abuse, more children living in the home, living with a biological/step-parent, or having a caregiver who abused alcohol, was depressed, lacked social support, or had limited economic resources. Youth who were reunified were more likely to experience multiple re-reports. However, it was notable and unexpected that children with all types of permanent placement, including adoption, relative and non-relative foster care, were represented in the trajectory groups that continued to experience maltreatment re-reports across the 8-year follow-up period.

In a second study, Proctor et al. (2011) utilized a data reduction procedure (Classification and Regression Tree Analyses) to examine stability (age 6 to 8) across a variety of permanent placements (e.g., adoption, reunification, non-relative and relative foster caregivers), and to begin identifying potential predictors of stability at a range of ecological levels; for example, individual, caregiver, family. One out of seven children experienced caregiver instability over this 2-year period. The strongest factor differentiating those who remained with the same caregiver versus those who did not was a permanent adoptive placement. Additional family (e.g., father involvement, expressiveness within the family) and child (e.g., intellectual functioning, externalizing behavior problems) factors differentiated those who remained with the same caregiver versus those who did not across the other types of permanent placement. Thus, early adoptions appear to be relatively stable over this 2-year period of time. It was also encouraging to find that a number of modifiable family and individual factors appeared to be related to stability in the other placements.

Two related longer-term prospective studies continued to examine the trauma of instability and exposure to other adversities in our cohort as they aged. Using a latent variable modeling approach, Villodas, Litrownik, Newton, and Davis (2016) identified four stable and two unstable placement trajectories for our cohort during their childhood (age 4–12). The stable trajectories included those who were adopted, remained in kinship care, lived with their biological parent, and those who lived with the same non-relative foster parent. The two unstable trajectories comprised children who had been reunified at some time, but returned to substitute care, and those who moved within non-relative foster care. Though more than 80% of the children were in a stable group, nearly one-third of those who were reunified or placed in non-relative care experienced multiple caregiver changes during their childhood.

The continuing instability of placements was evidenced in a second study (Villodas, Cromer, et al., 2016) that followed youth in these placement trajectory classes over a 2-year period (i.e., to the age of 14, or first adolescent interview). Almost one in five changed caregiver from age 12 to 14. This compares to the one in seven who changed caregiver from age 6 to 8 (Proctor et al., 2011), and is again disappointing. It is also interesting to note that changes occurred across all six of the childhood placement trajectories, with several unexpected trends. First, many of the unstable reunified group appeared to settle into a relatively stable living situation, while the unstable foster group continued to experience a lack of stability. Second, more than one in four of the stable relative care group experienced a caregiver change between the ages of 12 to 14. And finally, a number of the stable adopted group no longer lived with their adoptive parents at age 14. In fact, when we looked at where adopted youth lived at subsequent ages, we found that almost 30% no longer lived with their adoptive parents at age 16, while this percentage ballooned to almost 50% at age 18. Interestingly, some of the youth who experienced caregiver changes were later found to be living with their biological parent.

Not only were these children continuing to experience the trauma of multiple caregiver changes well after they were removed from their home at an early age, but they were also experiencing other multiple adversities. Specifically, eight adversities (i.e., caregiver mental health problem, family member substance abuse, incarceration, witnessed family violence, neglect, physical, sexual, and emotional abuse) from the Adverse Childhood Experiences (ACE) study (Felitti et al., 1998) were defined using data obtained from the LONGSCAN study for ages 4 to 12. The mean number of adversities (range=0–8) based on these data collected prospectively from age 4 to age 12 ranged from a high of 4.4 in the unstable groups to a low of 1.4 in the stable adoptive group. Finally, qualitative data or statements from youth participating in the focus group and NIDA study further highlight the extent of continuing adversities (e.g., "I was exposed to a lot of stuff that kids probably shouldn't be exposed to, like drugs and violence and criminals." "I would see my mom's boyfriend beat the crap out of her until she was bleeding everywhere." "My mom would get so high she would piss herself."); lack of stability in the lives of foster youth (e.g., "I didn't have a home." "I just stayed with relatives, like . . . I did go from different relatives like all the time." "We've moved, oh my gosh, 30 times in the last 12 years or something."); and their impact on them (e.g., "It was difficult to make friends and switching . . . if I did actually manage to talk to someone and make a friend, we would move the next week and go to a different school and start all over." "It was a horrible, horrible, horrible nightmare.").

Long-Term Socioemotional Development

As indicated, the San Diego Foster Care Study provided an opportunity not only to continue to identify trauma exposure during out-of-home care and following exits from care, but also to determine how youth were doing as they aged. There is much data suggesting that youth of all ages who become involved with the Child Welfare System, and certainly those who enter out-of-home care as a result, evidence more socioemotional problems initially. Some researchers (e.g., Berger et al., 2009; Goemans, van Geel, & Vedder, 2015) have concluded that in the short term, foster care has neither a positive nor negative effect on foster children as a group, or after controlling for prior functioning. However, we would argue that the most meaningful research questions are those that address the long-term socioemotional functioning of current and former foster youth and identify factors (e.g., risk, mediating, moderating) that could inform our attempts to promote well-being.

The San Diego Foster Care cohort evidenced significant socioemotional problems shortly after entering care, and these problems continued throughout the period that we followed them. For example, almost 44% of the cohort was identified as having at least one diagnosis at age 14, and a little more than 38% at age 18 on the Diagnostic Interview Schedule for Children and Young Adults (DISC). These percentages are not only higher than those found in the multi-site Methods for the Epidemiology of Child and Adolescent Mental Disorders (MECA) study (Shaffer et al., 1996) which assessed 9 to 17 year olds (i.e., 32%), but also for those from other LONGSCAN samples (age 18 range=22% to 31%).

While a number of the continuing socioemotional problems are probably due to the early trauma experienced by these youth prior to their removal, there is much evidence suggesting that subsequent trauma and/or adversities also play a role. For example, Proctor, Skriner, Roesch, and Litrownik (2010) utilized Growth Mixture Modeling to identify three internalizing and four externalizing trajectories of problem behaviors in the San Diego cohort over an 8-year period (age 6 to 14). Consistent with earlier findings, critical predictors of membership in the adjustment or increasing adjustment groups included caregiver stability and the absence of a physical abuse report during the 8-year period.

Additionally, we found that previously identified Unstable Placement Groups were more likely than the Stable Relative/Non-relative group to be in the clinical range at age 12 for both self- and caregiver-reported Externalizing Problems, and for self-reported Internalizing Problems, after controlling for age 4 baseline scores on the CBCL (Villodas, Litrownik et al., 2016). We also noted that the Stable Reunified group was more likely to be in the clinical range than the Stable Relative/Non-relative group. This finding seems to suggest that those youth who are reunified, even those who remain reunified over time, may continue to be at risk for more behavioral problems. Another finding which added to some earlier concerns about the touted benefits of adoption (e.g., stability during adolescence), indicated that the Stable Adopted group was almost four times more likely to be in the clinical range on the CBCL Externalizing Scale than the Stable Relative/Nonrelative group, again after controlling for earlier Externalizing Behavior Problem scores on the CBCL. Finally, the relationship between the stability groups and socioemotional problems at age 12 and age 14 appeared to be mediated by Adverse Childhood Experiences (Villodas, Cromer et al., 2016).

As mentioned previously, there have been a number of findings that do not support the unequivocal benefits of adoption as a desired exit from care (see also Simmel, Barth, & Brooks, 2007). Though adoption from the Child Welfare System has been a major focus in the last three decades, there has been much less attention to providing services to children and families after adoption, much less any long-term follow-up of children and their adoptive families, except for data coming from the San Diego LONGSCAN Foster Care Study. Specifically, we utilized longitudinal data on caregiver-rated behavior problems (CBCL) from age 4 to age 14, based on who the youth were living with at each interview (adopted, reunified, relative, non-relative). Confirming earlier work, the adopted youth were rated by their caregivers as having fewer behavior problems at the age 4 and 6 interviews. By the age 8 interview, and continuing at age 10, this advantage was no longer observed. And finally, by age 14, the adopted youth were now being rated as having significantly more internalizing and externalizing problems. To confirm these unexpected findings, we examined data obtained from the DISC at the age 14 interview. We found that the adopted youth not only had significantly more symptoms of disruptive behavior disorders than those who were reunified or remained in substitute care, but also more disruptive behavior disorder diagnoses. Following these analyses, we went back and re-read a number of life event narratives for adopted youth. The narratives were consistent with the quantitative data in that a number of adopted youth evidenced severe disruptions in their living situation during adolescence.

These unique and unexpected findings suggest that adoption from foster care may not prevent children from being exposed to subsequent challenges, nor protect them from developing disorders. We have not identified the specific challenges they faced, but hypothesize that they are likely to include preprogrammed vulnerabilities (i.e., genetic, constitutional, early adversities), and dealing with the normal challenges of adolescent identity (i.e., demands of parents, peer group identification, and interest in their biological parents and implications for their development) (see van der Vegt et al., 2009, for example).

Summary and Recommendations

LONGSCAN Findings: What we Know from a Life Course Perspective

Based on LONGSCAN findings, supported by data from other sources, we can confidently state that we know:

1. As the science of child abuse and neglect is developing (Institute of Medicine & National Research Council, 2014), it has become clear that maltreatment can be characterized along a

number of dimensions (e.g., timing, chronicity, severity, type) to help us better understand the problem, its precursors, and myriad sequelae (see also Jackson et al., 2014), and that multiple sources of information about its occurrence are needed. Child abuse and neglect do not occur in isolation; rather, different types may co-occur, and are often associated with other adverse childhood experiences (e.g., family instability and chaos) impacting development. These adversities are even more critical when they are experienced early in life (see also Casanueva et al., 2014).
2. Young children make up the majority of those who enter foster care (see U.S. Department of Health & Human Services, 2015), and they are likely to have been exposed to multiple risk factors, in addition to abuse and neglect prior to entering care.
3. Though removing children may protect them from adversities faced in their former home, they will necessarily be presented with new challenging stressors (i.e., the removal process). Given these stressors and prior adversities, it is not surprising that young children enter care with multiple socioemotional problems.
4. Young children removed from the home and placed in foster care are at risk for experiencing violence, maltreatment, chaotic living situations, as well as changes in their primary caregiver, both during their time in formal care, as well as after they exit care (see also Havlicek & Courtney, 2016).
5. Again, it is not surprising to find that youth who have been in foster care continue to present with a host of socioemotional problems as they develop through childhood, adolescence, and emerging adulthood, due not only to the trauma that led them to be removed initially, but also to the trauma experienced during removal, while in care, and thereafter.
6. The specific type of initial formal placement in family foster care (e.g., relative, non-relative) does not guarantee that subsequent trauma will be avoided, much less ensure that young children will not have subsequent socioemotional problems (see also Font, 2015; Institute of Medicine & National Research Council, 2014). The same can be said for different types of permanent placement at time of exit (see also Institute of Medicine & National Research Council, 2014). Research findings on the advantages, both short- and long-term, of different placements is mixed.
7. Though there is some evidence indicating that minority populations are more likely to come into contact with the Child Welfare System as well as experience different dispositions (e.g., Institute of Medicine & National Research Council, 2014), we have, as yet, found little evidence to suggest that foster care is anything but an equal opportunity marker for problematic socioemotional outcomes.

Implications

These conclusions have a number of implications for research, practice, and policy if our aim is to promote the well-being of children and youth who enter foster care. They can be organized, or thought of as existing in several categories, varying from the general to more specific.

The *first* general overarching implication is that we need to take a life course perspective when considering future research, practice, and policy as it relates to foster children and their well-being. In terms of research, the most informative studies will be those that examine well-being over time, allowing us to take into account changes over time, due both to development, as well as to intervening trauma or protective factors. Such a life course perspective is also critical when considering how to intervene with those who enter substitute care. Those responsible for implementing practice in the Child Welfare System must recognize that promotion of well-being requires that foster children and youth be followed not only during their formal involvement in the Child Welfare System, but also after their exit. In other words, the responsibility of the system does not end at the point of exit or realization of the permanent plan, but rather continues through to the age of majority and beyond (e.g., linking emerging adults with other service systems, supports, etc.). It is also the case that psycho-social interventions require long-term follow-up to ensure maintenance and generalizability of effects as well as alerting practitioners when new issues or problems arise that may be a function of changing developmental challenges (see Litrownik, 2012; Litrownik & Castillo-Canez, 2000). Finally, our policies need to recognize the responsibility that is assumed when children or youth are removed from the care of their parent(s). Again, if our interest is in promoting well-being, then the continued involvement of the corporate parent (see Courtney, 2009) is required beyond a permanent placement and the age of majority, and we would need to assess well-being. Though the Adoption and Safe Families Act of 1997 requires an annual report to Congress (e.g., Children's Bureau of the U.S. Department of Health & Human Services, 2016), it is remarkable that data on a number of desired outcomes (e.g., reduce recurrence of child abuse and/or neglect, increase permanency for children in foster care, increase placement stability) are presented, but nothing on well-being is provided. A first step in promoting healthy outcomes in current and former foster youth would be to require that data on well-being be included in reports to Congress, necessitating adequate funding for assessments. If the needed resources are not forthcoming, one potential option that has at least led to changes in short-term funding (i.e., litigation) could be considered (see Ryan & Gomez, 2016).

A *second* general implication of what we know is that there is not a simple answer for how best to promote well-being. We would suggest that it is time to move beyond attempts to establish one best option or approach. For example, this is reflected in prior research on permanent placement types and their outcomes that have both positive and negative effects (e.g., Lau et al., 2003), and reports that even when a significant relationship has been found, there is much individual variability.

The appropriate research questions are those that ask how best to promote well-being and prevent or avoid negative outcomes. As a result, our future research efforts are much more likely to have meaning if they focus on potential moderators of relationships; that is, identifying individual, family, and system factors that interact with given attempts to promote well-being. Our practice will also benefit from such an approach. Rather than aiming for a particular permanent placement outcome, such as exit to adoption, and then assuming once it is accomplished, that the responsibility of the system has been fulfilled, efforts to ensure that the permanent placement does in fact lead to well-being would be more beneficial. This would include continued monitoring, identification of needed supports, provision of those supports, and assessment of their effects. Thus, specific interventions (e.g., parent training, therapeutic foster parenting, mentoring) that have been developed and found to be effective (e.g., Chamberlain et al., 2008; N'zi, Stevens, & Eyberg, 2016; Taussig & Culhane, 2010) can be tailored for a given individual. Within the context of a life course perspective, such individual tailoring of interventions would require an approach that would parallel what the Institute of Medicine (2001) identified as Evidence-Based Practice (i.e., integration of research evidence, clinical expertise, and patient values).

As effective programs are identified or approaches developed, methods to disseminate them and ensure their implementation will be required (see Lutzker & Casillas, 2016). Not only will such evidence-informed programs need to be disseminated to Child Welfare workers, but also workers will need to be trained to be: a) good consumers of the empirical literature or information made available to them; b) able to formulate case conceptualizations; c) sensitive to individual and cultural differences; and d) able to identify the most appropriate course of action, and how to assess its impact. The possession of such skills would necessarily require that they be viewed as professionals, not simply "workers." Finally, as suggested above, additional resources would be needed to accomplish these ends; that is, appropriate training, and ensuring that a specific exit does in fact promote well-being.

A *third* general implication is that we need to listen to the voices of those whom we care for (i.e., current and former foster children or youth). Their voices are critical in the research arena, as they are likely to help us frame the most relevant research questions on the one hand, and on the other, facilitate the interpretation of quantitative relationships that are found. A number of former foster youth have told us and others (e.g., Mariscal, Akin, Lieberman, & Washington, 2015) that they wish they had been asked about what they wanted, that they were listened to, and that their concerns, desires, and recommendations were heeded, or at least considered. We need to continue to provide former and current foster youth with the opportunity to make their voices heard both formally (e.g., The Congressional Coalition on Adoption Institute's Foster Youth Internship Program) and informally.

A *fourth*, more specific, implication relates to conceptualizing stability. In terms of policy and practice in the Child Welfare System, stability has referred to the consistency of where a foster child is placed. There has been some recognition that stability might be a concern after exit from care, but for the most part, stability has been operationalized as the formal or official living situation or arrangement. Given what we know about chaotic, dysfunctional family situations—informal changes, people coming in and out of the home, caregiver problems—and their potential impact on child/youth well-being (Evans & Wachs, 2010), our thinking about stability needs to be expanded. This has specific implications for research efforts, moving beyond placement stability to caregiver stability, to chaos and dysfunction, when considering its impact on well-being. And, of course, efforts to promote well-being in foster children and youth must necessarily consider more than simple changes in placement when trying to find a "stable" living situation. If we are interested in addressing "stability" beyond placements, our policies for communication between service agencies (e.g., housing, mental health, educational, child welfare) need to be improved.

The bottom line is that what we know suggests that we can do a better job of promoting both the short-, and more importantly, the long-term well-being of foster children and youth. Though requiring a commitment of time, energy, and resources to meet our responsibilities, there is room for thinking outside the box. For example, longitudinal prospective studies are the gold standard for research, but can be expensive and the findings delayed. One potential creative approach, utilized by the Centers for Disease Control (CDC) in addressing the impact of safe, stable, and nurturing environments on children's development, was to identify relevant research questions, and then ask investigators familiar with longitudinal datasets to operationalize variables and address the research questions in each of their longitudinal studies (see Litrownik, 2013; Merrick, Leeb, & Lee, 2013). There are a number of longitudinal datasets available (e.g., National Data Archive on Child Abuse and Neglect at Cornell University) that include children and youth who have come into contact with the Child Welfare System (e.g., LONGSCAN—both the San Diego and Seattle site studies; NSCAW) which have the advantage of using many, if not all, of the same measures.

Finally, there is a new, exciting approach to how we might think about effecting positive changes that identifies what are called "wise" interventions (see Walton, 2014). Criteria for such a label include having a specific intervention that is brief, recursive, has long-term effects, and is based on theory. One such example in the maltreatment arena comes from our attempt to provide non-offending caregivers of suspected child sexual abuse victims with an approach to "help" their children deal with the abuse. These caregivers were shown a brief 20-minute videotape during the time that their children were going through an evidentiary interview. The video aimed to normalize problems that they might observe in their children, and more importantly, to identify and demonstrate for caregivers how they could help their children by believing them, supporting them, talking to them, and seeking help for them (see Jinich & Litrownik, 1999). There are a number of other critical periods in the life of a foster child when information (e.g., appropriate expectations) and examples of how to negotiate new challenges could be provided to children/youth as well as others in their life (e.g., when a child is first removed, exits care to adoptive parents, etc.).

In sum, there is reason to be optimistic. With a stated policy and emphasis on the importance of well-being, recognition that we need to take a life course perspective, and the developing empirical literature, we anticipate that the next generation of foster children and youth is more likely to receive appropriate support in their pursuit of happiness, and to become productive members of society.

Acknowledgments

Supported by grants #90CA1566, 90CA1676, and 90CA1748 (PI: A. Litrownik) from the U.S. Department of Health & Human Services, Administration for Children and Families; #1R01HD039689 (PI: D. Runyan) from the National Institute of Child Health and Human Development; #1R01DA031189 (PI: H. Dubowitz) and #7R21DA034834-03 (PI: L. Proctor) from the National Institute of Drug Abuse; and from the Doris Duke Charitable Foundation (LONGSCAN: From Science to Practice [PI: E. Knight]).

References

Aarons, G.A., James, S., Monn, A.R., Raghavan, R., Wells, R.S., & Leslie, L.K. (2010). Behavior problems and placement change in a national child welfare sample: A prospective study. *Journal of the American Academy of Child & Adolescent Psychiatry, 49*, 770–780. https://doi.org/10.1016/j.jaac.2009.09.005

Achenbach, T. (1991). *Manual for Child Behavior Checklist/4–18 and 1991 profile*. Burlington: University of Vermont, Department of Psychiatry.

Barnett, D., Manly, J.T., & Cicchetti, D. (1993). Defining child maltreatment: The interface between policy and research. In D. Cicchetti & S.L. Toth (Eds.), *Advances in applied developmental psychology: Child abuse, child development and social policy* (pp. 7–73). Norwood, NJ: Ablex Publishing Corp.

Berger, L.M., Bruch, S.K., Johnson, E.I., James, S., & Rubin, D. (2009). Estimating the "impact" of out-of-home placement on child well-being: Approaching the problem of selection bias. *Child Development, 80*, 1856–1876. https://doi.org/10.1111/j.1467-8624.2009.01372.x

Besinger, B., Garland, A., Litrownik, A., & Landsverk, J. (1999). Caregiver substance abuse among maltreated children placed in foster care. *Child Welfare, 78*, 221–239.

Black, M.M., Oberlander, S.E., Lewis, T., Knight, E.D., Zolotor, M.D., Litrownik, A.J., . . . English, D.E. (2009). Sexual intercourse among adolescents maltreated before age 12: A prospective investigation. *Pediatrics, 124*, 941–949. https://doi.org/10.1542/peds.2008-3836

Bronfenbrenner, U. (1993). Ecological systems theory. In R. Wozniak & K. Fisher (Eds.), *Specific environments: Thinking in contexts*. Hillsdale, NJ: Erlbaum.

Casanueva, C., Dozier, M., Tueller, S., Dolan, M., Smith, K., Webb, M.B., . . . Harden, B.J. (2014). Caregiver instability and early life changes among infants reported to the child welfare system. *Child Abuse & Neglect, 38*(3), 498–509. https://doi.org/10.1016/j.chiabu.2013.07.016

Catalano, R.F. & Hawkins, J.D. (1996). The social development model: A theory of antisocial behavior. In J.D. Hawkins (Ed.), *Delinquency and crime* (pp. 149–197). New York: Cambridge University Press.

Chamberlain, P., Price, J., Leve, L., Laurent, H., Landsverk, J., & Reid, J. (2008). Prevention of behavior problems for children in foster care: Outcomes and mediation effects. *Prevention Science, 9*, 17–27. https://doi.org/10.1007/s11121-007-0080-7

Children's Bureau of the U.S. Department of Health & Human Services. (2016). *Child welfare outcomes 2010–2013: Report to Congress: Safety, permanency, well-being*. Retrieved from www.acf.hhs.gov/cb/resource/cwo-10-13

Clausen, J.M., Landsverk, J., Ganger, W., Chadwick, D., & Litrownik, A. (1998). Mental health problems of foster children in three California counties. *Journal of Child and Family Studies, 7*, 283–296. https://doi.org/10.1023/A:1022989411119

Courtney, M. (2009). The difficult transition to adulthood for foster youth in the US: Implications for the State as corporate parent. *Social Policy Report: Giving Child and Youth Development Knowledge Away, 23*, 1–18.

Dubowitz, H., Pitts, S., Litrownik, A., Cox, C.E., Runyan, D., & Black, M. (2005). Defining child neglect based on Child Protective Services data. *Child Abuse & Neglect, 29*, 493–511. https://doi.org/10.1016/j.chiabu.2003.09.024

Dubowitz, H., Villodas, M.T., Litrownik, A.J., Pitts, S.C., Hussey, J.M., Thompson, R., . . . Runyan, D.K. (2011). Psychometric properties of a youth self-report measure of neglectful behavior by parents. *Child Abuse & Neglect*, *35*(6), 414–424. https://doi.org/10.1016/j.chiabu.2011.02.004

English, D.J., Graham, J.C., Litrownik, A.J., Everson, M., & Bangdiwala, S.I. (2005). Defining maltreatment chronicity: Are there differences in child outcomes? *Child Abuse & Neglect*, *29*(5), 575–595. https://doi.org/10.1016/j.chiabu.2004.08.009

English, D., Upadhyaya, M., Litrownik, A.J., Marshall, J., Dubowitz, H., Runyan, D., & Graham, J.C. (2005). Maltreatment's wake: The relationship of maltreatment dimensions to child outcomes. *Child Abuse & Neglect*, *29*(5), 597–619. https://doi.org/10.1016/j.chiabu.2004.12.008

Evans, G.W., & Wachs, T.D. (2010). *Chaos and its influence on children's development: An ecological perspective*. Washington, DC: American Psychological Association.

Everson, M.D., Smith, J.B., Hussey, J.M., English, D., Litrownik, A.J., Dubowitz, H., . . . Runyan, D.K. (2008). Concordance between adolescent reports of childhood abuse and Child Protective Service determinations in an at-risk sample of young adolescents. *Child Maltreatment*, *13*, 14–26. https://doi.org/10.1177/1077559507307837

Fanshel, D., Finch, S.J., & Grundy, J.F. (1990). *Foster children in a life course perspective*. New York: Columbia University Press.

Felitti, V.J., Anda, R.F., Nordenberg, D., Williamson, D.F., Spitz, A.M., Edwards, V., . . . Marks, J.S. (1998). Relationship of childhood abuse and household dysfunction to many of the leading causes of death in adults: The Adverse Childhood Experiences (ACE) Study. *American Journal of Preventive Medicine*, *14*(4), 245–258. https://doi.org/10.1016/S0749-3797(98)00017-8

Flaherty, E.G., Thompson, R., Litrownik, A.J., Zolotor, A.J., Dubowitz, H., Runyan, D.K., . . . Everson, M.D. (2009). Adverse childhood exposures and reported child health at age 12. *Academic Pediatrics*, *9*, 150–156. https://doi.org/10.1016/j.acap.2008.11.003

Font, S.A. (2015). Is higher placement stability in kinship foster care by virtue or design? *Child Abuse & Neglect*, *42*, 99–111. https://doi.org/10.1016/j.chiabu.2015.01.003

Goemans, A., van Geel, M., & Vedder, P. (2015). Over three decades of longitudinal research on the development of foster children: A meta-analysis. *Child Abuse & Neglect*, *42*, 121–134. https://doi.org/10.1016/j.chiabu.2015.02.003

Havlicek, J. & Courtney, M.E. (2016). Maltreatment histories of aging out foster youth: A comparison of official investigated reports and self-reports of maltreatment prior to and during out-of-home care. *Child Abuse & Neglect*, *52*, 110–122. https://doi.org/10.1016/j.chiabu.2015.12.006

Hussey, J.M., Marshall, J.M., English, D.J., Knight, E.D., Lau, A.S., Dubowitz, H., & Kotch, J.B. (2005). Defining maltreatment according to substantiation: Distinction without a difference? *Child Abuse & Neglect*, *29*(5), 479–492. https://doi.org/10.1016/j.chiabu.2003.12.005

Institute of Medicine. (2001). *Crossing the quality chasm: A new health system for the 21st century*. Washington, DC: The National Academies Press.

Institute of Medicine & National Research Council. (2014). *New directions in child abuse and neglect research*. Washington, DC: The National Academies Press.

Jackson, Y., Gabrielli, J., Fleming, K., Tunno, A.M., & Makanui, P.K. (2014). Untangling the relative contribution of maltreatment severity and frequency to type of behavioral outcome in foster youth. *Child Abuse & Neglect*, *38*, 1147–1159. https://doi.org/10.1016/j.chiabu.2014.01.008

Jinich, S., & Litrownik, A.J. (1999). Coping with sexual abuse: Development and evaluation of a videotape intervention for nonoffending parents. *Child Abuse & Neglect*, *23*, 175–190. https://doi.org/10.1016/S0145-2134(98)00120-3

Jones, D.J., Lewis, T., Litrownik, A., Thompson, R., Proctor, L., Isbell, T., . . . Runyan, D. (2013). Linking childhood sexual abuse and early adolescent risk behavior: The intervening role of internalizing and externalizing problems. *Journal of Abnormal Child Psychology*, *41*, 139–150. https://doi.org/10.1007/s10802-012-9656-1

Knudsen, D.D. (1989). Duplicate reports of child maltreatment: A research note. *Child Abuse & Neglect*, *13*, 41–43.

Kotch, J.B., Lewis, T., Hussey, J.M., English, D., Thompson, R., Litrownik, A.J., . . . Dubowitz, H. (2008). Importance of early neglect for childhood aggression. *Pediatrics*, *121*, 725–731.

Lau, A., Litrownik, A., Newton, R., & Landsverk, J. (2003). Going home: The complex effects of reunification on the psychosocial adjustment of children in foster care. *Journal of Abnormal Child Psychology*, *31*, 345–358. https://doi.org/10.1023/A:1023816000232

Lau, A.S., Leeb, R.T., English, D., Graham, J.C., Briggs, E.C., Brody, K.E., & Marshall, J.M. (2005). What's in a name? A comparison of methods for classifying predominant type of maltreatment. *Child Abuse & Neglect*, *29*(5), 533–551. https://doi.org/10.1016/j.chiabu.2003.05.005

Lewis, T., Kotch, J.B., Wiley, T.R., Litrownik, A.J., English, D.J., Thompson, R., . . . Dubowitz, H. (2011). Internalizing problems: A potential pathway from child maltreatment to adolescent smoking. *Journal of Adolescent Health, 48,* 247–252. https://doi.org/10.1016/j.jadohealth.2010.07.004

Lewis, T., Thompson, R., Kotch, J.B., Proctor, L.J., Litrownik, A.J., English, D.J., . . . Dubowitz, H. (2012). Parent–youth discordance about youth-witnessed violence: Associations with trauma symptoms and service use in an at-risk sample. *Child Abuse & Neglect, 36*(11–12), 790–797. https://doi.org/10.1016/chiabu.2012.09.009

Litrownik, A.J. (2012). A longitudinal perspective on mental health services for foster youth: Continued risk and the challenge of chaotic caregiving environments. *American Psychological Association: CYF News, Winter 2012,* 17–19.

Litrownik, A.J. (2013). Advances in understanding intergenerational transmission of parenting practices and the role of safe, stable, and nurturing relationships: Comments on a promising approach, practical application, and some cautions. *Journal of Adolescent Health, 53,* 42–43. https://doi.org/10.1016/j.jadohealth.2013.07.040

Litrownik, A.J. & Castillo-Canez, I. (2000). Childhood maltreatment: Treatment of abuse/incest survivors. In C.R. Snyder & R.E. Ingram (Eds.), *Handbook of psychological change: Psychotherapy processes and practices for the 21st century* (pp. 520–545). New York: Wiley.

Litrownik, A.J., Lau, A., English, D., Briggs, E., Newton, R., Romney, S., & Dubowitz, H. (2005). Measuring the severity of child maltreatment. *Child Abuse & Neglect, 29*(5), 553–573. https://doi.org/10.1016/j.chiabu.2003.08.010

Litrownik, A.J., Newton, R., Hunter, W.M., English, D., & Everson, M.D. (2003). Exposure to family violence in young at-risk children: A longitudinal look at the effects of victimization and witnessed physical and psychological aggression. *Journal of Family Violence, 18,* 59–73. https://doi.org/10.1023/A:1021405515323

Litrownik, A.J., Newton, R., Mitchell, B.E., & Richardson, K.K. (2003). Long-term follow-up of young children placed in foster care: Subsequent placements and exposure to family violence. *Journal of Family Violence, 18,* 19–28. https://doi.org/10.1023/A:1021449330344

Lutzker, J.R. & Casillas, K.I. (Eds.). (2016). Issues and solutions in the implementation of evidence-informed Child Welfare Practices [Special Issue]. *Child Abuse & Neglect, 53,* 1–146. https://doi.org/10.1016/j.chiabu.2016.01.005

Mariscal, E.S., Akin, B.A., Lieberman, A.A., & Washington, D. (2015). Exploring the path from foster care to stable and lasting adoption: Perceptions of foster care alumni. *Children and Youth Services Review, 55,* 111–120. https://doi.org/10.1016/j.childyouth.2015.05.017

McLaughlin, K.A. & Sheridan, M.A. (2016). Beyond cumulative risk: A dimensional approach to childhood adversity. *Current Directions in Psychological Science, 25,* 239–245. https://doi.org/10.1177/0963721416655883

Merrick, M.T., Leeb, R.T., & Lee, R.D. (2013). Examining the role of safe, stable, and nurturing relationships in the intergenerational continuity of child maltreatment—Introduction to the Special Issue. *Journal of Adolescent Health, 53*(4), 1–3. https://doi.org/10.1016/j.jadohealth.2013.06.017

Merrick, M.T., Litrownik, A.J., Margolis, B., Wiley, T., Everson, M.D., Dubowitz, H., & English, D. (2015). Sexualized behaviors partially mediate the link between maltreatment and delinquent behaviors. *Journal of Child and Family Studies, 24,* 2217–2228. https://doi.org/10.1007/s10826-014-0024-3

Myers, J.B. (2008). A short history of child protection in America. *Family Law Quarterly, 42*(3), 449–463.

National Research Council. (1993). *Understanding child abuse and neglect.* Washington, DC: National Academy Press.

Newton, R., Litrownik, A.J., & Landsverk, J.A. (2000). Children and youth in foster care: Disentangling the relationship between problem behaviors and number of placements. *Child Abuse & Neglect, 24*(10), 1363–1374. https://doi.org/10.1016/S0145-2134(00)00189-7

Nooner, K.B., Litrownik, A.J., Thompson, R., Margolis, B., English, D., Knight, E.D., . . . Roesch, S. (2010). Youth self-report of physical and sexual abuse: A Latent Class Analysis. *Child Abuse & Neglect, 34*(3), 146–154. https://doi.org/10.1016/j.chiabu.2008.10.007

N'zi, A.M., Stevens, M.L., & Eyberg, S.M. (2016). Child Directed Interaction Training for young children in kinship care: A pilot study. *Child Abuse & Neglect, 55,* 81–91. https://doi.org/10.1016/j.chiabu.2016.03.001

Proctor, L.J., Aarons, G.A., Dubowitz, H., English, D.J., Lewis, T., Thompson, R., . . . Roesch, S.C. (2012). Trajectories of maltreatment re-reports from ages 4 to 12: Evidence for persistent risk after early exposure. *Child Maltreatment, 17,* 207–217. https://doi.org/10.1177/1077559512448472

Proctor, L.J., Lewis, L., Roesch, S., Thompson, R., Litrownik, A.J., English, D., . . . Dubowitz, H. (2017). Child maltreatment and age of alcohol and marijuana initiation in high-risk youth. *Addictive Behaviors, 75,* 64–69. https://doi.org/10.1016/j.addbeh.2017.06.021

Proctor, L.J., Randazzo, K.V.D., Litrownik, A.J., Newton, R.R., Davis, I.P., & Villodas, M. (2011). Factors associated with caregiver stability in permanent placements: A Classification Tree Approach. *Child Abuse & Neglect, 35*(6), 425–436. https://doi.org/10.1016/j.chiabu.2011.02.002

Proctor, L.J., Skriner, L.C., Roesch, S., & Litrownik, A.J. (2010). Trajectories of behavioral adjustment following early placement in foster care: Predicting stability and change over 8 years. *Journal of the American Academy of Child and Adolescent Psychiatry, 49*, 464–473. https://doi.org/ 10.1016/j.jaac.2010.01.022

Raudenbush, S.W. & Bryk, A.S. (2002). *Hierarchical linear models: Applications and data analysis methods* (2nd ed.). Thousand Oaks, CA: Sage Publications.

Roesch, S.C., Villodas, M.T., & Villodas, F. (2010). Latent Class/Profile Analysis in maltreatment research: A commentary on Nooner et al., Pears et al., and looking beyond. *Child Abuse & Neglect, 34*(3), 150–160. https://doi.org/10.1016/j.chiabu.2010.01.003

Romney, S.C., Litrownik, A.J., Newton, R.R., & Lau, A. (2006). The relationship between child disability and living arrangement in Child Welfare. *Child Welfare, 85*, 965–984.

Runyan, D.K., Cox, C.E., Dubowitz, H., Newton, R.R., Upadhyaya, M., Kotch, J.B., . . . Knight, E. (2005). Describing maltreatment: Do child protective service reports and research definitions agree? *Child Abuse & Neglect, 29*(5), 461–477. https://doi.org/10.1016/j.chiabu.2004.06.015

Ryan, T.N. & Gomez, R.J. (2016). Trends in state budgets and child outcomes during and post child welfare class action litigation. *Children and Youth Services Review, 62*, 49–57. https://doi.org/10.1016/j.childyouth.2016.01.017

Samuels, B. (2012). *Information Memorandum: Promoting social and emotional well-being for children and youth receiving Child Welfare Services.* Administration for Children and Families, U.S. Department of Health & Human Services. Issued April 17, 2012.

Shaffer, D., Fisher, P., Dulcan, M., Davies, M., Piacentini, J., Schwab-Stone, M., . . . Regier, D. (1996). The NIMH Diagnostic Interview Schedule for Children (DISC-2): Description, acceptability, prevalence, and performance in the MECA study. *Journal of the American Academy of Child & Adolescent Psychiatry, 35*, 865–877. https://doi.org/10.1097/00004583-199607000-00012

Simmel, C., Barth, R.P., & Brooks, D. (2007). Adopted foster youths? Psychosocial functioning: A longitudinal perspective. *Child & Family Social Work, 12*(4), 336–348. https://doi.org/10.1111/j.1365-2206.2006.00481.x

Taussig, H.N., & Culhane, S.E. (2010). Impact of a mentoring and skills group program on mental health outcomes for maltreated children in foster care. *Archives of Pediatric Adolescent Medicine, 164*(8), 739–746. https://doi.org/10.1001/archpediatrics.2010.124

Thompson, R., Jones, D.J., Litrownik, A.J., English, D.J., Kotch, J.B., Lewis, T., & Dubowitz, H. (2014). Linking mother and youth parenting attitudes: Indirect effects via maltreatment, parent involvement, and youth functioning. *Child Maltreatment, 19*, 233–246. https://doi.org/10.1177/1077559514547263

Thompson, R., Lewis, T., Neilson, E.C., English, D.J., Litrownik, A.J., Margolis, B., . . . Dubowitz, H. (2017). Child maltreatment and risky sexual behavior: Indirect effects through trauma symptoms and substance use. *Child Maltreatment, 22*, 69–78. https://doi.org/10.1177/1077559516674595

Thompson, R., Litrownik, A.J., Isbell, P., Everson, M.D., English, D.J., Dubowitz, H., . . . Flaherty, E.G. (2012). Adverse experiences and suicidal ideation in adolescence: Exploring the link using the LONGSCAN samples. *Psychology of Violence, 2*, 211–225. https://doi.org/10.1037/a0027107

Thompson, R., Tabone, J.K., Litrownik, A.J., Briggs, E.C., Hussey, J.M., English, D.J., & Dubowitz, H. (2011). Early adolescent risk behavior outcomes of childhood externalizing behavioral trajectories. *Journal of Early Adolescence, 31*, 234–257. https://doi.org/10.1177/0272431609361203

Tripp De Robertis, M. & Litrownik, A.J. (2004). The experience of foster care: Relationship between foster parent disciplinary approaches and aggression in a sample of young foster children. *Child Maltreatment, 9*, 92–102. https://doi.org/10.1177/1077559503260402

U.S. Department of Health & Human Services. (1992). *National Child Abuse and Neglect Data System: Working Paper 2: 1991 Summary Data Component.* Retrieved from www.ncjrs.gov/pdffiles1/Digitization/144419NCJRS.pdf

U.S. Department of Health & Human Services. (2015). *The AFCARs report. Preliminary FY 2014 estimates as of July 2015. No. 22.* Retrieved from www.acf.hhs.gov/cb/resource/afcars-report-22

van der Vegt, E.J.M., Tieman, W., van der Ende, J., Ferdinand, R.F., Verhuist, F.C., & Tiemeier, H. (2009). Impact of early childhood adversities on adult psychiatric disorders: A study of international adoptees. *Social Psychiatry and Psychiatric Epidemiology, 44*, 724–731. https://doi.org/10.1007/s00127-009-0494-6

Villodas, M.T., Cromer, K.D., Moses, J.O., Litrownik, A.J., Davis, I., & Newton, R.R. (2016). Unstable child welfare permanent placements and early adolescent physical and mental health: The roles of adverse childhood experiences and post-traumatic stress. *Child Abuse & Neglect, 62*, 76–88. https://doi.org/10.1016/j.chiabu.2016.10.014

Villodas, M.T., Litrownik, A.J., Jones, D.J., Thompson, R., Block, S., Hussey, J., . . . Roesch, S. (2015). Developmental transitions in presentations of externalizing problems among boys and girls at-risk for child maltreatment. *Development and Psychopathology, 27,* 205–219. https://doi.org/10.1017/S0954579414000728

Villodas, M.T., Litrownik, A.J., Newton, R.R., & Davis, I.P. (2016). Long-term placement trajectories of children who were maltreated and entered the Child Welfare System at an early age: Consequences for physical and behavioral well-being. *Journal of Pediatric Psychology, 41,* 46–54. https://doi.org/10.1093/jpepsy/jsv031

Villodas, M.T., Litrownik, A.J., Thompson, R., Roesch, S.C., English, D.J., Dubowitz, H., . . . Runyan, D.K. (2012). Changes in youth's experiences of child maltreatment across developmental periods in the LONGSCAN consortium. *Psychology of Violence, 2*(4), 325–338. https://doi.org/10.1037/a0029829

Walton, G.M. (2014). The new science of wise psychological interventions. *Current Directions in Psychological Science, 23,* 73–82. https://doi.org/10.1177/0963721413512856

5

Foster Youth Voices

An Exploratory Study on their Challenges and Strengths

Nancy Trevino-Schafer and Elizabeth Trejos-Castillo

I appreciate you all doing this ...
not a lot of people want to know ... at least from our side

("Joseph")

Introduction

Adolescents today face an ever-changing world, one that is significantly different from the world of earlier generations. Today's adolescents are faced with a different economy where a college degree does not guarantee a higher-paying job, and where many of their interactions are based on social media platforms rather than traditional face-to-face contact. But no matter how the world changes, society's building blocks are still the family and home life. Adolescents have consistently reported that their families, especially their parents, influences their decisions (Bednar & Fisher, 2003; Commendador, 2010; Guilamo-Ramos, Lee, & Jaccard, 2016; Luster & Small, 1994; Wilks, 1986). For youth who have been raised in state care and have had their decisions managed by child protective services, navigating society and decision-making can be even more challenging, especially for a significant number of these youth aging out of care without support from family members or other caring permanent adults (Singer, Berzin, & Hokanson, 2013; Winter, Brandon-Friedman, & Ely, 2016).

During adolescence, there are multiple biological, emotional, cognitive, social, and relational changes occurring at the same time which collectively, over time and in conjunction with the surrounding context, shape an adolescent into an adult (Biro & Dorn, 2006; Blakemore, Burnett, & Dahl, 2010; Blakemore & Mills, 2014; Graber, Nichols, & Brooks-Gunn, 2010; Rosenthal, Smith, & de Visser, 1999; Sartor & Youniss, 2002). For most young people, the transition to adulthood is a gradual process, sometimes even lasting until the age of 25 (Furstenberg, Rumbaut, & Settersten, 2005; Goldschieder, F. & Goldscheider, C., 1999; Tanner & Arnett, 2016); however, for foster youth, it is a very different situation as they age out of care, usually at age 18 but this varies from state to state (Winter et al., 2016). In fact, the U.S. Department of Health & Human Services (2006; cited henceforth as USDHHS) has noted that these youth who age out of care are too old to be a part of the child welfare system, but are usually not ready to live as independent young adults. Many of these youth have not been prepared to live on their own and often lack appropriate educational attainment, and living and social skills (Osgood, Foster, & Courtney, 2010; Winter et al., 2016). To better prepare youth in foster care, some states have opted to extend foster care until age 19, 20, or 21, and during this time, they offer youth additional education and training (USDHHS [Children's Bureau], 2017a), which was allowed through provisions in the Fostering Connections to Success and Increasing Adoptions Act of 2008 (see P.L. 110-351). This extension of services for youth aging out of foster care is not offered consistently across all states, and in some states may not be available at all. According to the 2016 AFCARS Report, there were 20,789 foster youth who were transitioning out of foster care during fiscal year (FY) 2015, many of whom had no access to any extended services (USDHHS [Children's Bureau], 2016).

Not only do these foster youth have a different experience as they make the transition to independent living and adulthood, they have also had a different experience during adolescence. Youth who enter foster care placements do so because they have experienced some form of maltreatment or neglect (Thompson & Auslander, 2011; USDHHS [Children's Bureau], 2016). Often, it takes multiple reports from the community before child welfare becomes involved (Healey & Fisher, 2011), prolonging the maltreatment and/or neglect of children and youth. Some of the reasons for child removal might include: neglect, physical abuse, sexual abuse, child behavior problems, parental alcohol or drug abuse, inadequate housing (USDHHS [Children's Bureau], 2016; USDHHS [Child Welfare Information Gateway], 2016). Youth who are in care are required not only to face the problems that all adolescents face, but also the unique challenges of being in state care, including but not limited to, changing contexts (i.e., school, neighborhoods, placements, friends), working with numerous child welfare staff, service providers, and foster parents to coordinate approvals, services, and other paper work required by the state (Ahrens, Spencer, Bonnar, Coatney, & Hall, 2016; Pryce & Samuels, 2010; Svoboda, Shaw, Barth, & Bright, 2012). Foster youth also experience the numerous challenges of being in state care (Riebschleger, Day, & Damashek, 2015; Salazar, Keller, Gowen, & Courtney, 2013). These include unstable placements (Riebschleger et al., 2015), limited ability to participate in extracurricular activities (Pears, Kim, Fisher, & Yoerger, 2013), and a non-normative upbringing with few opportunities to have continued contact with friends outside school and across placements (Conn, Calais, Szilagyi, Baldwin, & Jee, 2014; Singer et al., 2013; Unrau, Seita, & Putney, 2008).

Previous research has suggested that young adults emerging out of foster care are at greater risk for negative outcomes, and more problem behaviors than those who were not in foster care (Farruggia, Greenberger, Chen, & Heckhausen, 2006; Mersky & Janczewski, 2013; Rosenthal & Curiel, 2006; Smith, Clark, & Nigg, 2015; Sullivan, Jones, & Matiesen, 2010). These include poorer physical health (Ahrens, Garrison, & Courtney, 2014; Szilagyi, Rosen, Rubin, & Zlotnik, 2015), disparities in reproductive health, with higher rates of teen pregnancy and teen parenting (Aparicio, Pecukonis, & O'Neale, 2015; Smith et al., 2015), poorer mental health, with higher rates of depression (Valdez, Bailey, Santuzzi, & Lilly, 2014), anxiety and aggression issues (Bradley, 2000), unhealthy relationships (Kim & Cicchetti, 2010; Smith et al., 2015; Storer et al., 2014; Thompson & Auslander, 2011), loss of self-esteem (Unrau et al., 2008), higher rates of Post-Traumatic Stress Disorder (PTSD; Salazar, Keller, Gowen, & Courtney, 2013), and adjustment problems (Healey & Fisher, 2011). Research findings also suggest that these youth are ill-equipped to navigate these issues, and display negative coping skills, such as non-suicidal self-injury (Swannell et al., 2012) and more frequent attempts to self-medicate: these contribute to greater substance abuse in former foster youth, higher rates of substance use disorder diagnoses, more illicit drug and alcohol use, more polydrug use (i.e., alcohol and marijuana), and earlier initiation of substance use (Havlicek, Garcia, & Smith, 2013; Thompson & Auslander, 2011).

In addition, former foster youth have consistently been found to have worse educational outcomes, including higher school drop-out rates (Berger, Cancian, Han, Noyes, & Rios-Salas, 2015; Chapple & Vaske, 2010; Geiger, Hanrahan, Cheung, & Lietz, 2016). These are thought to have lasting economic effects (Currie & Widom, 2010), including higher rates of unemployment (Stewart, Kum,

Barth, & Duncan, 2014), living in poverty and homelessness (Dion, Dworsky, Kauff, & Kleinman, 2014; Dworsky, Napolitano, & Courtney, 2013), and higher rates of involvement in the criminal justice system (Bilchik, 2010; Herz & Ryan, 2008; Lambie & Randell, 2013; Petro, 2007; Ryan & Testa, 2005).

Sadly, research has suggested that many of these issues continue into adulthood (Thompson & Auslander, 2011). However, the long-term effects of experiencing child maltreatment do not always determine how well or poorly the youth will be adjusted. Indeed, some studies have reported no significant differences in adjustment and developmental outcomes across foster and non-foster youth (Fallesen, 2013; Farruggia et al., 2006). Other studies have even found that youth with a history of foster care can show resiliency after aging out of care (Batsche et al., 2014; Hass & Graydon, 2009; Healey & Fisher, 2011; Shpiegel, 2016; Strolin-Goltzman, Kollar, & Trinkle, 2010).

Previous studies have found important favorable outcomes in foster youth; namely, emotional regulation and school adjustment (Healey & Fisher, 2011). Emotional regulation has been linked to overall positive adjustment (McMillen et al., 2015; Morris, Silk, Steinberg, Myers, & Robinson, 2007), emotional competence (Littlefield, Cavanagh, Knapp, & O'Grady, 2017), healthy relationship development (Denham, 2003; Nesmith & Christophersen, 2014; Pears, Kim, & Fisher, 2016), and emotional responses and behavior control (Garon, Bryson, & Smith, 2008; Jackson, Gabrielli, Fleming, Tunno, & Makanui, 2014; Ladd, Birch, & Buhs, 1999; McClelland, Morrison, & Holmes, 2000). Emotional responses contribute to adaptation in social environments (Shipman, Edwards, Brown, Swisher, & Jennings, 2005); and, when lacking, can contribute to dysfunctional behaviors like those often reported among children and youth in foster care, including anxiety, withdrawal, aggression, and even bullying (Bradley, 2000; Cicchetti & Toth, 2005; Racusin, Maerlender, Sengupta, Isquith, & Straus, 2005). Furthermore, school adjustment, including academic achievement and social and behavioral functioning, has been found to be representative of long-term functioning (Courtney et al., 2014; Lynch, Dickerson, Pears, & Fisher, 2017), with school success as early as kindergarten being linked to higher educational attainment (Lynch et al., 2017; Pears et al., 2013), employment (Stewart et al., 2014), and overall psychosocial adjustment (Forsman, Brännström, Vinnerljung, & Hjern, 2016; Nadeem et al., 2017).

Though scholarship on foster youth has continued to grow during the past two decades, the majority of research has centered on the child welfare system itself, or those providing services and care for foster youth, including but not limited to placements and services (Ayasse, 1995; Berrick, 1997; Cautley & Aldridge, 1975; Doelling & Johnson, 1990; Frerer, Sosenko, Pellegrin, Manchik, & Horowitz, 2013; Kerker & Dore, 2006; Leathers & Testa, 2006; Packard, Delgado, Fellmeth, & McCready, 2008; Palmer, 1996; Wulczyn, Kogan, & Harden, 2003); foster and adoptive parents (Cooley, Farineau, & Mullis, 2015; Denby, Rindfleisch, & Bean, 1999; Fees et al., 1998; Festinger & Baker, 2013; Herczog, van Pagee, & Pasztor, 2001; Nash & Flynn, 2016; Orme, Buehler, McSurdy, Rhodes, & Cox, 2003; Rodger, Cummings, & Leschied, 2006; Stone, N. M. & Stone, S. F., 1983; Suter, Baxter, Seurer, & Thomas, 2014; Touliatos & Lindholm, 1981); and perspectives of social workers or caseworkers about foster youth (Hess, 1988; Lindsey, 1992; Nesmith, Patton, Christophersen, & Smart, 2017; Smith, 1996; Zima, Bussing, Yang, & Belin, 2000).

Similarly, the field has relied mostly on quantitative methodological approaches to capture only a small portion of the experience of youth in foster care. Some quantitative datasets that are widely used include: the National Youth in Transition Database (NYTD; see USDHHS [Children's Bureau], 2017b); National Child Abuse and Neglect Data System (NCANDS; see USDHHS [Children's Bureau], 2017c); National Incidence Study (NIS; see USDHHS [Child Welfare Information Gateway], n.d.); National Survey of Child and Adolescent Well-Being (NSCAW; see USDHHS [Office of Planning, Research & Evaluation], 2014); and Adoption and Foster Care Analysis and Reporting System (AFCARS; see USDHHS [Children's Bureau], 2017d). Although quantitative data have provided extensive knowledge about foster youth, and even with "enormous advances in quantitative statistical approaches, arguably especially in regard to the longitudinal methods" (Lerner, 2005, p. 23), they have only provided a limited understanding on the individual experiences of foster youth and their trajectories through the child welfare system.

One recent report, *A National Look at the Use of Congregate Care in Child Welfare*, used a mixed-method approach by collecting quantitative data about foster youth at their entry into care and at another point in time, and also included a qualitative section. The focus of these qualitative data was not the perspective of foster youth, but rather comprised data from states regarding promising practices to reduce reliance on congregate care (USDHHS [Children's Bureau], 2015). However, to improve child welfare services for those most affected, it is important to accurately capture and include the voices of those who are currently or have previously been involved in state care. Capturing this kind of information can be done by utilizing qualitative methods. Lerner reminds us that, "there has been an increased appreciation of the importance of qualitative methods, both as valuable tools for the analysis of the life course and as a means to triangulate quantitative appraisals of human development" (2005, p. 24). To date, foster youth's voices and reflections on their unique challenges and strengths remain understudied. New research techniques (i.e., mixed methods, including developmental data) and wider data gathering (i.e., from multiple sources, including current and former foster youth, social workers, biological and foster family members) have suggested a more complex experience for those who are or have been involved with the foster care system. A limited body of recent research has also shifted its focus to include the perspective of youth currently or previously in foster care, covering topics such as transitioning out of care (Cunningham & Diversi, 2013; Liabo, McKenna, Ingold, & Roberts, 2017; Nesmith, 2017); visitation (Salas Martínez, Fuentes, Bernedo, & García-Martín, 2016); participation in foster care (Bijleveld, Dedding, & Bunders-Aelen, 2015); participating in therapy (Mersky, Topitzes, Janczewski, & McNeil, 2015); and caseworker attrition (Strolin-Goltzman et al., 2010).

More recent research has also moved away from emphasizing foster youth deficits and highlighting their issues, with the aim of capturing not only the challenges of foster youth, which are widely documented and discussed in this volume, but also the strengths of those who have been in the foster care system (Britner, Randall, & Ahrens, 2013; Stott, 2012). Positive Youth Development (PYD) is a strength-based perspective, which takes into account the individual's complex background, individual characteristics, and environmental factors contributing to individual development (Damon, 2004). Without disregarding negative influences on individual development, PYD emphasizes the developmental successes, and the influences of individual characteristics and contextual factors (i.e., socio-political, familial, non-familial, etc.) to prevent negative outcomes, and promote positive well-being and resiliency in youth (Catalano, Berglund, Ryan, Lonczak, & Hawkins, 2004; Lerner et al., 2013; Moore, Lippman, & Brown, 2004). Lerner et al. (2005) conceptualized PYD by operationalizing the Five Cs—competence, confidence, character, connection, caring, all of which have been identified in youth who are considered to be thriving, or having measurable positive developmental outcomes. The PYD perspective is useful for exploring adolescence, a period in which there are "socially important changes" (Lerner, 2005, p. 54). Our current study is informed by PYD, and will provide insights on the strengths, challenges, and current or future goals identified by youth during and after aging out of care, using an exploratory approach. We aim to generate new knowledge about foster youth's individual experiences while in care as well as transitioning out of care to independent living.

Methodology

Recruitment and Data Collection Procedures

This exploratory study was conducted in collaboration with a state-wide recognized non-governmental agency working with foster youth in the state of Texas. Data were collected over a period of 3 years in conjunction with two transitioning centers for youth aging out of care in Bexar County and West Texas. The qualitative portion of this study is part of a larger study that includes approximately 750 foster youth thus far (data collection in progress). Four focus groups were conducted with a total number of 24 participants, aged 18–22 (33% females) who transitioned out of care during the last 5 years. Foster youth were recruited using flyers giving information about the study, and with the support of caseworkers and centers' staff members providing services to the youth. Staff members at the transition centers facilitated the collection of participant assent forms and helped to coordinate the four focus groups that were conducted at the centers for the convenience of the participants. All data collection protocols were approved by the full review board of a university institutional ethics and human subjects' committee. Focus groups lasted from 45 to 80 minutes, had about five to seven participants per group, and used the same set list of guiding questions. All participants were asked to use an "alias" during the focus groups for confidentiality and anonymity purposes. Data were voice recorded, transcribed, and checked for accuracy by the Principal Investigators and supporting doctoral students.

Plan of Analyses

Data were coded following Thematic Network Analysis procedures described by Attride-Stirling (2001), informed by Grounded Theory (Glaser & Strauss, 1967; Grbich, 2007), and supported by Atlas.ti 7 software to examine the associations across themes emerging across focus groups. For simplicity purposes in the current study, quotations are provided in lieu of graphical representations.

Results and Discussion

Accomplishments

> You have to plan out your life—beginning, middle, and end
>
> ("Alicia")

School and Grades

When foster youth were asked what their main accomplishments were, there were some answers that we would expect to receive from any individual between the ages of 18 and 21, such as graduating from high school, getting good grades, and going to college. Two of the respondents were particularly proud of their academic achievements, one for being the first in her family to earn her Associate's degree and another who had maintained a 4.0 grade point average (GPA). These are "normal" young adult responses. Of the foster youth who participated in the focus groups, several were in the General Education Development (GED) preparation classes and had not yet taken the GED exam. A report entitled *Secondary School Completion and Dropouts in Texas Public Schools for 2012–13* (Texas Education Agency, 2014) stated that 88% of the Class of 2013 graduated and 0.8% had earned their GEDs. Educational research suggests that youth involved in the foster care system often experience unstable placements, with frequent moves and subsequent changes of school. This negatively impacts educational attainment, including repeating courses or grade levels, overrepresentation in special education programs, while many youth drop out of school altogether (Courtney, 2009; Jonson-Reid & Barth, 2000; Leathers, 2006; Macomber, 2009).

One of our participants said, "education is forever, when everything else is materialistic and it can't be taken from you," suggesting that no matter the challenges linked to education, foster youth recognize the merits of education and desire to do well in school and even attend college. Participants often shared that they had a desire to further their education or were currently preparing for higher education (i.e., buying books, filling out paperwork for tuition assistance); this is consistent with prior research which found that a majority of foster youth reported a desire to go to college (Dworsky & Pérez, 2009; Tzawa-Hayden, 2004). Those who age out of the foster care system and complete high school, by earning either their high school diploma or GED, become eligible for a tuition waiver to any public institution which makes them able to attend any public institution of their choice. In some states, former foster youth also have access to local agencies for scholarship application assistance and year-round or holiday dorm access (Kirk & Day, 2011). Those youth who leave care before the age of 18 become ineligible and lose all of these benefits; however, some foster youth report that they did not even know that they were eligible, and have lost these resources, which could have helped them change their future and stop the cycle of CPS intervention with their family.

Family Planning

Not only are these former foster youth working to make "good" grades in school and receive job training, they are also seriously planning their lives and futures, including the timing of childbearing.

> My biggest accomplishment that I am trying to get towards is college, a career, a stable environment ... breaking the cycle of my family that has been going on for a long time and set a future for my kids when I have them ... so, the things that are the biggest cycle would have to be foster care. My mom had her kids taken away. My older sister has had her kids taken away. My brother, a 21 year old, had his kids ... kid taken away and got back. I'm gonna break that cycle because I'm gonna make sure I do right to and make sure that the things I do revolve around what my kids do when I have kids. Doing the right thing, having a good environment, put them in school when they need to be in school, have shot records taken care of, taken care of in a good way, not let them bein' around drugs and weed and alcohol all their lives, being around gang violence, and and bang poppers,... and things like that.

As we expected, the participants in our study, like other young people in this same stage in life, identified family planning as an important accomplishment. Even though family planning primarily delayed childbearing, it was discussed as an accomplishment. It was primarily discussed with negative comparisons to their biological family members who did not delay childbearing and were already parenting as adolescents and young adults. As one participant offered:

> I can honestly say I have a lot um—graduating in high school is one, but also passing the age of 16 without having a child. Due to the fact that every girl in my family's been 16 with a baby or with a baby on the way.

These negative comparisons between themselves and their biological family members that came up in this discussion were unexpected.

It is important for teens and young adults to have comprehensive sexual education information so that they can make responsible, healthy reproductive choices when they decide to begin engaging in sex (Boonstra, 2009; Dworsky & Courtney, 2010; Smith et al., 2015). This is important for foster youth, especially in the light of the reproductive health disparities that have been found consistently among current and former foster youth. These include: earlier ages of sexual initiation (i.e., by age 13), a greater number of sexual partners, less likelihood of using contraception methods, higher rates of teen pregnancy and parenting, increased risk of exposure to HIV by engaging in greater sexual risk-taking, increased rates of HIV and STIs during and after care, and repeat pregnancies (Aparicio et al., 2015; Cheung, Montgomery, & Benjamins, 2014; Dworsky & Courtney, 2010; Shpiegel,

Cascardi, & Dineen, 2017; Smith et al., 2015). The participants in the focus groups felt that choosing to delay childbearing was an accomplishment, and they took this decision very seriously; one participant stated, "I don't have any kids either, I don't plan to in a while, I have a bird and I am happy with it."

Relational Issues

There was a wide range of relational issues that came up during the focus groups, including anger management, emotional closure, and romantic relationships. This was not unexpected, as individuals with a history of state care have also been found to have poorer social relationships (Storer et al., 2014).

ANGER MANAGEMENT

Participants at each location, both males and females, mentioned that one of their major accomplishments was to have overcome anger issues and learned to manage their anger and/or temper. Anger management and emotional regulation issues could lead to foster youth being perceived as hostile, aggressive, or defiant (Cicchetti & Toth, 2005; Kim & Cicchetti, 2010). If foster parents perceive the foster youth in their care as having anger issues, a hostile temperament, or display excessive defiant behaviors, this could lead to a worse placement "fit", or a possible change in placement, and can be predictive of abusive and neglectful behavior from the foster parents and greater peer rejection (Doelling & Johnson, 1990; Kim & Cicchetti, 2010; Trickett, Negriff, Ji, & Peckins, 2011).

EMOTIONAL CLOSURE

During our focus groups, the concept of emotional closure was brought up by a few of the participants. One of these former foster youth discussed how they had forgiven their father for failing to be an involved dad while they were in foster care. Another participant discussed how he realized that he had emotional closure at the time of his father's death. Jack decided that he would disconnect emotionally from his father, not allowing any more pain in his life from that relationship. Jack struggled for words, but said, "Losing feeling, like I guess feeling to care about stuff . . . recently my father passed . . . and . . . like I didn't cry . . . I kinda lost that feeling." Emotional closure has been discussed in previous research as a survival mechanism used to try to fit into the foster family placement, but which can often lead to feelings of disloyalty to biological parents (Butler & Charles, 1999; Holland & Crowley, 2013; Unrau et al., 2008). Emotional closure with a father figure or other paternal figures was discussed by a couple of the focus group participants, but none of the participants, including those who discussed paternal closure, discussed the same level of emotional closure with their maternal figures (i.e., mothers, grandmothers, aunts). One possible explanation for this found by research is that former foster youth often maintain contact with their biological mothers into adulthood (Courtney, 2009).

ROMANTIC RELATIONSHIPS

Several participants identified cohabitating, or finding a romantic partner who "gets" them, as one of their accomplishments. This can be a major accomplishment, since research studies have found that relationship patterns can be transmitted intergenerationally, with youths' relationships mirroring those of their parents and caregivers; for youth involved in foster care, the models of relationships they have been exposed to in their family environments have often been abusive, neglectful, and generally unhealthy ones (Bryant & Conger, 2002; Cicchetti & Toth, 2005; Hare, Miga, & Allen,

2009). Youth who are in care may not have seen their parents involved in positive romantic relationships, and often, foster youth themselves become involved in negative, abusive, or exploitive romantic relationships. These can contribute to re-victimization, including rape, human trafficking, and sex work, all factors that increase HIV risk behaviors, such as substance use and engaging in sex without a condom (Courtney et al., 2011; Elze, Auslander, McMillen, Edmond, & Thompson, 2001; Smith et al., 2015; Thompson & Auslander, 2011; Winter et al., 2016). In addition, youth who have been in foster care have higher rates of teen pregnancy, repeat pregnancy, and more reports of engaging in sexual risk-taking behaviors (Aparicio et al., 2015; Courtney et al., 2011; Thompson & Auslander, 2011; Wilson et al., 2014). This may suggest that these youth want to be loved, but they may not know how to have healthy romantic and intimate relationships (Hare et al., 2009; Trickett et al., 2011; Winter et al., 2016). It seems as though these former foster youth are trying to have committed, adult, romantic relationships by engaging in adult behaviors, such as sexual intercourse, and building long-term relationships including cohabitating, but may not have positive relationship models; however, the youth in our focus groups have overcome these obstacles, and were engaging in romantic relationships that they felt were positive and caring.

Challenges

> They don't understand that we've done what we've done to help ourselves
>
> ("Joseph")

Foster youth come into the child welfare system at a disadvantage, most with histories of abuse, neglect, family instability and disruption, deficits in education, and sometimes even mental health issues (Elze, Auslander, Stiffman, & McMillen, 2005; Jonson-Reid & Barth, 2000; Manlove, Welti, McCoy-Roth, Berger, & Malm, 2011; Thompson & Auslander, 2011). The focus group participants shared some normative challenges that we expected individuals in their transitional phase to face, whether or not they have a history of foster care involvement, such as enrolling or preparing for higher education and training (i.e., buying books, registering for courses), finding a job or choosing a career path, and balancing a budget. As with accomplishments, these youth shared challenges that we did not expect (i.e., terminating parental rights). These youth shared their difficult experiences in a reflexive manner that helped us to gain a better understanding of the challenges of foster youth and former foster youth, and gave us insights into the impact of foster care on these youth as they transition out of care.

Decision to Terminate Parental Rights

One of the challenges that was discussed was the decision to terminate their parents' legal rights. This is not a decision that the average adolescent will have to make, but it is a decision that many older adolescents in foster care may have to make, or be asked to offer their perspective on during the legal process required to terminate their parents' legal rights. There has been legislation during the last two decades aimed at providing legal permanency for children and youth involved in the foster care system through legal adoption or a guardianship home (Rolock & White, 2016). The majority of youth who participated in our focus groups did not discuss experiences with adoption. Emancipation (i.e., aging out of care) usually becomes the case plan goal for youth who will not be reunified with family, released into the care of another adult, or adopted (USDHHS [Children's Bureau], 2016). If a youth remains in the foster care system for long enough, or 15 of the past 22 months, the courts can terminate parental rights (Wulczyn, Chen, & Hislop, 2006). Two of the participants discussed how one of their biggest challenges was the decision to terminate their parents' rights. One participant, Joseph, the youngest sibling in his biological family, said the following about the struggle with the decision to terminate his mother's rights:

> In the long run, all they [parents] are doing is pulling and tugging their kid's hearts. And that's what hurt me the most. And when I was trying to get adopted by this family, my mom's rights had to be terminated. So I got my mom's rights terminated so I could continue living my life. So she could stop hurting me, and thinking, you know, I'm going home you know but I'm not. You know and that was the hardest thing, seeing people I lived with, people in the house—12 people, you know. The hardest thing I was the youngest one there [group home] when I went, and I ended up being the oldest one there when I left. And seeing all these kids go back home and you know leaving and coming and coming back again—like we did, you know. That killed me, you know, I mean, that's hard—that was the hardest.

The participant talked about leaving, and then returning to care again, meaning that his mother complied with CPS service requirements for unification with her children, but then she would "mess up" (i.e., drugs and alcohol abuse—according to him); as a result, she would be in non-compliance with CPS reunification rules, and have her children removed from her care and placed in foster care again. We do not know Joseph's exact age when he terminated his mother's rights. In general, very little is known about parents' service experience and how it impacts foster care case outcomes, including termination of parental rights, reunification, and subsequent re-entry into foster care (Alpert, 2005).

We also heard from another youth about the process of terminating his mother's parental rights. He had been in and out of the system for several years. He said:

> I don't ever hold anything against my family—not my mom, not my stepdad, not my dad. I thank them instead for doing the best they could. I would never feel anything against them; in fact, I wish that I could have a good relationship with them sometimes . . . Whatever my mom did, or whatever she did, you know,—any physical, you know, the injuries—you know, burns and bruises and blood—it all heals. The scars, they eventually disappear from the body. But after several years, when I was 17 and a half, I took it upon myself to go ahead and terminate her rights, and just stay in the system since then. I mean I had been in the system on and off, but at that point that was when I stayed until I aged out at 18. . . . So it's more about internal challenge to know that I lost, not only the relationship with her and my stepdad and my little sister—but also my cousins, my uncles, my aunts, everybody, my grandma . . . Everybody that I've met in my life, you know, everybody that was closer to me, because ultimately everybody listens to her word more than mine, naturally. And that internal challenge, I think is—I think it's far, far more—creates far more damage than anything else external.

The decision to remove the legal bond to their parent has probably crossed every teen's mind at some fleeting moment of frustration; however, foster youth have serious reasons (i.e., history of abuse, neglect, and potential for adoption) and sometimes the legal necessity to carry out that decision. This is not a decision that these youth took lightly, and the decision to terminate their parents' legal rights was usually only acted on after many years of pain—physical, emotional, and psychological—as was expressed in the statement above. This decision can cost them not only the legal connection to their biological parent, but also contact with their extended biological family members. Many foster youth have socioemotional issues of abandonment and attachment in the light of their early experiences with caregivers, which was often a major contributor to their involvement with the foster care system (Lind, Raby, Caron, Roben, & Dozier, 2017; Muller-Ravett & Jacobs, 2012; Noonan & Burke, 2005; Thompson, Greeson, & Brunsink, 2016). Youth whose parental rights have been terminated often find themselves moving from foster placement to foster placement (Hong, Ryan, Hernandez, & Brown, 2014).

Foster Care System

ISSUES WITH CASEWORKERS

During the course of our focus groups, a number of concerns with the foster care system were shared. Concerns ranged from foster youth feeling like "just another number" to not understanding the rules (e.g., assigned caseworker, rules, curfew, check-in, standards of placement, termination in the program, etc.), especially as they pertained to the new program allowing foster youth to "return to care." Youth discussed how caseworkers are responsible for advocating for the foster youth's needs, but are also viewed as a major part of "The System" which often does not meet their needs. One complaint was that their caseworkers grew to be difficult to work with and seemed indifferent to the youth:

> I was like so he was just so against everything I wanted to do. Originally I wanted to do what he wanted to do but then when I started to have a mind of my own and ... I ummm ... I was speaking out for myself again, that I didn't do before, that was when he was really against me. When he would, he would be like [deep audible sigh] every time he saw me or spoke to me or anything.

Caseworkers are important to the health and well-being of foster youth, as they are responsible for assuring that youth are safe, and have stability and permanence in their lives; limited research also suggests that interactions between caseworkers and foster youth are significant and can determine future life outcomes for foster youth (Strolin-Goltzman et al., 2010). Further, caseworkers who have low caseloads and frequent contact with foster youth have higher rates of discharging youth within 2 years of involvement with the child welfare system; and when caseworkers leave, foster youth are negatively impacted emotionally and physically through loss of trust and stability (Strolin-Goltzman et al., 2010).

PLACEMENT PROBLEMS

There were also many concerns discussed about placements within the foster care system. Those complaints ranged from placements having too high a ratio of foster children/youth to adults responsible for their care, to a complaint of a foster youth who was perceived as "troubled" being inappropriately placed in a state-run facility that worked with military veterans. Others talked about changing placements numerous times, and subsequently not being advocated for at their schools by the people in charge of their new placements. Placement problems should be given more attention, because foster youth who age out of the child welfare system have, on average, changed placements eight times during their last 5 years in state care, and older youth are often placed in institutional placements rather than foster home placements (Berzin, Rhodes, & Curtis, 2011; Stott, 2012; USDHHS [Children's Bureau], 2012). Youth even reported that foster parents would sow discord in placements between the biological family members and the foster youth (Jo), and others reported that further abuse and neglect (e.g., locking foster youth in a closet, feeding dog food to foster youth) occurred in their out-of-home placements. Sadly, these were not isolated experiences for our participants; it has been documented that foster youth in state placements have experienced further abuse (verbal, physical, sexual) and trauma, while in state care, from caregivers and even from other children in their placements (Euser, Alink, Tharner, van IJzendoorn, & Bakermans-Kranenburg, 2013; Riebschleger et al., 2015; Salazar, Thomas, et al., 2013; Samuels & Pryce, 2008; Unrau et al., 2008). Some youth also voiced concerns about the laws and policies regarding foster care placements and the treatment of foster youth in general, stating that these areas of "The System" needed to be revised, including adding better guidance for more effective discipline strategies used with foster youth.

STIGMA OF BEING A "BAD KID"

In addition, some participants discussed the challenge of having to deal with the stigmatization of youth in foster care as "bad kids."

> But a lot of the foster parents, and a lot of people in foster care, the government. They have all these bad kids and they don't know what to do with them. Well my thing is . . . if you have all these bad kids, why are they bad in the first place? Why do they think . . . They never sit down and try to get to understand these people, . . . they never try to get to understand what's going through their mind or hear what they have to say, they just jump to conclusions because they think, "Oh, look at this record, oh my god this person's this, and this, and that." Why do they do it in the first place? Like with me, they think I'm a troubled kid, they think when I returned to Back to Care, they didn't think I was going to make it, and that I was going to leave, but I'm still there.

This stigma of being "bad" and the negative perceptions of foster youth are problems that have been studied infrequently. However, there are some studies which support the view that foster youth are being perceived as more aggressive, less cooperative, and generally worse than their same-age peers (Brown & Bednar, 2006; Gramkowski et al., 2009; Trickett et al., 2011). It is important to recognize that many of the negative externalizing behaviors that foster youth often display which get them labeled as "bad" are not due to defaults in their personality or character, but rather are rooted in emotional dysregulation linked to child maltreatment (Kim & Cicchetti, 2010). Sarge discussed how he feels a significant challenge to overcome the stigma of being a foster youth. Youth in foster care also have significantly higher rates of mental health needs, and both needing mental health care and being involved in the foster care system can contribute to a double stigmatization (Jee, Conn, Toth, Szilagyi, & Chin, 2014; Winter et al., 2016).

Mixed Bag

> I believe that, even those persons, even those people who do not influence us positively . . . I think we can learn from them positively.
>
> ("Miguel")

A surprising find with the focus groups was that some of the topics which participants discussed did not fit neatly into one category or the other, but rather they were a "mixed bag." Some of the participants offered discussion on a topic framed as an accomplishment, and other participants offered discussion on the same topic, but framed it as a challenge. Three such topics were housing, self-reliance, and interactions with biological family.

Housing

In general, we expect people between the ages of 18 and 21 to be more involved with making decisions about their living arrangements than they had previously been because during this stage, individuals are beginning to find their own place in the world. However, we do not expect people of this age group to be overly worried about housing. Some of these youth had, at times in the past, been lacking the basic necessity of housing.

> There has to be a strong distinction between what is the real world and what is not. Um, the worst thing that can happen when you don't pay your bills is—you have nowhere to go, and you don't eat. But it doesn't get any worse than that. And if we've already been through it, then there's nothing to, you know, worry about in the real world.... I mean you learn to detach from that so you can know your very basic stuff—what you actually need when you actually age out. You know, I mean somewhere to sleep, somewhere to take a shower, somewhere to go to the restroom and eat. And I mean, if you have that, you're pretty much well off.

Sometimes the previous experience with homelessness or inadequate housing was due to their history of family instability, as has been discussed in Jonson-Reid and Barth (2000) and Elze and colleagues (2005). However, it seemed, at least for our participants, that this previous housing experience made them re-prioritize their housing needs. Many discussed how, having recently transitioned out of care, they had limited resources, and that a shared apartment or dorm rather than their very own house was more realistic. One example of this was a young woman who reported that a caseworker who taught one of the Preparation for Adult Living (PAL) program classes helped her to prioritize and implement the curriculum material into her life:

> [S]he helped me realize!—That I have to budget and work and save up for a car, and make sure that—she said, she was like, "The smartest thing to do is live in the dorms for this long, save up, and then get your apartment, and you know, make sure you're financially stable...." The PAL classes really did help me prepare for the real world.

Sometimes, the experience of homelessness was recent or occurred during the transition to independent living. One factor that contributes to homelessness for former foster youth is the "aging out" transition that can leave many foster youth displaced. One participant said:

> When I turned 18, they [foster family] packed my stuff and put it on the porch and told me I had to go. If I didn't leave the house by midnight, they would call the sheriff and they would have me arrested ... so I worked over there and made $550 and paid $310 for a ticket to [town in Texas] and that's how I got here. I had no money and none of my family members even let me stay with them.

This young person is not alone in experiencing homelessness. Studies have found that foster youth often experience homelessness, which can be contributed to by a number of factors that foster youth experience at higher rates. These include lower educational attainment which can mean employment earning lower wages, poverty, and lacking or only having limited support, such as help in filling out rental agreements or providing required references (Dworsky et al., 2013; Fowler, Marcal, Zhang, Day, & Landsverk, 2017).

Some of the foster youth found housing to be an accomplishment they were proud of, a milestone toward complete self-sufficiency; others found housing to be a great challenge, lacking one of the most basic necessities of life. But most often, youth discussed housing as both an accomplishment and a challenge. One youth mentioned that he found himself in a situation that made it extremely difficult to pay his rent:

> I thought I was going to get my raise. And—so I was going to give up my lease, I was going to break my lease, and they [non-government organization staff] said ... "You're not breaking your lease, you're not giving up your truck, you're not. No." So, it feels good.... When you're about to give up on everything ... Cause I have a queen size mattress that fits in the back of my [truck] bed, I have a tent ... I just cannot lose my job, you know?! But everything worked out, cause you know, they gave a check to my apartment, ... and I received my raise, you know.

This young man considered not paying his rent and breaking his lease, to instead allocate his limited resources to make his truck payment, which he needed for transportation to his job, but which could also provide temporary housing. The previous quote exemplifies the challenges that former foster youth are faced with when learning the balance of being self-sufficient, where limited resources and support can end in homelessness or other negative consequences that are usually far less severe for their same-age peers with a larger support system and more resources (Bender, Yang, Ferguson, & Thompson, 2015; Dworsky et al., 2013; Fowler et al., 2017).

Self-Reliance

Self-reliance, which came in different forms, was discussed as both an accomplishment and a challenge. One participant reported that he had a job and provided for himself financially. Another participant shared that he had completed writing the first three chapters of what he called his "ground breaking story," which could help him provide for himself when it was completed. Another participant shared that he had to depend on only himself, and had realized that he could not depend on any of his biological family members, which was emotionally troubling and difficult for him. One female participant who was enrolled in college and living in a student dorm said that providing for herself and all her needs was a challenge. Another participant shared that she was proud of being able to differentiate between her needs and her wants; this helps her to make better decisions. She went on to share that she had decided to enroll in the "return to care" program; she wants to be completely self-sufficient one day, but recognized that she was unable to provide for herself at the time of the study. The statements that youth shared during the focus group support what research has suggested about former foster youth possibly being unprepared for the transition to self-sufficiency, and needing the programs implemented in many states to extend assistance for foster youth until age 21, rather than age 18 (Samuels & Pryce, 2008; Winter et al., 2016).

Biological Families

Foster youth discussed complex relationships with their families, presenting these as both an accomplishment and a challenge. Participants said that reconnecting or rebuilding relationships with their biological family was an accomplishment; specifically, one participant reported getting an uncle to speak to him as an accomplishment. After aging out of care, some former foster youth will live with a biological family member, maintain weekly contact with biological family members, report feeling close to biological family members, and even depend on family members for concrete assistance (i.e., childcare), but research on these family relationships needs more attention (Courtney et al., 2007). In addition, participants reported challenges with their biological family members. One participant had lost many relationships with his biological family members when he terminated his mother's rights, and another reported that family members only came around when they were looking for his benefits; namely housing, food, and money. Also, a small number of children are involved with foster care because of a death (USDHHS [Children's Bureau], 2016). One such participant shared that he had had to provide care for his grandfather with Alzheimer's before being placed in foster care; about a year after he was placed in care, very closely following the death of his biological father, his grandfather passed away and he had to remain in care until he aged out, a challenge for him. Another participant's mother passed away when he was 9 years old, leaving him everything in her will, which caused much friction between him and his older siblings. Some participants also mentioned having engaged in physical altercations with biological family members in the past, which was a challenge. Others discussed remaining distant from their biological family members, usually siblings, for long periods of time, and they stated that this was a challenge for them.

Conclusions

It is important to listen to the voices of young people, as this can show them respect and promote their development (Gilligan, 2000). The voices of the young people who participated help us to get a truer picture of their experiences within the foster care system, transitioning to adulthood, and living independently, allowing us to get information beyond what is usually reported, such as pregnancy and parenting rates, incarceration rates, and utilization of services. The accomplishments that these youth stated are impressive for anyone their age, especially when you consider the lingering effects that child maltreatment can have, and the limited resources and supports that these young people have (Ahrens et al., 2014; Courtney, 2009; Courtney et al., 2011; Trickett et al., 2011). These youth hold themselves to very high standards in school, and they have made alternate "families" that support them in their development. Some of the challenges that these youth have identified, including terminating parental rights and the lack of satisfaction with the foster care system, are unique to former foster youth. These are challenges that were difficult to hear and after each focus group we conducted, we had to hold a session to debrief.

As we conducted the focus groups, transcribed and analyzed the data, the voices of the foster youth stood out to us. One of the strongest statements shared was: "I'm a survivor." This is the sentiment that many of the former foster youth revealed in their stories and the experiences they chose to share with us during the course of this study. No matter how complicated the lives and decisions of these foster youth have been, many have managed to keep a positive outlook. One participant statement said it best:

> [I]f you look at it, there's a lot of kids that come and go, but if you look at it, there be kids and people not in foster care and in foster care that have it worse than you, and yet you're complaining what you don't got.

These former foster youth shared their experiences in care and transition out of care, and offered insights on what they identified as their greatest accomplishments and challenges, and we must reflect on their words to develop ways to implement practical policy changes to better the daily lives of the youth in state care.

Strengths and Limitations

As previously discussed, much of the research regarding foster care has been from the perspective of those providing care or services for foster youth, including foster parents, caseworkers, administrators, and health care providers. We consider that the focus on the voices of foster youth, which have not been heard before, is a strength of the current study. This study has allowed us to hear a different perspective on aging out of the foster care system—from the voices of foster youth who are experts on their experiences. The focus group participants were asked to use aliases. We believe this allowed them the freedom to speak candidly and honestly. This ability to discuss openly their experiences in their own words has offered us the ability to understand more clearly the complicated relationships that foster youth have with biological family members after aging out of care. In addition, our participants offered glimpses of how policies directly impact foster youth, not by numbers and rates, but by sharing their personal stories.

No study is perfect, and ours is no exception. We would have liked the opportunity to conduct individual extended interviews with all participants. However, we were limited by the amount of time available, resources, and mobility issues. All of the focus group participants were preparing to age out of foster care, or had recently done so; some had returned to care by enrolling in the extended foster care program, and others were only utilizing benefits (i.e., educational benefits) that they were eligible for because they had aged out of foster care. Many of the participants were new to living on their own, including some who had only very recently aged out of the system. It seemed as though living on their own was still too new for many of these individuals for them really to have a grasp of how living independently was similar to, and different from, what they thought it would be like, or to have a deep understanding of the challenges that come with long-term independent living. It is also important to note that some of the challenges that participants discussed were recent, some were unresolved, with the youth continuing to work through them at the time of their participation. While the study was originally set up to include foster youth 12 years old and over, and though human subjects' and agencies/care workers' authorizations were approved, we were not allowed to use the data after they were collected due to state provisions that remain unresolved.

Future Directions

More data will be collected from additional focus groups, and if time allows, from in-depth interviews. We would also like to conduct additional research with former foster youth who have been living independently for longer periods of time, to see if they identify different challenges and accomplishments that may be more long-term. One of the interesting things that we found during our study (both qualitative and quantitative) was the idea of alternative family and mentors who are accessible to the youth through the non-government agency. The quantitative data collected aimed to evaluate the curriculum used to prepare youth for independent living, but we found out, as Miguel said, "Um, I think for me, more than the program—is the faculty." We would like to explore this relationship further.

Final Remarks

From the limited research regarding foster youth, we find that they often have worse outcomes, including higher rates of teen pregnancy and parenting, more substance use and abuse, lower educational attainment, and more experiences with homelessness and living in poverty, a much more bleak future when compared to their peers who have not been involved in foster care. In addition, foster youth are often not free to practice the same decision-making skills which their same-age peers develop during adolescence, such as participating in school sports, spending time outside school with friends, or making other daily choices; however, foster youth often have more difficult decisions to make, such as terminating parental rights so that they might be adopted in the future, and planning to make the transition out of state care with very limited support. In order to help these youth be more successful, we must listen to the voices of experts; namely, the youth transitioning out of foster care and those who are involved with the foster care system. It is our deepest desire that the voices of the foster youth provided in this chapter will help to improve the foster care system for youth who might, one day, be placed in foster care.

Acknowledgment

This research is funded in part by the U.S. Department of Health & Human Services, Administration on Children, Youth and Families, Personal Responsibility Education Program (PREP) Competitive Grants under the Affordable Care Act (ACA) HHS-2012-ACF-ACYF-AK-0284. We would like to deeply thank all the staff, community partners, foster youth, and other supporting individuals who made this study possible. We appreciate the instrumental work you do every day, your invaluable insights for this study, and your trust in us to continue generating new knowledge for the benefit of all youth in care.

References

Ahrens, K. R., Garrison, M. M., & Courtney, M. E. (2014). Health outcomes in young adults from foster care and economically diverse backgrounds. *Pediatrics, 134*(6), 1067–1074.

Ahrens, K. R., Spencer, R., Bonnar, M., Coatney, A., & Hall, T. (2016). Qualitative evaluation of historical and relational factors influencing pregnancy and sexually transmitted infection risks in foster youth. *Children and Youth Services Review, 61*, 245–252.

Alpert, L. T. (2005). Research review: Parents' service experience—a missing element in research on foster care case outcomes. *Child & Family Social Work, 10*(4), 361–366.

Aparicio, E., Pecukonis, E. V., & O'Neale, S. (2015). "The love that I was missing": Exploring the lived experience of motherhood among teen mothers in foster care. *Children and Youth Services Review, 51*, 44–54.

Attride-Stirling, J. (2001). Thematic networks: An analytic tool for qualitative research. *Qualitative Research, 1*(3), 385–405.

Ayasse, R. H. (1995). Addressing the needs of foster children: The foster youth services program. *Children & Schools, 17*(4), 207–216.

Batsche, C., Hart, S., Ort, R., Armstrong, M., Strozier, A., & Hummer, V. (2014). Post-secondary transitions of youth emancipated from foster care. *Child & Family Social Work, 19*(2), 174–184.

Bednar, D. E., & Fisher, T. D. (2003). Peer referencing in adolescent decision making as a function of perceived parenting style. *Adolescence, 38*(152), 607–621.

Bender, K., Yang, J., Ferguson, K., & Thompson, S. (2015). Experiences and needs of homeless youth with a history of foster care. *Children and Youth Services Review, 55*, 222–231.

Berger, L. M., Cancian, M., Han, E., Noyes, J., & Rios-Salas, V. (2015). Children's academic achievement and foster care. *Pediatrics, 135*(1), e109–e116.

Berrick, J. D. (1997). Assessing quality of care in kinship and foster family care. *Family Relations, 46*, 273–280.

Berzin, S. C., Rhodes, A. M., & Curtis, M. A. (2011). Housing experiences of former foster youth: How do they fare in comparison to other youth? *Children and Youth Services Review, 33*(11), 2119–2126.

Bijleveld, G. G., Dedding, C. W., & Bunders-Aelen, J. F. (2015). Children's and young people's participation within child welfare and child protection services: A state-of-the-art review. *Child & Family Social Work, 20*(2), 129–138.

Bilchik, S. C. (2010). *Addressing the needs of youth known to both the Child Welfare and Juvenile Justice systems.* National Center for State Courts. Retrieved from https://cdm16501.contentdm.oclc.org/digital/collection/famct/id/305

Biro, F. M., & Dorn, L. D. (2006). Puberty and adolescent sexuality. *Psychiatric Annals, 36*, 685–690.

Blakemore, S. J., Burnett, S., & Dahl, R. E. (2010). The role of puberty in the developing adolescent brain. *Human Brain Mapping, 31*(6), 926–933.

Blakemore, S. J., & Mills, K. L. (2014). Is adolescence a sensitive period for sociocultural processing? *Annual Review of Psychology, 65*, 187–207.

Boonstra, H. D. (2009). The challenge in helping young adults better manage their reproductive lives. *Guttmacher Policy Review, 12*, 13–18.

Bradley, S. J. (2000). *Affect regulation and the development of psychopathology.* New York, NY: Guilford Press.

Britner, P. A., Randall, K. G., & Ahrens, K. R. (2013). Youth in foster care. In D. L. DuBois & M. J. Karcher (Eds.), *The handbook of youth mentoring* (2nd ed.; pp. 341–354). Thousand Oaks, CA: Sage.

Brown, J. D., & Bednar, L. M. (2006). Foster parent perceptions of placement breakdown. *Children and Youth Services Review, 28*(12), 1497–1511.

Bryant, C. M., & Conger, R. D. (2002). An intergenerational model of romantic relationship development. In A. L. Vangelisti, H. T. Reis, & M. A. Fitzpatrick (Eds.), *Advances in personal relationships: Stability and change in relationships* (pp. 57–82). Cambridge: Cambridge University Press.

Butler, S., & Charles, M. (1999). The past, the present, but never the future: Thematic representations of fostering disruption. *Child and Family Social Work, 4*, 9–20.

Catalano, R. F., Berglund, M., Ryan, J. M., Lonczak, H. S., & Hawkins, J. (2004). Positive Youth Development in the United States: Research findings on evaluations of Positive Youth Development programs. *Annals of the American Academy of Political and Social Science, 591*, 98–124. doi: 10.1177/0002716203260102

Cautley, P. W., & Aldridge, M. J. (1975). Predicting success for new foster parents. *Social Work, 20*, 48–53.

Chapple, C. L., & Vaske, J. (2010). Child neglect, social context, and educational outcomes: Examining the moderating effects of school and neighborhood context. *Violence and Victims, 25*(4), 470–485. http://dx.doi.org/10.1891/0886-6708.25.4.470

Cheung, K. K., Montgomery, D., & Benjamins, L. J. (2014). Prevalence of sexually transmitted infections among adolescents entering child protective services. *Journal of Pediatric and Adolescent Gynecology, 28*(5), 324–326. http://dx.doi.org/10.1016/j.jpag.2014.09.011

Cicchetti, D., & Toth, S. L. (2005). Child maltreatment. *Annual Review of Clinical Psycholy, 1*, 409–438.

Commendador, K. A. (2010). Parental influences on adolescent decision making and contraceptive use. *Pediatric Nursing, 36*(3), 147–156.

Conn, A. M., Calais, C., Szilagyi, M., Baldwin, C., & Jee, S. H. (2014). Youth in out-of-home care: Relation of engagement in structured group activities with social and mental health measures. *Children and Youth Services Review, 36*, 201–205.

Cooley, M. E., Farineau, H. M., & Mullis, A. K. (2015). Child behaviors as a moderator: Examining the relationship between foster parent supports, satisfaction, and intent to continue fostering. *Child Abuse & Neglect, 45*, 46–56.

Courtney, M. E. (2009). The difficult transition to adulthood for foster youth in the U.S.: Implications for the State as a corporate parent. *Social Policy Report, 23*(1), 3–19.

Courtney, M. E., Charles, P., Okpych, N. J., Napolitano, L., Halsted, K., Courtney, M. E., . . . Hall, C. (2014). *Findings from the California Youth Transitions to Adulthood Study (CalYOUTH): Conditions of foster youth at age 17*. Chicago: Chapin Hall at the University of Chicago.

Courtney, M., Dworsky, A., Brown, A., Cary, C., Love, K., & Vorhies, V. (2011). *Midwest Evaluation of the Adult Functioning of Former Foster Youth: Outcomes at age 26*. Chicago: Chapin Hall at the University of Chicago.

Courtney, M. E., Dworsky, A. L., Cusick, G. R., Havlicek, J., Perez, A., & Keller, T. E. (2007). *Midwest Evaluation of the Adult Functioning of Former Foster Youth: Outcomes at age 21*. Chicago: Chapin Hall at the University of Chicago.

Cunningham, M. J., & Diversi, M. (2013). Aging out: Youths' perspectives on foster care and the transition to independence. *Qualitative Social Work, 12*(5), 587–602.

Currie, J., & Widom, C. S. (2010). Long-term consequences of child abuse and neglect on adult economic well-being. *Child Maltreatment, 15*(2), 111–120. http://dx.doi.org/10.1177/1077559509355316

Damon, W. (2004). What is positive youth development? *The Annals of the American Academy of Political and Social Science, 591*, 13–24. doi: 10.1177/0002716203260092

Denby, R., Rindfleisch, N., & Bean, G. (1999). Predictors of foster parents' satisfaction and intent to continue to foster. *Child Abuse & Neglect, 23*, 287–303.

Denham, S. A. (2003). Relationships between family rituals, family routines, and health. *Journal of Family Nursing, 9*(3), 305–330.

Dion, R. M., Dworsky, A., Kauff, J., & Kleinman, R. (2014, May). *Housing for youth aging out of foster care*. SSRN. Available at https://papers.ssrn.com/sol3/papers.cfm?abstract_id=2446532

Doelling, J. L., & Johnson, J. H. (1990). Predicting success in foster placement: The contribution of parent–child temperament characteristics. *American Orthopsychiatric Association, 60*, 585–593.

Dworsky, A., & Courtney, M. E. (2010). The risk of teenage pregnancy among transitioning foster youth: Implications for extending state care beyond age 18. *Children and Youth Services Review, 32*(10), 1351–1356. http://dx.doi.org/10.1016/j.childyouth.2010.06.002

Dworsky, A., Napolitano, L., & Courtney, M. (2013). Homelessness during the transition from foster care to adulthood. *American Journal of Public Health, 103*(S2), S318–S323.

Dworsky, A., & Pérez, A. (2009). *Helping former foster youth graduate from college: Campus support programs in California and Washington State*. Chicago: Chapin Hall at the University of Chicago.

Elze, D. E., Auslander, W., McMillen, C., Edmond, T., & Thompson, R. (2001). Untangling the impact of sexual abuse on HIV risk behaviors among youths in foster care. *AIDS Education and Prevention, 13*(4), 377–389.

Elze, D. E., Auslander, W. F., Stiffman, A., & McMillen, C. (2005). Educational needs of youth in foster care. In G. P. Mallon & P. Hess (Eds.), *Child welfare for the twenty-first century: A handbook of practices, policies, and programs* (pp. 185–204). New York, NY: Columbia University Press.

Euser, S., Alink, L. R., Tharner, A., van IJzendoorn, M. H., & Bakermans-Kranenburg, M. J. (2013). The prevalence of child sexual abuse in out-of-home care: A comparison between abuse in residential and in foster care. *Child Maltreatment, 18*(4), 221–231.

Fallesen, P. (2013). Time well spent: The duration of foster care and early adult labor market, educational, and health outcomes. *Journal of Adolescence, 36*(6), 1003–1011.

Farruggia, S. P., Greenberger, E., Chen, C., & Heckhausen, J. (2006). Perceived social environment and adolescents' well-being and adjustment: Comparing a foster care sample with a matched sample. *Journal of Youth and Adolescence, 35*, 349–358.

Fees, B. S., Stockdale, D. F., Crase, S. J., Riggins-Caspers, K., Yates, A. M., Lekies, K. S., & Gillis-Arnold, R. (1998). Satisfaction with foster parenting: Assessment one year after training. *Children and Youth Services Review, 20,* 347–363.

Festinger, T., & Baker, A. J. (2013). The quality of evaluations of foster parent training: An empirical review. *Children and Youth Services Review, 35*(12), 2147–2153.

Forsman, H., Brännström, L., Vinnerljung, B., & Hjern, A. (2016). Does poor school performance cause later psychosocial problems among children in foster care? Evidence from national longitudinal registry data. *Child Abuse & Neglect, 57,* 61–71.

Fowler, P. J., Marcal, K. E., Zhang, J., Day, O., & Landsverk, J. (2017). Homelessness and aging out of foster care: A national comparison of child welfare-involved adolescents. *Children and Youth Services Review, 77,* 27–33.

Frerer, K., Sosenko, L. D., Pellegrin, N., Manchik, V., & Horowitz, J. (2013). *Foster youth stability: A study of California foster youths' school and residential changes in relation to educational outcomes.* Berkeley, CA: Center for Social Services Research and Institute for Evidence-Based Change.

Furstenberg, F. F., Rumbaut, R. G., & Settersten, R. A. (2005). On the frontier of adulthood: Emerging themes and new directions. In R. Settersten, F. F. Furstenberg, & R. G. Rumbaut (Eds.), *On the frontier of adulthood: Theory, research, and public policy* (pp. 3–25). Chicago: University of Chicago Press.

Garon, N., Bryson, S. E., & Smith, I. M. (2008). Executive function in preschoolers: A review using an integrative framework. *Psychological Bulletin, 134*(1), 31–60.

Geiger, J. M., Hanrahan, J. E., Cheung, J. R., & Lietz, C. A. (2016). Developing an on-campus recruitment and retention program for foster care alumni. *Children and Youth Services Review, 61,* 271–280.

Gilligan, R. (2000). Adversity, resilience and young people: The protective value of positive school and spare time experiences. *Children & Society, 14*(1), 37–47.

Glaser, B., & Strauss, A. (1967). *The discovery of Grounded Theory: Strategies for qualitative research.* New York, NY: Aldine de Gruyter.

Goldscheider, F., & Goldscheider, C. (1999). *The changing transition to adulthood: Leaving and returning home.* Thousand Oaks, CA: Sage Publications.

Graber, J. A., Nichols, T. R., & Brooks-Gunn, J. (2010). Putting pubertal timing in developmental context: Implications for prevention. *Developmental Psychobiology, 52,* 254–262. doi: 10.1002/dev.20438

Gramkowski, B., Kools, S., Paul, S., Boyer, C. B., Monasterio, E., & Robbins, N. (2009). Health risk behavior of youth in foster care. *Journal of Child and Adolescent Psychiatric Nursing, 22*(2), 77–85.

Grbich, C. (2007). *Qualitative data analysis: An introduction.* Thousand Oaks, CA: Sage Publications.

Guilamo-Ramos, V., Lee, J. J., & Jaccard, J. (2016). Parent–adolescent communication about contraception and condom use. *JAMA Pediatrics, 170*(1), 14–16.

Hare, A. L., Miga, E. M., & Allen, J. P. (2009). Intergenerational transmission of aggression in romantic relationships: The moderating role of attachment security. *Journal of Family Psychology, 23*(6), 808–818.

Hass, M., & Graydon, K. (2009). Sources of resiliency among successful foster youth. *Children and Youth Services Review, 31*(4), 457–463.

Havlicek, J. R., Garcia, A. R., & Smith, D. C. (2013). Mental health and substance use disorders among foster youth transitioning to adulthood: Past research and future directions. *Children and Youth Services Review, 35*(1), 194–203.

Healey, C. V., & Fisher, P. A. (2011). Young children in foster care and the development of favorable outcomes. *Children and Youth Services Review, 33*(10), 1822–1830.

Herczog, M., van Pagee, R., & Pasztor, E. M. (2001). The multinational transfer of competency-based foster parent assessment, selection, and training: A nine-country case study. *Child Welfare, 80,* 631–643.

Herz, D. C., & Ryan, P. J. (2008). *Bridging two systems: Youth involved in the child welfare and juvenile justice systems.* Washington, DC: Georgetown University, Center for Juvenile Justice Reform.

Hess, P. (1988). Case and context: Determinants of planned visit frequency in foster family care. *Child Welfare, 67*(4), 311–326.

Holland, S., & Crowley, A. (2013). Looked-after children and their birth families: Using sociology to explore changing relationships, hidden histories and nomadic childhoods. *Child & Family Social Work, 18*(1), 57–66.

Hong, J. S., Ryan, J. P., Hernandez, P. M., & Brown, S. (2014). Termination of parental rights for parents with substance use disorder: For whom and then what? *Social Work in Public Health, 29*(6), 503–517.

Jackson, Y., Gabrielli, J., Fleming, K., Tunno, A. M., & Makanui, P. K. (2014). Untangling the relative contribution of maltreatment severity and frequency to type of behavioral outcome in foster youth. *Child Abuse & Neglect, 38*(7), 1147–1159.

Jee, S. H., Conn, A. M., Toth, S., Szilagyi, M. A., & Chin, N. P. (2014). Mental health treatment experiences and expectations in foster care: A qualitative investigation. *Journal of Public Child Welfare, 8*(5), 539–559.

Jonson-Reid, M., & Barth, R. P. (2000). From placement to prison: The path to adolescent incarceration from child welfare supervised foster or group care. *Children and Youth Services Review, 22*, 493–516. doi: 10.1016/S0190-7409(00)00100-6

Kerker, B. D., & Dore, M. M. (2006). Mental health needs and treatment of foster youth: Barriers and opportunities. *American Journal of Orthopsychiatry, 76*(1), 138–147.

Kim, J., & Cicchetti, D. (2010). Longitudinal pathways linking child maltreatment, emotion regulation, peer relations, and psychopathology. *Journal of Child Psychology and Psychiatry, 51*(6), 706–716.

Kirk, R., & Day, A. (2011). Increasing college access for youth aging out of foster care: Evaluation of a summer camp program for foster youth transitioning from high school to college. *Children and Youth Services Review, 33*(7), 1173–1180.

Ladd, G. W., Birch, S. H., & Buhs, E. S. (1999). Children's social and scholastic lives in kindergarten: Related spheres of influence? *Child Development, 70*(6), 1373–1400.

Lambie, I., & Randell, I. (2013). The impact of incarceration on juvenile offenders. *Clinical Psychology Review, 33*(3), 448–459.

Leathers, S. J. (2006). Placement disruption and negative placement outcomes among adolescents in long-term foster care: The role of behavior problems. *Child Abuse & Neglect, 30*, 307–324.

Leathers, S. J., & Testa, M. F. (2006). Foster youth emancipating from care: Caseworkers' reports on needs and services. *Child Welfare, 85*(3), 463–498.

Lerner, R. M. (2005, September). Promoting positive youth development: Theoretical and empirical bases. In *White paper prepared for the workshop on the science of adolescent health and development, national research council/institute of medicine.* Washington, DC: National Academies of Science.

Lerner, J. V., Bowers, E. P., Minor, K., Boyd, M. J., Mueller, M. K., Schmid, K. L., . . . Lerner, R. M. (2013). Positive youth development: Processes, philosophies, and programs. In R. M. Lerner, M. A. Easterbrooks, J. Mistry, & I. B. Weiner (Eds.), *Handbook of psychology: Developmental psychology* (pp. 365–392). Hoboken, NJ: John Wiley.

Lerner, R. M., Lerner, J. V., Almerigi, J., Theokas, C., Phelps, E., Gestsdottir, S., . . . von Eye, A. (2005). Positive youth development, participation in community youth development programs, and community contributions of fifth grade adolescents: Findings from the first wave of the 4-H Study of Positive Youth Development. *Journal of Early Adolescence, 25*(1), 17–71.

Liabo, K., McKenna, C., Ingold, A., & Roberts, H. (2017). Leaving foster or residential care: A participatory study of care leavers' experiences of health and social care transitions. *Child: Care, Health and Development, 43*(2), 182–191.

Lind, T., Raby, K. L., Caron, E. B., Roben, C. K., & Dozier, M. (2017). Enhancing executive functioning among toddlers in foster care with an attachment-based intervention. *Development and Psychopathology, 29*(2), 575–586.

Lindsey, D. (1992). Reliability of the foster care placement decision: A review. *Research on Social Work Practice, 2*(1), 65–80.

Littlefield, L., Cavanagh, S., Knapp, R., & O'Grady, L. (2017). KidsMatter: Building the capacity of Australian primary schools and early childhood services to foster children's social and emotional skills and promote children's mental health. In E. Frydenberg, A. J. Martin, & R. J. Collie (Eds.), *Social and emotional learning in Australia and the Asia-Pacific* (pp. 293–311). Singapore: Springer Singapore.

Luster, T., & Small, S. A. (1994). Factors associated with sexual risk-taking behaviors among adolescents. *Journal of Marriage and the Family, 56*, 622–632.

Lynch, F. L., Dickerson, J. F., Pears, K. C., & Fisher, P. A. (2017). Cost effectiveness of a school readiness intervention for foster children. *Children and Youth Services Review, 81*, 63–71.

Macomber, J. (2009). The impact of ASFA on the permanency and independence for youth in foster care. In *Intentions and results: A look back at the Adoption and Safe Families Act* (pp. 83–92). Washington, DC: Urban Institute. Retrieved from http://affcny.org/wp-content/uploads/IntentionsandResults.pdf

Manlove, J., Welti, K., McCoy-Roth, M., Berger, A., & Malm, K. (2011). Teen parents in foster care: Risk factors and outcomes for teens and their children. *Child Trends Research Brief, No. 28*.

McClelland, M. M., Morrison, F. J., & Holmes, D. L. (2000). Children at risk for early academic problems: The role of learning-related social skills. *Early Childhood Research Quarterly, 15*(3), 307–329.

McMillen, J. C., Narendorf, S. C., Robinson, D., Havlicek, J., Fedoravicius, N., Bertram, J., & McNelly, D. (2015). Development and piloting of a treatment foster care program for older youth with psychiatric problems. *Child and Adolescent Psychiatry and Mental Health, 9*(1), 23.

Mersky, J. P., & Janczewski, C. (2013). Adult well-being of foster care alumni: Comparisons to other child welfare recipients and a non-child welfare sample in a high-risk, urban setting. *Children and Youth Services Review, 35*(3), 367–376.

Mersky, J. P., Topitzes, J., Janczewski, C. E., & McNeil, C. B. (2015). Enhancing foster parent training with parent–child interaction therapy: Evidence from a randomized field experiment. *Journal of the Society for Social Work and Research, 6*(4), 591–616.

Moore, K., Lippman, L., & Brown, B. (2004). Indicators of child well-being: The promise for Positive Youth Development. *Annals of the American Academy of Political and Social Science, 591*, 125–145. doi: 10.1177/0002716203260103

Morris, A. S., Silk, J. S., Steinberg, L., Myers, S. S., & Robinson, L. R. (2007). The role of the family context in the development of emotion regulation. *Social Development, 16*, 361–388. doi: 10.1111/j.1467-9507.2007.00389.x [PubMed: 19756175]

Muller-Ravett, S., & Jacobs, E. (2012). *After foster care and juvenile justice: A preview of the Youth Villages Transitional Living evaluation.* MDRC Policy brief. Retrieved from http://files.eric.ed.gov/fulltext/ED531545.pdf

Nadeem, E., Waterman, J., Foster, J., Paczkowski, E., Belin, T. R., & Miranda, J. (2017). Long-term effects of pre-placement risk factors on children's psychological symptoms and parenting stress among families adopting children from foster care. *Journal of Emotional and Behavioral Disorders, 25*(2), 67–81.

Nash, J. J., & Flynn, R. J. (2016). Foster and adoptive parent training: A process and outcome investigation of the preservice PRIDE program. *Children and Youth Services Review, 67*, 142–151.

Nesmith, A. (2017). Coping with change: Using the Bridge's Transitions Framework with foster youth. *Children and Youth Services Review, 78*, 41–47.

Nesmith, A., & Christophersen, K. (2014). Smoothing the transition to adulthood: Creating ongoing supportive relationships among foster youth. *Children and Youth Services Review, 37*, 1–8.

Nesmith, A., Patton, R., Christophersen, K., & Smart, C. (2017). Promoting quality parent–child visits: The power of the parent–foster parent relationship. *Child & Family Social Work, 22*(1), 246–255.

Noonan, K., & Burke, K. (2005). Termination of parental rights: Which foster care children are affected? *The Social Science Journal, 42*(2), 241–256.

Orme, J. G., Buehler, C., McSurdy, M., Rhodes, K. W., & Cox, M. E. (2003). The Foster Parent Potential Scale. *Research on Social Work Practice, 13*, 181–207. doi: 10.1177/1049731502250405

Osgood, D. W., Foster, E. M., & Courtney, M. E. (2010). Vulnerable populations and the transition to adulthood. *The Future of Children, 20*(1), 209–229.

Packard, T., Delgado, M., Fellmeth, R., & McCready, K. (2008). A cost–benefit analysis of transitional services for emancipating foster youth. *Children and Youth Services Review, 30*(11), 1267–1278.

Palmer, S. E. (1996). Placement stability and inclusive practice in foster care: An empirical study. *Children and Youth Services Review, 18*, 589–601.

Pears, K. C., Kim, H. K., & Fisher, P. A. (2016). Decreasing risk factors for later alcohol use and antisocial behaviors in children in foster care by increasing early promotive factors. *Children and Youth Services Review, 65*, 156–165.

Pears, K. C., Kim, H. K., Fisher, P. A., & Yoerger, K. (2013). Early school engagement and late elementary outcomes for maltreated children in foster care. *Developmental Psychology, 49*(12), 2201–2211.

Petro, J. (2007). *Juvenile justice and child welfare agencies: Collaborating to serve dual jurisdiction youth survey report.* Washington, DC: Child Welfare League of America, Research and Evaluation Division.

Pryce, J. M., & Samuels, G. M. (2010). Renewal and risk: The dual experience of motherhood and aging out of the child welfare system. *Journal of Adolescent Research, 25*(2), 205–230.

Racusin, R., Maerlender, A., Sengupta, A., Isquith, P., & Straus, M. (2005). Psychosocial treatment of children in foster care: A review. *Community Mental Health Journal, 41*, 199–221. doi: 10.1007/s10597-005-2656-7 [PubMed: 15974499]

Riebschleger, J., Day, A., & Damashek, A. (2015). Foster care youth share stories of trauma before, during, and after placement: Youth voices for building trauma-informed systems of care. *Journal of Aggression, Maltreatment & Trauma, 24*(4), 339–360.

Rodger, S., Cummings, A., & Leschied, A. W. (2006). Who is caring for our most vulnerable children? The motivation to foster in child welfare. *Child Abuse & Neglect, 30*, 1129–1142.

Rolock, N., & White, K. R. (2016). Post-permanency discontinuity: A longitudinal examination of outcomes for foster youth after adoption or guardianship. *Children and Youth Services Review, 70*, 419–427.

Rosenthal, D. A., Smith, A. M. A., & de Visser, R. (1999). Personal and social factors influencing age at first sexual intercourse. *Archives of Sexual Behavior, 28*, 319–333.

Rosenthal, J. A., & Curiel, H. F. (2006). Modeling behavioral problems of children in the child welfare system: Caregiver, youth, and teacher perceptions. *Children and Youth Services Review, 28*, 1390–1408.

Ryan, J. P., & Testa, M. K. (2005). Child maltreatment and juvenile delinquency: Investigating the role of placement and placement instability. *Children and Youth Services Review, 27*, 227–349.

Salas Martínez, M. D., Fuentes, M. J., Bernedo, I. M., & García-Martín, M. A. (2016). Contact visits between foster children and their birth family: The views of foster children, foster parents and social workers. *Child & Family Social Work, 21*(4), 473–483.

Salazar, A. M., Keller, T. E., Gowen, L. K., & Courtney, M. E. (2013). Trauma exposure and PTSD among older adolescents in foster care. *Social Psychiatry and Psychiatric Epidemiology, 48*(4), 545–551. doi: 10.1007/s00127-012-0563-0

Samuels, G. M., & Pryce, J. M. (2008). "What doesn't kill you makes you stronger": Survivalist self-reliance as resilience and risk among young adults aging out of foster care. *Children and Youth Services Review, 30*(10), 1198–1210.

Sartor, C. E., & Youniss, J. (2002). The relationship between positive parental involvement and identity achievement during adolescence. *Adolescence, 37*, 221–234.

Shipman, K. L., Edwards, A., Brown, A., Swisher, L., & Jennings, E. (2005). Managing emotion in a maltreating context: A pilot study examining child neglect. *Child Abuse and Neglect, 29*, 1015–1029. doi: 10.1016/j.chiabu.2005.01.006 [PubMed: 16159666]

Shpiegel, S. (2016). Resilience among older adolescents in foster care: The impact of risk and protective factors. *International Journal of Mental Health and Addiction, 14*(1), 6–22.

Shpiegel, S., Cascardi, M., & Dineen, M. (2017). A social ecology analysis of childbirth among females emancipating from foster care. *Journal of Adolescent Health, 60*(5), 563–569.

Singer, E. R., Berzin, S. C., & Hokanson, K. (2013). Voices of former foster youth: Supportive relationships in the transition to adulthood. *Children and Youth Services Review, 35*(12), 2110–2117.

Smith, M. C. (1996). An exploratory survey of foster mother and caseworker attitudes about sibling placement. *Child Welfare, 75*(4), 357–375.

Smith, T., Clark, J. F., & Nigg, C. R. (2015). Building support for an evidence-based teen pregnancy and sexually transmitted infection prevention program adapted for foster youth. *Hawaii Journal of Medicine & Public Health, 74*(1), 27–32.

Stewart, C. J., Kum, H. C., Barth, R. P., & Duncan, D. F. (2014). Former foster youth: Employment outcomes up to age 30. *Children and Youth Services Review, 36*, 220–229.

Stone, N. M., & Stone, S. F. (1983). The prediction of successful foster placement. *Social Casework: The Journal of Contemporary Social Work, 83*, 11–17.

Storer, H. L., Barkan, S. E., Stenhouse, L. L., Eichenlaub, C., Mallillin, A., & Haggerty, K. P. (2014). In search of connection: The foster youth and caregiver relationship. *Children and Youth Services Review, 42*, 110–117.

Stott, T. (2012). Placement instability and risky behaviors of youth aging out of foster care. *Child and Adolescent Social Work Journal, 29*(1), 61–83. http://dx.doi.org/10.1007/s10560-011-0247-8

Strolin-Goltzman, J., Kollar, S., & Trinkle, J. (2010). Listening to the voices of children in foster care: Youths speak out about child welfare workforce turnover and selection. *Social Work, 55*(1), 47–53.

Sullivan, M. J., Jones, L., & Matiesen, S. (2010). School change, academic progress, and behavior problems in a sample of foster youth. *Children and Youth Services Review, 32*, 164–170.

Suter, E. A., Baxter, L. A., Seurer, L. M., & Thomas, L. J. (2014). Discursive constructions of the meaning of "family" in online narratives of foster adoptive parents. *Communication Monographs, 81*(1), 59–78.

Svoboda, D. V., Shaw, T. V., Barth, R. P., & Bright, C. L. (2012). Pregnancy and parenting among youth in foster care: A review. *Children and Youth Services Review, 34*(5), 867–875.

Swannell, S., Martin, G., Page, A., Hasking, P., Hazell, P., Taylor, A., & Protani, M. (2012). Child maltreatment, subsequent non-suicidal self-injury and the mediating roles of dissociation, alexithymia and self-blame. *Child Abuse & Neglect, 36*(7), 572–584.

Szilagyi, M. A., Rosen, D. S., Rubin, D., & Zlotnik, S. (2015). Health care issues for children and adolescents in foster care and kinship care. *Pediatrics, 136*(4), e1142–e1166.

Tanner, J. L., & Arnett, J. J. (2016). The new life stage between adolescence and young adulthood. In A. Furlong (Ed.), *Routledge handbook of youth and young adulthood* (2nd ed.; pp. 34–40). New York: Routledge.

Texas Education Agency. (2014). *Secondary school completion and dropouts in Texas public schools, 2012–13* (Document No. GE14 601 07). Austin, TX: Author.

Thompson, R. G. Jr., & Auslander, W. F. (2011). Substance use and mental health problems as predictors of HIV sexual risk behaviors among adolescents in foster care. *Health & Social Work, 36*(1), 33–43.

Thompson, A. E., Greeson, J. K., & Brunsink, A. M. (2016). Natural mentoring among older youth in and aging out of foster care: A systematic review. *Children and Youth Services Review, 61*, 40–50.

Touliatos, J., & Lindholm, B. W. (1981). Measurement of potential for foster parenthood. *The Journal of Psychology, 109*, 255–263.

Trickett, P. K., Negriff, S., Ji, J., & Peckins, M. (2011). Child maltreatment and adolescent development. *Journal of Research on Adolescence, 21*, 3–20. doi:10.1111/j.1532-7795.2010.00711.x

Tzawa-Hayden, A. (2004). Take me higher: Helping foster youth pursue higher education. *Child Law Practice, 23*(10), 163–166.

Unrau, Y. A., Seita, J. R., & Putney, K. S. (2008). Former foster youth remember multiple placement moves: A journey of loss and hope. *Children and Youth Services Review, 30*(11), 1256–1266.

U.S. Department of Health & Human Services [USDHHS]. (2006). *The AFCARS report: Preliminary estimates for FY 2005 as of September 2006 (13)*. Washington, DC: Children's Bureau. Retrieved from www.acf.hhs.gov/sites/default/files/cb/afcarsreport13.pdf

U.S. Department for Health & Human Services [USDHHS] (Children's Bureau). (2012). *The AFCARS report. Preliminary FY 2011 estimates as of July 2012. No. 19*. Available at www.acf.hhs.gov/programs/cb/resource/afcars-report-19

U.S. Department of Health & Human Services [USDHHS] (Children's Bureau). (2015). *A national look at the use of congregate care in child welfare*. Retrieved from www.acf.hhs.gov/cb/resource/congregate-care-brief (PDF retrieved from: www.acf.hhs.gov/sites/default/files/cb/cbcongregatecare_brief.pdf).

U.S. Department of Health & Human Services [USDHHS] (Children's Bureau). (2016). *Trends in foster care and adoption: FY 2006–FY2015 (Based on data submitted by States as of June 8, 2016)*. AFCARS (Adoption Foster Care Analysis Reporting System). Retrieved from www.acf.hhs.gov/cb/resource/trends-in-foster-care-and-adoption-fy15 (PDF retrieved from www.acf.hhs.gov/sites/default/files/cb/trends_fostercare_adoption2015.pdf).

U.S. Department of Health & Human Services [USDHHS] (Children's Bureau). (2017a). *Extension of foster care beyond age 18*. Retrieved from: www.childwelfare.gov/topics/systemwide/laws-policies/statutes/extensionfc/ (PDF retrieved from www.childwelfare.gov/pubPDFs/extensionfc.pdf).

U.S. Department of Health & Human Services [USDHHS] (Children's Bureau). (2017b). *National Youth in Transition Database*. Retrieved from www.acf.hhs.gov/cb/research-data-technology/reporting-systems/nytd

U.S. Department of Health & Human Services [USDHHS] (Children's Bureau). (2017c). *National Child Abuse and Neglect Data System*. Retrieved from www.acf.hhs.gov/cb/research-data-technology/reporting-systems/ncands

U.S. Department of Health & Human Services [USDHHS] (Children's Bureau). (2017d). *Adoption and Foster Care Analysis and Reporting System*. Retrieved from www.acf.hhs.gov/cb/research-data-technology/statistics-research/afcars

U.S. Department of Health & Human Services [USDHHS] (Child Welfare Information Gateway). (n.d.). *The National Incidence Study*. Retrieved from www.childwelfare.gov/topics/systemwide/statistics/nis/#n4

U.S. Department of Health & Human Services [USDHHS] (Child Welfare Information Gateway). (2016). *Definitions of child abuse and neglect*. Retrieved from www.childwelfare.gov/topics/systemwide/laws-policies/statutes/define/

U.S. Department of Health & Human Services [USDHHS] (Office of Planning, Research & Evaluation). (2014). *National Survey of Child and Adolescent Well-Being*. Retrieved from www.acf.hhs.gov/opre/research/project/national-survey-of-child-and-adolescent-well-being-nscaw

Valdez, C. E., Bailey, B. E., Santuzzi, A. M., & Lilly, M. M. (2014). Trajectories of depressive symptoms in foster youth transitioning into adulthood: The roles of emotion dysregulation and PTSD. *Child Maltreatment, 19*(3–4), 209–218.

Wilks, J. (1986). The relative importance of parents and friends in adolescent decision making. *Journal of Youth and Adolescence, 15*(4), 323–334.

Wilson, E., Casanueva, C., Smith, K. R., Koo, H., Tueller, S. J., & Webb, M. B. (2014). Risk of early sexual initiation and pregnancy among youth reported to the child welfare system. *Child Welfare, 93*(1), 127–147.

Winter, V. R., Brandon-Friedman, R. A., & Ely, G. E. (2016). Sexual health behaviors and outcomes among current and former foster youth: A review of the literature. *Children and Youth Services Review, 64*, 1–14.

Wulczyn, F. H., Chen, L., & Hislop, K. B. (2006). Adoption dynamics and the Adoption and Safe Families Act. *Social Service Review, 80*(4), 584–608.

Wulczyn, F., Kogan, J., & Harden, B. J. (2003). Placement stability and movement trajectories. *Social Service Review, 77*, 212–236.

Zima, B. T., Bussing, R., Yang, X., & Belin, T. R. (2000). Help-seeking steps and service use for children in foster care. *The Journal of Behavioral Health Services and Research, 27*(3), 271–285.

Part III
Impact of Foster Care on Youth's Overall Health

6
Assessment of Youth in Foster Care

Jeffrey N. Wherry

The need for assessment of abused and neglected youth arises from the work which has established that behavioral (Kaplan, Pelcovitz, & Labruna, 1999; Petrenko, Friend, Garrido, Taussig, & Culhane, 2012) and mental health problems (Cicchetti & Toth, 2005) are prevalent among abused and neglected youth removed from the custody of a caregiver. For example, post-traumatic stress disorder is more prevalent among foster care youth than in the general population (English et al., 2005). Sadly, based on this author's reading of thousands of reports, most psychologists do not individualize the assessments or psychological evaluations which they conduct. Literally, for decades, youth and adolescents have been completing cognitive assessments (formerly described as IQ tests), academic achievement tests, and often two or more "tests" designed to assess emotional and behavioral functioning. Unfortunately, these test batteries were administered without any logical rationale and without specific referral questions. A medical analogy involving youth entering foster care would be to administer a magnetic resonance imaging (MRI) scan of the brain, an electroencephalograph (EEG), a blood panel, and a test for diabetes to all youth regardless of specific concerns, complaints, or history.

Child welfare caseworkers, Court-Appointed Special Advocates (CASAs), attorneys, and judges are not trained in the differences among the various tests and assessments, and unfortunately, psychologists do not receive training to design or tailor an evaluation/assessment specific to the youth's needs. Some misguided and well-funded sites seem proud of their extensive work-ups involving some of the aforementioned assessments and more, but with no or little thought to what is helpful, what is necessary, and what even could be harmful. Let us start with harmful; how could a test be harmful? One way is if a youth is administered a test of cognitive or intellectual functioning (e.g., the Wechsler Intelligence Scale for Children–Fifth Edition; Wechsler, 2014). The nature of these tests makes it extraordinarily difficult to perform better than you are able to. However, if a youth is assessed immediately following a disruptive separation from a parent, or is assessed while other siblings in care are participating in a favorable activity, the youth's motivation and attitude may be less than stellar, and the youth under-performs. While the person conducting the assessment may note the lack of motivation, rarely is the test score *not* reported. Then, for the droves of people who carelessly read the report looking only for scores, the youth's poor performance, which represents under-performing during that single session on a single day, becomes etched in stone as the whole truth about the youth's capability. In this way, harm is done.

What we Know

Newsflash! Children or youth removed from the custody of their parents almost all the time have a family member who has neglected, physically abused, emotionally abused, or sexually abused their youth.

Newsflash 1

These forms of youth maltreatment often are co-morbid. Therefore, youth should be formally asked about these other forms of maltreatment, which are different from the event that was referred for investigation. For those child protective services (CPS) upper-level managers who assert that youth are routinely asked about other forms of youth maltreatment, this author would ask, "When are they asked?" Is it in the presence of the parent? Is it in the middle of the night, after law enforcement has separated two quarreling, inebriated parents? If he or she is removed in the late night or early morning hours, the youth may witness caregivers who are placed in separate patrol cars; then a well-meaning social worker in a separate car questions the youth. What is the likelihood that the youth will talk candidly at that moment? As far as the youth knows, mom and dad (now in patrol cars) are to be taken to jail forever, and the youth will be without parents for the remainder of his or her life. Thus, after the youth has been removed, and the youth's world has returned to some degree of normalcy, a trained professional with some relationship with the youth should ask questions about other forms of youth maltreatment.

Newsflash 2

There are some fairly predictable symptoms which abused youth may experience, including post-traumatic stress, dissociation, sexualized behavior, anger or aggressive behavior, anxiety, and depression and suicidal behavior (Lanktree et al., 2012). Most of these symptoms are not assessed effectively or efficiently with the cognitive assessment, an achievement test, a sentence completion task, the Rorschach Inkblots, a storytelling task (e.g., the Thematic Apperception Test; TAT), or even with a great unidimensional measure like the Children's Depression Inventory—2 (Kovacs, 2010) or a respectable broad-band rating scale like the Child Behavior Checklist (CBCL; Achenbach & Rescorla, 2001). Most of the tests/measures/ratings listed above are irrelevant, and none of them assess trauma-related symptoms or sexualized behavior. Moreover, Cashel (2002) identified the 30 most frequently administered assessments, and none of the measures recommended in this chapter are on that list.

Newsflash 3

There are two broad-band assessments and two broad-band screening measures which assess relevant symptoms (post-traumatic stress, dissociation, depression, anxiety, anger, and sexual concerns) and are reliable, valid, and normed. Moreover, when the two assessments (i.e., Trauma Symptom Checklist for Children [TSCC; Briere, 1996]/Trauma Symptom Checklist for Young Children [TSCYC; Briere, 2005]) are utilized, the perspective of both the youth and a knowledgeable caregiver (i.e., someone familiar with the youth and not merely someone who has spent several days with the youth) are assessed. Similarly, the two screening measures (the TSCC—Screening Form and the TSCYC—Screening Form; Briere & Wherry, 2016) allow for less time-intensive screening of youth, utilizing self-report and knowledgeable caregiver reports.

Newsflash 4

Perhaps counter-intuitively, if you are thinking confidently that you are above the crowd because you assess post-traumatic stress (PTS) symptoms, consider that *not* all youth are traumatized by their abuse or even by the separation from the family. For example, some young children or youth are not traumatized (Kolko et al., 2010), perhaps because the alleged perpetrator has his/her sexual needs gratified in ways which are deceiving, but not physically painful; in fact, the whole ploy may be to present the abuse as a game. So, if a unidimensional measure of PTS symptoms is administered, an array of other possible symptoms may be ignored.

The Problem

Mental health providers continue to use the same old irrelevant test batteries which provide precious little information about symptoms which are common responses to abuse (e.g., PTS, depression, anxiety, dissociation, anger, suicidal thinking, sexualized behavior). The problem is compounded by the fact that universities are teaching courses on assessment that rarely, if ever, mention, let alone teach, the administration, scoring, and interpretation of relevant measures (e.g., the TSCC or TSCYC).

A second problem resulting from the first problem is the limited training available to those already licensed. Like evidence-based treatment, evidence-based assessment is best learned outside of graduate practica, when it is part of a learning collaborative where training is followed by a consultation component. Otherwise, trainers focus on scores alone, with little attention to more nuanced issues in interpretation and differential diagnosis. Learning these skills takes more than a seminar or "lunch and learn."

A third problem or "straw man" argument is that these existing measures cost too much. True, the instruments are not free, but then mammograms are not free either, but they are necessary and a good investment. So, because the reliable, valid, and normed measures are not free, clinicians often advocate for the use of measures which are in the public domain (i.e., free). Some of these public domain measures, while not maliciously designed, are misused by those looking for an inexpensive alternative.

Backtracking

Theory

One challenge facing the field of abuse, foster care, and assessment is the relatively slow pace of advancement in terms of tools for use with youth. Most measures cited in research are measures developed by a researcher, but are merely established as reliable, or maybe even valid, but are not standardized. Standardization is essential so that clinicians can determine if a specific behavior or symptom is out of the range of the normal distribution for a youth of a specific age and gender. The process of standardization or norming is akin to bringing a new drug to market by a pharmaceutical company. It is an expensive proposition sampling thousands of individuals—especially when there is no certainty that the assessment will be valuable and marketable.

Some of these research instruments may assess constructs which are more theoretically based (e.g., in attachment theory or cognitive theory); however, without standardization, the measures have little practical value and would be considered lacking in basic psychometric properties as promulgated by the American Psychological Association (APA, 2014).

However, a conceptual model for understanding the impact of abuse on youth generally (if not specifically for foster youth) has been offered by Spaccarelli (1994). Spaccarelli postulated that in addition to the nature of the abuse, there are issues associated with the investigation process that might impact the development of clinical symptoms. The model examines factors related to the abuse of the youth as well as factors associated with the investigation (i.e., disclosure events) and events that may occur subsequent to, and because of, the investigation (e.g., related events like placement outside the home and court hearings). Specifically, placement outside the home could theoretically have a traumatic impact (e.g., when a youth is removed following an episode of witnessed domestic violence between parents with both parents being incarcerated) or little negative impact (e.g., when a young child is removed from a neglectful parent who has ignored the youth's emotional and physical needs). In the second scenario, placement in a foster home might represent the first placement where the youth's emotional, physical, and safety needs are met.

Age, sex, and personality factors are also identified as possible moderating variables that have the potential to impact the expression of a youth's symptomatology. Finally, previous coping styles and cognitive appraisal schemes influence the way a youth organizes and understands events in his or her world. Individually and collectively, these factors influence expression of traumatic-related symptoms (e.g., PTS and dissociation), as well as helplessness and hopelessness (often leading to depression or suicidality), sexualized behavior, and anxieties about the future.

The value of such a transactional model lies not so much in the identification of symptoms, but rather, when the symptoms are identified by some other means (e.g., the TSCC or TSCYC), they can be linked to the transactional events with implications for intervention. For example, a youth is identified as being anxious after placement. Perhaps the anxiety is rooted in some misunderstanding in a young child's mind about the nature and duration of a foster care placement. One possible intervention might be repeated, age-appropriate explanations of the reason for placement and reiterating the ultimate goal of reunification. With the exception of understanding cognitive appraisals of the placement and the abuse/neglect, this transactional model assists in identifying issues, if not symptoms, and allowing for the application of other theory-based interventions (e.g., family systems theory, behavioral theory) or even atheoretical problem-solving in the form of case management.

Terms

Now that you are interested, there is a need to address more mundane issues. Specifically, there is confusion about various terms. Often these terms are used interchangeably when they should not be, or in some cases, the difference in terms is insignificant. Terms used to describe assessment which are largely interchangeable include: psychosocial, clinical intake, assessment, intake, and biopsychosocial. All refer to an assessment of sorts, which can be provided and written by almost any mental health professional with a graduate degree, training in assessment, and a license to practice in their state. Terms like "psychiatric evaluation" and "psychological evaluation" can only be used by their respective disciplines. Furthermore, there are some assessments or psychological tests, which can be purchased and administered only by certain disciplines (e.g., psychologists). Finally, there are three terms or procedures that are often used in confusing ways—screening, mental status exam, and the Child and Adolescent Needs and Strengths.

When professionals speak of screening, they may be referring to screening of symptoms or screening for abusive/traumatic events. Identifying traumatic events is an important prerequisite to identifying symptoms. For example, some youth experience multiple traumatic events prior to placement in foster care (e.g., domestic violence, a suicide attempt by a parent, sexual abuse, and neglect). However, the "referral event" (i.e., that which leads to placement into foster care) may be physical neglect identified by police during a domestic call to a residence. By identifying these additional forms of youth maltreatment, a more comprehensive response which ensures family safety is made possible. Additionally, in some situations, the additional traumatic event may not involve youth maltreatment (e.g., being attacked by a dog). This becomes relevant because the youth might experience the dog attack as more traumatic than some of the abusive episodes. Thus, the dog attack might also warrant treatment. If professionals do not screen for additional, potentially traumatic events, a youth may not offer those events spontaneously. Screening of symptoms is equally important, so that clinicians do not merely identify one part of the problem, when additional problems might be more important or more urgent. As an example, it is common among sexually abused youth to have trauma-related symptoms (e.g., PTS symptoms or dissociative symptoms) and, in some cases, sexualized behavior. For a 7-year-old boy in foster care, the sexualized behavior in a home with younger youth may demand immediate attention to prevent the additional sexualization of other youth in the home or at school. Screening measures inherently are shorter and thus sacrifice consistency (reliability) and validity for brevity. Reliability is one of the basic psychometric qualities of any good assessment, and refers to the consistency of answers across raters (e.g., between parents and teachers), the consistency of items within a purported scale or construct (e.g., anxiety), or consistency over time (i.e., test-retest reliability) (Kline, 2013). Validity is an important attribute that is achievable only if the test is reliable, but is altogether a separate issue. Validity is the degree to which a test in fact measures what it purports to measure (Kline, 2013). For example, is an item on a test that purports to measure anxiety actually measuring anxiety or some related construct like depression?

A second term which can be confusing is the term "mental status exam," which is a semi-structured clinical interview often taught to psychiatrists. It is *not* a test and is no more reliable or valid than any other semi-structured or even unstructured interviews.

Finally, a third term or procedure used now in many states is the Child and Adolescent Needs and Strengths (CANS; Kisiel, Blaustein, Fogler, Ellis, & Saxe, 2009). Needs and *strengths* certainly have their appeal; however, all versions of the CANS currently are not assessment measures, but rather are information *integration* tools. When used correctly, the CANS can be immensely helpful; however, the integrated information is only as good as the individual "pieces" of information and the method, reliability, validity, and understanding related to normative behavior. More coarsely put, if the data gathered are unreliable or invalid, then the integration of the same data will be unreliable and invalid. Of course, this concern applies to all techniques and tools—anything can be used inappropriately. It is the misperception of many, though, that the CANS is an assessment tool that makes its potential for misuse a concern.

Special Characteristics of Youth Entering the Foster Care System

Polyvictimization

Exposure to multiple forms of abuse or trauma (also known as polyvictimization) occurs in 20% to 48% of all youth who report abuse (Finkelhor, Ormond, & Turner, 2007). In virtually all cases where youth are placed into foster care by the authority of the state, the placement has been precipitated by some form of child maltreatment—neglect, physical abuse, sexual abuse, or some combination. While it is not uncommon for there to be a combination of different forms of child abuse ("polyvictimization"), it is rare for youth to volunteer additional forms of maltreatment while in the middle of the removal process. Moreover, London, Bruck, Ceci, and Shuman (2005) found that the modal rate of disclosure by child sexual abuse victims during childhood was 33%, and even then, the reporting may have occurred months or years after the event. While there are no studies which focus on incremental disclosures by youth in foster care, it has been this author's experience as a clinician to review a record for a youth placed in care and to learn of neglect as the precipitating event leading to removal from the home and placement in foster care. However, once safe from the abuser, many of these clinical cases make incremental disclosures of additional forms and episodes of abuse. This is sometimes difficult for the public, the courts, and even professionals to understand; however, at the point that youth are separated from their family, the chief concern often is, "How do I get back to my family?" It may be weeks or months before a youth can trust one of the new adults in their world (e.g., caseworkers, foster parents, teachers), and tell them about additional maltreatment. Ultimately, youth should be asked directly about their abuse experience in clinical settings since, otherwise, a significant number of abuse victims may go unrecognized (Ungar, Barter, McConnell, Tutty, & Fairholm, 2008).

Complex Trauma

Often as a result of polyvictimization, youth exhibit symptoms of complex trauma as contrasted with simple or a single episode of trauma. To the experienced caseworker or therapist, this notion is nothing novel; however, for those new to the field, consider the reaction of a youth to one episode of sexual abuse—say genital touching. While that single episode may result in severe symptoms like post-traumatic stress, imagine daily abuses—sexual, physical, and emotional, plus witnessing domestic violence and enduring neglect. Youth who live in these circumstances often have complex trauma. In complex trauma, domains effected may include attachment (e.g., distrust of others, attunement to the emotional states of others, and interpersonal difficulties), biological and affective regulation (e.g., medical problems with or without a psychological component, poor emotional self-regulation), cognition (e.g., concentration, executive function, accurate processing of events, stimuli, interactions), dissociation (e.g., depersonalization, derealization, altered states of consciousness), behavioral control (e.g., modulation of impulses, sleep problems, pathological self-soothing, self-destructive behavior), and self-concept (e.g., low self-esteem, shame and guilt, disturbances of body image) (Cook, Blaustein, Spinazzola, & van der Kolk, 2003).

Misdiagnosis

When clinicians are unaware of polyvictimization or even the extent of recent, limited episodes of parental abuse, they may assign a diagnosis which is phenomenologically accurate (e.g., attention deficit hyperactivity disorder [ADHD] or depression to account for concentration difficulties when the more accurate diagnosis is PTSD), but fails to consider the comprehensive impact of the abuse on the child/adolescent (Weinstein, Staffelbach, & Biaggio, 2000). Often the diagnosis is a "missed" diagnosis inasmuch as symptoms are "misidentified" (e.g., vivid re-experiencing symptoms of post-traumatic stress misidentified as hallucinations; Graham, Nurcombe, Sheridan, & McFarland, 2007). Another example could be a youth who appears to exhibit symptoms of separation anxiety (clinging to a parent) when the clinging serves the function of avoiding an abusive individual (a symptom of post-traumatic stress avoidance).

Separation Issues

The aforementioned separation anxiety is an excellent illustration of how interpersonal relationships and interactions may be mischaracterized in the absence of context and knowledge about abuse. In a quite functional manner, youth may cling to a safe caregiver, and be misdiagnosed with separation anxiety disorder or labeled with school refusal or as "truant" (Wherry & Marrs, 2008). Alternatively, the youth placed in foster care who was neglected by a parent may be preoccupied by notions of reunification. While fostering a youth is designed to create a safe and predictable environment for an abused and/or neglected youth, parents remain parents, and the sanctity of "mom" leaves many youth uncertain about their future and willing to risk the predictability of the abusive past over an uncertain future. This challenge of fitting in with a foster family while waiting on the return of the struggling parent is reviewed by Biehal (2014). That is, separation from a biological parent who intermittently delivers nurturing and then neglectful or abusive messages to the youth can leave a youth ambivalent about even the safest of foster placements. Thus, the youth may be reluctant to fully trust the foster family, all the while holding on to the hope of reunifying with a parent.

Assessing and Enhancing Family Motivation

Courts, fostering agencies, and Court-Appointed Special Advocates are comprised of well-intentioned individuals who choose their professional or volunteer time with the hope of helping others. However, preconceived notions about youth, about abuse, and about abusive or neglectful parents can result in either: (a) premature reunification; or (b) a failure to engage and align with biological parents and thus be predisposed to termination. Thus, assuming motivation or lack of motivation can be a significant mistake. Motivational interviewing with the purpose of addressing a parent's ambivalence and counting the cost can be the beginning of engagement. Studies have shown (e.g., Chaffin et al., 2009) that even with the use of an evidence-based treatment like Parent–Child Interaction Therapy (PCIT; McNeil & Hembree-Kigin, 2010), parents referred by child protective services (CPS) must be motivated.

Record Review

Youth who are placed in foster care sometimes have families with a history of CPS involvement and services. That is, there may be multiple reports of abuse and investigations. Thus, at times, there are records of previous investigations, assessments, or treatments. While those records can provide important clues or direct answers to concerns, the challenge can lie in identifying relevant records and securing their release. However, a simple request may yield helpful information and reduce unnecessary assessments, while simultaneously allowing more youth who need complete assessments to be served. An example is school records. Often, a youth performs well in regular classes and scores well on routinely administered, group achievement tests. If records, including grades and standardized test scores administered by the school, are available, they may reveal normal functioning and performance until a specific grade that might be associated with the onset of abuse, domestic violence, and removal from the home. If there is a precipitous decline in school results, then perhaps the decline is *not* due to a learning disability, but more likely a response to traumatic events.

Records also can provide corroboration or clues which assist in confirming or disconfirming hypotheses related to symptoms associated with abuse. For example, perhaps a youth begins to exhibit problems with concentration at age 8. Simultaneously, there is a decline in math performance. Usually, the onset of ADHD symptoms is earlier than age 8; however, occasionally a very bright youth "gets by," despite concentration difficulties, during the early grades. However, if a history of abuse is discovered, and the onset of the abuse coincides with the onset of concentration problems, then perhaps the concentration difficulties are best explained as a post-traumatic stress symptom of arousal. In turn, the math problems may not reflect a learning disability in math, but rather a decline associated with the difficulty in concentrating. In math, the negative impact can occur quickly since each new skill depends on a previously learned skill. As a student, if I was "checked out" for a few weeks while learning the basics of fractions or subtraction with borrowing, I may need to be re-taught those skills because they might be outside my repertoire or learned incorrectly. That is, sometimes students have rules which govern their math or reading skills; they are just not the correct rules.

Often stakeholders or referring agents have specific questions about a youth, and seek out an assessment to address those "referral questions." Sometimes the answer to a referral question, or at least a clue, can be found in the review of existing records.

Evaluation of Records and Reports

When records are obtained, how can a caseworker, CASA, or therapist evaluate the quality of these documents? An exact algorithm for determining useful documents may be elusive; however, for the experienced clinician, bad reports and records are often obvious. For example, if a clinician writes a report and fills the report with jargon rather than offering understandable explanation for symptoms present, then the clinician may be "hiding" behind the jargon—leading inexperienced individuals to feel uninformed while the clinician actually is unable to explain symptoms and the origins in everyday language. Occasionally, a bad assessment includes numerous "rule outs" with regard to a diagnosis, showing a degree of uncertainty which may be linked to a poor understanding by the clinician or sacrificing accuracy for efficiency (i.e., spending limited time and being unable to draw conclusions). Another potential sign of inadequate clinical conceptualization or poor diagnostic skills is the enumeration of multiple, complete diagnoses (e.g., seven separate diagnoses) for virtually every symptom or cluster of symptoms. Sometimes a parsimonious and simple understanding of diverse symptoms results in more direct treatment of the most important issues for youth and families involved with foster care.

Referral Questions

Almost any assessment is enhanced when it has a clear purpose—that is, a specific referral question that the examiner is tasked with addressing. Early in training, my supervisor related his frustration with pediatric residents who routinely failed to articulate referral questions when making referrals of youth receiving care on one of the pediatric service units. The residents routinely wrote the following on their referral paperwork: "Please see and evaluate." After months of working with residents and hours of coaching, the supervisor resorted to writing the following on the consultation forms: "Child seen and evaluated." Ultimately, this led to lessons learned by the residents, but training consumers, stakeholders, caseworkers, teachers, and agency staff to articulate meaningful and helpful referral questions is a challenge.

Poor referral questions are often vague and poorly formulated. A helpful referral question will be helpful to the client, the referring agent, and the person conducting the assessment. Therefore, the more specific a referral question can be, usually the more helpful it will be. Examples of poor referral questions include: (a) Would this child benefit from therapy? (Ask them directly as a first step.) or (b) Is this child at risk to _____? (The best predictor of the future is the past.) Better referral questions include: (a) Are the concentration problems at school the result of ADHD, depression, or PTSD? or (b) Is the mood dysregulation the result of a mood disorder, exposure to a chaotic, dysregulated environment, substance abuse, or some combination?

If you are someone who does assessments, take the time to train your referral sources. Those who make referrals are then more likely to ask specific questions, and then a good assessment will provide specific answers.

Moving Forward with the Assessment

With a referral question, and background information gathered from existing records, now you are ready to formulate a strategy for assessment. The most common responses to child abuse include trauma responses which may include PTSD, Acute Stress Disorder, and/or some dissociative symptoms along a continuum. That continuum may include mild dissociation (e.g., appearing to be in a fog) to pathological dissociation (which represents a smaller percentage of youth and may include a very small percentage who report vivid imaginary companions, or the child has two distinct personalities one of which seemingly takes control during the dissociative state). However, not all youth who have been abused have been traumatized by their abuse (see Newsflash 4). While abuse is seldom pleasant, it may be merely stressful and not traumatic; that is, the fight or flight response is not elicited because there was no pain or intense fear. For some youth who have been sexually abused, the symptoms may be sexual reactivity (e.g., Silovsky & Larissa, 2002). Finally, for yet others, there is evidence of behavioral problems (e.g., anger/aggression) or negative affectivity (e.g., anxiety or depression). Specifically, among abused youth, suicidal thoughts may occur in one-third or more clients based on youth or caregiver rating (e.g., Wherry, Baldwin, Junco, & Floyd, 2013). Assessment of these common response patterns should occur with all youth who enter the foster care system because we know that they have either been abused, neglected, or exposed to drugs or domestic violence. A subset of youth may have no retrievable memory because the abuse occurred in those years prior to the language development—making retrieval of memories difficult (Bauer, 2015). Nonetheless, the entire field of human development would contend that these early experiences, as an infant, affect formulations related to predictability, security, attachment, trust in others, and a youth's view of the world and people in it.

A Note to Stakeholders/Case Managers about Reports

Over many years as a clinician, researcher, and trainer, I have found that many individuals who are in a position to refer clients for assessment frequently utilize familiar resources when making referrals for assessment. However, if you as a referring agent do not understand every aspect of the written report, you should not be impressed; rather, you should insist that the professional completing the assessment report change the format and style, so that you can use it in planning. Often, stakeholders settle for professionals who meet one important benchmark—completing the assessment and report in a timely fashion. A medical analogy is in order: Merely because a physician can quickly schedule and complete an exam or lab, is not reason enough to repeatedly use the physician as a resource. One would hope that their interpretation and recommendations are "on point," bring relief, and ultimately, are understandable.

Methods Used in Assessment

As noted, a good start in any assessment is a review of existing records. While a clinician will undoubtedly benefit from the context and assessment provided, there is no obligation to unthinkingly carry forward a diagnosis assigned (or mis-assigned) by a previous clinician. Whenever possible, caregiver ratings should be used. This is especially true when assessing younger children or youth, since their self-awareness and meta-cognition are, based on their development, limited (see Kuhn, 2000). Caregiver input should include multiple informants like biological parents, foster parents, and teachers. Biological parents may over-report misbehavior in their own children as if to justify to themselves and others the physical abuse which may have been inflicted on the youth. However, ratings by biological parents can nonetheless supplement the observations of foster parents. Ironically, non-kinship foster parents may over-report symptoms of children or youth (Handwerk, Larzelere, Soper, & Friman, 1999; Shore, Sim, Le Prohn, & Keller, 2002) in some situations like non-kinship care or for externalizing behaviors (e.g., disobedience of adults, hitting others), while under-reporting might occur early in the foster relationship. For example, the foster parent who has worked with ten foster youth may have a slightly different "benchmark" for what is considered usual, typical, or normal in children or youth. If the foster parents have recently fostered very challenging youth with significant behavioral problems, a new, relatively well-behaved youth who is still in a "honeymoon" phase with foster parents may be described quite positively. While there were no identified studies to support teacher ratings, it may be possible that the perspective of teachers provides a solid reference point because they have seen many youth from a variety of home situations. Thus, their rating may be accurately influenced by their broad exposure to a variety of youth.

Whether measures are completed by caregivers or by children or adolescents, there are three ways of possibly construing rating forms. There are unidimensional measures which assess a single construct (e.g., depression, ADHD, or PTSD). These measures have value, but usually that value is realized only if one of these single disorders or domains is suspected. Rating scales have been developed for

PTSD symptoms (e.g., the UCLA PTSD Index [Pynoos, Rodriguez, Steinberg, Stuber, & Frederick, 1998)]; the Child PTSD Symptom Scale [CPSS; Foa, Johnson, Feeny, & Treadwell, 2001]); however, while these scales have been found to be reliable and valid, they have not been normed. Another unidimensional measure of a common abuse-related symptom is the Child Sexual Behavior Inventory (CSBI; Friedrich, 1997). When sexual concerns or sexualized behaviors are suspected, reported, or of concern, these 38 items from the CSBI can help a clinician to understand the extent of sexualized behavior. However, elevations should never be considered as proof for a history of sexual abuse, inasmuch as other events may explain sexualized behavior (e.g., watching movies, visiting Internet sites). One disadvantage of the CSBI is the fact that the normative data were collected prior to common access by the public to the Internet, and well before the advent of smart phones where every youth is potentially a few "clicks" away from pornography on their smart phone.

Another variation is broad-band rating scales. These are comprehensive and may cover a broad range of behaviors (e.g., picking at skin) to serious symptoms (e.g., possible visual hallucination). Often scores are summarized as either internalizing or externalizing symptoms, and empirically derived (not diagnostic) dimensions are assigned T scores which allow comparisons to a normative group. Examples include the Child Behavior Checklist (CBCL; Achenbach & Rescorla, 2001) or the Behavior Assessment System for Children (BASC; Reynolds & Kamphaus, 1998).

A third option is a multidimensional measure which assesses domains of behavior commonly evident in a specific population (e.g., abused youth). An example of a parent measure assessing multiple domains of symptoms common in abuse is the Traumatic Symptom Checklist for Young Children (TSCYC; Briere, 2005). It assesses symptoms in the domains of depression, anxiety, anger, post-traumatic stress (PTS), dissociation, and sexual concerns. Scores are based on normative samples and are reported as raw scores, T scores, and percentiles. A similar measure of multiple, relevant domains completed by youth aged 8 to 16 is the Trauma Symptom Checklist for Children (TSCC; Briere, 1996) which assesses the same broad domains as the TSCYC.

Clinical interviewing as a follow-up to caregiver ratings and self-reports is an important procedure. Often, timely follow-up to endorsed items from an assessment measure may yield additional details or embellishments which enrich the interpretation of behaviors and the understanding of the larger picture of all symptoms exhibited by a child or adolescent. The use of a structured clinical interview may not be necessary since they often are time-consuming and offer less flexibility. That is, the entire interview protocol is strictly scripted. Semi-structured interviews may combine comprehensiveness with some flexibility; however, an experienced clinician often can be more efficient using an unstructured clinical interview. However, clinical interviewing alone may not be sufficient. Notably, according to Meyer et al. (2001), clinicians who rely solely on clinical interviews are prone to incomplete understanding of their clients. For example, in a review of current clinical practices, Cashel (2002) discovered that 71% of psychologists used clinical interviews, while 69.8% of psychologists also used IQ or cognitive assessments, but tests of trauma symptoms were not identified for use with adults, let alone youth.

The aforementioned measures (the TSCC, TSCYC, CSBI) are well suited for assessing abuse-related symptoms common to youth in foster care. All three measures also have the added value of being reliable, valid, and normed. Traditional batteries should be avoided (e.g., cognitive assessments) unless there is some genuine concern not better explained by other factors. In addition, other measures which sometimes are part of a generic battery include the aforementioned cognitive assessment, academic achievement tests, a sentence completion task, a Minnesota Multiphasic Personality Inventory (MMPI)—Adolescent form (Butcher et al., 1992), a projective storytelling task (e.g., Thematic Apperception Test), and the Rorschach. While some of these procedures may have value for specific youth with specific referral questions, their use in a battery administered to all youth placed in foster care is often without a rationale.

Feedback to Youth and Families

Professionals conducting assessments have an obligation to share findings with clients, family members, and referral sources when consents are properly executed, and individuals are available to participate in a feedback session. Moreover, the ideal feedback is to a youth in the presence of adults involved in his/her life. The information should be honest, accurate, and depathologized when possible. Depathologizing is especially important for adolescents and children who have been in the foster care system for a long time. The initial fear of, and later the disdain for evaluations arise because the youth become cynical with the thought that all of the assessments are done because the adults think they are "crazy." As an example, post-traumatic stress disorder (PTSD) is a diagnosis that is commonly appropriate for some abused youth in foster care. An explanation of this "disorder," its symptoms, the function of the symptoms, and the course with and without treatment can be explained in a manner which is respectful and depathologizes or normalizes symptoms. For example, PTSD can be presented as a "hard-wired" natural response to an unnatural, frightening, or painful event. Many of the initial symptoms (e.g., arousal and re-experiencing) are functional and serve a purpose. Explaining the symptoms as originally functional can make treatment more palatable to youth and family members. A prognostic statement might include the fact that if PTSD symptoms are present and left untreated, what once was functional in an abusive context may evolve into a cluster of symptoms which become dysfunctional—leading to impairment and a "shrinking" of the client's world as they seek to avoid all stimuli or triggers associated with the abuse or trauma.

Challenges in the Assessment Process

Lack of Agreement by Raters

It is not uncommon for youth and adults to disagree on the frequency or intensity of specific behaviors (Lee, Elliott, & Barbour, 1994; Rescorla et al., 2013). For example, parents and caregivers often provide a more accurate picture of behavior problems or externalizing behaviors. Conversely, youth often are better informants of symptoms which are internal (internalizing) and not apparent to adults (e.g., depression or anxiety). Thus, when youth and adult raters do not agree, they may either complement each other, or the true extent of symptomatology may be somewhere between the extremes reported by a caregiver or youth.

Time Constraints

Unfortunately, some clinicians are taught in graduate and professional training that assessment is not necessary. Rather, it has been recommended that they move directly to treatment without assessment. For this author, such a practice would be like an orthopedic surgeon who jumps directly to shoulder surgery without first imaging the shoulder (e.g., through x-ray and then an MRI). Realistically, a clinician could spend too much time in endless administration of unidimensional measures—one after the other. In the end, just enough evaluation should be done to answer referral questions and to provide a cogent understanding of the youth, their strengths, and challenges.

Expense

A common complaint by clinicians, insurance companies, and agencies is the expense of certain measures which have been researched and found to be reliable and valid, and which are normed—all psychometric properties essential to any assessment measure (Conradi, Wherry, & Kisiel, 2011). While it is true that normed measures do cost more, the reason is simple. Research and development of good measures is like research and development of an effective and safe medication. Test developers and publishing companies invest much time and money in developing measures, without any promise that their labor will result in something useful or marketable. The complaints that "greedy companies" are exploitive is tiresome and a sign of the times. As the adage says, "Sometimes you get what you pay for." Also, complaints about the cost of assessment measures reflect the fact that mental health has not yet achieved parity with traditional health care. For example, no one would ever say that an x-ray is too expensive when an arm is broken.

It should be mentioned that there are a variety of measures which are available at little or no expense which are in the public domain. The developers of these instruments deserve accolades for their efforts, but none of the extant measures currently meet all of the following characteristics: (a) reliability of the measure, (b) validity of the measure, (c) establishment of norms for the instrument, (d) multiple domains common to abused youth are assessed, (e) multiple informants can complete comparable measures, and (f) thoughts of self-harm or suicidality are assessed. Only two measures meet those criteria when combined—the TSCC and the TSCYC. However, it should be noted that these two measures are not without their drawbacks. First, while caregiver and youth complete the TSCYC and TSCC, respectively, the TSCYC is normed for completion by caregivers for youth at ages 3 to 12, and the TSCC is normed for self-report by children and youth at ages 8 to 16. Thus, the ages of overlap are between 8 and 12. A second "shortcoming" comes more in the way of careless reading and false expectations by users. Neither measure is diagnostic. Like many measures (other than structured or semi-structured interviews), the TSCC and the TSCYC scores do not map directly to specific diagnoses. Rather, the scales are empirically derived. So, a great example of a possible dilemma is the case of PTS symptoms. An elevation on the PTS scale could mean that on follow-up interview, a diagnosis of PTSD is confirmed. Conversely, the PTS scale might not be elevated (e.g., on the TSCC) where PTS is represented empirically by PTS re-experiencing symptoms, primarily because those are the symptoms recognized and reported in the development of the measure. Only one re-experiencing symptom is required for a diagnosis of PTSD, so it is important to follow-up on the PTSD criteria if any symptom is endorsed. Finally, it is important to note that suicide and self-harm are far from irrelevant among abused youth who often are placed in foster care. Even in an outpatient sample of abused youth living with their parents, Wherry et al. (2013) found that 34% of an outpatient children's advocacy center treatment-seeking sample experienced suicidal thinking or thoughts of self-harm.

Using the Assessment to Make Treatment Recommendations

Assessment measures are best used when the administering clinician is familiar with evidence-based treatments that address identified symptoms common among abused youth in foster care. Then specific recommendations can be made to address symptoms or symptom clusters. Assessment reports with recommendations that merely name modalities (e.g., "Individual therapy," "Group therapy," and/or "Family therapy"), rather than offering specific recommendations, are of little use.

Many of the existing evidence-based treatments include treatment components which are common across many therapies or at least trauma-related therapies (e.g., psychoeducation, stress management, exposure therapy, cognitive processing, affect regulation). It will be an important, though expensive and arduous, process to perform dismantling studies in order to determine which components of these evidence-based treatments might be necessary and sufficient for the treatment of certain symptomatic presentations.

One common complaint by therapists is that some foster parents will not participate in the treatment of the youth. Moreover, Weiner, Schneider, and Lyons (2009) found substantial challenges engaging foster parents, with participation linked to treatment retention. Like the issue of paying for assessments, this issue may be another example of low expectations, a self-fulfilling prophecy, and settling for less than what is ideal. Generally, caregiver involvement—foster and biological caregivers—is an essential component of treatment, especially if reunification is the goal. Merely "settling" for foster parents who drop kids off for therapy or parents who secure their own supportive therapy with an individual therapist is a low bar in terms of expectations. Youth deserve better, and we should insist upon better participation by the adults in their lives. Engagement strategies for evidence-based treatments of abused youth have been identified and improve completion rates (e.g., Dorsey et al., 2014).

One final observation can be made about treatment of youth in foster care. Many states, in effect, require youth to participate in therapy during the entire duration of foster care. That is, the duration of services is dictated by your placement and not by your symptoms. Placement for many years may be a function of a parent's sporadic involvement and progress, rather than symptoms driving treatment needs. These needs and related policies deserve closer scrutiny and problem-solving. It is a waste of resources in some instances. Furthermore, for the youth who has lost motivation for treatment or never has been motivated for treatment, that youth may have low expectations for therapy in the future—even in the event that he/she becomes motivated to address questions, issues, or challenges.

Using Assessment Measures for Evaluating Outcomes/Programs

Gone are the days when reports of outputs ("millions served") meet the expectations of state agencies and funding sources. Consumers and payers want to know that the effort and expense are of value. Standardized assessments which serve as baseline measures when complemented by re-assessment (either periodically or at discharge) can inform agencies, treatment providers, and clients if progress is being made. Moreover, Hersen (2004) recommends that assessment occur before, during, and after treatment. These data also can confirm the worth of a payer's investment, whether the dollars are personal (philanthropic) or based on government expenditures (taxes paid by individual citizens). When assessment measures are utilized, they are considered most frequently as the dependent variable in the evaluation. Most certainly, there are other factors (independent variables) which may influence outcomes, including the nature of the treatment; the motivation and involvement of parent, youth, and foster parent; demographic differences (e.g., age); duration of placement; and the nature of the abuse. Thus, these and other factors should be considered when drawing conclusions about these outcomes.

Cultural Considerations

One of the basic requirements in the field of assessment is standardization of norms using a representative sample based on sex, age, and race/ethnicity. The reason for norming is that a young Hispanic female may exhibit aggressive behavior far less frequently than an adolescent Caucasian male. The development of norms allows us to convert rated raw scores into standardized scores so that comparisons can be made using T scores. So, in the example provided, we might find that young Hispanic females are less aggressive, normatively, than adolescent Caucasian males. If that is the case, then the interpretation of the same rating of frequency will be adjusted with normative data. Many instruments have not been standardized, while others (e.g., the CSBI) were standardized on a primarily Caucasian sample. Standard interpretations of T scores are appropriate when the family/youth is among the racial or ethnic groups included in the sample. Unfortunately, for less-represented cultures (i.e., non-Caucasian, non-African-American, and non-Hispanic), the availability of appropriate, normed measures is scant.

Principles of cultural competence deserve mention. First, interpretation of any behavior should be neither ethnocentric (i.e., based on the majority cultural norm) nor completely relative to the culture (i.e., cultural relativism). However, there often is as much variability within a racial group as between racial groups. Thus, it is important to learn about global and idiosyncratic cultural beliefs and practices related to child-rearing, family structure, sex roles, and religious beliefs, as well as levels of acculturation.

Finally, there are other cultural considerations that may be particularly salient in the case of youth maltreatment. Cultural concerns historically have included (a) disproportionate representation of some racial/ethnic groups in the child welfare system, (b) differences in rates of substantiation and out-of-home placement, and (c) greater likelihood of other system involvement for many youth of color. However, as noted by some researchers and public policy-makers (Alliance for Racial Equality in Child Welfare, 2011; Bartholet, 2009; Drake et al., 2011), these are very complex issues, which are confounded by factors, such as socioeconomic status (SES) and higher rates of youth maltreatment among some racial/ethnic groups, which may account for this apparent disproportionality. Nonetheless, this speaks to the importance of cultural sensitivity and awareness in the assessment process.

Innovative Use of Technology

It seems that the social sciences are frequently late in adopting the use of technology (again, a combined problem of parity and low, self-fulfilling expectations). Electronic health care records hold potential for integrating assessment measures in meaningful ways for tracking progress for individuals and for programs. A continuous improvement feedback loop then may result in modifications to programs on the whole or in treatments specifically offered to the individual.

Web-based platforms for assessment, scoring, and entry into data sets should soon be widely available—though at some cost. Using measures at the point of check-in and discussing progress can inform ongoing treatment. While technology will lend efficiency to some processes, the effectiveness of the assessment will always be contingent on engaging the client and family, explaining the process and its rationale, and then using the results in a thoughtful and purposeful way—prioritizing needs and addressing those needs using evidence-based treatments, which can be efficiently implemented in communities.

Conclusions

Our understanding of assessment with abused youth is increasing, but the challenge of doing research with a vulnerable population during the crisis of an abuse investigation is significant. Similar issues affect our ability to concentrate our research efforts with foster youth, since as "wards of the state," they deserve and receive a special level of protection from research which might be either invasive or unhelpful in the moment. However, if we are to better serve youth in various forms of foster care, researchers must partner collaboratively with state agencies, biological families, foster families, and youth. The availability and implementation of evidence-based treatments have increased; however, the implementation of evidence-based assessments lags behind. Legislators and policy-makers should resist the temptation to "get by" using less expensive or free measures which do not assess relevant constructs in a reliable and valid manner. Ultimately, any measure should be normed with samples which are representative of different ages, genders, and ethnicities. Finally, education and implementation are the key. Until practitioners performing and referring youth for assessments are educated in graduate and professional training, youth will continue to receive less than individualized care.

References

Achenbach, T. M., & Rescorla, L. A. (2001). *Manual for the ASEBA School-Age Forms & Profiles*. Burlington: University of Vermont, Research Center for Children, Youth, and Families.

Alliance for Racial Equality in Child Welfare. (2011). *Disparities and disproportionality in child welfare: Analysis of the research*. Washington, DC: Center for the Study of Social Policy and the Annie E. Casey Foundation.

American Psychological Association. (2014). *Standards for educational and psychological testing*. Washington, DC: APA.

Bartholet, E. (2009). Racial disproportionality. *Arizona Law Review, 51*, 871–932.

Bauer, P. J. (2015). A complementary processes account of the development of childhood amnesia and a personal past. *Psychological Review, 122*(2), 204–231.

Biehal, N. (2014). A sense of belonging: Meanings of family and home in long-term foster care. *British Journal of Social Work, 44*(4), 955–971.

Briere, J. (1996). *The Trauma Symptom Checklist for Children*. Odessa, FL: Psychological Assessment Resources, Inc.

Briere, J. (2005). *The Trauma Symptom Checklist for Young Children*. Odessa, FL: Psychological Assessment Resources, Inc.

Briere, J., & Wherry, J. (2016). *Development and validation of the TSCC Screening Form and the TSCYC Screening Form*. Odessa, FL: Psychological Assessment Resources, Inc.

Butcher, J. N., Williams, C. L., Graham, J. R., Archer, R. P., Tellegen, A., Ben-Porath, Y. S., & Kaemmer, B. (1992). *Minnesota Multiphasic Personality Inventory—Adolescent (MMPI)*. Minneapolis: University of Minnesota Press.

Cashel, M. L. (2002). Child and adolescent psychological assessment: Current clinical practices and the impact of managed care. *Professional Psychology: Research and Practice, 33*(5), 446–453.

Chaffin, M., Valle, L. A., Funderburk, B., Gurwitch, R., Silovsky, J., Bard, D., . . . Kees, M. (2009). A motivational intervention can improve retention in PCIT for low-motivation child welfare clients. *Child Maltreatment, 14*(4), 356–368.

Cicchetti, D., & Toth, S. L. (2005). Child maltreatment. *Annual Review of Clinical Psychology, 1*, 409–438.

Conradi, L., Wherry, J., & Kisiel, C. (2011). Linking child welfare and mental health using trauma-informed screening and assessment practices. *Child Welfare, 90*(6), 129–147.

Cook, A., Blaustein, M., Spinazzola, J., & van der Kolk, B. (Eds.). (2003). Complex trauma in children and adolescents. National Child Traumatic Stress Network. Retrieved from www.nctsnet.org/nctsn_assets/pdfs/edu_materials/ComplexTrauma_All.pdf

Dorsey, S., Pullmann, M. D., Berliner, L., Koschmannd, E., McKaye, M., & Deblinger, E. (2014). Engaging foster parents in treatment: A randomized trial of supplementing Trauma-focused Cognitive Behavioral Therapy with evidence-based engagement strategies. *Child Abuse & Neglect, 38*(9), 1508–1520.

Drake, B., Jolley, J. M., Lanier, P., Fluke, J., Barth, R. P., & Jonson-Reid, M. (2011). Racial bias in child protection? A comparison of competing explanations using national data. *Pediatrics, 127*(3), 471–478.

English, D. J., Upadhyaya, M. P., Litrownik, A. J., Marshall, J. M., Runyan, D. K., Graham, J. C., & Dubowitz, H. (2005). Maltreatment's wake: The relationship of maltreatment dimensions to child outcomes. *Child Abuse & Neglect, 29*(5), 597–619.

Finkelhor, D., Ormrod, R. K., & Turner, H. A. (2007). Polyvictimization and trauma in a national cohort. *Developmental Psychopathology, 19*, 149–166.

Foa, E. B., Johnson, K. M., Feeny, N. C., & Treadwell, K. R. (2001). The Child PTSD Symptom Scale: A preliminary examination of its psychometric properties. *Journal of Clinical Child Psychology, 30*(3), 376–384.

Friedrich, W. N. (1997). *The Child Sexual Behavior Inventory professional manual*. Odessa, FL: Psychological Assessment Resources, Inc.

Graham, S. J., Nurcombe, B., Sheridan, J., & McFarland, M. (2007). Hallucinations in adolescents with post-traumatic stress disorder and psychotic disorder. *Australasian Psychiatry, 15*(1), 44–48.

Handwerk, M. L., Larzelere, R. E., Soper, S. H., & Friman, P. C. (1999). Parent and child discrepancies in reporting severity of problem behaviors in three out-of-home settings. *Psychological Assessment, 11*(1), 14–23.

Hersen, M. (2004). *Psychological assessment in clinical practice: A pragmatic guide*. New York: Brunner-Routledge.

Kaplan, S., Pelcovitz, D., & Labruna, V. (1999). Child and adolescent abuse and neglect research: A review of the past 10 years. Part 1: Physical and emotional abuse and neglect. *Journal of American Academy of Child and Adolescent Psychiatry, 38*(10), 1214–1221.

Kisiel, C. L., Blaustein, M., Fogler, J., Ellis, H., & Saxe, G. (2009). Treating children with traumatic experiences: Understanding and assessing needs and strengths. In J. S. Lyons & D. A. Weiner (Eds.), *Behavioral health care: Assessment, service planning and total clinical outcomes management* (pp. 17:1–15). Kingston, NJ: Civic Research Institute.

Kline, P. (2013). *Handbook of psychological testing*. New York: Routledge.

Kolko, D. J., Hurlburt, M. S., Zhang, J., Barth, R. P., Leslie, L. K., & Burns, B. J. (2010). Posttraumatic stress symptoms in children and adolescents referred for child welfare investigation: A national sample of in-home and out-of-home care. *Child Maltreatment, 15*(1), 48–63.

Kovacs, M. (2010). *Children's Depression Inventory–2*. San Antonio, TX: NCS Pearson, Inc.

Kuhn, D. (2000). Metacognitive development. *Current Directions in Psychological Science, 9*(5), 178–181.

Lanktree, C. B., Briere, J., Godbout, N., Hodges, M., Chen, K., Trimm, L., . . . Freed, W. (2012). Treating multi-traumatized, socially marginalized children: Results of a naturalistic treatment outcome study. *Journal of Aggression, Maltreatment & Trauma, 21*(8), 813–828.

Lee, S. W., Elliott, J., & Barbour, J. D. (1994), A comparison of cross-informant behaviour ratings in school-based diagnosis. *Behavioural Disorders, 19*, 87–97.

London, K., Bruck, M., Ceci, S. J., & Shuman, D. W. (2005). Disclosure of child sexual abuse: What does the research tell us about the ways that children tell? *Psychology, Public Policy, and Law, 11*, 194–226.

McNeil, C. B., & Hembree-Kigin, T. L. (2010). *Parent–child interaction therapy* (2nd ed.). New York: Springer.

Meyer, G. J., Finn, S. E., Eyde, L. D., Kay, G. G., Moreland, K. L., Dies, R. R., . . . Reed, G. M. (2001). Psychological testing and psychological assessment: A review of evidence and issues. *American Psychologist, 56*(2), 128–165.

Petrenko, C. L. M., Friend, A., Garrido, E. F., Taussig, H. N., & Culhane, S. E. (2012). Does subtype matter? Assessing the effects of maltreatment on functioning in pre-adolescent youth in out-of-home care. *Child Abuse & Neglect, 36*(9), 633–644.

Pynoos, R., Rodriguez, N., Steinberg, A., Stuber, M., & Frederick, C. (1998). *UCLA PTSD Index for DSM-IV*. Los Angeles: University of California, Los Angeles.

Rescorla, L.A., Ginzburg, S., Achenbach, T. M., Ivanova, M. Y., Almqvist, F., Begovac, I., . . . Verhulst, F. C. (2013). Cross-informant agreement between parent-reported and adolescent self-reported problems in 25 societies. *Journal of Clinical Child and Adolescent Psychology, 42*, 262–273.

Reynolds, C. R., & Kamphaus, R. W. (1998). *BASC: Behavior assessment system for children: Manual*. Circle Pines, MN: American Guidance Service.

Shore, N., Sim, K. E., Le Prohn, N. S., & Keller, T. E. (2002). Foster parent and teacher assessments of youth in kinship and non-kinship foster care placements: Are behaviors perceived differently across settings? *Children and Youth Services Review, 24*(1), 109–134.

Silovsky, J. F., & Larissa, N. (2002). Characteristics of young children with sexual behavior problems: A pilot study. *Child Maltreatment, 7*(3), 187–197.

Spaccarelli, S. (1994). Stress, appraisal, and coping in child sexual abuse: A theoretical and empirical review. *Psychological Bulletin, 116*(2), 340–362.

Ungar, M., Barter, K., McConnell, S. M., Tutty, L. M., & Fairholm, J. (2008). Patterns of abuse disclosure among youth. *Qualitative Social Work, 8*, 341–356.

Wechsler, D. (2014). *Wechsler Intelligence Scale for Children–Fifth Edition*. San Antonio, TX: NCS Pearson, Inc.

Weiner, D. A., Schneider, A., & Lyons, J. S. (2009). Evidence-based treatments for trauma among culturally diverse foster care youth: Treatment retention and outcomes. *Children and Youth Services Review, 31*, 1199–1205.

Weinstein, D., Staffelbach, D., & Biaggio, M. (2000). Attention-deficit hyperactivity disorder and posttraumatic stress disorder: Differential diagnosis in childhood sexual abuse. *Clinical Psychology Review, 20*(3), 359–378.

Wherry, J. N., Baldwin, S., Junco, K., & Floyd, B. (2013). Suicidal thoughts/behaviors in sexually abused children. *Journal of Child Sexual Abuse, 22*(5), 534–551.

Wherry, J. N., & Marrs, A. S. (2008). Anxious school refusers and symptoms of PTSD in abused children. *Journal of Child and Adolescent Trauma, 1*(2), 109–117.

7
Physical Health and Foster Youth

Yo Jackson and Lindsay Huffhines

Youth are placed in foster care when their biological home is deemed unsafe by the state social services authority. Foster care is intended to provide youth with a new living environment where their mental and physical health needs can be met (U.S. Department of Health & Human Services, 2016). In actual practice, it is often a challenge to determine whether foster care is effective at providing for the mental and physical health needs of youth. Studies of youth in care usually indicate that the rates of mental and physical health problems among youth who enter foster care are significantly higher than rates for youth in the general population (Rosenbach, 2000). That is, as many as 80% of youth enter foster care with a significant mental health issue (Szilagyi, 2012). Youth in care have many unique mental health needs, but the physical health of foster youth also needs to be examined.

Almost half of youth in foster care have a chronic medical problem(s) *not related to a mental health diagnosis* (Lopez & Allen, 2007). Research on the physical health of youth in foster care suggests that *almost all* youth (87% to 95%) enter foster care with at least one physical health diagnosis, and most have numerous physical health problems (Leslie et al., 2005). The purpose of the current chapter is to summarize the nature of the data on physical health problems, service use, and barriers to care, and the role of factors like placement type, age, and gender on the physical health needs of youth in foster care.

Scope of Physical Health Problems among Youth in Foster Care

Evidence for the disproportionately high levels of poor physical health among youth in foster care is widespread; data from self-report, child welfare administrative and national medical databases, and both state and nationwide surveys consistently report a similar negative health trend. Theoretically, the approach to understanding why youth in foster care evidence poor health status, compared to their non-foster peers, is primarily grounded in ecological approaches. First developed by Bronfenbrenner (1979), the Ecological System Theory suggests that youth development is best understood in the context of their environment (i.e., relationships with family members, school quality, community resources, culture) and how those different levels of environment interact with each other. Youth health, then, is dependent on not only their biological makeup, but also on the direct and indirect experiences with other people and institutions throughout their lifespan. Applied to youth in foster care, most research that addresses the rationale for poor health outcomes surmises that most are due in part to the living and parenting conditions that youth experience prior to placement in care. Specifically, being exposed to experiences like poverty, limited prenatal care, parental substance use, family and community violence, and parental mental illness would place any child at risk for deficient health and health care (Miller, Chen, & Parker, 2011).

Some research, however, takes more of a developmental approach as a framework for understanding the health status of youth in foster care. The focus is on the age of the child and the relevant emotional and social needs that change as a child gets older. Because the majority of youth who enter care as victims of child abuse and neglect are age 5 or younger, a period of time when attentive, nurturing, and consistent childcare is critical for healthy development (Child Welfare Information Gateway, 2016), it should be expected that the majority of youth in care will likely demonstrate developmental delays and physical challenges.

Consistent with this notion that age matters, some evidence points to later-age entry into care as a risk factor. That is, youth who entered foster care as school-age children typically have more physical health problems than youth who entered care as very young children (Tarran-Sweeny, 2008). Although those of preschool age, and younger, also demonstrate significant health problems, the author suggests that youth who enter care later in childhood may have worse physical health than do younger youth because of the longer length of time that school-age youth may have spent in their families of origin, where sub-optimal care and exposure to child maltreatment may have been significant (Tarran-Sweeny, 2008). The physical vulnerabilities of youth, exposure to abuse and neglect, and the disadvantageous family environments in which maltreatment occurs is likely to have a negative impact on youths' physical health trajectory. Even when rates of poor physical health prior to entry into care are documented, the data on the health of youth while in care are striking and suggest that this population is in rather dire need of attention and quality services by health professionals.

As far back as the early 1970s, research has documented the poor health status of youth in foster care. In a review of 668 youth who had been in foster care for a year in 1973 in New York, Kavaler and Swire (1983) found that 45% had one or more chronic health problem and 37% required referral and treatment by a specialist. Kavaler and Swire also found that about a third of their sample met criteria for a developmental disability, and that over half of the school-age youth had IQ scores in the borderline or mild mental retardation range. Thirty years later, a review by the Council of Family and Child Caring Agencies (2013) of youth in foster care in New York, the evidence suggests that little preventative care is provided to youth prior to admission to foster care. In a given year, only 15.7% of youth had at least one well-child visit to a medical professional prior to entry into care, a number that increased by a small percentage to only 25.2% during the youths' time in care. The data from other regions of the United States indicate similar findings.

For example, in a sample of over 5,000 youth in foster care in Chicago, over a 22-month period, 44% had a documented medical problem such as anemia, acute infections, and lead poisoning (Flaherty & Weiss, 1990). In other large metropolitan areas like Baltimore, it was found that in a sample of 2,419 youth in foster care, 92% had at least one physical health concern, with respiratory problems reported by 66%. Almost a quarter of the younger portion of the sample was not meeting developmental expectations, and at least half of the sample required referrals to specialists for additional medical care (Chernoff, Combs-Orme, Risley-Curtiss, & Heisler, 1994). Leslie et al. (2005) studied a sample of 1,551 early childhood-aged youth in San Diego. Results revealed that 31.5% of youth had at least one significant physical health problem, 25.4% had three or more problems, with 65% of those reviewed having a dermatological problem followed by 22% reporting a respiratory problem.

It is important to note that it is not clear from the data if the physical health problems documented in samples of youth in foster care are exclusively the result of foster care, or a combination that includes evidence of preexisting conditions in the poor health of youth enrolled in foster care. Evidence also suggests that youth who were suspected victims of child abuse and neglect, and were not removed from their biological homes, have similarly high rates of physical health and developmental problems to youth placed in foster care (Leslie et al., 2005). Youth in foster care, however, are more likely to become pregnant, almost 2.5 times more likely to become pregnant by age 19 than youth without a history of foster care (Love, McIntosh, Rosst, & Tertzakian, 2005). Moreover, almost half of youth transitioning out of foster care experience a pregnancy before the age of 20, compared to the national average of 31% (Courtney & Dworsky, 2006), suggesting that the physical health needs of older youth in care for pregnancy and prenatal care may continue long past their time in foster care.

Physical Health Status in Foster Youth

Research has consistently demonstrated that youth in foster care have higher rates of physical health problems in general (Rubin, Halfon, Raghavan, & Rosenbaum, 2005). Youth in foster care also have more chronic health conditions than their non-foster, Medicaid-eligible peers (Hansen, Mawjee, Barton, Metcalf, & Joye, 2004; Jee et al., 2006). Moreover, youth in families who have been investigated by child protective services, yet whose children remain at home, tend to have health problems at similar rates and of similar types to those youth who are placed in foster care, especially for those under the age of 6 (Ringeisen, Casanueva, Urato, & Cross, 2008). These findings make it hard to know how much of the physical health challenges that youth in care experience is a product of pre-foster care conditions and how much is a product of placement in foster care (Jee et al., 2006; Ringeisen et al., 2008).

As a result of the consistent and negative physical health reports, youth in foster care have been designated by the American Academy of Pediatrics (AAP) as a group of youth who have increased physical health needs compared with youth from similar socioeconomic or high environmental risk backgrounds (e.g., low-income, high-crime neighborhoods; Deutsch & Fortin, 2015). Significant differences in health outcomes were found in a comparison of three groups of Medicaid-eligible youth aged 1 to 17 years: those receiving Aid to Families with Dependent Children (AFDC) who did not enter foster care; those receiving AFDC who subsequently entered foster care; and those in foster care (Bilaver, Jaudes, Koepke, & Goerge, 1999).

In the comparison of the two groups of youth receiving AFDC, 27% of the youth who eventually entered foster care had a diagnosis of at least one chronic condition, compared to 21% of the youth who never entered care. In contrast, over 40% of the youth in foster care had a diagnosis of at least one chronic condition. Youth in foster care were significantly more likely to have a diagnosis in nearly all of the condition categories than were the youth who subsequently entered foster care. These findings support the hypothesis that youth in foster care have significantly more health problems than both youth who more recently entered care and youth living in poverty. The American Academy of Pediatrics (2005) reported that other studies using nationally representative data have also found that between 35% and 50% of youth in foster care have chronic health conditions, compared with less than 20% of the general population.

Prevalence rates may vary based on whether chronic health conditions are assessed using health professionals' judgements, medical records, or caregiver report. Studies using data from medical records, including the aforementioned investigations, tend to report higher prevalence rates than studies using caregiver report. For example, Bilaver et al. (1999), using data from the National Survey of Child and Adolescent Well-Being, where caregivers reported on chronic conditions, reported that the prevalence of chronic conditions among youth in foster care for one year were 30%. However, in Jee et al. (2006), 20% of foster caregivers reported that their foster child had one chronic condition, 3.8% reported two chronic conditions, and 3.1% reported three or more. In addition, approximately 3% of caregivers reported that their child had a chronic condition, but did not identify the condition.

The type of health conditions that youth in foster care experience range from failure to obtain preventative care (e.g., routine physicals and well-checks) to serious diseases. Although health conditions might also encompass injuries sustained from abuse, the focus of most research is on medical conditions that could, but do not necessarily, have a direct link to negligent caregiving (i.e., respiratory conditions). Failure to obtain preventative care, or care that is inconsistent (e.g., missing follow-up appointments), is a substantial issue for youth in foster care. First, foster youth may experience medical neglect from caregivers. Second, this population is largely transient compared to non-foster youth and may experience multiple moves over the course of their lives, interrupting routine health care. Finally, many biological parents investigated by social service agencies for child abuse and neglect also experience substance use problems, domestic violence, or other parental mental health issues, making effective organization of primary care for their youth or attention to preventative care difficult to manage (Casanueva, Martin, & Runyan, 2009).

Lapses in preventative care include missed immunizations, missed vision and hearing screenings, lack of routine dental care, and lack of routine laboratory screening (e.g., screening for anemia; lead levels; Deutsch & Fortin, 2015). At entry into foster care, 90% of youth had an abnormality in at least one body system, such that 25% failed the vision screen, 15% failed the hearing screen, 12% required an antibiotic, and over 50% needed urgent or non-urgent referrals for medical services (Chernoff et al., 1994). Merely 12% of the youth in the sample were current with health care and required only routine follow-up care. More recent research has shown similar findings: 87% to 95% of youth came into foster care with at least one physical health diagnosis; most had numerous physical health problems (Leslie et al., 2005). Another study examining the dental health of foster youth found that only 43% utilized any professional dental services, and even fewer utilized diagnostic (41%), preventative (39%), restorative (11%), or complex (5%) services (Melbye, Chi, Milgrom, Huebner, & Grembowski, 2014).

In addition to lapsed health care, youth in foster care are at risk for a number of serious, chronic health conditions. Although definitions vary as to what a chronic health condition is, common themes include persistent and recurring health problems, a duration measured in months and years instead of days and weeks, and significant disruption to daily life and activities, such as schooling (Goodman, Posner, Huang, Parekh, & Koh, 2013). For the most part, chronic conditions are lasting diseases that impact physical and mental health, well-being, and quality of life (Van Cleave, Gortmaker, & Perrin, 2010). The most common chronic condition diagnoses as reported by foster caregivers in the National Survey of Child and Adolescent Well-Being were asthma (32.8%), other respiratory problems (12.8%), and a category including severe allergies, repeated ear infections, and recurrent eczema (6%) (Jee et al., 2006). Jaudes, Bilaver, and Champagne (2015) also found a high prevalence of asthma in their foster care sample, with youth in foster care demonstrating a significantly higher prevalence of asthma symptoms (19.8% versus 14.7%) and persistent asthma (9.4% versus 5.0%) than income-eligible Medicaid youth who were not in state care.

In a sample of foster youth aged 8 to 18, 49% had a diagnosis of a chronic condition listed in their medical record, with chronic pain being the most common diagnosis (44%), followed by asthma (30%), constipation/enuresis (12%), obesity (11%), and sleep disorder (2%) (Jackson et al., 2016). Youth could have more than one condition and thus may have contributed to more than one category. Steele and Buchi (2008) found that dental problems or being overweight/obese were the most common chronic health conditions experienced by a sample of foster youth. In this sample, 35% of youth in foster care had a body mass index (BMI) in the overweight range, and 18% had a BMI in the obese range. These percentages were significantly higher than the 15% to 20% of youth in the general population in the overweight/obese range. Another study of Hispanic youth aged 2 to 18 in foster care or receiving child welfare services found that approximately 40% of the participants in the study were overweight/obese (Schneiderman, Arnold-Clark, Smith, Duan, & Fuentes, 2013). Interestingly, polyvictimization (i.e., experiencing multiple types of abuse and/or neglect), compared with having only one maltreatment type, did not significantly increase or decrease the likelihood of being in the overweight/obese categories for girls in this sample. However, boys who experienced polyvictimization were less likely to be overweight or obese. Further, abuse did not put girls or boys at increased risk of being overweight/obese, as compared with neglect.

These findings suggest that it may be useful for future studies to parse out the effects of foster care placement, abuse, and neglect on weight status in foster youth. Finally, one study including 106 foster youth found that 81% of youth had a BMI in the typical range, or the 9th to 91st percentile, when they entered foster care, with a trend to obesity the longer they stayed in care (Hadfield & Preece, 2008). Specifically, 60% of youth remained within the 9th to 91st percentile, while 36% were in the >91st percentile category. Only one youth was obese prior to entering foster care. After 3 years in care, eight youths were classified as obese. The percentage of youth in the overweight and obese group compared with the whole study population ranges from 8.1% prior to entering foster care to 35.9% in those in care for over 3 years. Together, these findings demonstrate some support for the relation between placement in foster care and overweight/obesity conditions. This is problematic given that as BMI increases, so do blood pressure, cholesterol, triglycerides, blood sugar, and inflammation; these changes translate into greater risk for coronary heart disease, stroke, and cardiovascular death (Guh et al., 2009).

The majority of studies on the physical health of foster youth have examined one or two domains of health (i.e., chronic condition and or health service use). Assessing multiple domains appears to be an important next step for the field to obtain a more complete health profile of youth in foster care. One longitudinal study examined health outcomes of adolescents (ages 11 to 18) in foster care, using the Child Health and Illness Profile–Adolescent Edition (CHIP–AE), which is a self-report, multi-domain measure of six dimensions of health, including satisfaction with health, discomfort, disorders, risks, resilience, and achievement (Kools, Paul, Jones, Monasterio, & Norbeck, 2013). *Satisfaction with health* measured youths' perceptions of their health and well-being, *discomfort* measured physical and emotional sensations associated with health status, *disorders* were chronic health conditions, *risks* were potential health-altering behaviors, *resilience* assessed behaviors with potential to decrease likelihood of illness or injury, and *achievement* assessed youths' standing on developmental milestones.

Kools et al. (2013) developed health profiles based on scores on four of these dimensions: satisfaction with health, risks, resilience, and discomfort. Scores on these four dimensions were combined to arrive at four health status rankings: 1—Best Health Status (average or excellent health in all four domains), 2—Fair Health Status (poor health in one domain), 3—Poor Health Status (poor health in two domains), and 4—Worst Health Status (poor health in three or four domains). Most youth in the sample fell into the Best Health Status category (38.9%), followed by Fair Health Status (30.5%), Poor Health Status (17.6%), and finally, Worst Health Status (13.0%). Although health status rankings were similar to a sample of youth in the general population, the general population sample had fewer youth in the Worst Health Status category (10.3%).

This study by Kools et al. (2013) represents a different and potentially useful method for measuring the physical health of foster youth. It may be useful for future studies to include multiple domains of health. However, each of the domains included in this study was derived from adolescent self-report. Youth self-report of their physical health is a fairly unusual method for collecting health history information, primarily due to concerns regarding one's ability (youth or adult) to recall one's history of doctor visits and illness or injuries accurately. It is important to note, however, that most studies which include youth self-report, primarily adolescents, tend to find mixed patterns of health findings. For example, Kools, Paul, Norbeck, and Robbins (2009) found that when adolescents in foster care were asked about their physical health, overall, the sample reported average levels of satisfaction and relatively low levels of physical discomfort. When the data were examined by gender, however, girls reported significantly lower scores on satisfaction, self-esteem, and physical discomfort (compared to a non-foster norm sample). In contrast, another study with adolescent youth in foster care indicated that overall, the sample reported significantly poor health, with boys reporting significantly worse physical health status than girls (Farruggia & Sorkin, 2009). Although self-report is a rather novel way of collecting health information among youth in foster care—but likely has its merits for representing how youth feel—it may be the case that a more complete health profile should include data from paid claims and medical records, health care professionals, youth, and caregivers. Moreover, to the authors' knowledge, no other research has been conducted on youths' perspectives of their own needs, and experiences in regard to physical health. Such research would greatly contribute to giving foster youth a voice as well as a better understanding of their needs, challenges, and strengths in their own eyes.

Possible Moderators of Health Status: Gender, Age, Ethnicity, and Placement Type

The examination of potential moderators of physical health outcomes has been another way in which researchers have learned more about the health status of foster youth, and which youth in particular are most at risk for poor health. Statistically significant moderators have included gender, age, ethnicity, and placement status. For instance, Kools and colleagues (2013) found that adolescent girls reported significantly worse health than adolescent boys. Specifically, 82.6% of the Poor Health Status group and 70.6% of the Worst Health Status group was made up of girls. In a sample of adults who had been placed in foster care as youth, men were 38% more likely to have better health than women (Villegas, Rosenthal, O'Brien, & Pecora, 2011). In summary, these studies suggest that females may be at greater risk for poor health outcomes than males, but additional studies are needed to examine the effects of gender.

In regard to age, the study by Kools et al. (2013) indicated that 11 to 13 year olds were the most likely age group to be in the Best Health Status group. Youth aged 14 to 16 were represented in higher proportions as the health status ranking worsened. For example, 49% of the Best Health Status group were 11 to 13 year olds, while 14 to 16 year olds made up 50.0% of the Fair, 56.5% of the Poor, and 82.4% of the Worst Health Status groups. The pattern of poorer health outcomes in older youth was also demonstrated in Schneiderman et al.'s (2013) study of obesity in foster youth, with the highest prevalence of being overweight/obesity observed among youth aged 12 to 18 (47.7%). Youth aged 6 to 18 were at increased risk of being overweight/obese, compared with youth at ages 2 to 5 years. These findings suggest that older age and potentially longer stays in foster care may be risk factors for negative health outcomes and obesity beyond simple placement in foster care.

Few studies have examined ethnicity and health status in foster youth. Specifically, Kools et al. (2013) found no significant differences in racial or ethnic groups among the four health status groups. Similarly, ethnicity was not related to chronic health problems in adults who had been placed in foster care as youth (Villegas et al., 2011). Schneiderman et al. (2013), on the other hand, found that Hispanic youth were more likely to be overweight/obese than non-Hispanic youth. Given that little research has been conducted in this area, and that the majority of youth in care are ethnic minorities, additional studies are needed to examine the relation between ethnicity and health status in foster youth.

Placement type, number of placements, and length of time in foster care have been some of the most commonly investigated possible moderators of health status for youth in foster care. Importantly, results have varied between studies. Kools et al. (2013) found no statistically significant differences in age at first placement, length of time in foster care, or type of placement (foster family, relative/kinship placement, group home) between the four health status groups (i.e., Best, Fair, Poor, and Worst). In Jaudes et al.'s (2015) study of asthma in youth in foster care, using Medicaid claims data, results suggest that youth in group home settings had significantly higher rates of having an asthma-related emergency room visit than youth in foster homes or income-eligible Medicaid youth (home settings: 6.3%; income-eligible youth: 7.6%; and group homes: 10.1%). This finding may be due in large part to the fact that the youth in group home settings had fewer preventative and routine visits for asthma than the youth in traditional foster home settings. This likely led to more emergency care use for asthma. Specifically, youth in group home settings were hospitalized for asthma at nearly four times the rate of income-eligible Medicaid youth (6.5% versus 1.7%). The pattern of worse health outcomes for youth in group homes was consistent when examining overweight/obesity as well. Schneiderman et al. (2013) found that youth placed in a group home had the highest prevalence of being overweight (60%) and of obesity (43%) compared to other types of placement. In another study of youth in foster care, no differences were found between weight diagnoses or type of medical diagnoses by placement type, although youth with three or more medical diagnoses were more likely to live with kin, and a longer stay in foster care was positively related with having a medical diagnosis (Schneiderman, Leslie, Arnold-Clark, McDaniel, & Xie, 2011). Length of time in care was also related to an increasing proportion of youth in the overweight/obese group in another study, but age at entry into care or the number of placements while in care was not (Hadfield & Preece, 2008).

All aspects of trauma history, including type of abuse and neglect, severity of experiences, and chronicity of maltreatment, appear to be important predictors of health status, but these have not been examined very often in samples of foster youth. For example, some research points to specific differences related to type of abuse and health outcome. Kools et al. (2013) found that for youth who were exposed to sexual abuse, the health status ranking was worse than for other kinds of child maltreatment. That is, a greater percentage of those with Worst Health Status had a history of sexual abuse (35.3%), whereas the percentage of those with Best Health Status that reported sexual abuse was 7.8%. Most research on type of abuse (or severity, age at time of abuse) has shown a fairly consistent negative relation to either mental health or developmental outcomes (English et al., 2005). Additional studies are needed in order to examine variables associated with foster youths' specific types of trauma histories and physical health outcomes.

The health problems among youth in foster care often do not stop in childhood, but persist into young adulthood and later life, making factors associated with foster care a risk factor for lifelong disease and health service utilization. For example, in a longitudinal study of young adults transitioning out of foster care, 25% reported having a health condition that prevented them from engaging in vigorous physical activity (Courtney & Dworsky, 2006). Approximately 33% reported having gone to the emergency room at least three times in the last 5 years. The most frequent physical health conditions reported by young adults were stomach aches, skin problems, muscle or joint aches, and trouble sleeping. Further, Reilly (2003) found that 30% of a sample of former foster youth aged 18 to 25 had experienced a serious health problem since exiting care. Youth in the study had been out of care for 6 months to 3 years. Only 54% of this sample rated their health as *very good* or *excellent*. Other studies demonstrated detrimental health consequences even later in life. Individuals born in 1970 who had experienced foster care during childhood were more likely to have poor physical health than were those individuals who had never been placed in foster care (Viner & Taylor, 2005). Finally, Carpenter and Clyman (2004) compared health outcomes for women who had and who had not experienced kinship foster care during childhood. The experience of kinship care predicted poorer self-reported adult health in bivariate analyses. Women in the group with a history of kinship care were more likely to be obese and to be current smokers.

Scope of Health Service Use by Youth in Foster Care

While youth are in foster care, social services and foster parents are required to provide youth in their charge with adequate physical health care; however, many youth in foster care experience poor access to and insufficient use of appropriate health care services (Simms, Dubowitz, & Szilagyi, 2000). Most of the data on service use by youth in foster care come from analyses of data from Medicaid, the primary insurer of youth in state custody (Child Welfare Information Gateway, 2015). It is important to note that the consistent health care of youth in foster care can be challenging, at least in part due to the transient nature of the population. Moreover, foster parents and medical providers have to coordinate with caseworkers, sort out consent procedures and confidentiality, work with limited and sometimes absent medical history information, and endure long waiting times for services (Hilen & Gafson, 2015). For many youth in care, the emergency room is the primary provider of physical health services. Due to inconsistent record keeping across placements, foster parents and caseworkers may lack the necessary knowledge and expertise to wisely navigate and coordinate the health needs of youth with complex medical histories (Rubin, O'Reilly, Luan, & Localio, 2007).

Health Service Use

A recent review from 2005 to 2012 across the state of New York is a good example of common findings from state providers to youth in foster care. The review, prepared for the Council of Family and Child Caring Agencies in 2013, compares rates of use of health services by youth before, during, and after time spent in foster care (Johnson, Silver, & Wulczyn, 2013). The results are concerning, but given the high rates of physical health problems, perhaps not surprising. For example, the review indicated that the state spent 2.6 billion dollars to serve 73,000 youth in foster care. Moreover, youth in foster care used emergency room services more often, had fewer well-child checkups, and less preventative care than youth in the general population. Service use of any kind was higher while the youth were in care (compared to pre and post care) and the majority of Medicaid dollars were spent on psychological rather than physical health problems (Johnson et al., 2013). It is not clear if the higher rates of Medicaid dollars spent while youth are in foster care (compared to pre/post care) represent greater attention to the health needs of youth in care by foster parents and social service agencies, or is a response to an actual increase in health problems while youth are in foster care. More research is needed to determine if youth are actually more likely to be ill while in foster care, or if the greater use of services while in care represents an increase in attention to their physical health when more adults (i.e., caseworkers, foster parents) are involved, and provide consistent advocacy regarding the youth's health needs.

Data from reviews in earlier decades echo this pattern. For example, Halfon, Berkowitz, and Klee (1992) found in a survey of health service use in California, that youth in foster care accounted for more cost and utilization of medical services than youth receiving any other kind of medical assistance coverage. The primary expense was for hospitalization services to address perinatal conditions (i.e., health problems stemming from birth complications) and infectious diseases, as well as a myriad of mental health problems. Another survey in the 1990s (Takayama, Bergman, & Connell, 1994) showed that for children (ages 0–7 years) in the state of Washington, compared to youth who received Aid to Families with Dependent Children (AFDC), the mean expenditure by the state for health care on youth in foster care was five times the amount spent for youth receiving AFDC. Moreover, twice as many youth in foster care required medical equipment, specialist services, or hospitalization. Thirteen percent of foster youth required a physical therapist or visiting nurse (compared to 1% of youth on AFDC).

Emergency Service Use

Although physical and psychiatric diagnoses are common to youth in foster care, most studies find that these youth are seen in emergency rooms (ER) at an even higher rate than expected (Chartier, Walker, & Naimark, 2007). It is likely that the need for emergency services is linked to the rather low rates of regular checkups and consistent medical care (e.g., care provided by one consistent provider, or a medical home). Moreover, the ER is often the primary care provider for youth and adults with chronic health problems, particularly for low-income families (Johnson et al., 2013; Medford-Davis, Eswaran, Shah, & Dark, 2015). Not all foster youth, however, come from low-income families. Thus, it may be that ERs are used in place of a primary care provider when youth move to a new placement, given that their foster family may know little about their health history or are unsure of where to take their youth for care. The use of the ER is also common when youth, foster or otherwise, have complex health problems and fail to receive attention from multiple providers, adding risk for inconsistent care and crises in physical health.

In a review of ER use by youth in care, 36% of school-age foster youth had not seen a primary care provider for annual physical exams or well-child checkups in the course of a year, and use of the ER was high (e.g., three to four times in a given year; Almgren & Marcenko, 2001). Many of the youth in the sample visited the ER because of psychiatric problems. Psychiatric and not physical health conditions were the main contributors to high ER use; however, among physical health problems, respiratory and pulmonary conditions were the only medical conditions significantly correlated with high ER use in the foster care sample.

In a study using Wave 1 data from the National Survey of Child and Adolescent Well-Being for youth aged 1 to 14 from 1999 to 2000, 31% of youth in foster care had been to the ER (Jee, Antonucci, Aida, Szilagyi, M. A., & Szilagyi, P. G., 2005). Analyses indicated that in the presence of a chronic condition, youth who were younger, specifically under age 6, and youth whose foster parents were younger than 54 years, were significantly more likely to use the ER. The authors concluded that the need for a medical home model for youth in foster care is supported by findings like these, emphasizing the importance of coordination of care so that the ER is less likely to be the primary care provider for youth in care. Other research supports this notion, including a study by Rubin, Alessandrini, Feudtner, Localio, and Hadley (2004) which examined rates of ER use by youth in foster care in the context of placement changes. Using Medicaid data on 2,358 youth, over the course of a year, and comparing use of the ER with use by youth not in foster care, the results indicated that youth who experienced more placement changes (≥2) over the course of a year also had a higher rate of ER use than youth who did not change placements or youth who were not in foster care. The study also found that of the 1,206 visits to the ER among the youth in care, almost 75% occurred in the period immediately after a placement change (i.e., within 3 weeks). This finding suggests that the period following a placement change is particularly likely to result in use of the ER.

Barriers to Care

Expected physical health in youth requires that medical services are easily accessible, comprehensive, and allow for continuity of care across providers (Szilagyi, Rosen, Rubin, & Zlotnik., 2015). Most state agencies have policies to ensure that the youth in their care are provided with medical care consistent with these goals. In actual practice, however, the experience of receiving proper medical attention is often limited, given the myriad obstacles in the structure of the foster care system. According to the AAP (2015), there are several barriers to consistent, effective health care for youth in foster care (Szilagyi, 2012). In its 2015 report, the AAP suggested that the core of the problem is the transient nature of foster care; that is, the notion that youth move placements, and move in and out of state custody, making it hard for there to be a "primary provider," either a parent or medical professional who is sufficiently familiar with a given child's medical needs and history. The report goes on to highlight four features of foster care that make addressing physical health a challenge. Each of the following problems could account for the significant rates of medical concerns in samples of foster youth.

The first is the lack or unavailability of the youth's complete medical history at the time of placement in foster care. Given that some biological parents may not be cooperative, it is not always possible for caseworkers to collect accurate information on the youth's medical history status, both for those youth who have had multiple contacts with medical professionals and for those who have had limited to no contact with medical professionals. If previous medical providers are known, it may be up to the new foster parents or caseworkers to reach out to those medical professionals to fully understand the child's medical needs. To ensure proper care, foster parents and caseworkers need to know the youth's record of health screenings, vision and dental checkups, history of hospitalization, injuries, allergies, surgeries, chronic illnesses, and medications. The latter is perhaps the most important, given that most youth in foster care receive three times the number of medications (usually behavioral medications) and at higher doses than do youth in the general population (Rubin et al., 2012) making record keeping on medication history perhaps more challenging than the tracking required for yearly vision checkups.

The second concern highlighted in the AAP (2015) report was the confusion that can sometimes occur over who has the ability to consent for medical care for youth in the foster care system (Leslie, Kelleher, Burns, Landsverk, & Rolls, 2003). Despite youth being in the legal custody of the state, the rules vary from state to state on who can consent for medical care and the process by which consent is determined. For example, in some states, biological parents retain the right for consent for medical services; and in others, biological parents must sign a consent form for the state and foster parents to provide routine care (but events like surgery or mental health evaluations are not included). Even when foster parents are given the power by the social service agency to consent for their foster youth's medical care, in some states, a court proceeding is necessary to establish guardianship and to make this power official. When biological parents are not cooperative and refuse to sign over their consent for medical treatment of their child, another court proceeding may be required to give consenting rights to the state agency and/or the new foster parent. Although on a case-by-case basis, the process can be different for each child in foster care, for immediate medical needs, for the most part, foster parents have the ability to consent for treatment. Given that identifying who can and cannot consent for a given treatment or procedure can be complex, it is imperative that medical professionals and foster care providers engage in what can be a time-consuming process and be up to date on the laws governing consent practices for foster youth in their care.

The third issue involves the nature of how health care for youth in foster care is financed. Although it is not clear just how many youth are covered, Medicaid is the primary health coverage payer for youth in foster care (Halfon & Klee, 1987). The quality and accessibility of services provided by Medicaid to youth in care have proven to be a considerable barrier to quality health care that meets the needs of a given youth. Often coverage provided by state-run Medicaid programs does not provide sufficient services to meet the health needs of youth in foster care (Leslie et al., 2003). In a survey of 14 counties in California, Halfon and Klee (1987) found that foster parents and social workers complained both of difficulty in finding providers and frequent delays in obtaining authorization for physical health care services. More recently, research has found that youth with Medicaid, which is the majority of youth in foster care, face longer waiting times and difficulty scheduling appointments with specialty care providers (Bisgaier & Rhodes, 2011). It is possible that these kinds of challenges make it more likely that foster parents will rely on ER or outpatient facilities, where continuing health care services may not be offered.

The final issue identified in the AAP (2015) report was the lack of coordination of care and communication between care providers, both foster and medical. For foster youth with physical health problems, multiple evaluation and treatment services from a variety of providers may be required. Although this is also true for physically compromised youth who are not in foster care, it is especially difficult for foster parents when accessing and documenting services require coordination with caseworkers and medical professionals, and multiple appointments can place a burden on the personal resources of the foster parent. If foster parents do not have permission to consent for unexpected medical treatment, the question as to who can give consent is often a point of confusion requiring input and approval from state authorities which then must determine if the procedure or treatment is justified in terms of both cost and benefit to the child. As a result, medical care for youth in foster care can be delayed; this could result in exacerbation of medical health problems that could have been easily addressed if treated immediately.

It is also important to note that despite best efforts, part of the challenge in addressing the physical health of youth in foster care appears to lie with the system of foster care itself. That is, administrative procedures, frequent caseworker turnover, and the demands of foster care can lead to a series of social welfare providers being assigned responsibility for a child's case. Nearly a quarter of youth in foster care experience three or more foster home placements, usually involving a change in health care providers as well (Jackson et al., 2016). Therefore, unlike youth who have no experience of foster care, youth in foster care may lack the expected stable relationships with adults who are familiar with their needs and who can effectively advocate to protect their health and well-being. Moreover, there is no consistently adopted training program for social welfare professionals and foster parents that would assist these providers in making adequate plans for the health of a given foster youth. Even when a complete medical file is available, without medical guidance, foster parents and caseworkers may not be fully equipped to understand the file or all of the youth's physical health needs, which could lead to a lack of recognition of the youth's problems. Unless all youth entering care are systematically screened, only those with the most severe and obvious problems will likely receive medical attention. As a result, in the short term, this may mean that a minority of youth will get the medical services needed, and in the long term, there is a missed opportunity to develop prevention strategies to promote wellness for the majority of youth in foster care.

Addressing the Barriers: Recommendations for the Assessment and Provision of Health Needs for Youth in Foster Care

In 2006, the AAP developed a task force on foster care with the goal of raising the awareness, knowledge, and skills of pediatricians and other relevant partners regarding the physical health needs of youth in foster care. The result of the task force was a policy statement and a set of guidelines for medical professionals and service providers to improve the physical (and mental) health of youth in foster care. Later, in 2011, the task force was merged with other relevant sections of the AAP, and the Council on Foster Care, Adoption, and Kinship Care (COFCAKC) was formed. In 2015, the COFCAKC published both a policy statement and a technical report (AAP, 2015) identifying the health needs of youth in foster care and a set of best practices for improving both physical health and assessment of health needs (Szilagyi et al., 2015).

To address the barriers to quality health care for youth in foster care, the AAP (2015) suggested that the medical home model be adopted to serve youth in foster care. By definition, a medical home is a "system of coordinated health care that is continuous over time, compassionate, culturally sensitive, competent, trauma-informed, family centered, and child focused" (Szilagyi et al., 2015, p. e1151). The authors go on to state that, for youth in foster care, the medical home should also include:

1. an understanding by medical personnel of the effects of child abuse and neglect, childhood trauma, and removal from family on the child, birth family, and foster/kinship family;
2. a collaborative relationship with child welfare and the legal system on behalf of the child;
3. coordination of care with other community-based resources, including Early Intervention, mental and dental health professionals, Head Start, schools, and childcare providers;
4. team-based care that ideally would include a child welfare liaison officer, mental health expert, and health care monitoring manager;
5. mental health integration into the medical home or a referral network of trauma-informed mental health providers.

Several examples of how social service systems have put the medical home model in place are worth noting. For foster youth in Illinois, Utah, and Vermont, the state social service agencies have developed preferred provider models, operating from a centralized system where the youth's health is monitored, and where the child's health data are shared, collated, and tracked electronically by health care managers within the child protective services agency. Other states, like Texas and New Jersey, have a team of health professionals who coordinate and meet regularly with child welfare workers to manage the physical health of foster youth. The focus is the coordination of services and the management of care, and the cooperation between health care providers and the social service agency to ensure the health of the child. A collaborative and cooperative partnership between social services staff, medical personnel, and foster and birth parents is critical for the continuous and effective delivery of medical care for youth in foster care. When health care is coordinated, especially for youth who change placements, and when the trauma-informed professionals are involved, the result is improved quality of care and tracking of physical health needs for youth in foster care (Ziring et al., 1999).

Finally, the American Academy of Pediatrics (2005) provides practice parameters for primary care providers, which can be downloaded at no cost at the Healthy Foster Care America website. The guidelines state that fundamentally, youth in foster care should be seen *early and often* in the context of a medical home model where the medical professionals are trauma-informed. Youth should be seen ideally three times over the first 3 months of foster care so that caregivers and medical professionals can become familiar with the physical health needs of the youth. Moreover, some youth, especially those with chronic medical conditions, may require more frequent and comprehensive assessments over time, especially to monitor any health changes that may occur in conjunction with placement changes or reunification efforts with biological parents. The manual also identifies steps and goals for preventative health care based on the age of the child and could serve as a good resource for medical professionals and child welfare or foster caregivers alike.

Future Directions and Next Steps

In the field of physical health and foster youth, there is generally little argument that youth in foster care have more medical problems than their non-foster youth peers, and that their exposure to medical care is limited, inconsistent, and not likely as effective as needed. Although the data detailing the nature of physical health problems among youth in foster care are consistent, professional attention to the physical health needs of youth in care is not. That is, most services for youth in care, outside of incidents of major physical injury, are focused on remediating the rather abundant mental health problems so commonly identified in this population. The physical health of any child is important, and perhaps especially so for the more than 400,000 youth who reside in foster care each year (Administration for Children and Families, 2014). Despite the rather dark portrait for health the data provide, there is some cause for optimism. Recent efforts by the AAP and state and local government social service agencies to provide guidance and implementation of best practices for improving the physical health of foster youth may soon begin to show signs of hope that the physical health status for future generations of foster youth will have little resemblance to the current data.

One approach that appears to have the most promise is the use of the medical home model, where care is coordinated across state and family caregivers and where medical professionals are a consistent part of the child welfare team (AAP, 2014). Policy makers have taken note of this idea, as recent amendments to the Child Abuse Prevention and Treatment Act (CAPTA) in 2003 recommended that state social service agencies work to collaborate with public health providers to address the comprehensive health and developmental needs of youth in foster care. Moreover, in 2008, with the passage of the Fostering Connections to Success and Increasing Adoptions Act, all states are mandated to find a cost-effective way to provide oversight and coordination of health care services for all youth in foster care, including guaranteeing continuity of care. The clearest example of this law in practice has been the implementation of the medical home model. Jaudes, Champagne, Harden, Masterson, and Bilaver (2012) reported great success using this approach across the state of Illinois, one of the first efforts in the United States to apply the medical home model to target the health needs of foster youth specifically.

By forming a network of primary care providers, the state social service agency was able to establish a role for medical history data collection across 19 health departments, and created a "Health Passport" or medical file that traveled with the youth as the youth moved residences. The results, based on 28,934 youth in state care, over the course of several years, compared to non-foster Medicaid-only youth, and controlling for demographic differences, showed that youth in foster care were three times more likely to have had a well-child visit and to have seen a dentist, and a greater proportion were up to date on their immunizations than the youth in the Medicaid-only group. Although youth in foster care had a higher rate of ER use, they also tended to have more chronic medical conditions than did the comparison group (youth not in care). Thus, youth in foster care may have greater need for medical attention, above and beyond what Medicaid can provide.

Another approach that directly focuses on the health needs of youth in foster care is the foster-care-specific clinic. The CHECK (Comprehensive Health Evaluations for Cincinnati's Kids) Foster Care Center is an outpatient program at the Cincinnati Children's Hospital that is specifically designed to assist with the medical needs of youth in foster care. The staff consists of trauma-informed medical providers who provide initial and comprehensive assessments of youth new to foster care. The staff also create a complete medical file for the youth so that the foster care provider, social service agency, and the medical staff have accurate and complete medication information. The clinic also arranges for any additional medical services for any specialty care the youth may require, and is seen as a resource for continuity of care while the youth is in foster care.

Recommendations

Given that the number of youth in foster care has not changed substantially over the past decade, it is clear that the physical and mental health needs of this population will continue to pose challenges to standard modes of health provision. Data and policy both point to several shared ideas that provide substantial support to any efforts to make systemic change that addresses the health needs of youth in foster care. First, all youth entering foster care should have an initial physical examination to identify any medical concern that may require monitoring by both the immediate caregivers and the broader social service agency. Second, findings from any medical or psychiatric assessment should be shared with all relevant parties (i.e., the court, biological parents, foster parents, and caseworkers). Further, communication and coordination of services, and changes in the youth's condition, should be tracked and updated regularly. How the youth is doing physically and psychologically should be a mandatory component of that youth's court-approved social service plan. Third, regular meetings with medical professionals should take place to discuss the youth's health. Social service staff and foster care providers should have access to medical professionals to make sure that they clearly understand the youth's diagnoses, medications, and plan for well-being. Moreover, any change in caseworker or placement should be shared with the medical provider. This is also an important time for an updated assessment on the youth's adjustment.

Fourth, all providers, including teachers, foster parents, and medical caregivers should be educated in and practice trauma-informed care. Youth in foster care are not the only youth who experience trauma, so it is likely this education would benefit many more youth than only those in care. For those who are in care, however, it is critical that those seeking to maintain healthy functioning of the youth be informed regarding how trauma, both old and new, chronic and acute, can negatively impact the otherwise healthy trajectory of youth. Fifth, providers and caretakers should consider that youth in foster care might require more assessments and preventative services than typically developing youth who live in stable home environments. Foster caretakers should be prepared for longer appointments with health care providers, and caseworkers should be present at these meetings so that all relevant information can be reviewed collectively. Care providers for youth in foster care should consider adopting a long-term view of health status for youth in care so that changes in behavior and health can be evaluated with a broad view of the child's history and experiences.

References

Administration for Children and Families. (2014). *Trends in foster care*. Retrieved from www.acf.hhs.gov/sites/default/files/cb/trends_fostercare_adoption2014.pdf

Almgren, G., & Marcenko, M. O. (2001). Emergency room use among a foster care sample: The influence of placement history, chronic illness, psychiatric diagnosis, and care factors. *Brief Treatment and Crisis Intervention, 1*, 55–64.

American Academy of Pediatrics (Council on Foster Care, Adoption, and Kinship Care, Committee on Adolescence, & Council on Early Childhood). (2015). Health care issues for children and adolescents in foster care and kinship care. *Pediatrics, 136*(4), e131–136. doi: 10.1542/peds.2015-2655

American Academy of Pediatrics (District II New York State Task Force on Health Care for Children in Foster Care). (2005). *Fostering health: Health care for children and adolescents in foster care*. Retrieved from www.aap.org/en-us/advocacy-and-policy/aap-health-initiatives/healthy-foster-care-america/Pages/Fostering-Health.aspx

American Academy of Pediatrics (The National Center for Medical Home Implementation). (2014). *What is a medical home?* Retrieved from https://medicalhomeinfo.aap.org/overview/pages/whatisthemedicalhome.aspx

Bilaver, L. A., Jaudes, P. K., Koepke, D., & Goerge, R. M. (1999). The health of children in foster care. *Social Service Review, 73*, 401–417.

Bisgaier, J., & Rhodes, K. V. (2011). Auditing access to specialty care for children with public insurance. *New England Journal of Medicine, 364*, 2324–2333.

Bronfenbrenner, U. (1979). *The ecology of human development: Experiments by nature and design*. Cambridge, MA: Harvard University Press.

Carpenter, S., & Clyman, R. (2004). The long-term emotional and physical wellbeing of women who have lived in kinship care. *Children and Youth Services Review, 26*, 673–686.

Casanueva, C., Martin, S., & Runyan, D. K. (2009). Repeated referrals for child maltreatment among intimate partner violence victims: Findings from the National Survey of Child and Adolescent Well-Being. *Child Abuse & Neglect, 33*, 84–93.

Chartier, M. J., Walker, J. R., & Naimark, B. (2007). Childhood abuse, adult health, and health care utilization: Results from a representative community sample. *American Journal of Epidemiology, 165*, 1031–1038.

Chernoff, R., Combs-Orme, T., Risley-Curtiss, C., & Heisler, A. (1994). Assessing the health status of children entering foster care. *Pediatrics, 93*, 594–601.

Child Abuse Prevention and Treatment Act [CAPTA] of 2003, Pub. L. 108-36, 117 STAT. 800, codified as amended at 42 U.S.C. 5101. (2003).

Child Welfare Information Gateway. (2015). *Health-care coverage for youth in foster care—and after*. Issue Brief. Retrieved from www.childwelfare.gov/pubPDFs/health_care_foster.pdf

Child Welfare Information Gateway. (2016). *Foster care statistics 2015*. Retrieved from www.childwelfare.gov/pubs/factsheets/foster/

Council of Family and Child Caring Agencies. (2013). *Raising the bar for health and mental health services for children in foster care: Developing a model of managed care*. Retrieved from www.cofcca.org/pdfs/FosterCareManagedCare-FinalReport.pdf

Courtney, M. E., & Dworsky, A. (2006). Early outcomes for young adults transitioning from out-of-home care in the USA. *Child and Family Social Work, 11*, 209–219.

Deutsch, S. A., & Fortin, K. (2015). Physical health problems and barriers to optimal health care among children in foster care. *Current Problems in Pediatric and Adolescent Health Care, 45*, 286–291.

English, D. J., Upadhyaya, M. P., Litrownik, A. J., Marshall, J. M., Runyan, D. K., Graham, J. C., & Dubowitz, H. (2005). Maltreatment's wake: The relationship of maltreatment dimensions to child outcomes. *Child Abuse & Neglect, 29*, 597–619.

Farruggia, S. P., & Sorkin, D. H. (2009). Health risks for older US adolescents in foster care: The significance of important others' health behaviors on youths' health and health behaviors. *Child: Care, Health and Development, 35*, 340–348.

Flaherty, E. G., & Weiss, H. (1990). Medical evaluation of abused and neglected children. *American Journal of the Disabled Child, 144*, 330–334.

Fostering Connections to Success and Increasing Adoptions Act of 2008, H. R. 6893 §§ 102-601. (2008).

Goodman, R. A., Posner, S. F., Huang, E. S., Parekh, A. K., & Koh, H. K. (2013). Defining and measuring chronic conditions: Imperatives for research, policy, program, and practice. *Prevention of Chronic Disease, 10*, 120–239.

Guh, D. P., Zhang, W., Bansback, N., Amarsi, Z., Birmingham, C. L., & Anis, A. H. (2009). The incidence of co-morbidities related to obesity and overweight: A systematic review and meta-analysis. *BMC Public Health, 9*, 88.

Hadfield, S. C., & Preece, P. M. (2008). Obesity in looked after children: Is foster care protective from the dangers of obesity? *Child: Care, Health and Development, 34*, 710–712.

Halfon, N., Berkowitz, G., & Klee, L. (1992). Children in foster care in California: An examination of Medicaid reimbursed health services utilization. *Pediatrics, 89*, 1230–1237.

Halfon, N., & Klee. L. (1987). Health and development services for children with multiple needs: The child in foster care. *Yale Law and Policy Review, 9*, 71–96.

Hansen, R. L., Mawjee, F. L., Barton, K., Metcalf, M. B., & Joye, N. R. (2004). Comparing the health status of low income children in and out of foster care. *Child Welfare, 83*, 367–380.

Hilen T., & Gafson, L. (2015). Why good placements matter: Pre-placement and placement risk factors associated with mental health disorders in pre-school children in foster care. *Clinical Child Psychology and Psychiatry, 20*, 486–499.

Jackson, Y., Cushing, C. C., Gabrielli, J., Fleming, K., O'Connor, B. M., & Huffhines, L. (2016). Child maltreatment, trauma, and physical health outcomes: The role of abuse type and placement moves on health conditions and service use for youth in foster care. *Journal of Pediatric Psychology, 41*, 28–36.

Jaudes, P. K., Bilaver, L. A., & Champagne, V. (2015). Do children in foster care receive appropriate treatment for asthma? *Children and Youth Services Review, 52*, 103–109.

Jaudes, P. K., Champagne, V., Harden, A., Masterson, J., & Bilaver, L. A. (2012). Expanded medical home model works for children in foster care. *Child Welfare, 91*, 9–33.

Jee, S. H., Antonucci, T. C., Aida, M., Szilagyi, M. A., & Szilagyi, P. G. (2005). Emergency department utilization by children in foster care. *Ambulatory Pediatrics, 5*, 102–106.

Jee, S. H., Barth, R. P., Szilagyi, M. A., Szilagyi, P. G., Aida, M., & Davis, M. M. (2006). Factors associated with chronic conditions among children in foster care. *Journal of Health Care for the Poor and Underserved, 17*, 328–341.

Johnson, C., Silver, P., & Wulczyn, F. (2013). *Raising the bar for health and mental health services for children in foster care: Developing a model of managed care*. Council of Family and Child Caring Agencies. Retrieved from www.cofcca.org/pdfs/FosterCareManagedCare-FinalReport.pdf

Kavaler, F., & Swire, M. R. (1983). *Foster-child health care*. Lexington, MA: Lexington Books.

Kools, S., Paul, S. M., Jones, R., Monasterio, E., & Norbeck, J. (2013). Health profiles of adolescents in foster care. *Journal of Pediatric Nursing: Nursing Care of Children and Families, 28*, 213–222.

Kools, S., Paul, S. M., Norbeck, J. S., & Robbins, N. R. (2009). Dimensions of health in young people in foster care. *International Journal of Adolescent Medicine and Health, 21*, 221–233.

Leslie, L. K., Gordon, J. N., Meneken, L., Premji, K., Michelmore, K. L., & Ganger, W. (2005). The physical, developmental, and mental health needs of young children in child welfare by initial placement type. *Journal of Developmental Behavioral Pediatrics, 26*, 177–185.

Leslie, L. K., Kelleher, K. J., Burns, B. J., Landsverk, J., & Rolls, J. A. (2003). Foster care and Medicaid managed care. *Child Welfare, 82*, 367–392.

Lopez, P., & Allen, P. J. (2007). Addressing the health needs of adolescents transitioning out of foster care. *Pediatric Nursing, 33*, 345–355.

Love, L. T., McIntosh, J., Rosst, M., & Tertzakian, K. (2005). *Fostering hope: Preventing teen pregnancy among youth in foster care*. Washington, DC: National Campaign to Prevent Teen Pregnancy.

Medford-Davis, L. N., Eswaran, V., Shah, R. M., & Dark, C. (2015). The Patient Protection and Affordable Care Act's effect on emergency medicine: A synthesis of the data. *Annals of Emergency Medicine, 66*, 496–506.

Melbye, M. L. R., Chi, D. L., Milgrom, P., Huebner, C. E., & Grembowski, D. (2014), Washington state foster care: Dental utilization and expenditures. *Journal of Public Health Dentistry, 74*, 93–101.

Miller, G. E., Chen, E., & Parker, K. J. (2011). Psychological stress in childhood and susceptibility to the chronic diseases of aging: Moving towards a model of behavioral and biological mechanisms. *Psychological Bulletin, 137*, 959–997.

Reilly, T. (2003). Transition from care: Status and outcomes of youth who age out of foster care. *Child Welfare, 82*, 727–746.

Ringeisen, H., Casanueva, C., Urato, M., & Cross, T. (2008). Special health care needs among children in the child welfare system. *Pediatrics, 122*, e232–e241.

Rosenbach, M. (2000). *Children in foster care: Challenges in meeting their health care needs through Medicaid.* Princeton, NJ: Mathematica Policy Research, Inc.

Rubin, D. M., Alessandrini, E. A., Feudtner, C., Localio, A. R., & Hadley, T. (2004). Placement changes and emergency department visits in the first year of foster care. *Pediatrics, 114*, e354–e360.

Rubin, D., Halfon, N., Raghavan, R., & Rosenbaum, S. (2005). *Protecting children in foster care: Why proposed Medicaid cuts harm our nation's most vulnerable children.* Seattle, WA: Casey Family Programs.

Rubin, D. M., Matone, M., Huang, Y.-S., dosReis, S., Feudtner, C., & Localio, R. (2012). Interstate variation in trends of psychotropic medication use among Medicaid-enrolled children in foster care. *Children and Youth Services Review, 34*, 1492–1499.

Rubin, D. M., O'Reilly, A. L., Luan, X., & Localio, A. R. (2007). The impact of placement stability on behavioral well-being for children in foster care. *Pediatrics, 119*, 336–344.

Schneiderman, J. U., Arnold-Clark, J. S., Smith, C., Duan, L., & Fuentes, J. (2013). Demographic and placement variables associated with overweight and obesity in children in long-term foster care. *Maternal and Child Health Journal, 17*, 1673–1679.

Schneiderman, J. U., Leslie, L. K., Arnold-Clark, J. S., McDaniel, D., & Xie, B. (2011). Pediatric health assessments of young children in child welfare by placement type. *Child Abuse & Neglect, 35*, 29–39.

Simms, M. D., Dubowitz, H., & Szilagyi, M. A. (2000). Health care needs of children in the foster care system. *Pediatrics, 106*, 909–918.

Steele, J. S., & Buchi, K. F. (2008). Medical and mental health of children entering the Utah foster care system. *Pediatrics, 122*, e703–e709.

Szilagyi, M. (2012). The pediatric role in the care of children in foster and kinship care. *Pediatrics in Review, 33*, 496–507.

Szilagyi, M. A., Rosen, D. S., Rubin, D., & Zlotnik, S. (2015). Health care issues for children and adolescents in foster care and kinship care. *Pediatrics, 136*, e1142–e1166.

Takayama, J., Bergman, A. B., & Connell, F.A. (1994). Children in foster care in the state of Washington. Health care utilization and expenditures. *Journal of the American Medical Association, 15*, 1850–1855.

Tarran-Sweeney, M. (2008). The mental health of children in out-of-home care. *Current Opinion in Psychiatry, 21*, 345–349.

U.S. Department of Health & Human Services. (2016). *Foster care.* Retrieved from www.acf.hhs.gov/cb/focus-areas/foster-care

Van Cleave, J., Gortmaker, S. L., & Perrin, J. M. (2010). Dynamics of obesity and chronic health conditions among children and youth. *Journal of the American Medical Association, 303*, 623–630.

Villegas, S., Rosenthal, J. A., O'Brien, K., & Pecora, P. J. (2011). Health outcomes for adults in family foster care as children: An analysis by ethnicity. *Children and Youth Services Review, 34*, 110–117.

Viner, R. M., & Taylor, B. (2005). Adult health and social outcomes of children who have been in public care: Population-based study. *Pediatrics, 115*, 894–899.

Ziring, P. R., Brazdziunas, D., Cooley, W. C., Kastner, T. A., Kummer, M. E., Gonzalez de Pijem, L., . . . Perrin, J. M. (1999). American Academy of Pediatrics, Committee on Children with Disabilities. Care coordination: integrating health and related systems of care for children with special health care needs. *Pediatrics, 104*, 978–981.

8

The Sexual and Reproductive Health of Youth in Foster Care

Amy Dworsky

The Adoption and Safe Families Act of 1997 established three federal child welfare goals: permanency, safety, and well-being (Children's Bureau, 2014). Although the goals of permanency and safety were not new, the emphasis on well-being was. Over the past two decades, growing attention has been paid to promoting the social, emotional, physical, behavioral, and cognitive development of children and youth in foster care (Biglan, 2014). More recently, their sexual and reproductive health has also begun to receive attention. This attention comes in response to growing evidence that youth in foster care are engaging in early and unprotected sexual behavior, becoming pregnant, and giving birth to or fathering children at higher rates than their same-age peers who are not in foster care (Dworsky & Courtney, 2010; James, Montgomery, Leslie, & Zhang, 2009; Ramseyer Winter, Brandon-Friedman, & Ely, 2016; Svoboda, Shaw, Barth, & Bright, 2012).

This chapter provides an overview of what we know about sexual behavior, pregnancy, and parenting among this population. It discusses the sexual and reproductive health care needs of this population and how those needs are (or are not) being addressed by federal and state policies. Finally, it examines the state of the evidence on interventions aimed at preventing pregnancy and improving parenting among youth in foster care.

Sexual Risk Behavior among Youth in Foster Care

Sexual risk behaviors are behaviors that put individuals at risk of an unplanned pregnancy or a sexually transmitted infection (STI). A number of studies have found high rates of sexual risk behaviors among youth in foster care, such as initiating sexual intercourse at an early age, having multiple sexual partners, and infrequently or inconsistently using contraception (James et al., 2009; Ramseyer Winter et al., 2016). However, differences in samples and methodology make it difficult to compare estimated rates. Moreover, a number of these studies suggest that rates of sexual risk behaviors are higher among youth in foster care than among their non-foster care peers in the general population.

Some of our knowledge about sexual risk behaviors among this population comes from two longitudinal studies of youth transitioning out of foster care: the Midwest Evaluation of the Adult Functioning of Former Foster Youth (i.e., the Midwest Study) and the California Youth Transitions to Adulthood Study (i.e., CalYOUTH). The Midwest Study followed a sample of more than 700 young people from Illinois, Iowa, and Wisconsin as they transitioned out of foster care and into adulthood. Baseline data were collected from Midwest Study participants when they were 17 or

18 years old (Courtney, Terao, & Bost, 2004). The CalYOUTH Study is currently following approximately 2,500 current and former foster youth from 51 of California's 58 counties. Baseline data were collected from CalYOUTH Study participants when they were 17 years old (Courtney, Charles, Okpych, Napolitano, & Halsted, 2014). Both studies collected the second wave of data at age 19 (Courtney et al., 2005; Courtney et al., 2016).

Additionally, many of the questions used by the Midwest Study and the CalYOUTH Study to measure sexual behavior came from the National Longitudinal Study of Adolescent to Adult Health (Add Health). Add Health is a longitudinal study of a nationally representative sample of adolescents who were in grades 7 to 12 during the 1994/95 school year (Harris et al., 2009).[1] Four waves of data have been collected, most recently in 2008, when study participants were between 24 and 32 years old. Using the Add Health questions meant that there were data from a nationally representative sample to which the Midwest Study and the CalYOUTH Study results could be compared.

By age 19, 88 percent of the Midwest Study participants and 86 percent of the CalYOUTH Study participants had had sexual intercourse, and the median age at first sexual intercourse for youth in both studies was 15 years. By comparison, 79 percent of 19 year olds in the nationally representative sample had ever had sexual intercourse, and their median age at first sexual intercourse was 16 years. These differences are not large and a majority of young people in all three samples had had sex for the first time by their mid-teens, although it occurred 1 year earlier, on average, among the young people who were currently or formerly in foster care.

Particularly troubling was the high percentage of 19-year-old study participants who reported having sexual intercourse at least once during the past year without using condoms (63 percent of the Midwest Study participants and 76 percent of the CalYOUTH Study participants) and without using birth control (55 percent of the Midwest Study participants and 67 percent of the CalYOUTH Study participants). Likewise, far too many of these 19 year olds reported not using condoms (42 percent of the Midwest Study participants and 58 percent of the CalYOUTH Study participants) or not using birth control (32 percent of the Midwest Study participants and 47 percent of the CalYOUTH Study participants) the last time they had sexual intercourse.

Both the Midwest Study and the CalYOUTH Study looked at the prevalence of other risky sexual behaviors. At age 19, 14 percent of the Midwest Study participants and 9 percent of the CalYOUTH Study participants who had ever had sexual intercourse reported having a sexual partner with a sexually transmitted infection (STI), compared to 6 percent of the Add Health Study participants; 5 percent of the Midwest Study participants and 6 percent of the CalYOUTH Study participants reported ever being paid to have sex, compared to 2 percent of the Add Health Study participants; and 2 percent of the Midwest Study participants and 5 percent of the CalYOUTH Study participants reported having sex with someone who took street drugs using a needle, compared to 2 percent of the Add Health Study participants.

Because the Midwest Study and CalYOUTH Study participants were at least 17 years old when the studies began, neither study provides much information on sexual behavior among youth in foster care early in adolescence. Another frequently cited source of information about the prevalence of sexual risk behaviors among youth in foster care does. The National Survey of Child and Adolescent Well-Being (NSCAW) is a federally funded longitudinal study of a nationally representative sample of children who were the subjects of a Child Protective Services (CPS) investigation (NSCAW Research Group, 2010). The purpose of the study is to examine how the outcomes of those children and their families are related to their experiences with the child welfare system, child and family characteristics, and other factors.

Two cohorts of children have been enrolled in the study. The NSCAW 1 cohort includes 6,231 children, at ages birth to 15 years, who were selected from 92 Primary Sampling Units (PSUs) in 97 counties across the United States. Eighty-eight percent (n = 5,504) of those children had contact with Child Protective Services between October 1999 and December 2000. The other 12 percent (n = 727) were children who had been in foster care for approximately 12 months when the sample was drawn (NSCAW Research Group, 2001). Because the foster care sample, which included children placed in non-relative and kinship foster homes, group homes, residential treatment facilities, and other out-of-home care settings, is relatively small, drawing conclusions from these data about youth in foster care should be done with caution.

One analysis of the NSCAW I data focused on the prevalence of health risk behaviors among a sample of 933 youth who were between 11 and 15 years old at the first wave of data collection. Seventy-two percent of these youth were between the ages of 12 and 14, with a mean age of 12.7, 57 percent were female, and 12 percent were in foster care when the first wave of data was collected. Twenty-six percent of all the youth—but 29 percent of 12 to 14 year olds—had engaged in sexual intercourse, compared to 17 percent of the 7th and 8th Graders in the Add Health Study (Leslie et al., 2010).[2]

Another analysis of NSCAW I data focused specifically on the prevalence of sexual risk behaviors among a sample of 877 youth who were between 14 and 18 years old when the fourth wave of data was collected 36 months post-baseline (James et al., 2009). The mean age of the youth was 15.3 years, 54 percent were female, and 23 percent had been placed in foster care (n = 202). Youth were asked if they had ever had sexual intercourse, and if they gave an affirmative response, they were also asked about forced and unforced sex. Although most of these youth were too young to legally consent to having sex, 50 percent of all the youth reported having engaged in consensual (i.e., unforced) sexual intercourse.[3]

To contextualize their results, James et al. (2009) compared some of their findings to data collected as part of the Youth Risk Behavior Surveillance System (YRBSS) in the late 1990s. The YRBSS is a survey of a nationally representative sample of high school students in grades 9 through to 12 that is conducted every 2 years by the Centers for Disease Control and Prevention. The survey includes questions about a variety of health risk behaviors, including sexual behaviors related to unplanned pregnancy and sexually transmitted infections (Centers for Disease Control and Prevention, 2017).[4] Although youth in the NSCAW sample reported having engaged in consensual sexual intercourse at about the same rate as high school students in the YRBSS, youth in the NSCAW sample reported being 7.2 months younger, on average, than their YRBSS peers when they first had consensual sexual intercourse. In fact, 20 percent of the NSCAW sample reported first having consensual sex prior to the age of 14, compared with 8 percent of the YRBSS sample, even though the YRBSS sample was somewhat older on average. Finally, 68 percent of the youth in the NSCAW sample who were sexually active reported using "protection" often or always during consensual sex.[5]

The NSCAW I data were also used to examine the relationship between sexual risk behaviors and a host of psychosocial factors that were measured at baseline (James et al., 2009). However, different psychosocial factors predicted different sexual risk behaviors. For example, delinquency and deviant peers increased the odds of sexual intercourse, behavior problems increased the odds of early onset of sexual intercourse, and deviant peers increased the odds of pregnancy. Perhaps the most notable finding was the lack of a relationship between engagement in sexual risk behaviors and placement in out-of-home care. Although youth who had been placed in foster care had higher rates of sexual intercourse and onset of sexual activity prior to age 14 than those who remained in their home following a child maltreatment investigation, those differences were not statistically significant after controlling for other factors. This could indicate that youth who have been involved with the child welfare system are a vulnerable population when it comes to sexual risk behaviors, regardless of whether they are placed in foster care.

The NSCAW II data have also been used to examine the prevalence of sexual risk behaviors among youth who had a history of child welfare involvement. The NSCAW II cohort includes 5,872 children, at ages from birth to 17.5 years, who had been the subject of a CPS investigation within a 15-month period between February 2008 and April 2009 in 81 counties across the United States.

The sample was selected from substantiated and unsubstantiated CPS investigations that were closed during that 15-month period. Because only 13 percent of the sample was in some type of out-of-home care when the first wave of data was collected, caution should be exercised in drawing conclusions from these data about the prevalence of sexual risk behaviors among youth in foster care (Dolan, Smith, Casanueva & Ringeisen, 2011).[6]

At the first wave of NSCAW II data collection, 28 percent of all the females and 31 percent of all the males aged 11 to 17 reported having ever had sex, while 24 percent of the females and 22 percent of the males reported having sex in the past 12 months. However, those percentages varied widely by age. For females, the percentage who had ever had sex rose from 7 percent among 11 and 12 year olds, to 29 percent among 13 and 14 year olds, to 49 percent among 15 to 17 year olds. For males, the percentage who had ever had sex rose from 13 percent among 11 and 12 year olds, to 16 percent among 13 and 14 year olds, to 60 percent among 15 to 17 year olds.

These rates of sexual activity are considerably higher than the rates among adolescents in the general population. For example, the National Center for Health Statistics (NCHS) conducts the National Survey of Family Growth (NSFG). The NSFG collects data on factors that affect the formation, growth, and dissolution of families from a nationally representative sample of women and men aged 15 to 49 years. Topics covered include marriage, divorce, and cohabitation; contraception, sterilization, and infertility; and pregnancy and births.[7] Twenty-seven percent of 15- to 17-year-old females and 28 percent of 15- to 17-year-old males who participated in the 2006–2010 NSFG reported ever having had sexual intercourse, while 25 percent of 15- to 17-year-old females and 25 percent of 15- to 17-year-old males reported having sex in the past 12 months (Martinez, Copen, & Abma, 2011).

Among adolescents in NSCAW II who reported having sexual intercourse in the past year, 30 percent of females and 14 percent of males reported using no contraception (e.g., oral or injectable contraceptives), while 40 percent of females and 25 percent of males reported not using a condom the last time they had sex. By comparison, 14 percent of sexually active 15- to 19-year-old females and 8 percent of sexually active 15- to 19-year-old males who participated in the 2006–2010 NSFG reported not using contraception or a condom the last time they had sex (Martinez et al., 2011).

By the third wave of NSCAW II data collection, study participants were 14 to 20.5 years old. Overall, 53 percent of the males and 64 percent of the females reported ever having had consensual sex, while 44 percent of the males and 59 percent of the females reported having had sex in the past year. However, there were large age-related differences. The 18- to 20-year-old males were much more likely to report ever having had consensual sex than the 14- to 17-year-old males (78 percent versus 33 percent), and much more likely to report having had sex in the past year (67 percent versus 26 percent). Likewise, the 18- to 20-year-old females were much more likely to report ever having had consensual sex than the 14- to 17-year-old females (92 percent versus 42 percent), and much more likely to report having had sex in the past year (83 percent versus 39 percent). Many of the youth had also begun having sex at an early age. Forty-nine percent of the males and 49 percent of the females who were at least 18 years old reported having had sex before the age of 16.[8] Finally, among those youth who reported having had sex in the past year, 66 percent of the males and 63 percent of the females reported that they or their partner had used contraception (including condoms) the last time they had sex (Wilson et al., 2014).

Other studies have also examined predictors of sexual risk behaviors among youth in foster care. In one cross-sectional study, youth who exhibited externalizing problems (i.e., delinquent and aggressive behaviors) engaged in significantly more HIV-risk behaviors (e.g., sex without using a condom, sex while under the influence of alcohol or other drugs, and sex in exchange for money, drugs, or shelter) than youth who did not exhibit those problems, even after controlling for demographic characteristics. Moreover, and contrary to expectations, a history of sexual abuse was not associated with engaging in more HIV-risk behaviors (Auslander et al., 2002). Similarly, a longitudinal study found that older age and behavior problems when the first wave of data was collected predicted engagement in sexual risk behaviors when the second wave of data was collected, although being sexually abused did not (Taussig, 2002).

In sum, research suggests that youth in foster care engage in sexual behaviors that put them at risk of an unplanned pregnancy or a sexually transmitted infection (STI) at higher rates than their non-foster care peers.

Factors Contributing to Sexual Risk Behaviors among Youth in Foster Care

Several predictors of sexual risk behaviors have been identified, and each of these predictors is prevalent among youth in foster care. One is a history of neglect, abuse, or other traumatic experiences. Childhood maltreatment has been linked to a variety of sexual risk behaviors (Fortenberry, 2013), including early initiation of sexual intercourse (Black et al., 2009) and multiple sexual partners (Noll, Haralson, Butler, & Shenk, 2011). Much of the research on the relationship between child maltreatment and sexual risk behaviors has focused on sexual abuse (Senn, Carey, & Vanable, 2008). However, other types of maltreatment, including physical abuse and neglect, have also been linked to sexual risk behaviors, including early initiation of sexual intercourse (Black et al., 2009; Wilson & Widom, 2008).

One explanation for this relationship between childhood maltreatment and sexual risk behaviors is that childhood abuse and neglect disrupt multiple developmental pathways (Briere, 1996), and these disruptions can lead to delays in the development of motor, emotional, behavioral, language, social, and cognitive skills (De Bellis, 2001). Disruption of these developmental pathways can also have adverse effects on healthy sexual development (Schloredt & Heiman, 2003) and the cultivation of healthy relationships (Anthonysamy & Zimmer-Gembeck, 2007; Kim & Cicchetti, 2010; Trickett, Noll, & Putnam, 2011). Most youth in foster care have experienced neglect, abuse, or other trauma, and these experiences may contribute to their high rate of sexual risk behaviors.

A second predictor of sexual risk behaviors is mental and behavioral health problems, including depression, post-traumatic stress disorder (PTSD), and substance abuse (Brown et al., 2010). Specifically, some research suggests that mental and behavioral health problems may lead to sexual risk behaviors by impairing judgment and increasing impulsivity (Donenberg & Pao, 2005). Youth in foster care have higher rates of mental and behavioral health problems than adolescents in the general population (McMillen et al., 2005; Shin, 2005). If mental and behavioral health problems lead to sexual risk behaviors by impairing judgment and increasing impulsivity, then higher rates of mental and behavioral health problems among youth in foster care might account, at least in part, for their higher rates of sexual risk behaviors.

A third predictor of sexual risk behavior is a lack of supportive relationships with parents or other adults. Research has found that parents or other adults play an important role in the decisions that youth make about engaging in sexual activity. In particular, having a supportive relationship with a parent or other adult is associated with a delay in the onset of sexual activity, and higher rates of contraceptive use (Miller, Benson, & Galbraith, 2001; Parkes, Henderson, Wight, & Nixon, 2011). Placement in foster care can disrupt existing relationships and frequent placement changes can make it difficult for new relationships to be built (Constantine, W., Jerman, & Constantine, N., 2009; Love, McIntosh, Rosst, & Tertzakian, 2005). Some of the sexual risk behavior observed among youth in foster care may be attributed to their lack of supportive relationships with caring adults.

Consequences of Sexual Risk Behaviors among Youth in Foster Care

For youth in foster care, as for adolescents generally, the three major consequences of engaging in risky sexual behaviors are sexually transmitted infections (STIs), pregnancy, and early parenthood. Each of these risks is discussed in turn below.

Sexually Transmitted Infections (STIs)

Youth in foster care are more likely to engage in sexual behaviors associated with an increased risk of STIs (Courtney et al., 2007; Courtney et al., 2016), such as having sex without using a condom, having sex with a partner who has an STI, exchanging sex for money, or having sex with an injection drug user. However, few studies have looked at the rate of STIs among youth in foster care. One exception is the CalYOUTH Study. At age 19, 19 percent of the young women and 5 percent of the young men in the CalYOUTH Study reported ever having an STI (Courtney et al., 2016).

Another exception is a study that used data from the National Longitudinal Study of Adolescent to Adult Health (Add Health) to compare STI rates among male and female youth who had been in foster care to rates among their peers (Aherns et al., 2010). Bio-specimens were collected from study participants and tested for three sexually transmitted infections: trichomonas, gonorrhea, and chlamydia. Less than 3 percent of the female study participants and 2 percent of the male study participants had ever been in foster care, and very few were still in foster care when the bio-specimens were collected. Nevertheless, female study participants who had been in foster care were significantly more likely to test positive for trichomonas, but not for gonorrhea or chlamydia; and male study participants who had been in foster care were significantly more likely to test positive for gonorrhea and chlamydia (but not trichomonas), compared with their peers. The authors of the study noted that the increased risk for STIs was not necessarily attributable to out-of-home care placement per se. Rather, the increase may be attributable to preexisting factors such as high rates of early adverse exposures, or to the mental or behavioral health problems that can result from that exposure.

Pregnancy

Despite precipitous drops in the U.S. teenage pregnancy rate over the past few decades (Kost & Maddow-Zimet, 2016), pregnancy rates among young women in foster care have remained persistently high (see Svoboda et al. [2012] for a review). For example, 20 percent of the 14- to 18-year-old young women in the NSCAW sample reported ever being pregnant. Thirty-three percent of the young women in the Midwest Study and 26 percent of the young women in the CalYOUTH Study had been pregnant at least once prior to baseline (Courtney et al., 2014; Dworsky & Courtney, 2010). By age 19, 51 percent of the young women in the Midwest Study and 49 percent of the young women in the CalYOUTH Study had been pregnant at least once (Courtney et al., 2016; Dworsky & Courtney, 2010). Although racial and ethnic differences between the Midwest Study sample and the nationally representative Add Health sample appear to explain some of the difference in pregnancy rates, Dworsky and Courtney (2010) found that the difference remained statistically significant even after controlling for differences in race/ethnicity. Another recent longitudinal study that examined pregnancy rates among a sample of 325 Missouri youth in foster care found even higher pregnancy rates. At age 17, 20 percent of the young women reported ever being pregnant. By age 19, that figure had increased to 55 percent (Oshima, Narendorf, & McMillen, 2013). By comparison, only 20 percent of 19-year-old young women in a nationally representative sample (Dworsky & Courtney, 2010) had ever been pregnant.

Equally troubling is the high rate of repeat pregnancy among young women in foster care. At baseline, 23 percent of the young women in the Midwest Study and 30 percent of the young women in the CalYOUTH Study who had been pregnant had been pregnant more than once (Courtney et al., 2014; Dworsky & Courtney, 2010). By age 19, the repeat pregnancy rate had risen to 46 percent and 49 percent, respectively (Courtney et al., 2016; Dworsky & Courtney, 2010). By comparison, 17 percent of the young women in a nationally representative sample (Dworsky & Courtney, 2010) who had been pregnant by age 17 and 34 percent of the young women who had been pregnant by age 19 had had a repeat pregnancy.

Although youth in foster care appear to be at a very high risk for getting pregnant, remaining in foster care might be a protective factor (Courtney et al., 2005; Dworsky & Courtney, 2010). The Midwest Study found that youth who were still in foster care at age 19 were less likely to have become pregnant since the baseline data were collected than their peers who left care (Dworsky & Courtney, 2010). Likewise, the CalYOUTH Study found that young women who were still in care at age 19 were less likely than young women who had exited care to have ever been pregnant.[9] Why remaining in care appears to reduce the risk of teenage pregnancy is not entirely clear. One possibility is that young women who are still in care simply have fewer "opportunities" to become pregnant, due to the supervision that their foster parents or other caregivers provide. Another is that young women who are still in care may be given more advice about risky behaviors to avoid or more encouragement to engage in positive activities. Understanding this relationship will require more research.

Births

Teenage birth rates in the United States have fallen sharply in recent years (Kost & Maddow-Zimet, 2016; Ventura, Hamilton, & Mathews, 2014). However, birth rates among youth in foster care continue to be high (see Svoboda et al. [2012] for a review). One study found that the birth rate between 2000 and 2009 for 15- to 19-year-old female foster youth in Maryland was nearly three times higher than the birth rate for their peers who were not in foster care, although the birth rate for the female foster youth did appear to be trending downward over time (Shaw, Barth, Svoboda, & Shaikh, 2010). In California, the birth rate for 15- to 17-year-old female foster youth was 59 percent higher than the birth rate for their peers between 2006 and 2010 (King, Putnam-Hornstein, Cederbaum, & Needell, 2014). Additionally, 12 percent of the 17-year-old young women who were in foster care between 2003 and 2007 gave birth at least once before age 18, and 28 percent gave birth at least once before age 20 (Putnam-Horstein & King, 2014).

Other studies, based on survey data, have also reported high rates of childbearing among young women in foster care. For example, 19 percent of the young women in the Midwest Study and 9 percent of the young women in the CalYOUTH Study had given birth to at least one child prior to the baseline interviews (Courtney et al., 2014; Dworsky & Courtney, 2010). By age 19, 32 percent of the young women in the Midwest Study and 27 percent of the young women in the CalYOUTH Study had given birth to at least one child, compared with 12 percent of 19-year-old young women in the general population (Courtney et al., 2016; Dworsky & Courtney, 2010).

Another source of information about childbearing rates among youth in foster care is the National Youth in Transition Database (NYTD). The Foster Care Independence Act of 1999, which established the John H. Chafee Foster Care Independence Program, required the Administration for Children & Families to create a National Youth in Transition Database to track the independent living services that states provide to youth in foster care; the characteristics of the youth who receive those services; and youth outcomes related to educational attainment, employment, welfare dependency, homelessness, non-marital childbirth, incarceration, and high-risk behaviors (Dworsky & Crayton, 2009).[10] States collect baseline outcome data from youth in foster care at age 17 and collect follow-up outcome data from those same youth at ages 19 and 21. The follow-up data are collected regardless of whether the youth are still in foster care.[11] The baseline data are collected from a new cohort of 17 year olds every 3 years. Ten percent of the 17-year-old females from whom baseline data were collected in Fiscal Year (FY) 2011 reported that they had given birth to at least one child, and 17 percent of the 19-year-old females from whom follow-up data were collected in FY 2013 reported giving birth to at least one child in the past 2 years (Children's Bureau, 2014).[12]

Fatherhood

Although most of the attention paid to pregnancy and childbearing among youth in foster care has focused on young women, there is some data on the percentage of young men in foster care who get their partner pregnant or father a child. For example, 12 percent of the 17-year-old males in the CalYOUTH Study reported ever getting a partner pregnant. By age 19, this had risen to 21 percent (Courtney et al., 2014; Courtney et al., 2016). Likewise, the percentage of the young men in the Missouri study who reported getting a partner pregnant rose from 4 percent at age 17 to 23 percent at age 19 (Oshima et al., 2013). The percentage of young men in foster care who get their partner pregnant may be higher than these data suggest because some young men whose partners become pregnant may not know about the pregnancy.

Somewhat more is known about the percentage of young men in foster care who have fathered a child. The results from several studies suggest that young men in foster care are more likely than their peers in the general population to become fathers at an early age, but the difference between them is much smaller than the difference between their female counterparts. By age 19, 14 percent of the young men in the Midwest Study and 9 percent of young men in the CalYOUTH Study (Courtney et al., 2005; Courtney et al., 2016) had fathered at least one child, compared to 7 percent of 19-year-old males in the nationally representative Add Health Study sample (Courtney et al., 2005).

The NYTD data also provide information about the percentage of young men in foster care who have fathered a child. Four percent of the 17-year-old males from whom baseline data were collected in FY 2011 reported that they had fathered at least one child, and 6 percent of the 19-year-old males from whom follow-up data were collected in FY 2013 reported fathering at least one child in the past 2 years (Children's Bureau, 2014).[13]

Factors Contributing to the High Pregnancy and Birth Rate among Youth in Foster Care

The high rate of pregnancy and parenthood among youth in foster care can probably be attributed to a confluence of several factors. Although some of these are similar to the factors that motivate other adolescents to become pregnant (or perhaps more precisely to not avoid pregnancy), others may be especially salient for youth in foster care.

For some youth in foster care, becoming pregnant and bearing a child may be a way to create the family they did not have growing up (Constantine et al., 2009; Love et al., 2005; Shaw et al., 2010). Creating their own family may also fill an emotional void because a child is someone they can love unconditionally, and be unconditionally loved by (Constantine et al., 2009; Love et al., 2005).

Youth in foster care who can't envision a future much different from their past may not perceive adolescent childbearing as an adverse outcome to be avoided or delayed, but as an opportunity to demonstrate that they can be a better parent to their child than their parents had been to them (Constantine et al., 2009; Love et al., 2005; Shaw et al., 2010). Moreover, many youth in foster care come from families and communities in which adolescent pregnancy and parenthood are more the norm than the exception. Becoming pregnant and then a parent are thus accepted rather than stigmatized (Constantine et al., 2009; Shaw et al., 2010).

As noted above, youth in foster care are more likely to have experienced abuse, neglect, or other traumas during childhood than other adolescents. This childhood trauma can disrupt multiple developmental pathways, including those related to healthy sexuality and relationships (Cook et al. 2005; Putnam, 2003). This, in turn, can lead youth to engage in sexual risk behaviors, including early and unprotected sexual intercourse.

Research suggests that youth in foster care are, on average, younger than their peers the first time that they have sexual intercourse. Sex education may come "too late" for youth in foster care who are already sexually active (Gowen & Aue, 2011; Love et al., 2005). However, youth in foster care who are sexually active could still benefit from sex education if the curriculum is comprehensive—that is, it provides information about the importance of using contraception and condoms; an "abstinence only" curriculum is unlikely to resonate.

Research also indicates that parents play an important role in the decisions youth make about engaging in sexual activity, and that supportive relationships with parents or other adults are associated with a delay in the onset of sexual activity and higher rates of contraceptive use. All too often, youth in foster care don't have close relationships with their parents or other caring and trusted adults (Constantine et al., 2009; Love et al., 2005).

Some research suggests that youth in foster care lack access to information about sexual and reproductive health, including contraception (Hudson, 2012).[14] For example, 55 percent of the 17- and 18-year-old Midwest Study participants reported that they had *not* received information about birth control (Courtney et al., 2004). Another study conducted in Illinois found that knowledge of contraception among youth in foster care is often inaccurate or incomplete, and that many youth in foster care desire additional information about contraceptive methods (Love at al., 2005). However, other studies suggest that a lack of access to information may be less of a problem. Only 3 percent of the 17-year-old CalYOUTH Study participants reported *not* receiving any information about sexual health and only 8 percent reported *not* receiving any information about family planning (Courtney et al., 2014). This difference could reflect the fact that the studies did not take place in the same states, or that the data were collected more than a decade apart, a decade during which heightened attention was being paid to the high rate of pregnancy among youth in foster care.

Although some research suggests that access to condoms and birth control is not a barrier to pregnancy prevention among youth in foster care (Love et al., 2005), other studies have found that accessing sexual and reproductive health care services can be a challenge. For example, youth in foster care may not be aware of community-based clinics where they can obtain condoms and birth control (Constantine et al., 2009). Finally, even when youth are educated about their sexual and reproductive health and understand the risks of engaging in sexual activity, they may not act on that knowledge (Constantine et al., 2009; Love et al., 2005).

Consequences of Early Pregnancy and Parenthood

There are several reasons to be concerned about the high rates of pregnancy and parenthood among youth in foster care. First, compared with pregnant women in their twenties, pregnant adolescents—including adolescents in foster care—are less likely to receive early prenatal care and are more likely to experience pregnancy complications. Their babies are more likely to be born premature and/or at a low birthweight (Jaffee, Caspi, Moffitt, Belsky, & Silva, 2001; Levine, Emery, & Pollak, 2007). Second, many adolescent parents lack basic parenting skills and their limited knowledge about child development can lead to unrealistic expectations of child behavior (Borkowski, Whitman, & Farris, 2007). Normal adolescent egocentrism can also make it difficult for teenage parents to recognize and respond to their children's needs and feelings (Coley & Chase-Lansdale, 1998; Noria, Weed, & Keogh, 2007). Youth in foster care may be even less prepared for early parenthood than other adolescents due to the impacts of the abuse, neglect, or other trauma they have experienced on their development and their lack of exposure to positive parenting.

Third, prior research suggests that children born to mothers who first gave birth as teens are at increased risk of experiencing child maltreatment compared with children whose mothers were older when their first child was born (Connelly & Straus, 1992; Goerge, Harden, & Lee, 2008; Stier, Leventhal, Berg, Johnson, & Mezger, 1993). There is also evidence that children whose adolescent mothers were neglected or abused are at greater risk of being maltreated than children whose adolescent mothers have no childhood abuse or neglect history (Bartlett & Easterbrooks, 2012; Putnam-Horstein, Cederbaum, King, & Needell, 2013).

Although very little is known about child welfare services' involvement among children whose parents were in foster care when they were born, at least one recent study found that the rate of child welfare services' involvement among the children of youth in foster care is higher than the rate among children of adolescent parents in the general population. Specifically, an analysis of child welfare administrative data from Illinois revealed that 39 percent of the children born to parents who were in foster care when their first child was born were the subject of at least one CPS investigation, 17 percent had at least one indicated report, and 11 percent were placed in the care of the Department of Child and Family Services care at least once before their 5th birthday (Dworsky, 2015).

Finally, the adverse consequences of teenage parenthood on economic well-being have been well-documented (Hoffman, 2006). Several studies have found that teenage mothers are less likely to complete high school and graduate from college than their peers with no children (Levine & Painter, 2003; Perper, Peterson, & Manlove, 2010). Research also indicates that adolescent childbearing has a negative effect on future employment and earnings, even after controlling for other factors that might explain differences in labor market outcomes between young women who were teenage mothers and their peers who delayed becoming parents (Fletcher & Wolfe, 2009; Lee, 2010). Some argue that young women who were teenage mothers experience poor labor market outcomes because adolescent childbearing impedes human capital accumulation (Becker 1993). However, others argue that these adverse outcomes are an artifact of the disadvantaged backgrounds from which most teenage mothers come (Geronimus, 1991; Geronimus, Korenman, & Hillemeier, 1994). Regardless of the reason, teenage parenthood is associated with high rates of poverty and receiving public assistance (Ng & Kaye, 2012). Although this research on the adverse economic consequences of teenage parenthood has not focused specifically on youth in foster care, teenage mothers who are also in foster care would seem to have an additional strike against them because youth in foster care tend to fare more poorly than their peers with respect to education and employment (Courtney et al., 2007; Courtney, Dworsky, Lee, & Raap, 2010).

Barriers to Educating Youth in Foster Care about Sexual and Reproductive Health

There are several barriers to educating youth in foster care about their sexual and reproductive health and providing them with the skills and resources to address their sexual and reproductive health care needs. First, for many youth, school-based sex education programs are an important source of medically accurate and developmentally appropriate information about sexual and reproductive health. Unfortunately, youth in foster care often change schools when they change placements. Because different schools teach sex education in different grades or at different times during the year, these disruptions in their schooling mean that youth in foster care may miss all or part of the school-based sex education curriculum to which their peers are exposed (Becker & Barth, 2000; Constantine et al., 2009; Gowen & Aue, 2011).

Second, sex education curricula are often not inclusive of either youth of color or youth who identify as lesbian, gay, bisexual, transgender, or questioning/queer (LGBTQ) (Fine & McClelland, 2006; Hillier & Mitchell, 2008). Exclusion of these groups is problematic because they are over-represented among youth in foster care (Sullivan, Sommer, & Moff, 2001). Curricula that are not inclusive of these youth and that do not reflect their experiences are unlikely to be effective (Shaw et al., 2010).

Third, sex education curricula have not been developed or adapted to meet the unique needs of youth in foster care. In particular, the types of child maltreatment or other traumas that many youth in foster care have experienced are generally not considered in the design of sex education curricula (Fava & Bay-Cheng, 2013; Lamb & Plocha, 2011). Hence, youth in foster care may inadvertently be retraumatized by curricula that do not recognize the developmental impacts of child maltreatment and other traumas.

Fourth, youth in foster care experience a great deal of instability due to frequent changes in their placements and in their caseworkers. One consequence of this instability is a lack of trusting long-term relationships with adults, and youth in foster care may not feel comfortable discussing sexual and reproductive health with caseworkers, foster parents, or other caregivers who have not yet earned their trust, particularly if they have concerns about the confidentiality of what they share (Gowen & Aue, 2011; Love et al., 2005; Shaw et al., 2010).

Finally, child welfare workers, foster parents, and other caregivers do not always talk with youth in foster care about their sexual and reproductive health (Love et al., 2005). Several factors may contribute to this failure. One is a lack of comfort on the part of many child welfare workers, foster parents, and other caregivers when it comes to talking with youth in foster care about sexual and reproductive health (Constantine et al., 2009; Dworsky & DeCoursey, 2009). Unfortunately, few curricula exist for training child welfare workers, foster parents, or other caregivers on how to talk with youth in foster care about pregnancy prevention or sexual and reproductive health (Dworsky & Dasgupta, 2014) so most child welfare workers, foster parents, and other caregivers do not receive that type of training (Constantine et al., 2009; Shaw et al., 2010).

Another factor contributing to the failure of some child welfare workers, foster parents, and other caregivers to talk with youth in foster care about sexual and reproductive health is religious or moral beliefs (Constantine et al., 2009; Shaw et al., 2010). For example, some faith-based or religiously affiliated child welfare agencies expressly prohibit staff from discussing certain issues, such as contraception, with youth in foster care. Likewise, foster parents or other caregivers may believe that having those discussions sends youth the "wrong message."

Also contributing to the failure of child welfare workers, foster parents, and other caregivers to talk with youth in foster care about sexual and reproductive health is the lack of clear policies or protocols related to who should have those conversations and what they should include (Constantine et al., 2009; Gowen & Aue, 2011; Shaw et al., 2010). The absence of formal guidance for child welfare workers, foster parents, or other caregivers may mean that no one takes responsibility for talking with youth in foster care about healthy sexual development or how to protect themselves against an unwanted pregnancy or sexually transmitted infection.

Use of and Access to Sexual and Reproductive Health Care Services

There are no national or state-level data on the receipt of sexual and reproductive health care services among youth in foster care. Much of what we do know comes from just two studies. Fifteen percent of the 17- and 18-year-old Midwest Study participants and 26 percent of the 17-year-old CalYOUTH Study participants reported that they had received family planning services. Additionally, 24 percent of the Midwest Study participants and 23 percent of the CalYOUTH Study participants reported being tested or treated for an STI (Courtney et al., 2004; Courtney et al., 2014). By comparison, 8 percent of a nationally representative sample of their same-age peers in the general population had received family planning services and 7 percent had been tested or treated for an STI (Courtney et al., 2004).

These data suggest that youth in foster care were more likely to receive family planning services and more likely to have been tested or treated for an STI than a nationally representative sample of their peers. However, the high rate of teenage pregnancy among the female study participants suggests that youth in foster care were also more likely to have been engaging in risky sexual behavior, and hence, were in greater need of services.

Pregnancy Prevention and Sexual Risk Reduction Programs

According to the Office of Adolescent Health, 44 dozen pregnancy prevention programs are currently identified as evidence-based (U.S. Department of Health & Human Services, 2017). However, few evidence-based programs have been developed or adapted for youth in foster care. This is important because cognitive-behavioral and skill-based interventions, which have been shown to be effective with adolescents in the general population, may be less effective with youth in foster care. More specifically, the prevalence of mental health problems and educational deficits, the absence of supportive families or social networks, and high rates of exposure to abuse or other traumas among youth in foster care may compromise their effectiveness.

One important exception is POWER Through Choices (PTC) 2010 (Oklahoma Institute for Child Advocacy & University of Oklahoma National Resource Center for Youth Services, 2010). This comprehensive sexual health, pregnancy prevention, and risk reduction curriculum was specifically designed to address the unique needs of and the risk factors faced by youth in foster care. The PTC 2010 curriculum is an updated version of POWER Through Choices, a curriculum developed in the mid-1990s by the Family Welfare Research Group (FWRG) at the University of California, Berkeley, in response to an unmet need among this population for sexual health education (Becker & Barth, 2000). While the curriculum was never rigorously evaluated, one study found positive effects on knowledge, attitudes, and intentions related to safe sex (Becker & Barth, 2000).

Grounded in four psychosocial theories of behavior (i.e., the health belief model, self-regulation theory, the theory of reasoned action, and social and cognitive learning theory), PTC 2010 aims to empower youth to make healthy, positive choices related to sexual behavior; build contraceptive knowledge and skills; develop and practice effective communication skills; and learn how to locate and access available resources. These short-term outcomes are thought to have long-term effects on a range of behavioral outcomes, including delayed onset of sexual activity, fewer sexual partners, increased use of contraception, and increased condom use. The ultimate goals of the program are to reduce the incidence of teen pregnancy and STIs.

The PTC 2010 curriculum can be used with youth in a wide variety of out-of-home care settings. Ten 90-minute program sessions are delivered once or twice a week for 5 to 10 weeks. The interactive approach engages youth through role-playing activities, group discussion, and other hands-on activities. Compared to the original curriculum, PTC 2010 includes updated data and resource information and is more inclusive with respect to sexual orientation (Meckstroth, Barry, Keating, Kisker, & Andrews, 2014).

As part of the national Evaluation of Adolescent Pregnancy Prevention Approaches (PPA) funded by the Office of Adolescent Health, PTC 2010 was implemented in 44 group homes in Oklahoma, California, and Maryland for youth involved with the child welfare and/or juvenile justice systems. Ninety-seven cohorts of 13 to 18 year olds who were predominantly male (79 percent of the sample) were randomly assigned either to a treatment group (n = 518) that received PTC 2010 or a control group (n = 520) that did not, between January 2012 and June 2014. The evaluation used a "cluster" random assignment design such that all youth in the same group home were assigned to the same condition. Survey data were collected at baseline, after the end of the ten sessions (i.e., short-term), 6 months post-enrollment and 12 months post-enrollment (i.e., long-term).

Approximately 90 percent of the study participants in both the treatment and control groups reported having had sexual intercourse, approximately 70 percent reported having had sexual intercourse by the age of 14, and more than a third reported having been pregnant or having got a partner pregnant. Nevertheless, exposure to the PTC 2010 program had large and statistically significant positive short-term impacts: on receipt of information related to reproductive health; knowledge about reproductive health; perceived ability to communicate with a partner and to avoid unprotected sex; and intentions to avoid unprotected sex by using condoms.

The evaluation also demonstrated a number of significant long-term impacts (Covington et al., 2016). Youth who received the PTC 2010 curriculum were less likely than those who had not received the curriculum to report ever being or having got someone pregnant. The former were also more knowledgeable about STIs, HIV, and methods of birth control; felt more confident about their ability to communicate with a partner about sex; were more likely to report that they planned to use condoms or other methods of birth control and more aware of where to obtain them. However, youth in the treatment group were no less likely than those in the control group to report having had sex without using a condom and having had sex without using other methods of birth control.

Further analysis revealed not only that the negative effects on pregnancy were primarily among youth who were 17 or 18 at baseline, but also that exposure to the PTC 2010 curriculum reduced the likelihood of having had sex in the past 3 months and having had sex without using birth control among those youth. Consequently, PTC 2010 is now identified as an evidence-based program by the U.S. Department of Health & Human Services' Office of Adolescent Health.

Unlike PTC 2010, which was specifically developed with the needs of youth in foster care in mind, Making Proud Choices! is an example of a program that has been adapted for this population. Making Proud Choices! is an interactive, evidence-based sexual health curriculum designed to help adolescents understand behaviors that put them at risk for pregnancy and STIs, and to empower them to reduce this risk through healthy decision making. In 2011, the National Campaign to Prevent Teen and Unplanned Pregnancy began a 3-year project in partnership with the American Public Human Services Association (APHSA) aimed at reducing teen pregnancy rates among youth involved with the child welfare system. With support from the Annie E. Casey Foundation, numerous adaptations to Making Proud Choices! were made (Finley, Antonishak, Suellentrop, & Griesse, 2014). These included recognizing various "family" structures that youth in care may have; emphasizing the role of healthy relationships; providing tips for facilitating the curriculum with youth in care: strengths-based approach, trauma-informed facilitation, respect for diversity, including LGBTQ youth, and preparation for handling disclosures and making referrals.

Five teams of state and local child welfare professionals received technical assistance to implement the ten-module adapted curriculum, Making Proud Choices! for Youth in Out-of-Home Care. The five teams—located in Alameda County (CA), Minnesota, North Carolina, Rhode Island, and Hawaii—established critical partnerships between public health and child welfare organizations and participated in a process evaluation. The curriculum was implemented differently in different sites, and the evaluators were unable to observe the sessions to assess fidelity. However, 85 to 90 percent of the youth who participated in the program reported that they enjoyed it and that they learned more about pregnancy and STI prevention (Finley et al., 2014). Making Proud Choices! for Youth in Out-of-Home Care is also being implemented by some California counties as part of the California Foster Youth Pregnancy Prevention Institute.

Another evidence-based intervention that has been demonstrated to be effective with youth in foster care is Treatment Foster Care Oregon (TFCO), formerly Multidimensional Treatment Foster Care (MTFC). Grounded in social learning theory, TFCO was developed as a community-based alternative to congregate care (e.g., group homes, residential treatment, incarceration) for adolescents with chronic behavior problems. Youth are placed in a structured yet supportive family setting with foster parents who implement a behavior management system, while the caregivers to whom the youth will return develop the skills necessary to maintain the youth at home. Two randomized controlled trials examined the effects of TFCO on female juvenile offenders in Oregon who had been placed in out-of-home care due to chronic delinquency. The average age of the female offenders in both studies was 15 years. Two years after random assignment, the pregnancy rate was approximately 40 percent lower among youth in the TFCO group than among youth in the control group (Kerr, Leve, & Chamberlain, 2009; Leve, Kerr, & Harold, 2013).

Finally, although most pregnancy prevention and sexual risk reduction interventions have targeted youth in foster care, an alternative approach is to focus on the adults who care for and supervise those youth. Dworsky and Dasgupta (2014) published a report detailing the implementation of a training initiative developed by the Illinois Department of Children and Family Services to help both caseworkers and foster parents talk with foster youth about sexual health and pregnancy prevention.

This training has also been implemented as part of the California Foster Youth Pregnancy Prevention Institute by some California counties. An evaluation of the curriculum in Illinois revealed modest increases in comfort in talking about sexual health-related topics, but did not measure the impact on caseworker and foster parent behaviors or foster youth outcomes.

Sexual and Reproductive Health of Youth in Foster Care: Policy Context

Although states across the United States have begun to implement strategies to prevent pregnancy and otherwise improve sexual and reproductive health outcomes among youth in foster care, the impacts of those strategies have yet to be evaluated. More importantly, perhaps, many states lack explicit policies regarding the sexual and reproductive health of youth in foster care. Among the types of policies many states are lacking are the following:

- policies that require caseworkers, foster parents, and other caregivers to provide youth in foster care with age-appropriate and medically accurate information about sexual and reproductive health;
- policies that require caseworkers, foster parents, and other caregivers to help youth in foster care access sexual and reproductive health care services including contraception;
- policies regarding the rights of youth in foster care to consent to and receive sexual and reproductive health care and to have autonomy over decisions about their sexual and reproductive health;
- policies that require training to help caseworkers, foster parents, and other caregivers talk with youth in foster care about sexual and reproductive health;
- policies that require the provision of services and supports that address the needs of pregnant and parenting youth in foster care.

The absence of policies regarding the provision of services and supports for pregnant and parenting youth merits particular attention given the growing number of youth aged 18 and older who are currently in foster care. The Fostering Connections to Success and Increasing Adoptions Act of 2008 (P. L. 110-351) extended Title IV-E eligibility to youth in foster care until their 21st birthday. To qualify, youth must be either enrolled in school, employed, participating in a training program designed to remove barriers to employment, or have a documented medical condition that limits their ability to work or attend school. States are not required to allow youth to remain in foster care beyond the age of 18. However, as of April 2017, 24 states plus the District of Columbia had federally-approved plans to extend Title IV-E foster care to age 21 under the Fostering Connections to Success and Increasing Adoptions Act of 2008.[15]

Because pregnancy and childbearing are more common among adolescents aged 18 and older than among adolescents under the age of 18 (Kost & Maddow-Zimet, 2016; Martin, Hamilton, Osterman, Driscoll, & Mathews, 2017), an increasing number of young women will become pregnant and give birth and an increasing number of young men will father children while in foster care. In the past, many of these youth would already be living on their own by the time they became parents and the child welfare agency would not have been responsible for providing them with services or supports. The extension of federal foster care to age 21 in nearly half the U.S. states, including six of the eight states with the largest foster care populations, means that that is no longer the case.[16]

Finally, because the federal government had not required states to report the number of youth in foster care who are pregnant and/or parents, most states' child welfare agencies do not have a system to track this information. Fortunately, this is likely to change for two reasons. First, the Preventing Sex Trafficking and Strengthening Families Act (P. L. 113-183), which President Obama signed into law in 2014, requires the collection and reporting of state-level data on the number of children in foster care who are pregnant or parenting as part of the annual Child Welfare Outcomes Report to Congress beginning in FY 2016.

Second, the Administration for Children & Families has made several changes to the data that states are required to report to the Adoption and Foster Care Reporting System (AFCARS). These changes include three new elements related to pregnant and parenting youth that states would be required to report: (1) if a female youth in foster care is or was *pregnant*; (2) if a female or male youth in foster care is a *minor parent* (i.e., ever gave birth to or fathered a child); and (3) the number of children living with any *minor parent*. Notice of these proposed rules was issued in February 2015, and a final announcement about their adoption was made in December 2016. Moreover, although the rule refers to minor parents, it also states that a youth in foster care who is aged 18 or older is a "minor parent" if she or he has children. State Title IV-E agencies have two fiscal years to comply with the changes, which means that collection of the new AFCARS data elements will begin October 1, 2019 (Children's Defense Fund, 2017).

Recommendations for Policy and Practice

States need comprehensive pregnancy prevention and sexual risk reduction strategies. These strategies should include a number of different components:

- States need to ensure that youth in foster care receive comprehensive, trauma-informed sex education that includes age-appropriate, medically accurate information about sexual and reproductive health. As already noted, it cannot be assumed that youth in foster care will receive this information from school-based sex education programs. Hence, it is incumbent upon child welfare caseworkers, foster parents, or other caregivers to provide that information. However, in the absence of a clear policy, child welfare caseworkers, foster parents, and other caregivers may choose not to take on that responsibility.
- States need to ensure that youth in foster care have access to sexual and reproductive health care services, including contraceptives. Youth must also be informed about the availability of those health care services and know how to access them.
- States must have clear policies regarding the rights of youth in foster care to consent to and receive sexual and reproductive health care and to have autonomy over decisions about their sexual and reproductive health. These policies should also clarify the right of foster youth to confidentiality when it comes to their receipt of sexual and reproductive health care.
- Caseworkers and caregivers should be required to promote sexual health and help youth in foster care to access sexual and reproductive health care services, including contraception. In the absence of such a requirement, caseworkers and caregivers, including foster parents, may decide that helping youth in foster care to access sexual and reproductive health care is not their responsibility; or they may choose not to help youth in foster care access sexual and reproductive health care, because doing so would be contrary to their moral or religious beliefs.
- Caseworkers and caregivers (foster parents and group care staff) should be trained to talk about sexual and reproductive health and risky sexual behaviors with youth in foster care. Foster parents and caseworkers need training to develop competencies in talking with foster youth about pregnancy prevention and other issues related to sexual health.
- States need to provide pregnant and parenting youth in foster care with comprehensive services and support that address their developmental needs and help them with the adult responsibilities of being a parent. This includes connecting pregnant and parenting youth in foster care with home-visiting programs that have been demonstrated to be effective in reducing child abuse, improving health outcomes, preparing children for school, and linking families to needed services

- States need to implement interventions to youth in foster care to reduce high-risk sexual behaviors, promote good sexual decision making, and help youth to avoid early pregnancy and STIs. This may require making adaptations to sex education curricula to ensure materials are inclusive and meet the needs of over-represented subpopulations, such as youth of color and youth who identify as LGBTQ. These interventions must help youth overcome the antecedents of teenage pregnancy: low self-esteem, low expectations for the future, disengagement from school, growing up in poor and violent neighborhoods, lack of role models and caring relationships with adults, and lack of information about and access to birth control. Moreover, because placement instability can make it more difficult to reach youth in care with pregnancy prevention services, these interventions must be flexible enough to accommodate youth in different placement settings and frequent placement changes.

Areas for Future Research

As alluded to throughout this chapter, there are critical gaps in our knowledge about the sexual and reproductive health of youth in foster care. Each of these gaps represents an opportunity for future research. Some of these opportunities are briefly discussed below.

Need for Additional Data Collection

To date, estimates of pregnancy and birth rates among youth in foster care have come from a limited number of studies and none of those estimates has been national in scope. One approach that has been used to estimate state-specific birth rates for youth in foster care is to link child welfare data to vital statistics records. Moving forward, states will be required to track and report the number of youth in foster care who are pregnant and the number who are parents. Researchers can use these data to identify predictors of pregnancy and parenthood. With this information, pregnancy prevention interventions can be targeted to those at greatest risk.

More data are also needed on the use of sexual and reproductive health care services by youth in foster care and on barriers to accessing those services. These data could be used to identify subgroups of youth in foster care who are not receiving sexual and reproductive health care services. Once these subgroups have been identified, strategies to increase their access to sexual and reproductive health care services could be developed and implemented.

Apart from a relatively small number of studies, most notably the National Survey of Child and Adolescent Well-Being (NSCAW), not much is known about the prevalence of sexual risk behaviors among youth in foster care. Likewise, few studies have examined the prevalence of STIs among this population. Collecting additional data on the prevalence of sexual risk behaviors and STIs among youth in foster care should be a priority so that interventions can be targeted at youth who are most likely to engage in risky sexual behaviors or to contract an STI.

Finally, although states across the United States have begun to implement strategies to prevent pregnancy and otherwise improve sexual and reproductive health outcomes among youth in foster care, the strategies they are implementing have not been systematically documented. Documenting those strategies is important for two reasons. First, unless those strategies are documented, they cannot be evaluated. Second, states cannot learn from one another in the absence of documentation.

Sexual and Reproductive Health among Over-Represented Subpopulations

Youth of color and youth who identify as LGBTQ are over-represented among youth in foster care. However, differences in sexual and reproductive behaviors based on race/ethnicity or sexual orientation have not been a focus of research. Although the need for more inclusive sexual education curricula has been recognized, studies have not examined the sexual and reproductive health care needs of youth of color or youth who identify as LGBTQ. Nor has sufficient attention been paid to the unique challenges *that* youth of color or youth who identify as LGBTQ may face *in* accessing sexual and reproductive health care services.

Evaluation

Although the Office of Adolescent Health has begun to fund evaluations of pregnancy prevention and sexual risk reduction programs targeting youth in foster care, there are relatively few programs that have been shown to be effective at preventing pregnancy or reducing sexual risk behaviors among this population. This is important because evidence-based programs will not necessarily be effective when implemented with youth in foster care, or may only be effective if some adaptations are made.

Increasingly, the need for training aimed at helping caseworkers, foster parents, and other caregivers to promote the sexual and reproductive health of youth in foster care is being recognized. However, there are currently no evidence-based training programs for caseworkers, foster parents, or other caregivers. As programs are developed to train caseworkers, foster parents, and other caregivers to talk with youth in foster care about their sexual and reproductive health and to help those youth access sexual and reproductive health care, the implementation and impact of those training programs should be evaluated.

Youth Voice

It is important for future research on the sexual and reproductive health of youth in foster care to incorporate the voices of youth. Capturing the perspectives of youth is critical in studies that seek to understand the sexual and reproductive health care needs of this population, the reasons they engage in (or do not avoid) sexual risk behaviors, and their motivations for becoming pregnant (or for not avoiding pregnancy). Incorporating youth voice is best accomplished with qualitative methods such as focus groups or in-depth interviews. Researchers could even use a timeline narrative approach to examine how the sexual behavior of youth in foster care changes over time and in response to other life circumstances.

Development of Theoretical Framework

Finally, some studies of sexual and reproductive health behavior among youth in foster care have been informed by theoretical frameworks that incorporate our understanding of adolescent development (i.e., developmental theory) with existing knowledge about the effects of various risk and protective factors at individual, family, peer, community, and systems levels (i.e., ecological theory). That said, much of the research in this area has not been theory-driven. This a-theoretical approach to research is not unique to research on the sexual and reproductive health behaviors of youth in foster care. Rather, it is characteristic of child welfare research on youth in foster care more generally. To move the field forward, future research should be guided by theoretical frameworks that have been used to understand adolescent sexual and reproductive health behaviors from a developmental perspective.

Conclusion

Growing evidence that youth in foster care are engaging in early and unprotected sexual behavior, becoming pregnant, and giving birth to or fathering children at higher rates than their same-age peers who are not in foster care has led to increased attention to their sexual and reproductive health. Despite some progress, there are still critical gaps in federal and state policies to address the sexual and reproductive health care needs of youth in foster care, in the evidence-base for interventions aimed at preventing pregnancy and promoting sexual health among this population, and in our understanding of their sexual and reproductive health behaviors.

Notes

1. Additional information about the Add Health research design can be found at www.cpc.unc.edu/projects/addhealth/design
2. Results were not reported separately by gender.
3. Results were not reported separately for youth who had been in foster care.
4. Youth Risk Behavior Surveillance System overview: www.cdc.gov/healthyyouth/data/yrbs/overview.htm
5. The YRBSS asks about condom and contraceptive use during last sexual intercourse, so the rates cannot be compared.
6. Nine percent were placed in a non-relative or kinship foster home, a group home, or a residential treatment setting. The other 4 percent were living informally with relative or non-relative caregivers.
7. About the National Survey of Family Growth: www.cdc.gov/nchs/nsfg/about_nsfg.htm
8. These percentages include youth who had never had consensual sex.
9. The percentage of young women who had become pregnant since the baseline interview was not reported separately for those who were still in care and those who were no longer in care.
10. Additional information about NYTD can be found at www.acf.hhs.gov/cb/resource/about-nytd?page=all
11. States with a large number of youth in foster care may collect the follow-up data from a random sample of the youth from whom baseline data were collected at age 17.
12. The cumulative percentage of 19-year-old females in the NYTD sample who had given birth was not reported.
13. The cumulative percentage of 19-year-old males in the NYTD sample who had fathered a child was not reported.
14. See discussion below about barriers to educating youth in foster care about sexual and reproductive health.
15. States with federally-approved plans for extended foster care (EFC) include Alabama, Arkansas, California, Connecticut, District of Columbia, Hawai'i, Illinois, Indiana, Maine, Maryland, Massachusetts, Michigan, Minnesota, Nebraska, New York, North Dakota, Oregon, Pennsylvania, Tennessee, Texas, Virginia, Washington, West Virginia, and Wisconsin. Indiana only extended foster care to age 20. Tennessee and West Virginia limit EFC to youth completing high school or pursuing postsecondary education, and Wisconsin limits EFC to youth completing high school. North Carolina is in the process of obtaining approval of its plan.
16. The eight states with the largest foster care populations in 2015 were California, Texas, Florida, New York, Arizona, Indiana, Illinois, and Pennsylvania. Child Trends analysis of data from the Adoption and Foster Care Analysis and Reporting System (AFCARS), made available through the National Data Archive on Child Abuse and Neglect. Retrieved July 5, 2017 from http://datacenter.kidscount.org/data/tables/6243-children-in-foster-care#detailed/2/2-52/false/573,869,36,868,867/any/12987

References

Adoption and Safe Families Act [ASFA], Public Law 105-89. (1997).
Aherns, K., Richardson, L., Courtney, M., McCarty, C., Simoni, J., & Katon, W. (2010). Laboratory-diagnosed sexually transmitted infections in former foster youth compared with peers. *Pediatrics, 126*(1), 97–103.
Anthonysamy, A., & Zimmer-Gembeck, M. J. (2007). Peer status and the behaviors of maltreated children and their classmates in the early years of school. *Child Abuse & Neglect, 31*, 971–991.
Auslander, W., McMillen, J. C., Elze, D., Thompson, R., Jonson-Reid, M., & Stiffman, A. (2002). Mental health problems and sexual abuse among adolescents in foster care: Relationship to HIV risk behaviors and intentions. *AIDS & Behavior, 6*(4), 351–359.
Bartlett, J., & Easterbrooks, A. (2012). Links between physical abuse in childhood and child neglect among adolescent mothers. *Children and Youth Services Review, 34*, 2164–2169.
Becker, G. S. (1993). *Human capital: A theoretical and empirical analysis with special reference to education.* Chicago: University of Chicago Press.
Becker, M., & Barth, R. (2000). Power through choices: The development of a sexuality education curriculum for youths in out-of-home care. *Child Welfare, 79*(3), 269–282.

Biglan, A. (2014). *A comprehensive framework for nurturing the well being of children and adolescents.* Washington, DC: Children's Bureau.

Black, M., Oberlander, S., Lewis, T., Knight, E., Zolotor, A., Litrownik, A., . . . English, D. (2009). Sexual intercourse among adolescents maltreated before age 12: A prospective investigation. *Pediatrics, 124*(3), 941–949.

Borkowski, J., Whitman, T., & Farris, J. (2007). Adolescent mothers and their children: Risks, resilience, and development. In J. Borkowski, J. Farris, T. Whitman, S. Carothers, K. Weed, & D. Keogh (Eds.), *Risk and resilience: Adolescent mothers and their children grow up* (pp. 1–34). Mahwah, NJ: Lawrence Erlbaum.

Briere, J. (1996). A self-trauma model for treating adult survivors of severe child abuse. In J. Briere, L. Berliner, J. Bulkley, C. Jenny, & T. Reid (Eds.), *The APSAC handbook on child maltreatment* (pp. 175–203). Thousand Oaks, CA: Sage.

Brown, L., Hadley, W., Stewart, A., Lescano, C., Whiteley, L., Donenberg, G., & DiClemente, R. (2010). Psychiatric disorders and sexual risk among adolescents in mental health treatment. *Journal of Consulting and Clinical Psychology, 78*(4), 590–597.

Centers for Disease Control and Prevention. (2017). *Youth Risk Behavior Surveillance System (YRBSS) overview.* Atlanta, GA: Division of Adolescent and School Health, National Center for HIV/AIDS, Viral Hepatitis, STD, and TB Prevention.

Children's Bureau. (2014). *National Youth in Transition Database data brief #4: Comparing outcomes reported by young people at ages 17 and 19 in NYTD Cohort 1.* Washington, DC: Children's Bureau.

Children's Defense Fund. (2017). *The Adoption and Foster Care Analysis and Reporting System (AFCARS): Final rule.* Washington, DC: Children's Defense Fund.

Coley, R., & Chase-Lansdale, L. (1998). Adolescent pregnancy and parenthood. Recent evidence and future directions. *American Psychologist, 53*(2),152–166.

Connelly, C., & Straus, M. (1992). Mother's age and risk for physical abuse. *Child Abuse & Neglect, 16*(5), 709–718.

Constantine, W., Jerman, P., & Constantine, N. (2009). *Sex education and reproductive health needs of foster and transitioning youth in three California counties.* Oakland, CA: Center for Research on Adolescent Health and Development, Public Health Institute.

Cook, A., Spinazzola, J., Ford, J., Lanktree, C., Blaustein, M., Cloitre, M., . . . van der Kolk, B. (2005). Complex trauma in children and adolescents. *Psychiatric Annals, 35*(5), 390–398.

Courtney, M., Charles, P., Okpych, N., Napolitano, L., & Halsted, K. (2014). *Findings from the California Youth Transitions to Adulthood Study: Conditions of foster youth at age 17.* Chicago: Chapin Hall at the University of Chicago.

Courtney, M., Dworsky, A., Lee, J., & Raap, M. (2010). *Midwest Evaluation of the Adult Functioning of Former Foster Youth: Outcomes at ages 23 and 24.* Chicago: Chapin Hall at the University of Chicago.

Courtney, M., Dworsky, A., Ruth, G., Havlicek, J., Perez, A., & Keller, T. (2007). *Midwest Evaluation of the Adult Functioning of Former Foster Youth: Outcomes at age 21.* Chicago: Chapin Hall at the University of Chicago.

Courtney, M., Dworsky, A., Ruth, G., Keller, T., Havlicek, J., & Bost, N. (2005). *Midwest Evaluation of the Adult Functioning of Former Foster Youth: Outcomes at age 19.* Chicago: Chapin Hall at the University of Chicago.

Courtney, M., Okpych, N., Charles, P., Mikell, D., Stevenson, B., Park, K., . . . Feng. H. (2016). *Findings from the California Youth Transitions to Adulthood Study: Conditions of youth at age 19.* Chicago: Chapin Hall at the University of Chicago.

Courtney, M., Terao, S., & Bost, N. (2004). *Midwest Evaluation of the Adult Functioning of Former Foster Youth: Conditions of youth preparing to leave state care.* Chicago: Chapin Hall at the University of Chicago.

Covington, R. D., Goesling, B., Tuttle, C., Crofton, M., Manlove, J., Oman, R., & Vesely, S. (2016). *Final impacts of the POWER Through Choices program.* Washington, DC: U.S. Department of Health & Human Services, Office of Adolescent Health.

De Bellis, M. (2001). Developmental traumatology: The psychobiological development of maltreated children and its implications for research, treatment, and policy. *Development and Psychopathology, 13*, 537–561.

Dolan, M., Smith, K., Casanueva, C., & Ringeisen, H. (2011). *NSCAW II baseline report: Introduction to NSCAW II* (OPRE Report #2011-27a). Washington, DC: Office of Planning, Research and Evaluation, Administration for Children and Families, U.S. Department of Health & Human Services.

Donenberg, G., & Pao, M. (2005). Youth and HIV/AIDS: Psychiatry's role in a changing epidemic. *Journal of the American Academy of Child and Adolescent Psychiatry, 44*, 728–747.

Dworsky, A. (2015). Child welfare services involvement among the children of young parents in foster care. *Child Abuse & Neglect, 45*, 68–79.

Dworsky, A., & Courtney, M. E. (2010). The risk of teenage pregnancy among transitioning foster youth: Implications for extending state care beyond age 18. *Children and Youth Services Review, 32*, 1351–1356.

Dworsky, A., & Crayton, C. (2009). *National Youth in Transition Database: Instructional guidebook and architectural blueprint*. Washington, DC and Chicago: American Public Human Services Association, Chapin Hall at the University of Chicago, and Center for State Foster Care and Adoption Data.

Dworsky, A., & Dasgupta, D. (2014). *Preventing pregnancy and promoting sexual health among youth in care: Results from the evaluation of a training for caregivers and child welfare workers*. Chicago: Chapin Hall at the University of Chicago.

Dworsky, A., & DeCoursey, J. (2009). *Pregnant and parenting foster youth: Their needs, their experiences*. Chicago: Chapin Hall at the University of Chicago.

Fava, N., & Bay-Cheng, L. (2013). Trauma-informed sexuality education: Recognizing the rights and resilience of youth. *Sex Education: Sexuality, Society and Learning, 13*(4), 383–394.

Fine, M., & McClelland, S. (2006). Sexuality education and desire: Still missing after all these years. *Harvard Educational Review, 76*(3), 297–338.

Finley, C., Antonishak, J., Suellentrop, K., & Griesse, R. (2014). Making MPC+ matter. *Policy & Practice, 72*(6), 16–19.

Fletcher, J., & Wolfe, B. (2009). Education and labor market consequences of teenage childbearing. *Journal of Human Resources, 44*, 303–325.

Fortenberry, J. D. (2013). Puberty and adolescent sexuality. *Hormones and Behavior, 64*(2), 280–287.

Foster Care Independence Act of 1999, Public Law 106-169. (1999).

Geronimus A. (1991). Teenage childbearing and social reproductive disadvantage: The evolution of complex questions and the demise of simple answers. *Family Relations, 40*, 463–471.

Geronimus, A., Korenman, S., & Hillemeier. M. (1994). Does young maternal age adversely affect child development? Evidence from cousin comparisons in the United States. *Population and Development Review, 20*(3), 585–609.

Goerge, R., Harden, A., & Lee, B. (2008). Consequences of teen childbearing for child abuse, neglect, and foster care placement. In S. Hoffman & R. Maynard (Eds.), *Kids having kids: Economic costs and social consequences of teen pregnancy* (pp. 257–288). Washington, DC: The Urban Institute Press.

Gowen, L., & Aue, N. (Eds.). (2011). *Sexual health disparities among disenfranchised youth*. Portland, OR: Public Health Division, Oregon Health Authority and Research and Training Center for Pathways to Positive Futures, Portland State University.

Harris, K., Halpern, C., Whitsel, E., Hussey, J., Tabor, J., Entzel, P., & Udry, J. (2009). *The National Longitudinal Study of Adolescent to Adult Health: Research design*. Retrieved 7/3/2017 from www.cpc.unc.edu/projects/addhealth/design.

Hillier, L., & Mitchell, A. (2008). It was as useful as a chocolate kettle: Sex education in the lives of same-sex-attracted young people in Australia. *Sex Education, 8*(2), 211–224.

Hoffman, S. (2006). *By the numbers: The public costs of teen childbearing*. Washington, DC: National Campaign to Prevent Teen and Unplanned Pregnancy.

Hudson, A. (2012). Where do youth in foster care receive information about preventing unplanned pregnancy and sexually transmitted infections? *Journal of Pediatric Nursing, 27*(5), 443–450.

Jaffee, S., Caspi, A., Moffitt, T., Belsky, J., & Silva, P. (2001). Why are children born to teen mothers at risk for adverse outcomes in young adulthood? Results from a 20-year longitudinal study. *Developmental Psychopathology, 13*(2), 377–397.

James, S., Montgomery S., Leslie, L., & Zhang, J. (2009). Sexual risk behaviors among youth in the child welfare system. *Children and Youth Services Review, 31*(9), 990–1000.

Kerr, D., Leve, L., & Chamberlain, P. (2009). Pregnancy rates among juvenile justice girls in two randomized controlled trials of Multidimensional Treatment Foster Care. *Journal of Consulting and Clinical Psychology, 77*, 588–593.

Kim, J., & Cicchetti, D. (2010). Longitudinal pathways linking child maltreatment, emotion regulation, peer relations, and psychopathology. *Journal of Child Psychology and Psychiatry, 51*(6), 706–716.

King, B., Putnam-Hornstein, E., Cederbaum, J. A., & Needell, B. (2014). A cross-sectional examination of birth rates among adolescent girls in foster care. *Children and Youth Services Review, 36*, 179–186.

Kost, K., & Maddow-Zimet, I. (2016). *U.S. teenage pregnancies, births and abortions, 2011: National and state trends and trends by age, race and ethnicity*. New York, NY: Guttmacher Institute.

Lamb, S., & Plocha, A. (2011). The underlying ethics in sex education: What are the needs of vulnerable groups? In D. J. deRuyter & S. Miedema (Eds.), *Moral education and development* (pp. 163–177). Rotterdam: Sense.

Lee, D. (2010). The early socioeconomic effects of teenage childbearing. *Demographic Research, 23*, 697–736.

Leslie L., James, S., Monn, A., Kauten, M., Zhang, J., & Aarons, G. (2010). Health-risk behaviors in young adolescents in the child welfare system. *Journal of Adolescent Health, 47*(1), 26–34.

Leve, L., Kerr, D., & Harold, G. (2013). Young adult outcomes associated with teen pregnancy among high-risk girls in a randomized controlled trial of Multidimensional Treatment Foster Care. *Journal of Child & Adolescent Substance Abuse, 22*(5), 421–434.

Levine, D., & Painter, G. (2003). The schooling costs of teenage out-of-wedlock childbearing: Analysis with a within-school propensity-score-matching estimator. *Review of Economics and Statistics, 85*, 884–900.

Levine, J., Emery, C., & Pollack, H. (2007), The well-being of children born to teen mothers. *Journal of Marriage and Family, 69*, 105–122.

Love, L., McIntosh, J., Rosst, M., & Tertzakian, K. (2005). *Fostering hope: Preventing teen pregnancy among youth in foster care.* Washington, DC: National Campaign to Prevent Teen and Unplanned Pregnancy.

Martin, J., Hamilton, B., Osterman, M., Driscoll, A., & Mathews, T. (2017). *Births: Final data for 2015.* National Vital Statistics Reports, Vol. 66, No. 1. Hyattsville, MD: National Center for Health Statistics.

Martinez, G., Copen, C., & Abma, J. (2011). *Teenagers in the United States: Sexual activity, contraceptive use, and childbearing, 2006–2010 National Survey of Family Growth.* Vital and Health Statistics Series, Vol. 23. Washington, DC: National Center for Health Statistics.

McMillen, J. C., Zima, B., Scott, L., Auslander, W., Munson, M., Ollie M., & Spitznagel, E. (2005). Prevalence of psychiatric disorders among older youths in the foster care system. *Journal of the American Academy of Child & Adolescent Psychiatry, 44*(1), 88–95.

Meckstroth, A., Barry, B., Keating, B., Kisker, E., & Andrews, K. (2014). *Addressing teen pregnancy risks for youth living in out-of-home care: Implementing POWER Through Choices 2010.* Washington, DC: Office of Adolescent Health, U.S. Department of Health & Human Services.

Miller, B., Benson, B., & Galbraith, K. (2001). Family relationships and adolescent pregnancy risk: A research synthesis. *Developmental Review, 21*(1), 1–38.

Ng, A., & Kaye, K. (2012). *Why it matters: Teen childbearing, education, and economic wellbeing.* Washington, DC: National Campaign to Prevent Teen and Unplanned Pregnancy.

Noll, J., Haralson, K., Butler, E., & Shenk, C. (2011). Child maltreatment, psychological dysregulation and risky sexual behaviors in female adolescents. *Journal of Pediatric Psychology, 36*(7), 743–752.

Noria, C., Weed, K., & Keogh, D. (2007). The fate of adolescent mothers. In J. Borkowski, J. Farris, T. Whitman, S. Carothers, K. Weed, & D. Keogh (Eds.), *Risk and resilience: Adolescent mothers and their children grow up* (pp. 35–68). Mahwah, NJ: Lawrence Erlbaum.

NSCAW Research Group. (2001). *National Survey of Child and Adolescent Well-Being (NSCAW) description and information.* Ithaca, NY: Cornell University, National Data Archive on Child Abuse and Neglect.

NSCAW Research Group. (2010). *National Survey of Child and Adolescent Well-Being: Overview of NSCAW and NSCAW II, and main findings of NSCAW.* Ithaca, NY: Cornell University Summer Research Institute.

Oklahoma Institute for Child Advocacy, & University of Oklahoma National Resource Center for Youth Services. (2010). *POWER Through Choices: Sexuality education for youth in foster and group care.* Oklahoma City, OK: OICA & NRCYS.

Oshima, K., Narendorf, S., & McMillen, J. C., (2013). Pregnancy risk among older youth transitioning out of foster care. *Children and Youth Services Review, 35*(10), 1760–1765.

Parkes, A., Henderson, M., Wight, D., & Nixon, C. (2011). Is parenting associated with teenagers' early sexual risk-taking, autonomy and relationship with sexual partners? *Perspectives on Sexual and Reproductive Health, 43*(1), 30–40.

Perper, K., Peterson, K., & Manlove, J. (2010). *Diploma attainment among teen mothers.* Fact Sheet, #2010-01. Washington, DC: Child Trends.

Putnam, F. (2003). Ten-year research update review: Child sexual abuse. *Journal of the American Academy of Child and Adolescent Psychiatry, 43*, 269–278.

Putnam-Horstein, E., Cederbaum, J., King, B., & Needell, B. (2013). *California's most vulnerable parents: When maltreated children have children.* Agoura Hills, CA: Conrad Hilton Foundation.

Putnam-Hornstein, E, & King, B. (2014). Cumulative teen birth rates among girls in foster care at age 17: An analysis of linked birth and child protection records from California. *Child Abuse & Neglect, 38*(4), 698–705.

Ramseyer Winter, V., Brandon-Friedman, R., & Ely, G. (2016). Sexual health behaviors and outcomes among current and former foster youth: A review of the literature. *Children and Youth Services Review, 64*, 1–14.

Schloredt, K., & Heiman, J. (2003). Perceptions of sexuality as related to sexual functioning and sexual risk in women with different types of childhood abuse histories. *Journal of Traumatic Stress, 16*(3), 275–284.

Senn, T., Carey, M., & Vanable, P. (2008). Childhood and adolescent sexual abuse and subsequent sexual risk behavior: Evidence from controlled studies, methodological critique, and suggestions for research. *Clinical Psychology Review, 28*(5), 711–735.

Shaw, T., Barth, R., Svoboda, D., & Shaikh, N. (2010). *Fostering safe choices: Final report.* Baltimore, MD: University of Maryland, Baltimore, School of Social Work, Ruth H. Young Center for Families and Children.

Shin, S. (2005). Need for and actual use of mental health service by adolescents in the child welfare system. *Children and Youth Services Review, 27*(10), 1071–1083.

Stier, D., Leventhal, J., Berg, A., Johnson, L., & Mezger, J. (1993). Are children born to young mothers at increased risk of maltreatment? *Pediatrics, 91,* 642–648.

Sullivan, C., Sommer, C., & Moff, J. (2001). *Youth in the margins: A report on the unmet needs of lesbian, gay, bisexual, and transgender adolescents in foster care.* New York, NY: Lambda Legal Defense and Education Fund.

Svoboda, D., Shaw, T., Barth, R., & Bright, C. (2012). Pregnancy and parenting among youth in foster care: A review. *Children and Youth Services Review, 34,* 867–875.

Taussig, H. (2002). Risk behaviors in maltreated youth placed in foster care: A longitudinal study of protective and vulnerability factors. *Child Abuse & Neglect, 26*(11), 1179–1199.

Trickett, P., Noll, J., & Putnam, F. (2011). The impact of sexual abuse on female development: Lessons from a multigenerational, longitudinal research study. *Development and Psychopathology, 23*(2), 453–476.

U.S. Department of Health & Human Services (Office of Adolescent Health). (2017). *Evidence-based teen pregnancy prevention programs at a glance.* Washington, DC: Office of Adolescent Health.

Ventura, S., Hamilton, B., & Mathews, T. (2014). *National and state patterns of teen births in the United States, 1940–2013.* National Vital Statistics Reports, Vol. 63, No. 4. Hyattsville, MD: National Center for Health Statistics.

Wilson, E., Casanueva, C., Smith, K., Koo, H., Tueller, S., & Webb, M. (2014). Risk of early sexual initiation and pregnancy among youth reported to the child welfare system. *Child Welfare, 93,* 127–147.

Wilson, H., & Widom, C. (2008). An examination of risky sexual behavior and HIV among victims of child abuse and neglect: A thirty-year follow-up. *Health Psychology, 27,* 149–158.

9

Substance Use and Addiction Problems in Foster Youth

Jordan M. Braciszewski

Introduction

Annually, reports of abuse and neglect affect over 7 million youth (U.S. Department of Health & Human Services, 2017). Due to the profound impact this can have on a person's life trajectory, public health officials have asserted that maltreatment, in its various forms (e.g., physical abuse, sexual abuse, neglect), warrants as much research attention as other concerns affecting young people, such as HIV/AIDS, smoking, and obesity (Butchart, Harvey, Mian, & Furniss, 2006). Although maltreatment is related to myriad negative outcomes, it appears to have a uniquely strong relationship with alcohol and drug use (Dube et al., 2003; Dube et al., 2006). Exposure to Adverse Childhood Experiences (ACEs)—including physical/emotional neglect, physical/sexual/emotional abuse, domestic violence, parental substance use, parental mental illness, parental separation, and parental incarceration—is strongly related to youth substance use. While exposure to any one ACE corresponds to a significantly increased likelihood of using alcohol or drugs, the cumulative exposure to multiple ACEs exponentially increases risk for youth substance use (Dube et al., 2003; Dube et al., 2006).

As can be expected, ACEs are significantly more common and accumulate more frequently among youth in foster care (Stambaugh et al., 2013). For example, exposure to four or more ACEs is 50 times more likely among foster youth than among young people raised in two-parent families (Bramlett & Radel, 2014). It follows, then, that substance use among foster youth may happen earlier (Gabrielli, Jackson, & Brown, 2016) and involves higher prevalence rates of both "hard" drug use and substance use disorders (Braciszewski & Stout, 2012).

Comprehensive knowledge about foster youth substance use, however, is limited, with several barriers to accurate data collection (Braciszewski & Stout, 2012; Brook, Rifenbark, Boulton, Little, & McDonald, 2015). This chapter presents an overview of the extant literature, applies a theoretical framework to foster youth substance use, and offers steps that the child welfare system, researchers, and others can take to bridge the gap between knowledge and service.

Status of the Field

Youth in Care

There is little doubt that foster youth are at increased *vulnerability* for developing substance use problems. In addition to the high prevalence of ACEs, caregiver alcohol and drug use are also highly prevalent in this population, with parental substance abuse rates ranging from 16% to 61% (Courtney et al., 2014; Young, Boles, & Otero, 2007). As a result, foster youth may develop positive social norms about substance use (Haight, Ostler, Black, Sheridan, & Kingery, 2007)—feeling that substance use is normative and accepted—which is subsequently associated with increased likelihood of alcohol and drug use (Borsari & Carey, 2003; Neighbors, Geisner, & Lee, 2008). Academic success is related to a lower likelihood of substance use (D'Amico, Ellickson, Collins, Martino, & Klein, 2005); however, educational attainment among foster youth is low, as recently reported rates of high school graduation have ranged from 45% (Frerer, Sosenko, & Henke, 2013) to 66% (Courtney et al., 2016), well below the national rate of 88% (Harris et al., 2009). Although the relationship between academic achievement and substance use can be reciprocal, with early substance use leading to poor academic outcomes (King, Meehan, Trim, & Chassin, 2006) and school struggles predicting substance use disorders (Fothergill et al., 2008), attention to the low rates of academic success among foster youth is paramount.

While strong evidence exists for increased vulnerability for substance abuse, actual measurement of substance use among foster youth is varied. Specifically, few studies have used a common age range or developmental period (e.g., younger adolescents, older adolescents, all adolescents), time frame (e.g., past month, 3 months, year), substance (e.g., alcohol, marijuana, all drugs, all "hard" drugs), outcome (e.g., use, diagnosis), or matched comparison group. This substantial measurement variability across studies has led to mixed findings on whether foster youth actually *engage* in substance use at a level beyond that of their general population peers.

Two nationally-representative, general population studies often serve as the gold standard for epidemiological data on youth substance use and are, thus, useful for comparison with foster youth. Monitoring the Future (MTF) began in 1975 and is an ongoing annual study of alcohol, drug, and tobacco use among 40,000 to 50,000 8th, 10th, and 12th Graders across the United States, sponsored by the National Institute on Drug Abuse. The National Survey on Drug Use and Health (NSDUH) is sponsored by the Substance Abuse and Mental Health Services Administration (SAMHSA) and collects substance use and mental health data on approximately 70,000 randomly selected U.S. citizens each year. While a number of methodological differences exist between these two studies, contributing to their variable estimates, they are still widely considered to be the preeminent studies of youth substance use (SAMHSA, 2012).

With regard to lifetime alcohol use (i.e., having ever drunk alcohol in one's life, usually more than just a sip), rates have ranged from 40% to 65% among youth in foster care (Kohlenberg, Nordlund, Lowin, & Treichler, 2002; McDonald, Mariscal, Yan, & Brook, 2014; Siegel, Benbenishty, & Astor, 2016; Zhan, Smith, Warner, North, & Wilhelm, 2016). When compared to the above referenced nationally-representative studies, foster youth seem similar to MTF participants (46%; Johnston, O'Malley, Miech, Bachman, & Schulenberg, 2016),[1] but report much higher rates than NSDUH participants (28%; Center for Behavioral Health Statistics and Quality [CBHSQ], 2016). A similar pattern is seen with recent alcohol use (defined loosely as during the past 6 or 12 months); 34% to 40% of youth in foster care have drunk recently (Kohlenberg et al., 2002; Pilowsky & Wu, 2006; Shin, 2004; Thompson & Auslander, 2007; Vaughn, Ollie, McMillen, Scott, & Munson, 2007), which is similar to MTF respondents (40%) and more than NSDUH participants (23%). A more detailed examination of NSDUH data indicated that respondents who had a history of foster care placement were significantly more likely to have drunk in the past year (Pilowsky & Wu, 2006). Current drinking (within the past month), however, seems to occur less often among youth in care (7% to 13%; Kohlenberg et al., 2002; Zhan et al., 2016) compared to MTF (22%) and NSDUH (9.6%) respondents. While slightly higher rates have been reported (32%), they were not significantly different from a matched comparison group (30%; McDonald et al., 2014). Indeed, only one study has demonstrated more frequent alcohol use in the past month among youth in care (35% versus 23%; Siegel et al., 2016).

When examining marijuana use, the same pattern emerges; higher lifetime and recent marijuana use rates for youth in foster care compared to the general population. Specifically, lifetime marijuana use is reported by 16% and 30% of NSDUH and MTF respondents, respectively, while past year rates are 13% and 24% (CBHSQ, 2016; Johnston et al., 2016). Among youth in foster care, 38% to 46% have smoked marijuana in their lifetime, while recent use falls between 20% and 68% (Kohlenberg et al., 2002; McDonald et al., 2014; Pilowsky & Wu, 2006; Smith, Chamberlain, & Eddy, 2010; Thompson & Auslander, 2007; Vaughn et al., 2007; Zhan et al., 2016). However, just as with alcohol, examination of current marijuana use suggests that foster youth are at the same level (Kohlenberg et al., 2002; McDonald et al., 2014) or significantly lower (Zhan et al., 2016) than their general population counterparts.

Data on non-marijuana drug use are also scant, particularly with regard to research that directly compares foster youth and young people without such a history. Non-statistical comparisons with a matched sample by Kohlenberg et al. (2002) indicated that lifetime use of hallucinogens, stimulants, non-street opioids, and cocaine were all higher among foster youth. Comparing these data, as well as reports from Vaughn et al. (2007), to NSDUH data indicates a shockingly high lifetime prevalence of "hard" drug use. Specifically, Kohlenberg et al. (2002) and Vaughn et al. (2007) indicated use of hallucinogens (12%–13.5%), stimulants (12.1%), opioids/heroin (6% to 9.8%), cocaine (5.5% to 7%), and amphetamines (16%), all of which were substantially higher than NSDUH respondents' reports, where lifetime prevalence rates were less than 1% for these drugs. Recent drug use is also high among foster youth, with Thompson and Auslander (2011) reporting rates of heroin, cocaine, and hallucinogen use at least twice as high as NSDUH participants. In an analysis of NSDUH data that directly compared foster and non-foster youth drug use, foster youth were significantly more likely to have used drugs in the past year (34% versus 18%; Pilowsky & Wu, 2006). A more recent study indicated that foster youth were more likely to report lifetime and current use of inhalants, ecstasy, hallucinogens, cocaine, methamphetamines, steroids, and heroin compared to non-foster youth (McDonald et al., 2014).

In terms of substance use disorders (SUDs), the outlook remains grim. Again, using NSDUH data, Pilowsky and Wu (2006) reported that foster youth were almost five times more likely than non-foster youth to meet criteria for substance dependence in the past year (9.8% versus 2.2%). When all past year substance use diagnoses (i.e., alcohol or any other drug, abuse or dependence) were considered, foster youth were between two and four times more likely to meet diagnostic criteria. In one of the largest studies of foster youth (the Midwest Study), Keller, Salazar, & Courtney (2010) interviewed 732 youth in care and reported lifetime rates of alcohol abuse (9.8%), alcohol dependence (4%), and substance dependence (4.8%) were all higher than corresponding national general population data (CBHSQ, 2016). Finally, the Casey Field Office Mental Health Study (White, Havalchak, Jackson, O'Brien, & Pecora, 2007) examined mental health disorders among 188 foster youth (age 14–17) being served by Casey Family Programs, a national leader in foster care services and advocacy. In addition to youth assessments, authors provided a weighted comparison between their data on foster youth and the National Comorbidity Survey–Adolescent (NCS–A) survey, a nationally-representative sample of 10,148 youth aged 13 to 17. Casey Study participants had significantly higher rates of lifetime alcohol dependence (3.6% versus 1.1%), substance abuse (14.1% versus 8.8%), and substance dependence (4.2% versus 1.8%) diagnoses. Past year diagnostic rates in this study were either equal between foster youth and the general population or, in one case (substance abuse), significantly lower.

Information on predictors of substance use among youth in foster care is not clear. Although Midwest Study data indicated an increased risk of substance misuse among Caucasians (Keller, Blakeslee, Lemon, & Courtney, 2010), other studies have not demonstrated differences based on race/ethnicity (Thompson & Auslander, 2007; Zhan et al., 2016). Gender has also not been a significant predictor of substance use among older youth in care (Keller, Salazar, et al., 2010; Thompson & Auslander, 2007; Zhan et al., 2016). A comprehensive review of predictors indicates that more than 15 variables accounted for substance use among foster youth (e.g., older age, neglect, behavior problems, mobility, low academic performance, lack of commitment to school), with little continuity across studies (Braciszewski & Stout, 2012); thus, more work is needed in this area so that interventions can be appropriately tailored to the population.

Taken together, the studies reported here tend to indicate significantly more substance misuse among foster youth than within general population adolescents. This discrepancy is even more pronounced when examining recent and lifetime data or when considering substances other than alcohol. This trend is surprising; that is, foster youth report higher rates of lifetime and recent (i.e., past 6–12 months) substance use compared to their general population peers, yet similar levels of current substance use. Although this is not contradictory, such a pattern (i.e., admitting to past use, but denying current use) is unusual. One interpretation is that foster youth may engage with substances earlier than their general population peers (Gabrielli et al., 2016), given their heightened risk. Early initiation may then lead to a "graduation" to harder drugs and a higher propensity for substance use problems (i.e., diagnoses). Indeed, the non-linear relationship between exposure to ACEs and severity of substance use is stronger at younger ages (Dube et al., 2003). Alternatively, foster youth may be more likely to experiment with drugs such as cocaine, amphetamines, and heroin, but only on a limited basis, which would elevate their lifetime rates of use, but explain the similarity to the general population on current rates.

At the same time, the data noted above indicate that rates of current SUDs among foster youth are equal to those for the general population, while lifetime rates are very high. Thus, it is possible that foster youth mature out of substance use problems in a fashion similar to normative populations, albeit a process that starts earlier for this vulnerable group. Finally, foster youth may be reluctant to admit to current use. Homeless young adults with a foster care history reported that, while in care, they did not disclose substance use because they feared a change of placement (Meyers, White, Whalen, & DiLorenzo, 2007). Thus, youth may be comfortable admitting to past substance use (i.e., use that won't get them in trouble), but refrain from talking about current alcohol or drug use. This hypothesis—that there are significant, population-specific barriers to substance use disclosure—is addressed more fully later in this chapter.

Former Foster Youth

As the focus of this chapter (and book) is on current foster youth, attention to the available data on substance use among former foster youth is paramount. That is, we need to understand the ramifications of our current approach to addressing substance use within the foster care system. Youth who have exited care experience high rates of unemployment, unstable housing, and both psychiatric and physical health issues (Courtney et al., 2005; Pecora et al., 2006). Evidence-based programs are needed within the child welfare system to improve the foundation from which these young people can exit care and build their transition to adulthood.

To that end, the chances of successful independence are increased if substance use is not a major concern. Unfortunately, substance use continues to escalate after exit from care. Two studies have compared former foster youth to matched, nationally-representative samples (Pecora, White, Jackson, & Wiggins, 2009; White, C. R., O'Brien, White, J., Pecora, & Phillips, 2008). Results suggested that foster care alumni had significantly higher rates of past year and lifetime alcohol and substance use dependence diagnoses. Even more concerning is the rapid increase in new SUDs after youth exit foster care. Longitudinal data have indicated an increase of 11% and 13% for alcohol and substance use disorders, respectively, within 1 year of emancipation (Courtney et al., 2005). Comparative rates for this age group in the general population are approximately 1% to 4% (CBHSQ, 2016). It is plausible that once youth leave care, many do not have robust coping mechanisms to navigate young adulthood independently, thus relying on maladaptive tools like substance use. Indeed, others have stated that lack of access to appropriate mental health services may lead to (maladaptive) self-medicating with alcohol and other drugs (White et al., 2008). More generally, exposure to ACEs and other traumatic events have been linked to using substances as a means to cope (Rothman, Edwards, Heeren, & Hingson, 2008).

As with youth currently in care, the few studies of foster care alumni have not delineated clear predictors of substance use. White et al. (2008) reported relationships between alcohol dependence and both school and residential mobility, as well as length of time in foster care. One study has examined the role of race/ethnicity, finding that African-American alumni were less likely to develop a substance use disorder compared to White, non-Hispanics (Dworsky et al., 2010). However, too few studies have been completed on former foster youth to draw any distinct conclusions about predictors of substance use. Clearly, attention to alcohol and drug misuse and creation of empirically-based interventions are needed while youth remain in care to staunch this surge in problematic substance use post-exit.

Substance Use Screening, Assessment, and Treatment in Care

The availability of substance use screening, assessment, and treatment services is critical during adolescence and young adulthood, as young people lay the foundation for their independence. Despite the need for such resources, less than 10% of U.S. general population adolescents who misuse substances receive appropriate services (CBHSQ, 2016). For foster youth, the gap between the need for services and actual receipt is even wider; a strange phenomenon given their access to government-supported health insurance and being enveloped in a system of care (Casanueva, Stambaugh, Urato, Fraser, & Williams, 2011).

Screening and assessment of substance use appears to be rare across child welfare systems (McCarthy, Van Buren, & Irvine, 2007). Entry into foster care is a potentially critical access point for determining the health and needs of young people, yet in the few states where screening and assessment are occurring, the procedures are not comprehensive (McCarthy et al., 2007). Provision of treatment, furthermore, has been reported as under-resourced (McCarthy et al., 2007). Taken together, foster youth represent a population at significant risk of misusing alcohol and drugs, yet few safeguards have been constructed to identify and mitigate this issue.

In addition to policies that require screening, assessment, and referral to treatment, significant individual, family, and structural issues must also be considered. Foster youth face many of the same barriers that prevent most adolescents from seeking and receiving substance use services. For example, many teens do not perceive the need for help, stating that experimenting with alcohol and drugs is normal for their age (Wu & Ringwalt, 2006). Young people have also indicated that, once they have identified the need for help, they do not know where to turn (CBHSQ, 2016). Confidentiality and stigma are significant issues for adolescents (Rickwood, Deane, & Wison, 2007), decreasing the likelihood that they seek help. Finally, many young people have difficulty articulating their troubles to adult service providers, feeling that adults do not understand their lives (Rice & Dolgin, 2008).

Foster youth face these and other significant barriers to receiving mental health and substance use care. First, by virtue of their placement in foster care, these young people have had mildly to severely challenging relationships with people in authority. Not only does this materialize through abuse and neglect, but also through the frequent mobility that foster youth experience. Over half (53%) of Midwest Study youth had experienced more than three school changes as a result of being in foster care, and over one-third had more than five school changes (Courtney, Terao, & Bost, 2004). In this same sample, over half (53%) had three or more placements during their time in foster care; 16% had seven or more. Thus, this frequent rotation of homes, schools, case managers, caregivers, and health providers may result in significant skepticism about divulging personal information to someone who may soon be out of their lives.

Braciszewski, Moore, and Stout (2014) reported that foster care staff and parents are mindful of this instability and subsequent lack of trust in adults. Specifically, the authors proposed brief interventions, delivered by either health care staff or former foster youth, as an approach for mitigating foster youth substance use. Brief interventions are often rooted in Motivational Interviewing (Miller & Rollnick, 2013), are carried out over one or two 30-minute sessions, and have been effective at reducing substance use in myriad populations (D'Amico, Miles, Stern, & Meredith, 2008; Mitchell et al., 2012; Spirito et al., 2004). Responding to these proposed methods, foster parents, staff, and administrators were unsure whether a solid bond could be formed between youth and interventionist in such a short amount of time. In addition, they expressed strong concern about developing such a bond, only for the interventionist to eventually leave, as many foster youth have had recurring patterns of important adults exiting their lives. Thus, even with the best screening and assessment tools and a policy mandate to collect such information, foster youth may be reluctant to divulge information without significant rapport building and safeguards against abandonment.

In addition, case managers, foster parents, group home providers, and other foster care stakeholders do not often receive adequate training in recognizing and addressing substance use. The field of social work education has acknowledged that substance use training is largely absent (Schroeder, Lemieux, & Pogue, 2008). Furthermore, the American Academy of Pediatrics (2002) has reported a lack of awareness in child welfare about the availability of community-based treatment programs, reducing service access for young people. In addition to system stakeholders, foster parents may also need assistance in identifying and addressing substance use. For example, a recent survey of foster parents indicated that while 40% had fostered a youth with an SUD, only 61% of those parents had received any training for parenting a youth with these unique needs (Meyers, Kaynak, Clements, Bresani, & White, 2013), adding to the stress of fostering. Over one-quarter of these parents admitted that their contact agency was not helpful in dealing with issues that arose as a result of their foster youth's SUD, further complicating a challenging home environment. Taken together, strong measurement tools and trust can only move us so far; without an awareness of and training in substance misuse by important stakeholders, opportunities to intervene with foster youth in need will be missed.

Finally, as mentioned, foster youth are often very mobile, which can negatively impact the delivery of health care through rotating providers and inaccurate reporting of health histories. Furthermore, consent for treatment sometimes remains with the young person's biological parent(s) (Simms, Dubowitz, & Szilagyi, 2000), which can cause delays in service provision. Given these factors, it is not surprising that foster care status was related to decreased continuity of care relative to teen Medicaid patients who were not in foster care (DiGiuseppe & Christakis, 2003). Thus, even with improved measurement quality, a secure alliance where youth feel empowered to talk about substance use, and a keen awareness of substance use issues among child welfare staff and case managers, there are clear structural breaks in the chain from screening to assessment to treatment where foster youth will still fall through the cracks.

Adolescent substance use is a not a straightforward phenomenon to study, assess, or treat. There are many biological, psychological, social, developmental, cultural, and contextual factors involved in the initiation and continuation of alcohol and drug use. The picture is further complicated by the foster care setting, as additional families, authority figures, systems, and other stakeholders are involved and should be considered as interventions are developed. In order to further our understanding of foster youth substance use and implement a system of care that can acknowledge this multifaceted context, a solid theoretical guideline should be explored.

A Theoretical Approach to Foster Youth Substance Use

Four considerations are important when adopting a theory of foster youth substance use. First, the theory should take a developmental approach, which accounts for the rapid and distinct changes seen during adolescence. Second, the theory should account for the amplified risk faced by this vulnerable group. Third, the theory needs to address the interconnected contextual factors associated with foster care. Finally, not all youth are doomed to an adulthood of homelessness, unemployment, poor physical health, and mental illness (Courtney, Hook, & Lee, 2012). Thus, the theory should also attend to protective factors that push youth to be resilient in the face of amplified risk.

Structural Ecosystems Theory (SET; Szapocznik & Coatsworth, 1999) synthesizes the complex body of work on adolescent substance use, highlighting the individual and social risk and protective mechanisms that occur within a young person's ecology. Structural Ecosystems Theory addresses both context and development as the influences on an adolescent's behavior ebb and flow over time.

The authors of the theory argue that previous approaches to understanding adolescent substance use have focused too narrowly on individual risk and protective factors (e.g., the role of parental monitoring versus deviant peers), rather than on their interconnectedness. In reality, behavior is influenced by multiple, related factors that influence each other over time; thus, attention to any one characteristic over others will overestimate the importance of that factor.

In short, SET integrates four major areas of study: the social ecology model (Bronfenbrenner, 1979), structural family therapy (Minuchin, 1974), Multisystemic Therapy (Henggeler & Borduin, 1990), and a lifespan development approach. As such, it places family at the center of the young person's social ecology. Given that the major goals of foster care are reunification and, if necessary, adoption into a nurturing family, a focus on the family's role in alcohol and substance use is important. In addition, because youth in foster care are embedded within dynamically shifting settings, with many interacting stakeholders, SET's multi-layered approach and focus on development within those contexts are an excellent match for decreasing substance use in this population. Specific approaches, within an SET framework, are now presented.

Implications for Child Welfare Health Policy

Substance Use Screening and Assessment

As previously mentioned, youth in foster care are at significant risk for a number of poor social and health outcomes. Of the issues most salient to foster youth, substance use is among the more serious; however, little attention has been paid to screening, assessment, prevention, or treatment of these problems. The ramifications of this inattention are stark, with rapid increases in substance use disorder diagnoses once youth exit the system. To combat this, routine screening for and assessment of substance use should be implemented throughout child welfare agencies. Indeed, the Children's Bureau of the Administration for Children and Families issued such a call for all youth in out-of-home care. In addition, child welfare leaders created guidelines which call for: (1) screening of mental health and substance use issues within 72 hours of entry into foster care; (2) more comprehensive screening of needs and functioning within 30 days of placement; (3) a comprehensive assessment within 60 days of screening; and (4) ongoing, informal assessment of needs at each case manager visit (Romanelli et al., 2009).

The detailed Children's Bureau recommendations dovetail with SET (Szapocznik & Coatsworth, 1999), as they call for measurement of individual behavior, family, caregiver risk factors, academic variables, peer influences, and community-level factors. For example, assessments should capture data on caregiver involvement in the school, school–community bonds, relationships between biological and/or foster caregivers and the local child welfare system, and the amount of contact that caregivers have with the young person's peers, as these relationships will have an indirect impact on youth outcomes. Caregivers should also be asked about their support systems, work stressors, and locus of control at work. It would also be important to understand relationships between caregivers and case managers, as well as institutional stressors for case managers, given the impact of burnout on quality of care. Such a focus may bolster both instrumental and perceived support for adolescents in foster care.

Romanelli et al. (2009) also support the use of evidence-based measurement and intervention. The Child and Adolescent Needs and Strengths (CANS) assessment is a comprehensive screening tool designed for child welfare agencies to determine functioning across a range of risk and protective factors (Lyons, J. S., Weiner, Lyons, M. B., & Mariush, 2004). The CANS is primarily used for decision support; that is, determining the need for services in a particular domain using data collected across multiple sources. Its focus on strengths is certainly an advantage over many other screening tools, particularly when working with a population often described in terms of its weaknesses. Others have noted that the CANS is well-suited to the child welfare population because these youth are often at the extremes of most clinical rating scales (Winters, Collett, & Myers, 2005); the CANS, rather, provides context to descriptions of functioning. With regard to substance use, utility of the CANS depends on the goals of the user. If the goal is to determine placement into substance use services, the CANS appears to be a good candidate for treatment placement and monitoring of outcomes. For monitoring lower-level use, more rapid changes in use, or clinical "grey areas" (e.g., the kind that might result in a brief intervention, rather than treatment), the CANS may not be the best option. The CANS also involves rigorous training and extensive user support, a double-edged sword. Child welfare staff can become reliable and valid users, but only if their agency supports initial training, implementation strategies, ongoing monitoring of fidelity, and the associated financial costs.

Many substance use screening tools used in non-foster care populations are readily available, can be self-administered, and would require little adaptation for this population. For example, the National Institute on Alcohol Abuse and Alcoholism (NIAAA) has created a two-question screen for problematic alcohol use for youth from ages 9 to 18 (NIAAA, 2011). Responses are used to place the youth in a risk category that corresponds to intervention recommendations. The Brief Screening Instrument for Adolescent Tobacco, Alcohol, and Drug Use (BSTAD; Kelly et al., 2014) builds upon the NIAAA measure by adding items on tobacco, marijuana, cocaine, heroin, amphetamines, hallucinogens, inhalants, and prescription medications. The BSTAD is psychometrically sound and has cut-offs that correspond to the *Diagnostic and Statistical Manual of Mental Disorders' (DSM)* criteria for SUDs. The Screening to Brief Intervention (S2BI; Levy et al., 2014) instrument has also demonstrated excellent psychometric properties in the assessment of alcohol, tobacco, and other drugs, discriminating on SUD severity (e.g., moderate, severe). Like the NIAAA measure, these results are translated into actionable intervention categories. Finally, the CRAFFT (Knight et al., 1999) is among the most popular screening tools for adolescent substance use and measures consequences of use (e.g., Have you gotten in TROUBLE while using alcohol or drugs?).

Most of these measures, however, do not assess tobacco use, the single most preventable cause of morbidity and premature mortality (U.S. Department of Health & Human Services, 2014). Although cigarette use has declined among general population youth, smoking is now increasingly concentrated among high-risk groups (Garrett, Dube, Babb, & McAfee, 2014), such as foster youth. As a result, these vulnerable young people will bear a disproportionate burden of tobacco-related disease and death. Indeed, rates of lifetime smoking among foster youth are over four times that of general population adolescents (Siegel et al., 2016); smoking in the past month is over three times national rates (Braciszewski & Colby, 2015; Siegel et al., 2016), while daily smoking is nearly four times more prevalent (Braciszewski & Colby, 2015). Despite this health disparity, very little attention has been paid to tobacco assessments and interventions among youth in foster care (Leslie et al., 2003). Although reports indicate a recent dip, electronic cigarette use has been on the rise among young people since 2011 (Miech, Johnston, O'Malley, Bachman, & Schulenberg, 2016), surpassing cigarettes as the most commonly used tobacco product among youth (Murthy, 2017). Preliminary data indicate that e-cigarette use among young adults who have recently left foster care is not substantial (Braciszewski & Colby, 2017); however, more data are needed to accurately assess potential harms. Thus, it is imperative that substance use screening and assessment include questions about all forms of tobacco.

Substance Use Interventions

Once the need for services is identified, evidence-based interventions must be delivered in a timely, reliable, and acceptable fashion. As previously mentioned, there are a number of population-specific barriers to delivering substance use services that particularly impede on the last issue, acceptability. Earlier in the chapter, barriers such as difficulties with alliance development, lack of training on the part of case managers and foster parents around substance use, and frequent mobility of foster youth were outlined. In addition, youth in foster care sometimes fear tangible, negative repercussions for admitting to substance use (Meyers et al., 2007), as other resources in the child welfare system can sometimes be predicated upon abstinence (Braciszewski et al., 2014). A potential loss of a resource provides a disincentive for youth to seek help with problematic substance use. To navigate these issues, a two-tiered approach to intervention is recommended.

First, Screening, Brief Intervention, and Referral to Treatment (SBIRT; Babor et al., 2007) utilizes routine screening of substance use and, based on the results, a recommendation for further intervention. Brief interventions (BIs) are suggested for individuals with low/moderate severity of use. This approach would involve one to two short sessions (20–30 minutes), often rooted in Motivational Interviewing (Miller & Rollnick, 2013). The goal of BIs is to increase insight and awareness about a youth's substance use, while also attempting to increase motivation to change. Those who screen in the higher range receive a referral to treatment. The SBIRT approach has been endorsed for use in a variety of service systems (Bernstein, E., Bernstein, J. A., Stein, & Saitz, 2009) and has been successful in reducing adolescent substance use in emergency departments (Spirito et al., 2004), pediatric clinics (D'Amico et al., 2008), and schools (Mitchell et al., 2012).

Yet, the aforementioned issues remain; as Braciszewski et al. (2014) report, gaining the trust of a youth in foster care within a short time frame can be difficult. If that bond is formed, it could be detrimental to the young person if the interventionist then exits the youth's life. To address these issues, the author of this chapter and his team have been developing the first brief substance use intervention designed specifically for foster youth (Braciszewski et al., 2016). iHeLP (Interactive Healthy Lifestyle Preparation) is a two-part intervention, delivered completely using technology. It begins with a computerized screening and brief intervention (SBI) that targets reductions in substance use. The SBI is programmed using Computerized Intervention Authoring Software (CIAS; Ondersma, Chase, Svikis, & Schuster, 2005), a sophisticated intervention development tool where researchers can modify and deliver screening, assessment, and intervention, all of which are individually personalized for participants. The CIAS utilizes an animated narrator to deliver intervention content. The narrator can talk, move, gesture, display emotional reactions, and make empathic reflections that parallel those of a person-to-person interaction and can be disarming for people who are reluctant to share such personal information.

As with SBIRT, the computerized SBI in iHeLP addresses substance use by using an approach consistent with Motivational Interviewing (Miller & Rollnick, 2013). Motivation for change, however, fluctuates over time, and these dynamic changes should be addressed when designing interventions that seek to increase motivation (Resnicow & Page, 2008). To account for these changes, the second iHeLP component uses daily text messaging and weekly "poll questions" to assess major outcomes and readiness to change over 6 months. Specifically, participants are asked the Readiness Ruler question, "On a scale from 0 to 10, how ready are you to cut down/quit using your drug of choice?" each week. Depending on their answers, they are thought to fall into one of three stages of change, as defined by the Transtheoretical Model (Prochaska & DiClemente, 1992): precontemplation (not ready), contemplation (on the fence), or preparation/action (ready). Participants then receive text message content that is written for someone in that stage of change. Each week, however, they are asked the Readiness Ruler question again; if participants respond in a way that alters their stage of change, the content of their messages reflects that change. This design allows more up-to-the-minute tailoring of message content, rather than relying on baseline or follow-up data collected months apart.

The design of iHeLP has been carried out with the assistance of youth who are exiting the foster care system. Indeed, because few interventions have incorporated the preferences and voices of current or transition-age foster youth, a central goal of iHeLP development was to collect participant feedback throughout all study phases. During the initial focus group phase of iHeLP development, participants (age 18 to 19, recently removed from foster care, and who were engaged in risky substance use) were asked about previous barriers to substance use care, and how they would design a substance use intervention; one that would reflect the best-case scenario of how they would want to be treated. Group members consistently reported a history of feeling judged for using substances, rather than receiving compassion or empathy (Braciszewski, Tzilos, Moore, & Stout, 2015), highlighting the need for interventions to have a non-judgmental stance. Participants also reported a preference for some type of interaction (i.e., not just receiving information) and respect for autonomy and individuality, all of which were consistent with the outline for iHeLP. Participants were also heavily involved in providing direct feedback on pre-written text message content (Braciszewski et al., 2017), as well as writing messages, themselves, that were incorporated into the larger study text bank. One surprising result was that a non-trivial number of participants disliked messages related to accessing social support for help in reducing substance use. In particular, youth indicated that they often did not have such supports, and that a reminder to use these resources made them feel ashamed and isolated, increasing their desire to use alcohol or drugs (Braciszewski et al., 2017). Given that social support for abstinence is one of the most robust predictors of successful recovery (Kelly, Hoeppner, Stout, & Pagano, 2012), more research is needed in this area.

An open trial of iHeLP using the same inclusion criteria demonstrated acceptability and feasibility (Braciszewski et al., 2015), with all participants rating the computer as easy to work with and indicating that the narrator was non-judgmental. During the open trial, text messages were followed with a question about the relevance/likability of that day's message; results indicated a 92% approval rating for the messages. The weekly poll question response rate was 87%, which is high, given the duration of the intervention. Exit interviews were exceedingly positive, with many participants noting advantages over traditional means of intervention (e.g., face-to-face contact with a physician, nurse, counselor, or case manager).

Although iHeLP seems to show promise, brief interventions will not carry the day for the many foster youth who struggle with multiple mental and physical health issues. Prevalence rates of trauma and subsequent Posttraumatic Stress Disorder (PTSD), for example, are high among foster youth, with studies reporting diagnostic rates in the range of 14% to 16% (Courtney et al., 2004; McMillen et al., 2005), a level that is twice as high as the general population (Merikangas et al., 2010). As PTSD is strongly associated with substance use (Giaconia et al., 2000), interventions for foster youth would be wise to incorporate material on trauma, a recommendation supported by others (Romanelli et al., 2009).

More comprehensive interventions could be further informed by SET (Szapocznik & Coatsworth, 1999). Using SET as a framework for intervention development, approaches could focus on caregiver (e.g., biological and/or foster parent/guardian) social support, improving relationships between caregivers and schools and/or caregivers and peers, or peer involvement in community development efforts, for example. Structural Ecosystems Theory advises the creation of interventions that target these interactions, rather than factors in isolation. For instance, rather than providing tutoring for foster youth, a more comprehensive (and likely more effective) approach would engage caregivers in tutoring. This can help to improve the relationship between the caregiver and young person, boost the self-efficacy of the caregiver, and strengthen the linkages between the caregiver and the school, all of which are individually associated with reductions in substance use. Indeed, a school readiness program that involved foster youth and caregivers was found to decrease positive attitudes toward drinking (Pears, Kim, & Fisher, 2016), a risk factor for drinking intentions (Nargiso, Friend, & Florin, 2013) and alcohol use (Borsari & Carey, 2003).

Conclusions and Next Steps

Youth in foster care represent a unique, at-risk population. As a function of growing up in the foster care system, they encounter great instability, with new placements, schools, guardians, and case managers, sometimes more than once per year. Their experiences preceding and during foster care place them at increased vulnerability for a host of negative outcomes, all of which are a challenge to address comprehensively. Structural Ecosystems Theory, as a framework for understanding foster youth substance use, allows for the simultaneous acknowledgment of more than one barrier to successful development, while also identifying protective factors from which to create interventions. As foster care agencies continue to implement wraparound services for the families they service, an SET framework may augment those efforts.

This chapter suggests a need to focus on several areas within the domains of practice and research. First, child welfare agencies are encouraged to promote: (1) universal screening of substance use, probably starting at age 12; (2) ongoing assessment of service needs and functioning; and (3) collaboration across agencies that serve this population. Early screening of substance use and associated risk factors can help to prevent substance use initiation and escalation. Such efforts may also reduce the likelihood of other negative outcomes associated with early initiation of alcohol and drug use. However, data collection cannot end at screening. Youth who endorse substance use should receive comprehensive follow-up assessments and placement into a level of care commensurate with their level of use. Finally, states would be wise to create interagency alliances to prevent redundant work and promote data sharing, so that youth can be served properly and efficiently. Child welfare agencies, schools, community mental health, and Medicaid (among other service agencies) do not often have a way to connect, despite serving the same population. Guardianship also plays a role in information portability, as foster parents and group home leaders may not have the legal authority to provide treatment consent or release of records. As a result, obtaining consent from biological parents can delay service provision. Policies that promote collaboration across service agencies have the potential to lighten the load on all providers, while augmenting services for youth. This is especially prudent for older foster youth, as they make the transition to the adult care system. Through grant-funded efforts (SAMHSA, 2016), many states are supporting multi-agency transition-aged care systems that serve the unique needs of this developmental period. Such collaborative efforts would be especially beneficial for foster youth, so that they are not left alone to navigate the adult services world.

Second, more research on foster youth substance use is desperately needed, with an emphasis on (1) predictors of substance use and (2) population-tailored interventions. Among a small body of literature on substance use among foster youth, no robust predictors have emerged, and our gaps in understanding are both wide and deep. Researchers have tended to use instruments, time frames, predictors, and outcomes that have very little overlap; thus, few conclusions can be made about the general population of foster youth, much less subgroups such as racial/ethnic minorities, LGBTQ individuals, and youth at different developmental stages. To date, assessment of substance use has predominantly been a domain of functioning attached to a host of other outcomes being assessed within large studies. Thus, there have been no theoretically-driven, longitudinal inquiries that focus solely on understanding substance use, mechanisms of initiation, use over time, and development of substance use disorders.

Such an effort would augment attempts to create effective interventions, particularly those aimed at subgroups of youth. In lieu of epidemiological data, intervention development should take place alongside youth. Indeed, current literature suggests that programs developed with youth input are more likely to appeal to diverse groups of young people (D'Amico & Edelen, 2007). Thus, if the strategies suggested here are to be pursued, they would likely be optimized if the voice of foster youth is involved. Furthermore, the barriers described throughout this chapter indicate that technology-based screening and assessment (and, possibly, intervention) may be the most acceptable and efficacious form of collecting data. Specifically, the lack of screening and assessment in foster care is often the result of high financial cost (Casanueva et al., 2011). Technology-based assessments can drastically reduce those costs (Newman, Szkodny, Llera, & Przeworski, 2011), while delivering the screening or assessment with perfect reliability. Use of technology to report health issues may also increase willingness to disclose sensitive information (Butler, Villapiano, & Malinow, 2009).

While computers and phones, even with an animated narrator, may not develop the same alliance which can be nurtured with a health provider, technology-based strategies may increase awareness of problematic substance use and change youths' minds about seeking professional help. Finally, access to technology is nearly ubiquitous; thus, even within a consistently mobile population, a technology-based approach would allow for continuity of care and ease of access, relative to in-person meetings. In sum, utilization of technology can tailor data collection to this population in a way that makes information gathering personal, acceptable, accessible, and reliable, all of which make it more likely that a comprehensive, in-person intervention would be more palatable. It is clear that youth in foster care face a number of health disparities, including substance use. If we are to reduce such disparities, collaboration among foster youth, researchers, child welfare agencies, and other affiliated service providers is needed and would constitute a comprehensive effort to deliver healthier outcomes in this vulnerable population.

Note

1   Data from MTF are averaged across 8th, 10th, and 12th Grade to provide a relative comparison.

References

American Academy of Pediatrics. (2002). Health care of young children in foster care. *Pediatrics, 109*(3), 536–541.
Babor, T. F., McRee, B. G., Kassebaum, P. A., Grimaldi, P. L., Ahmed, K., & Bray, J. (2007). Screening, Brief Intervention, and Referral to Treatment (SBIRT): Toward a public health approach to the management of substance abuse. *Substance Abuse, 28*(3), 7–30.
Bernstein, E., Bernstein, J. A., Stein, J. B., & Saitz, R. (2009). SBIRT in emergency care settings: Are we ready to take it to scale? *Academic Emergency Medicine, 16*(11), 1072–1077.
Borsari, B., & Carey, K. B. (2003). Descriptive and injunctive norms in college drinking: A meta-analytic integration. *Journal of Studies on Alcohol, 64*(3), 331–341.
Braciszewski, J. M., & Colby, S. M. (2015). Tobacco use among foster youth: Evidence of health disparities. *Children and Youth Services Review, 58*, 142–145.
Braciszewski, J. M., & Colby, S. M. (2017). A comprehensive examination of tobacco use among youth exiting foster care. Poster presented at the Society for Research on Nicotine and Tobacco, Florence, Italy.
Braciszewski, J. M., Moore, R. S., & Stout, R. L. (2014). Rationale for a new direction in foster youth substance use disorder prevention. *Journal of Substance Use, 19*(1–2), 108–111.
Braciszewski, J. M., & Stout, R. L. (2012). Substance use among current and former foster youth: A systematic review. *Children and Youth Services Review, 34*(12), 2337–2344.
Braciszewski, J. M., Stout, R. L., Tzilos, G. K., Moore, R. S., Bock, B. C., & Chamberlain, P. (2016). Testing a dynamic automated intervention model for emerging adults. *Journal of Child & Adolescent Substance Abuse, 25*(3), 181–187.
Braciszewski, J. M., Tran, T. B., Moore, R. S., Bock, B. C., Tzilos, G. K., Chamberlain, P., & Stout, R. L. (2017). Developing a tailored texting intervention: A card sort methodology. *Journal of Applied Biobehavioral Research, 22*(2), e12060.
Braciszewski, J. M., Tzilos, G. K., Moore, R. S., & Stout, R. L. (2015). iHeLP: A collaborative approach to substance use prevention for foster youth. Paper presented at the Society for Community Research and Action, Lowell, MA.

Bramlett, M. D., & Radel, L. F. (2014). Adverse family experiences among children in nonparental care, 2011–2012. *National Health Statistics Report, 74*(4), 1–8.

Brook, J., Rifenbark, G. G., Boulton, A., Little, T. D., & McDonald, T. P. (2015). Risk and protective factors for drug use among youth living in foster care. *Child and Adolescent Social Work Journal, 32*(2), 155–165.

Bronfenbrenner, U. (1979). Contexts of child rearing: Problems and prospects. *American Psychologist, 34*(10), 844–858.

Butchart, A., Harvey, A. P., Mian, M., & Furniss, T. (2006). *Preventing child maltreatment: A guide to taking action and generating evidence.* Geneva: World Health Organization.

Butler, S. F., Villapiano, A., & Malinow, A. (2009). The effect of computer-mediated administration on self-disclosure of problems on the Addiction Severity Index. *Journal of Addiction Medicine, 3*(4), 194–203.

Casanueva, C., Stambaugh, L., Urato, M., Fraser, J. G., & Williams, J. (2011). Lost in transition: Illicit substance use and services receipt among at-risk youth in the child welfare system. *Children and Youth Services Review, 33*(10), 1939–1949.

Center for Behavioral Health Statistics and Quality [CBHSQ]. (2016). *2015 National Survey on Drug Use and Health: Detailed tables.* Rockville, MD: Substance Abuse and Mental Health Services Administration.

Courtney, M. E., Charles, P., Okpych, N. J., Napolitano, L., Halsted, K., Courtney, M., . . . Hall, C. (2014). *Findings from the California Youth Transitions to Adulthood Study (CalYOUTH): Conditions of foster youth at age 17.* Chicago: Chapin Hall Center for Children at the University of Chicago.

Courtney, M. E., Dworsky, A., Ruth, G., Keller, T., Havlicek, J., & Bost, N. (2005). *Midwest Evaluation of the Adult Functioning of Former Foster Youth: Outcomes at age 19.* Chicago: Chapin Hall Center for Children at the University of Chicago.

Courtney, M. E., Hook, J. L., & Lee, J. S. (2012). Distinct subgroups of former foster youth during young adulthood: Implications for policy and practice. *Child Care in Practice, 18*(4), 409–418.

Courtney, M. E., Okpych, N. J., Charles, P., Mikell, D., Stevenson, B., Park, K., . . . Courtney, M. (2016). *Findings from the California Youth Transitions to Adulthood Study (CalYOUTH): Conditions of youth at age 19.* Chicago: Chapin Hall Center for Children at the University of Chicago.

Courtney, M. E., Terao, S., & Bost, N. (2004). *Midwest Evaluation of the Adult Functioning of Former Foster Youth: Conditions of youth preparing to leave state care.* Chicago: Chapin Hall Center for Children at the University of Chicago.

D'Amico, E. J., & Edelen, M. O. (2007). Pilot test of Project CHOICE: A voluntary afterschool intervention for middle school youth. *Psychology of Addictive Behaviors, 21*(4), 592–598.

D'Amico, E. J., Ellickson, P. L., Collins, R. L., Martino, S., & Klein, D. J. (2005). Processes linking adolescent problems to substance-use problems in late young adulthood. *Journal of Studies on Alcohol, 66*(6), 766–775.

D'Amico, E. J., Miles, J. N., Stern, S. A., & Meredith, L. S. (2008). Brief motivational interviewing for teens at risk of substance use consequences: A randomized pilot study in a primary care clinic. *Journal of Substance Abuse Treatment, 35*(1), 53–61.

DiGiuseppe, D. L., & Christakis, D. A. (2003). Continuity of care for children in foster care. *Pediatrics, 111*(3), e208–e213.

Dube, S. R., Felitti, V. J., Dong, M., Chapman, D. P., Giles, W. H., & Anda, R. F. (2003). Childhood abuse, neglect, and household dysfunction and the risk of illicit drug use: The adverse childhood experiences study. *Pediatrics, 111*(3), 564–572.

Dube, S. R., Miller, J. W., Brown, D. W., Giles, W. H., Felitti, V. J., Dong, M., & Anda, R. F. (2006). Adverse childhood experiences and the association with ever using alcohol and initiating alcohol use during adolescence. *Journal of Adolescent Health, 38*(4), e1–e10.

Dworsky, A., White, C. R., O'Brien, K., Pecora, P., Courtney, M., Kessler, R., . . . Hwang, I. (2010). Racial and ethnic differences in the outcomes of former foster youth. *Children and Youth Services Review, 32*(6), 902–912.

Fothergill, K. E., Ensminger, M. E., Green, K. M., Crum, R. M., Robertson, J., & Juon, H.-S. (2008). The impact of early school behavior and educational achievement on adult drug use disorders: A prospective study. *Drug and Alcohol Dependence, 92*(1), 191–199.

Frerer, K., Sosenko, L. D., & Henke, R. R. (2013). *At greater risk: California foster youth and the path from high school to college.* San Francisco: Stuart Foundation.

Gabrielli, J., Jackson, Y., & Brown, S. (2016). Associations between maltreatment history and severity of substance use behavior in youth in foster care. *Child Maltreatment, 21*(4), 298–307.

Garrett, B. E., Dube, S. R., Babb, S., & McAfee, T. (2014). Addressing the social determinants of health to reduce tobacco-related disparities. *Nicotine & Tobacco Research, 78*(8), 892–897.

Giaconia, R. M., Reinherz, H. Z., Hauf, A. C., Paradis, A. D., Wasserman, M. S., & Langhammer, D. M. (2000). Comorbidity of substance use and post-traumatic stress disorders in a community sample of adolescents. *American Journal of Orthopsychiatry, 70*(2), 253–262.

Haight, W., Ostler, T., Black, J., Sheridan, K., & Kingery, L. (2007). A child's-eye view of parent methamphetamine abuse: Implications for helping foster families to succeed. *Children and Youth Services Review, 29*(1), 1–15.

Harris, K. M., Halpern, C. T., Whitsel, E., Hussey, J., Tabor, J., Entzel, P., & Udry, J. R. (2009). *The National Longitudinal Study of Adolescent Health: Study design.* Retrieved from www.cpc.unc.edu/projects/addhealth/design

Henggeler, S. W., & Borduin, C. M. (1990). *Family therapy and beyond: A multisystemic approach to treating the behavior problems of children and adolescents.* Pacific Grove, CA: Thomson Brooks/Cole.

Johnston, L. D., O'Malley, P. M., Miech, R. A., Bachman, J. G., & Schulenberg, J. E. (2016). *Monitoring the Future national survey results on drug use, 1975–2015: Overview, key findings on adolescent drug use.* Ann Arbor: Institute for Social Research, University of Michigan.

Keller, T. E., Blakeslee, J. E., Lemon, S. C., & Courtney, M. E. (2010). Subpopulations of older foster youths with differential risk of diagnosis for alcohol abuse or dependence. *Journal of Studies on Alcohol and Drugs, 71*(6), 819–830.

Keller, T. E., Salazar, A. M., & Courtney, M. E. (2010). Prevalence and timing of diagnosable mental health, alcohol, and substance use problems among older adolescents in the child welfare system. *Children and Youth Services Review, 32*(4), 626–634.

Kelly, J. F., Hoeppner, B., Stout, R. L., & Pagano, M. E. (2012). Determining the relative importance of the mechanisms of behavior change within Alcoholics Anonymous: A multiple mediator analysis. *Addiction, 107*(2), 289–299.

Kelly, S. M., Gryczynski, J., Mitchell, S. G., Kirk, A., O'Grady, K. E., & Schwartz, R. P. (2014). Validity of Brief Screening Instrument for Adolescent Tobacco, Alcohol, and Drug Use. *Pediatrics, 133*(5), 819–826.

King, K. M., Meehan, B. T., Trim, R. S., & Chassin, L. (2006). Marker or mediator? The effects of adolescent substance use on young adult educational attainment. *Addiction, 101*(12), 1730–1740.

Knight, J. R., Shrier, L. A., Bravender, T. D., Farrell, M., Vander Bilt, J., & Shaffer, H. J. (1999). A new brief screen for adolescent substance abuse. *Archives of Pediatrics & Adolescent Medicine, 153*(6), 591–596.

Kohlenberg, E., Nordlund, D., Lowin, A., & Treichler, B. (2002). *Alcohol and substance use among adolescents in foster care in Washington State: Results from the 1998–1999 Adolescent Foster Care Survey.* Rockville, MD: Center for Substance Abuse Treatment.

Leslie, L. K., Hurlburt, M. S., Landsverk, J., Rolls, J. A., Wood, P. A., & Kelleher, K. J. (2003). Comprehensive assessments for children entering foster care: A national perspective. *Pediatrics, 112*(1), 134–142.

Levy, S., Weiss, R., Sherritt, L., Ziemnik, R., Spalding, A., Van Hook, S., & Shrier, L. A. (2014). An electronic screen for triaging adolescent substance use by risk levels. *JAMA Pediatrics, 168*(9), 822–828.

Lyons, J. S., Weiner, D. A., Lyons, M. B., & Mariush, M. (2004). Measurement as communication in outcomes management: The Child and Adolescent Needs and Strengths (CANS). In M. Mariush (Ed.), *The use of psychological testing for treatment planning and outcomes assessment. Volume 2: Instruments for children and adolescents* (pp. 461–476). Mahwah, NJ: Lawrence Erlbaum Associates.

McCarthy, J., Van Buren, E., & Irvine, M. (2007). *Child and family services reviews: 2001–2004: A mental health analysis.* Washington, DC: Georgetown University.

McDonald, T. P., Mariscal, E. S., Yan, Y., & Brook, J. (2014). Substance use and abuse for youths in foster care: Results from the Communities that Care normative database. *Journal of Child & Adolescent Substance Abuse, 23*(4), 262–268.

McMillen, J. C., Zima, B. T., Scott, L. D., Auslander, W. F., Munson, M. R., Ollie, M. T., & Spitznagel, E. L. (2005). Prevalence of psychiatric disorders among older youths in the foster care system. *Journal of the American Academy of Child & Adolescent Psychiatry, 44*(1), 88–95.

Merikangas, K. R., He, J.-p., Burstein, M., Swanson, S. A., Avenevoli, S., Cui, L., . . . Swendsen, J. (2010). Lifetime prevalence of mental disorders in US adolescents: Results from the National Comorbidity Survey Replication–Adolescent Supplement (NCS–A). *Journal of the American Academy of Child & Adolescent Psychiatry, 49*(10), 980–989.

Meyers, K., Kaynak, Ö., Clements, I., Bresani, E., & White, T. (2013). Underserved parents, underserved youth: Considering foster parent willingness to foster substance-using adolescents. *Children and Youth Services Review, 35*(9), 1650–1655.

Meyers, K., White, T., Whalen, M., & DiLorenzo, P. (2007). *Aged-out and homeless in Philadelphia.* Philadelphia, PA: The Greater Philadelphia Urban Affairs Coalition.

Miech, R. A., Johnston, L. D., O'Malley, P. M., Bachman, J. G., & Schulenberg, J. E. (2016). Vaping, hookah use by US teens declines for first time [Press release]. Available at www.monitoringthefuture.org

Miller, W. R., & Rollnick, S. (Eds.). (2013). *Motivational interviewing: Helping people change.* New York: The Guilford Press.

Minuchin, S. (1974). *Families and family therapy.* Cambridge, MA: Harvard University Press.

Mitchell, S. G., Gryczynski, J., Gonzales, A., Moseley, A., Peterson, T., O'Grady, K. E., & Schwartz, R. P. (2012). Screening, Brief Intervention, and Referral to Treatment (SBIRT) for substance use in a school-based program: Services and outcomes. *The American Journal on Addictions, 21*(s1), S5–S13.

Murthy, V. H. (2017). E-cigarette use among youth and young adults: A major public health concern. *JAMA Pediatrics, 171*(3), 209–210.

Nargiso, J. E., Friend, K., & Florin, P. (2013). An examination of peer, family, and community context risk factors for alcohol use and alcohol use intentions in early adolescents. *The Journal of Early Adolescence, 33*(7), 973–993.

National Institute on Alcohol Abuse and Alcoholism [NIAAA]. (2011). *Alcohol screening and brief intervention for youth: A practitioner's guide.* (NIH Publication No. 11–7805). Retrieved from http://pubs.niaaa.nih.gov/publications/Practitioner/YouthGuide/YouthGuide.pdf

Neighbors, C., Geisner, I. M., & Lee, C. M. (2008). Perceived marijuana norms and social expectancies among entering college student marijuana users. *Psychology of Addictive Behaviors, 22*(3), 433–438.

Newman, M. G., Szkodny, L. E., Llera, S. J., & Przeworski, A. (2011). A review of technology-assisted self-help and minimal contact therapies for drug and alcohol abuse and smoking addiction: Is human contact necessary for therapeutic efficacy? *Clinical Psychology Review, 31*(1), 178–186.

Ondersma, S. J., Chase, S. K., Svikis, D. S., & Schuster, C. R. (2005). Computer-based brief motivational intervention for perinatal drug use. *Journal of Substance Abuse Treatment, 28*(4), 305–312.

Pears, K. C., Kim, H. K., & Fisher, P. A. (2016). Decreasing risk factors for later alcohol use and antisocial behaviors in children in foster care by increasing early promotive factors. *Children and Youth Services Review, 65*, 156–165.

Pecora, P. J., Kessler, R. C., O'Brien, K., White, C. R., Williams, J., Hiripi, E., . . . Herrick, M. A. (2006). Educational and employment outcomes of adults formerly placed in foster care: Results from the Northwest Foster Care Alumni Study. *Children and Youth Services Review, 28*(12), 1459–1481.

Pecora, P. J., White, C. R., Jackson, L. J., & Wiggins, T. (2009). Mental health of current and former recipients of foster care: A review of recent studies in the USA. *Child & Family Social Work, 14*(2), 132–146.

Pilowsky, D. J., & Wu, L. T. (2006). Psychiatric symptoms and substance use disorders in a nationally representative sample of American adolescents involved with foster care. *Journal of Adolescent Health, 38*(4), 351–358.

Prochaska, J. O., & DiClemente, C. C. (1992). Stages of change in the modification of problem behaviors. In M. Hersen, R. M. Eisler, & P. M. Miller (Eds.), *Progress in behavior modification* (Vol. 28, pp. 183–218). Sycamore, IL: Sycamore Press.

Resnicow, K., & Page, S. E. (2008). Embracing chaos and complexity: A quantum change for public health. *American Journal of Public Health, 98*(8), 1382–1389.

Rice, F. P., & Dolgin, K. G. (2008). *The adolescent: Development, relationships, and culture* (12th ed.). Boston, MA: Pearson.

Rickwood, D. J., Deane, F. P., & Wison, C. J. (2007). When and how do young people seek professional help for mental health problems? *Medical Journal of Australia, 187*, S35–S39.

Romanelli, L. H., Landsverk, J., Levitt, J. M., Leslie, L. K., Hurley, M. M., Bellonci, C., . . . Jensen, P. S. (2009). Best practices for mental health in child welfare: Screening, assessment, and treatment guidelines. *Child Welfare, 88*(1), 163–188.

Rothman, E. F., Edwards, E. M., Heeren, T., & Hingson, R. W. (2008). Adverse childhood experiences predict earlier age of drinking onset: Results from a representative US sample of current or former drinkers. *Pediatrics, 122*(2), e298–e304.

Schroeder, J., Lemieux, C., & Pogue, R. (2008). The collision of the Adoption and Safe Families Act and substance abuse: Research-based education and training priorities for child welfare professionals. *Journal of Teaching in Social Work, 28*(1–2), 227–246.

Shin, S. H. (2004). Developmental outcomes of vulnerable youth in the child welfare system. *Journal of Human Behavior in the Social Environment, 9*(1), 39–56.

Siegel, A., Benbenishty, R., & Astor, R. A. (2016). A comparison of adolescents in foster care and their peers in high school: A study of substance use behaviors and attitudes. *Journal of Child & Adolescent Substance Abuse, 6*, 530–538.

Simms, M. D., Dubowitz, H., & Szilagyi, M. A. (2000). Health care needs of children in the foster care system. *Pediatrics, 106*(4), 909–918.

Smith, D. K., Chamberlain, P., & Eddy, J. M. (2010). Preliminary support for Multidimensional Treatment Foster Care in reducing substance use in delinquent boys. *Journal of Child and Adolescent Substance Abuse, 19*(4), 343–358.

Spirito, A., Monti, P. M., Barnett, N. P., Colby, S. M., Sindelar, H., Rohsenow, D. J., . . . Myers, M. (2004). A randomized clinical trial of a brief motivational intervention for alcohol-positive adolescents treated in an emergency department. *The Journal of Pediatrics, 145*(3), 396–402.

Stambaugh, L., Ringeisen, H., Casanueva, C., Tueller, S., Smith, K., & Dolan, M. (2013). *Adverse childhood experiences in NSCAW*. (OPRE Report# 2013-26). Washington, DC: US Department of Health & Human Services.

Substance Abuse and Mental Health Services Administration [SAMHSA]. (2012). *Comparing and evaluating youth substance use estimates from the National Survey on Drug Use and Health and other surveys*. (HHS Publication No. SMA 12-4727.) Rockville, MD: Author.

Substance Abuse and Mental Health Services Administration [SAMHSA]. (2016). Healthy Transitions grant program. Retrieved from www.samhsa.gov/nitt-ta/healthy-transitions-grant-information

Szapocznik, J., & Coatsworth, J. D. (1999). An ecodevelopmental framework for organizing the influences on drug abuse: A developmental model of risk and protection. In M. Glantz & C. R. Hartel (Eds.), *Drug abuse: Origins and interventions* (pp. 331–366). Washington, DC: American Psychological Association Press.

Thompson, R. G., & Auslander, W. F. (2007). Risk factors for alcohol and marijuana use among adolescents in foster care. *Journal of Substance Abuse Treatment, 32*(1), 61–69.

Thompson, R. G., & Auslander, W. F. (2011). Substance use and mental health problems as predictors of HIV sexual risk behaviors among adolescents in foster care. *Health & Social Work, 36*(1), 33–43.

U.S. Department of Health & Human Services. (2014). *The health consequences of smoking—50 years of progress: A report of the Surgeon General*. Atlanta, GA: Author.

U.S. Department of Health & Human Services. (2017). *Child maltreatment 2015*. Washington, DC: U.S. Government Printing Office.

Vaughn, M. G., Ollie, M. T., McMillen, J. C., Scott, L. Jr., & Munson, M. (2007). Substance use and abuse among older youth in foster care. *Addictive Behaviors, 32*(9), 1929–1935.

White, C. R., Havalchak, A., Jackson, L., O'Brien, K., & Pecora, P. J. (2007). *Mental health, ethnicity, sexuality, and spirituality among youth in foster care: Findings from the Casey Field Office Mental Health Study*. Seattle, WA: Casey Family Programs.

White, C. R., O'Brien, K., White, J., Pecora, P. J., & Phillips, C. M. (2008). Alcohol and drug use among alumni of foster care: Decreasing dependency through improvement of foster care experiences. *Journal of Behavioral Health Services & Research, 35*(4), 419–434.

Winters, N. C., Collett, B. R., & Myers, K. M. (2005). Ten-year review of rating scales, VII: Scales assessing functional impairment. *Journal of the American Academy of Child & Adolescent Psychiatry, 44*(4), 309–338.

Wu, L.-T., & Ringwalt, C. L. (2006). Use of alcohol treatment and mental health services among adolescents with alcohol use disorders. *Psychiatric Services, 57*(1), 84–92.

Young, N. K., Boles, S. M., & Otero, C. (2007). Parental substance use disorders and child maltreatment: Overlap, gaps, and opportunities. *Child Maltreatment, 12*(2), 137–149.

Zhan, W., Smith, S. R., Warner, L. C., North, F., & Wilhelm, S. (2016). Cigarette, alcohol, and marijuana use among adolescents in foster family homes. *Children and Youth Services Review, 69*, 151–157.

Part IV
Foster Youth Development in Context

10

Natural Mentoring to Support the Establishment of Permanency for Youth in Foster Care

John Paul Horn and Renée Spencer

Introduction

It is well-known that young people aging out of foster care are at risk for a variety of negative outcomes related to leaving foster care; some of these outcomes are thought to be the result of lacking specific types of support which one typically receives from family during the transition to adulthood. Because not every eligible young person who enters foster care is adopted or placed in a permanent guardianship/kinship arrangement, child welfare professionals are tasked with finding innovative solutions to connect youth with caring, non-parent adults who can provide the kind of permanency and lifelong support that all youth need, especially during this period of transition to adulthood. Natural mentoring for current and former foster youth is emerging as one potentially promising way to address these important permanency needs.

Natural mentors are important non-parent adults, such as teachers, coaches, neighbors, and extended family members, from whom a young person receives support and guidance (Zimmerman, Bingenheimer, & Behrendt, 2005). There have been many studies that have examined the psychosocial and economic impacts of important non-parent adults for youth aging out of care. Thompson, Greeson, and Brunsink (2016) completed a meta-analysis of existing studies on the role of natural mentors for foster youth and found support for what child welfare practitioners have long recognized: relationships matter for everyone and young people aging out of foster care can experience better outcomes if they have a strong relationship with at least one important adult. Such relationships with non-parent adults can provide young people with much-needed support as they begin their transition into adulthood.

Many young people naturally form relationships with an array of important non-parent adults in their schools and communities. However, experiences of trauma/marginalization combined with continued disruptions in these youths' lives can make maintaining and forming new relationships with key adults difficult. Child welfare professionals and others who work with young people aging out of foster care are tasked, both legislatively and professionally, with helping these vulnerable youth to seek out and preserve important relationships so that they may secure lifelong connections with adults who will support them through their emergence into adulthood and beyond.

To help youth develop nurturing relationships with supportive adults, those who work with youth can gain insight by understanding the policy context governing foster youth entering adulthood and their developmental needs and assets. Child welfare workers, and others who work with foster youth,

Table 10.1 Domains of Social Work Practice

Micro-level	Mezzo-level	Macro-level
Interventions targeted toward individuals, couples, and families. Focus is on the person(s) involved in the intervention and the nature of relationships.	Interventions targeted toward less intimate relationships and places where those relationships are built, such as school settings, therapy groups, work places, or neighborhoods. Focus is on the group process which facilitates/hinders relationship building along these domains.	Interventions targeted toward larger system structures, such as communities or organizations, further removed from individuals. Focus is on program development, policy intervention, and administration.

Source: Adapted from Hepworth, Rooney, R. H., Rooney, G. D., Strom-Gottfried, & Larsen, 2010

must understand the federal policies related to child welfare that seek to promote these lifelong relationships with supportive adults and the rationale behind enacting them. Understanding prevailing thought about the issues confronting young people as they make the transition to adulthood can also help practitioners to situate the specific needs of youth aging out of foster care and the role(s) that natural mentors play in supporting them as they move in, and through, this important developmental stage. Finally, practitioners will also benefit from a knowledge of established and emerging strategies to promote connections with supportive adults.

We begin this chapter with a present snapshot of foster youth and common issues faced by young people aging out of foster care, specifically with regard to transition issues related to relationships and social capital. We then offer a review of some common theoretical lenses that support the development of relationships among youth aging out of foster care, as well as some related theories about the importance of these types of relationships for social and vocational development. Relevant federal legislation related to the ideas of permanency and mentoring among foster youth is discussed, as the promotion of permanent connections has gained particular importance within this legislation. We then consider social work practices at the macro-, mezzo-, and micro-levels that engage youth in identifying these supportive adults, and highlight ways that child welfare professionals can help young people to develop and maintain these relationships. Finally, we offer specific guidance on using mentoring programs, in particular what is being called *youth initiated mentoring* (YIM; Schwartz, Rhodes, Spencer, & Grossman, 2013; Spencer, Tugenberg, Ocean, Schwartz, & Rhodes, 2016), as a way for practitioners to help in meeting the needs of youth exiting foster care by accessing and enlisting the support of caring adults.

A Primer on Foster Youth and Permanency

The Children's Bureau, an office of the Administration for Children and Families through the U.S. Department of Health & Human Services (henceforth, USDHSS), compiles statistical information related to foster care in the United States in the form of the Adoption and Foster Care Analysis and Reporting System (AFCARS) report. According to the most recent AFCARS report (Fiscal Year [FY] 2015), there were an estimated 427,910 youth in foster care (USDHSS, 2016). Just under a quarter of these youth in care (111,820) were waiting to be adopted, meaning that their case goal plan was not to be returned to their biological families, but to await adoption or another planned permanency arrangement (i.e., legal guardianship, kinship care, emancipation—only for youth under 16).[1] *Emancipation* refers to legally exiting the child welfare system due to reaching the age of 18. Roughly 86% of youth had some goal that denoted creating or maintaining a permanent type of relationship (e.g., family reunification with extended family or with parents, primary caretakers, or other relatives; adoption, or legal guardianship), while 7% of the remaining youth had *long-term foster care* or emancipation as their case goal plan (USDHHS, 2016).

Placement types for the vast majority of foster youth (79%) were in non-relative foster homes (45%), extended family foster homes (30%), and pre-adoptive homes (4%); the remaining 21% of youth in care were in institutions (8%), group homes (6%), trial home visits (5%), and supervised independent living settings (1%), with the final 1% representing runaway (or missing) youth (USDHHS, 2016). At least 51% of youth in care had spent over 1 year in foster care (M = 20.4 months; median = 12.6 months), indicating a trend toward shorter times in care for the majority of youth in FY 2015 (USDHHS, 2016). The majority of children in care were male (52%), with children of color (Black or African-American, Hispanic, Asian, American Indian, Two or More Races) accounting cumulatively for 55% of the foster care population (USDHHS, 2016).

In FY 2015, an estimated 243,060 foster youth exited care. A large number (88%) of these youth were reunified with parents or other relatives, had been adopted, or had some other type of permanent living arrangement. This indicates that an overwhelming majority of foster youth had plans for some type of permanent connection. Nine percent of these youth emancipated from foster care (USDHHS, 2016). It is these 9% of emancipated youth for whom the following outcomes are focused.

Outcomes of Youth Exiting Care

Many studies have examined outcomes for youth aging out of care, but there are two popular studies that dominate the child welfare literature: the Northwest Foster Care Alumni Study (henceforth, Northwest Alumni Study) (Pecora et al., 2005) and the Midwest Evaluation of the Adult Functioning of Former Foster Youth (henceforth, Midwest Study) (Courtney et al., 2011). These two studies examined large samples (Northwest Alumni Study, n = 479; Midwest Study, n = 723) of former foster youth, asking a variety of questions on outcomes related to education, housing, family relationships, and the mental health of each population. Both studies used a comparison group of young adults of a similar age (not involved in foster care) based on other, outside existing datasets. However, the Midwest Study is cited more frequently in the literature with regard to former foster youth outcomes, has a larger and more robust set of outcomes due to its longitudinal nature, and is more reflective of the national foster care population with regard to sex than the Northwest Alumni Study. Further, the findings from the Midwest Study are comparable to similar findings in the Northwest Alumni Study (Courtney et al., 2011; Pecora et al., 2005). For this reason, more focus on the Midwest Study statistics will be used in this chapter.

The Midwest Study is the largest and longest longitudinal study of the outcomes of former foster youth. It began in 1999 when researchers at Chapin Hall at the University of Chicago were interested in examining the effects of the Foster Care Independence Act of 1999 (FCIA). The research team surveyed 723 foster youth from three Midwestern states (Iowa, Wisconsin, and Illinois), beginning at age 17 or 18, and followed this cohort onward to age 26 (Wave 4). By the final wave, 596 foster youth were interviewed, representing a follow-up response rate of 83%. The sample was representative of the sexes in a national sample of foster youth (48.4% male), but less so for race; the sample in the Midwest Study was comprised of 68.6% persons of color, larger than the 55% represented in the AFCARS data (Courtney et al., 2011; USDHHS, 2016). Many questions asked of this population were also asked of the general population in a separate, outside study, the National Longitudinal Study of Adolescent to Adult Health (henceforth, Add Health), which allowed for a comparison of this foster youth cohort to the general population (Courtney et al., 2011). The Add Health study is a national longitudinal study of 20,745 adolescents from Grades 7 to 12. The Add Health study has followed these youth to their mid-20s in the most recent wave (Wave 4) (Harris, 2013). The Add Health study represents an ideal comparison group, as the study is longitudinal and uses nearly identical measures with a population that is the natural comparison for foster youth.

According to the most recent wave of the Midwest Study (Courtney et al., 2011), which looked at the outcomes of former foster youth at age 26, former foster youth were more likely to experience negative outcomes in the transition to adulthood than their non-foster-care peers across a variety of domains, including housing instability, educational interruptions, economic difficulties, and poorer physical and mental health. With regard to housing, Courtney and colleagues (2011) found that, by age 26, at least 31% of former foster youth reported being homeless or having couch surfed for at least one night since their most recent interview, at ages 23 and 24. Of those who had experienced at least one night of homelessness or couch surfing, more than 60% had done so more than once since entering adulthood. It was noted that former foster youth were more likely to report being homeless or experiencing homelessness than their non-foster youth peers in the Add Health study as well (Courtney et al., 2011). Former foster youth were also found to fare poorly in educational and vocational outcomes. By age 26, they had lower rates of educational attainment than youth who had not been in foster care. They were ten times less likely to have completed a 4-year college degree and were more than three times less likely to have completed high school (Courtney et al., 2011). They fared worse vocationally and economically as well, with lower rates of employment, lower earnings, and higher rates of economic hardships (e.g., not enough money for rent or facing eviction). These youth were more likely to rate their physical and mental health as *fair* or *poor* and were less likely to be covered by health and dental insurance. They reported greater disruptions in their close relationships, with higher rates of intimate partner violence and of having their own children living in out-of-home care (i.e., foster care, kinship care). Finally, they were more disconnected from their communities, with lower rates of civic engagement and higher rates of arrest and incarceration (Courtney et al., 2011).

These negative outcomes in multiple domains demonstrate that former foster youth face significantly greater challenges in adulthood than their non-foster youth peers (Courtney et al., 2011). At the same time, signs of resilience among former foster youth have been identified. The former foster youth in the Midwest Study (Courtney et al., 2011) generally reported feeling supported by important people in their lives across multiple domains, including emotional support (e.g., people listening to them and providing affirmative support during times of crisis), informational support (e.g., providing job leads or other advice on further educational or employment efforts), tangible support (e.g., providing access to monetary or other resources in order to help youth meet needs), and companionship (e.g., spending time with the youth). These youth were as likely as their non-foster-care peers to access mental health resources (Courtney et al., 2011). Finally, 68% of the sample reported maintaining a positive relationship with a caring, non-parent adult (a proxy for *mentor*) since age 14. The large majority (72.8%) of those with caring, non-parent adults reported feeling very close to their mentors, and 67.1% reported at least monthly contact, either via e-mail or telephone; these rates were somewhat lower for in-person contact (54.6%). Only 1.7% of these former foster youth reported having stable, mentoring-type relationships with volunteer mentors (such as Big Brothers/Big Sisters). The remaining former foster youth who indicated maintaining positive relationships with caring adults reported that their stable, mentoring-type relationships were with people like extended kin and siblings, teachers, counselors, coaches, clergy members, neighbors/friends of parents, and social workers (Courtney et al., 2011). This indicated that the majority of mentoring-type relationships for former foster youth occurred outside recognized mentoring programs.

The findings related to family connections and mentoring are indicative of the importance of permanent connections for this population and their reliance on these relationships for support. These findings also indicate that former foster youth largely develop relationships with individuals outside structured mentoring programs, such as Big Brothers/Big Sisters. This means that child welfare practitioners should examine a variety of options when attempting to help youth develop these important adult relationships.

A (Very) Brief History of Federal Policy for Foster Youth Entering Adulthood

The existing legislation addressing the needs of youth aging out of foster care (entering legal adulthood and exiting foster care) offers an important context for understanding the role that macro-level social work interventions play in helping to establish permanent connections. A number of federal policies have been created to address the negative outcomes of foster youth leaving care, to increase the positive impacts of employment, and education, and to reduce reliance on federally-funded programs (e.g., Supplemental Nutrition and Access Program [SNAP], Temporary Assistance for Needy Families [TANF], and other social welfare programs). This chapter will address four key pieces of legislation which have attempted to address some of these issues: Consolidated Omnibus Budget Reconciliation Act (COBRA) of 1985; Foster Care Independence Act of 1999 (FCIA); Promoting Safe and Stable Families Amendments of 2001 (PSSFA), and Fostering Connections to Success and Increasing Adoptions Act of 2008 (FCSIAA).

COBRA of 1985 and Independent Living Programs

Title XII, Subtitle C of the Consolidated Omnibus Budget Reconciliation Act (COBRA) of 1985 provided for the creation of independent living programs (ILPs) (COBRA, 1986). It was the first law to provide federal guidance and funding for programs serving young people leaving foster care. The law allowed states to receive financial assistance in creating programs to help older youth in foster care, who had reached the age of 16, make the transition from foster care to independent living. Specific program components required by the legislation included: helping participants seek a high school diploma (or its equivalent) and take part in vocational training programs; providing training for daily living skills (e.g., budgeting, locating housing, and career planning); providing individual and group counseling; integrating service coordination; establishing outreach programs to attract eligible youth; and providing each youth who receives services with a written transition plan, based on a needs assessment of the youth (COBRA, 1986).

The focus of this legislation was creating a program that helped youth who had not been adopted and were expected to leave foster care at age 18 to learn the skills needed to live independently; missing from this legislation was a focus on permanent connections or mentoring. This legislation also did not provide any services to youth above the age of 18. Subsequent legislation refined the legislative intent of the ILP program.

Foster Care Independence Act of 1999

The first substantial reform to ILPs occurred more than 10 years later, with the passage of the Foster Care Independence Act of 1999 (FCIA, 1999). The law used findings from prior research which justified the improvement of independent living programs. Specifically, these findings concluded that foster youth aging out of care experienced difficulty making the transition to adulthood, and had high rates of homelessness, poverty, criminal involvement, and non-marital childbearing (FCIA, 1999).

The law added language about specific ILP training topics (e.g., high school completion, vocational training, budgeting, financial management skills) and added programming on substance abuse prevention, job placement and retention, and preventative health activities. It also encouraged programs "to provide personal and emotional support to children aging out of foster care, through mentors and the promotion of interactions with dedicated adults" [FCIA, 1999, § 477(a)(4)]. Programs were expanded to serve those who had emancipated from care to age 21. Congress renamed the Independent Living Programs, now calling them the John H. Chafee Foster Care Independence Program (FCIA, 1999).

Promoting Safe and Stable Families Amendments of 2001

In 2001, Congress passed the Promoting Safe and Stable Families Amendments (PSSFA, 2002). This law provided a number of supports to encourage permanent connections for youth and increase positive outcomes for youth aging out of foster care. First, the law provided grant funding to states in order to improve post-adoption services and family preservation services, indicating a prevention approach to working with families involved with child welfare services. These services included family support services and family preservation services (to prevent removal), time-limited family reunification services (to help families regain custody of their children), and adoption promotion and support services (to increase adoption and prevent adoption failure) (PSSFA, 2002). The law also provided specific funding to mentoring programs for children of prisoners because "[e]mpirical research demonstrates that mentoring is a potent force for improving children's behavior across all risk behaviors affecting health" [PSSFA, 2002, § 439 (a)(1)(e)]. The law specifically named Big Brothers/Big Sisters programs as effective at helping to reduce negative behaviors among young people, and allowed budget appropriations for other mentoring agencies to provide services specifically for children of incarcerated parents (PSSFA, 2002). Finally, the law encouraged the successful completion of postsecondary education among foster youth by enacting the Education and Training Voucher (ETV) program and allowing states to provide these vouchers to youth who aged out of foster care (PSSFA, 2002).

Fostering Connections to Success and Increasing Adoptions Act of 2008

In 2008, Congress passed the Fostering Connections to Success and Increasing Adoptions Act (FCSIAA), which sought to increase kinship and guardianship options for youth in care. This was accomplished by providing grant funding for kinship- and guardianship-focused programs for youth in care, mandating that child welfare agencies seek out adult relatives of all children in care, and allowing states to increase the age of foster care to 21 years of age (if the youth is already in care prior to age 18). This extension of foster care services also extended to certain youth in kinship or guardianship arrangements (FCSIAA, 2008). The definition of "child" for the purposes of foster care was expanded to include those who had been in foster care prior to their 18th birthday, or who had been receiving adoption or kinship/guardianship assistance after their 16th birthday, provided they met one of the following criteria: enrollment in a high school completion or General Education Development (GED) program; enrollment in a postsecondary or vocational training program; participation in a program to remove barriers to employment; employment for at least 80 hours per month; being incapable of meeting the previously described criteria due to disability (FCSIAA, 2008).

The law also focused on improving transition planning for youth who were to age out of foster care, with a stated focus on mentors, and included language to allow the transition plan to be "as detailed as the child may elect" [FCSIAA, 2008, § 202 (3)]. The Act also included language that helped to provide educational stability for youth in care and required that states take into account the suitability of educational settings when determining placement, in order to help prevent educational disruption (FCSIAA, 2008). However, the law did not define suitability for the purposes of practice. This ambiguity may create issues in practice, because the standards for suitability vary across jurisdiction, meaning that no consistency in maintaining educational stability exists for youth.

This law appeared to stress the importance of promoting and preserving relationships with family and others who wished to create permanent ties to the youth. It sought to increase positive outcomes by extending the age of foster care to 21 so that former foster youth could focus on increasing their educational attainment or employment opportunities. Finally, the law also provided specific language that encouraged mentoring and set the youth as the person who determined when their transition plan was detailed enough for their needs.

Factors Informing How Efforts to Promote Permanent Connections Are Enacted

The ways in which these legislative efforts are translated into practice depend on a number of factors. As indicated in the previous section related to federal policy, placement settings, case plan goals, age, length of time in care, and reason for exiting foster care are primary indicators of what types of services youth might be eligible for and what types of resources might be offered (COBRA, 1986; FCSIAA, 2008). Further, racial and sexual/gender identities or presence of a serious mental health condition or developmental disability may complicate the focus toward developing permanency. Studies have found that non-White foster youth are less likely to achieve legal permanency (reunification, guardianship, or adoption) than White youth (Akin, 2011; Becker, Jordan, & Larsen, 2007); these same studies found that youth with mental health conditions or developmental disabilities had similar outcomes to other populations less likely to achieve legal permanency. Other studies found that lesbian, gay, bisexual, transgender, or questioning/queer (LGBTQ) youth have difficulty achieving legal permanency (Mallon, Aledort, & Ferrera, 2002); the posited causes for this lack of permanency are group home placements, reasons for entering care (i.e., family rejection based on sexual orientation/gender identity), and age at time of entry into care (Mallon, 2011). Children who are eligible for adoption are more likely to receive services (e.g., adoption incentives provided by federal and state governments) that will encourage caring adults to either adopt them or gain legal guardianship (PSSFA, 2002; FCSIAA, 2008). Children and youth who are newly involved in the foster care system are also given services to identify appropriate kinship placements (PSSFA, 2002). Both of these services are designed to establish permanent connections for these youth by connecting them with family and other permanent adults at an early stage during their time in care. Independent Learning Program services are generally not provided to children and youth who are not expected to remain in foster care until emancipation.

Older youth who are expected to age out of foster care through emancipation are more likely to be offered an array of services designed for independent living, because federal policy mandates that these particular youth receive services that focus on reducing the negative outcomes associated with foster care (FCIA, 1999). Federal legislation expects ILP services to be provided to youth older than age 16 who are expected to age out of foster care (COBRA, 1986), though some states may offer services to youth earlier. However, federal legislation also articulates a clear expectation that these youth be connected with a mentor or other caring adult in order to encourage positive outcomes, even without establishing a legal familial/parental bond like that of adoption or guardianship (FCIA, 1999; PSSFA, 2002; FCSIAA, 2008).

Theoretical Frameworks Pertinent to Foster Youth Exiting Care

While many theories could be used to describe the sometimes forced emergence of former foster youth into adulthood, three theoretical frameworks pertinent to promoting interdependence and empowerment exist within the context of youth in foster care: Relational–Cultural Theory; Social Support, Network, and Capital Theory(ies); and Positive Youth Development. These theories assume that the youth are not entirely independent actors in their social world and that needs are met through interactions with others; relationships become important for meeting their social, biological, psychological, spiritual, and cultural needs. An overview of these different theories is provided.

Relational–Cultural Theory

Relational–Cultural Theory (RCT) was developed by Miller and her colleagues at the Stone Center in response to the lack of developmental theories which adequately captured the experiences of women and other oppressed groups (Jordan, 2010; Miller & Stiver, 1997). Central to this theory is that psychological health is promoted by meaningful and mutual relationships with others throughout the life span, and that issues arise when individuals are unable to maintain connections to others. *Connections*, *disconnections*, and *reconnections* in relationships are viewed as core developmental processes (Miller, 1988; Miller & Stiver, 1997). As all youth benefit from stable relationships (Spencer, 2000), this specific theory helps to provide a framework for understanding why it is important to encourage and promote stable relationships for youth aging out of care.

Miller (1988) describes five important outcomes of relational *connections*: 1) both parties feel a greater sense of energy as a result of their relationship; 2) as a result of being active in the relationship, both parties feel more capable of acting within the world and do so; 3) participating in the relationship provides each person with a greater sense of self as well as a better sense of the other; 4) connections lead to a greater sense of self-worth; and 5) people in connected relationships are motivated to seek out more connections with others. Disconnections are understood to have different consequences which are the opposite of those resulting from experiences of connections. Individuals feel less energy, less capable, have less understanding of others and self, are less sure of themselves and their worth, and are less motivated to seek relationships with others. These *disconnections*, if left unrepaired, can lead to feelings of isolation and cause feelings of shame within the self, leading to a belief that one is unworthy and unvalued (Miller, 1988). These constant feelings of condemned isolation can lead to the changing of the self, or the exclusion of the whole self, in order to maintain relationships, leading to psychological isolation and pathology. This persistent isolation leads a person to fear connecting with others, forming what Miller and Stiver (1997) called *the central paradox*, which is when the skills one employs to participate in these isolating relationships prevent a person from fully engaging in new relationships (Spencer, 2000). These skills are often employed to prevent feelings of rejection and marginalization within relationships, but they also contribute to continued isolation (Miller & Stiver, 1997).

Reconnections are the situations where disconnections in a relationship have been repaired and transformed into new, deeper connections. The issues causing disconnection between two individuals have been addressed and a deeper understanding of the other is able to take place. Connections, disconnections, and reconnections are seen as normal, natural processes in all relationships along the life span (Spencer, 2000). Some challenges to reconnections occur when structural violence/marginalization exists to perpetuate the disconnections and increase the need for self-protection by engaging in self-isolating behaviors (Comstock et al., 2008). A challenge to reconnections may be the result of youth in care developing a self-protection mechanism called a *veneer of self-reliance*, where the youth develops an unhealthy, fierce focus on self-reliance and complete independence, actively avoiding relationships that can help to address problems during their transition to adulthood (Kools, 1999).

The crux of the theory is that authenticity and mutuality in relationships matter for both parties; that is, psychologically healthy relationships occur because both parties believe that the other has value, has the ability to meaningfully contribute, has an understanding of the other, and feels positively about the relationship (Jordan, 1991). When mutuality is missing, either through interpersonal interaction or structural issues with the environment, relationships can contribute to continued feelings of isolation rather than being supportive and beneficial. This offers important insights for fostering permanency, as it suggests that for relationships to become growth-promoting relationships, experiences of mutuality and authenticity may be critical.

Social Networks, Social Capital, and Social Support

Three different theories develop the foundation for understanding how foster youth can use strong, mutual relationships with caring adults to successfully transition to adulthood: Social Network

Theory, Social Capital Theory, and Social Support Theory. While related in many ways, each theory explains one component of how people engage their environments to meet their needs. *Social network theory* holds that groups and larger social structures form as a result of a series of interactions between actors within the group (Wasserman & Faust, 2009). *Social capital theory* specifies that individuals within these networks inherit most relationships from their families, and use these relationships to advance their positions in the social world (e.g., economic, social standing, etc.) by seeking help from others in their inherited and created social networks (Bourdieu, 1986). *Social support theory* further refines these theories by asserting that aid provided by supportive individuals within a social network is specialized to meet a specific need (emotional, informational, instrumental, or companionship) and may be sought from a variety of individuals within a network, based on perceived need (Langford, Bowsher, Maloney, & Lillis, 1997). Thus, seeking social support requires that individuals possess the ability to leverage their social capital within their networks to receive specialized support for their needs.

Central to these concepts is the idea that one is a part of a larger network, and that one is active within this network in order to get one's needs met. Langford and colleagues (1997) argue that three things must be present to receive social support: first, that individuals belong to a social network that provides for the giving and receiving of support; second, that persons are socially embedded in their networks (e.g., that strong ties exist between members of a network); and third, that the social climate of the environment allows for the exchange of support between individuals. Fundamentally, this network must exist within a climate that allows for assistance in order for social support to be given (Langford et al., 1997). Because social resources are often inherited from parents or families (Bourdieu, 1986), foster youth are at risk for lacking these supportive relationships as their access to these resources is often limited by their being separated from their biological families, limiting access to inherited social networks (Avery, 2010). Social support is often described as three or four distinct types of support: emotional support, instrumental support, informational support, and appraisal support (Langford et al., 1997). *Emotional support* describes the feeling that one is loved, valued, and belongs, without condition. *Instrumental support* describes the provision of concrete assistance that one may need, such as housing or financial resources. *Informational support* describes the provision of problem-solving help during a time of need. *Appraisal support* describes the process of providing approval of another's actions or statements (Langford et al., 1997). In some literature, *emotional support* and *appraisal support* are merged together to describe one specific type of support (as in Courtney et al., 2011).

A small but growing body of research has examined social support among young people aging out of foster care and found that building supportive relationships with adults using structured programming can aid young people in the important transition to adulthood (Geenen et al., 2015; Hass & Graydon, 2009; Nesmith & Christophersen, 2014). Curry and Abrams (2015) reviewed research that specifically examined the role of social support with regard to housing for former foster youth, and identified two types of social support in their review: informal social support systems that were the result of relationships; and formal social support systems that were the result of formalized connections to organizations that provide services. From their review, they determined that helping youth to develop and maintain sources of social support may lead to better outcomes in adulthood (Curry & Abrams, 2015).

However, Lee and Berrick (2014) state that social support and social capital measures are imperfect proxies with which to study permanent connections. This is because youth who are able to seek social support and utilize social capital are better connected with adults and these connections may be influenced by having a better sense of belonging. Simply having resources available is not enough; youth must also have the sense that they can engage with their sources of support. This rationale aids the idea that developing strong, mutual relationships is necessary for youth to seek out and accept help from supportive adults.

Positive Youth Development

Positive youth development represents a philosophical approach to working with young people that starts with the assumption that youth are at the center of meeting their social, emotional, intellectual, and/or physical needs, and are capable of making positive, informed choices about how to meet such needs (Lerner, R. M., Lerner, J. V., & Benson, 2011). This theory holds that youth are agents in their own development who can be positively influenced by adults and other social institutions in order to make good decisions about their own needs, or ones which promote their growth and development (Lerner et al., 2005). In order for positive youth development to occur, youth must be actively engaged in decisions about activities that impact their own growth and development. Lofquist (1989) describes three ways in which youth are often viewed by adults in any key decision-making processes: as objects, recipients, and/or resources.

Applying these ideas to the child welfare worker–foster youth relationship, when practitioners view youth as *objects*, youth have little to no power in the decision-making process about activities and experiences which affect them (Lofquist, 1989). No meaningful or significant input or participation in decision making occurs when youth are viewed as objects (Lofquist, 1989). In practice, viewing youth as objects means holding the belief that child welfare practitioners know what is best for young people in all instances, and that youth must be protected from making mistakes which might endanger their placement stability or outcomes after leaving care. This view is disempowering to the youth as it prevents youth from being actively involved and consulted about their experiences in foster care and how these experiences may impact their futures.

When viewed as *recipients* by child welfare practitioners, youth are invited to make decisions about their activities or experiences, but the focus is on preparing young people to learn to become adults (Lofquist, 1989). From an engagement standpoint, decisions and responsibilities given to youth in this viewpoint generally involve simple tasks that hold little to no importance (Lofquist, 1989). In practice, viewing youth as recipients would mean that child welfare practitioners believe that youth have the ability to contribute to decisions about their care, but their contributions are valued less than those of the adults around them. This view also treats youth as *tokens*; that is, youth may be asked to participate in decision making as a courtesy, but without the intention of having their viewpoint seriously considered. Both of the previous approaches to working with youth conflict with the legislative mandate that youths' transitions plans should be as detailed as they elect (FCSIAA, 2008).

The final view is that of youth as a *resource* for child welfare practitioners. When viewed as resources, youth are seen as contributing members of their care team, and their opinions and views of their experiences and activities are given serious consideration. Youth are seen as equal partners in making decisions that impact their development and their time in foster care (Lofquist, 1989). In practice, engaging with youth as resources entails giving youth increasing responsibility in making meaningful decisions about their activities and experiences in care. Discretion must be exercised by knowledgeable, caring adults to ensure that decisions are developmentally appropriate to the youths' age or level of competence and do not place them at immediate risk. In this way, child welfare workers cultivate youths' abilities to make informed choices that will impact their futures.

One application of positive youth development theory encourages working with youth to promote the development of protective assets (Benson, Scales, Roehlkepartain, & Leffert, 2011). This theory identifies 40 assets that youth develop and utilize to avoid negative outcomes such as substance abuse, criminal justice system involvement, and failed educational opportunities (Benson et al., 2011). These assets are both internal (e.g., commitment to learning, positive values, social competencies, and positive identity) and external (e.g., support, empowerment, boundaries/expectations, and constructive use of time) (Benson et al., 2011). Diehl, Howse, and Trivette (2011) examined developmental assets and their relationships with youths' feelings toward adoption and mentoring; youth who perceived more control in their lives were less likely to desire a mentor, but all youth, regardless of risk level (low/high), had positive attitudes about mentoring.

Interventions for Youth Aging Out of Care—Micro, Mezzo, and Macro

A variety of intervention approaches are needed in order to address the permanency needs for foster youth aging out of foster care. Table 10.1, provided earlier, explains the various levels of intervention in which practitioners may engage. At the micro-level, practitioners should be aware of existing and emerging interventions for youth preparing to exit care. At the mezzo-level, child welfare practitioners should be aware of the impact that administration issues at the organizational level have on modeling and maintaining these types of permanent relationship among foster youth and those leaving care. Finally, while some legislative efforts exist to help youth to gain permanent connections, more can be done to influence federal policy that addresses developing these relationships at the macro-level.

Micro-Level: Mentoring as an Intervention for Youth Aging Out of Care

Mentoring provides youth with opportunities to develop long-lasting relationships with caring adults. While many mentoring relationships are thought of as official relationships supported by formal programs, natural mentors are often involved in the lives of young people in foster care. *Formal mentoring* takes place when a mentor and youth are matched together without knowing each other prior to the match, usually in recognized mentoring programs (e.g., Big Brothers/Big Sisters.) *Natural mentors* are non-parent adults to whom youth turn for support outside a formal mentoring relationship. These relationships result from daily interactions with adults in the youths' lives and often include teachers and coaches at school, employers at after-school jobs, spiritual leaders, and those who run community centers (Timpe & Lunkenheimer, 2015). As indicated by the Midwest Study, most youth aging out of foster care described having at least one caring non-parent adult to whom they were close, and almost all of these relationships were with individuals who were not volunteers from formal mentoring programs (Courtney et al., 2011).

Greeson (2013) gives preference to natural mentoring over formal mentoring for youth in care because these relationships develop gradually, the youth is more likely to trust the adult, and the youth and mentor are already a part of each other's social networks, increasing the likelihood that the relationship is able to continue over time. The quality of these relationships matters to former foster youth. Munson and colleagues (2010) found that former foster youth with natural mentors described these relationships as consistent and enduring relationships. These former foster youth also described these mentors as approachable and understanding of their unique experiences as foster youth. Greeson and Bowen (2008) also examined the role of natural mentors among young women of color aging out of care, and found that trust and emotional support were important in those relationships. The research demonstrates that not only do youth seek out adults they can trust, but this special trust and consistent, enduring provision of support are important indicators of healthy, lasting relationships for foster youth.

Natural mentoring relationships yield positive outcomes for youth aging out of foster care. Munson and McMillen (2009) found that foster youth in natural mentoring relationships lasting at least 1 year reported fewer symptoms of depression, lower levels of stress, increased life satisfaction, and lower arrest rates during the transition-aged time period (age 18 to 19). A small cross-section of the youth from this sample indicated that the natural mentors provided instrumental, informational, and tangible support to the former foster youth (Munson et al., 2010). Ahrens, DuBois, Richardson, Fan, and Lozano (2008) found that former foster youth who were mentored during adolescence had better educational and general health outcomes and lower rates of suicide risk than non-mentored youth in care, though the differences in risk reductions were relatively small between populations.

The findings of these qualitative and quantitative studies involving former foster youth echo other literature surrounding mentoring relationships among youth without foster care experiences. Studies have found that youth engaged in mentoring, from middle school to college, valued trust and fidelity, role-modeling and identification, non-judgmental support, and mutuality in their mentoring relationships (Eller, Lev, & Feurer, 2014; Liang, Spencer, Brogan, & Corral, 2008). Youth have described feeling empowered as a result of these relationships (Liang et al., 2008). Rhodes, Spencer, Keller, Liang, and Noam (2006) posit that youth engaged in mentoring relationships receive a variety of benefits, including the promotion of social and emotional, cognitive, and identity development. DuBois and Silverthorn (2005) found that mentoring relationships between youth and mentors from outside the extended family systems were more likely to yield better educational and health outcomes, particularly when mentors had backgrounds in education or other helping professions (e.g., child welfare workers, clergy, coaches, physicians).

Taken together, these findings among former foster youth and non-foster-care youth indicate that youth in higher-quality and more enduring relationships tend to derive an array of positive outcomes. Such relationships encourage the growth-promoting connections identified in Relational–Cultural Theory. By establishing trusting, caring, and mutual relationships with natural mentors, youth transitioning out of foster care may be more apt to see themselves as capable of establishing similar types of relationships with other adults and peers (Miller, 1988). This could serve to reduce the isolation experienced by many of these youth and increase their social networks. Large, stable, reciprocal social networks are essential for garnering sufficient social support (Avery, 2010; Langford et al., 1997), helping these youth to achieve more positive outcomes after transitioning out of foster care (Curry & Abrams, 2015; Geenen et al., 2015; Hass & Graydon, 2009; Nesmith & Christophersen, 2014).

Mezzo-Level: Removing Barriers within Care to Encourage Relationships

The administration of foster care can be a barrier to establishing long-lasting relationships for youth. Multiple placements prevent foster youth from developing and maintaining relationships, especially because youth may move frequently and without prior warning (Pecora, 2012). Since many natural mentors could be accessed through educational and other social institution settings, it is important that placement permanence be a priority for child welfare practitioners. Avoiding placement disruption can provide opportunities for youth to develop and maintain important relationships.

Another area in which agencies can improve practices is by employing a positive youth development framework in transition planning. As discussed earlier, federal legislation provides specific language that places control over the detail of transition plans with the child; that is, "as detailed as the *child* may elect" [FCSIAA, 2008, § 202 (3)]. This legislative mandate, combined with positive youth development principles, indicates that youth should have meaningful power and control over the details of their transition plans and be consulted about important non-parent adults in their lives. Avery (2010) encourages practice models that rely on youth to identify and involve significant adults, related or otherwise, in permanency plan development. The Iowa Department of Human Services (2011) has already instituted this practice in helping youth to develop their transition plans with the *Iowa Blueprint for Forever Families 2011*.

Child welfare worker turnover, described as a restraining force (National Resource Center for Youth Development, 2000), is another barrier to establishing permanency among youth aging out of care. Aside from the practical issue of workers needing time to learn about their new cases, relational aspects of the child welfare worker/foster youth relationship may be overlooked due to the focus on relationships outside the child welfare agency. Child welfare worker/foster youth relationships are ultimately still adult/child relationships. They represent, at their core, an opportunity for foster youth to develop trusting relationships with adults. When foster youth were asked to describe their experiences with worker turnover and change, many youth felt that these relationship losses mirrored those they had experienced prior to entering care, and described the difficulty in establishing trust with the new workers assigned to them (Strolin-Goltzman, Kollar, & Trinkle, 2010). Because these relationships are models for how youth perceive relationships with other adults, more care should be taken in preventing unnecessary worker transition for youth in care.

Macro-Level: Remembering Mentors as Part of the Transition Process

Federal policy suggests that mentoring and other efforts to establish permanent relationships should be a priority for youth expected to exit care as a result of emancipation. However, much of the language within the current legislation prioritizes connecting youth to adoptive families or other kinship/guardianship arrangements in order to establish permanency. While these efforts may be ideal for younger youth and/or youth likely to reunify with family, these efforts may not be effective for foster youth unlikely to be adopted or to reunify with family. These youth require specific programming within legislation that promotes relationship-building with caring, non-parent adults.

Greeson (2013) asserts that the promotion of natural mentoring relationships is a promising alternative to legal permanence for older youth in care, and that more federal legislation is needed to provide increased funding to organizations focusing on natural mentoring support. To that end, child welfare practitioners and others who work with youth aging out of care should advocate for federal policies that identify specific practices (e.g., focus on developing enduring, high-quality relationships) to support and promote youths' relationship development with non-relative adults who can guide youth as they enter emerging adulthood. Rather than using ILPs for this purpose, separate programs that could serve foster youth populations should be allowed to draw down federal funding to focus on mentoring relationships. These programs should also utilize a positive youth development approach that prioritizes youths' opinions about which non-parent adults are important, especially because youth exiting care are already developing relationships with these types of adults outside recognized mentoring programs.

One such practice that is emerging within the field of mentoring is youth initiated mentoring. *Youth initiated mentoring* (YIM) is an approach to formal mentoring that capitalizes and builds on naturally occurring connections that youth have with supportive adults (Schwartz et al., 2013; Spencer et al., 2016). A hybrid of formal and natural mentoring, mentoring programs employing YIM work with youth to identify positive adults within their existing support networks with whom a more formal mentoring relationship could be established. The program then recruits, screens, and trains the identified mentor, and formalizes the relationship. Monitoring and ongoing support are provided, as with any structured mentoring program.

Although only a handful of programs have implemented this approach, it is highly promising for its potential to redress some long-standing problems faced by many mentoring programs, such as volunteer attrition and premature match closures (Grossman & Rhodes, 2002; Herrera, Grossman, Kauh, & McMaken, 2011; Schwartz et al., 2013).

Further, the encouragement of youth voice and choice in YIM may be especially important for youth in foster care, as these youth have often endured a series of short-lived or tumultuous relationships with adults of varying responsiveness and dependability. These can result in youth feeling fatigued, wary about forming relationships, and doubtful about the helpfulness of new relationships with adults who are strangers to them (Kupersmidt, Stump, Stelter, & Rhodes, 2017; Zilberstein & Spencer, 2017). Preliminary findings from a descriptive qualitative study of YIM that included former foster youth who are making the transition to adulthood indicated that this approach can help youth to form strong, meaningful, and potentially long-lasting connections with supportive adults (Spencer, Gowdy, Drew, Horn, & Rhodes, 2017). This is important because evidence is mounting that both formal and informal mentoring relationships that persist, and in which youth feel close to their mentors, tend to be of the greatest benefit (Grossman & Rhodes, 2002; Hiles, Moss, Wright, & Dallos; 2013; Hurd & Sellers, 2013; Liang, Tracy, Taylor, & Williams, 2002; Parra, DuBois, Neville, Pugh-Lilly, & Povinelli, 2002). The youth selected adults in whom they already experienced some level of trust and whom they thought would be helpful without being judgmental. The adults selected entered into these newly formalized mentoring relationships with high levels of commitment to the youth and a strong desire to be a source of significant and ongoing support to them. Although this descriptive study points to the potential power of this approach in promoting more permanent, supportive relationships between adults and foster youth, further research is needed to determine whether and to what degree YIM is effective in promoting positive outcomes.

Conclusion

Although all young people need supportive non-parent adults to make the transition from adolescence to early adulthood, this is especially true for foster youth, who have experienced significant instability and disruptions in their primary relationships with adults. The promotion of mentoring relationships is a promising strategy for cultivating the kinds of permanent connections deemed so critical to the success of transitioning foster youth. For mentoring to be successful at serving the needs of foster youth, however, youth must be meaningfully engaged and viewed as resources in the process of identifying and engaging important adults in their lives. Child welfare workers may begin by simply asking youth to reflect on adults who have been important to them, and in whom they have felt some sense of trust, in order to generate a list of potential adults with whom these youth can foster enduring relationships. Those adults who meet both the safety standards of the welfare agency and relational standards of the youth could be encouraged to maintain an active involvement in the lives of the transitioning foster youth. For this to happen, however, agencies and courts would need to allow these adults to maintain contact and visit with the youth. This would require policy changes that allow for the continuation of these types of relationship, especially because establishing a more traditional formal mentoring program within the child welfare system may be a difficult task (Spencer, Collins, Ward, & Smashnaya, 2010).

Youth initiated mentoring (YIM) may be particularly well suited to meeting the permanency needs of transitioning foster youth. As a new approach to mentoring, the evidence base examining its effectiveness is limited. However, Relational–Cultural Theory and the research on positive youth development, social support, and social capital support the core elements of YIM; namely, youth voice and choice in the mentor selection process. This helps youth to identify potential mentors from among their existing pool of adults, with whom they have already experienced trusting, caring, and understanding interactions.

Although some evidence already in hand clearly points to important ways that informal mentors may promote more positive outcomes for transitioning foster youth, more work in this area is sorely needed. First, more evaluation research should be completed of programs that support YIM approaches among foster youth, to explore the effectiveness of these programs. Second, a more substantial review should be conducted of how ILPs are meeting the mentoring needs of foster youth, to see if there are natural ways that child welfare organizations could support these needs. Finally, research should be conducted on child welfare agencies and their use of existing mentoring programs, in order to examine the feasibility of incorporating mentoring into the youths' already large array of services, especially because child welfare organizations generally have increased administrative considerations and safety concerns due to the nature of the population served. Finally, more theoretically-driven research is needed, particularly employing the strengths-based perspectives considered in this chapter. By learning more about the effectiveness of these emerging mentoring programs and organizational processes that can support the youths' access to said programs, researchers can help child welfare practitioners to find quality mentoring that meets the unique needs of the youth with whom they work.

Note

1 The AFCARS does not include youth over 16 years of age with a case plan goal of "emancipation" and whose parental rights have been terminated in their numbers of "youth waiting to be adopted."

References

Ahrens, K. R., DuBois, D. L., Richardson, L. P., Fan, M., & Lozano, P. (2008). Youth in foster care with adult mentors during adolescence have improved adult outcomes. *Pediatrics, 121*(2), e246–e252. https://doi.org/10.1542/peds.2007-0508

Akin, B. A. (2011). Predictors of foster care exits to permanency: A competing risk analysis of reunification, guardianship, and adoption. *Children and Youth Services Review, 33*(6), 999–1011. https://doi.org/10.1016/j.childyouth.2011.01.008

Avery, R. J. (2010). An examination of theory and promising practice for achieving permanency for teens before they age out of care. *Children and Youth Services Review, 32*(3), 399–408. https://doi.org/10.1016/j.childyouth.2009.10.011

Becker, M. A., Jordan, N., & Larsen, R. (2007). Predictors of successful permanency planning and length of stay in foster care: The role of race, diagnosis and place of residence. *Children and Youth Services Review, 29*(8), 1102–1113. https://doi.org/10.1016/j.childyouth.2007.04.009

Benson, P. L., Scales, P. C., Roehlkepartain, E. C., & Leffert, N. (2011). *A fragile foundation: The state of developmental assets among American youth* (2nd ed.). Minneapolis, MN: Search Institute. Retrieved from http://files.eric.ed.gov/fulltext/ED431040.pdf

Bourdieu, P. (1986). The forms of capital. In J. G. Richardson (Ed.), *Handbook on theory and research for the sociology of education* (pp. 241–258). New York, NY: Greenwood Press.

Comstock, D. L., Hammer, T. R., Strentzsch, J., Cannon, K., Parsons, J., & Salazar, G. (2008). Relational–Cultural Theory: A framework for bridging relational, multicultural, and social justice competencies. *Journal of Counseling & Development, 86*(3), 279–287. doi: 10.1002/j.1556-6678.2008.tb00510.x

Consolidated Omnibus Budget Reconciliation Act of 1985 [COBRA], Pub. L. No. 99-272, 100 Stat. 82. (1986).

Courtney, M. E., Dworsky, A., Brown, A., Cary, C., Love, K., & Vorhies, V. (2011). *Midwest Evaluation of the Adult Functioning of Former Foster Youth: Outcomes at age 26* [Report]. Chicago: Chapin Hall at the University of Chicago. Retrieved from www.chapinhall.org/sites/default/files/Midwest%20Evaluation_Report_4_10_12.pdf

Curry, S. R., & Abrams, L. S. (2015). Housing and social support for youth aging out of foster care: State of research literature and directions for future inquiry. *Child and Adolescent Social Work Journal, 32*(2), 143–153. https://doi.org/10.1007/s10560-014-0346-4

Diehl, D. C., Howse, R. B., & Trivette, C. M. (2011). Youth in foster care: Developmental assets and attitudes towards adoption and mentoring. *Child & Family Social Work, 16*(1), 81–92. doi: 10.1111/j.1365-2206.2010.00716.x

DuBois, D. L., & Silverthorn, N. (2005). Characteristics of natural mentoring relationships and adolescent adjustment: Evidence from a national study. *The Journal of Primary Prevention, 26*(2), 69–90. https://doi.org/10.1007/s10935-005-1832-4

Eller, L. S., Lev, E. L., & Feurer, A. (2014). Key components of an effective mentoring relationship: A qualitative study. *Nurse Education Today, 34*(5), 815–820. https://doi.org/10.1016/j.nedt.2013.07.020

Foster Care Independence Act of 1999 [FCIA], Pub. L. No. 106-169, 113 Stat. 1822. (1999)..

Fostering Connections to Success and Increasing Adoptions Act of 2008 [FCSIAA], Pub. L. No. 110-351, 122 Stat. 3949. (2008).

Geenen, S., Powers, L. E., Phillips, L. A., Nelson, M., McKenna, J., Winges-Yanez, N., . . . Swank, P. (2015). Better Futures: A randomized field test of a model for supporting young people in foster care with mental health challenges to participate in higher education. *The Journal of Behavioral Health Services & Research, 42*(2), 150–171. https://doi.org/10.1007/s11414-014-9451-6

Greeson, J. K. P. (2013). Foster youth and the transition to adulthood: The theoretical and conceptual basis for natural mentoring. *Emerging Adulthood, 1*(1), 40–51. https://doi.org/10.1177/2167696812467780

Greeson, J. K. P., & Bowen, N. K. (2008). "She holds my hand": The experiences of foster youth with their natural mentors. *Children and Youth Services Review, 30*(10), 1178–1188. https://doi.org/10.1016/j.childyouth.2008.03.003

Grossman, J., & Rhodes, J. (2002). The test of time: Predictors and effects of duration in youth mentoring relationships. *Journal of Community Psychology, 30*(2), 198–219. doi: 10.1023/A:1014680827552

Harris, K. M. (2013). *The Add Health Study: Design and accomplishments* [Report]. Chapel Hill, NC: Carolina Population Center. Retrieved from www.cpc.unc.edu/projects/addhealth/documentation/guides/DesignPaperWIIV.pdf

Hass, M., & Graydon, K. (2009). Sources of resiliency among successful foster youth. *Children and Youth Services Review, 31*(4), 457–463. https://doi.org/10.1016/j.childyouth.2008.10.001

Hepworth, D. H., Rooney, R. H., Rooney, G. D., Strom-Gottfriend, K., & Larsen, J. (2010). *Direct social work practice: Theory and skills* (8th ed.). Belmont, CA: Brooks and Cole.

Herrera, C., Grossman, J. B., Kauh, T. J., & McMaken, J. (2011). Mentoring in schools: An impact study of Big Brothers Big Sisters school-based mentoring. *Child Development, 82*(1), 346–361. doi: 10.1111/j.1467-8624.2010.01559.x

Hiles, D., Moss, D., Wright, J., & Dallos, R. (2013). Young people's experience of social support during the process of leaving care: A review of the literature. *Children and Youth Services Review, 35*(12), 2059–2071. https://doi.org/10.1016/j.childyouth.2013.10.008

Hurd, N. M., & Sellers, R. M. (2013). Black adolescents' relationships with natural mentors: Associations with academic engagement via social and emotional development. *Cultural Diversity and Ethnic Minority Psychology, 19*(1), 76–85. http://dx.doi.org/10.1037/a0031095

Iowa Department of Human Services. (2011). *Iowa's blueprint for forever families 2011* [Handbook]. Retrieved from www.ifapa.org/pdf_docs/BlueprintforPermanency.pdf

Jordan, J. V. (1991). *The movement of mutuality and power*. Paper No. 53, Work in Progress series. Wellesley, MA: Stone Center.

Jordan, J. V. (2010). *Relational–Cultural Therapy*. Washington, DC: American Psychological Association.

Kools, S. M. (1999). Self-protection in adolescents in foster care. *Journal of Child and Adolescent Psychiatric Nursing, 12*(4), 139–152. doi: 10.1111/j.1744-6171.1999.tb00063.x

Kupersmidt, J. B., Stump, K. N., Stelter, R. L., & Rhodes, J. E. (2017). Predictors of premature match closure in youth mentoring relationships. *American Journal of Community Psychology, 59*(1–2), 25–35. doi: 10.1002/ajcp.12124

Langford, C. P. H., Bowsher, J., Maloney, J. P., & Lillis, P. P. (1997). Social support: A conceptual analysis. *Journal of Advanced Nursing, 25*(1), 95–100. doi: 10.1046/j.1365-2648.1997.1997025095.x

Lee, C., & Berrick, J. D. (2014). Experiences of youth who transition to adulthood out of care: Developing a theoretical framework. *Children and Youth Services Review, 46*, 78–84. https://doi.org/10.1016/j.childyouth.2014.08.005

Lerner, R. M., Lerner, J. V., Almerigi, J. B., Theokas, C., Phelps, E., Gestsdottir, S., . . . von Eye, A. (2005). Positive youth development, participation in community youth development programs, and community contributions of fifth-grade adolescents: Findings from the first wave of the 4-H study of positive youth development. *The Journal of Early Adolescence, 25*(1), 17–71. https://doi.org/10.1177/0272431604272461

Lerner, R. M., Lerner, J. V., & Benson, J. B. (2011). Positive youth development. Research and applications for promoting thriving in adolescence. *Advances in Child Development and Behavior, 41*, 1–17. https://doi.org/10.1016/B978-0-12-386492-5.00001-4

Liang, B., Spencer, R., Brogan, D., & Corral, M. (2008). Mentoring relationships from early adolescence through emerging adulthood: A qualitative analysis. *Journal of Vocational Behavior, 72*(2), 168–182. https://doi.org/10.1016/j.jvb.2007.11.005

Liang, B., Tracy, A., Taylor, C., & Williams, L. (2002). Mentoring college-age women: A relational approach. *American Journal of Community Psychology, 30*(2), 271–315. doi: 10.1023/A:1014637112531

Lofquist, W. (1989). *The technology of prevention workbook*. Tucson, AZ: AYD Publications.

Mallon, G. P. (2011). Permanency for LGBTQ youth. *Protecting Children, 26*(1), 49–57.

Mallon, G. P., Aledort, N., & Ferrera, M. (2002). There's no place like home: Achieving safety, permanency, and well-being for lesbian and gay adolescents in out-of-home care. *Child Welfare, 81*(2), 407–439.

Miller, J. B. (1988). *Connections, disconnections and violations*. Paper No. 33, Work in Progress series. Wellesley, MA: Stone Center.

Miller, J. B., & Stiver, I. P. (1997). *The healing connection*. Boston, MA: Beacon Press.

Munson, M. R., & McMillen, J. C. (2009). Natural mentoring and psychosocial outcomes among older youth transitioning from foster care. *Children and Youth Services Review, 31*(1), 104–111. https://doi.org/10.1016/j.childyouth.2008.06.003

Munson, M. R., Smalling, S. E., Spencer, R., Scott, L. D. Jr., & Tracy, E. M. (2010). A steady presence in the midst of change: Non-kin natural mentors in the lives of older youth exiting foster care. *Children and Youth Services Review, 32*(4), 527–535. https://doi.org/10.1016/j.childyouth.2009.11.005

National Resource Center for Youth Development. (2000). *Permanency planning: Creating lifelong connections: What does it mean for adolescents* [Report]. Tulsa, OK: University of Oklahoma, National Resource Center for Youth Development. Retrieved from http://files.eric.ed.gov/fulltext/ED478788.pdf

Nesmith, A., & Christophersen, K. (2014). Smoothing the transition to adulthood: Creating ongoing supportive relationships among foster youth. *Children and Youth Services Review, 37*, 1–8. https://doi.org/10.1016/j.childyouth.2013.11.028

Parra, G. R., DuBois, D. L., Neville, H. A., Pugh-Lilly, A. O., & Povinelli, N. (2002). Mentoring relationships for youth: Investigation of a process-oriented model. *Journal of Community Psychology, 30*(4), 367–388. doi: 10.1002/jcop.10016

Pecora, P. J. (2012). Maximizing educational achievement of youth in foster care and alumni: Factors associated with success. *Children and Youth Services Review, 34*(6), 1121–1129. https://doi.org/10.1016/j.childyouth.2012.01.044

Pecora, P. J., Kessler, R. C., Williams, J., O'Brien, K., Downs, A. C., English, D., . . . Holmes, K. (2005). Improving family foster care: Findings from the Northwest Foster Care Alumni Study. Seattle, WA: Casey Family Programs. Retrieved from http://cdn.casey.org/media/AlumniStudies_NW_Report_FR.pdf

Promoting Safe and Stable Families Amendments of 2001 [PSSFA], Pub. L. No. 107-133, 115 Stat. 2413. (2002).

Rhodes, J. E., Spencer, R., Keller, T. E., Liang, B., & Noam, G. (2006). A model of the influence of mentoring relationships on youth development. *Journal of Community Psychology, 34*(6), 691–707. doi: 10.1002/jcop.20124

Schwartz, S. E. O., Rhodes, J. E., Spencer, R., & Grossman, J. B. (2013). Youth initiated mentoring: Investigating a new approach to working with vulnerable adolescents. *American Journal of Community Psychology, 52*(1), 155–169. doi: 10.1007/s10464-013-9585-3

Spencer, R. (2000). *A comparison of relational psychologies.* Paper No. 5, Project Report series. Wellesley, MA: Stone Center.

Spencer, R., Collins, M. E., Ward, R., & Smashnaya, S. (2010). Mentoring for young people leaving foster care: Promise and potential pitfalls. *Social Work, 55*(3), 225–234. https://doi.org/10.1093/sw/55.3.225

Spencer, R., Gowdy, G., Drew, A. L., Horn, J. P., & Rhodes, J. E. (2017, January)."It just helps to have someone there": Youth initiated mentorship for former foster care youth. Paper presented in symposium (G. Gowdy, Chair) on Natural Mentorship for Foster Care Youth: Prevalence, Impact, and Programmatic Support at the Conference of the Society for Social Work and Research, New Orleans, LA.

Spencer, R., Tugenberg, T., Ocean, M., Schwartz, S. E. O., & Rhodes, J. E. (2016). "Somebody who was on my side": A qualitative examination of youth initiated mentoring. *Youth & Society, 48*(3), 402–424. https://doi.org/10.1177/0044118X13495053

Strolin-Goltzman, J., Kollar, S., & Trinkle, J. (2010). Listening to the voices of children in foster care: Youths speak out about child welfare workforce turnover and selection. *Social Work, 55*(1), 47–53. https://doi.org/10.1093/sw/55.1.47

Thompson, A. E., Greeson, J. K. P., & Brunsink, A. M. (2016). Natural mentoring among older youth in and aging out of foster care: A systematic review. *Children and Youth Services Review, 61*, 40–50. https://doi.org/10.1016/j.childyouth.2015.12.006

Timpe, Z. C., & Lunkenheimer, E. (2015). The long-term economic benefits of natural mentoring relationships for youth. *American Journal of Community Psychology, 56*(1–2), 12–24. doi: 10.1007/s10464-015-9735-x

U.S. Department of Health & Human Services [USDHSS] (Administration for Children and Families, Children's Bureau). (2016). *The AFCARS report: Preliminary FY 2015 estimates as of June 2016.* No. 23. Washington, DC: U.S. Department of Health & Human Services. Retrieved from www.acf.hhs.gov/sites/default/files/cb/afcarsreport23.pdf

Wasserman, S., & Faust, K. (2009). *Social network analysis: Methods and applications* (19th ed.). New York, NY: Cambridge University Press.

Zilberstein, K., & Spencer, R. (2017) Breaking bad: An attachment perspective on youth mentoring relationship closures. *Child & Family Social Work, 22*(1), 67–76. doi: 10.1111/cfs.12197

Zimmerman, M. A., Bingenheimer, J. B., & Behrendt, D. E. (2005). Natural mentoring relationships. In D. L. Dubois & M. J. Karcher (Eds.), *Handbook of youth mentoring* (pp. 143–157). Newbury Park, CA: Sage Publications.

11

Youth in Foster Care Relationships with Biological, Foster, and Adoptive Families

Armeda Stevenson Wojciak and Nathan A. Hough

Within this book, you have learned the most recent statistics on the youth who are living in foster care, the impact which that system has on their mental health and physical health, and their cognitive and emotional development, as well as some of the potential challenges that youth face aging out of the foster care system. In this chapter, our focus is on the context of relationships that youth in foster care have, what we know empirically about these relationships, and how youth navigate these relationships within the complex foster care system.

Overview of Relationships within the Context of Foster Care

The mere placement in foster care signifies an important shift in the youth's familial relationships. Placement in foster care is the consequence of a family's involvement with the child welfare system due to suspected abuse and neglect of the child (Weisz, Wingrove, Beal, & Faith-Slaker, 2011). As a result of the investigation into suspected abuse and neglect, the courts can deem the youth's maltreatment at home to be too dangerous for them to continue living there and authorize the removal of the child from the parent(s)' custody and temporary placement into foster care (Lee & Whiting, 2008). Youth are often not involved in the decision-making process and consequently report confusion surrounding their placement in foster care and mistrust of the legal system (Festinger, 1983). The confusion that youth experience is complicated by the fact that youth are removed from the home and relationships that they knew, and are placed into an unknown setting, potentially with people that they do not know. In traditional foster care, youth are placed in an unfamiliar home with strangers and have to forge new relationships with their foster parents. This home may have other children who are now their foster siblings. Their foster care placement means that their biological parents are not caring for them, and there is a possibility that their biological sibling(s) may not be placed with them (Herrick & Piccus, 2005). Youth have to navigate what living with a foster family means and how that influences the relationships they have with their biological family members. Following their child's placement in the foster care system and the rehabilitative work that parents have to do to be reunified with their children, some parents may not successfully complete their case plan and may consequently lose their parental rights (Weisz et al., 2011). Permanency is a primary goal of the child welfare system. If parents are unable to fulfill their case plan in a timely manner, their child(ren) would be eligible for adoption through the child welfare system. This chapter provides a glimpse into the complex relationships that youth in foster care may have. Further, we will explore the unique relationship considerations within three different relational contexts: youth's relationships with their biological family, their foster families, and adoptive families. While the majority of children in foster care reside in foster families, this chapter does not explore the relationships of youth who may live in kinship care or group homes. Within these two contexts, there are myriad other factors that influence the complexity of relationships, needing further investigation and understanding that is outside the scope of this chapter.

Biological Family Relationships

There is a long history highlighting the importance of biological relationships to child development. John Bowlby's (1969) Attachment Theory emphasizes the significance of the parent–child relationship in developing a sense of safety and security in the world of a child, allowing them to explore and learn about the environment around them, as well as experiencing the reliability of their needs being met. Bowlby theorized that when a parental caregiver consistently meets the needs of a child (i.e., feeding, changing diapers, comforting when distressed), a secure attachment is developed and the child knows they can depend upon their parental caregiver for safety, allowing them to explore the world around them without fear. In contrast, children who develop an insecure attachment did not have their needs met consistently by a parental care provider, and thus have difficulties developing a sense of security to explore and make sense of the world around them. Even in families that are considered at risk, separation from their attachment figures can have significant effects on the mental health of the children, resulting in distress and anxiety (Howe, Brandon, Hinnings, & Schofield, 1999; Lowenthal, 1999; McWey, Acock, & Porter, 2010; McWey & Mullis, 2004). Bowlby (1982) further asserted that even when the caregiver is replaced with a capable care provider, children exhibit distress.

Although there is a large amount of literature that describes the significance of parent–child attachment, there is a scant amount of literature that discusses attachment between biological siblings. Sibling relationships play a significant role in foster care due to the loss of the connection between the children and their biological parents. Bank and Kahn (1982) stated that

> the hunger for affection, contact, and relatedness is so strong in early life that we are willing to settle for substitutes, on the principle that a little bit of attachment or an unhappy attachment is better than none at all.
>
> (Bank & Kahn, 1982, p. 27)

These peer-like relationships offer opportunities such as negotiating social and cognitive challenges (i.e., conflict resolution) and skill development that are similar to opportunities offered by parental attachment figures (Richardson & Yates, 2014). The literature also states that sibling relationships may often act as a buffer toward the stress of life events (Gass, Jenkins, & Dunn, 2007). Gass et al. (2007) also asserted that a positive relationship with their sibling mitigated life stressors even in the presence of marital conflict between their biological parents and child disturbance such as removal from the family home. When siblings are placed into foster care, the roles in which they identified within the biological family, such as golden child, forgotten child, sibling care provider, or one of three siblings must shift to accommodate the creation of new roles within the foster family. The siblings may then take on a new role as attachment figures, providing what Bank and Kahn (1982) considered to be a "life giving force" (p. 28). These relationship shifts change the previous roles of siblings from fostering social skills into a relationship that creates a sense of safety and emotional continuity (Shlonsky, Bellamy, Elkins, & Ashare, 2005).

Adding to the complexity that biological families must endure when entering the child welfare system, parents are issued with a permanency plan that details goals for the reunification with the biological family or adoption for the child. In understanding the importance of maintaining a relationship with the biological family, the child welfare system upholds visitations between the children in foster care and their biological parents. There is a divide in the literature stating whether or not these visits are beneficial to the well-being of children in foster care. In 1975, Littner stated, "For better or worse, they are his roots to the past, his support and foundation. When he is separated from them, he feels that he has lost a part of himself" (p. 177). He further reported that should children be denied the opportunity to visit their families, they may develop unrealistic images of their biological parents (Littner, 1975). Other studies reported positive correlations between visitations with the biological parents and children's current well-being by helping to foster a greater sense of security and greater overall adjustment into foster care (Cantos, Gries, & Slis, 1997; McWey & Mullis, 2004). In contrast, many studies have shown that visitations with the biological parents are detrimental to the child's well-being. Haight, Black, Workman, and Tata (2001) reported that ideal visitations would be comprised of an enriched environment and parents would be emotionally supportive; however, visits are often not *ideal*. These less than ideal situations often develop due to the youth having conflicting loyalties between biological and foster parents, or a lack of understanding of the purpose of supervised visits, often causing aggression during visits and conflict between the foster family and biological parents (Fuentes-Pelaez, Amoros, Mateos, Balsells, & Violant, 2013). Among younger youth in foster care, negative outcomes due to visits with biological families include aggression such as arguing, physical altercations, destruction of property, hyperactivity and attention problems; while older youth experience depression, anxiety, and psychosomatic symptoms (Steinhauer, 1991). Despite these negative outcomes, several studies on visitations indicated that an overwhelming number of foster youth reported significant feelings of anxiety, they wanted more frequent visits or greater contact with their biological parents regardless of the youth's age (Fernandez, 2009; Morrison, Mishna, Cook, & Aitken, 2011; Sinclair, Wilson, & Gibbs, 2005). The literature on biological parental visitation therefore is conflictual, some arguing that these visits are beneficial to children in foster care; others that they are more detrimental to foster children's development. However, the existing literature on sibling relationships supports the need to keep siblings together as they are placed into foster care. Reasons for placing siblings together are that they provide one another with a sense of belonging, shared history, connection, and love (Wojciak, 2017).

To assist in the reunification process and improve the benefits of visitations, organizations from the United States and Europe, such as Parent Mutual Aid Organizations, the Child Welfare Information Gateway, and the Council of Europe have established psycho-educational and support-based parenting programs as well as peer mentoring to help the facilitation of skills that biological parents need to be reunified with their children (Frame, Conley, & Berrick, 2004). The Council of Europe developed a national law in Spain that established the importance of positive parenting on the development of children. The law states that parents have responsibilities in health, educational, and social responsibilities toward their children. It also states that the government has a responsibility in providing incentives, and establishing guidelines for parents to obtain the resources to engage in what they consider to be positive parenting, in an effort to reduce the potential negative outcomes from separating children from their biological parents (Council of Europe, 2006).

Foster Family Relationships

Foster families are a vital part of the foster care system. For youth in foster care, foster parents play two important roles: a) bureaucratic, in the sense that they are agents of the state who are ensuring youth's well-being; and b) familial, in that they are substitute parents and fulfill all the roles and characteristics that effective parents should embody (Berrick, 2015). Given these roles, foster families operate on a supply and demand system (Wojciak, 2014a); more foster families are needed when more children are involved in the foster care system. Social service agencies struggle with recruiting and retaining quality foster families (Cox, Orme, & Rhodes, 2002). Foster parent licensing varies by state, but is often highly regulated upon the physical safety of the placement (Berrick, 2015). Shlonsky and Berrick (2001) argued that minimal standards of safety are not sufficient for children in foster care, as children often have emotional and behavioral problems that need to be *parented* in a way that promotes the child's well-being. It is within this context that consideration needs to be applied to youth in foster care, particularly understanding of the youth's relationships with foster families.

As previously mentioned, youth in foster care have been removed from their home because the court has said it is too dangerous for the child to live there (Lee & Whiting, 2008). The child has experienced maltreatment at the hands of the person or people who should be ensuring their well-being, their parents. Child maltreatment that deems removal from the home may be categorized as complex trauma. Complex trauma is defined as "a combination of early and later-onset, sometimes invasive adverse events, usually of an ongoing, interpersonal nature" (Lanktree & Briere, 2017, p. 5). Complex trauma at the hands of those who care for youth often has long-term consequences. Youth who have experienced complex trauma may have impairments in multiple domains, such as attachment, affect regulation, behavioral problems, dissociation, cognitive functioning, and lack of self-confidence (Cook et al., 2005).

The above-mentioned list of possible impairments as a result of complex trauma all have the ability to influence the youth's experience while in foster care, and specifically in the way in which they interact with foster families. For instance, if we just take one domain, attachment, Cook and colleagues (2005) state that youth may experience impairments with boundaries, difficulty understanding another person's perspective, may isolate themselves from others, have a distrust/suspiciousness of others (particularly adults), may have problems interacting with others, and experience difficulty in attuning to others' emotions. From an attachment perspective, these responses reflect the consequences of the maltreatment the child experienced at the hands of their parent and first attachment figure (Bowlby, 1969). Bowlby proposes that children develop an unconscious blueprint of attachment style based on their relationship with their primary caregiver that they use for all relationships later in life (Whelan, 2003); he called this an internal working model. Internal working models are thought to be fully formed by the age of 5, but can change based on the child's caregiving experiences. If the child has attachment impairments as a result of their relationship with their biological parent, they may transfer their working model of attachment onto their foster parents. That child may be suspicious of the foster parent's best effort to try and make the child feel welcome in their home. How would the child know if the foster parent is someone they could trust? Milan and Pinderhughes (2000) reported that the mother–child relationship that a youth had with their biological mother was significantly predictive of the youth's view of their foster mothers. Youth are trying to react in the best way they know how to, given their previous living environment and relationships. Fortunately, internal working models can be modified, but require work from foster parents. Kelly and Salmon (2014) offer a relational learning framework to help foster parents understand the child's experiences and perspective, in order to inform the way they interact with the children in their home.

Youth in foster care may not only have to navigate new relationships with foster parents, but also relationships with other children in the foster home. Foster parents may have their own biological children living with them as well as other children living in foster care. Each child in the home brings their own experiences and their internal working models of attachment. Youth in foster care might exhibit distrust and suspicion of the other children, difficulty understanding their perspective, and interpersonal difficulties. Youth have to negotiate their role within the new home and with each new child that may enter it. Given the abuse or neglect youth had prior to placement, youth may not have the best tools, models, or examples of how to solve interpersonal problems. The interpersonal differences among the children, as well as with the foster parents, may make it difficult for foster parents to manage the behaviors of the children in their home. Attachment difficulties, particularly for younger youth, are associated with placement instability (Pasalich, Fleming, Oxford, Zheng, & Spieker, 2016). Attachment disorders have been associated with externalizing behaviors, which are also often associated with placement instability (Strijker, Knorth, & Knot-Dickscheit, 2008). Difficulties with attachment might be challenging for foster parents and foster families and can influence youth outcomes. To foster parents who do not fully understand the youth's internal working model of attachment, the youth's responses may make it seem like the placement is not a good fit. If the youth is removed from that home, it strengthens the youth's existing working model of attachment and can perpetuate greater social isolation and self-protective behaviors which could potentially jeopardize the youth's placement. Not surprisingly, a greater number of placements is associated with increased externalizing behaviors (Newton, Litrownik, & Landsverk, 2000; Strijker et al., 2008), and placement instability is associated with poorer long-term outcomes for youth in foster care (Barth et al., 2007).

The attachment impairments discussed highlight the potential effects of one of the possible seven impairments that Cook and colleagues (2005) described of the effects of complex trauma. Attachment was chosen as it is the most pressing when conceptualizing the complexities and nuances of relationships that youth in foster care experience. Now imagine the interplay of consequences if the youth has experienced impairments in more than one of the domains of complex trauma. How would that influence the youth's relationships with foster families? It would make it much more difficult to navigate these relationships.

Further complicating the relational experiences of youth in foster care is the fact that the youth may not be the only child in the home. There may be multiple children in the foster family's home who are experiencing these same challenges, which consequently influence the interactions youth have with one another and with their foster families. Furthermore, foster parents may have their own adversity or trauma history that they are working through. While there is limited research examining foster parents' own trauma history, in her dissertation, McLain (2008) reported that the majority, 97% of her sample of 201 foster parents, reported a personal history of trauma as assessed by the Stressful Life Events Screening Questionnaire. Further, given the information that we know from Felitti and colleagues' (1998) work surrounding adverse childhood experiences, we know that adverse childhood experiences are fairly common within the general population. The youth's trauma history, the impact of the trauma history of other youth in the home, and the foster parents' possible trauma history have the potential to create a *complex relational spider web within foster families that can become quite intricate*.

The complexity of all the relationship dynamics and consequent behaviors that can occur in foster homes highlights the need identified by Shlonsky and Berrick (2001), for foster parents trained in understanding and working with youth with emotional and behavioral problems. Often, youth can be *labeled* with a diagnosis or problem behaviors; however, if we understand where the basis of these behaviors comes from and the influence it has on the youth's relationships, a shift can occur in how foster families respond to the youth's behaviors. For instance, Sullivan, Murray, and Ake (2015) examined the usefulness of the Resource Parent Curriculum, a curriculum designed to increase understanding of youth who have experienced trauma. They found that it significantly helped kinship and traditional foster parents increase their knowledge of trauma-informed parenting and their confidence in parenting children with trauma. Trainings like this and an integration of trauma-informed care practices into foster parent training could be helpful in making a shift that can help to improve youth relationships and placement outcomes.

Adopted Family Relationships

As stated earlier, two concurrent permanency goals are established once children are placed in foster care. The first is reunification with their biological parents and the second goal is typically adoption. Approximately 59% of all adoptions in the United States are from the child welfare system and are often considered special-needs adoption (Forbes & Dziegielewski, 2003; Smith, Howard, Garnier, and Ryan, 2006). According to the Adoption and Foster Care Analysis and Reporting System (AFCARS) (U. S. Department of Health & Human Services, 2016), approximately 53,549 children were adopted through the utilization of child welfare agencies. Criteria for what is considered special-needs adoptions are set by each state and can vary from state to state; however, most states incorporate in their definition of special needs: children with severe mental, emotional, or cognitive disabilities; children who need to be placed with siblings; children who have histories of abuse, neglect, or exposure to drugs or alcohol during fetal development. Once the children are adopted, the parents must adjust their parenting techniques to compensate for these *special needs* of their children. This adjustment must also take into consideration everything the adopted children bring into their home from current issues to the entirety of their past (Forbes & Dziegielewski, 2003). In special-needs adoptions, normative developmental family tasks and dynamics are often affected by psychosocial problems unique to this type of adoption (Brodzinsky, 1990). When a family adopts special-needs children, there can be a disruption in the family dynamics; for example, fewer resources available to the biological children, changes in family member roles, or loss of intimacy between the adoptive parents. These can create an imbalance within already established family roles and stress, potentially leading to disruption of the adoption where the children return to foster care (Foli, South, Lim, & Jarnecke, 2016; Forbes & Dziegielewski, 2003).

There are significant strains that are placed on a family when an adoption occurs. The most common reason found for adoptive families terminating adoptions was that these families were unable to access the services needed to support the adopted children (U.S. Government Accountability Office, 2015). These families, once they feel they have exhausted their resources, may turn to the dissolution of the adoption. The Children's Bureau defines adoption dissolution as

> the legal relationship between the adoptive parents and adoptive child is severed, either voluntarily or involuntarily, after the adoption is legally finalized. This results in the child's return to (or entry into) foster care or placement with new adoptive parents.
> (Child Welfare Information Gateway, 2012, p. 1)

Over the past several decades, researchers have found that the most significant factor associated with adoption dissolution is the age of a child at placement into foster care as well as at adoption—older children are more likely to have the adoption dissolved (Festinger, 2002; Jones & LaLiberte, 2010; Rolock & White, 2016; Rosenthal, 1993). Rolock and White (2016) further asserted that when children aged 8.7 and younger enter adoption into the same household, there is a greater risk for adoption disruption or dissolution. Other factors that have been found to impact adoption dissolution were gender and race, with the highest risk being among African-American males (Coakley & Berrick, 2008). Public opinion regarding adoption dissolution has been found to be significantly unsupportive of adoptive parents returning their adopted children to the child welfare system. Hollingsworth (2003) found that individuals over the age of 30 with some college education were more likely to support the dissolution of adoption; however, 58% of the participants still believed that adoptive parents should not be allowed to change their mind and should be "required to keep the child" (p. 164). Although there is research on adoption dissolution, little is known about the outcomes that siblings experience after dissolution has occurred. Outcomes such as attachment issues, behavioral issues, effects on cognitive development, and long-term relational issues have not been studied.

Not only are there significant issues that adoptive parents must deal with, there are also social stigmas, as well as grief and loss, that affect the mental well-being of the parents, especially the adoptive mother. Culturally, mature womanhood is directly linked to a woman producing biological children. March and Miall (2000) wrote that the dominant culture's social belief that adoption is inferior to natural birth often has significant effects, possibly causing the social isolation of adoptive mothers. The government has attempted to reduce this social stigma by requiring a new birth certificate to be issued for each adopted child that lists the adoptive parents as their legal *biological* parents; however, the dominant culture still does not regard adoption as being the same as biological families (Forbes & Dziegielewski, 2003; Johnson, 2002; Miall, 1996). Miall (1987) found the existence of three major cultural stigmas: 1) it is assumed that biological ties are significant in fostering bonding and love, therefore adoptive families are considered second rate; 2) adoptive children are further considered second rate because there is little known about their biology; and 3) adoptive parents are not considered as real parents because they are not biologically related to their children.

Forbes and Dziegielewski (2003) asserted that families often go through a honeymoon stage, and afterward become shocked by the nature of their adopted children's needs. They also wrote that adoptive mothers experience great loss when they come to the realization that the ability to have natural children is not a reality. This reality continues to exacerbate many mental health issues experienced by adoptive parents. It is well understood that when a mother is depressed, her ability to tend to the needs of her children diminishes significantly. In 2010, Payne, Fields, Meuchel, Jaffe, and Jha reported that approximately 27.9% of adoptive mothers experienced post-adoption depression within the first year after the adoption was finalized. Little is known about the adoptive father's experience. However, as adoptive mothers experience external stressors related to the adoption, adoptive fathers experience internal forms of stress, most of which is due to questioning their masculinity based on their infertility (Baumann, 1999). Foli, South, Lim, and Hebdon (2013) reported that 18% to 26% of mothers and 11% to 24% of fathers experience post-adoption depression within the first year after adoption. Despite the negative responses to adoption, adoptive parents do go through a claiming process in which the adopted children are viewed as though they are completely a member of the family, and characteristics of the children begin to resemble those of the adoptive parents, such as temperament, physical appearance, and behaviors (Baumann, 1999).

Adoptive parents are not the only members of the family who suffer from issues that arise because of the adoption; the biological and adoptive children suffer as well. Biological children will respond to the adoption of a new sibling in many ways, and often in a negative fashion. Children who are in middle childhood may be excited about their new sibling entering their home, but as the time approaches for the adoption to occur, they will begin to suffer fear of abandonment which can result in intense anxiety that they feel they cannot express to their parents (Phillips, 1999). Whereas adolescents who are beginning to develop their own sense of identity begin to question the loyalty of their adoptive parents; they begin to wonder about their biological parents, asking why did they give me up for adoption or why did they not want me anymore (Phillips, 1999). Currently there is a scant amount of literature that focuses on the experiences of biological children of adoptive parents.

Adopted children deal with their own set of feelings, such as abandonment and grief from severed relationships with their biological family. Johnson (2002) stated that there are potential advantages to being adopted versus being biologically born to one's parents. Such benefits might include being adopted into a higher socioeconomic status (SES), being offered better nutrition, and having parents with a higher level of education (Hoksbergen, 1999; Johnson, 2002). Studies of adopted children in the United Kingdom and Canada showed that although children had significant developmental delays, all adopted children in their studies showed significant improvement in their developmental quotients, scaled on the Denver Developmental Quotient (Ames, 1997; Johnson, 2002). This scale specifically looks at development in the following domains: fine motor-adaptive, gross motor, personal-social, and language skills (Ringwalt, 2008). Despite these positive outcomes for adoptive children, there are also ones that have a negative impact on both the individual and sibling(s) due to the adoption, such as externalized behaviors, increased mental health issues, and attachment issues. When the attachment from a child's parental caregiver is broken, the child suffers from indiscriminate sociability that lasts for a significant period of time after adoption. More specifically, these children have difficulties attaching to their adoptive parents due to the loss of their biological parents (van den Dries, Juffer, van IJzendoorn, & Bakermans-Kranenburg, 2010; Zeanah, 2000).

Furthermore, when thinking of adoption, children who are adopted are not only separated from their biological parents, but they may also be separated from their siblings. Children who are adopted with or without their siblings must navigate new relationships and find new attachment figures they can bond with in order to feel a sense of security in their new home. They may also experience a shift in family roles, new or different sibling relationships and sibling placement, and many other significant factors that affect the child's attachment (Cossar & Neil, 2013; Hipple & Haflich, 1993). For instance, an older child in their biological family may now be the middle child in their adopted family. This change in the family structure causes instability in the relationships and disruptions in attachments for all family members. The biological children of the adoptive parents must grieve the loss of the family they grew up in and learn how to navigate their new position within the family.

Resilience Theory and Foster Care

Youth in foster care are at risk for myriad negative outcomes. Researchers have reported that youth in foster care have higher instances of mental health issues compared to peers in similar socioeconomic backgrounds (Harmon, Childs, & Kelleher, 2000), educational shortcomings (Courtney et al., 2007; Pecora et al., 2003), increased rates of pregnancy (Love, McIntosh, Rosst, & Tertzakian, 2005), incarceration (Massinga & Pecora, 2004), and chance of being homeless (Massinga & Pecora, 2004). However, despite these statistics, we know that many youth in foster care experience good outcomes. Resilience theory provides a strengths-based framework for understanding how some youth who have experienced adversity still experience healthy development and positive outcomes (Fergus & Zimmerman, 2005). Resilience is a dynamic process that can be targeted for intervention (Kolar, 2011). In fact, Fergus and Zimmerman state that resilience theory enables researchers to identify ways to interview and to encourage resilience with two types of promotive factors: assets and resources. Assets are positive factors that are inherent in the individual; examples of assets include self-esteem and self-efficacy. Resources are positive factors outside the individual that can support the youth; these factors can include support from a youth's parents and mentors, as well as programming designed to support youth and their development. Assets and resources work together to promote resilience within youth.

For children who have experienced abuse and neglect, besides fixed factors such as race and gender, length of placement and social support were the biggest predictors of resilience (DuMont, Widom, & Czaja, 2007). DuMont and colleagues state that a longer length of time in placement or in a stable, two-parent home may be correlated with social support as youth who live with the same people continuously over time are able to develop more supportive relationships throughout adolescence and early adulthood. The Center of the Developing Child at Harvard University states that having a reliable adult is the single most important predictor of resilience for children. These two factors, placement stability and adult support, are incrementally important for understanding resilience for youth in foster care. Think of the attachment examples described thus far: it is clear that the experiences youth have prior to entering foster care and while in care have the potential to influence their behaviors. Previous harmful experiences that youth have may influence their attachment with their foster families and/or adoptive families.

Attachment difficulties are associated with externalizing behaviors like aggression with peers (Groh, Fearon, van IJzendoorn, Bakermans-Kranenburg, & Roisman, 2017). Externalizing behaviors are associated with placement instability (Pasalich et al., 2016; Strijker et al., 2008). Greater numbers of placements are associated with lower levels of resilience (DuMont et al., 2007). Yet, resilience theory posits that interventions can occur to help shift promotive factors in youth (Fergus & Zimmerman, 2005). Supportive relationships and placement stability are predictors of resilience for youth who have experienced child maltreatment (DuMont et al., 2007). Consequently, interventions designed to improve supportive relationships between youth and their foster caregivers can have the potential to increase resilience in these youth. Within this chapter, our focus is on relationships. In order to intervene and improve relationships, we need to understand relationships with biological, foster, and adoptive families from the youth's perspective. The following sections will explore what we know empirically about these relationships from the youth's perspective. Learning from them can help us to target more effectively ways to promote these relationships in order to promote resilience and, ultimately, better outcomes.

Youth Perspective of Biological Families

In a study conducted by Johnson, Yoken, and Voss (1995), they found that most children in foster care were uncertain about why they were placed in foster care. They further stated that before these children were removed from their homes, relatives attempted to help the biological families with their problems; however, these attempts were refused, ignored, or not accepted by the biological parents. Of the children who understood why they were removed from their homes, the most common responses were: parents were addicted to drugs, one or both parents were deceased, or there was an illness in the family (Baker, Creegan, Quinones, & Rozelle, 2016; Fuentes-Pelaez et al., 2013). Further studies showed that despite the positive or negative experience, most children in foster care expressed a desire to return to their families and missed them very much (Aldgate & McIntosh, 2006; Selwyn, Saunders, & Farmer, 2010). In a qualitative study by Johnson and colleagues (1995) almost all of the children had advice they wanted to give to their parents such as: "a child needs someone to raise them, someone to take care of them," and in reference to biological parents maintaining contact, "children need to know them and parents need to know what the child's life is like in the foster home" (p. 967).

Once a child is removed from their birth home, they continue to have contact with their biological parents. These points of contact occur through phone calls, physical visitations, letters, etc. Although the foster children report both positive and negative aspects to the visits with their biological parents, there is a lot of confusion that occurs during these visits. Fuentes-Pelaez et al. (2013) conducted a qualitative study to understand foster children's perceptions about their biological visits, reporting that many foster children in kinship care question who is in charge: "Who is in charge, my grandmother or my mother? . . . Yes, I want visits, why do they have to control them?" (p. 351). Among the different types of foster care, kinship care is the one in which children have the most contact with their biological parents due to their grandparents, aunt, uncle, or other family member obtaining legal guardianship. Among the confusion of how birth parents, foster parents, and social workers rank in authority regarding youth in placement, the desire to be back home with their parents, and the confusion as to why they are in foster care all contribute to the trauma that foster children experience, affecting behaviors, mental health, and social/personal relationships. McWey and Mullis (2004) indicated that youth who had more frequent contact with their biological parents had stronger levels of attachment to their parents and fewer behavioral problems, compared to youth who had less frequent visitation with biological parents. These results indicate that contact is important for maintaining attachment to biological parents when reunification is the primary permanency goal. Further research needs to be conducted through phenomenological and narrative studies to get a better understanding of the perspectives of biological siblings and parent–child relationships from the youth perspective.

Youth's Perspective of Foster Families

Ambiguous loss is a way to understand the complicated emotions, perceptions, and behaviors of unresolved loss that people experience (Boss, 1999). Ambiguous loss has been used to conceptualize the feelings that youth often describe of their time living in foster care (Lee & Whiting, 2008;

Samuels, 2009; Wojciak, McWey, & Helfrich, 2013). An example of ambiguous loss is that children are not living in the same household as their biological family, but they are still family and still influence each other (Whiting & Lee, 2003). In ambiguous loss terms, they are psychologically present, but physically absent. A participant in Samuels' (2009) qualitative study who experienced three different foster homes discussed the difficulty and the toll that multiple moves take on a child. This youth shared the difficulty they had navigating different family systems (rules, roles, and relationship dynamics) in addition to what they were experiencing with their own biological family since being in the foster care system. Another youth in the study shared how they would go to all "them different foster homes" and would become family, but would keep getting "pulled and pulled and pulled out of placements" (Samuels, 2009, p. 1233). Youth in foster care report not only losing connections with their biological families as a result of their placement in foster care, but if they move placements while in foster care, they may also lose connections with previous foster families.

Despite the ambiguous loss that youth feel, researchers have examined youth's satisfaction with their placement in foster care. Jones (2015) summarized existing studies that examined foster youth satisfaction, and indicated that the majority of studies found that youth thought they had a better quality of life in their foster home, greater safety, and better neighborhoods than they did with their biological families. In a qualitative study exploring whether or not removal from the home was necessary, 80% of youth who aged out of foster care reported that it was necessary that they were removed from their biological families (Jones, 2015). There were five major themes the youth reported for why removal was necessary:

1. There were parental deficits such as abusive parents, parents who abused substances, and parents who could not take care of their children.
2. Removal from the home made them a better person. Youth stated that they were stronger and better able to take care of themselves.
3. The education they received as a result of being removed—youth stated that they wouldn't have gone to school, their biological parents didn't support education. They received more help with school as a result of being placed in foster care. A few youth reported that they didn't think they would be in college if they had not been placed in foster care and received the support they did for their education.
4. There were multiple problems in their biological home, such as family members who were in prison, homelessness, and poor living conditions.
5. Foster care provided safety. Youth shared how they would probably have ended up in jail, pregnant, become a runaway, homeless, or dead if they hadn't been placed in foster care.

Similarly, Johnson et al. (1995) interviewed children between 11 and 14 years old; 58% stated that they felt that removal from their home was necessary. They stated that if they had not been removed, their life (including their living situation, family relationship, abuse/neglect) would have stayed the same or would have got worse. Sixty percent of the kids thought that traditional foster families were good and reported similar reasons to Jones's study: foster families provide a safe home, food, nicer neighborhoods and greater educational support.

Foster Parents

Qualitative and quantitative investigations have shed light on youth's perceptions of foster parents. The youth in Johnson et al. (1995) identified characteristics that make up a *good* and *bad* foster parent. A *good* foster parent likes kids and wants to listen and understand the child. A *good* foster parent is there to teach them right from wrong and does not have favorites. Youth in this study, as well as Samuels' (2009) study, shared the notion that you had a good foster family if you could invite people over, relax, and go to the refrigerator and get food. This concept of belonging, and the sentiment of being able to relax and invite people over were almost identical in the two different studies. This highlights the youth's desire for normalcy within the foster care context. In contrast to that, the youth in Johnson et al.'s study indicated that a *bad* foster parent was someone who did not care for kids and yelled and hit them. The youth recommended ways to improve relationships. They suggested that foster parents should get to know the child, find out why they are in foster care, learn about their personality, what their likes and dislikes are, what things would hurt their feelings. Essentially, the youth want foster parents who want to get to know them and take the time to do so. In qualitative interviews of nine focus groups, youth identified four key elements of supportive foster parent–foster youth relationships: guidance, structure/boundaries, genuine interest, and sense of belonging (Storer et al., 2014). The findings from this study reinforce previous reports of what youth consider *good* foster parents.

In a national sample of youth in foster care, a warm relationship with a foster parent was a significant moderator in the youth's report of trauma symptoms and internalizing behaviors; more specifically, youth who reported a warmer relationship reported a weaker relationship between trauma symptoms like nightmares or flashbacks and internalizing behaviors like depression (Wojciak, Thompson, & Cooley, 2016). Youth's perception of their relationship with their caregiver was also predictive of youth reports of internalizing behaviors (Cooley, Wojciak, & Farineau, 2014). These findings are important, particularly when considering predictors of placement instability, attachment, and externalizing behaviors (Pasalich et al., 2016; Strijker, et al., 2008). Leathers (2005) reported that when there was a warm relationship between the youth and their caregiver, the youth had a sense of belonging in the foster family, and was less likely to have a placement disruption. Better communication between youth in foster care and their foster parents was also indicative of lower behavioral problems in youth (Vuchinin, Ozretich, Pratt, & Kneedler, 2002). These findings highlight the importance of the relationship between the youth and the foster parent, and identify a place for intervention to promote resilience in these youth, via a supportive relationship with a caring adult.

Siblings

While in foster care, foster parents are important, but the relationships that youth have with other youth in their foster home can also make an impact. Youth who are removed from their home may also have biological siblings. For myriad logistic (i.e., space, child with special needs) and relational (i.e., sibling abuse) reasons, members of sibling groups may be placed in different homes without their sibling once they enter foster care. Reasons for separation may include violence between siblings, a sibling group that is too large and lack of a foster home that can accommodate the sibling set, and siblings who enter the system at different times. In fact, studies have reported ranges of 10% to 82% of siblings in foster care who are separated from at least one biological sibling (Leathers, 2005; Wulczyn & Zimmerman, 2005). Furthermore, sibling placements are not systematically tracked within the foster care system (Herrick & Piccus, 2005). Despite these difficulties, results from studies examining youth outcomes and sibling placement highlight the positive role that siblings can play while in foster care. For instance, Hegar and Rosenthal (2011) reported that siblings who were placed together for the duration of their time in foster care had lower levels of internalizing and externalizing behaviors, and had better academic outcomes compared to sibling sets that were separated. Siblings also offer one another a sense of belonging within a foster home and provide a continuity of relationships while in care (Leathers, 2005).

Recently, researchers have started to examine sibling relationship quality, regardless of whether or not siblings are placed together. Wojciak et al. (2013) found that a warm relationship with their sibling significantly mediated the association between trauma symptoms and internalizing behaviors. The authors argued that for youth in foster care, the sibling relationship is a protective factor that is often overlooked and understudied. Further, researchers are investigating the role that siblings can play in promoting resilience for youth in foster care. Richardson and Yates (2014) reported that for youth who have aged out of foster care, siblings placed with one another offer a relational mechanism to promote resilience; the authors advocate for efforts to maintain sibling relationships for youth in foster care. Wojciak (2014b) investigated the predictive role of warm sibling relationships for youth in foster care. A warm sibling relationship was identified as having a sibling whom you could turn to, who cared for you and you cared for them. Findings from this study indicated that warm sibling relationships were a significant predictor of individual resilience. These studies underline the importance of promoting biological sibling relationships for youth in foster care.

Promotion of these sibling relationships is highly variable. States often vary in the requirements and how they support the maintenance of biological sibling relationships. It wasn't until the Fostering Connections to Success and Increasing Adoptions Act of 2008 that a federal policy dictated anything about maintaining sibling relationships. In this policy, it states that "reasonable efforts" should be made to place siblings with one another, and if that is not possible, "reasonable efforts" should be made to maintain sibling relationships [42 U.S.C.A. § 671(a)(31)]. While the policy addresses siblings, it does not specify how to implement "reasonable efforts." Additionally, many states do not have state policy regarding sibling placement and visitation. The lack of policy has great implications for sibling relationships.

Gardner (1996) conducted an experiential activity of closeness for children living in foster care. She asked youth to create a picture of their family and to depict their level of closeness by proximity of family members to themselves. In this study, youth in foster care identified other youth living in their foster home as siblings. Furthermore, youth reported feeling closer to the other children in their foster home than they did to their biological siblings when they were separated. Bank and Kahn (1982) state that sibling relationships require proximity and closeness. For youth in foster care, this may not be able to happen and this can greatly impair their relationship with their sibling(s).

In a qualitative study of youth living in foster care, Wojciak (2017) shared youth's perspectives of what their sibling means to them while living in foster care. The majority of youth reported that their sibling played a positive role in their life. Specifically, youth reported that their sibling meant everything to them, that they were their *world*. The participants had a shared history and experienced the reality of the challenges associated with being separated from their sibling and the impact it has on their relationship. One youth reported that you only know what your sibling tells you about themselves, you don't really know them. That viewpoint highlights the struggle that some youth experience with their sibling relationships. Others shared the sadness they experience as a result of the uncertainty they have in knowing when they will see their sibling again. Given the research indicating the protective role of siblings, and the reality that sibling relationships are not always effectively promoted within the foster care system, more needs to be done to explicitly state how sibling relationships can be maintained, even if for very real logistical reasons, siblings have to be separated.

Adoptive Family Perspectives

Children who are adopted from foster care have an interesting relational journey. To put the relationship and experience in perspective, in order for youth to be eligible for adoption through the foster care system, the youth's biological parents had to have their parental rights terminated. Termination of parental rights may occur if biological parents do not fulfill all the requirements in their permanency plan and/or they have been found to be unfit to parent their children (Child Welfare Information Gateway, 2016). Termination of parental rights and the consequences of this decision can influence the youth's relationships indefinitely. Those whose parents had their rights terminated reported mixed influences. For instance, some youth reported that the termination of their parental rights negatively impacted their relationships as they isolated themselves from peers, foster parents, and other important social relationships (Durousseau, 2009). The isolation is attributed to the negative view that youth had of themselves as a result of the termination. Other youth reported that the termination of parental rights was positive in that it allowed them to build more stable relationships with others.

Youth who are adopted from foster care not only have the impact of this influencing their relationships with their adoptive parents; they may also have been part of previous foster homes which influence their relationships. Neil (2012) highlighted the complexity of emotions that youth who are adopted from foster care report. In her qualitative study, she stated that the majority of the youth feel positively about their adoptive parents and report being integrated into their adoptive home. However, youth who are adopted also have to differentiate between their biological families and adoptive families. Neil (2012) stated that half of her sample reported complicated emotions such as grief, rejection, and sadness over their biological families.

Given the abuse and neglect children may have experienced prior to adoption, and the complicated emotions (fear, anger, and confusion) they may feel due to the adoption, efforts to enhance this important adoptive relationship have been studied. Faver and Alanis (2012) examined a program that promotes empathy and communication between youth who have been adopted and their adoptive parents. Empathy and communication are promoted through shared stories. These stories addressed relevant topics for adoption—fear, attachment, and trust. Adoptive parents and youth were able to take the perspective of those in the study. Further, Johnstone and Gibbs (2010) explored how adoptive parents in New Zealand helped to build relationships and attachment with children recently adopted from Russian orphanages, arguably having attachment difficulties. The strategies these parents used could easily be applied to adoptive parents of those who have lived in the foster care system. The New Zealand parents reported that they needed to spend quality time with the youth, play with them, and to care for them in a nurturing way, as well as the use of support groups for them, and leaning on their own family for support.

Implications

As humans, we know that we are relational beings and consequently care about relationships. This chapter has provided a nuanced view of the relationships that youth in foster care navigate. We discussed research that examined the youth's perspective, showcasing the thoughts and knowledge of youth themselves. Listening to the youth who are served in the foster care system is important. The youth reported that they wanted foster parents to get to know them (Samuels, 2009). It is through relationships that resilience can be promoted. Resilience is a dynamic process and something that can respond to intervention (Fergus & Zimmerman, 2005). Across all of the relational domains covered in this chapter, there were positive and protective factors that were discussed. For providers who work with these youth, it is imperative to get to know them and understand their relationships. Understanding their relationships helps us to understand their attachment style, what their interpersonal strengths and weaknesses are, and with whom they are able to build/maintain strong relationships. It is through these relationships that we can help to promote resilience.

Implications for Research

The study of relationships that youth in foster care have in the myriad settings in which they live is in its infancy. Rightfully so, attachment theory has been a leading theme in the majority of the research presented in this chapter. Attachment theory offers a solid base with which to understand the relationships, but research using systems theory (Becvar, D. S., & Becvar, R. J., 1999) and Bronfenbrenner's ecological theory (2009) may help guide investigations into the complexity and interconnection of these relationships within multiple systems. The child welfare system is set up to protect and ensure the well-being of children. This is an admirable mission. The literature surrounding youth perspectives is growing, but as can be gleaned from this chapter, there is a dearth of knowledge about the perspectives of biological parents whose children are involved in the foster care system, and the complexity and difficulties that foster parents encounter when building relationships and managing the relationships of youth in their care. A theoretical orientation toward systems theory would encourage researchers to elicit perspectives from multiple informants, in order to create a more complete picture of the impact that placement in foster care has on biological, foster, and adoptive families. Further, a social justice lens should be added to these investigations to examine diverse issues such as race, gender, and sexual orientation. A systems orientation and social justice lens that give voice to all involved could identify nuances which could greatly inform child welfare practice and policy.

Conclusion

Youth involved with the child welfare system have myriad experiences that led to their placement in foster care. Attachment theory provides a conceptual framework for those working with youth in foster care to understand how their relationships can be influenced by their first experiences with their primary caregiver(s). Abuse and neglect at the hands of one's parents have lasting effects that can influence later relationships. Working from a perspective of listening to the youth and trying to understand the way in which the trauma they experienced and attachment impairments has affected the youth's current relationships could be helpful for all involved.

References

Aldgate, J., & McIntosh, M. (2006). *Looking after the family: A study of children looked after in kinship care*. Edinburgh, UK: Social Work Inspection Agency.

Ames, E. W. (1997). *The development of Romanian orphanage children adopted to Canada*. Burnaby, BC: Simon Fraser University.

Baker, A. J. L., Creegan, A., Quinones, A., & Rozelle, L. (2016). Foster children's views of their birth parents: A review of the literature. *Children and Youth Services Review, 67*, 177–183.

Bank, S. P., & Kahn, M. D. (1982). *The sibling bond*. New York: Basic Books.

Barth, R. P., Lloyd, E. C., Green, R. L., James, S., Leslie, L. K., & Landsverk, J. (2007). Predictors of placement moves among children with and without emotional and behavioral disorders. *Journal of Emotional and Behavioral Disorders, 15*, 45–55.

Baumann, C. (1999). Adoptive fathers and birthfathers: A study of attitudes. *Child and Adolescent Social Work Journal, 16*, 373–391.

Becvar, D. S., & Becvar, R. J. (1999). *Systems theory and family therapy: A primer*. Lanham, MD: University Press of America.

Berrick, J. D. (2015). Research and practice with families in foster care. In S. Browning & K. Pasley (Eds.), *Contemporary families: Translating research into practice* (pp. 54–69). New York, NY: Routledge.

Boss, P. (1999). *Ambiguous loss*. Cambridge, MA: Harvard University Press.

Bowlby, J. (1969). *Attachment and loss: Vol 1. Attachment*. New York, NY: Basic Books.

Bowlby, J. (1982). Attachment and loss: Retrospective and prospective. *American Journal of Orthopsychiatry, 52*, 664–678.

Brodzinsky, D. M. (1990). A stress and coping model of adoption adjustment. In D. M. Brodzinsky & M. D. Schechter (Eds.), *The psychology of adoption* (pp. 3–24). New York, NY: Oxford University Press.

Bronfenbrenner, U. (2009). *The ecology of human development: Experiments by nature and design*. Cambridge, MA: Harvard University Press.

Cantos, A. L., Gries, L. T., & Slis, V. (1997). Behavioral correlates of parental visiting during family foster care. *Child Welfare, 76*, 309–329.

Child Welfare Information Gateway. (2012). *Adoption disruption and dissolution*. Washington, DC: U.S. Department of Health & Human Services, Children's Bureau.

Child Welfare Information Gateway. (2016). *Grounds for involuntary termination of parental rights*. Retrieved from www.childwelfare.gov/pubPDFs/groundtermin.pdf#page=2&view=Grounds for termination of parental rights

Coakley, J. F., & Berrick, J. D. (2008). Research review: In a rush to permanency: Preventing adoption disruption. *Child and Family Social Work, 13*, 101–112.

Council of Europe. (2006). *Recommendation Rec(2006)19 of the Committee of Ministers to member states on policy to support positive parenting*. Retrieved from https://search.coe.int/cm/Pages/result_details.aspx?ObjectID=09000016805d6dda

Cook, A., Spinazzola, J., Ford, J., Lanktree, C., Blaustein, M., Cloitre, M., & Van der Kolk, B. (2005). Complex trauma in children and adolescents. *Psychiatric Annals, 35*, 390–398.

Cooley, M., Wojciak, A. J., & Farineau, H. (2014). Behaviors and relationships with caregivers of youth in foster care: A child and caregiver perspective. *Journal of Social Work Practice, 29*, 205–221. doi: 10.1080/02650533.2014.933405

Cossar, J., & Neil, E. (2013). Making sense of siblings: Connections and severances in post-adoption contact. *Child and Family Social Work, 18*, 67–76.

Courtney, M. E., Dworsky, A., Cusick, G. R., Havlicek, J., Perez, A., & Keller, T. (2007). *Midwest Evaluation of the Adult Functioning of Former Foster Youth: Outcomes at age 21*. Chicago: Chapin Hall Center for Children at the University of Chicago.

Cox, M. E., Orme, J. G., & Rhodes, K. W. (2002). Willingness to foster special needs children and foster family utilization. *Children and Youth Services Review, 24*, 293–318.

DuMont, K. A., Widom, C. S., & Czaja, S. J. (2007). Predictors of resilience in abused and neglected children grown-up: The role of individual and neighborhood characteristics. *Child Abuse & Neglect, 31*, 255–274.

Durousseau, R. (2009). *Termination of parental rights: Recall of attachment experiences among adults who were legally separated from their parents*. Dissertation Abstracts International: Section B: The Science and Engineering, Vol. 69.

Faver, C. A., & Alanis, E. (2012). Fostering empathy through stories: A pilot program for special needs adoptive families. *Children and Youth Services Review, 34*, 660–665.

Felitti, V. J., Anda, R. F., Nordenberg, D., Williamson, D. F., Spitz, A. M., Edwards, V., . . . Marks, J. S. (1998). Relationship of childhood abuse and household dysfunction to many of the leading causes of death in adults. The Adverse Childhood Experiences (ACE) Study. *American Journal of Preventative Medicine, 14*, 245–258.

Fergus, S., & Zimmerman, M. A. (2005). Adolescent resilience: A framework for understanding healthy development in the face of risk. *Annual Review of Public Health, 26*, 399–419.

Fernandez, E. (2009). Children's wellbeing in care: Evidence from a longitudinal study of outcomes. *Children and Youth Services Review, 31*, 1092–1100.

Festinger, T. (1983). *No one ever asked us . . . A postscript to foster care*. New York: Columbia University Press.

Festinger, T. (2002). After adoption: Dissolution or permanence? *Child Welfare, 81*, 515–533.

Foli, K. J., South, S. C., Lim, E., & Hebdon, M. (2013). Depression in adoptive fathers: An exploratory mixed methods study. *Psychology of Men & Masculinity, 14*(4), 411–422.

Foli, K. J., South, S. C., Lim, E., & Jarnecke, A. M. (2016). Post-adoption depression: Parental classes of depressive symptoms across time. *Journal of Affective Disorder, 200*, 293–302.

Forbes, H., & Dziegielewski, S. (2003). Issues facing adoptive mothers of children with special needs. *Journal of Social Work, 3*, 301–320.

Fostering Connections to Success and Increasing Adoptions Act of 2008, P.L. 110-351. (2008).

Frame, L., Conley, A., & Berrick, J. D. (2004). "The real work is what they do together": Peer support and birth parent change. *The Journal of Contemporary Social Services, 87*(4), 509–520.

Fuentes-Pelaez, N., Amoros, P., Mateos, A., Balsells, M. A., & Violant, V. (2013). The biological family from the perspective of kinship fostered adolescents. *Psicothema, 25*(3), 349–354.

Gardner, H. (1996). The concept of family: Perceptions of children in family foster care. *Child Welfare, 75*, 161–182.

Gass, K., Jenkins, J., & Dunn, J. (2007). Are sibling relationships protective? A longitudinal study. *Journal of Child Psychology and Psychiatry, 48*, 167–175.

Groh, A. M., Fearon, R. M. P., van IJzendoorn, M. H., Bakermans-Kranenburg, M. J., & Roisman (2017). Attachment in the early life course: Meta-analytic evidence for its role in socioemotional development. *Child Development Perspectives, 11*, 70–76.

Haight, W., Black, J., Workman, C., & Tata, L. (2001). Parent–child interaction during foster care visits: Implications for practice. *Social Work, 46*, 325–338.

Harmon, J. S., Childs, G. E., & Kelleher, K. J. (2000). Mental health care utilization and expenditures by children in foster care. *Archive of Pediatric Adolescent Medicine, 154*, 1114–1117.

Hegar, R. L., & Rosenthal, J. A. (2011). Foster children placed with or separated from siblings: Outcomes based on a national sample. *Children and Youth Services Review, 33*, 1245–1253.

Herrick, M. A., & Piccus, W. (2005). Sibling connections: The importance of nurturing sibling bonds in the foster care system. *Children and Youth Services Review, 27*, 845–861.

Hipple, L., & Haflich, B. (1993). Adoption's forgotten clients: Birth siblings. *Child and Adolescent Social Work Journal, 10*, 53–65.

Hoksbergen, R. A. C. (1999). The importance of adoption for nurturing and enhancing the emotional and intellectual potential of children. *Adoption Quarterly, 3*, 29–41.

Hollingsworth, L. D. (2003). When an adoption disrupts: A study of public attitudes. *Family Relations, 52*, 161–166.

Howe, D., Brandon, M., Hinings, H., & Schofield, G. (1999). *Attachment theory, child maltreatment and family support*. Basingstoke, UK: Macmillan.

Johnson, K. (2002). Politics of international and domestic adoption in China. *Law and Society Review, 1*, 379–396.

Johnson, P. R., Yoken, C., & Voss, R. (1995). Family foster care placement: The child's perspective. *Child Welfare: Journal of Policy, Practice, and Program, 74*, 959–974.

Johnstone, J., & Gibbs, A. (2010). "Love them to bits; spend time with them; have fun with them": New Zealand parents' views of building attachments with their newly adopted Russian children. *Journal of Social Work, 12*, 225–245.

Jones, A. S., & LaLiberte, T. (2010). *Adoption disruption and dissolution report*. University of Minnesota, School of Social Work, Center for Advanced Studies in Child Welfare. Retrieved from http://cascw.umn.edu/wp-content/uploads/2014/04/AdoptionDissolutionReport.pdf

Jones, L. P. (2015). "Was taking me out of the home necessary?": Perspectives of foster youth on the necessity for removal. *Families in Society: The Journal of Contemporary Social Services, 96*, 108–115.

Kelly, W., & Salmon, K. (2014). Helping foster parents understand the foster child's perspective: A relational learning framework for foster care. *Clinical Child Psychology and Psychiatry, 19*, 535–547.

Kolar, K. (2011). Resilience: Revisiting the concept and its utility for social research. *International Journal of Mental Health and Addiction, 9*, 421–433.

Lanktree, C. B., & Briere, J. N. (2017). *Treating complex trauma in children and their families: An integrated approach*. New York: Sage.

Leathers, S. J. (2005). Separation from siblings: Associations with placement adaptation and outcomes among adolescents in long-term foster care. *Children and Youth Services Review, 27*, 793–819.

Lee, R. E., & Whiting, J. B. (2008). Introduction: The culture and environment of foster care. In R. E. Lee, & J. B. Whiting (Eds.), *Foster care therapist handbook* (pp. 1–16). Arlington, VA: Child Welfare League of America Press.

Littner, N. (1975). The importance of natural parents to the child in placement. *Child Welfare, 54*, 175–181.

Love, L. T., McIntosh, J., Rosst, M., & Tertzakian, K. (2005). *Fostering hope: Preventing teen pregnancy among youth in foster care*. Washington, DC: National Campaign to Prevent Teen and Unplanned Pregnancy.

Lowenthal, B. (1999). Effects of child maltreatment and ways to promote children's resiliency. *Childhood Education, 2*, 204–209.

March, C., & Miall, C. E. (2000). Adoption as a family form. *Family Studies, 49*, 359–362.

Massinga, R., & Pecora, P. J. (2004). Providing better opportunities for older children in the child welfare system. *The Future of Children, 14*, 150–173.

McLain, K. B. (2008). *The impact of burnout, compassion fatigue, and compassion satisfaction on foster parenting*. Retrieved from ProQuest Dissertations Publishing.

McWey, L. M., Acock, A., & Porter, B. E. (2010). The impact of continued contact with biological parents upon the mental health of children in foster care. *Children and Youth Services Review, 32*, 1338–1345. doi: 10.1016/j.childyouth.2010.05.003

McWey, L. M., & Mullis, A. (2004). Improving the lives of children in foster care: The impact of supervised visitation. *Family Relations, 53*, 293–300.

Miall, C. E. (1987). The stigma of adoptive parent status: Perceptions of community attitudes toward adoption and the experience of informal social sanctioning. *Family Relations, 36*, 34–39.

Miall, C. E. (1996). The social construction of adoption: Clinical and community perspectives. *Family Relations, 45*, 309–317.

Milan, S. E., & Pinderhughes, E. E. (2000). Factors influencing maltreated children's early adjustment in foster care. *Development and Psychopathology, 12*, 63–81.

Morrison, J., Mishna, F., Cook, C., & Aitken, G. (2011). Access visits: Perceptions of child protection workers, foster parents, and children who are crown wards. *Children and Youth Services Review, 33*, 1476–1482.

Neil, E. (2012). Making sense of adoption: Integration and differentiation from the perspective of adopted children in middle childhood. *Children and Youth Services Review, 34*, 409–416.

Newton, R. R., Litrownik, A. J., & Landsverk, J. A. (2000). Children and youth in foster care: Disentangling the relationship between problem behaviors and number of placements. *Child Abuse & Neglect, 24*, 1363–1374.

Pasalich, D. S., Fleming, C. B., Oxford, M. L., Zheng, Y., & Spieker, S. J. (2016). Can parenting intervention prevent cascading effects from placement instability to insecure attachment to externalizing problems in maltreated toddlers. *Child Maltreatment, 21*, 175–185.

Payne, J. L., Fields, E. S., Meuchel, J. M., Jaffe, C. J., & Jha, M. (2010). Post adoption depression. *Archives of Women's Mental Health, 13*, 147–151.

Pecora, P. J., Williams, J., Kessler, R. C., Downs, A. C., O'Brien, K., Hiripi, E., . . . Holmes, K. E. (2003). *Assessing the effects of foster care: Early results from the Casey National Alumni Study.* Seattle, WA: Casey Family Programs.

Phillips, N. K. (1999). Adoption of a sibling: Reactions of biological children at different stages of development. *American Journal of Orthopsychiatry, 69*(1), 122–126.

Richardson, S. M., & Yates, T. M. (2014). Siblings in foster care: A relational path to resilience for emancipated foster youth. *Children and Youth Services Review, 47*, 378–388.

Ringwalt, S. (2008). *Developmental screening and assessment instruments with an emphasis on social and emotional development for young children ages birth through five.* Chapel Hill, NC: University of North Carolina, National Early Childhood Technical Assistance Center. Retrieved from www.nectac.org/~pdfs/pubs/screening.pdf

Rolock, N., & White, K. R. (2016). Post-permanency discontinuity: A longitudinal examination of outcomes for foster youth after adoption or guardianship. *Children and Youth Services Review, 70*, 419–427.

Rosenthal, J. A. (1993). Outcomes of adoption of children with special needs. *The Future of Children, 3*(1), 77–88.

Samuels, G. M. (2009). Ambiguous loss of home: The experience of familial (im)permanence among young adults with foster care backgrounds. *Children and Youth Services Review, 31*, 1229–1239.

Selwyn, J., Saunders, H., & Farmer, E. (2010). The views of children and young people on being cared for by an independent foster-care provider. *British Journal of Social Work, 403*, 696–731.

Shlonsky, A., Bellamy, J., Elkins, J., & Ashare, C. J. (2005). The other kin: Setting the course for research, policy, and practice with siblings in foster care. *Children and Youth Services Review, 27*, 697–716.

Shlonsky, A., & Berrick, J. D. (2001). Assessing and promoting quality in kin and nonkin foster care. *Social Service Review, 75*, 60–83.

Sinclair, I., Wilson, K., & Gibbs, I. (2005). *Foster placements: Why they succeed and why they fail.* London: Jessica Kingsley.

Smith, S. L., Howard, J. A., Garnier, P. C., & Ryan, S. D. (2006). Where are we now? A post-ASFA examination of adoption disruption. *Adoption Quarterly, 9*(4), 19–44.

Steinhauer, P. D. (1991). *The least detrimental alternative: A systematic guide to case planning and decision making for children in care.* Toronto, ON: University of Toronto Press.

Storer, H. L., Barkan, S. E., Stenhouse, L. L., Eichenlaub, C., Mallillin, A., & Haggerty, K. P. (2014). In search of connection: The foster youth and caregiver relationship. *Children and Youth Services Review, 42*, 110–117.

Strijker, J., Knorth, E. J., & Knot-Dickscheit, J. (2008). Placement history of foster children: A study of placement history and outcomes in long-term family foster care. *Child Welfare, 87*, 107–124.

Sullivan, K. M., Murray, K. J., & Ake, G. S. (2015). Trauma-informed care for children in the child welfare system. *Child Maltreatment, 21*, 147–155.

U.S. Department of Health & Human Services. (2016). *The AFCARs report. Preliminary FY 2015 estimates as of June 2016. No. 23.* Retrieved from www.acf.hhs.gov/sites/default/files/cb/afcarsreport23.pdf

U.S. Government Accountability Office (2015, September). *Child welfare: Steps have been taken to address unregulated custody transfers of adopted children.* Report to Congressional Requesters. (GAO-15-733).

van Den Dries, L., Juffer, F., van IJzendoorn, M. H., & Bakermans-Kranenburg, M. J. (2010). Infants' physical and cognitive development after international adoption from foster care or institutions in China. *Journal of Developmental & Behavioral Pediatrics, 31*(2), 144–150.

Vuchinich, S., Ozretich, R., Pratt, C., & Kneedler, B. (2002). Problem-solving communication in foster families and birth families. *Child Welfare, 81*, 571–595.

Weisz, V., Wingrove, T., Beal, S. J., & Slaker-Faith, A. (2011). Children's participation in foster care hearings. *Child Abuse & Neglect, 35*, 267–272.

Whelan, D. J. (2003). Using attachment theory when placing siblings in foster care. *Child and Adolescent Social Work Journal, 20*(1), 21–36.

Whiting, J. B., & Lee, R. E. (2003). Voices from the system: A qualitative study of foster children's stories. *Family Relations, 52*, 288–295.

Wojciak, A. S. (2014a) Foster families. In M. J. Coleman, & L. H. Ganong, (Eds.), *The social history of the American family: An encyclopedia*. Thousand Oaks, CA: Sage Publications.

Wojciak, A. S. (2014b). *Exploring sibling relationships among youth in foster care* (Doctoral dissertation). Florida State University. Retrieved from ProQuest Dissertations Publishing.

Wojciak, A. S. (2017). "It's complicated": Exploring the meaning of sibling relationships of youth in foster care. *Child and Family Social Work, 22*, 1283–1291.

Wojciak, A. S., McWey, L., & Helfrich, C. (2013). Sibling relationships on internalizing symptoms of youth in foster care. *Children and Youth Services Review, 35*, 1071–1077.

Wojciak, A. S., Thompson, H. M., & Cooley, M. E. (2016). The relationship between caregivers and youth in foster care: Examining the relationship for mediation and moderation effects on youth behaviors. *Journal of Emotional and Behavioral Disorders, 25*(2), 96–106.

Wulczyn, F., & Zimmerman, E. (2005). Sibling placement in longitudinal perspective. *Children and Youth Services Review, 27*, 741–763.

Zeanah, C. (2000). Disturbances of attachment in young children adopted from institutions. *Journal of Developmental and Behavioral Pediatrics, 21*, 230–236.

12

Factors Affecting the Educational Trajectories and Outcomes of Youth in Foster Care

Katherine C. Pears, Hyoun K. Kim, Kimbree L. Brown

Youth in foster care often perform worse in school than their peers who are not in foster care across a number of domains, including academic, social, and behavioral adjustment (Blome, 1997; Scherr, 2007). They are likely to enter kindergarten without the skills needed to succeed in school (Pears, Heywood, Kim, & Fisher, 2011), and these skill deficits persist throughout the school years, resulting in higher rates of placement in special education, greater numbers of suspensions and expulsions, and much lower rates of high school completion and college attendance (Blome, 1997; Scherr, 2007). Conversely, for youth at high risk for poor adjustment, success in school appears to confer a number of protective advantages, including better overall educational, occupational, and income attainment and better physical and mental health (Campbell et al., 2014; Jones, Greenberg, & Crowley, 2015; Naccarato, Brophy, & Courtney, 2010; Reynolds, Temple, Ou, Arteaga, & White, 2011). Thus, ensuring educational success for youth in foster care may contribute to their long-term health and psychosocial well-being.

Although past studies have done the important work of establishing the typical educational outcomes for youth in foster care, very little research has investigated the factors that influence and predict those outcomes over the course of youth's development (Mehana & Reynolds, 2004). A good deal of the past research has been retrospective (e.g., asking young adults who were formerly in care to recall events from their school years) and focused either only on describing outcomes or explaining how single factors might be linked to outcomes (Mehana & Reynolds, 2004). While such research has been very helpful in illuminating the poor educational outcomes that many youth in foster care experience, it has also been largely atheoretical. Thus, the field lacks a coherent conceptual model specifying the behaviors, experiences, and contextual factors that predict poor school experiences and the mechanisms by which these predictors independently and cumulatively influence youth's outcomes. Importantly, in order to be able to understand how and when to most effectively prevent negative educational trajectories, such conceptual models must also be longitudinal in nature, illustrating which predictors are most influential at each of the developmental stages.

In order to synthesize the past research and begin to develop a more theory-informed approach, this chapter presents a longitudinal model of the predictors and processes involved in the development of educational outcomes for youth in foster care. The model takes a developmental stages approach, recognizing that the effects of experiences during one developmental stage are likely to carry forward into and impact the next stage (Cicchetti & Rogosch, 2002). The model also takes an ecological systems approach (Bronfenbrenner, 1989), focusing not only on the intra-individual factors, but also

Educational Trajectories and Outcomes

the interpersonal and contextual factors that might influence youth's educational trajectories and outcomes. This is intended to represent the beginning of what, it is hoped, will be a larger effort across the field to develop a comprehensive model of the pathways to varied educational outcomes for youth in foster care, which can be used to tailor effective interventions to promote positive youth outcomes. With that goal in mind, in the latter portion of this chapter, several promising prevention efforts targeting critical factors at each developmental stage in the proposed model are reviewed.

A Model of Factors Affecting the Educational Outcomes of Youth in Foster Care

Figure 12.1 outlines the proposed model of factors that may contribute to poor educational outcomes for youth in foster care. The model begins with experiences of maltreatment and consequent placement in foster care. Because they so frequently co-occur (U.S. Department of Health & Human Services, 2016) and it is beyond the scope of this chapter to separate out the individual effects of these

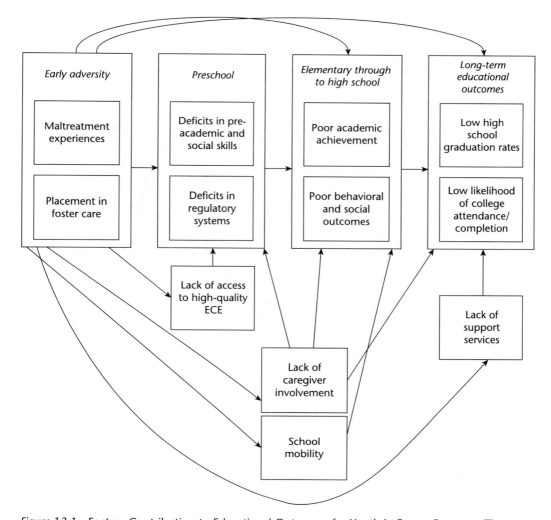

Figure 12.1 Factors Contributing to Educational Outcomes for Youth in Foster Care over Time

209

early adverse experiences, they are considered together here. The effects of these experiences on educational outcomes, as well as the factors that might mediate the effects of these experiences, are shown across prekindergarten and the K–12 school years. These factors then cumulatively predict the long-term educational outcomes of youth in foster care. Each stage in the model is reviewed in detail below.

Prekindergarten Readiness for School

Deficits in Pre-Academic and Social Skills

From the beginning of their school careers, youth in foster care may have greater difficulties than their peers who are not in foster care. Well-developed pre-academic skills—literacy and numeracy—are essential to school readiness and continuing school success. Early literacy skills are positively linked to later reading and math outcomes across elementary and middle school (Duncan et al., 2007), and youth who read proficiently by Grade 3 are consequently more likely to graduate from high school (Hernandez, 2012). Early numeracy, although less studied than early literacy, is also positively linked to academic achievement (Duncan et al., 2007). Conversely, poor early reading and math abilities predict behavioral difficulties and a greater likelihood of grade retention across elementary and middle school (Halonen, Aunola, Ahonen, & Nurmi, 2006; McIntosh, Reinke, Kelm, & Sadler, 2013).

Maltreatment and foster care placement negatively impact youth's early academic skills. For example, youth in foster care demonstrate deficits in critical pre-reading skills when compared to low-income youth who were not in foster care (Pears et al., 2011). Such deficits might arise from histories of neglect, during which parents were unlikely to have engaged in activities with the youth such as reading to them and teaching them critical pre-academic skills (e.g., counting, letter naming; Manly, Lynch, Oshri, Herzog, & Wortel, 2013). Additionally, experiences of abuse and neglect may have resulted in injuries or developmental delays that might interfere with youth's abilities to learn new skills at the same rate as non-maltreated youth (Pears & Fisher, 2005a).

Youth's abilities to get along with adults and peers are also critical to school readiness. Key prosocial behaviors that predict positive peer and teacher relationships include entering peer groups, sharing materials, cooperating, and maintaining social interactions (Ladd, Birch, & Buhs, 1999; Pianta & Stuhlman, 2004). Accurately interpreting the emotions of others (i.e., emotion understanding) is also central to reacting appropriately to peers (Denham et al., 2002). Over time, individuals who show greater prosocial skills at school entry are more likely to graduate from high school, complete college, and obtain full and stable employment in young adulthood—as well as avoid problem behaviors such as involvement in criminality and excessive alcohol use (Jones et al., 2015).

The social skills of preschool-aged children in foster care appear to lag behind those of their peers. For example, youth in foster care have more difficulties recognizing and interpreting the thoughts and emotions of others, which are key social skills (Harden, Morrison, & Clyman, 2014; Pears & Fisher, 2005b). Once they enroll in school, youth in foster care generally score lower on ratings of social skills than their peers who are not in foster care (Almas et al., 2012; Leve, Fisher, & DeGarmo, 2007).

Deficits in Regulatory Systems

In addition to pre-academic skills, youth's abilities to regulate emotions and behaviors to prevent themselves from disrupting academic performance and social relationships are essential to school readiness. Inhibitory control, an executive function that overlaps with self-regulation, involves voluntarily inhibiting dominant attentional or behavioral responses (e.g., yelling out an answer in class) to perform a different response (e.g., raising one's hand before speaking). These skills influence the acquisition of early literacy skills; higher levels of inattention are associated with lower levels of early literacy, even after accounting for cognitive abilities (Lonigan et al., 1999; Walcott, Scheemaker, & Bielski, 2010). Proficiency in emotional and behavioral self-regulation and inhibitory control also predicts better engagement in learning, higher academic achievement, and better social skills (Brock, Rimm-Kaufman, Nathanson, & Grimm, 2009; Graziano, Reavis, Keane, & Calkins, 2007; Howse, Calkins, Anastopoulos, Keane, & Shelton, 2003).

A number of studies have demonstrated the negative effects of early adversity on the regulatory systems of youth in foster care. Specifically, preschool-aged children who are in foster care show deficits in inhibitory control, which appear to be closely associated with changes in caregivers (Lewis, Dozier, Ackerman, & Sepulveda, 2007; McDermott, Westerlund, Zeanah, Nelson, & Fox, 2012; Pears, Bruce, Fisher, & Kim, 2010). Early difficulties in inhibitory control then contribute to poorer functioning in elementary school (Pears, Fisher, Bruce, Kim, & Yoerger, 2010).

The functioning of the physiological stress regulatory systems is an underlying aspect of emotional and behavioral self-regulation that may be particularly important to youth who have experienced early adversity. The hypothalamic pituitary adrenal (HPA) axis, a stress-sensitive neurobiological system (Gunnar, 1998; Hertsgaard, Gunnar, Erickson, & Nachmias, 1995; Jacobson, Bihun, & Chiodo, 1999; Levine, Lyons, & Schatzberg, 1997), functions interdependently with other systems to mobilize bodily resources in response to real or perceived threat. Its functioning is often measured by the amount of cortisol—the end product of HPA activity—secreted by an organism. Cortisol displays a diurnal rhythm typically characterized by levels that peak around 30–45 minutes after awakening and decline to near zero by bedtime (Kirschbaum, Steyer, Patalla, Schwenkmezger, & Hellhammer, 1990). Response to and recovery from environmental challenges are necessary for well-regulated HPA axis functioning (McEwen, 1998), and school can present a number of challenges to young children—including the demands of entering a new environment, learning new rules and routines, adjusting to the signals and responses of a new group of peers, and complying with requests from unfamiliar adults.

Previous research (Bruce, Davis, & Gunnar, 2001) has shown that typically developing children demonstrate an HPA axis response to the start of school characterized by a steeper diurnal cortisol slope (or greater change in cortisol levels across the day) on the first day of school compared to later in the school year. This may indicate an appropriate HPA axis response to the normative stressor of starting school (Bruce et al., 2001). In one of the only studies to examine prediction of outcomes from the HPA axis response to the start of school, a steeper cortisol slope on the first day of school was linked to higher teacher ratings of learning behaviors through the fall term of kindergarten (Graham, Pears, Kim, Bruce, & Fisher, 2017).

Youth who are in foster care display dysregulation in their HPA axis functioning (Bernard, Butzin-Dozier, Rittenhouse, & Dozier, 2010; Bruce, Fisher, Pears, & Levine, 2009; Gunnar & Vazquez, 2001). For example, maltreated youth in foster care failed to show an increased diurnal cortisol slope across the first day of school compared to non-maltreated youth (Graham et al., 2011). This may signify a lack of responsivity to the transition, such that these youth fail to pick up on important aspects of the new school environment and to modify their behavior to the demands of that environment, which may then lead to skills deficits (Graham et al., 2017).

Lack of Access to High-Quality Early Childhood Education

In low-income youth, school readiness deficits have been linked to the lack of quality early childhood programming and other experiences such as exposure to books and high levels of vocabulary (Alexander & Entwisle, 1988; Chazan-Cohen et al., 2009). Given that many youth in foster care experienced low incomes in their families of origin (Barth, Wildfire, & Green, 2006), it is likely that a lack of early learning experiences contributes to their low school readiness skills as well. The limited research on the early childhood education (ECE) experiences of youth in foster care suggests that they may be enrolled in programs targeted at high-risk children, like Head Start, at lower rates than their peers (National Working Group on Foster Care and Education, 2014). Furthermore, when these youth are in childcare, that care may be of lower quality than that of even their low-income peers (Lipscomb & Pears, 2011). This lower rate of high-quality ECE usage might be partially attributable to the fact that youth in foster care, even preschoolers, can be highly mobile.

Although experiences of early adversity can have negative effects on prekindergarten educational outcomes, there is also research illustrating that academic and social skills, as well as ECE experiences, can buffer the negative effects of early adversity on outcomes for youth in foster care. For example, in a study examining the effects of foster care on later adjustment, researchers found that early social competence and cognitive ability predicted patterns of stable or increasing behavioral adjustment across time (Proctor, Skriner, Roesch, & Litrownik, 2010). Another study found that participation in Head Start programming predicted better subsequent academic scores for girls and youth with older caregivers in foster care (Lee, 2016). Thus, one potential point of intervention to prevent later educational difficulties might be to strengthen prekindergarten academic, social, and regulatory skills through quality programming.

Youth in Foster Care in Elementary through to High School

Poor Academic, Behavioral, and Social Functioning

There is evidence that youth's earlier deficits in school readiness and regulatory skills contribute to continuing problems with academic, social, and behavioral adjustment—considered together here because they often influence one another—throughout the school years (Pears, Fisher, et al., 2010). One meta-analysis found that youth in foster care were almost five times more likely to be placed in special education classes than their peers who were not in care (Scherr, 2007). The majority of youth involved with child welfare services who were in special education had received a diagnosis of emotional disturbance—a pattern of behavior associated with difficulties in learning and displaying inappropriate social behaviors toward others—which was associated with higher rates of emergency room visits and juvenile delinquency (Lee & Jonson-Reid, 2009). Higher rates of special education placement may adversely affect the opportunities of these youth for educational attainment because, compared to students in general education, foster youth in special education earn fewer credits toward graduation (Geenen & Powers, 2006). Such poor outcomes for foster youth in special education have led some researchers to question whether such placements might be overly restrictive for some of these youth (see Zetlin, 2006).

In addition to higher rates of special education placement, youth in foster care are more likely to be held back in a grade than their peers (Burley & Halpern, 2001; Flynn & Biro, 1998; Scherr, 2007). One study found a 32% difference between the percentages of youth in foster care who had repeated a grade (41%) and the percentage of youth not in care (9%) who had done so (Flynn & Biro, 1998). Youth in foster care are also more likely than their peers to receive sanctions for poor behavior in school. Rates of suspensions and expulsions are consistently higher for youth in foster care than for their peers (McMillen, Auslander, Elze, White, & Thompson, 2003; Scherr, 2007; Smithgall, Gladden, Howard, Goerge, & Courtney, 2004; Zima et al., 2000). Time missed from school is likely to negatively affect achievement.

Lack of Caregiver Involvement

Decades of research show that caregiver involvement is critical for youth's positive school adjustment (Barnard, 2004; Christenson, 2004). Caregivers can provide practical assistance (e.g., helping with homework and advocating for the youth at school), emotional support, and may pass on their views on the value of education (Barnard, 2004; Chazan-Cohen et al., 2009; Miedel & Reynolds, 1999). There is very little research on caregiver involvement in school for youth in foster care, specifically, but the extant studies suggest that involvement is poorer for these youth (Pears, Fisher, et al., 2010). For example, 65% of foster youth in high school reported that their caregivers had never attended a teacher conference, 73% reported that their caregivers had never visited their class, and 70% reported that their caregivers had never volunteered at school (Blome, 1997).

Multiple placement changes are likely to interfere with caregiver involvement in schooling in several ways (Storer et al., 2014). The caregiver may not receive adequate information about the youth's academic history. For example, one study found that information on past academic performance was missing from 53% of foster youth's school records (Parrish et al., 2001). Additionally, if the duration of a placement is short (e.g., 1–2 months), caregivers may not have the opportunity to become involved with the schooling of the youth in their care. A recent study demonstrated that while foster caregivers clearly believed that involvement in school was an important part of their role, most caregivers never, or only occasionally, participated in activities at their foster youth's schools. By contrast, over 80% were involved at home through asking about homework or what was happening at school, although only 55%–57% reported actually helping with homework activities (Beisse & Tyre, 2013).

Caregiver involvement in schooling may buffer youth in foster care from some of the negative effects of early adversity. In one study of school outcomes through to Grade 2, higher caregiver involvement predicted better academic competence (Pears, Fisher et al., 2010). In another study of youth aged between 10 and 15 years, higher home-based caregiver involvement (e.g., helping with homework, talking about problems at school) and higher academic expectations predicted academic success (Cheung & Pomerantz, 2012). Interestingly, caregiver involvement in school activities (e.g., field trips or parent–teacher association meetings) was not significantly associated with academic success (Cheung, Lwin, & Jenkins, 2012).

School Mobility

Youth in foster care change schools frequently, and these changes often occur in the middle of the school year (Barrat, 2013; Pears, Kim, Buchanan, & Fisher, 2015). Studies have shown that moving between schools puts all youth (not only those in foster care) at a disadvantage in a number of ways (Grigg, 2012; Mehana & Reynolds, 2004; Sullivan, Jones, & Mathiesen, 2010). Mobile youth may miss considerable amounts of classroom instructional time, causing them to fall behind their nonmobile peers. Some researchers have estimated that mobile students are about 4 months behind in reading and math achievement (Mehana & Reynolds, 2004). Once in the new school, youth may continue to lose time in appropriate instruction because it may take teachers time to establish the correct placement for the student. More important for youth in foster care, lack of records may interfere with teachers' abilities to provide students with the appropriate level of instruction and services (Grigg, 2012). Finally, because school mobility is likely to disrupt social relationships (Sullivan et al., 2010), youth establishing new ties with peers and adults at their new school may become distracted from academic studies.

Studies on school mobility, specifically on youth in foster care, generally find negative effects of such mobility (Conger & Finkelstein, 2003; Ferguson & Wolkow, 2012; Ward, 2009). However, many of these have been based on retrospective reports from youth exiting foster care, and thus were not able to show directionality of associations. More recently, a prospective study of youth in foster care demonstrated that school mobility in early elementary school adversely affected social-emotional adjustment in Grades 3 through to 5 (Pears et al., 2015), but only for youth who had had poorer academic skills at kindergarten entry. The youth who had better early academic skills did not experience negative effects even when they changed schools, once again highlighting a potential point of intervention (Pears et al., 2015).

Long-Term Educational Outcomes for Youth in Foster Care

Low Rates of High School Graduation and College Attendance/Completion

Although youth in foster care frequently aspire to go to college, they are between one-third to one-half less likely to graduate from high school than even their highest-risk, most impoverished peers (Barrat, 2013; Burley & Halpern, 2001; Wolanin, 2005). Those youth who do graduate from high school are less likely to go to college, and those who do attend college perform more poorly and are more likely to drop out than their peers (Day, Dworsky, Fogarty, & Damashek, 2011; Gillum, Lindsay, Murray, & Wells, 2016; Unrau, Font, & Rawls, 2012). Not surprisingly, studies that have followed foster care alumni across late adolescence and early adulthood have documented that completion rates for secondary education are very low (Gillum et al., 2016). Such low educational attainment may contribute to the finding that the average earnings of foster care alumni were not enough to raise them above the poverty threshold (Naccarato et al., 2010).

Continuing Effects of Caregiver Involvement and School Mobility

As with performance in school, high school graduation and the pursuit of higher education are affected by both caregiver involvement and school mobility (Burley & Halpern, 2001). In a study of over 1000 foster care alumni, the higher the number of placement changes that a youth had experienced, the lower was the likelihood that the youth would graduate from high school (Pecora, 2012). Other reports on foster youth aging out of care highlight the youths' continuing reliance on relationships with their former foster caregivers to help them navigate the developmental milestones of young adulthood, including college attendance (Courtney, Piliavin, Grogan-Kaylor, & Nesmith, 2001).

Support Services

Studies on youth who have aged out of foster care have shown that the use of support services—such as financial aid, assistance with housing, and academic advising—increase the likelihood that they will complete higher education programs and obtain post-high-school degrees (Lovitt & Emerson, 2008; Merdinger, Hines, Osterling, & Wyatt, 2005). Additionally, federal legislation provides for Education and Training Vouchers (ETVs; Promoting Safe and Stable Families Amendments of 2001) for eligible foster care alumni to enroll in postsecondary vocational, technical, or academic programs. However, these studies also note that many youth do not know about the existence of these services or how to access them (Lovitt & Emerson, 2008; Merdinger et al., 2005). There also appears to be wide variation in how individual states allocate funding for ETVs, as well as whether additional funds beyond the ETVs are available to foster care alumni (Simmel, Shpiegel, & Murshid, 2013).

The Buffering Effects of Better Educational Outcomes

Throughout the proposed model of educational outcomes for youth in foster care, there is evidence that better academic, social, and behavioral outcomes and contextual factors at any one stage can help to buffer youth against negative outcomes in later stages. For example, as is noted above, youth in foster care who had better skills at the start of school did not appear to be adversely affected by school mobility in the same way as foster youth who had poorer early skills (Pears et al., 2015). Youth whose caregivers were more involved in kindergarten were likely to have better outcomes in elementary school than youth with less-involved caregivers (Pears, Fisher et al., 2010). Finally, youth who complete some part of a 4-year college program or obtain an Associate's degree earn 50% more than former foster youth with lower educational attainment (Naccarato et al., 2010). The higher the level of educational attainment, the more likely the foster alumni are to have employment and housing, and the less likely they are to be involved in criminal activities or to have severe mental and physical health problems (Courtney, Hook, & Lee, 2012). Taken together, these findings suggest possible points of intervention to protect youth at each stage from negative outcomes in the next. They also highlight the critical importance of ensuring that youth in foster care have support to attain the highest levels of educational attainment that they can achieve in order to promote healthy adult outcomes.

Interventions to Improve the Educational Outcomes of Youth in Foster Care

This section explores interventions to improve educational outcomes for youth in foster care that target particular points in youth's educational trajectories. It should be noted that there are a number of intervention programs to promote better school adjustment—such as Head Start—that include youth in foster care. This section, however, focuses on programs designed specifically for youth in foster care. This is not an exhaustive review, but rather an overview of the types of program that might help to prevent negative educational outcomes. Further, it should be noted that very few of these programs have been rigorously tested, with the exception of the Kids in Transition to School (KITS) Program detailed below.

Intervening on School Readiness to Improve Educational Outcomes

Decades of research have demonstrated the utility of intervening before formal schooling begins in order to prepare youth for success in school and into adulthood (Ramey, Campbell, & Blair, 1998; Reynolds & Bezruczko, 1993; Reynolds & Temple, 2008). For youth in foster care, such intervention may be particularly important because it may buffer the effects of later events such as school mobility. Preparing youth in foster care to enter school with the skills necessary to succeed in kindergarten and promote subsequent positive school adjustment is the aim of the KITS Program (Pears et al., 2013). It features a series of 24 school readiness groups for children in which they learn and practice early literacy, numeracy, prosocial, and self-regulation skills. The program also focuses on promoting caregiver involvement in early learning and school through a series of 12 workshops for caregivers that occur concurrently with the school readiness groups. These workshops feature discussions on such topics as how caregivers may teach critical early academic skills through everyday activities, how they may become involved at school, as well as positive parenting techniques to help children learn new skills and regulate behaviors that may interfere at school and home. The program duration is relatively short (12–16 weeks) in order to decrease the potential of mobility interfering with children receiving the full dosage of the intervention.

The KITS Program has been tested in a randomized controlled trial with 192 children in foster care who were entering kindergarten and their caregivers. The youth were followed through to their Fifth-Grade year. Results from that study show immediate positive effects of the KITS Program on children's early literacy and self-regulation skills just before kindergarten entry (Pears et al., 2013). Positive effects on children's teacher-rated behavior at the end of kindergarten have also been demonstrated (Pears, Kim, & Fisher, 2012). Finally, the program continues to have positive effects on youth's self-competence through to the Third Grade, 4 years after the intervention was delivered. Additionally, the program decreases youth's positive views of alcohol use and antisocial behavior, for which youth in foster care are at high risk, as well as the likelihood that they will be involved with deviant peers (Pears, Kim, & Fisher, 2016).

Intervening to Reduce the Negative Effects of Mobility in Elementary through to High School

As is noted above, school mobility has negative effects on the academic, social, and behavioral adjustment of youth in foster care (Conger & Finkelstein, 2003; Ferguson & Wolkow, 2012; Pears et al., 2015; Ward, 2009). Thus, efforts to reduce school mobility seem warranted. The Fostering Connections to Success and Increasing Adoptions Act (2008) requires that state child welfare agencies create plans to ensure educational stability for youth in foster care. Such plans should allow the youth to remain in the same school that he or she attended at the time of placement unless it is not in the youth's best interest. In practice, this may be difficult for agencies to do, especially if youth move between school districts during placement changes. The McKinney-Vento Homeless Education Assistance Improvements Act (1987) requires districts to provide transportation for youth who are homeless to their schools of origin. This has led some districts to develop novel approaches that could be replicated or expanded for youth in foster care. Such efforts do require the support of a range of school personnel, as well as endorsement by the family (James & Lopez, 2003).

When changes in schools cannot be prevented, efforts to ensure that records and other information about the youth are quickly transferred to the new school become critically important. Various efforts have been made by states or localities to develop systems by which to do this. One example is the Foster Care Passport Program in Washington State. Through this program, youth's dental, medical, behavioral, psychological, and educational records are summarized in one set of documents and given to the foster care provider at the youth's entry into foster care (Burley & Halpern, 2001). In this way, the caregiver would be able to provide a new school with information about the youth's past educational history, placement, and any special services. However, as noted in their review of the program, Burley and Halpern (2001) found that educational information was not always available to be included in the passports. Further, passports may not be available for all youth entering care (Children's Administration of the State of Washington, 2016). Thus, although this could be a promising way to reduce the length of time that it takes for records to reach new schools, it remains to be determined how all of the relevant information can be collected in one place as well as how records will be updated over time (Burley & Halpern, 2001). Additionally, the efficacy of this method in helping to improve school outcomes would still need to be rigorously tested.

Intervening to Improve Attendance and Completion of Secondary Education

Given that attendance in post-high-school training and academic programs may confer advantages on former foster youth (Courtney, Hook, & Lee, 2010; Naccarato et al., 2010), efforts to increase the success of youth in these programs could be critical for their adult functioning. As is noted above, at a national level, youth who have been involved in foster care may receive ETVs, and many states have individual tuition waiver or scholarship programs (Simmel et al., 2013). However, as Dworsky and Pérez (2010) note, although these programs may help ease some of the financial burden, they do not actually offer the social, academic, and logistical supports that former foster youth may need to successfully navigate and complete postsecondary programs.

Campus support programs specifically targeted at youth with a history of foster care offer a promising approach to increasing the likelihood that they will attain post-high-school education. Examples of services include financial support, assistance choosing courses, study-skills training, and mentoring. In one of the only studies of multiple campus-support programs in California and Washington (Dworsky & Pérez, 2010), the majority of program recipients who responded to a survey reported high satisfaction with the programs. Many youth appreciated the sense that there was somewhere that they could go for support and to meet with peers who shared their experiences. Although the researchers noted that these programs are promising, they also pointed out that most programs do not yet have a way to track the progress of the participants through college. A critical next step in the development of such programs will be to rigorously evaluate their effects.

Future Directions in Improving Educational Outcomes for Youth in Foster Care

The interventions described above are not the only programs that may help to improve the educational outcomes of youth who have been in foster care. However, given the unique sets of circumstances faced by youth in foster care, such as maltreatment and separation from the biological family, programs tailored to the needs of these youth may prove to be the most effective (Dworsky & Pérez, 2010). In order to determine if this is the case, interventions that specifically target youth in foster care need to be evaluated using rigorous tests, such as randomized controlled trials with long-term follow-up.

Additionally, in order to give youth in foster care a voice in determining their experiences and outcomes, interventions should focus on the youths' satisfaction with programs and their feedback about potential ways to adapt and improve those programs. Although in a few cases, such as the study of campus-support programs cited above (Dworsky & Pérez, 2010), youth have been interviewed about their experiences with an intervention, this is relatively rare in the literature. Future research should clarify what components and types of program the youth themselves find helpful and easy to access.

As shown in Figure 12.1, the educational trajectories of youth in foster care span multiple developmental stages, with the outcomes in each stage affecting those in the next. Although the factors shown are not the only ones that are likely to affect that trajectory, research has shown them to be salient for youth in foster care. As such, they provide points at which to intervene to improve the educational outcomes of these youth. Further research to identify other potential intervention targets is needed.

Because youth in foster care are likely to have experienced a number of severe forms of early adversity, the deficits that they exhibit may require intervention across time and developmental stages. Thus, they are likely to benefit most from multiple programs across their educational trajectories that build on past successes, rather than one "single bullet" program at any one stage. Research should focus on how efficacious interventions might be combined to additively increase positive educational outcomes across time.

Critically, because there has been very little research on how educational trajectories and outcomes vary by gender and ethnicity, future research must consider these factors. Admissions into foster care are higher for minority youth (Wulczyn & Lery, 2007), suggesting that these youth may be disproportionately at risk for poorer educational outcomes. This is particularly important as the limited research on potential gender and ethnic disparities in service usage by youth in foster care shows that minority youth are less likely to utilize mental health services than non-minority youth (Leslie et al., 2000). Thus, in addition to understanding whether differences in trajectories and outcomes by gender and ethnicity exist, future studies will need to examine whether there are also differences in availability and usage of interventions to promote positive educational outcomes for these youth. Finally, it will also be important to tailor interventions to different groups depending on their differential experiences and their own input about which programs might be most "user-friendly" and efficacious.

Conclusion

Youth in foster care appear to have significantly reduced chances of such positive educational outcomes as finishing high school or completing a degree in secondary education. In order to change these outcomes for the better, we need to understand the factors affecting their educational trajectories at different stages of their school careers. We also need to examine how individual characteristics, skill levels, and behaviors, as well as contextual factors, may interact to produce differing outcomes over time. Through understanding the risk and protective factors for negative educational outcomes and using those factors to build testable, theoretical models, researchers and practitioners will be better able to effectively increase positive educational trajectories for youth in foster care.

Acknowledgments

Support for this chapter was provided by the following grants: R01 DA021424 and P30 DA023920 Division of Epidemiology, Services and Prevention Research, Prevention Research Branch, National Institute on Drug Abuse (NIDA), U.S. Public Health Service. The content of this chapter is solely the responsibility of the authors and does not necessarily represent the official views of the funding organizations. Katherine Pears is a co-developer of the Kids in Transition to School (KITS) Program. The authors would like to thank Sally Schwader for editorial assistance.

References

Alexander, K. L., & Entwisle, D. R. (1988). Achievement in the first 2 years of school: Patterns and processes. *Monographs of the Society for Research in Child Development, 53*, 1–157. doi:10.2307/1166081

Almas, A. N., Degnan, K. A., Radulescu, A., Nelson, C. A. III, Zeanah, C. H., & Fox, N. A. (2012). Effects of early intervention and the moderating effects of brain activity on institutionalized children's social skills at age 8. *Proceedings of the National Academy of Sciences of the United States of America, 109*(Suppl. 2), 17228–17231. doi:10.1073/pnas.1121256109

Barnard, W. M. (2004). Parent involvement in elementary school and educational attainment. *Children and Youth Services Review, 26*(1), 39–62. doi:10.1016/j.childyouth.2003.11.002

Barrat, V. X. (2013). *The invisible achievement gap, Part 1: Education outcomes of students in foster care in California's public schools.* San Francisco: WestEd.

Barth, R. P., Wildfire, J., & Green, R. L. (2006). Placement into foster care and the interplay of urbanicity, child behavior problems, and poverty. *American Journal of Orthopsychiatry, 76*(3), 358–366. doi:10.1037/0002-9432.76.3.358

Beisse, K., & Tyre, A. (2013). Caregiver involvement in the education of youth in foster care: An exploratory study. *School Social Work Journal, 37*, 1–20.

Bernard, K., Butzin-Dozier, Z., Rittenhouse, J., & Dozier, M. (2010). Cortisol production patterns in young children living with birth parents vs children placed in foster care following involvement of child protective services. *Archives of Pediatrics & Adolescent Medicine, 164*(5), 438–443. doi:10.1001/archpediatrics.2010.54

Blome, W. W. (1997). What happens to foster kids: Educational experiences of a random sample of foster care youth and a matched group of non-foster care youth. *Child and Adolescent Social Work Journal, 14*(1), 41–53. doi:10.1023/A:1024592813809

Brock, L. L., Rimm-Kaufman, S. E., Nathanson, L., & Grimm, K. J. (2009). The contributions of 'hot' and 'cool' executive function to children's academic achievement, learning-related behaviors, and engagement in kindergarten. *Early Childhood Research Quarterly, 24*(3), 337–349.

Bronfenbrenner, U. (1989). Ecological systems theory. In R. Vasta (Ed.), *Six theories of child development: Revised formulations and current issues* (pp. 187–249). Greenwich, CT: JAI Press.

Bruce, J., Davis, E. P., & Gunnar, M. R. (2001). Individual differences in children's cortisol response to the beginning of a new school year. *Psychoneuroendocrinology, 27*(6), 635–650. doi:10.1016/S0306-4530(01)00031-2

Bruce, J., Fisher, P. A., Pears, K. C., & Levine, S. (2009). Morning cortisol levels in preschool-aged foster children: Differential effects of maltreatment type. *Developmental Psychobiology, 51*(1), 14–23. doi:10.1002/dev.20333

Burley, M., & Halpern, M. (2001). *Educational attainment of foster youth: Achievement and graduation outcomes for children in state care.* Olympia, WA: Washington State Institute for Public Policy.

Campbell, F. A., Conti, G., Heckman, J. J., Moon, S. H., Pinto, R., Pungello, E., & Pan, Y. (2014). Early childhood investments substantially boost adult health. *Science, 343*, 1478–1485. doi:10.1126/science.1248429

Chazan-Cohen, R., Raikes, H., Brooks-Gunn, J., Ayoub, C., Pan, B. A., Kisker, E. E., . . . Fuligni, A. S. (2009). Low-income children's school readiness: Parent contributions over the first five years. *Early Education and Development, 20*(6), 958–977. doi:10.1080/10409280903362402

Cheung, C., Lwin, K., & Jenkins, J. M. (2012). Helping youth in care succeed: Influence of caregiver involvement on academic achievement. *Children and Youth Services Review, 34*(6), 1092–1100. doi:10.1016/j.childyouth.2012.01.033

Cheung, C. S.-S., & Pomerantz, E. M. (2012). Why does parents' involvement enhance children's achievement? The role of parent-oriented motivation. *Journal of Educational Psychology, 104*(3), 820–832. doi:10.1037/a0027183

Children's Administration of the State of Washington. (2016). *Foster care passport program*. Retrieved from www.skagitcounty.net/departments/healthfamily/fosterpassport.htm

Christenson, S. L. (2004). The family–school partnership: An opportunity to promote the learning competence of all students. *School Psychology Review, 33*(1), 83–104.

Cicchetti, D., & Rogosch, F. A. (2002). A developmental psychopathology perspective on adolescence. *Journal of Consulting and Clinical Psychology, 70*(1), 6–20. doi:10.1037/0022-006X.70.1.6

Conger, D., & Finkelstein, M. J. (2003). Foster care and school mobility. *The Journal of Negro Education, 72*(1), 97–103.

Courtney, M. E., Hook, J. L., & Lee, J. S. (2010). *Distinct subgroups of former foster youth during young adulthood: Implications for policy and practice*. Issue Brief, March 2010. Chicago: Chapin Hall at the University of Chicago.

Courtney, M. E., Hook, J. L., & Lee, J. S. (2012). Distinct subgroups of former foster youth during young adulthood: Implications for policy and practice. *Child Care in Practice, 18*(4), 409–418. doi:10.1080/13575279.2012.718196

Courtney, M. E., Piliavin, I., Grogan-Kaylor, A., & Nesmith, A. (2001). Foster youth transitions to adulthood: A longitudinal view of leaving care. *Child Abuse & Neglect, 80*(6), 685–717.

Day, A., Dworsky, A., Fogarty, K., & Damashek, A. (2011). An examination of post-secondary retention and graduation among foster care youth enrolled in a four-year university. *Children and Youth Services Review, 33*(11), 2335–2341. doi:10.1016/j.childyouth.2011.08.004

Denham, S. A., Caverly, S., Schmidt, M. H., Blair, K., DeMulder, E., Caal, S., ... Mason, T. (2002). Preschool understanding of emotions: Contributions to classroom anger and aggression. *Journal of Child Psychology and Psychiatry, 43*(7), 901–910. doi:10.1111/1469-7610.00139

Duncan, G. J., Dowsett, C. J., Claessens, A., Magnuson, K., Huston, A. C., Klebanov, P., ... Japel, C. (2007). School readiness and later achievement. *Developmental Psychology, 43*(6), 1428–1446.

Dworsky, A., & Pérez, A. (2010). Helping former foster youth graduate from college through campus support programs. *Children and Youth Services Review, 32*(2), 255–263. doi:10.1016/j.childyouth.2009.09.004

Ferguson, H. B., & Wolkow, K. (2012). Educating children and youth in care: A review of barriers to school progress and strategies for change. *Children and Youth Services Review, 34*(6), 1143–1149. doi:10.1016/j.childyouth.2012.01.034

Flynn, R. J., & Biro, C. (1998). Comparing developmental outcomes for children in care with those for other children in Canada. *Children & Society, 12*, 228–233.

Fostering Connections to Success and Increasing Adoptions Act of 2008 U.S.C, Pub. L. No. 110-351, 3949 Stat. (2008).

Geenen, S., & Powers, L. E. (2006). Are we ignoring youths with disabilities in foster care? An examination of their school performance. *Social Work, 51*(3), 233–241. doi:10.1093/sw/51.3.233

Gillum, N. L., Lindsay, T., Murray, F. L., & Wells, P. (2016). A review of research on college educational outcomes of students who experienced foster care. *Journal of Public Child Welfare, 10*(3), 291–309. doi:10.1080/15548732.2016.1172056

Graham, A. M., Pears, K. C., Kim, H. K., Bruce, J., & Fisher, P. A. (2017). Effects of a school readiness intervention on HPA axis functioning and school adjustment for children in foster care. *Development and Psychopathology: Advanced Online Publication*. doi:10.1017/S0954579417001171

Graham, A. M., Yockelson, M., Kim, H. K., Bruce, J., Pears, K. C., & Fisher, P. A. (2011). Effects of maltreatment and early intervention on diurnal cortisol across the start of school: A pilot study. *Child Abuse & Neglect, 36*(9), 666–670. doi:10.1016/j.chiabu.2012.07.006

Graziano, P. A., Reavis, R. D., Keane, S. P., & Calkins, S. D. (2007). The role of emotion regulation in children's early academic success. *Journal of School Psychology, 45*(1), 3–19. doi:10.1016/j.jsp.2006.09.002

Grigg, J. (2012). School enrollment changes and student achievement growth: A case study in educational disruption and continuity. *Sociology of Education, 85*(4), 388–404. doi:10.1177/0038040712441374

Gunnar, M. R. (1998). Quality of early care and buffering of neuroendocrine stress reactions: Potential effects on the developing human brain. *Preventive Medicine: An International Journal Devoted to Practice & Theory, 27*(2), 208–211. doi:10.1006/pmed.1998.0276

Gunnar, M. R., & Vazquez, D. M. (2001). Low cortisol and a flattening of expected daytime rhythm: Potential indices of risk in human development. *Development and Psychopathology, 13*(3), 515–538. doi:10.1017/S0954579401003066

Halonen, A., Aunola, K., Ahonen, T., & Nurmi, J. E. (2006). The role of learning to read in the development of problem behavior: A cross-lagged longitudinal study. *British Journal of Educational Psychology, 76*(3), 517–534. doi:10.1348/000709905X51590

Harden, B. J., Morrison, C., & Clyman, R. B. (2014). Emotion labeling among young children in foster care. *Early Education & Development, 25*, 1180–1197. doi:10.1080/10409289.2014.907694

Hernandez, D. J. (2012). *Double jeopardy: How third-grade reading skills and poverty influence high school graduation.* Baltimore, MD: Annie E. Casey Foundation.

Hertsgaard, L., Gunnar, M. R., Erickson, M., & Nachmias, M. (1995). Adrenocortical responses to the strange situation in infants with disorganized/disoriented attachment relationships. *Child Development, 66*, 1100–1106.

Howse, R. B., Calkins, S. D., Anastopoulos, A. D., Keane, S. P., & Shelton, T. L. (2003). Regulatory contributors to children's kindergarten achievement. *Early Education and Development, 14*, 101–119. doi:10.1207/s15566935eed1401_7

Jacobson, S. W., Bihun, J. T., & Chiodo, L. M. (1999). Effects of prenatal alcohol and cocaine exposure on infant cortisol levels. *Development and Psychopathology, 11*(2), 195–208.

James, B. W., & Lopez, P. D. (2003). Transporting homeless students to increase stability: A case study of two Texas districts. *Journal of Negro Education, 72*(1), 126–140. doi:10.2307/3211296

Jones, D. E., Greenberg, M., & Crowley, M. (2015). Early social-emotional functioning and public health: The relationship between kindergarten social competence and future wellness. *American Journal of Public Health, 105*(11), 2283–2290. doi:10.2105/AJPH.2015.302630

Kirschbaum, C., Steyer, M., Patalla, U., Schwenkmezger, P., & Hellhammer, D. (1990). Cortisol and behavior: 2. Application of a latent state-trait model to salivary cortisol. *Psychoneuroendocrinology, 15*(4), 297–307.

Ladd, G. W., Birch, S. H., & Buhs, E. S. (1999). Children's social and scholastic lives in kindergarten: Related spheres of influence? *Child Development, 70*(6), 1373–1400. doi:10.1111/1467-8624.00101

Lee, K. (2016). Head Start's impact on cognitive outcomes for children in foster care. *Child Abuse Review, 25*(2), 128–141. doi:10.1002/car.2413

Lee, M. Y., & Jonson-Reid, M. (2009). Needs and outcomes for low income youth in special education: Variations by emotional disturbance diagnosis and child welfare contact. *Children and Youth Services Review, 31*(7), 722–731. doi:10.1016/j.childyouth.2009.01.005

Leslie, L. K., Landsverk, J., Ezzet-Lofstrom, R., Tschann, J. M., Slymen, D. J., & Garland, A. F. (2000). Children in foster care: Factors influencing outpatient mental health service use. *Child Abuse & Neglect, 24*(4), 465–476.

Leve, L. D., Fisher, P. A., & DeGarmo, D. S. (2007). Peer relations at school entry: Sex differences in the outcomes of foster care. *Merrill-Palmer Quarterly, 53*(4), 557–577.

Levine, S., Lyons, D. M., & Schatzberg, A. F. (1997). Psychobiological consequences of social relationships. *Annals of the New York Academy of Science, 807*, 210–218. doi:10.1111/j.1749-6632.1997.tb51922.x

Lewis, E., Dozier, M., Ackerman, J., & Sepulveda, S. (2007). The effect of placement instability on adopted children's inhibitory control abilities and oppositional behavior. *Developmental Psychology, 43*(6), 1415–1427. doi:10.1037/0012-1649.43.6.1415

Lipscomb, S. T., & Pears, K. C. (2011). Patterns and predictors of early care and education for children in foster care. *Children and Youth Services Review, 33*, 2303–2311. doi:10.1016/j.childyouth.2011.08.002

Lonigan, C. J., Bloomfield, B. G., Anthony, J. L., Bacon, K. D., Phillips, B. M., & Samwel, C. S. (1999). Relations among emergent literacy skills, behavior problems, and social competence in preschool children from low- and middle-income backgrounds. *Topics in Early Childhood Special Education, 19*(1), 40–53. doi:10.1177/027112149901900104

Lovitt, T., & Emerson, J. (2008). *Foster youth who have succeeded in higher education: Common themes.* Minneapolis, MN: National Center on Secondary Education and Transition.

Manly, J. T., Lynch, M., Oshri, A., Herzog, M., & Wortel, S. N. (2013). The impact of neglect on initial adaptation to school. *Child Maltreatment, 18*, 155–170. doi:10.1177/1077559513496144

McDermott, J. M., Westerlund, A., Zeanah, C. H., Nelson, C. A., & Fox, N. A. (2012). Early adversity and neural correlates of executive function: Implications for academic adjustment. *Developmental Cognitive Neuroscience, 2*(Suppl. 1), S59–S66. doi:10.1016/j.dcn.2011.09.008

McEwen, B. S. (1998). Protective and damaging effects of stress mediators. *The New England Journal of Medicine, 338*(3), 171–179. doi:10.1056/NEJM199801153380307

McIntosh, K., Reinke, W. M., Kelm, J. L., & Sadler, C. A. (2013). Gender differences in reading skill and problem behavior in elementary school. *Journal of Positive Behavior Interventions, 15*(1), 51–60. doi:10.1177/1098300712459080

McKinney-Vento Homeless Education Assistance Improvements Act 101, U.S.C., Pub. L. No. 100-77 § 101(a), 482 Stat. (1987).

McMillen, C., Auslander, W. F., Elze, D., White, T., & Thompson, R. (2003). Educational experiences and aspirations of older youth in foster care. *Child Welfare, 82*(4), 475–495.

Mehana, M., & Reynolds, A. J. (2004). School mobility and achievement: A meta-analysis. *Children and Youth Services Review, 26*, 93–119. doi:10.1016/j.childyouth.2003.11.004

Merdinger, J. M., Hines, A. M., Osterling, K. L., & Wyatt, P. (2005). Pathways to college for former foster youth: Understanding factors that contribute to educational success. *Child Welfare, 84*(6), 867–896.

Miedel, W. T., & Reynolds, A. J. (1999). Parent involvement in early intervention for disadvantaged children: Does it matter? *Journal of School Psychology, 37*(4), 379–402.

Naccarato, T., Brophy, M., & Courtney, M. E. (2010). Employment outcomes of foster youth: The results from the Midwest Evaluation of Adult Functioning in Former Foster Youth. *Children and Youth Services Review, 32*, 551–559. doi:10.1016/j.childyouth.2009.11.009

National Working Group on Foster Care and Education. (2014, January). Fostering success in education: National factsheet on the educational outcomes of children in foster care. *Research Highlights on Education and Foster Care,* 1–20.

Parrish, T., Delano, C., Dixon, D., Webster, D., Berrick, J. D., & Bolus, S. (2001). *Education of foster group home children, whose responsibility is it? Study of the educational placement of children residing in group homes*. Palo Alto, CA: American Institutes of Research.

Pears, K. C., Bruce, J., Fisher, P. A., & Kim, H. K. (2010). Indiscriminate friendliness in maltreated foster children. *Child Maltreatment, 15*, 64–75. doi:10.1177/1077559509337891

Pears, K. C., & Fisher, P. A. (2005a). Developmental, cognitive, and neuropsychological functioning in preschool-aged foster children: Associations with prior maltreatment and placement history. *Journal of Developmental and Behavioral Pediatrics, 26*, 112–122.

Pears, K. C., & Fisher, P. A. (2005b). Emotion understanding and theory of mind among maltreated children in foster care: Evidence of deficits. *Development and Psychopathology, 17*, 47–65. doi:10.1017/S0954579405050030

Pears, K. C., Fisher, P. A., Bruce, J., Kim, H. K., & Yoerger, K. (2010). Early elementary school adjustment of maltreated children in foster care: The roles of inhibitory control and caregiver involvement. *Child Development, 81*(5), 1550–1564. doi:10.1111/j.1467-8624.2010.01491.x

Pears, K. C., Fisher, P. A., Kim, H. K., Bruce, J., Healey, C. V., & Yoerger, K. (2013). Immediate effects of a school readiness intervention for children in foster care. *Early Education and Development, 24*(6), 771–791. doi:10.1080/10409289.2013.736037

Pears, K. C., Heywood, C. V., Kim, H. K., & Fisher, P. A. (2011). Prereading deficits in children in foster care. *School Psychology Review, 40*(1), 140–148.

Pears, K. C., Kim, H. K., Buchanan, R., & Fisher, P. A. (2015). Adverse consequences of school mobility for children in foster care: A prospective longitudinal study. *Child Development, 86*(4), 1210–1226. doi:10.1111/cdev.12374

Pears, K. C., Kim, H. K., & Fisher, P. A. (2012). Effects of a school readiness intervention for children in foster care on oppositional and aggressive behavior in kindergarten. *Children and Youth Services Review, 34*(12), 2361–2366. doi:10.1016/j.childyouth.2012.08.015

Pears, K. C., Kim, H. K., & Fisher, P. A. (2016). Decreasing risk factors for later alcohol use and antisocial behaviors in children in foster care by increasing early promotive factors. *Children and Youth Services Review, 65*, 156–165. doi:10.1016/j.childyouth.2016.04.005

Pecora, P. J. (2012). Maximizing educational achievement of youth in foster care and alumni: Factors associated with success. *Children and Youth Services Review, 34*, 1121–1129. doi:10.1016/j.childyouth.2012.01.044

Pianta, R. C., & Stuhlman, M. W. (2004). Teacher–child relationships and children's success in the first years of school. *School Psychology Review, 33*(3), 444–458.

Proctor, L. J., Skriner, L. C., Roesch, S. C., & Litrownik, A. (2010). Trajectories of behavioral adjustment following early placement in foster care: Predicting stability and change over 8 years. *Journal of the American Academy of Child and Adolescent Psychiatry, 49*, 464–473. doi:10.1016/j.jaac.2010.01.022

Promoting Safe and Stable Families Amendments of 2001 U.S.C., Pub. L. No. 107-133 § 201, 2413 Stat. (2002).

Ramey, C. T., Campbell, F. A., & Blair, C. (1998). Enhancing the life course for high-risk children: Results from the Abecedarian Project. In J. Crane (Ed.), *Social programs that work* (pp. 163–183). New York: Russell Sage Foundation.

Reynolds, A. J., & Bezruczko, N. (1993). School adjustment of children at risk through fourth grade. *Merrill-Palmer Quarterly, 39*(4), 457–480.

Reynolds, A. J., & Temple, J. A. (2008). Cost-effective early childhood development programs from preschool to third grade. *Annual Review of Clinical Psychology, 4*, 109–139. doi:10.1146/annurev.clinpsy.3.022806.091411

Reynolds, A. J., Temple, J. A., Ou, S.-R., Arteaga, I. A., & White, B. A. B. (2011). School-based early childhood education and age-28 well-being: Effects by timing, dosage, and subgroups. *Science, 333*(6040), 360–364. doi:10.1126/science.1203618

Scherr, T. G. (2007). Educational experiences of children in foster care. *School Psychology International, 28*(4), 419–436. doi:10.1177/0143034307084133

Simmel, C., Shpiegel, S., & Murshid, N. S. (2013). Foster care alumni and funding for postsecondary education: Examining variation in state support. *Journal of Policy Practice, 12*(1), 43–61. doi:10.1080/15588742.2012.739132

Smithgall, C., Gladden, R. M., Howard, E., Goerge, R., & Courtney, M. (2004). *Educational experiences of children in out-of-home care.* Chicago: Chapin Hall Center for Children at the University of Chicago.

Storer, H. L., Barkan, S. E., Stenhouse, L. L., Eichenlaub, C., Mallillin, A., & Haggerty, K. P. (2014). In search of connection: The foster youth and caregiver relationship. *Children and Youth Services Review, 42,* 110–117. doi:10.1016/j.childyouth.2014.04.008

Sullivan, M. J., Jones, L., & Mathiesen, S. (2010). School change, academic progress, and behavior problems in a sample of foster youth. *Children and Youth Services Review, 32*(2), 164–170. doi:10.1016/j.childyouth.2009.08.009

Unrau, Y. A., Font, S. A., & Rawls, G. (2012). Readiness for college engagement among students who have aged out of foster care. *Children and Youth Services Review, 34,* 76–83. doi:10.1016/j.childyouth.2011.09.002

U.S. Department of Health & Human Services. (2016). *Child maltreatment 2014.* Washington, DC: Author.

Walcott, C. M., Scheemaker, A., & Bielski, K. (2010). A longitudinal investigation of inattention and preliteracy development *Journal of Attention Disorders, 14*(1), 79–85.

Ward, H. (2009). Patterns of instability: Moves within the care system, their reasons, contexts and consequences. *Children and Youth Services Review, 31*(10), 1113–1118. doi:10.1016/j.childyouth.2009.07.009

Wolanin, T. R. (2005). *Higher education opportunities for foster youth: A primer for policymakers.* Washington, DC: The Institute for Higher Education Policy.

Wulczyn, F., & Lery, B. (2007). *Racial disparity in foster care admissions.* Chicago: Chapin Hall Center for Children at the University of Chicago.

Zetlin, A. (2006). The experiences of foster children and youth in special education. *Journal of Intellectual and Developmental Disability, 31*(3), 161–165. doi:10.1080/13668250600847039

Zima, B. T., Bussing, R., Freeman, S., Yang, X., Belin, T. R., & Forness, S. R. (2000). Behavior problems, academic skill delays, and school failure among school-aged children in foster care: Their relationship to placement characteristics. *Journal of Child and Family Studies, 9*(1), 87–103. doi:10.1023/A:1009415800475

SECTION II

Part V

Aging Out of Foster Care into Independent Living

Challenges and Opportunities

13

Self-Sufficiency

Employment, Earnings, and Receipt of Public Benefits by Former Foster Youth

Loring P. Jones

The Transition to Adulthood in an American Context

Despite the policy mandate to reunify children with their family of origin, many young people remain in the system until they reach the age of 18. What these youth share with all emerging adults is that they have common needs to become employed, to be financially independent, to acquire the skills that enable them to live autonomously, to develop satisfying relationships with others, and to be integrated into the community as productive and valued members. Mastering the tasks of becoming independent and financially stable is a challenge for most young people. However, youth in foster care face challenges in fulfilling these tasks. These challenges begin before they enter the child welfare system. Children and youth are in care because of maltreatment in their own home. They have never known the love and security that come from a stable family life. These children are disproportionately poor and are often racial and ethnic minorities, particularly African-American (U.S. Department of Health & Human Services, 2014; Wildeman & Emanuel, 2014). They are likely to have grown up in poverty, and they have probably experienced homes where there has been parental dysfunction (mental health problems, substance abuse disorders, domestic violence, incarceration, etc.) (Crosson-Towers, 2007). They have experienced the emotional trauma and mental health difficulties caused by abuse and loss, and the potential disruption of family and community ties inherent in the removal from the home.

Entering the child welfare system should provide some benefits for the child or adolescent. First, children and youth are removed from abusive and neglectful environments that are a threat to their development, and are given social workers who provide services to address the multiple needs that they might have. They have access to health care, including mental health services, that they may not have had before. However, the removal from the home does pose a number of additional challenges to add to those previously mentioned. Children may not receive the protection promised them. Abuse by foster parents is not unknown, and many children do not receive the services they need (Kortenkamp & Ehrle, 2002; Mech, 2002). Some aspects of care, such as frequent placement changes, have detrimental effects on youth (Ryan & Testa, 2005). Numerous placement changes result in educational deficits and psychological distress because foster children may also be required to attend a different school in the middle of a school year. The socio-economic disadvantages that preceded foster care can also have a negative effect even after years in care. In fact, some research suggests that despite the efforts of child welfare agencies, former foster youth are in no better, or perhaps in worse condition, to cope with the transition to adulthood than youth with similar socio-economic statuses (Berzin, 2008; Buehler, Orme, Post, & Patterson, 2000; Kerman, Wildfire, & Barth, 2002). The last challenge they face on leaving care is the possible abrupt termination of care and support at age 18 or 19. Not only do they potentially lose services and benefits such as Medicaid; foster parents and social workers do not have a mandate to continue providing foster youth with support.

Achieving financial independence and establishing a household separate from the family of origin were identified as markers of adulthood throughout much of the second half of the twentieth century. Emerging adulthood, as defined by Arnett (2000), connotes a changing notion of adulthood where it is taking longer than it once did to become an adult in U.S. society. Arnett describes this time in a young person's life as a new developmental stage that occurs from age 18 to the mid- to late twenties where the youth is "in-between the restrictions of adolescence and the responsibilities of adulthood" (2000, p. 14). This prolonged period of preparation for adulthood has meant that youth are depending on their parents and family for support over a much longer time than had been the custom in U.S. society. Arnett's theory has been influential in informing the approach to developing services for youth leaving care, and in the provision of services after youth leave foster care (Avery & Freundlich, 2009).

Foster youth do not have the luxury of this extended period of preparation that is inherent in the concept of emerging adulthood. No one expects youth to become adults overnight, but that is what often does happen, as state support for basic living needs can end abruptly for a youth leaving care. Foster youth not only lose state support at emancipation, but they may also not have the sources of support from parents or family that are available to non-foster youth when they encounter difficulties adjusting to adulthood. Many youth return home after leaving care, but often their families have multiple problems and limited resources to provide them with assistance (Iglehart & Becerra, 2002). Youth are expected to take care of themselves without parental support or any other safety net. In short, these youth risk leaving care without the same help that most young people, who have not spent part of their childhood in out-of-home care, need, depend upon, and receive. The dismal outcomes noted for former foster youth in the research are undoubtedly partially a result of this lack of support.

The cumulative research suggests that public policy hurries youth leaving foster care into adulthood before they are ready to function on their own and without the supports that other youth in this society can count on during the transition to adulthood. Policies have an underlying assumption that youth leaving care would shortly attain financial self-sufficiency and emotional independence. Until the passage by Congress of the Fostering Connections to Success and Increasing Adoptions Act (P.L. 110-351; sometimes referred to as Chafee) in 2008, the expectation was that foster youth would leave care to live on their own with little or no support. Even today, youth often leave care with just a garbage bag containing their belongings, a referral to a homeless shelter, or bus fare to their parental home, and possibly, if they are fortunate, some essential documents like a social security card and some cash. Only 40% of youth leave care with at least $250 in cash, only one in three have a driver's license, and most do not have either the resources or skills to establish an independent residence (American Bar Association Commission on Youth at Risk, 2011; Delgado, 2013). Often they leave care without a high school education, a job, or a connection to a single caring adult. All of these challenges are made worse by the socio-economic disadvantage that preceded foster care, and in many cases follows youth into adulthood.

The transition to adulthood is a crucial opportunity that ought not to be missed, because it represents a chance to address the disadvantages that a youth brings into care. We are missing that opportunity to provide services that would ease the transition for too many youth. The state has assumed responsibility for these youth by removing them from their family home and placing them in foster care. This responsibility includes providing the best possible preparation for their charges on leaving care. This support is what most youth in this society expect from those who are responsible for them.

Courtney (2009) borrowed the term "corporate parenting" from the United Kingdom to describe the responsibility of the state in helping foster youth to make a successful transition to emerging adulthood. In this role, the state assumes responsibility for children when it takes them into custody. While the child is in care, the state acts as a good parent; that is, as a guide and resource toward a successful transition. The state would replicate as closely as possible what good parents do to assist their child to become an independent adult, which includes extending assistance after the child leaves home. The state cannot actually parent, but it can make sure, before it disengages from foster youth, that it has found supportive adults who will carry out that function with the former foster youth. The state can bring together the resources of the various service systems that a youth needs to emerge as a successful adult. Courtney (2009) asserts that this role widens the responsibility for assuring a successful transition for emancipated foster youth to include not only the child welfare system, but also to involve other relevant systems (education, employment assistance, health, public assistance, housing, etc.).

This chapter examines the post-discharge employment and financial experiences of former foster youth, and a subset of these youth called emancipated foster youth. The purpose of this examination is to increase the knowledge base on how foster youth are prepared for self-sufficiency, and to suggest improvements to the current policy and programming since self-sufficiency is a crucial component of making the transition into adulthood in America.

Two groups of youth are of concern in this chapter. The first group is the broad category of former foster youth (FFY). Former foster youth are those who have had foster care experience, but did not exit through emancipation; or the particular study discussed does not make a distinction on how youth exited care. Those youth who exit care through reaching the age of majority will be referred to as emancipated foster youth (EFY). Emancipation in the general population means that youth have reached the age where their parents are no longer legally responsible for their behavior, and the emerging adult does not need to answer to the parents. The same is true for EFY who have "aged out" of the system. They are no longer required to answer to the child welfare system, and the system will disengage its support from the youth. Parents are also no longer legally required to support their emancipated offspring, but most parents do provide considerable assistance to their transitioning offspring. The number of older foster youth, who exit before emancipation, is substantially greater than just youth who "age out." Much of the research reported upon in this chapter does not make this distinction, and uses the terms EFY and FFY interchangeably. As far as possible, I will try to use the terms as defined here.

Employment and Earnings of Former Foster Youth

The school-to-work transition is a crucial component of the movement into adulthood, and in the public policy interest in self-sufficiency for former foster youth. The cumulative findings on employment are that many youth leave foster care without the work training or skills to acquire a job, and when employed, they work in unskilled low-wage jobs that result in continual job and income insecurity. See the research listed in Table 13.1.

Undoubtedly, these poor outcomes are linked to the low levels of educational attainment documented for foster youth. Studies show that FFY lag behind their counterparts in the general population in completing high school. The cumulative research reports a range of high school graduation rates from 33% to 85% for youth leaving care (Barnow et al., 2015; Berzin, 2008; Buehler et al., 2000; Courtney & Dworsky, 2006; Harris, Jackson, O'Brien, & Pecora, 2009; Pecora, Kessler

Table 13.1 Employment, Finances, and Receipt of Public Benefits

Author(s)	Study Type	Purposes & Predictors	Employment Outcomes	Public Assistance Receipt	Financial Situation
Courtney, M.; Dworsky, A.; Brown, A.; Cary, C.; Love, K.; & Vorhies, V. (2011)	Mid-West Evaluation of Adult Functioning of Former Foster Youth Longitudinal, retrospective	Outcomes at age 26	Ever held a job: 94% Currently employed: 46% Not currently employed: 48% Worked in the past year: 25% Last worked more than a year ago: 23%	Unemployment insurance: (F=13%, M=15%) SSI: (F=17%, M=12%) Food Stamps: (F=68%, M=42%) TANF: (F=19%, M=2%) WIC: (F=34%) Received any means-tested program benefits: (F=87%, M=40%)	70% earned income in the past year. 38% had an income of less than $5K a year. 16% had an income of between $5K and $10K. 2.5% earned more than $50K. Median income: $8,950. 9.4% own a residence. 47% had a banking account. 48% owned a vehicle.
Courtney, M.; Dworsky, A.; Lee, J.; & Rapp, M. (2010)	Mid-West Evaluation of Adult Functioning of Former Foster Youth	Outcomes at ages 23 and 24	84% reported they had had a job since leaving foster care. 45% were currently employed. On average, youth worked 37 hours a week with a median hourly wage of $9.45. The Add Health comparison group workers had a 76% employment rate and earned $4 more an hour.	70% of females and 29% of males received at least one needs-based government program. 75% of women, 89% of custodial mothers, 33% of custodial males had received benefits from one or more government program.	Median income of $8,000 a year. 50% of youth experienced at least 1 of 5 material hardships (not enough money to pay rent; not enough money to pay a utility bill; had a utility cut off or phone service disconnected; or had been evicted). 29% had low or very low food security. 40% had been homeless or couch surfed since leaving foster care.

Author(s)	Study Type	Purposes & Predictors	Employment Outcomes	Public Assistance Receipt	Financial Situation
Courtney, M.; Dworsky, A; Cusick, G.; Havlicek, J.; Perez, A.; & Keller, T. (2009)	Mid-West Evaluation of Adult Functioning of Former Foster Youth	Outcomes at age 21	70% reported working in the previous year. One-half of youth were currently employed, working (mean 7 hours a day) 35 hours a week on average for $8.85 per hour. More men than women reported employment. Women worked less (34 hrs. vs 38 hrs. a week) and were paid less than males ($8.10 vs. $9.92 an hour).	Unemployment insurance: (F=7%, M=8%) SSI: (F=13%, M=13%) Food Stamps: (F=63%, M=22%) TANF: (F=20%, M=6%) WIC: (F=78%) 33% of females and 22% of males received at least one needs-based government program.	49.5% had at least one economic hardship. Mean number of hardships: 1.05
Courtney, M.; & Dworsky, A. (2005)	Mid-West Evaluation of Adult Functioning of Former Foster Youth	Outcomes at age 19	47% of those discharged were employed vs. 58% of the Add Health Sample. Worked on average 33 hours a week at $7.54. No difference in hours worked from Add Health sample. 75% earned less than $5K a year. 90% earned less than $10K. 49% of females and 25% of males received at least one needs-based government program.	49% of females & 25% had received at least one benefit.	One-quarter was food insecure. 12% of sample said they could not pay rent; 45% could not pay utility bill. Youth who remained in care at age 19 were much less likely to experience a material hardship. 46% had a savings account vs. 82% in Add Health sample. Youth who remained in care experienced fewer economic hardships than those youth who left.

(continued)

Table 13.1 Employment, Finances, and Receipt of Public Benefits (continued)

Author(s)	Study Type	Purposes & Predictors	Employment Outcomes	Public Assistance Receipt	Financial Situation
Courtney, M.; Terao, S.; & Bost, N. (2004)	Mid-West Evaluation of Adult Functioning of Former Foster Youth	Outcomes at age 17 to 18	48% had ever been employed; 35% were employed at the time of the interview. Most worked part-time (76%). 3% were in job Corps.	n.a.	n.a
Courtney, M.; Zinn, A.; Koralek, R.; Bess, R.; Stagner, M.; Pergamit, M.; & Johnson, H. (2011)	Evaluation of the Massachusetts Adolescent Outreach Program for Youths in Intensive Foster Care	ILS Evaluation	Treatment group and control had no differences on employment.	n.a.	n.a.
Barnow, B.; Buck, A.; O'Brien, K.; Pecora, P.; Ellis, M.; & Steiner, E. (2015)	Casey Foster Alumni Study N=1058 16–21 year olds in transition programs 71% of sample were African-American.	How well did youth do in transition programs? What services and demographics contributed to favorable outcomes? Longitudinal	Length of stay in the program is a contributor to success. 35% of the youth obtained employment.	n.a.	n.a.
Barth, 1980	Retrospective; no comparison group, purposive sampling N=55 former foster youth, ages 17 to 26 (53% female, 72% White, 13% Black, 9% Latino)	How well discharged youth fare after foster care	75% of youth were employed; 87% had a job before being discharged from care.	n.a.	53% reported serious money problems. 33% had engaged in criminal activity for money.

Author(s)	Study Type	Purposes & Predictors	Employment Outcomes	Public Assistance Receipt	Financial Situation
Benedict, M.; Zuravin, S.; & Stallings (1996)	Random sample of EFY in Baltimore after leaving care	Kin vs. non-kin foster care and employment	44% were working; 25% were "keeping house"; 7% were incarcerated; 16.3% were looking for work or in school; 2% had physical or mental disabilities which precluded working; 5% were "doing nothing."	n.a.	n.a.
Buehler, C.; Orme, J.; Post, J.; & Patterson, D. (2000)	National Survey of Families and Households (NSFH) National probability sample of 13,017 families in 1987–1988	Examined long-term correlates of experiencing family foster care before age 19.	95% of FFY reported working at some point vs. 91% of matched group (foster care vs. non-foster care, but with similar SES characteristics), and vs. 94% of the random sample (chosen from among all youth in the sample). No statistical differences between groups	n.a.	FFY had lower levels of economic well-being than the random group.
Havalchak, A.; White, C. R.; & O'Brien, K. (2008, March)	Casey Young Adult Services Extant literature as a comparison.	Post-foster care adaptation	82% were in the workforce.	38% received Medicaid; 25% Food Stamps; 19% WIC.	A little less than 75% had a banking account. 84% had income above the poverty line which is considered a living wage.
Cook, R. J. (1994) (sometimes referred to as the Westat Study)	National random sample Longitudinal	ILS effectiveness	49% were employed (43% of females & 56% of males). 38% were able to maintain a job for a year.	30% of youth used public assistance such as AFDC, Medicaid, Food Stamps. Of those using aid, 64% were female.	n.a.

(continued)

Table 13.1 Employment, Finances, and Receipt of Public Benefits (continued)

Author(s)	Study Type	Purposes & Predictors	Employment Outcomes	Public Assistance Receipt	Financial Situation
Daining, C. & DePanfilis, D. (2007)	Survey of youth leaving foster care	Resiliency	52% were employed. 81% of those employed worked full-time. 92% held a job for at least 3 months. 7% of youth were unemployed and never had the same job for 3 months.	n.a.	n.a.
Dworsky, A. (2005)	Administrative data from the State of Wisconsin Longitudinal	Examined self-sufficiency	80% of youth employed in at least one quarter after discharge. Females were more likely than males to be employed (83% vs. 78%).	17% (mostly female) were recipients of AFDC. TANF. Females were more likely than males to collect Food Stamps (43% vs. 25%).	Mean & median for all 8 quarters were $5,170 & $2,322. Income was at the poverty level.
Fallesen (2013)	Danish administrative data (N=7220)	Duration of foster care and its effects	Children in foster care were more dependent on welfare than children without that experience. Duration of care was a factor. Longer time in care increases adult income & labor force attachment.	See previous cell.	n.a.

Author(s)	Study Type	Purposes & Predictors	Employment Outcomes	Public Assistance Receipt	Financial Situation
Goerge, R.; Bilaver, L.; Joo Lee, B.; Needell, B.; Brookhart, A.; & Jackman, W. (2002)	Multistate Foster Care Data Archive Administrative data in three states Longitudinal	Employment and earnings of EFY	No more than 45% of FFY had earnings in any of the 13 quarters. Reunified youth did better than aging out youth. Low-income youth without foster care did slightly better (50%). Youth who worked before their 18th birthday were more likely to be working at the time of the interview than those who had not.	n.a.	Income levels were below poverty levels.
Greeson, J.; Usher, L.; & Grinstein-Weiss, M. (2010)	Add Health	Mentoring & asset accumulation	n.a.	n.a.	Having a mentor was associated with having a bank account.
Hook, J. & Courtney (2011)*	Mid-West Evaluation of Adult Functioning of Former Foster Youth Youth at age 23	Human capital framework	Correlates of employment: education (+), reading competence (+), criminal justice involvement (-), neglect (+), family foster care (+), placement change (-). For each year of care past 18, the likelihood of being employed increases 18%. 8.1% higher wages for staying in care until 21.*	n.a.	n.a.

(continued)

Table 13.1 Employment, Finances, and Receipt of Public Benefits (continued)

Author(s)	Study Type	Purposes & Predictors	Employment Outcomes	Public Assistance Receipt	Financial Situation
Kimberlin, S. & Lemley, A. (2012)	Exit outcomes for former foster youth participating in California's THP Plus transitional supportive housing programs	Program evaluation Pre- and post-test, but no comparison group N=552	41% of youth worked at entrance to the program. 43% were working at exit.	Public benefits (Food Stamps, CalWorks, SSI, etc.). Usage increased from 24% to 36% during the study period.	29% entered the program with zero income. The mean income for youth with yearly income was $8,274. The number of youth with a bank account during the program ranged from 52% to 72%.
Leathers, S. & Testa, M. (2006)	Random sample of Illinois youth in foster care Caseworker responded for youth	Needs assessment	44% of youth aged 18 and older were employed. 32% worked part-time. 28% were both attending school and working. 40% earned the minimum wage. 22% earned less than the minimum wage. Special needs youth and African-American youth were more likely to be unemployed. Youth who remained in care until age 19 had fewer behavioral problems, educational and job skills deficits.	n.a.	n.a.

Author(s)	Study Type	Purposes & Predictors	Employment Outcomes	Public Assistance Receipt	Financial Situation
Lenz-Rashid, S. (2006)	Cross-section (N=252) Comparison of foster (FFY) and non-foster youth who completed a job readiness program Asked about LGBT youth	Homeless youth FFY & non-foster comparisons Data gathered from staff and administrative data	Youth with mental health issues were less likely to be employed and had lower earnings.	n.a.	n.a.
Lindsey, E. & Ahmed, F. (1999)	ILP program evaluation & needs assessment	ILP	59% of ILP participants were employed vs. 44% non-participants employed.	ILP participants utilized public assistance (housing, AFDC, WIC, Emergency Assistance), possibly due to the larger number of females in the treatment group.	48% of the ILP participants had trouble paying their bills vs. 28% of the non-participants.
Mallon, G. P. (1998)	Pre & post quasi-evaluation	ILP	72% were employed at discharge. At follow-up, it was 78%.	n.a.	65% had a savings account at discharge. This had decreased to 39% at follow-up.
Macomber, J.; Kuehn, D.; McDaniel, M; Vericker, T.; Pergamit, M.; Cuccaro, S.; Needell, B.; Duncan, D.; Kum, H. K.; Stewart, J.; Kwon-Lee, C.; & Barth, R. (2008)	Midwest Evaluation of Former Foster Youth linked administrative databases in North Carolina, Minnesota, & California	Employment outcomes	Poor employment outcomes persist at age 24. Four categories of youth with connections to labor market: 0 to 10% were never connected to the job market and had zero income 16% to 25% were consistently connected to the job market (earnings: $1,080 to $1,575 a month);	n.a.	n.a.

(continued)

Table 13.1 Employment, Finances, and Receipt of Public Benefits (continued)

Author(s)	Study Type	Purposes & Predictors	Employment Outcomes	Public Assistance Receipt	Financial Situation
			22% to 46% were initially connected to the job market, but dropped out (earnings: $250 to $450 a month); 16% to 21% experienced a later connection to the labor market after initial difficulties (earnings, $750 to $905 a month).		
Mason, M.; Castrianno, L.; Kessler, C.; Holmstrand, L.; Huefner, J.; Payne, V.; Pecora, P.; Schmaltz, S.; Stenslie, S. (2003)	Post-income outcomes interview for alumni of four foster care agencies	Results from 46 emancipated youth	50% employed; 61% happy with work experience	n.a.	n.a.
McMillen, J. & Tucker, J. (1999)	Secondary data analysis Missouri Study Data Base		Association of placement instability with a reduced likelihood of employment.	n.a.	n.a.

Author(s)	Study Type	Purposes & Predictors	Employment Outcomes	Public Assistance Receipt	Financial Situation
Naccarato, T.; Brophy, M.; & Courtney, M. (2010)*	Midwest Evaluation of the Adult Functioning of Former Foster Youth	Employment & earnings	n.a.	n.a.	Range of earnings from $0 to $81K Mean=$8,603; median=$2,814 49% had no earnings at the time of the interview. 75% earned $15K or less. Only four youth earned more than $50K. Correlates of income: mental health problems (−), drugs & alcohol (+), education (+)*
National Youth in Transition Database (NYTD) (2012)	Administrative data from 50 states reporting requirements under Chafee	Employment, earnings, public assistance receipt, at age 17	28% report at least one employment experience.	18% received public aid of one kind or another.	n.a.
National Youth in Transition Database (NYTD) (2014)	Administrative data from 50 states reporting requirements under Chafee	Employment, earnings, public assistance receipt, at age 19 Youth in foster care compared with youth who left foster care	34% were employed. 12% of youth were employed full-time with 24% working part-time. Youth in care were more likely to be working part-time. Youth not in care were more likely to be working part-time.	44% reported receiving some form of public benefits other than public assistance. 36% of youth not in care received public benefits.	n.a.

(continued)

Table 13.1 Employment, Finances, and Receipt of Public Benefits (continued)

Author(s)	Study Type	Purposes & Predictors	Employment Outcomes	Public Assistance Receipt	Financial Situation
Pergamit, M. & Johnson, H. (2012)	Multi-site evaluation of Youth in Foster Care (Life Skills Training Program) & the California Child Welfare Services Case Management System	Benefits of extending care to age 21 Los Angeles	70% of youth worked in care between their 18th & 19th year; however, most of the youth did not work continuously. About one in three held a job for longer than 3 months. Only about one-quarter worked full-time. 23% had attended some sort of vocational program. The median income was $4,000.	One-fifth received Food Stamps with double that rate among females.	13% could not pay rent. About 5% had experienced a utility cut-off. 5% had been evicted. 20% had had their phone service discontinued. 13% said they were hungry and could not afford food. About half had a bank checking account.
Peters, C. M.; Sherraden, M.; & Kuchinski, A. M. (2016)	20 high savers and 10 low savers in the Operation Passport Program. (age 18)	Four unnamed sites in three states Qualitative	Most tended to work at minimum-wage jobs (fast food, retail, & temp agencies).	Youth reported receiving a variety of different types of public aid. Some received stipends for ILS participation and ETVs.	Earned Income Tax Credit and tax refunds were a big source of income. Most reported receiving stipends for school or training. Many reported debt & borrowing; use of pay day loans.

Author(s)	Study Type	Purposes & Predictors	Employment Outcomes	Public Assistance Receipt	Financial Situation
Needell, B.; Alamin, S. C.; Brookhart, A.; Jackman, W.; & Shlonsky, A. (2002)		Characteristics of emancipated foster youth	n.a.	25% of females were receiving TANF in each of the 6 yrs. following emancipation. 50% of females received TANF in at least 1 year. They are four times more likely to receive TANF than the general population.	n.a.
Pecora, P.; Kessler, R.C.; O'Brien, K.; White, C.R.; Williams, J.; Hiripi, E.; English, D.; White, J.; & Herrick, M.A.; (2006)	Northwest Foster Care Alumni Study	Educational and employment achievements	80% employment rate among alumni	17% received TANF.	Most alumni reported difficulties finding jobs that paid a living wage; one-third of households were below the poverty line.
Pecora, P.; Kessler, W.; Downs, A.C.; & O'Brien, K.; Hiripi, E.; & Morello, S. (2003)	Casey Family Alumni Study		88% were employed at the time of their interview.	n.a.	n.a.
Kerman, B.; Wildfire, J.; & Barth, R. (2002)	Casey National Foster Care Alumni Study Four groups: Adoption; Long-Term Foster Care; Extended Foster Care; Emancipated (Other)	Effects of foster care on adult functioning	Extended Foster Care & Adoption groups were more self-sufficient than the LTFC 2 groups. Adoption group did not do better than the Emancipated (Other) group.	n.a.	n.a.

(continued)

Table 13.1 Employment, Finances, and Receipt of Public Benefits (continued)

Author(s)	Study Type	Purposes & Predictors	Employment Outcomes	Public Assistance Receipt	Financial Situation
Reilly, T. (2003)	Cross-sectional; no comparison group, convenience sample	Explored post-discharge functioning	63% were employed. 26% had not had regular employment since leaving care. 55% had been terminated from a job. 24% supported themselves by dealing drugs. 11% had sex for money.	n.a.	60% made less than $10K a year. 34% were earning less than $5K a year. 41% said they did not have enough income to cover basic living expenses. The average pay was $7.25 per hour.
Salazar, A. (2013)	Casey National Foster Care Alumni Study N=329 Selected college graduates from the GSS, (a nationally representative sample), and the Panel Study of Income Dynamics	Examined the impact of having a BA degree	n.a.	n.a.	While no differences were found on individual earnings between Casey alumni BA holders, household income lagged behind those in the GSS nationally representative sample. Casey alumni were also half as likely as the national sample to own a home (25% vs. 50%).
Yates, T. & Grey, I. (2012)	Cross-sectional; no comparisons, convenience sample	Identifying profiles of risk and resilience	25% were employed.	n.a.	n.a.

Author(s)	Study Type	Purposes & Predictors	Employment Outcomes	Public Assistance Receipt	Financial Situation
Chantala, K. & Tabor, Y. (2010)	Nationally representative sample with adolescents Add Health		Ever held a job: 98% Currently employed: 80%	n.a.	94% earned income in the past year. 8% had an income of less than $5K a year; 8% had an income of between $5K and $10K; 13.5% earned more than $50K. Median income: $27,310 30.4% were homeowners. 27.5% had at least one economic hardship. Mean number of hardships: 0.46 One-eighth were food insecure.

Note: * + = positive relationship; - = negative relationship.

Key: SSI = Supplementary Security Income; TANF = Temporary Assistance for Needy Families; WIC = Women, Infants and Children program; ILS = Independent Living Services; AFDC = Aid for Dependent Children; GSS = General Social Survey.

et al., 2006). The graduation rate for all U.S. high school students in 2014 was 81% (National Center for Education Statistics, 2015).

One particular problem noted by Pecora, Williams et al. (2006) is that most studies do not distinguish between high school completion by a traditional diploma (HSD) or by a General Equivalency Diploma (GED). Data suggest that these two indicators of high school completion are very different items in terms of earning power and ability to pursue further education. Pecora and colleagues note that Casey alumni completed GEDs (19%) at almost four times the national rate. The drawbacks of having a GED versus earning an HSD are apparent in two areas: going on to secondary education and earnings from employment. In 2009, 73% of individuals with a high school diploma had at least some college education. Only 43% of GED recipients had any college education at all. One-third of all persons with an HSD have a Bachelor of Arts (BA) or Bachelor of Science (BS) degree. In stark contrast, only 5% of GED holders have earned a BA or BS degree. High school graduates also earned $1,600 more per month than GED recipients. Among those few GED holders who do go on to college and graduate with a BA, the GED still had a negative impact on their income. Recipients of the GED with a BA degree earned $1,400 a month less than other college graduates in 2009 (Ewart, 2012). However, both Pecora, Kessler et al. (2006) and Ewart (2012) emphasize that earning a GED is better than having nothing to indicate high school completion. Ewart (2012) estimates that having a GED may be worth at least $300 a month more than the earnings of a person with only an elementary school education. Researchers do agree that among the EFY who do go on to secondary education, only a small number actually earn a degree. Courtney, Dworsky et al. (2011) reported that at age 26, 5% of their sample had a college degree, and another 23% of the youth had completed a year of college. The Northwest Foster Care Alumni Study gathered data from FFY who had been in the care of several Pacific Northwest child welfare agencies (Pecora, Williams et al., 2006). This study found that about 40% of the alumni had attended college, university, or vocational training. However, as with most EFY research, this study revealed poor college completion rates. The Bachelor's degree completion rate of 2.7% was particularly low. Low levels of educational attainment indicate human capital deficits, and these deficiencies limit employment possibilities (Hook & Courtney, 2011; Leathers & Testa, 2006). In addition, EFY might experience additional problems such as mental health difficulties and substance use and abuse issues that are associated with employment problems (Lenz-Rashid, 2006).

The studies listed in Table 13.1 find 25% to 75% employment rate among EFY. Most studies agree with the Midwest Study estimate that around 50% of EFY were working at any time (Benedict, Zuravin, & Stallings, 1996; Cook, 1994; Courtney, Dworsky et al., 2011; Daining & DePanfilis, 2007; Goerge et al., 2002; Havalchak, White, & O'Brien, 2008; Leathers & Testa, 2006; Lindsey & Ahmed, 1999; Macomber et al., 2003; Mason et al., 2003; Naccarato, Brophy, & Courtney, 2010; Pecora, Kessler et al., 2006; Reilly, 2003; Yates & Grey, 2012). The Midwest Evaluation of the Adult Functioning of Former Foster Youth, sometimes referred to as the Midwest Study, as it is identified throughout this chapter, is probably the most important study to date in establishing the knowledge base for discharged foster children. At its inception, this study was the only large-scale investigation of emancipated foster children (Courtney, Piliavin, Grogan-Kaylor, & Nesmith, 2001; McDonald, Allen, Westerfelt, & Piliavin, 1993). This study was a longitudinal panel study that used a representative sample: 732 of the 758 foster youth who were age 17 on the verge of discharge from Illinois, Wisconsin, and Iowa, took part in the research. The three states in the study contained a rural, urban, and suburban mix, and thus were seen as broadly representative of the United States. Youth gave interviews at ages 17, 19, 23/24, and 26 (Courtney, Dworsky et al., 2011; Courtney, Terao, & Bost, 2004). Data suggest that females were more likely to be employed than males. This advantage with females was not found with young women who were pregnant or parenting (Courtney, Dworsky et al., 2011; Dworsky, 2005; National Youth in Transition Database, 2014). However, gender results are not consistent across studies. This difference is discussed later. The Midwest Study and other foster care research efforts used the National Longitudinal Study of Adolescent to Adult Health, which is commonly referred to as Add Health, as a comparison group. Add Health is the largest and most comprehensive survey of the health and social needs of adolescents in the United States completed to date. Add Health is a longitudinal study that began gathering data from a nationally representative sample of youth from when they were in Grades 7 through to 12. Youth were interviewed in their homes four times between the ages of 18 and 26. Youth were asked about factors that might impinge on their health, such as questions about their insurance status or alcohol use (Chantala & Tabor, 2010). Courtney and colleagues found that the EFY consistently lagged behind Add Health youth in employment rates and earnings. Add Health reports an 80% employment rate among all youth in their sample (Courtney, Dworsky et al., 2011). These same studies show that even when EFY are working, they do not earn enough to meet basic needs or to lift them out of poverty. The Midwest researchers at each interview queried youth about their employment status, and if unemployed, they asked the youth if they had worked since their last interview. The number of EFY who report that they had worked since the previous interview was always greater than the number of youth who said they were currently working at their most recent interview. Staying connected to the workforce seems to be a problem for EFY. Midwest youth have work histories which show that they cycle in and out of work in low-income jobs. This pattern may be a feature of low-income work, or it may mean that youth are not developing the skills to maintain employment.

A subset of studies that links state administrative data from a variety of sources provides another view of the economic well-being of foster youth, and are generally supportive of the employment and financial findings from studies that collected data directly from FFY. One example of these efforts is the Macomber et al. (2008) study which used administrative data from three states (California, Minnesota, and North Carolina) that linked child welfare records with unemployment insurance wage files and tracked youth over time. These wage files track a worker's payment into the insurance system when they are working and their drawdown of benefits when they are out of work. The receipt of unemployment benefits is viewed by researchers as a negative, while employment is seen as a positive adjustment to life after foster care. This study found that only 16% (North Carolina) to 25% (California) of youth maintained consistent employment between the time they left care and age 24. In addition, between 22% (North Carolina) and 33% (California) of youth did not have any connections to the labor market. These researchers compared their findings to results from the representative National Longitudinal Survey of Youth. Data from this survey were collected by the U.S. Office of Management and Budget, the U.S. Bureau of Labor Statistics, and the U.S. Census Bureau. Youth born between the years 1980 and 1984 and a corresponding parent completed 11 interviews between the years 1997 and 2007. The comparison of the two studies revealed that non-foster-care peers were more likely to be employed, and had substantially higher earnings than the FFY well into their twenties.

Buehler et al. (2000) report some more positive data on employment than other studies. These researchers used a nationally representative survey, the 1988 National Survey of Families and Households. The sample was divided into three groups for analysis: former foster youth (FFY group), a random sample of the general population group, and a low-income group with no foster care experience that was matched with the FFY group. No data were available to determine length of stay in care, or when the FFY exited care. This research also reported that over 90% of all adults in the database were working, with no statistical differences reported between groups on employment. The FFY in this sample were older than most studies of EFY, which may account for the higher employment rates found in this study. However, even though each group was employed at similar rates, the FFY and matched groups were more likely to be living in poverty than the nationally representative group. The matched group and the FFY group reported similar poverty rates; however, the FFY earned $2,000 a year less than the low-income disadvantaged group with no foster care experience. The researchers' conclusion was that having been in foster care carries a risk for economic well-being. We can also draw the conclusion from their research that foster youth, when it comes to economic well-being, have much more in common with poor children who did not grow up in foster care than they do with children in the general population.

Longitudinal investigations of EFY show an increase in income over time, but the additional income is never enough to provide for basic needs. Incomes mostly hovered around or below the poverty line (Courtney, Dworsky et al., 2011; Dworsky, 2005; Goerge et al., 2002; Naccarato et al., 2010). Thirty-six percent of youth participating in the Casey Young Adult Survey had incomes below the poverty line. Eighty-four percent of the Casey alumni had incomes that researchers considered to be less than a living wage. Casey researchers considered a living wage to be an income that was three times higher than the poverty line (Havalchak et al., 2008).

Courtney, Dworsky et al. (2011) reported that 38% of the Midwest sample at age 26 had incomes below $5,000 a year with a median income of $8,950. Pergamit and Johnson (2009) found a median income of $4,000 among 19-year-old EFY in Los Angeles. Dworsky (2005) used administrative data from the State of Wisconsin to track income and the receipt of public benefits by FFY over a period of eight fiscal quarters. She found that youth employment fluctuated across quarters. Total earnings by youth during the period under observation were less than a full-time minimum wage worker would earn if they worked continuously over the eight quarters. The comparison Add Health sample reported a median yearly income of $27,310. Salazar (2013) compared Casey alumni with BA degrees with college graduates drawn from the nationally representative General Social Survey (GSS) and found that individual income between her study groups was about the same, but household income was much higher in the GSS sample when compared to the FFY ($40,000 to $49,000 versus $25,000 to $29,999). The GSS is a nationally representative sample of adults (age 18 and older). The University of Chicago with National Science Foundation support has administered the survey on a biennial basis since 1994. The survey gathers demographic, behavioral, and attitudinal data with the intent of providing social scientists with a tool to track social trends over time. Approximately 60,000 persons have provided a face-to-face interview for the survey (NORC at the University of Chicago, 2017).

Twenty-nine percent of EFY participating in a transitional housing program in California did not have an income. Among youth with an income in that program, the mean yearly income was $8,724 (Kimberlin & Lemley, 2012). Courtney, Dworsky et al. (2011) also found that when EFY were working, it was in jobs that did not have benefits such as health insurance or paid vacations, when compared to the Add Health sample. For example, 77% of the Add Health sample had jobs that included paid vacations versus 52% of the Midwest sample workers with that benefit.

Goerge et al. (2002) analyzed administrative data from three states (Illinois, California, and South Carolina). They identified three groups from the data (EFY, FFY who were reunified with their family before emancipation, and a low-income group who had never been in foster care) for analysis. Only 45% of the EFY group, and 45% of the reunified with family group, had earnings in more than three of the 13 fiscal quarters assessed. The low-income youth group had earnings in 50% of the quarters. This finding supports Buehler et al.'s (2000) assertion that youth without foster care experience, but with similar socio-economic backgrounds to FFY, were doing slightly better than the FFY. This difference is surprising since these youth, who had never been in state care, presumably did not have the same access to services that foster youth have. Foster youth have social workers who seek out needed services for youth.

These researchers also found that working at an appropriate age during the teen years was positively associated with future employment and earnings. Youth were more likely to have earnings in the period examined if they had been working in the fiscal quarter prior to turning 18. If a youth did not have earnings in that quarter, they were less likely to have income in the next 2 years than were the youth who had that early work. Macomber et al. (2008) reported similar results—that youth who had a job between ages 16 and 18 were more likely to be consistently connected to the workforce at age 24. They note that this early work and consistent employment might not be program-related, but was a result of the internal characteristics of the youth such as their motivation to work. Nevertheless, many foster youth are not getting that early work experience. Only 34% of youth in the NYTD (2014) had an employment experience at age 17.

Some youth are able to demonstrate resiliency by completing high school, proceeding on to college, and finishing an AA, BA, or BS degree. We find that some youth were also able to show themselves to be resilient by maintaining consistent employment and increasing their earnings over time. These resilient youth left care with a job, were older at discharge, were female, had relatively long stays in foster care, and had completed high school (Barnow et al., 2015; Dworsky, 2005; Fallesen, 2013; Pecora, Williams et al, 2006).

Naccarato et al. (2010) in a secondary analysis of the Midwest Study data found that having a mental health problem was negatively associated with earnings, but curiously, alcohol and drug use were positively associated with an increase in income over the eight quarters examined by these researchers. Naccarato and colleagues explained this finding by suggesting that the income from work made the buying of substances possible, and/or maybe these youth were working to be able to afford substances. They also leave open the possibility that at the time of their interview, the youth were not using, but they had met the diagnostic criteria for substance use/abuse used in the study for the previous year. This diagnosis fit the youth before employment, but not when they were working. It is important to note that other studies have found the opposite; that drugs or alcohol adversely affect employment and earnings (Lenz-Rashid, 2006). More research is needed in this area.

Race, Ethnicity, Gender, LGBTQ, and Income

Race and Ethnicity

The Midwest Study showed employment disadvantages for African-Americans *who were EFY*. Forty percent of African-American youth in that study were employed at age 24 versus 60% of White youth. Dworsky (2005) also reports that being African-American or Hispanic predicted a decrease in earnings in her sample of FFY. She also found certain aspects of a youth's foster care history (placed in care voluntarily, running away from placement, or having had an institutional placement) were associated with lower earnings. On the other hand, when African-American youth were employed, they had higher wages than working White youth. She suggests that employed African-American youth are a select subgroup of EFY who have more human capital than the White youth. Human capital refers to educational and job skills and a skills set that a person might possess which equips them for success in the labor market, and is a determinant of their future income. Goerge et al. (2002) did not find consistent results on ethnicity across the states they studied. In California, Hispanic youth were more likely to work than other groups. Leathers and Testa (2006) report similar findings in their survey of Illinois caseworkers. These caseworkers said that African-American FFY were more likely than other FFY to have employment problems. Goerge and colleagues (2002) did not find race or gender effects on employment in South Carolina. However, African-American FFY had lower earnings than the other FFY in all three states investigated in that study. Macomber et al. (2008) found that non-Hispanic Whites had more employment stability and earnings than African-Americans did. Lenz-Rashid (2006) compared homeless youth with foster care experience with homeless youth without foster care experience. In her research, Hispanic FFY had higher earnings than Hispanic youth who had not experienced foster care. Lenz-Rashid concludes that foster care may provide a protective buffer in the area of earnings. Perhaps foster care provided access for Hispanic youth through Independent Living Services (ILS) to job-readiness skills. Foster care exposed them to services that helped those youth to obtain higher levels of human capital than they might have ordinarily achieved.

Harris et al. (2009) used the Casey alumni data to find in bivariate analysis that African-Americans were more likely to have incomes below the poverty line than White alumni. Two-thirds of Whites and only one-fifth of African-American alumni had incomes above the poverty line. However, multivariate analysis found that the effect of race/ethnicity on income was no longer significant when age at the time of interview, number of places lived prior to foster care, health of their birth father, having a learning disability, receipt of support services before or after leaving care, and the helpfulness of foster parents were all considered.

Based on previous research presented earlier in this chapter, it appears that African-American FFY are handicapped in finding employment during the transition. They must deal with racial bias in hiring practices. Some evidence exists in the literature to assert that African-American adolescents put more effort into job-seeking than Whites, but they are less likely to secure employment (Entwisle, Alexander, & Steffel-Olsen, 2000). African-American youth are also likely to live in areas where there is a dearth of jobs, and where there is considerable competition for these low-paying jobs. The differences in findings noted across states and geographic locales is explained by different contexts, economic conditions, demographic and socio-economic variations in the foster care population, and state policies that can differ on independent living preparation, age at discharge, and how much assistance is provided to a discharged foster youth.

Gender

Gender differences in income found by Dworsky (2005) were the result of the higher levels of education that females had relative to males. Females were more likely to be employed and had lower rates of incarceration than males. They were also more likely to have an income than males when not working, because they were eligible for public benefits due to the presence of children (Dworsky, 2005). Although income differences in Illinois were not found on gender by Goerge et al. (2002), in the other two states (Wisconsin and Iowa) that these researchers investigated, they found that males had higher earnings than females. Many of the youth in this sample were not EFY, and had been reunified with their families, or lived with relatives, or were adopted. These youth were more likely to work than the EFY. It may be that their parents or relatives were able to assist the reunified FFY with finding work, or families placed pressure on them to find jobs.

LGBTQ Youth

The previously discussed studies do not discuss the economic situation of lesbian, gay, bisexual, transgender, or questioning youth (LGBTQ). However, we can infer from two studies that examined self-identified LGBTQ among homeless shelter populations in San Francisco (Lenz-Rashid, 2006) and New York City (Nolan, 2006) that the financial situation of this group is not good. Both studies found FFY overrepresented among the shelter residents. About one-half of the residents in these studies were FFY. In San Francisco, 34% of the FFY was LGBTQ at intake. In New York, 92.5% of the youth said that they were LGBTQ. These studies are important because they are the only FFY studies that have focused on a LGBTQ FFY population. The samples are small and non-random, so caution should be exercised in drawing conclusions about the make-up of shelter populations. Nevertheless, these studies raise questions about how well these youths are supported during the transition. More research is needed to be completed with this population.

Capital and Employment

Hook and Courtney (2011) suggest human, personal, and social capital frameworks for explaining the poor employment and earnings outcomes. As was mentioned earlier, educational levels for FFY are quite low. Personal capital refers to behavioral and personal styles an individual has which might facilitate or hinder employment. Courtney, Hook, and Lee (2010) compared the Midwest Study sample with data from the National Youth in Transition Database (NYTD, 2014). The development of the NYTD was mandated by the Foster Care Independence Act (FCIA) of 1999 (P.L. 106-169) which required states to collect data on defined outcomes to determine the effectiveness of independent living programs. Outcome data included employment (status and skills), education, support from adults, homelessness, substance abuse, incarceration, pregnancy, and ILS receipt. Two methods were deployed to gather data. The first method was to track the delivery services in 14 independent living skills areas, information that is collected as part of the administration of programs. Second, outcome data were collected via interviews with said youth (Shpiegel & Cascardi, 2015). Youth are interviewed at age 17, 19, and 21. Results from the first two interviews have been reported. In 2013, 69% of eligible FFY participated, a rate which is respectable (N=7,845) (Shpiegel & Cascardi, 2015).

In examining findings from both the Midwest and NYTD studies, Courtney, Hook et al. (2010) concluded that male EFY have significant problems with the criminal justice system, including incarceration that limits their job prospects. They found that incarceration reduced employment by 25%. This difficulty is particularly problematic for African-American males, which may account for some of the employment difficulties noted earlier with this group. On the other hand, pregnancy, which is common among female EFY, creates complications in seeking work. Females, however, are more likely than males to be receiving public benefits because the presence of dependent children makes them eligible for these benefits. Lenz-Rashid (2006) also found that having a mental health problem is an important predictor on whether homeless FFY were working. Mental health difficulties are extensive in the FFY population.

Social capital refers to social networks that might link a person to job opportunities. The removal from the home may sever ties with family or neighbors who could help in the job search, but frequent moves in care, or group home placement, may hinder the development of ties with caring adults who could provide those social connections. Hook and Courtney (2011) found that each placement change was associated with a 7% reduction in earnings. They thought this finding was related to the behavioral problems associated with frequent placement changes. They found that youth who exited care from group homes or institutions were 63% less likely to be employed than youth in other out-of-home care situations. Youth who lived independently were also less likely to be working than youth who had been in family foster care, possibly because this type of living arrangement does not foster the development of social connections. Youth placed with relatives while in care were 30% less likely to be working after discharge than youth coming from a non-relative foster care placement.

Receipt of Public Benefits

A second aspect of self-sufficiency used by many researchers as an indicator of a successful transition is whether someone receives public benefits (Temporary Assistance for Needy Families [TANF], Supplementary Security Income [SSI], Supplementary Nutrition Assistance Program (SNAP), also known as Food Stamps, public housing, or Section 8 vouchers). On this standard, EFY demonstrate low levels of self-sufficiency. The three main sources of data for public assistance receipt are the Midwest Study, studies using state administrative data, and research completed with Casey Family Foundation support. These sources find that many EFY rely on public benefits for support. In the Midwest Study, at age 26, 77% of females and 48% of males received at least one of the following benefits during the previous year: Unemployment Insurance, Supplementary Security Income, Food Stamps, public housing or rental assistance, or Women, Infants and Children (WIC) benefits. The most common benefit received was Food Stamps (received by 68% of females and 41% of males). Fifteen percent of females and 2% of males received TANF. In this study, the collection of benefits declined by age 26, but is always high relative to the general population (Courtney, Dworsky et al., 2011). Other studies that examine the demographics of those who receive public assistance have also

Table 13.2 Receipt of Means-Tested Benefits

Program	Average Percentage of the U.S. Population Receiving the Benefits in Any One Month during 2012	% of Mid-West Study Receiving Benefits at Age 26 in the Past Year
Medicaid	15.3	Not reported
SNAP Food Stamps	13.4	56.5
Housing Assistance	4.2	9.3
SSI	3.0	14.4
TANF	1.0	17.9
Receiving at least one benefit	21.3	64.1

Source: Irving and Loveless, 2015.

Key: SNAP = Supplementary Nutrition Assistance Program; SSI = Supplementary Security Income; TANF = Temporary Assistance for Needy Families.

found similar results. Thirty to forty percent of EFY received benefits (Cook, Fleishman, & Grimes, 1991; Dworsky, 2005; Goerge et al., 2002; Havalchak et al., 2008; Kimberlin & Lemley, 2012; Needle, Alamin, Brookhart, Jackman, & Shlonsky, 2002). Table 13.2 shows national participation in means-tested programs compared with use in the Midwest Study.

The comparison shown in Table 13.2 does have some limitations. The dates covered in both columns do not quite match up. The Midwest Study includes just three states, and the measure used in the above table contains just 26 year olds, and not the entire population. However, Table 13.2 does give some estimate of how well the EFY are doing on self-sufficiency vis-à-vis the general population. Most studies view dependence on public assistance as an indicator of a youth failing to meet the federal policy goal, as expressed by the Fostering Connections to Success and Increasing Adoptions Act, of helping youth achieve self-sufficiency (Stott, 2013). Emancipated foster youth appear to be much more dependent on public benefit programs than the general population. Dworsky (2005) asserts that youth are discharged from state care to independence only to become dependent on that same state again. Youth must meet means-tested requirements (low income and sometimes having dependents) to qualify for benefits. Youth might not need these benefits if they had been better prepared for leaving care. It is possible to reframe the view of collecting benefits as a strength, indicating an ability to access needed resources that keep one housed, fed, and in school. These benefits may make it possible to achieve truer independence in the future.

Dworsky (2005) used administrative data to find that one-third of youth in Wisconsin received either cash assistance or Food Stamps in the first eight quarters after discharge. In multivariate analysis, she found that being male, White, having had a court-mandated child protection case, being transferred from an institutional setting, and having had longer lengths of stay in care were all associated in a hazard model with avoiding the utilization of public assistance (receipt of Food Stamps, Aid for Dependent Children [AFDC], and after 1993, TANF). Hazard analysis is a statistical analytic technique initially used in medical research to test how new procedures or medications contribute to the duration of patient survival. This method is used in the social sciences. The use of this method in the above research allowed researchers to identify factors that might reduce the need for the use of public benefits by FFY. While working at discharge showed strong positive associations with future employment and earnings, this relationship was not seen with receiving public assistance. Leaving care without a job did not mean that one collected TANF. It is also important to note that Dworsky's analysis was done at a time when the economy was relatively strong and was providing more abundant work (1992–1998). It is not surprising that TANF participation rates fell below the level of utilization of AFDC benefits, because of availability of work, and because of the stringent work requirements. Much of the work found by TANF participants was low-wage employment. Dworsky reports that rather than finding employment after the implementation of TANF, youth were relying more on Food Stamps to survive, following the pattern seen in the general population. Use of Food Stamps rose in the general population as they replaced cash assistance as the primary safety net (Yu, Lombe, & Nebbit, 2010). It is not surprising that non-Whites were more likely to receive assistance, given the documented problems that youth of color have with racism and the labor market. These problems were partially discussed earlier in this chapter. The overrepresentation of females in public assistance programs is a result of the presence of a large number of single-parenting females relative to male custodial parents.

Asset Accumulation

Assets provide the financial wherewithal to accomplish life goals and contribute to the overall economy (Greeson, Usher, & Grinstein-Weiss, 2010). The process of building up assets is an important part of transition and becoming a self-sufficient adult. As discussed previously, most youth can expect to receive aid, including financial assistance, from their parents in helping to ease the transition to adulthood, and to help youth begin accumulating assets. Typically, these assets include automobiles, education, homes, and small businesses. Many people in the political sector do not understand the employment and financial problems of disadvantaged youth. An example of this lack of understanding occurred in the 2012 presidential campaign, when candidate Mitt Romney counseled a group of college students to ask their parents for loans to start small businesses as an answer to diminished job prospects. He gave as an example a friend's son, who received an $80,000 loan from his parents to start a gourmet sandwich franchise (MSNBC, 2012). A more recent example was Donald Trump telling the story on the campaign trail of receiving $1 million from his father in what he called a small loan to get his business started (Snyder, 2015). Clearly, some youth are able to count on this aid from parents. Most youth do not have the kind of families that can provide even the sandwich franchise level of support. Reilly (2003) reported that EFY in Nevada left care with about $250. This amount is a weak foundation for starting up a household, and beginning asset accumulation. In the absence of monetary assistance, foster youth are handicapped in establishing financial stability. Assets provide the financial wherewithal to accomplish life goals and contribute to the overall economy (Greeson et al., 2010).

An increasing body of research links the building of assets not only with financial goals, but also with positive psychosocial benefits, particularly for low-income youth. These benefits include increased life satisfaction, decreased depression and alcohol abuse (Rohe & Stegman, 1994; Yadama & Sherraden, 1996), improved health status (Robert & House, 1996), more civic engagement and community revitalization (Van Zandt & Rohe, 2006), positive mental health during their childhood and adolescence, school completion, and avoidance of teenage pregnancy. Because of the demonstrated importance of asset development, it needs attention during the period of emerging adulthood as a means of promoting self-sufficiency, helping EFY reach their full potential, increasing their family's well-being, and contributing to the development of more vibrant communities in which youth reside.

The home is an American's largest financial asset. Courtney, Dworsky et al. (2011) found that at age 26, 9% of the Midwest Study sample owned a residence versus a 30% homeownership rate in the Add Health Study. Even Midwest Study college graduates lagged behind the rate of homeownership found in the comparison group. Both Casey Family studies (Pecora et al., 2003; Pecora et al., 2005) also examined asset building among FFY. Twenty-seven percent of the sample owned a home, which was half the rate of the GSS comparison sample (Salazar, 2013). Buehler et al. (2000) reported that youth who had been in foster care were not only less likely be home owners (40%) than the random sample they chose to represent the general population (64%), but also less likely to own a home than a matched sample of low-income non-foster youth (53%) All of these studies used a population that was much older than the typical foster youth study. Buehler and colleagues (2000) also found that FFY were more likely to live in apartments than in detached housing. In addition, Salazar (2013) found that just 47% of the EFY owned a vehicle and just 48% had bank accounts. Pergamit and Johnson (2009) found that only about one-half of Los Angeles EFY had a bank account. Youth reported in that study that the median amount of money that they had on hand when interviewed, including bank accounts, was $100. In comparison, 73% of the Add Health respondents owned a car, and 82% in the Add Health sample had a bank account. The lack of a bank account by EFY suggests saving deficiencies and cash liquidity problems which make EFY vulnerable to crisis. The lack of a car is likely to be a factor in not having the ability to obtain and keep employment.

Economic Hardships

The precarious financial circumstances of these emerging adults make them vulnerable to crisis. Most EFY are living in poverty or close to it. In order to document the economic vulnerability of this group, the Midwest Study collected data about five material hardships. These included an inability to pay a rent or utility bill, having their gas or electricity shut off, having their phone disconnected, or being evicted from a residence. About one-half of the youth at age 23 or 24 had experienced at least one of these hardships in the previous year versus 25% of the Add Health respondents who said that one of those events had happened to them (Courtney, Dworsky et al., 2010).

The most common economic hardship experienced was lost phone service (33%). Twenty-seven percent of the sample was not able to pay rent, and another 27% said they could not pay a utility bill. In contrast, only 9% of the Add Health youth could not pay rent, and 11% did not have the money for a utility bill (Courtney, Dworsky et al., 2010). Fifty percent of the Midwest Study sample reported experiencing at least one material hardship at all interviews. In addition, 25% of the youth reported that they did not always have access to sufficient quantities of nutritious and affordable food at age 21. This food insecurity was found at other measures (29% at ages 23/24). This means that youth were reporting that either sometimes or often they did not have enough food to eat. Pergamit and Johnson (2009) reported that 13% of their Los Angeles-based sample at age 19 was hungry at some point and could not afford food. The age 19 measure of the Midwest Study sample provides an interesting comparison on the benefits of extended care. Youth in Illinois, who had extended care, were less likely to experience any of the material hardships than youth in the other two states in that study which discharged youth at age 19. Only 4% of the youth still in care reported concerns about getting enough to eat; while 12% of youth living independently had those concerns (Courtney & Dworsky, 2006).

Improving Employment Outcomes

In summary, FFY are less likely to be employed than their peers in the general population who did not experience foster care. When they are working, they often work in jobs that are without benefits, and receive wages that often do not raise them out of poverty or provide sufficient income to meet basic needs, much less accumulate assets. In addition, these jobs are frequently unstable which means that many FFY do not have consistent incomes. The economic stress that many experience is seen in the reliance on public benefits for survival in larger proportions than their non-foster-care peers. The transition from foster care to emerging adulthood provides an opportunity to correct previous disadvantages through interventions that seek to ameliorate the intergenerational transmission of poverty among families. The following are suggested strategies for improving employment outcomes for EFY and FFY.

Extending Foster Care

Extending the time that states can claim Title IV-E federal reimbursement for EFY to age 25 would provide the stability needed by youth, and aid them in building up savings to meet some of the challenges of early adulthood. Although public child welfare agencies cannot provide support for former youth indefinitely, nor do youth want it, policy makers must recognize and respond to current social and economic trends, such as the increase in the age at which youth are leaving home in the general population, and the pattern of successive returns to the parental home (Baum, Ma, & Payea, 2013). An extended period of transitional services for all foster youth might help youth to cope with the challenges of emerging adulthood. Staying in care for a year or two longer is not enough to assure self-sufficiency for emerging adults. It is not much more realistic to expect someone to be self-sufficient at age 21 than it was at age 18. This extension might provide the same sort of supports afforded to youth in the general population, and would be congruent with the normative transition to adulthood in contemporary America (Osgood, Foster, & Courtney, 2010). The provision of services to former foster youth is conceptualized as a social investment because of the potential payoffs in future economic stability.

This extension would provide more assistance for the educational preparation needed for future self-sufficiency. Emancipated foster youth students are likely to be older than traditional college students because they are more likely than non-foster students to have repeated a grade, and they are often in need of remedial work that is taken without college credit. Emancipated foster youth are often forced to go to school part-time because of financial limitations and other factors such as parental responsibilities. Thus, EFY may need more time to complete school. This extension would put EFY on the same footing as non-foster youth, given the societal trends of remaining at home for a longer period.

Length of time in care has been associated with the likelihood of employment, and higher earnings (Courtney, Dworsky et al., 2011; Barnow et al. 2015; Fallesen, 2013; Hook & Courtney, 2011; Kerman et al., 2002). Specifically, Courtney, Hook, and Lee (2010) assert from their cost–benefit analysis that each additional year in care increases the likelihood of employment by 18%.

Minimum Provisions that Youth Need on Leaving Care for Employment

Youth should not leave care without an educational program and/or employment. After-care should have an assessment component to determine how well youth are faring with work and career development, and if help is needed to remove impediments to working, should include that assistance in their individualized independent living plan. Youth should be steered toward careers that provide an opportunity for income growth and have a career ladder. Independent Living Program Services staff need to think in terms of providing careers, and not just jobs. Macomber et al. (2008) said that one reason for the employment instability seen with EFY is that they are placed in low-income jobs. Employment in better-paying jobs might contribute to more stable employment. Finding well-paying jobs is difficult for this group because of their low level of human capital. One-half of the minimum-wage workers in the United States are aged 16 to 24 (Silver, 2014). This means that youth need to be encouraged to seek additional education beyond high school if they want to increase earnings. College is not the only option to consider, but also vocational training to gain the skills necessary for higher-paying jobs. Youth who do not have the interest nor the academic skills to pursue college should be encouraged to seek training in career-oriented employment that promises middle-class standards of pay.

Employment Outcomes and Participation in Independent Living Services (ILS)

Employment and vocational training services, work opportunities, and personal financial management should be major components of any ILS program. Research cited in this chapter indicates that youth who have early employment opportunities are more likely to be working and have higher incomes in their twenties. Youth should be assisted, beginning at age 16, with finding part-time employment, summer jobs, internships, apprenticeships, and job referrals. In addition, it is essential that youth complete high school, and if able and willing, that they have the means to pursue further education. These efforts would assure that youth have the human capital to achieve independence. The child welfare system needs to address its poor record in this area. Youth need opportunities to earn, save, and manage money before they leave care. Providing classroom education in these areas in an ILP may not be sufficient. Youth should have real-world opportunities to put these into practice (Peters, Sherraden, & Kuchinski, 2016). Work opportunities could be subsidized by federal ILP funds (Dworsky, 2005). Such opportunities will help students to gain work experience, and develop the confidence and maturity associated with employment. These experiences may be necessary since child welfare caseworkers report that keeping a job and going to work regularly were problem areas for FFY (Leathers & Testa, 2006). Emancipated foster youth not only need job-readiness skills, but they also need job-retention skills (Barth, 1980; Lenz-Rashid, 2006).

Youth are also eligible for employment and training services funded under the Workforce Investment Act of 1998 (P.L. 105-220) (U.S. Department of Labor, 2000). The use of tax credits as incentives for the hiring of FFY is another route to job creation for FFY that needs to be considered (Atkinson, 2008). States might also consider providing stipends for ILS participants who, on average, have little or no income after leaving care. California provides Chafee grants for youth who voluntarily enter their transitional housing program (Transitional Housing Plan). Youth receive assistance up to age 24. Youth receive a stipend and services. The stipend is $850 a month in the first year, and declines to $258 in the last year of eligibility. The stipend amount declines because of the assumption that the youth is making progress toward self-sufficiency (Kimberlin & Lemley, 2012).

The evidence on whether ILS programs make a difference in employment and incomes is mixed. Montgomery, Donkoh, and Underhill (2006) in a review of ILS evaluations conclude that there are benefits for employment outcomes if youth participate in the ILS programs. The more rigorous Multi-Site Evaluation of Foster Youth Programs, which used an experimental design, found no impact (Courtney, Zinn et al., 2011). Naccarato et al. (2010) did not find a relationship between receiving employment assistance during an ILS program and subsequent earnings. Courtney, Zinn and colleagues said that their findings were not surprising given that the evaluation was completed in an economically distressed area at the tail end of the Great Recession. It is important to note that most studies on FFY employment and earnings were completed during times of relatively low unemployment. However, it can be assumed that youth launched into the economy during the Great Recession (December 2007 to June 2009) would have difficulty finding work. Courtney, Zinn and colleagues also criticized the program for not engaging in the aggressive outreach that they thought was needed as a way of improving employment outcomes with EFY. Evaluations with experimental designs of programs are needed to find what works. Youth need better preparation for employment than is available through current services and policy.

Despite the lack of definitive data on the contributions of ILS programs to employment of emancipated foster youth, it appears that employment and training services are appropriate for them given the policy focus on self-sufficiency for former foster youth. Iglehart (1994) asserts that employment training may not be enough unless there are opportunities for real-world application of skills through internships, for example, and/or the linking to actual employment. Independent Living Services programs provide a means of teaching interview skills, resumé construction, and job maintenance skills. Job maintenance skills may be crucial given the instability of their work histories.

Emancipated foster youth also need to gain the skills to budget on a limited income, and they need knowledge of the common pitfalls of low-income consumers; such as warning them about the trap of pay day or title loans. Social workers, who work with these youth, need to know about these issues in order that they might better assist these youth. A few schools of social work have developed a curriculum to equip students with the skills they need for working with low-income clients. These curricula could be viewed as a start for planning education in this area (Jacobson, Sander, Svoboda, & Elkinson, 2011).

Mentoring and Job Coaching

Two types of intervention that help in job retention are mentoring and job coaching. Having a mentor who has a similar socio-economic background would provide a role model, as well as knowledge on the pathways to desired job opportunities. Job coaching is similar to mentoring, but focuses on helping youth to deal with issues with a specific job. Mentors focus on broader issues of career development over the period of emerging adulthood (Lenz-Rashid, 2006).

Vulnerable Groups and Employment

The literature points to a number of subgroups of FFY who need additional assistance. Naccarato et al. (2010) found that youth in the Midwest Study with mental health problems, specifically post-traumatic stress disorder (PTSD) and some affective disorders, had lower earnings than youth without those problems. These data suggest a need for mental health services before leaving care, as well as after leaving care. It also indicates a need for designing ILS program employment components to fit the needs of youth with mental health problems.

The research shows that FFY of color, particularly African-Americans, are vulnerable to adverse outcomes in early adulthood. Efforts need to be made to more adequately prepare these youth for work or school (Hook & Courtney, 2011). We need to ensure that ILS are culturally appropriate and relevant for this population. Aggressive outreach may be needed to ensure that these youth have these services. One group often left out of transition services are those adolescents who leave care prior to emancipation. Data also indicate poor employment outcomes for these foster youth. Dworsky (2005) urges including these youth in ILS through amending the Fostering Connections to Success and Increasing Adoptions Act of 2008.

Tangible Needs on Leaving Care

Casey Family Programs have developed Individual Development Accounts and Youth Opportunity Passports as an asset accumulation strategy. Beginning at age 14, youth set up savings accounts where Casey matches their savings to provide a nest egg when they leave care. Youth are provided with tangible resources when they leave care such as kitchen and dining utensils, driver's licenses, and other household needs like mattresses that would relieve some of the burden of setting up an independent household. They also receive financial literacy training. These items help them to find financial stability, and focus on their education program, and/or employment (Pecora, Kessler et al., 2006; Peters et al., 2016). These programs need rigorous evaluation to determine how they affect youth adaptation to the transition.

Financial and transportation problems were noted by EFY in a qualitative study as interfering with school attendance and the finding and maintaining of employment (Jones, 2014). Foster youth could benefit from the development of innovative programs, perhaps within public and private partnerships, to provide financial help in obtaining automobiles, car insurance, and housing. Such efforts would assist in asset building. In much of the United States, public transportation is underdeveloped. Napolitano and Courtney (2014) report that only two of the 35 EFY they interviewed in a qualitative study had access to a car, and most faced commutes of over an hour each way to employment. Therefore, maintaining a work or school schedule without a car can be difficult to impossible. Such help would enable youth to work and attend school. Consistent employment with a steady income would reduce some of the homelessness found among EFY.

Future Research Needs

The most effective way to examine the impact of foster care on future outcomes is to use random assignment, a type of research design that is not possible in most circumstances. However, this type of design is possible with the evaluations of ILS programs. These programs have the charge of preparing youth for life after foster care. After a little more than three decades of operation, we still do not have much of an idea of what an effective program would look like (Freundlich, Avery, & Padgett, 2007; Jones, 2014). The methodologies of most evaluations are weak. Demonstrations are needed that would allow innovative programs to establish their efficacy. We also need to know how to engage these youth in their preparation for emerging adulthood both prior to and after emancipation.

More longitudinal cohort studies with representative samples that utilize comparison groups are needed to determine relationships between a successful transition and the conditions of foster care, the adequacy of the preparation of youth to leave care, the supports provided upon leaving foster care, and the social and environmental contexts that contribute to success. Researchers should gather data from multiple sources: self-report, administrative data, observation, and collected from others in a subject's social network including family and social workers. The development of standardized measures and common definitions of outcomes would make the comparison of findings across studies more valid. Mixed-method research that utilizes qualitative methods would give voice to former foster youth. Studies are also needed that go beyond the late twenties and tell us more about the long-term effects of foster care.

Most of the research on FFY has shown negative outcomes. However, even these studies show that somewhere between 40% and 50% of youth are having a healthy and productive adaptation to emerging adulthood (Courtney, Hook et al., 2010). Studies of those youth would give policy and program planners insight into what type of interventions might lead to better outcomes.

It is important not to lay the blame for the poor outcomes noted with former foster youth solely on the child welfare system, though this system does have a responsibility for helping youth to make the best adaptation possible to emerging adulthood. These problems will only be remedied by a set of social policies that are well beyond the scope of the child welfare system's responsibilities and ability to make. Until we have a commitment to reducing poverty in U.S. society, and providing children with decent schools including early childhood education, these youth will continue having problems making the transition into a healthy adulthood. Their parents need educational and employment opportunities so they can take better care of their offspring. They need health care that includes family planning services to ensure that more children are born wanted, and access to substance abuse or mental health services if needed. All of these efforts would be a step toward really assuring child welfare.

References

American Bar Association Commission on Youth at Risk. (2011). *Report from a national summit on the Fostering Connections to Success Act*. New York: Roosevelt House Public Policy Institute at Hunter College.

Arnett, J. (2000). Emerging adulthood: A theory of development from the late teens through the twenties. *American Psychologist, 55*(5), 469–480.

Atkinson, M. (2008). Aging out of foster care: Towards a universal safety net for former foster youth. *Harvard Civil Rights—Civil Liberties Law Review, 43*, 183–212.

Avery, R. & Freundlich, M. (2009). You're all grown up now: Termination of foster care support at age 18. *Journal of Adolescence, 32*, 247–257.

Barnow, B., Buck, A., O'Brien, K., Pecora, P., Ellis, M., & Steiner, E. (2015). Effective services for improving education and employment outcomes for children and alumni of foster care services: Correlates and educational and employment outcomes. *Child and Family Social Work, 20*, 159–170.

Barth, R. P. (1980). On their own: The experiences of youth after foster care. *Child and Adolescent Social Work Journal, 7*(5), 419–440.

Baum, S, Ma, J., & Payea, K. (2013). *Education pays: The benefits of higher education for individuals and society*. Washington, DC: College Board.

Benedict, M., Zuravin, S., & Stallings (1996). Adult functioning of children who lived in kin vs. non-relative foster homes. *Child Welfare, 75*, 529–549.

Berzin, S. C. (2008). Difficulties in the transition to adulthood: Using propensity scoring to understand what makes foster youth vulnerable. *Social Service Review, 82*(2), 171–196.

Buehler, C., Orme, J., Post, J., & Patterson, D. (2000). The long-term correlates of family foster care. *Children and Youth Services Review, 22*(8), 595–625.

Chantala, K. & Tabor, J. (2010). *National Longitudinal Study of Adolescent Health: Strategies to perform a design-based analysis using ADD Health data.* Chapel Hill, NC: Carolina Population Center, University of North Carolina at Chapel Hill.

Cook, R. (1994). Are we helping foster care youth prepare for their future? *Children and Youth Services Review, 16*, 213–229.

Cook, R., Fleishman, E., & Grimes, V. (1991). *A national evaluation of Title IV-E foster care independent living program for youth: Phase 2, final report (Vol. 1).* Rockville, MD: Westat.

Courtney, M. (2009). *The difficult transition to adulthood for foster youth in the U.S.: Implications for the State as corporate parent.* Fairfax, VA.: Society for Research on Child Development.

Courtney, M. & Dworsky, A. (2005). *Midwest Evaluation of Adult Functioning of Former Foster Youth: Outcomes at age 19.* Chicago: Chapin Hall Center for Children at the University of Chicago.

Courtney, M. & Dworsky, A. (2006). Early outcomes for young adults transitioning from out-of-home care in the USA. *Social Work, 11*, 209–219.

Courtney, M., Dworsky, A., Brown, A., Cary, C., Love, K., & Vorhies, V. (2011). *Midwest Evaluation of Adult Functioning of Former Foster Youth: Outcomes at age 26.* Chicago: Chapin Hall Center for Children at the University of Chicago.

Courtney, M., Dworsky, A., Cusick, G., Havlicek, J., Perez, A., & Keller, T. (2009). *Midwest Evaluation of Adult Functioning of Former Foster Youth: Outcomes at age 21.* Chicago: Chapin Hall Center for Children at the University of Chicago.

Courtney, M., Dworsky, A., Lee, J., & Rapp, M. (2010). *Midwest Evaluation of Adult Functioning of Former Foster Youth: Outcomes at ages 23 and 24.* Chicago: Chapin Hall Center for Children at the University of Chicago.

Courtney, M., Hook, J., & Lee, J. (2010). *Distinct subgroups of former foster youth during young adulthood: Implications for policy and practice.* Chicago: Chapin Hall Center for Children at the University of Chicago.

Courtney, M., Piliavin, I., Grogan-Kaylor, A., & Nesmith, A. (2001). Foster youth transitions to adulthood. *Child Welfare, 80*, 685–717.

Courtney, M., Terao, S., & Bost, N. (2004). *Midwest Evaluation of Adult Functioning of Former Foster Youth: Conditions of youth preparing to leave care.* Chicago: Chapin Hall Center for Children at the University of Chicago.

Courtney, M., Zinn, A., Koralek, R., Bess, R., Stagner, M., Pergamit, M., & Johnson, H. (2011). *Evaluation of independent living—Employment services programs. Kern County, California. Final report.* Washington, DC: Office of Planning and Research Evaluation, U.S. Department of Health & Human Services.

Crosson-Towers, C. (2007). *Exploring child welfare: A practice perspective* (4th ed.). Boston, MA: Pearson Education, Inc.

Daining, C. & DePanfilis, D. (2007). Resilience of youth in transition from out-of-home care to adulthood. *Children and Youth Services Review, 29*, 1158–1178.

Delgado, M. (2013, December). *California's fostering connections: Ensuring that the AB 12 bridge leads to success for transition foster youth.* San Diego, CA: Children's Advocacy Center of the University of San Diego School of Law.

Dworsky, A. (2005). The economic self-sufficiency of Wisconsin former foster youth. *Children and Youth Services Review, 27*, 1085–1118.

Entwisle, D., Alexander, K. L., & Steffel-Olson, L. (2000). Early work histories of urban youth. *American Sociological Review, 65*(2), 279–297.

Ewart, S. (2012, February). What it's worth: Field of training and economic status in 2009. *Current Populations Reports*, 1–16.

Fallesen, P. (2013). Time spent well: The duration of foster care and early adult labor market, educational, and health outcomes. *Journal of Adolescence, 36*, 1003–1011.

Foster Care Independence Act [FCIA] of 1999, P.L. 106-169. (1999).

Fostering Connections to Success and Increasing Adoptions Act of 2008, P.L. 110-351. (2008).

Freundlich, M., Avery, R., & Padgett, D. (2007). Preparation of youth in care for independent living. *Child and Family Social Work, 12*, 64–72.

Goerge, R., Bilaver, L., Joo Lee, B., Needell, B., Brookhart, A., & Jackman, W. (2002). *Employment outcomes for youth aging out of foster care.* Chicago: Chapin Hall Center for Children at the University of Chicago.

Greeson, J., Usher, L., & Grinstein-Weiss, M. (2010). One adult who is crazy about you: Can natural mentoring relationships increase assets among young adults with and without foster care experience. *Children and Youth Services Review, 32,* 565–577.

Harris, M. S., Jackson, L., O'Brien, K., & Pecora, P. (2009). Disproportionality in education and employment outcomes of adult foster care alumni. *Children and Youth Services Review, 31,* 1150–1159.

Havalchak, A., White, C. R., & O'Brien, K. (2008, March). *Casey Young Adult Survey.* Seattle, WA: Casey Family Programs.

Hook, J. & Courtney, M. (2011). Employment outcomes of former foster youth as young adults. *Children and Youth Services Review, 33,* 1855–1865.

Iglehart, A. & Becerra, R. (2002). Hispanic and African-American youth: Life after foster care emancipation. *Journal of Ethnic Cultural Diversity in Social Work, 11*(1–2), 79–107.

Iglehart, A. P. (1994). Adolescents in foster care: Predicting readiness for independent living. *Children and Youth Services Review, 16*(3–4), 159–169.

Irving, S. K. & Loveless, T. A. (2015, May). Dynamics of economic well-being: Participation in government programs: 2009–2012, In S. K. Irving & T. A. Loveless, T.A. (Eds.), *Household economic studies* (pp. 70–141). Washington, DC: U.S. Census Bureau.

Jacobson, J. M., Sander, R., Svoboda, D., & Elkinson, A. (2011). *Defining the role and contributions of social workers in the advancement of economic stability and capability of individuals, family and community.* Madison, WI: Center for Financial Security, University of Wisconsin.

Jones, L. (2014). Former foster youth's perspectives on independent living preparation six months after discharge. *Child Welfare, 93*(1), 99–126.

Kerman, B., Wildfire, J., & Barth, R. (2002). Outcomes for young adults who experienced foster care. *Children and Youth Services Review, 24*(5), 319–344.

Kimberlin, S. & Lemley, A. (2012). *Exit outcomes for former foster youth participating in California's THP Plus transitional supportive housing programs.* San Francisco: John Burton Foundation.

Kortenkamp, K. & Ehrle, J. (2002). *The well-being of children involved with the child welfare system: A national overview.* Washington, DC: The Urban Institute.

Leathers, S. J. & Testa, M. F. (2006). Foster youth emancipating from care: Caseworkers report on needs and services. *Child Welfare, 85*(3), 463–498.

Lenz-Rashid, S. (2006). Employment experiences of young adults: Are they different for youth with a history of foster care. *Children and Youth Services Review, 28,* 235–259.

Lindsey, E. & Ahmed, F. (1999). The North Carolina Independent Living Program: A comparison of outcomes. *Children and Youth Services Review, 21*(5), 389–412.

Macomber, J., Kuehn, D., McDaniel, M., Vericker, T., Pergamit, M., Cuccaro, S., . . . Barth, R. (2008). *Coming of age: Employment outcomes for youth who age out of foster care through their middle twenties.* Presented at the 11th National Child Welfare Data and Technology Conference.

Mallon, G. P. (1998). After care, then where? Outcomes of an independent living program. *Child Welfare, 77*(1), 61–79.

Mason, M., Castrianno, L., Kessler, C., Holmstrand, L., Huefner, J., Payne, V., . . . Stenslie, S. (2003). A comparison of foster care outcomes across four child welfare agencies. *Journal of Family Social Work, 7*(2), 55–72.

McDonald, T. P., Allen, R. I., Westerfelt, A., & Piliavin, I. (1993). *Assessing the long term effects of foster care: A research synthesis.* Madison, WI: Institute for Research on Poverty.

McMillen, J. & Tucker, J. (1999). The status of older adolescents at exit from out-of-home care. *Child Welfare, 78*(3), 339–351.

Mech, E. (2002). *Uncertain futures: Foster youth in transition.* Washington, DC: CWLA.

Montgomery, P., Donkoh, C., & Underhill, K. (2006). Independent living programs for young people leaving the care system: The state of evidence. *Children and Youth Services Review, 28,* 1435–1448.

MSNBC (2012, April 27). Romney tells students to borrow money from their parents. *The Ed Show.* Retrieved from www.msnbc.com/the-ed-show/romney-tells-students-borrow-money

Naccarato, T., Brophy, M., & Courtney, M. (2010). Employment outcomes of foster youth: The results from the Midwest Evaluation of the Adult Functioning of Former Foster Youth. *Children and Youth Services Review, 32,* 551–559.

Napolitano, L. & Courtney, M. (2014). *Residential settings of young adults in extended foster care: A preliminary investigation.* Chicago: Chapin Hall Center for Children at the University of Chicago.

National Center for Education Statistics. (2015). *State non-fiscal survey of public elementary/secondary education.* Washington, DC: U.S. Department of Education.

National Youth in Transition Database (NYTD). (2012, September). *Highlights from the state reports to the National Youth in Transition Data Base, federal fiscal year 2011.* Washington, DC: Administration for Children and Youth.

National Youth in Transition Database (NYTD). (2014, September). *Comparing outcomes reported by young people at ages 17 and 19 in the NYTD Cohort 1*. Washington, DC: Administration for Children and Youth.

Needell, B., Alamin, S. C., Brookhart, A., Jackman, W., & Shlonsky, A. (2002). *Youth emancipating from foster care in California: Findings using linked administrative data*. Berkeley: Center for Social Services, University of California, Berkeley.

Nolan, T. (2006). Outcomes for transitional living programs serving LGBTQ youth in New York City. *Child Welfare, 85*(2), 385–406.

NORC at the University of Chicago. (2017). General Social Survey (2017). Retrieved May 12, 2017 from http://gss.norc.org/

Osgood, D. W., Foster, M., & Courtney, M. (2010). Vulnerable populations and the transition to adulthood. *Future of Children, 20*(1), 209–229.

Pecora, P. J., Kessler, W., Downs, A. C., & O'Brien, K., Hiripi, E., & Morello, S. (2003). *Early results from the Casey National Alumni Study*. Seattle, WA: Casey Family Foundation.

Pecora, P., Kessler, R. C., O'Brien, K., White, C. R., Williams, J., Hiripi, E., . . . Herrick, M. A. (2006). Educational and employment outcomes of adults formerly placed in foster care. *Children and Youth Services Review, 28*, 1469–1481.

Pecora, P., Kessler, L., Williams, J., O'Brien, K., Downs, A., English, D., & Holmes, K. (2005). *Improving family foster care: Findings from the Northwest Foster Care Alumni Study*. Seattle, WA: Casey Family Programs.

Pecora, P., Williams, J., Kessler, R., Hiripi, E., O'Brien, K., Emerson, J., . . . Torres, D. (2006). Assessing the educational achievements of adults who were formerly placed in family foster care. *Child and Adolescent Social Work, 11*, 220–231.

Pergamit, M. & Johnson, H. (2009). *Extending foster care to age 21: Implications and estimates of youth aging out of foster care in Los Angeles: Final Report to the Stuart Foundation*. Washington, DC: The Urban Institute.

Peters, C. M., Sherraden, M., & Kuchinski, A. M. (2016). From foster care to adulthood: The role of income. *Journal of Public Child Welfare, 10*(1), 39–58.

Reilly, T. (2003). Transition from care: Status and outcomes of youth who age out of foster care. *Child Welfare, 82*(6), 727–746.

Robert, S. & House, J. H. (1996). SES differential in health by age and alternative indicators of SES. *Journal of Aging and Health, 8*, 359–388.

Rohe, W. M. & Stegman, M. A. (1994). The effects of homeownership on self-esteem, perceived control and life satisfaction of low-income people. *Urban Affairs Quarterly, 30*, 152–172.

Ryan, J. & Testa, M. F. (2005). Child maltreatment and juvenile delinquency: Investigating the role of placement and placement instability. *Children and Youth Service Reviews, 27*, 227–249.

Salazar, A. (2013). The value of a college degree for foster care alumni: Comparisons with general population samples. *Social Work, 58*(1), 139–150.

Shpiegel, S. & Cascardi, M. (2015). Adolescent parents in the first wave of the National Youth in Transition Data Base. *Journal of Public Child Welfare, 9*, 277–298.

Silver, D. (2014, September 8). Who makes the minimum wage? Pew Research Center FACTTANK. Retrieved from www.pewresearch.org/fact-tank/2014/09/08/who-makes-minimum-wage/

Snyder, B. (2015, October 26). Here is the latest reason people are slamming Donald Trump. *Fortune*. Retrieved from http://fortune.com/2015/10/26/donald-trump-loan-dad/

Stott, T. (2013), Transitioning youth: Policies and outcomes. *Children and Youth Services Review, 35*, 218–227.

U.S. Department of Health & Human Services. (2014). *Adoption and foster care analysis and reporting system*. Washington, DC: Administration of Children and Families and Children's Bureau.

U.S. Department of Labor. (2000). *Employment status of the civilian non-institutional population by sex, age, race, and Hispanic origin: 2000 annual average*. Washington, DC: Bureau of Labor Statistics.

Van Zandt, S. & Rohe, W. M. (2006). Do first time homeowners improve their neighborhood quality? *Journal of Urban Affairs, 28*(5), 491–510.

Wildeman, C. & Emanuel, N. (2014). Cumulative risks of foster care placement by age 18 for U.S. children, 2000–2011. *PLOS One*. http://dx.doi.org/10.1371/journal.pone.0092785.

Workforce Investment Act of 1998, P.L. 105-220. (1998).

Yadama, G. N. & Sherraden, M. (1996). Effects of assets on attitudes and behaviors: Advance test of social policy proposal. *Social Work Research, 54*, 353–363.

Yates, T. & Grey, I. (2012). Adapting to aging out: Profiles of risk and resilience among emancipated foster youth. *Development and Psychopathology, 24*, 475–492.

Yu, M., Lombe, M., & Nebbit, V. (2010). Food Stamps program participation, informal supports, household food security and child food security: A comparison of African-American and Caucasian households in poverty. *Children and Youth Services Review, 32*, 767–773.

14

Supportive Housing Contexts and Educational Opportunities for Foster Youth Transitioning Out of Care

Harriett D. Romo and Sophia M. Ortiz

Young people with experience in the foster care system preparing to transition out of state care are a vulnerable youth population often overlooked when discussing housing and educational opportunities. These adolescents and young adults are more likely than youth from stable homes to experience challenges as they move into adulthood. Unstable housing conditions prevent the youth from pursuing higher education and employment. This chapter incorporates data from a 2-year mixed-methods study in which we (1) collaborated with a major agency serving foster youth in central Texas to identify gaps in foster care services; (2) made policy recommendations to support positive transitions out of foster care; and (3) offered research-based recommendations to improve services as youth leave the foster care system. Research questions guiding this study include: what are the issues related to housing available to foster youth and what promotes a successful transition to independence? What preparation for securing permanent housing is provided for youth making the transition out of care and where are the existing gaps in services?

Theoretical Framework

Bronfenbrenner's ecological systems theory provides a framework to examine systemic factors affecting youth transitions out of care. This theory suggests that an interaction among five distinct, yet interrelated, systems shapes and defines children's life experiences. These systems are the microsystem, mesosystem, exosystem, macrosystem, and chronosystem (Bronfenbrenner, 1979, 1994; Blankenhorn, Bayme, & Elshtain, 1990). Bronfenbrenner's theory provided contexts that help us to understand factors affecting youth as they transition out of state foster care. The microsystem is the layer closest to the youth and contains family, peer, and neighborhood structures, and processes that directly affect the youth. The microsystem encompasses relationships and interactions that a youth has with his or her immediate surroundings (Berk, 2000, pp. 23–38). Structures in the microsystem also include school and care environments (Bronfenbrenner, 1994). The microsystem of foster youth must also account for the non-normative process of entering into foster care, out-of-home placements, and social service agencies. These microsystems critically affect the youth's development over time. Much of a youth's behavior is influenced by the microsystem which in turn exerts increasing influence on lasting behavioral issues (Blankenhorn et al., 1990; Bronfenbrenner, 1994). For example, over half of foster youth run away at least once while in care, and nearly 70 percent of alumni of the foster care system have had at least one mental health problem at some point in their life (Courtney & Dworsky, 2006).

Youth with experience in the foster care system are also affected by the remaining four layers of the Ecological Model (Blankenhorn et al., 1990; Bronfenbrenner, 1994). The mesosystem is the layer that provides connection between the structures of the youth's microsystem (Berk, 2000). Examples include interconnections such as interactions between family and teachers, relationships among the youth's peers, and relations among a caseworker, the foster family, and/or the biological or extended family. Connections between teachers and foster parents, among religious institutions, schools, and neighborhoods influence a network of social support. Relationships are also influenced by state, local, and agency policies.

We acknowledge a microsystem of family or foster parent attachment or lack of attachment which may not adequately support the development of a youth with child welfare experiences. Adult connections may not provide mentoring, connections to community organizations, associations with religious and academic institutions, or other components of the socio-ecological system needed for independence (Bronfenbrenner, 1994). Nonetheless, this theoretical framework aids us in identifying gaps in services available to foster youth aging out of care in central Texas.

The exosystem is defined as the larger social system in which youth do not function directly, but which impacts the youth's development by interacting with some structure in his/her microsystem (Berk, 2000). Youth in the foster care system may not be involved directly in choosing housing arrangements, but they experience the forces involved with the interactions within this system. Thus, using Bronfenbrenner's exosystem as a model, foster youth who have been removed from their biological parents are dependent on foster parents or social service agencies for housing arrangements and are deeply affected by these placements. Although agencies and institutions are responsible for finding and maintaining stable placements that lead to positive transitions to adulthood, foster youth experience multiple placements, housing instability, and high rates of homelessness upon leaving care (Barth, 1990; Dworsky & Courtney, 2009). Foster youth are provided with some federal support such as the Chafee-funded Preparation for Adult Living (PAL) program and tuition waivers (Texas Department of Family and Protective Services, n.d.[a]), which is dictated by child welfare policies at the national or state level, but not all foster youth are aware of the resources available and are often left to navigate their lives without positive adult support.

A macrosystem may be considered the outermost layer in the youth's environment. This layer is comprised of cultural values, customs, and laws (Berk, 2000). The effects of larger principles defined by the macrosystem have major influences throughout the interactions of all other layers (Bronfenbrenner, 1994). The macrosystem has an especially high impact for foster youth who must deal with the cultures of agencies, foster families, or group homes, and the trauma of removal from biological families. Bronfenbrenner (1994) compares cultural context to socioeconomic status, poverty, and ethnicity and states that members of a cultural group share a common identity, heritage, and values. Youth growing up in a foster care system share a common status and identity as foster youth, which bears the stigma of a non-conventional macrosystem.

Youth in the foster care system lack macro-level protective factors, such as school stability and community support systems, which could buffer the negative effects of multiple placements and the stigma of foster care. Many leave the foster care system prematurely which prevents them from receiving benefits, such as educational stipends and other extended foster care supports (Berzin & Taylor, 2009; Burley & Halpern, 2001; Casey Family Programs, 2011; Courtney & Heuring, 2005).

The chronosystem encompasses the dimension of time as it relates to a youth's environments. Elements within this system can be either external, such as the timing of a parent's death or timing of the placement in foster care, or internal, such as the physiological changes that occur with the aging of a child. Length of time in the care of Child Protective Services (CPS) and the age of youth when entering and leaving foster care also affect youth outcomes. As youth in foster care mature, they may be more vulnerable to the restrictions of foster care that influence their well-being. The chronosystem encompasses the patterning of environmental events and transitions over the life course, as well as sociohistorical circumstances. Foster youth experience this layer as a non-traditional life-course change as they leave the foster care system without the supports available to youth making traditional transitions into adulthood. Acquiring safe and stable housing, as well as financial support and counseling which enable youth to remain in secure housing, are essential for young adults making the transition out of care (U.S. Department of Housing and Urban Development, 2012). Stability of housing allows youth to maintain permanent connections, promotes positive emotional well-being, and enables youth to participate in education and employment opportunities (see Figure 14.1).

Review of Literature

The U.S. Department of Health & Human Services (Administration on Children, Youth and Families, Children's Bureau) (2017) listed 238,230 foster youth who exited foster care services in the United States in 2014. The federal report collects case-level information from the state of Texas on all children in foster care and those who have been adopted, along with demographic information on foster children who "age out" of the system. In Texas, there are no data collected on outcomes of youth after they leave Child Protective Services, unless youth voluntarily return for assistance (U.S. Department of Health & Human Services [Administration on Children, Youth and Families, Children's Bureau], 2017). According to a study conducted by Portland State University, youth who are

> exiting foster care ideally receive comprehensive social support from a range of informal and formal sources, yet the social networks of transition-age foster youth are likely influenced over time by child welfare involvement, which can weaken or disrupt natural support relationships, while introducing service-oriented relationships that are not intended to last into adulthood.
> (Blakeslee, 2015, pp. 199–200)

Youth engaged with the foster care system have high numbers of foster care placements resulting in educational delays, few permanent connections, depression, and increased risk-taking behaviors (Fowler, Toro, & Miles, 2009; Salazar, Keller & Courtney, 2011). In the Scannapieco, Connell-Carrick, & Painter (2007) study, in which the researchers interviewed 72 participants in the Texas Department of Family and Protective Services foster care program, youth, their foster parents, and social workers discussed challenges in the foster care system and identified gaps in services. Scannapieco et al. (2007) found that youth often blamed themselves, felt guilty about their removal from their birth parents, and many wished to return to their birth parents even if they had experienced abuse or neglect from them. Youth reported feelings of being unwanted if awaiting adoption for a long time and felt helpless when they experienced numerous placements over time. They expressed conflicted emotions about foster parents, wanting to have positive relationships with them, but fearful of becoming too attached to them and then being moved to a different placement. They also felt insecure and uncertain about their futures (Scannapieco et al., 2007). These examples reinforce our argument that understanding youth with experiences in the foster care system requires the use of the full range of systems proposed by Bronfenbrenner (1979, 1994), but these understandings must be built with the acknowledgment that foster youth experience distinct systems compared to youth who transition to adulthood in stable biological families.

Housing Outcomes

Lack of stable housing is a main issue and an essential part of the mesosystem because where youth live influences access to good schools, safe neighborhoods, mentors, and friends. For example, researchers conducting the Midwest Study (Courtney et al., 2011), a longitudinal project undertaken

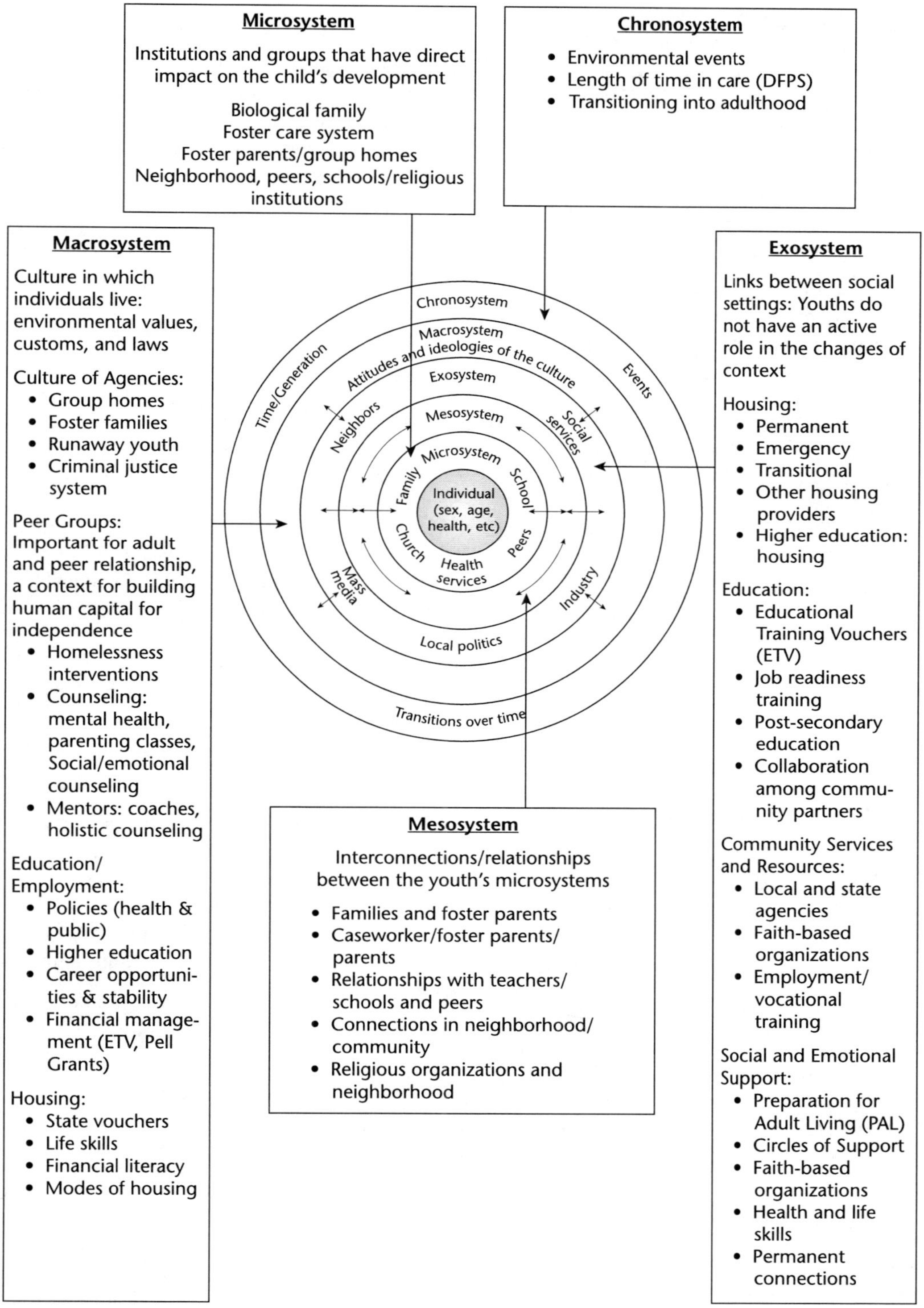
Microsystem
Institutions and groups that have direct impact on the child's development
Biological family
Foster care system
Foster parents/group homes
Neighborhood, peers, schools/religious institutions
Chronosystem
• Environmental events
• Length of time in care (DFPS)
• Transitioning into adulthood
Macrosystem
Culture in which individuals live: environmental values, customs, and laws
Culture of Agencies:
• Group homes
• Foster families
• Runaway youth
• Criminal justice system
Peer Groups: Important for adult and peer relationship, a context for building human capital for independence
• Homelessness interventions
• Counseling: mental health, parenting classes, Social/emotional counseling
• Mentors: coaches, holistic counseling
Education/ Employment:
• Policies (health & public)
• Higher education
• Career opportunities & stability
• Financial management (ETV, Pell Grants)
Housing:
• State vouchers
• Life skills
• Financial literacy
• Modes of housing
Chronosystem
Time/Generation
Events
Macrosystem
Attitudes and ideologies of the culture
Exosystem
Neighbors
Social services
Mesosystem
Microsystem
Family
School
Individual (sex, age, health, etc)
Church
Peers
Health services
Mass media
Industry
Local politics
Transitions over time
Exosystem
Links between social settings: Youths do not have an active role in the changes of context
Housing:
• Permanent
• Emergency
• Transitional
• Other housing providers
• Higher education: housing
Education:
• Educational Training Vouchers (ETV)
• Job readiness training
• Post-secondary education
• Collaboration among community partners
Community Services and Resources:
• Local and state agencies
• Faith-based organizations
• Employment/ vocational training
Social and Emotional Support:
• Preparation for Adult Living (PAL)
• Circles of Support
• Faith-based organizations
• Health and life skills
• Permanent connections
Mesosystem
Interconnections/relationships between the youth's microsystems
• Families and foster parents
• Caseworker/foster parents/ parents
• Relationships with teachers/ schools and peers
• Connections in neighborhood/ community
• Religious organizations and neighborhood

Figure 14.1 Bioecological System Theory

at Chapin Hall at the University of Chicago, reported that foster youth experienced housing instability after leaving state care, with most moving at least once. Almost 40 percent of the respondents in the Midwest Study reported two or more moves during the first 6 months after aging out of care (Dworsky & Courtney, 2010). Frequent moves made it difficult to establish friendships and hindered successful academic pursuits. Safe, secure housing provides a context for building human capital by connecting youth to internships or higher education and enables youth to manage various life challenges (Gewirtz, Hart-Shegos, & Medhanie, 2008; Rashid, 2004).

Housing stability allows youth access to better health care and social services and builds familiarity with their surroundings (Wade & Dixon, 2006). Many youth lack specific housing plans or independent living skills when they exit care (Texas Department of Family and Protective Services, n.d.[b]). According to a U.S. Department of Housing and Urban Development (2014) report, foster youth tend to depend on peer connections and cohabitation to enable them to live on their own. Only 31 percent of youth in the report had received Independent Living Services (ILS) after discharge, indicating that a great majority age out without accessing supportive services to help them find stable housing.

Perez and Romo (2011) found that even when youth were not currently homeless, they had experienced occasional homelessness and reverted to living conditions such as "couch surfing" or temporarily staying with acquaintances. Dworsky, Napolitano, and Courtney (2013) identified six predictors of homelessness among youth aging out of foster care: a history of delinquent behavior, being male, having mental health disorders, experience of physical abuse, a history of running away, or experience of numerous placement changes.

Despite the low ratio of youth with experience with CPS to the general U.S. young adult population (1:1200), the rate of homelessness among the foster youth population is three times higher than that of the general young adult population (National Health Care for the Homeless Council, 2016). Once foster youth age out of the system, one in five experiences homelessness within the first several years of independent living (Annie E. Casey Foundation, n.d.; Toro, Dworsky & Fowler, 2007). Information gathered from programs serving youth aged 14 to 17 in foster care indicated that single teen mothers and youth with less education, specifically those who have dropped out of high school, are more likely to be homeless than their peers (Dworsky & Courtney, 2009).

Harmful Behaviors and Housing

Lack of safe and stable housing can make youth more vulnerable to substance abuse, committing crimes, or becoming victims of crimes (Eyrich-Garg, Cacciola, Carise, Lynch, & McLellan, 2008; Fowler et al., 2009; Halley & English, 2008; Whitbeck, Hoyt, Yoder, Cauce, & Paradise, 2001). This is particularly the case for foster youth who have emotional, psychological, or behavioral problems (Avery, 2010; Avery & Freundlich, 2009; Dworsky et al., 2013). Due to dismal outcomes in education, employment, economic self-sufficiency, physical and mental health, and high rates of substance abuse and involvement in the criminal justice system, the likelihood of housing instability for youth with experiences in the foster care system greatly increases (Berzin, Singer, & Hokanson, 2014; Courtney & Heuring, 2005; Foster & Gifford, 2005). In spite of the ideals of out-of-home care, the realities of the microsystem of the foster care system significantly and negatively influence the pathways and outcomes of youth transitioning out of foster care (Courtney & Heuring, 2005; Institute of Medicine & National Research Council, 2015).

Educational Opportunities

A limited number of longitudinal studies of housing stability and educational achievement of former foster youth exists; however, previous research has consistently demonstrated that a lack of stable housing decreases chances of pursuing higher educational opportunities (Berzin, Rhodes, & Curtis, 2011; Courtney & Dworsky, 2006; Courtney et al., 2011; Perez & Romo, 2011). Foster youth have low rates of educational success and employment attainment which influence housing options and ability to pay for independent housing (Hass & Graydon, 2009). Placement instability heightens the risk that foster youth will change schools during the academic year, disrupting their educational instruction and social relationships, and resulting in missing transcripts and school records. While some training programs exist for older youth, students must meet certain eligibility and qualification criteria to be accepted into those programs, such as the Education and Training Voucher (ETV) program which can provide financial support for job training. However, unstable housing limits the ability of youth to take advantage of services available for them.

As one means of helping youth to make a successful transition out of foster care, the State of Texas offers the Preparation for Adult Living (PAL) program. However, classes and programs may not inform youth of the realities of independent living, such as the responsibilities of finding a co-signer and completing a lease, appropriate housekeeping tasks, the importance of paying rent on time, or other liabilities involved in managing independent housing. Moreover, the PAL classes may not explain the benefits of on-campus housing for youth pursuing post-secondary education (Dworsky & Pérez, 2010). The above descriptions demonstrate how social service agencies play a large role in the microsystem and mesosystem of foster youth. These youth are additionally affected in their social settings and living conditions by the remaining three layers of the Ecological Model (Blankenhorn et al., 1990) (see Figure 14.1).

Even though youth are in a subordinate position in society, they are active agents whose power and rights must be considered (Corsaro, 2015; Katz, 2014; Pugh, 2014). Supportive micro- and macrosystems help youth to mobilize their own resources by encouraging them to take on new roles and responsibilities. Despite troubled microsystems, foster youth can do well, as evidenced by tremendous resilience despite being the least well adapted in the domains of education, employment, and civic engagement (Yates & Grey, 2012). Much of the existing research we have reviewed on foster youth focused on the microsystem. In this chapter, we link the microsystem, mesosystem, exosystem, macrosystem, and chronosystem to illustrate how their interactions affect housing for foster youth transitioning out of state care.

Methodology

This study is based on a collaboration of the research team at the University of Texas at San Antonio Child and Adolescent Policy Research Institute and a major agency in Texas serving youth with experience in the child welfare system. The project was initiated by the U.S. Department of Health & Human Services, Administration for Children and Families' Planning Grants to Develop a Model Intervention for Youth/Young Adults with Child Welfare Involvement At-Risk of Homelessness. The research team and the agency spent 2 years gathering and analyzing data, reviewing evidence-based academic research, visiting sites identified as exemplary by the U.S. Department of Health & Human Services, and hosting task-force group meetings with agencies and institutions in the community serving youth preparing to exit foster care.

Foster youth are a vulnerable population, so the team focused on youth aged 18 or older who were preparing to transfer out of care or had recently transitioned out of care. The University of Texas at San Antonio Institutional Review Board (IRB) approved all research protocols. Meetings and discussions with agency staff and task-force group members focused on general services provided, not on personal experiences. Surveys and data provided by the agency contained no identifiable information. Youth participants received informational consent forms with details about the research and how information would be used, and the IRB allowed waivers of signed consent to protect the confidentiality of participants in focus group discussions and interviews. The research team encouraged all participants to ask questions about the project before beginning interviews, and told youth they did not have to answer any questions that made them feel uncomfortable.

The research approach of this chapter focuses on housing and how unstable housing affects a successful transition to independence for foster youth. Our qualitative-based mixed-methods study focused on three levels: (1) agencies that served youth aging out of the foster care system in central Texas; (2) housing providers which developed and implemented housing policies and programs for youth aging out of care; and (3) foster youth who accessed the various modes of available housing. We used "triangulation" in which we sought data and evidence from a wide range of different, independent sources (Berg, 2007, pp. 23–28; Hesse-Biber, 2017; Jick, 1979). Denzin (1978) argued that no single method can meet the requirements of interaction theory, and because each method reveals different aspects of empirical reality, multiple methods of observation must be employed. We gathered descriptions and explanations provided by youth, field notes from ongoing task-force group meetings with social workers and agencies, participant observations of programs, and analyses of agency data. Our approach aimed to understand how youth with experience with the child welfare system made meaning of their social world and how ecological systems affected their lives—an approach that is committed to multiple views of social reality (Hesse-Biber, 2017).

Agency staff assisted in recruiting focus group interview participants to ensure that the youth were over the age of 18 and transitioning out of foster care or had recently transitioned out of care. We also distributed surveys over a 2-year period at agency events asking youth and caretakers about the most important issues that concerned them, services they had received, services they wished they had received, and experiences with housing. No identifiable information appeared on the surveys. The surveys allowed us to provide a more robust understanding of the needs of youth transitioning out of care, to test the validity of qualitative findings on a wider sample, and to obtain a more representative sample (Hesse-Biber, 2017).

Youth Focus Groups

We held a series of focus group interviews with youth who had recently transitioned out of foster care to identify housing needs and look at the preparation youth received for securing permanent housing. The research team conducted six group interviews (six or seven youths per group) at agency offices, teen centers, and outreach programs. We recorded, transcribed, and analyzed the interviews to draw together similar themes as well as to draw attention to ideas that did not fit emerging themes. In the group interviews, we explored the perspectives of youth on effective and ineffective housing options. Participating youth preparing to transition out of care or who had recently transitioned out of care were purposefully selected and referred by collaborating foster youth agencies. We asked about perceptions of current modes of housing, housing policies, practices that youth believed contributed to housing success, preferred housing options, barriers encountered, how they acquired information about housing, where they went for assistance, and the youths' housing plans. Graduate research assistants who conducted the group interviews transcribed the focus group discussions. The Principal Investigator (PI) and graduate research assistants independently hand-coded the transcripts using combinations of inductive and deductive approaches (Berg, 2007; Hesse-Biber, 2017).

Observations of Programs

We analyzed components of local housing programs' policies concerning foster youth and identified the strengths and weaknesses of each mode of housing by interviewing agency officials and case managers who assisted youth with housing. We observed on-site transitional housing programs that the U.S. Department of Health & Human Services identified as exemplary in Philadelphia, Tennessee, and California, and talked with research staff and social workers at those sites about the strengths and weaknesses of the programs. We took field notes about the visits. At the invitation of youth and agency staff, we examined materials used as part of the Preparation for Adult Living (PAL) classes offered by the Texas Department of Family and Protective Services that focused on housing, and observed Circles of Support meetings for youth aging out of care.

Case Analyses

We conducted case analyses of services provided to 62 former foster youth, youth transitioning out of care, homeless youth, and youth in care who requested assistance with housing. Agency staff randomly selected the cases from a database used by the collaborating agency (Efforts to Outcomes [ETO] Software) and excluded all identifiable information. Case notes included information about the type of assistance the youth needed, services provided by the caseworker, and outcomes of services. The ETO database required staff to link their interactions with participants directly to measurable program outcomes.

Collaboration and Data Sharing among Agencies

In collaboration with the agency partner, we formed task-force groups based on the needs identified by the youth involved in focus groups and youth surveys conducted by the research team. The task-force groups met monthly for 2 years and addressed stable housing, permanent connections, social/emotional well-being, and education/employment. The housing task-force group included representatives from agencies that housed youth at independent living sites, emergency sites, educational/dorm housing, and permanent housing such as apartments or rental homes. The research team recorded field notes from the meetings, hand-coded and identified themes based on discussions, and recorded field notes from site visits to housing programs. We categorized emerging themes by needs/risks and protective factors related to housing.

Findings

Based on coding of the transcriptions of interviews and focus groups with youth, the research team identified the following key needs (see Table 14.1):

1. assistance with housing at independent living sites;
2. housing and financial management assistance before aging out of care;
3. a housing resource directory including strengths and weaknesses of different housing types;
4. housing plans that result in stable housing;
5. making employment and educational information readily available at housing sites and providing social opportunities to help youth establish friendships and peer support.

In our study, youth resilience and motivation were strong factors that led to effective negotiation skills pertinent to housing, education, employment, civic engagement, relationships, self-esteem, and mental health as youth aged out of care. Youth evidenced resilience skills despite exposure to incontrovertible adversities, vulnerability and loss, prolonged foster care, and lack of adequate preparation for aging out of care. Yates and Grey (2012) found that encouraging developing youth can enhance their resilience skills, independence, and knowledge of resources. With appropriate support across the interacting ecological systems affecting youth, young people with experience with the child welfare system can use resources to find housing and overcome other challenging adulthood transitions (Yates, Egeland & Sroufe, 2003).

Youth identified availability of job opportunities, access to smart phones and internet websites, additional resources after care, access to transportation, positive community connections, and adult support and guidance as protective factors. They wanted to be "treated like average youth" (i.e., youth not in foster care) and they wanted "hands-on experience" before exiting care (see Table 14.1).

Table 14.1 Needs and Protective Factors

	Needs/Risks	Protective Factors
Housing	<ul><li>Lack of affordable housing</li><li>Unrealistic goals</li><li>No housing plan</li><li>Limited options</li><li>Lack of staff knowledge</li><li>Inadequate foster parents</li><li>Limited information after age 18</li><li>Multiple placements</li><li>Special needs</li><li>Co-resident incompatibility</li><li>Loneliness</li><li>Inadequate income</li><li>Inadequate knowledge</li><li>Emergency assistance</li></ul>	<ul><li>Transitional living in urban areas/economic opportunity</li><li>Hands-on experiences</li><li>Independence</li><li>Smart phones</li><li>Access to the internet/websites</li><li>Private landlords/diverse housing options</li><li>Treated like average youth</li><li>More resources after care</li><li>Transportation access</li><li>Adult support and guidance</li><li>Community connections</li><li>Money management</li><li>Student rating system</li></ul>
Permanent Connections	<ul><li>Transportation</li><li>Lack of trust</li><li>Instability</li><li>Inadequate knowledge about organizations</li><li>Few positive adults</li><li>Numerous placements</li><li>Stigmatized identity</li><li>Lack of freedom</li><li>Staff turnover</li><li>Lack of follow-up</li><li>Staff overload</li><li>Staff burnout</li><li>Absence of normal life</li><li>Community perceptions/stereotypes</li><li>Restrictions</li><li>"Erased my existence"</li></ul>	<ul><li>Community connections</li><li>Circle of Support and Open Table</li><li>Mentoring</li><li>More social activities and events</li><li>Peer connections</li><li>Expanded social networks</li><li>Screening and training of foster parents</li><li>Staff competence</li><li>Religious connections</li><li>Support group/systems</li><li>Ongoing PAL courses</li><li>Community awareness of youth needs</li><li>Participation in extracurricular activities</li><li>Community activities (volunteering)</li><li>Accessibility</li></ul>
Social and Emotional Well-Being	<ul><li>"Treated like in jail"</li><li>Focus on negatives</li><li>Inconsistency of connections</li><li>Staff overload/unavailable</li><li>"Foster parents/staff in it for the paycheck"</li><li>"Can't depend on others"</li><li>Lack of trust</li><li>"Pity and babying"</li><li>Repetition of victim narrative</li><li>Lack of voice/choices</li><li>Don't know where to go</li><li>Little motivation</li></ul>	<ul><li>Support systems</li><li>Trust</li><li>Self-reliance/"It's all up to you"</li><li>Self-discipline</li><li>Patience</li><li>Learn by experience</li><li>Knowing about resources</li><li>Reinforcement of independence</li><li>Treated normally</li><li>Adoption</li><li>"Someone there for you"</li><li>"Place where youth can hang out/feel good"</li></ul>

	Needs/Risks	Protective Factors
Education and Employment	<ul><li>Inadequate information</li><li>Late entry into system</li><li>PAL too rushed/concentrated</li><li>Confusion about benefits</li><li>Age restrictions</li><li>Identification paperwork</li><li>"Not treated as normal"</li><li>Lack of professional opportunities</li><li>College readings</li><li>Quality of PAL instruction/instructors</li><li>Late intervention</li><li>Excessive paperwork</li><li>Disabilities</li><li>Staff lack of knowledge of opportunities/benefits</li><li>Lack of references</li><li>Access to technology</li></ul>	<ul><li>PAL follow-ups/refresher courses</li><li>Informational websites</li><li>More PAL centers</li><li>Hands-on activities/"learn by experience"</li><li>One-on-one contacts</li><li>PAL in-resident areas</li><li>Mentors/tutors</li><li>Positive support for success</li><li>Transportation</li><li>School stability</li><li>More college tours</li><li>Better employment opportunities</li><li>"How to keep a job"</li><li>Money management</li><li>Increased work/education experience</li><li>Foster parent engagement</li><li>Long-term plans</li><li>Better facilities</li></ul>

Too often, foster parents did not allow youth to experience independent living with support as they transitioned out of state care. One group discussed feeling that foster parents and agency staff treated them like they were "in jail," "erased their existence," and did not allow them to have a "normal life" because of restrictions and lack of freedom to participate in social and after-school activities like other youth. They also wanted other youth to rate housing options, so that they did not have to depend solely on adults' evaluations.

Youth noted protective factors similar to those identified by researchers (Valdez, Gibbard, Thompkins, & Woley, 2013), but they also felt that service agencies often had "unrealistic goals" of independent living and that staff "lacked the knowledge" needed to help youth transition out of care. Youth reported that high rates of staff turnover and staff "burnout" made it difficult for them to maintain connections with social workers who had helped them while in care. They knew few positive adults in the community whom they felt they could trust. Many had no housing plans, limited housing options, and inadequate income to acquire the few affordable housing units available in their community. Finding compatible co-residents presented challenges as well. Youth reported "loneliness" as a major risk once they left foster care. Several reported "inadequate foster parents" who made little effort to assist with transitions, or were "in it for the paycheck," and few who made efforts to establish long-term connections.

Housing Needs

Interviews and surveys with youth identified lack of housing as one of the biggest obstacles when transitioning from care. It was difficult for young people to cope with school or settle into a new job when they lived in inadequate housing or had difficulties finding somewhere to live. One youth told us:

> Lately, what I been doing, even though I been sleeping under the bridge, I still be getting up, looking for work, trying to go to the library, do a little studying here and there, trying to put a little more knowledge in my head, and stuff like that. You know it is hard when you age out of care. They take you away from the streets when you're a young age, but when you turn 18 they are throwing you back on the streets, you know. That's not cool. But we all have choices to make, that's life.

A critical issue identified by youth was insufficient staffing at agencies serving foster youth. Often this resulted from minimal state funding and high rates of staff turnover. Adequate staff to provide early interventions and support systems can prevent homelessness (Barrie, Casanova, & Romo, 2013). Youth needed strong and viable housing plans, fewer emergency housing crises, ongoing preparation for adult living, and increased opportunities to try out independent living in a supportive environment before being left on their own. Youth reported that the lessons of preparation for adult living came too late, were "too rushed" and "too concentrated." They complained of benefits requiring "excessive paperwork," having "age restrictions," and offered as "pity and babying" resources. One youth explained when we asked her to describe her living situation after she aged out:

> I had roommates, I was anxious . . . . everybody is itching to be an adult but once you're an adult you're itching to be a child again, like you want to go back, right? I had four roommates and we all shared an apartment.

Although there are various housing options for youth transitioning out of care, many are not aware of these resources. Youth complained about group homes located in areas that lacked adequate public transportation and offered limited access to educational or job opportunities. Our research team discovered that the research site, a major urban area, did not use Family Unification Program (FUP) vouchers for foster youth housing. The Housing Authority staff reported that foster youth returned

Housing Choice Vouchers (subsidized funding to find housing in the private market or in Section 8 project-based housing) or failed to apply for them because the youth felt inadequately supported to handle the requirements and paperwork demanded to apply for these funds. In focus groups, foster youth expressed the view that they often heard of services from another youth, rather than a caseworker, and many times had to seek information on their own. We found that agency staff mainly focused on youth in crises such as homelessness, drug use, or legal problems, neglecting youth who were reasonably well adjusted and doing well in school. These youth could have reached a greater potential with supports such as assistance with permanent housing, mentoring, and enrollment in educational and job training programs.

Congress passed the Education and Training Voucher (ETV) program in 2001 as an amendment to the Chafee Foster Care Independence Act of 1999 (Pub. L. 106-169). This established up to $5,000 per year to cover tuition, room and board, or other education-related costs for youth with experience in the child welfare system (Dworsky & Pérez, 2010), but this and other programs do not provide young people making the transition from foster care to college with assistance to address their non-financial needs. Many youth living in campus housing had nowhere to go during college breaks when dorms closed, or had no adult to co-sign leases or help with housing deposits. Housing providers often failed to recognize the issues confronted by youth without family supports. Youth reported that finding affordable housing near a college campus can be difficult, and transportation becomes an issue if a community lacks public transportation and youth must commute from far away. Dworsky & Pérez (2010) reported that on-campus housing often opened up access to other campus support services, such as tutoring and counseling. However, some youth eligible for campus programs do not want to be identified as former foster youth, thus limiting access to state or federal resources available for this group of students.

When youth experienced housing crises after transitioning out of care, all other aspects of their lives seemed to fall apart (Barrie et al., 2013; Yates & Grey, 2012). Perez & Romo (2011) found that many former foster youth in Texas experienced a period of homelessness after aging out of care. An extensive report on housing for foster youth (U.S. Department of Housing and Urban Development, 2012) cited only three Texas programs providing financial support for housing for youth aging out of care (all of which required youth financial contributions). The programs identified were Foster Youth Life Investment Partners, a public–private collaboration that provided some monthly rental assistance; Texas Aftercare Room and Board Assistance Program, which provided up to $500 per month with a $3000 lifetime limit; and Texas Transitional Living Allowance (with up to $1000 lifetime limit). While these are important resources, these housing subsidies fell short in meeting the housing costs in most urban areas.

Aside from housing needs, foster youth requested assistance in finding employment and educational opportunities, especially paid internships, that prepared them for jobs which would support affordable, high-quality, stable housing. One youth explained:

> It goes like this . . . I don't have a strong support system. Again, that is always going to be a factor, always for everything. You need a job to have a place to live, you need a place to live in order to take a shower, to eat, to do all that stuff. And therefore, you need those things to get an education. If you don't have that stuff, if you don't have a job to have a home and you don't have a home, how do you expect to get educated?

Modes of Housing

The effectiveness of different modes of housing for youth transitioning out of care varies depending on the strengths and needs of the youth. The main available housing categories reported by youth and the agencies providing housing services comprised:

- emergency housing;
- transitional housing, with social service supports and guidance;
- educational housing (dorms, boarding houses, etc.);
- permanent housing, which can include a return to biological or extended family, adoption, or long-term independent housing, such as apartments or rental housing on long-term leases.

Our research team found that transitional housing provided by agencies was very limited in our research site. When youth experienced homelessness, agencies relied on crisis housing, such as emergency shelters and residential treatment centers. While these services are crucial, one inadequacy of temporary housing is the short-term residency limitations, which mean that youth are likely to experience crisis housing needs again. Task-force group meetings with agency personnel who provided emergency housing also identified these problems.

Table 14.1 summarizes the challenges that youth identified as protective and risk factors impacting their housing experiences. Bronfenbrenner's ecological system theory helped us examine how the interactions of the various systems affect youth's self-sufficiency once leaving care, and the systemic components of foster care that either promote or inhibit self-sufficiency in the transition. The research team categorized the information collected by reference to housing, permanent connections, social and emotional well-being, or education and employment. Major risk factors leading to homelessness included the increased frequency of high-risk behaviors (drugs, sex, and alcohol), which has been supported by other studies (Rashid, 2004; Vaughn, Ollie, McMillen, Scott, & Munson, 2007; Whitbeck et al., 2001).

When youth lacked success in re-establishing biological or extended family relationships, survival became dependent upon peer social capital. Youth frequently moved between extended family and friends, eventually relying upon peers for support (Perez & Romo, 2011). Lack of knowledge of programs available to help with housing or lack of access to such programs pushed youth into couch surfing or homelessness. For example, one housing option required youth to work 15–20 hours per week or attend school within 30 days of entry into the program; the Salvation Army emergency shelter allowed residents to remain for only 10 days and youth had to be 18 or older to qualify; an independent housing program offered a 6-month stay, but required a monthly income of $650; a children's emergency home was open 24 hours, but licensed for emergency stays only; a prominent service agency had large caseloads that prevented social workers from providing one-on-one assistance. Case analysis of youth who reached out to the agency for help showed that youth contacted caseworkers when they experienced housing crises. Case managers referred them to emergency housing or shelters, but there was little follow-up to ensure that the youth found more permanent housing. Youth reported that staff lacked knowledge of stable housing options. Caseworkers said they could not provide adequate assistance for youth, with caseloads averaging 70+ youth to one case worker in Texas (Perez & Romo, 2011).

The results of the case analyses indicated that none of the factors of care alone fully explained youth's homelessness or self-sufficiency. The nature and content of the foster youth microsystem of peers, extended family or fictive kin, social workers, foster parents, or group homes have the potential to support or inhibit youth transitions into adulthood and independent living. Youth reported that they had inadequate plans for securing stable housing before leaving care and lacked transportation and access to the internet to explore housing options. Youth felt lonely in independent living arrangements, such as apartments, without support and guidance from adults or opportunities to establish positive peer friendships. Youth still in care complained that the general regulations of foster care limited their participation in independent activities, such as hanging out with friends, having their pictures included in athletic team photos, staying overnight at friends' homes, or other activities that could help them to develop a supportive peer group or community supports.

Permanent Connections and Social Well-Being

In our focus group interviews, youth identified an increased risk of experiencing anxiety as they faced coping with new responsibilities of budgeting, acquiring housing, and dealing with basic life skills on their own. Others stated that they had no desire to reconnect with the foster care system once they were old enough to leave, even if that meant that they would miss out on resources available to those who remained in care. Youth expressed the need for social support from friends, extended or biological family, religious institutions, and the community to establish strong relationships to help them find and maintain housing.

Having a coach/mentor to create permanent connections with positive adults can lead to a successful transition into stable housing while in the foster care system and as youth transition out of care (National Governors Association Center for Best Practices, 2007). Task-force group representatives from agencies that served youth in juvenile detention centers and in the juvenile justice system reported that lack of permanent connections became a major issue in finding housing when youth left care. Some agencies initiated efforts to reconnect youth with positive biological or extended family members. However, our observations of agency efforts to establish Circles of Support—a transition support team of mentors and caring adults as youth prepare to leave foster care—indicated that these efforts proved to be largely ineffective. One youth told us:

> I went to school and work at the same time, I did both. I made sure that I got all the records I need from my case worker. I called her on that because when I was in care we didn't have that Circle of Support and all those other things, so if I needed something I had to make sure to stay on somebody to get it.

Most of the adult connections at Circles of Support meetings we observed consisted of case managers and social service staff, rather than extended family or the natural mentors youth had identified. Helping youth to establish constructive relationships with a wide range of positive adults in the community beyond social service agency staff, before the youth transition out of care, might be more effective. Observations of successful programs helped us to identify potential role changes for social service staff, such as case managers serving as mentors and coaches instead of acting as social workers.

Employment and Education

Youth identified lack of employment opportunities while in care as another obstacle faced in maintaining stable housing. For example, when one youth was asked in what ways his current living situation affected higher education, he reported that he had little support to pursue higher education:

> It hasn't really been supported, it is basically me. But it made it a little difficult because it's a lot harder living with people that ain't going in the same path that you are, so everything I got to just do on my own. I don't get too much motivation from my family to go to school and all that, it's just me, because, I mean my mom didn't graduate school to be honest, man. My dad, he wasn't really in my life, so right now it's like there ain't too much good stuff going on right now.

Youth with access to stable housing are able to be more independent and can focus attention on furthering their education and being productive at work. Stable housing also allows youth to have better access to health care and social services (U.S. Department of Housing and Urban Development, 2012). Interviews we held with youth pertaining to the Preparation for Adult Living (PAL) curriculum identified a lack of housing information, few opportunities to try out real-life experiences, and minimal overall transition services in preparation for independent living. Youth reported that the programs should begin earlier and be ongoing. They complained that they forgot the details of life skills training received at age 16 by the time they were transitioning to independent living at age 17 or 18. For example, one youth discussed the lack of information about financing college, such as financial aid, grants, or scholarships:

> I always saw it on the TV but that is it ... It was like, do I have to pay that back? It's like you have a lot of questions in your head about which ones [loans, scholarships] you have to pay back and how much will it be, will there be interest? It's like they [the PAL program] tell you, you can get this much money ... what's the catch?

State reports demonstrated low PAL completion rates which strongly increases the risk of housing instability (Texas Department of Family and Protective Services, n.d.[c]). The agency we collaborated with fulfilled their state contract by offering PAL classes and enrolling the number of youth required by their contract. However, some youth aging out of care did not participate in PAL because of the lack of involvement of foster parents or agency staff in ensuring that youth attended the classes, minimal youth interest in the program, or inadequate information about availability of the program. Congress provides discretionary funds for PAL programs that must be appropriated each year. Youth must also meet certain eligibility criteria to participate. There is some evidence that youth who access Preparation for Adult Living (PAL) services have better outcomes than those who do not; however, not all youth access PAL, and it is clear from the high rates of homelessness and youth reports of housing instability upon leaving care that more services are needed (Kerman, Wildfire & Barth, 2002).

Theory of Change

Based on data collected from agency staff, task-force groups, and youth participating in the focus groups and surveys, the research team and agency staff formed a theory of change (see Figure 14.2, Theory of Change).

We anticipated that visualizing change would help youth to take full advantage of services provided and establish an awareness in the community that housing needs remain extremely high. Through strong collaborations, we identified gaps such as the lack of sufficient transitional housing. We recommended working with youth to develop detailed housing plans beginning at early ages, so youth have time to identify independent living opportunities. Through focus groups, youth informed us that beginning preparation for transition to adulthood at age 16 was too late. They requested earlier and ongoing independent living skills training. They identified a lack of social connections and the need for a stronger mesosystem to support financial literacy, coping skills, and decision-making to promote resiliency and successful independent living. Youth at all points lacked strong permanent connections and positive peer and adult support. The majority of youth we interviewed lacked feasible housing plans or needed additional support to implement their plans. The weak micro- and mesosystems throughout their experiences in the foster care system, and a macrosystem which assumes that foster parents and the foster care system are responsibly capable of raising children have meant that youth leave the foster care system lacking stable housing, self-efficacy and social skills, positive school and work experiences, family cohesion, and ongoing family connections (Courtney et al., 2011; Dion, Dworsky, Kauff, & Kleinman, 2014).

Conclusions

Our research identified stable housing as a major structural factor of the exosystem for foster youth. Stable housing is crucial for youth wanting to pursue educational opportunities, obtain jobs, and

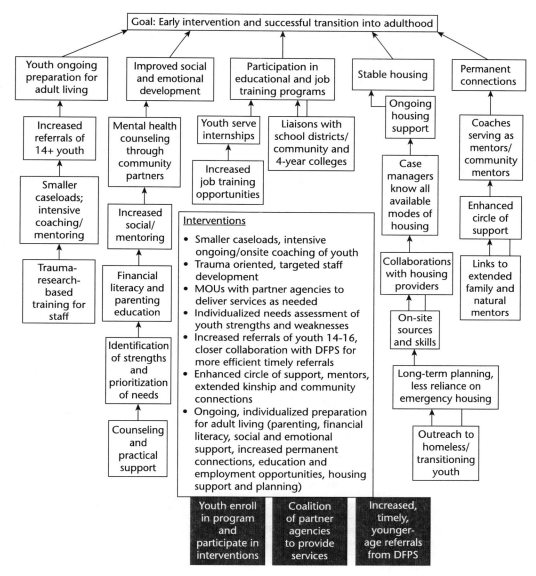

Figure 14.2 Theory of Change

establish permanent connections with positive adults who can support their efforts (Dworsky et al., 2013; Dworsky & Pérez, 2010; Wade & Dixon, 2006). Research shows high rates of homelessness among young adults involved in the foster care system and few evidence-informed housing interventions available to address the specific needs of this population (Institute of Medicine & National Research Council, 2015; Toro et al., 2007). Providing the necessary support to secure and maintain housing can help youth to achieve social-emotional well-being (Kushel, Yen, Gee & Courtney, 2007).

We propose that modes of housing; the neighborhoods where housing is located; adult assistance in locating and securing stable housing; the relationships among housing, education, and work opportunities; and agency and federal policies affecting youth aging out of foster care are important components of Bronfenbrenner's socio-ecological systems theory (see Figure 14.1). There are multiple interconnected layers nested together that influence the success of youth transitioning out of state care. Assisting a successful exit from foster care demands that we look at this transition as a process shaped by a complexity of interactions of actors and social systems. A more traditional micro- and mesosystem approach focused on the interactions of individuals within immediate nuclear families is insignificant in the foster care system. The child welfare system culture limits opportunities for youth to practice independence, includes a stigmatization of being in foster placements, and forces us to consider the diversity of youth experiences in foster care, youth adaptive practices, and a more nuanced complex of systems supporting transition to adulthood. One youth told us:

> By the way I was raised, you know, in CPS [Child Protective Services] my life feels like I was locked up, all my choices made for me. I had to be in bed at a certain time. I had to ask to use the bathroom. Staff has to know where I'm at all the time. You know, you just can't visit your family. You have to get like a year visit, you know. It kind of influenced me . . . in a way.

The microsystem refers to institutions and groups that most immediately and directly impact youth development. However, experiences with the foster care system influence the entire microsystem of the youth, including family, school, religious institutions, neighborhood, and peers. Youth in the foster care system experience multiple placements and frequent school and neighborhood transitions, which disrupt adult and peer support systems. Agencies and foster parents are attempting to provide a microsystem available to youth in family and community settings (Texas Department of Family and Protective Services, n.d. [b]), but according to the youth, these systems have not adequately prepared or supported the youth to make the transition to independent living.

Permanent Connections

The mesosystem includes peer relationships, employment, health care, and social support systems. Under current practice, the Circles of Support provided by the foster care system are largely comprised of professionals, caseworkers, therapists, and program staff rather than individuals whom the youth identify as positive connections and sources of support. Even while the federal government has asked states to create teams that best represent natural supports and permanent supportive systems for youth, teams are most often comprised of people whom a worker finds the easiest to engage, or of professionals already involved with the youth in a formal capacity who lack long-term commitment to the youth (Texas Department of Family and Protective Services, 2016). Weak microsystems and mesosystems mean that youth are not prepared for independent living and lack the protective factors to maintain social stability (Fowler et al., 2009; Gotbaum, 2005; Horwitz, Widom, McLaughlin & White, 2001; Keller, Salazar, & Courtney, 2010).

Housing

Housing has been neglected as part of the exosystem. Youth we interviewed reported that they had little preparation or support for finding appropriate stable housing. Although the macrosystem of youth in foster care services in Texas consists of the Chafee-funded Preparation for Adult Living (PAL) classes and the Texas Education and Training Voucher (ETV) program that allows youth to pursue higher education or job training, a court decision found that the Texas Department of Child Protective Services has not provided adequate care and resources to youth with experiences in foster care. The U.S. District Court declared the Texas program of foster care unconstitutional because of continuing reports of abuse and neglect. Plaintiffs claimed "the right to be reasonably safe from harm while in government custody" (M.D.; bnf Stukenberg v. Abbott, 2015). Fifty-six recommendations filed at the request of the judge proposed a series of operational changes to be imposed on the Texas Department of Family and Protective Services (Ward, 2016).

Although many foster youth plan to reunite with their families, few successfully meet that goal (Annie E. Casey Foundation, n.d.). Foster youth attributed lack of housing options, housing policies, and funding sources as barriers as they transitioned out of care. Housing agency personnel reported that foster youth did not apply for housing vouchers available as part of the macrosystem because the application system has become too complex (Texas Department of Family and Protective Services, n.d.[b]). Youth reported that housing funds did not arrive in a timely manner; they had no one to co-sign leases; and they did not have the financial literacy skills to manage a residence on their own. Inadequacies in the foster care system when youth are leaving the system often force them into a period of homelessness or cause them to return to care (U.S. Department of Housing and Urban Development, 2014). In Texas, there are few transitional housing sites providing on-site education and job training and ongoing life skills support.

Education and Employment

The fourth component, the macrosystem, includes social policy, health and public policy, and the wider environment. Foster youth are usually unaware of the updated policies and services affecting them. According to Weinberg, Oshiro, and Shea (2014), education liaisons can build relationships with the youth while they are still in the public school system and can provide support for youth transitioning out of care. Risk factors such as multiple home and school placement changes can intensify emotional and behavioral disorders which affect school success (Courtney, Terao, & Bost, 2004; Smithgall, Gladden, Howard, George, & Courtney, 2004). Data indicate that home and school instability, which often lead to school enrollment problems and grade retention, partially explain the poor educational performance of youth in foster care (Pecora, 2012; Webb et al., 2007; Zima et al., 2000).

Social and Emotional

The fifth component, the chronosystem, relates to the youth's developmental environment over time and how it changes based on surroundings, experiences, and events. Key fundamental life events include higher education, joining the workforce, military service, and parenting (Texas Department of Family and Protective Services, n.d.[c]). The structures in the chronosystem impact foster youth development by interacting with other systems over time (Berk, 2000). When youth lack transportation, skills for obtaining a driver's license, information about higher education, medical/health information, and housing stability over time, other systems are impacted. According to the Midwest Study (Kushel et al., 2007), housing status and homelessness were associated with being uninsured and having an unmet need for health care.

Our study indicated that within the current structure of foster care in Texas, the services provided are not achieving the core outcomes of increasing stable housing, establishing permanent connections, assuring positive education/employment outcomes, or supporting the social-emotional well-being of youth leaving the system. While some elements of the proposed interventions are present in one or more of the programs provided, nothing currently offers combined services that cover all the ecosystems to support youth in these core outcome areas (see Figure 14.1).

Our research documented the importance of housing collaborations to improve foster youth outcomes. Transitional housing, consisting of individual or peer-shared units, with educational opportunities and resources on-site and with some adult supervision, provided the best supportive environments for youth (Choca, Minoff, Angene, & Byrnes, 2004). In the past, most policy emphasis has been on emergency housing to address crisis needs rather than on transitional housing with supports that lead to long-term stable housing.

We explored housing modes, with reference to availability, youths' perceptions of the different modes of housing, housing stability, location to allow participation in community and work opportunities, and access to higher education. Supports offered at housing sites, affordability, and housing policies promote foster youth success. Our research identified the need for additional formal housing options made available through federal legislation (vouchers, transitional living apartments, dorms, etc.) and support for informal housing options identified by foster youth, such as return to their biological or extended families or co-residence with peers. Without stable housing, foster youth struggle at a level that prevents them from establishing themselves in society. New training for those who help this population, changes that address all levels of the youth's ecosystem, and policies addressing the lack of housing availability can help to establish positive youth transitions and can provide a chance for youth to become successful adults, regardless of their backgrounds.

Data collected in the collaboration between the university research team and the agency illustrated how foster youth frame their expectations about housing needs as they transition out of care. New policies must address the shortage of appropriate transitional housing options for youth leaving state care. Policy changes should be directed toward governmental agencies, non-profit organizations, and for-profit institutions to increase the availability of affordable housing and transitional housing units that allow youth to learn independent living skills with positive adult support. This will require making significant changes in the ecosystems affecting foster youth (see Figure 14.1).

In summary, the ecological model provides a framework from which to further understand the influences that social contexts have on the experiences of youth transitioning out of foster care. By incorporating multiple levels of influence to explain and support individual outcomes, the ecological model allows for a broader conceptualization of the various contextual influences on successful adulthood. The ecological systems of youth with experiences in Child Protective Services must incorporate the broader historical and temporal context of foster care, social service agencies, and local and national policies affecting the well-being of these youth.

Figure 14.2 illustrates how the ecosystems are linked and the interrelationships of the different systems that are essential to address the gaps in services to youth exiting foster care. Our findings (see Appendix) suggested smaller caseloads to allow intensive ongoing, on-site coaching of youth to support stronger links between the micro-, meso-, and macrosystems of foster youth transitioning out of care.

Administration of individual needs assessments to identify youths' strengths and weaknesses can ensure that the most needed interventions are provided. Earlier referrals of youth for services and closer collaboration of agencies servicing youth within Departments of Family and Protective Services will provide more timely referrals that allow youth to receive assistance as soon as they transition out of care. Micro- and mesosystems, including extended kinship connections and community connections, must be strengthened and expanded. The goal is for youth to have a successful transition into adulthood, fewer housing placements, and stable housing along with a continuation of support across all ecosystems.

Acknowledgments

This research was funded as part of a collaborative grant from the U.S. Department of Health & Human Services, funding opportunity HHS-2013-ACF-ACYF-CA-0636 Planning Grants to Develop a Model Intervention for Youth/Young Adults with Child Welfare Involvement At-Risk of Homelessness, to an agency serving foster youth transitioning out of care. Dr. Romo and her team of researchers helped to write the funded proposal and served as project evaluators of that grant. The information presented here represents the analyses of the authors and does not represent the views or opinions of the funding agency.

We would like to acknowledge the important support of student research assistants who helped in organizing meetings, data gathering, transcribing, data analysis, and the development of this chapter: Sabrina Agustsson, Courtney Barrie, Carlos Casanova, Saeni Castillo, Jorge Gonzalez, Edith Lopez, Christina Lopez-Mobilia, Janeth Martinez, and Marissa Mendoza.

References

Annie E. Casey Foundation. (n.d.). *Jim Casey Youth Opportunities Initiative.* Retrieved from www.aecf.org/work/child-welfare/jim-casey-youth-opportunities-initiative/

Avery, R. J. (2010). An examination of theory and promising practice for achieving permanency for teens before they age out of foster care. *Children and Youth Services Review, 32*(3). doi: 10.1016/j.childyouth.2009.10.011

Avery, R. J., & Freundlich, M. (2009). "You're all grown up now": Termination of foster care support at age 18. *Journal of Adolescence, 32*(2), 247–257. doi: 10.1016/j.adolescence.2008.03.009

Barrie, C. K., Casanova, C., & Romo, H. (2013). *Housing and access to higher education for former foster care youth.* Roundtable presentation at the American Sociological Association Annual Meeting, New York. Available at http://citation.allacademic.com/meta/p649892_index.html

Barth, R. P. (1990). On their own: The experience of youth after foster care. *Child and Adolescent Social Work, 7*(5), 419–440. doi: 10.1007/BF00756380

Berg, B. L. (2007). *Qualitative research methods for the social sciences* (6th ed.). Boston, MA: Pearson.

Berk, L. E. (2000). *Child development* (5th ed.). Boston, MA: Allyn and Bacon.

Berzin, C. S., Rhodes, A., & Curtis, M. (2011). Housing experiences of former foster youth: How do they fare in comparison to other youth? *Children and Youth Services Review, 33,* 2119–2126. doi: 10.1016/j.childyouth.2011.06.018

Berzin, C. S., Singer, E., & Hokanson, K. (2014). Emerging versus emancipating: The transition to adulthood for youth in foster care. *Journal of Adolescent Research, 29,* 616–638. doi: 10.1177/0743558414528977

Berzin, C. S., & Taylor, S. A. (2009). Preparing foster youth for independent living: Collaboration between county independent living programs and community-based youth-serving agencies. *Journal of Public Child Welfare, 3*(3), 254–274. doi: 10.1080/15548730903129848

Blankenhorn, D., Bayme, S., & Elshtain, J. B. (Eds.). (1990). *Rebuilding the nest: A new commitment to the American family.* Milwaukee, WI & Lewiston, NY: Manticore.

Blakeslee, J. E. (2015). Measuring the support networks of transition age foster youth: Preliminary validation of a social network assessment for research and practice. *Children and Youth Services Review, 52.* doi: 10.1016/j.childyouth.2015.03.014

Bronfenbrenner, U. (1979). *The ecology of human development: Experiments by nature and design.* Cambridge, MA: Harvard University Press.

Bronfenbrenner, U. (1994). Ecological models of human development. In *International encyclopedia of education, Vol. 3* (2nd. ed.). Oxford: Elsevier. [Reprinted from: M. Gauvain & M. Cole (Eds.). (1993). *Readings on the development of children* (2nd ed.; pp. 37–43). New York: Freeman.]

Burley, M. & Halpern, M. (2001). *Educational attainment of foster youth: Achievement and graduation outcomes for children in state care.* Washington State Institute for Public Policy. Retrieved from https://eric.ed.gov/?id=ED460220

Casey Family Programs. (2011). *Employment Programs and Life Opportunities for Youth (EmPLOY): Findings from a two-year national project.* Seattle, WA: Casey Family Programs.

Choca, M. J., Minoff, J., Angene, L., & Byrnes, M. (2004). Can't do it alone: Housing collaborations to improve foster youth outcomes. *Child Welfare, 83*(5), 469–492.

Corsaro, W. A. (2015). *The sociology of childhood* (4th ed.). Thousand Oaks, CA: Pine Forge Press.

Courtney, M. E., & Dworsky, A. (2006). Early outcomes for young adults transitioning from out-of-home care in the USA. *Child and Family Social Work, 11,* 209–219. doi: 10.1111/j.1365-2206.2006.00433.x

Courtney, M. E., Dworsky, A., Brown, A., Cary, C., Love, K., & Vorhies, V. (2011). *Midwest Evaluation of the Adult Functioning of Former Foster Youth: Outcomes at age 26.* Chicago: Chapin Hall Center for Children at the University of Chicago. Retrieved from www.chapinhall.org/sites/default/files/Midwest%20Evaluation_Report_4_10_12.pdf

Courtney, M. E., & Heuring, D. H. (2005). The transition to adulthood for youth "aging out" of the foster care system. In D. W. Osgood, E. M. Foster, C. Flanagan, & G. R. Ruth (Eds.), *On your own without a net: The transition to adulthood for vulnerable populations* (pp. 27–67). Chicago: University of Chicago Press.

Courtney, M., Terao, S., & Bost, N. (2004). *Midwest Evaluation of the Adult Functioning of Former Foster Youth: Conditions of youth preparing to leave state care.* Chicago: Chapin Hall at the University of Chicago. Retrieved from www.chapinhall.org/sites/default/files/CS_97.pdf

Denzin, N. K. (1978) *The research act.* New York, NY: McGraw-Hill.

Dion, R. M., Dworsky, A., Kauff, J., & Kleinman, R. (2014, May). *Housing for youth aging out of foster care.* Available at SSRN: http://dx.doi.org/10.2139/ssrn.2446532.

Dworsky, A., & Courtney, M. (2009). Homelessness and the transition from foster care to adulthood. *Child Welfare, 88*(4), 23–56.

Dworsky, A., & Courtney, M. (2010). *Does extending foster care beyond age 18 promote postsecondary educational attainment?* Issue Brief. Chicago: Chapin Hall at the University of Chicago. Retrieved from www.chapinhall.org/sites/default/files/publications/Midwest_IB1_Educational_Attainment.pdf

Dworsky, A., Napolitano, L., & Courtney, M. (2013). Homelessness during the transition from care to adulthood. *American Journal of Public Health, 103*(2), 318–323. doi: 10.2105/AJPH.2013.301455

Dworsky, A., & Pérez, A. (2010). Helping former foster youth graduate from college through campus support programs. *Children and Youth Services Review, 32*, 255–263. doi: 10.1016/j.childyouth.2009.09.004

Eyrich-Gang, K. M., Cacciola, J. S., Carise, D., Lynch, K. G., & McLellan, A. T. (2008). Individual characteristics of the literally homeless, marginally housed, and impoverished in a US substance abuse treatment-seeking sample. *Social Psychiatry and Psychiatric Epidemiology, 43*(10), 831–842. https://doi.org/10.1007/s00127-008-0371-8

Foster Care Independence Act of 1999, Pub.L. 106-169, 113 Stat. 1882. (1999).

Foster, E. M., & Gifford, E. J. (2005). The transition to adulthood for youth leaving public systems: Challenges to policies and research. In R. A. Settersten, Jr., F. F. Furstenberg, & R. G. Rumbaut (Eds.), *On the frontier of adulthood: Theory, research, and public policy* (pp. 501–534). Chicago: University of Chicago Press.

Fowler, P. J., Toro, P. A., & Miles, B. W. (2009). Pathways to and from homelessness and associated psychosocial outcomes among adolescents leaving the foster care system. *American Journal of Public Health, 99*(8), 1453–1458. doi: 10.2105/AJPH.2008.142547

Gewirtz, A., Hart-Shegos, E., & Medhanie, A. (2008). Psychosocial status of homeless children and youth in family supportive housing. *American Behavioral Scientist, 51*(6), 810–823. doi: 10.1177/0002764207311989

Gotbaum, B. (2005). *Children raising children: City fails to adequately assist pregnant and parenting youth in foster care.* The Public Advocate for the City of New York. Retrieved from www.nyc.gov/html/records/pdf/govpub/2708children_raising_children.pdf

Halley, M., & English, A. (2008). *Health care for homeless youth: Policy options for improving access.* Chapel Hill, NC & San Francisco: Center for Adolescent Health & the Law & Public Policy Analysis and Education Center for Middle Childhood, Adolescent, and Young Adult Health. Retrieved from http://nahic.ucsf.edu/wp-content/uploads/2009/02/2009-Homeless-Brief.pdf

Hass, M., & Graydon, K. (2009). Sources of resiliency among successful foster youth. *Children and Youth Services Review, 31*(4), 457–463.

Hesse-Biber, S. N. (2017). *The practice of qualitative research* (3rd ed.). Thousand Oaks, CA: Sage Publications.

Horwitz, A., Widom, C., McLaughlin, J., & White, J. (2001). The impact of childhood abuse and neglect on adult mental health: A prospective study. *Journal of Health and Social Behavior, 42*(2): 184–201.

Institute of Medicine & National Research Council. (2015). *Investing in the health and well-being of young adults.* Washington, DC: The National Academies. https://doi.org/10.17226/18869

Jick, T. D. (1979). Mixing qualitative and quantitative methods: Triangulation in action. *Administrative Science Quarterly, 24*(4), 602–611. doi: 10.2307/2392366

Katz, V. (2014). *Kids in the middle: How children of immigrants negotiate community interactions for their families.* New Brunswick, NJ: Rutgers University Press.

Keller, T., Salazar A., & Courtney, M. (2010). Prevalence and timing of diagnosable mental health, alcohol, and substance use problems among older adolescents in the child welfare system. *Children and Youth Services Review, 32*(4), 626–634.

Kerman, B., Wildfire, J., & Barth, R. (2002). Outcomes for young adults who experienced foster care. *Children and Youth Services Review, 24*, 319–344.

Kushel, M. B., Yen, I. H., Gee, L., & Courtney, M. E. (2007). Homelessness and health care access after emancipation. *Archives of Pediatrics & Adolescent Medicine, 161*(10), 986–993. doi: 10.1001/archpedi.161.10.986

M.D. bnf Stukenberg v. Abbott. 152 F. Supp. 3d 684. (S.D. Tx. 2015).

National Governors Association (NGA) Center for Best Practices. (2007). *State policies to help youth transition out of foster care.* Retrieved from www.nga.org/files/live/sites/NGA/files/pdf/2007/0701YOUTH.PDF

National Health Care for the Homeless Council [NHCHC]. (2016). *Annual report July 1, 2015 to June 30, 2016.* Retrieved from www.nhchc.org/wp-content/uploads/2016/10/fy16-annual-report-web-final.pdf

Pecora, P. J. (2012). Maximizing educational achievement of youth in foster care and alumni: Factors associated with success. *Children and Youth Services Review, 34*(6), 1121–1129.

Perez, B. F., & Romo, H. D. (2011). Couch surfing of Latino foster care alumni: Reliance on peers as social capital. *Journal of Adolescence, 34*, 239–248. doi: 10.1016/j.adolescence.2010.05.007

Pugh, A. (2014). The theoretical costs of ignoring childhood: Rethinking independence, insecurity, and inequality. *Theory and Society, 43*, 71–89.

Rashid, S. (2004). Evaluating a transitional living program for homeless former foster care youth. *Research on Social Work Practice, 14*(4), 240–248.

Salazar, A. M., Keller, T. E., & Courtney, M. E. (2011). Understanding social support's role in the relationship between maltreatment and depression in youth with foster care experience. *Child Maltreatment, 16*(2), 102–113. doi: 10.1177/1077559511402985

Scannapieco, M., Connell-Carrick, K., & Painter, K. (2007). In their own words: Challenges facing youth aging out of foster care. *Child and Adolescent Social Work Journal, 24*(5), 423–435. doi: 10.1007/s10560-007-0093-x

Smithgall, C., Gladden, R. M., Howard, E., George, R., & Courtney, M. (2004). *Educational experiences of children in out-of-home care*. Chicago: Chapin Hall at the University of Chicago. Retrieved from www.chapinhall.org/sites/default/files/old_reports/156.pdf

Texas Department of Family and Protective Services [TDFPS]. (n.d.[a]). *Preparation for Adult Living (PAL) program*. Retrieved from www.dfps.state.tx.us/Child_Protection/Youth_and_Young_Adults/Preparation_For_Adult_Living/

Texas Department of Family and Protective Services [TDFPS]. (n.d.[b]). *Transitional Living Services*. Retrieved from www.dfps.state.tx.us/Child_Protection/Youth_and_Young_Adults/Transitional_Living/

Texas Department of Family and Protective Services [TDFPS]. (n.d.[c]). *Regional Preparation for Adult Living (PAL) coordinators*. Retrieved from www.dfps.state.tx.us/Child_Protection/Youth_and_Young_Adults/Preparation_For_Adult_Living/PAL_coordinators.asp

Texas Department of Family and Protective Services [TDFPS]. (2016) *2016 Child and Family Services Plan VII*. Retrieved from www.dfps.state.tx.us/About_DFPS/Title_IV-B_State_Plan/2015_Progress_Report/2015_Texas_Title_IV-B_State_Plan.pdf

Toro, P., Dworsky, A., & Fowler, P. (2007). Homeless youth in the United States: Recent research findings and intervention approaches. Paper developed for the National Symposium on Homelessness Research, March 1–2 (pp. 6-1–6-33). Retrieved from www.huduser.gov/portal/publications/homeless/p6.html

U.S. Department of Health & Human Services (Administration on Children, Youth and Families, Children's Bureau). (2017). *Child welfare outcomes 2010–2014: Report to Congress*. Retrieved from www.acf.hhs.gov/sites/default/files/cb/cwo10_14.pdf

U.S. Department of Housing and Urban Development. (2012). *Housing for youth aging out of foster care: A review of the literature and program typology*. Retrieved from www.huduser.gov/publications/pdf/housingfostercare_literaturereview_0412_v2.pdf

U.S. Department of Housing and Urban Development. (2014). *Housing for youth aging out of foster care*. Retrieved from www.huduser.gov/publications/pdf/youth_hsg_main_report.pdf

Valdez, M., Gibbard, M., Thompkins, A., & Woley, M. (2013). *Comprehensive plan to prevent and end youth and young adult homelessness in King County by 2020: Homeless youth and young adult initiative*. Available at https://ncfy.acf.hhs.gov/library/2014/comprehensive-plan-prevent-and-end-youth-and-young-adult-homelessness-king-county-2020

Vaughn, M. G., Ollie, M. T., McMillen, J. C., Scott, L. D., & Munson, M. R. (2007). Substance use and abuse among older youth in foster care. *Addictive Behaviors, 32*, 1929–1935. http://dx.doi.org/10.1016/j.addbeh.2006.12.012

Wade, J., & Dixon, J. (2006). Making a home, finding a job: Investigating early housing and employment outcomes for young people leaving care. *Journal of Child & Family Social Work, 11*(3), 199–208. doi: 10.1111/j.1365-2206.2006.00428.x

Ward, M. (2016, November 4). Recommended foster care overhaul will carry steep price tag, officials say. *San Antonio Express News*. Retrieved from www.expressnews.com/news/local/article/Recommended-foster-care-overhaul-will-carry-steep-10594928.php

Webb, M. B., Frome, P., Harden, B. J., Baxter, R., Dowd, K., & Shin, S. H. (2007). Addressing the educational needs of children in child welfare services. In R. Haskins, F. Wulczyn, & M. B. Webb (Eds.), *Child protection: Using research to improve policy and practice* (pp. 243–258). Available at www.jstor.org/stable/pdf/10.7864/j.ctt6wpfh6.18.pdf

Weinberg, L. A., Oshiro, M., & Shea, N. (2014). Education liaisons work to improve educational outcomes of foster youth: A mixed methods case study. *Children and Youth Services Review, 41*(C), 45–52.

Whitbeck, L., Hoyt, D., Yoder, K., Cauce, A., & Paradise, M. (2001). Deviant behavior and victimization among homeless and runaway adolescents. *Journal of Interpersonal Violence, 16*(11), 1175–1204. Available at http://jiv.sagepub.com/cgi/content/abstract/16/11/1175

Yates, T. M., Egeland, B., & Sroufe, L. A. (2003). Rethinking resilience: A developmental process perspective. In S. S. Luthar (Ed.), *Resilience and vulnerabilities: Adaptation in the context of childhood adversities* (pp. 243–266). New York, NY: Cambridge University Press.

Yates, T. M., & Grey, I. K. (2012). Adapting to aging out: Profiles of risk and resilience among emancipated foster youth. *Development and Psychopathology, 24*, 475–492. doi: 10.1017/S0954579412000107

Zima, B. T., Bussing, R., Freeman, S., Yang, X., Belin, T. R., & Forness, S. R. (2000). Behavior problems, academic skill delays and school failure among school-aged children in foster care: Their relationship to placement characteristics. *Journal of Child and Family Studies, 9*(1), 87–103. Available at https://link.springer.com/content/pdf/10.1023%2FA%3A1009415800475.pdf

Appendix
Key Recommendations

- Housing and financial management assistance before aging out of care
- Ongoing preparation for adult living after transitions
- Smaller caseloads with staff as coaches rather than case managers
- Strategies and interventions tailored to each youth
- Transitional housing to prevent housing crises and homelessness often faced by former foster youth as they transition to adulthood
- A larger network of housing modes with on-site resources
- A housing resource directory including strengths and weaknesses of different housing types
- Support for youth in identifying housing availability
- A stronger circle of support in communities and institutions outside the foster care system to develop social capital to alleviate housing instability and enable independent living
- Employment and educational information readily available to youth at housing sites
- Social opportunities to help youth establish positive adult mentors, friendships, and peer support

15

Human Capital Accumulation
A Proposed Measure and Theoretical Framework for Foster Youth Job Placement Intervention Strategies

Toni Naccarato, Emily J. Bruce, Derek J. Stafford, and Nathaniel Hawkes

---

There are no means of disentangling the effects of economic change on social welfare issues in today's complex society. Historically, the theories of economists have evolved to account for changing economies driven by market forces and government interventions. Currently, one paradigm of choice focuses upon differences in productivity among the labor force. Three economists: Schultz (1961), Becker (1964), and Heckman (1974) believe that one key difference is the individual's human capital accumulation.

According to Becker (1993), human capital accumulation is an economic investment strategy that focuses on educational attainment, the development of employment skills, and protecting safeguards for health. Accumulating additional human capital is hypothesized to increase one's potential productivity and earnings. Those who do not accumulate sufficient human capital (i.e., physical and mental well-being, education, training, skills) are less likely to enter the workforce successfully, obtain competitive employment, and earn a living wage. Certain groups in the United States continue to lag behind in accumulating human capital. Adolescents in foster care are members of such a group (Naccarato, Brophy, & Courtney, 2010; Naccarato & Park, 2010).

This chapter discusses human capital as a measure and theoretical framework for evaluating interventions to support the transition for youth in foster care to become healthy and productive adults. One intervention to facilitate this transition is the federally mandated Independent Living Program (ILP), which was enacted in 1986. The ILP was initially intended to assist foster youth at ages 16 to 18 (P.L.99-272), but the program has now been extended in 11 states to cover ages 14 to 21 due to extended foster care legislation (Courtney, Dworsky, & Napolitano, 2013). The ILP is charged with helping foster youth in the transition from out-of-home care to independent adulthood. The program focuses on the development of life skills thought to be essential for basic living. The ILP seeks to boost the capacity of older foster youth to make the transition to independent adulthood by enhancing foster youth's productivity through education, employment, housing, and health care interventions (P.L. 99-272).

Social science research consistently documents a statistically significant relationship between higher educational achievement and success in adulthood related to employment and labor market productivity (Becker, 1993; Julian & Kominski, 2011). Yet, despite this research and the efforts of policy interventions, child welfare research has documented that foster youth, in comparison to youth in the general population, experience poor educational achievement and employment outcomes (Courtney & Dworsky, 2006; Courtney, Piliavin, Grogan-Kaylor, & Nesmith, 2001; Courtney, Terao, & Bost, 2004; Naccarato et al., 2010; Naccarato & DeLorenzo, 2008; Okpych & Courtney, 2014).

Within the last 25 years, economic opportunities for young people in the United States who have not graduated from high school or who only have a high school diploma or General Education Diploma (GED) have declined substantially. A generation ago, opportunities for young people with only a high school diploma were in sufficient existence (Julian & Kominski, 2011). Consequently, the economic opportunities for young people after high school without additional training are now extremely limited. It is in this context that concerns regarding the needs of young people leaving out-of-home care have grown exponentially. Thus, while increasingly elusive, adequate legal employment is seen as the most efficient pathway to self-sufficiency; and the most certain route to adequate legal employment appears to be via post-secondary educational opportunities and post-secondary vocational training (Pecora et al., 2006; Stewart, Kum, Barth, & Duncan, 2014). The traditional modes of transitioning from adolescence to adulthood include: 1) entering the workforce directly from high school, discussed above, 2) employment training programs, 3) military service, and/or 4) enrolling in college or vocational school.

Employment training opportunities include federal job skills training programs such as Job Corps and the efforts via the Workforce Investment Act (P.L. 105-220), which is now referred to as the Workforce Innovation and Opportunity Act (P.L. 113-128). Funding for these programs has declined and access has become more limited (Fabian, 2007). In addition, these potential post-secondary experiences have a different resonance for young people who are soon to be leaving placement in out-of-home care. Specifically, while the Job Corps is a useful program for many young people who have few resources, for many young people who have been in out-of-home care, the Job Corps can seem much like being in placement again.

Military service is another traditional way of making the transition from adolescence to adulthood. However, the military has become much more exclusive regarding who is accepted into military service (Christeson, Taggart, & Messner-Zidell, 2009). In the post-draft era, the military has become increasingly discriminating about who is selected from the enlistment pools. For many former foster youth who might have been interested in the military, the military may no longer be an available option—simply because many former foster youth do not have the educational foundation or the skills sought by the military; or because their records are likely to include mental health labels (Christeson et al., 2009).

The final way of making the transition from adolescence to adulthood is enrollment in a vocational program,[1] community college, 4-year college, or university. However, these options are becoming increasingly more expensive (Trombley, 2003), and thus less accessible. Many former foster youth indicate they have an interest in attending college; however, in general, many young people leaving care are severely limited in their abilities to make use of an opportunity to attend college. Many former foster youth find it a challenge, after being accepted into college, to stay in college (retention) and even fewer are able to complete a course of study (graduation) (Hernandez & Naccarato, 2010; McMillen, Auslander, Elze, White, & Thompson, 2003). Given these realities, the concern about sufficient educational and employment opportunities has become even more critical as employment opportunities have become increasingly competitive and severely limited in the 21st century.

This chapter proposes a strategy for foster youth to accumulate human capital, given the link between education and potential employment, vocational, and economic success. Current and former foster youth can be considered an at-risk population who are least likely to accumulate human capital. Thus, increasing the levels of a foster youth's human capital would help to decrease the levels of risk factors and mitigate the difficulties in the transition to adulthood.

Closely related to the topic of human capital is the topic of social capital (Coleman, 1990), which also will be discussed in this chapter, as it relates to the acquisition of human capital for this vulnerable population. Social capital is the cluster of resources related to a person's familial relationships, community, social organizations such as schools, and networks that provide social support (Coleman, 1990; Loury, 1981; Teachman, Paasch, & Carver, 1997).

The chapter provides a cohesive analytic framework to integrate child welfare policy and practice with economics, as well as the rationale explaining why human capital accumulation is an important theoretical framework to use in the measurement of predictors and outcomes for young people as they mature to adulthood, specifically regarding foster youth. In addition to the integrative approach to this analysis, the authors make recommendations for how to create job placement initiatives and interventions that reflect the human capital needed for the current technological and social realities of the 21st century.

The Foster Youth Population: Background and Significance

Foster care is a substitute living arrangement that includes relatives or kin, families previously unacquainted with the child (i.e., foster families), and various forms of residential and group care (Haskins, Wulczyn, & Webb, 2007). In 2016, the Adoption and Foster Care Analysis Reporting System (AFCARS) reported that there were 427,910 dependent children residing in foster care as of September 2015. According to AFCARS, 20,789 youth were discharged because of "emancipation" in 2015 (U.S. Department of Health & Human Services [cited henceforth as USDHHS], 2016).

Foster youth often experience a more disruptive transition to independence than non-foster youth, usually characterized by a lack of familial and/or social service system support (Courtney et al., 2007; Hernandez & Naccarato, 2010; Okpych & Courtney, 2014). Lack of support coupled with pervasive and challenging negative outcomes for foster youth provide the impetus for the development of more focused policy for this vulnerable population. There was, and there still is, a need for legislative mandates for services to help these youth become more successful, not only while they are in care, but also after discharge from the system. According to Hook and Courtney:

> The development of policy targeting foster youth at risk of aging-out of care is, to a large extent, a reflection of policymakers' acknowledgment of the moral imperative of not abandoning children who the state has arguably failed. Moreover, unlike other vulnerable youth in transition, including many who are significantly involved with public systems (e.g., youth served by the juvenile justice system and those served by the disabilities services systems), foster youth are literally the children of the state.
>
> (Hook & Courtney, 2011, p. 1855)

In order to try to assist foster youth to successfully transition from foster care to independent living, the federally-funded Independent Living Program (ILP), discussed above, was implemented in 1986 and was one of the first initiatives and interventions providing services to this specific population (P.L. 99-272).

Another form of intervention that has re-emerged for transition-age foster youth is the opportunity to live independently in supervised programs. These programs have become an important placement option for foster youth in those states that allow for the extension of foster care to age 21 or older (e.g., California, Illinois, and New York) (Courtney et al., 2013). The two top priorities of the child welfare system are to keep children from being placed in out-of-home care and to reduce the length of time a young person is in foster care. Many of the children entering the system will spend a substantial amount of their childhood living in out-of-home care (Wulczyn, Barth, Yuan, Jones-Harden, & Landsverk, 2005; Wulczyn & Goerge, 1992).

The average length of stay in foster care in 2015 was nearly 2 years (20.4 months), while nearly 52% (n = 222,150) of these children remained in foster care for 12 months or longer (USDHHS,

2016). Many youth who remain in care for longer periods are older adolescents, who tend to exit the foster care system at age 18 when they "age out" of foster care. Ideally, when these young people age out of placement, they have a plan and the resources to live on their own. According to AFCARS, of the 427,910 children in the American foster care system in 2015, 9% (20,789) of the 243,060 foster youth who exited from care emancipated out of the system (USDHHS, 2016).

Although the law in most states considers adolescents to be adults upon reaching their 18th birthday, most young people from intact supportive families continue to receive parental assistance beyond age 18. Financial, social, and emotional assistance are three major ways in which parents provide support to their young adult children. However, for youth who age out of the foster care system, the transition to adulthood is too often negatively anticipated, and represents an abrupt and traumatic event occurring on or near their 18th birthday. This abrupt change in status is characterized by the expectation that the former foster youth will live independently (Courtney et al., 2007).

Too few foster youth "age out" of the child welfare system with a high school diploma, employment skills, or vocational training (Okpych & Courtney, 2014). In fact, many studies have found that youth transitioning from out-of-home care have multiple risk factors that result in institutional challenges and difficulties. Frequently, the familial difficulties and dysfunction, which initially led to social service intervention, continue to place former foster youth at a disadvantage in terms of academic, employment, and vocational success (Naccarato & DeLorenzo, 2008; Okpych & Courtney, 2014). Thus, young adults who emancipate from out-of-home care face incredible barriers to self-sufficiency. Those barriers include, but are not limited to, prior abuse and/or neglect, multiple foster care placements, and gaps in their educational experiences prior to and during foster care. These barriers can contribute to poverty and overall lowered expectations in adulthood (Hines, Merdinger, & Wyatt, 2005).

There are varieties of risks that challenge transitioning foster youth. While these risks are not inevitable, they arise frequently and when they do, the magnitude of harm is substantial. The risks faced by transitioning foster youth include: school failure, unemployment, episodes of running away from placements, limited access to physical and behavioral health care, housing instability and homelessness, violence, teen parenthood, and high rates of involvement with the criminal justice system (Courtney & Barth, 1996; Courtney et al., 2007; Montgomery, Donkoh, & Underhill, 2006; Naccarato, Brophy, & Hernandez, 2008; Naccarato & DeLorenzo, 2008). Ultimately, these risks undermine the goal of academic achievement, vocational preparation, and successful employment outcomes, which subsequently results in a lowered accumulation of human capital for foster youth.

Legislative Efforts

To try to address these risk factors, the ILP was designed and implemented nationally. In 1986, the Consolidated Omnibus Budget Reconciliation Act of 1985, signed into law by President Reagan, incorporated the authorization for the federally-funded Independent Living Program (P.L. 99-272).

The ILP was designed specifically to assist children in foster care, aged 16 and over, to begin to plan and prepare for the transition from foster care to independent living, and ultimately to mitigate the risks that had been observed. Prior to the ILP, most child welfare agencies did not provide any specific services to help foster youth prepare for life after discharge from the system. In that context, youth were offered services: 1) to support graduation from high school (or completion of a GED); 2) to develop employment and daily living skills (e.g., grocery shopping, cooking, and laundry); 3) to gain money management skills; and 4) other forms of support, all designed to facilitate a successful transition from foster care to independent living.

A report prepared by the U.S. General Accounting Office (1999) regarding the effectiveness of independent living services for foster youth more than a decade after the ILP was implemented found little evidence that the outcomes for former foster youth were positively associated with ILP training and support. In fact, many state and local ILP administrators reported that they could not provide all of the needed supports to youth leaving care (Courtney & Dworsky, 2006; Naccarato & Park, 2010; USDHHS, 1999).

These issues regarding the implementation of the ILP led to subsequent federal legislation, the Foster Care Independence Act of 1999 (P.L. 106-169). This legislation increased the ILP fiscal allocation, authorizing entitlements from $70 million to $140 million, allowing for increased housing resources, lowering the age of eligibility to 14 years, and expanding Medicaid eligibility to all foster youth automatically as they left foster care (Nollan & Downs, 1999).

Due to the frequency and severity of negative outcomes for this vulnerable population, the federal government determined that even more legislative effort was needed. One such policy is the Promoting Safe and Stable Family Amendments of 2001 (P.L. 107-133). This legislation created Education and Training Vouchers (ETVs) for youth "aging out" of the foster care system. The ETV program provides money to help pay for college or specialized education. The ETV grants are funded by the federal government and administered by the states. Eligible students may receive grants of up to $5,000 per academic year in most states.

The Fostering Connections to Success and Increasing Adoptions Act of 2008 (P.L. 110-351) is a noteworthy piece of federal legislation designed to assist foster youth in their transition from care. This Act not only modified the original ETV program by supplementing the support for the transition out of foster care by extending the availability of ETVs, but also provided other substantial sources of support for transitioning foster youth from 18 to 21 years of age. This legislation, even with the lags in implementation across the states, corresponds to the notion of extending foster care beyond age 18 with a focus on youth pursuing post-secondary education programs as a new paradigm. In other words, no longer is the transition from foster care to adulthood framed as an abrupt and traumatic event; it is now characterized as a multi-year process.

It would be difficult to overemphasize the importance of this policy and accompanying operational changes for foster youth. The early data from the CalYOUTH study indicated that, at least in California, youth who are deciding to stay on in the foster care system past the age of 18 as *non-minor dependents* are receiving additional support and services (Okpych, Courtney, & Charles, 2015).

Initial research suggests that extending foster care beyond the age of 18 has had a positive impact in the areas of employment and education, in comparison to those youth who did not choose to remain in extended foster care (Okpych & Courtney, 2014). Data from the Midwest Evaluation of the Adult Functioning of Former Foster Youth (hereafter referred to as the Midwest Study) focusing on foster youth in Illinois also indicated that remaining in foster care past the age of 18 was a protective factor in terms of education and employment (Courtney et al., 2007). These legislative changes subsequently modified expectations regarding foster youth. Now these young people can be served longer in terms of educational and ILP opportunities, transitional housing, placement in foster care past 18 to 19 years of age (age depends on state), access to health insurance, and ongoing case management, to name a few of the services. Young people may now be expected to utilize these additional services and supports in order to accumulate the education and job skills necessary to become competitively employed (Okpych et al., 2015). Further, because of this policy change and the resulting additional services and support, there is a concomitant increased focus on technological advances and the human capital needed to utilize technology in the current U.S. economy.

Economics and Human Capital as a Theoretical Framework

Technology has altered certain types of mechanical equipment, production techniques, and other types of output. Economic growth and progress involve not only technological advancements to equipment and processes, but also people. Scientific and technical knowledge have raised the productivity of labor and other inputs in production. This focus on science and technology has greatly increased the value of college education, technical schooling, and on-the-job training, as this growth in knowledge and skill has become embodied in individuals who contribute to output (Becker, 1993). Further, an investment in people permits society to take advantage of technical progress and also sustain that progress. According to Weisbrod (1962), "Improvements in health make investment in education more rewarding by extending life expectancy. Investment in education expands and extends knowledge, leading to advances, which raise productivity and improve health" (p. 106). Further, key factors in human capital accumulation are formal schooling, informal learning, on-the-job training, social supports, public health, and soft-skills development (Dodge, 2003). Becker viewed these items as capital because they improve health and raise earnings while maintaining the concept of capital as an economic concept as traditionally defined. Expenditures on medical care, education, and training are investments in capital, but these result in human capital, not physical or financial capital. People cannot be separated from their knowledge, skills, health, or values in the way it is possible to separate financial and physical assets from their owners (Becker, 1993). "Education and training are the most important investments in human capital" (Becker, 1993, p. 17). His research has shown that having a high school and college education in the United States greatly raises a person's income, even after adjusting for more resourced family backgrounds and after netting out the direct and indirect costs of schooling (Becker, 1993).

Heckman (2000) discussed human capital as a combination of education, acquired skills, and innate ability as a stock that accumulates over time. To Heckman, human capital accumulation is a positive trajectory where the quantity of human capital increases across the lifespan. Foster youth have special needs for integrated education, physical health, behavioral health, social services, and Positive Youth Development (PYD)—a broad conceptualization of human capital. By extension, it is reasonable that the focus of interventions provided to youth in foster care should seek to increase human capital accumulation.

Few studies to date in the social welfare literature have variables that measure human capital accumulation as a clearly stated and defined variable, as compared to the economics field. One such study used that approach to assess data from the Midwest Study. Several research projects were implemented using data collected from this longitudinal panel, with data collected from this one cohort over three periods in time. Wave 1, the baseline, occurred when these young people were 17 to 18 years of age (n = 732); Wave 2 occurred when these young people were 19 to 20 years of age (n = 603); and Wave 3 occurred when these young people were 21 to 22 years of age (n = 591) (Courtney et al., 2004; Courtney et al., 2005; and, Courtney et al., 2007). Wave 4 occurred when these young people were ages 23 or 24 [n = 602] (Hook & Courtney, 2011).

With data from Wave 3, a Tobit analysis was used to test the statistical relationship between multiple factors (i.e., demographics, human capital, independent living services utilization, and yearly income for former foster youth). There were 591 youth who participated in Wave 3 of the project; 524 youth were age 21 [88.8%] and 66 youth were age 22 [11.2%] (Naccarato et al., 2010).

The variables that sought to measure human capital as it related to educational attainment were as follows: 1) repeating a grade; 2) the raw score from the Wide Range Achievement Test (WRAT); and 3) the education level. The variable regarding repeating a grade was used to determine if the youth were at or below grade level. The WRAT score was used as an addition to the Weschler–Bellevue Scales intelligence test (Wilkinson, 1993), and the primary purpose of the WRAT score was to assess the ability of a participant to learn basic skills in arithmetic, spelling, and reading. The youth were given the word recognition part of the test at the baseline interview. One point was given for each word that was properly pronounced. The total possible points were 42. The education-level variable has five categories: 1) some high school; 2) GED or high school equivalency diploma; 3) high school diploma; 4) some college; or 5) an Associate's degree (Naccarato et al., 2010). The results from the analysis of the Wave 3 data from the Midwest Study indicated that 46% of the youth reported having to repeat a grade (n = 273). The mean WRAT score was 21.27 (approximately 7th

Grade reading level—12 to 13 years old). Thirty-eight percent of the youth had completed a GED [n = 222]; 10% had received a high school diploma [n = 57]; and 30% of youth had attended some college or had obtained an Associate's degree [n = 175] (Naccarato et al., 2010).

The study findings also point out the benefits of educational attainment for this population. In this sample, many youth approached the age of majority being one or more grade levels behind. This limited their possibility of obtaining a high school diploma. Findings also indicated that when youth had some college education or an Associate's degree, their earnings were 50% greater than those youth who only had some high school education. Thus, in this study, increasing one's education was associated with higher earnings (Naccarato et al., 2010). This highlights the importance of increasing human capital accumulation for youth in foster care.

A second study that also used the longitudinal data from the Midwest Evaluation of the Adult Functioning of Former Foster Youth (n = 602) provided a view of employment outcomes of foster youth who were transitioning to adulthood over time. The authors used a theoretical framework based on Caspi, Wright, Moffitt, and Silva's (1998) work, which focused on human, personal, and social capital. Human capital was defined as an individual's education and skill set. Personal capital was defined as behavioral characteristics or personal styles. Social capital was defined as a youth's personal relationships and connections to social networks (Caspi et al., 1998; Hook & Courtney, 2011). Hook and Courtney (2011) used secondary data analyses with four waves of the longitudinal panel data, tracking a cohort of youth exiting the public child welfare system in Illinois (n = 474), Iowa (n = 63), and Wisconsin (n = 195).

Human capital in this study was again measured by the respondent's reading ability at baseline using the WRAT. In this sample, the average WRAT score was 39.5, which indicated that the youth exhibited reading skills corresponding to a 7th Grade reading level. Hook and Courtney (2011) then created "three dichotomous measures indicating a reading level of 6th to 8th grade, high school, and post-high school (less than 6th grade is the reference category)" (p. 1858). Hook and Courtney (2011) used "contemporaneous interviews" to assess the educational attainment of the study participants. Three categories were constructed: "less than high school, high school (this included a regular diploma, GED, other equivalency, or certificate of completion), and one year of college or more" (p. 1858).

The study findings indicated that human capital was strongly associated with youth employment. The youths' WRAT scores were related to the odds of employment. Youth who scored above Grade 6 were 40% to 70% more likely than youth scoring below Grade 6 to be employed for at least 20 hours per week. Employed youth who scored at a post-high-school level by age 17 earned 7% higher wages. Human capital, defined as educational attainment, was shown to be strongly associated with employment and wages (Hook & Courtney, 2011). Youth who had a high school diploma or GED were twice as likely to be employed when compared to youth who did not complete high school or get a GED. Youth who had some college attendance or an Associate's degree were approximately four times more likely to be employed. In the sample, at age 24 years, 20% had not completed high school, 46% had a high school diploma, GED, or equivalency, 28% had some college, and 6% had an Associate's degree. The findings from this multivariate analysis in this longitudinal study suggest that human capital plays a role in influencing the employment outcomes of foster youth in their transition to young adulthood. Youth who were not employed typically had lower educational attainment than employed youth. The study concluded that for foster youth, education appears critically important for employment and wages (Hook & Courtney, 2011).

A third study used logistic regression to analyze youth's attendance at one or more ILP services provided by five agencies, according to the youth's self-reported educational goal serving as a proxy for human capital accumulation (Naccarato & Park, 2010). The study examined whether there was a relationship between youth's stated educational goals, social workers' stated educational goals for youths, gender, ethnicity, placement type, ILP contract agency, and ILP *human-capital-related* session attendance (17 weeks of training). The dependent variables (human-capital-related ILP sessions) were as follows: attended one or more employment session, attended one or more education session, and attended one or more employment or education session (i.e., human-capital-related) (Naccarato & Park, 2010).

This study's findings indicated that youth in this sample (n = 365) had a low rate of attendance at ILP sessions in general. The mode for this sample for attendance at ILP sessions was zero. One argument to explain this low rate of attendance could be that youth participating in the study did not believe that ILP was a useful intervention. A second argument might be that youth were not aware of ILP as an intervention. However, it also might be argued that youth could have been receiving ILP services in an informal manner; for example, within their relatives' home or foster home placements. Finally, this study indicated that from a return-on-investment perspective, it is unclear and ambiguous whether ILP advances a foster youth's later educational success or any other areas of human capital accumulation such as employment or vocational training.

Economics and Social Capital as a Theoretical Framework

A topic closely related to human capital is *social capital*. According to Teachman et al. (1997), social capital is the cluster of resources that reside in "function-specific relationships in which individuals are embedded" (p. 1344). According to Loury (1981), social capital is the set of resources that reside in family relations and in community social organizations that can be useful for the social and cognitive development of a child or young person. These resources are different across people and can constitute an important advantage for children and adolescents in their development of human capital. In reaction to the influence of economic theory on sociology, Coleman (1990) argued that the concepts of financial capital and human capital should be supplemented with the concept of social capital when attempting to explain human actions.

Social capital may be represented by the density and consistency of educationally-focused relationships that exist between school, children, and parents (Teachman et al., 1997). A rudimentary hypothesis is that children who are embedded in richer and more consistent school-related relationships will achieve higher educational attainment. The thought is that youth with more social capital will more likely remain in school, perform better, and graduate in greater numbers (Teachman et al., 1997).

With specific regard to foster youth, it appears that they have less social capital than non-foster youth in the general population. There is research that indicates a statistical relationship between poverty, child abuse and neglect, and foster care placement (Barth, 1990; Cook, 1994). Furthermore, foster youth more often come from and remain in neighborhoods where crime and a lack of education are prevalent. In addition, foster youth are typically removed from, and appear more likely to remain estranged from, their classical networks of parents, friends, and extended family (Cromer, 2007).

The developmental impacts of challenging environments are associated with social capital for foster youth that can create risks such as lifelong trauma and hardship, and not just in the here and now. Undesirable outcomes stemming from adverse childhood experiences include incomplete and problematic transitions to adulthood (Osgood, Foster, & Courtney, 2010), as well as negative outcomes during adulthood. Negative outcomes include premature, preventable death (Corso, Edwards, Fang, & Mercy, 2008) and intergenerational child maltreatment (Anda, Butchart, Felliti, & Brown, 2010). Thus, when considering and analyzing interventions for youth in foster care, it is important to assess not only human capital accumulation, but also social capital accumulation.

Education Trajectories of Foster Youth

The potential difficulties prior to placement in out-of-home care, along with the issues that come with being placed in out-of-home care, can all combine to result in poor educational outcomes.

Far too many children and youth leave care without the necessary educational attainment. Researchers have consistently found evidence that children in out-of-home care do not acquire the skills necessary to establish a successful academic foundation. One possible key obstacle keeping children and youth who are in out-of-home care from satisfactory academic performance is transience. Out-of-home placements are often not stable, which results in a problematic level of instability in a child's academic context (Bruce, Naccarato, Hopson, & Morelli, 2010; Zetlin & Weinberg, 2004).

Generally, what is known about educational outcomes for foster youth is limited to high school completion rates. National estimates of the number of foster youth who leave care with a high school diploma range from 37% to 60% (Blome, 1997; Westat, 1991). Studies suggest that 30% to 40% of foster youth graduate from high school or pass the test necessary to earn a General Education Diploma (GED) or other high school equivalent diploma (McMillen & Tucker, 1999; Scannapieco, Schagrin, & Scannapieco, 1995; Westat, 1990). A Westat study (1991) of educational achievement for foster youth found a 54% graduation rate, and a Midwest study found a 64% graduation rate (Courtney et al., 2001). Pecora et al. (2006) looked at the adult functioning of 659 former foster youth. These researchers found that former foster youth obtained a GED instead of a high school diploma at a rate of nearly six times the rate of the general population (28.5% versus 5%). In a more recent study, Barrat and Berliner (2013) found that in the state of California, 58% of the 2,674, 17-year-old foster youth in the 2009/2010 academic year completed high school.

"[S]tates are [*currently*] required by the federal government to administer the National Youth in Transition Database (NYTD) survey to cohorts of foster youth at ages 17, 19 and 21" to attempt to measure the outcomes of youth transitioning out of foster care (USDHHS [Children's Bureau], 2014, p. 1). Outcomes regarding educational attainment reported by youth in the first NYTD cohort at ages 17 and 19 are now available. According to the USDHHS (Children's Bureau) (2014, p. 1), "response rates for both baseline (age 17) and follow-up (age 19) surveys varied widely by state."

The findings from the NYTD were that "in Federal Fiscal Year (FFY) 2011, 29,569 youth were identified as eligible to take the survey at age 17" (USDHHS [Children's Bureau], 2014, p. 2). Fifty-three percent (n = 15,597) of these 29,569 youths completed the survey. The numbers of youth who completed the survey from the states, which did submit findings indicated extensive variability in their respective response rates ("from 12% to 100%") (USDHHS [Children's Bureau], 2014, p. 1). Two years later, when the youth from the first cohort were age 19, less than half of the original cohort was eligible to participate in the follow-up survey (n = 11,712); and only 7,845 of these youths (67%) responded to the follow-up survey at age 19. Again, it was found that "state-level response rates . . . varied widely at follow-up, from 26% to 95%" (USDHHS [Children's Bureau], 2014, p. 1).

The findings from this initial cohort have some significant limitations in that a small unreported number of states did not take part in surveying 19-year-old current and/or former foster youth. This is what led to the wide range in the response rates reported from the states; thus "non-response bias is a concern" (USDHHS [Children's Bureau], 2014, p. 2). The demographic profile of the 17-year-old survey respondents was very similar to the demographic profile of the 19-year-old survey respondents, in terms of their gender and their ethnic background. An interesting observation was that this first cohort of survey participants was ethnically heterogeneous.

Because of the Fostering Connections to Success and Increasing Adoptions Act (P.L. 110-351, 2008), some of the survey participants had decided to remain in foster care at age 19. In fact, 36% of the 19-year-old survey participants (n = 2,824) had decided to remain in foster care. In addition, "[t]he NYTD survey asks young people to report their current status of enrollment in an educational program and the highest educational certification received" (USDHHS [Children's Bureau], 2014, p. 3). Understandably, when this first cohort was initially surveyed at age 17, most of the youth were still in school, and had not yet received a high school diploma or other certification. However, at age 19, when the follow-up survey was conducted, over half (55%; n = 4,315) of the respondents had completed a high school diploma (or GED). In addition, 54% of those 19-year-old survey participants still in care (n = 1,525) were engaged in some post-secondary education and/or training; and less than half of this group that was involved in ongoing education or training (49%; n= 747) had "a high school diploma or GED" (USDHSS [Children's Bureau], 2014, p. 4).

Employment Trajectories: Job Types, Potential Earnings, and Job Training

Historically, the assumption has been that high school graduates will gain and sustain meaningful employment. So, historically, once a foster youth either completed high school or failed to complete high school by age 18, the child welfare system's responsibility for these youth terminated. The assumption was that these former foster youth had become adults and the child welfare case should be closed. Early data from Okpych and Courtney (2014) have called this theory into question, and the extended foster care options in California and Illinois also suggest that these assumptions are not well-founded.

Images of foster youth moving on to adulthood in a successful manner at age 18 by pulling themselves up by their bootstraps seem to be implied in this policy and practice model, even though there is no evidence to support this notion. The employment outcomes for youth who have aged out of foster care amount to negative scenarios, including foster youth falling prey to human trafficking, substance abuse disorders, and criminal activity (Osgood et al., 2010). Although an identifiable number of those studied had obtained positive employment outcomes, foster youth generally had difficulty obtaining and keeping employment, and the employment they do obtain tends to skew toward low-wage jobs (Courtney et al., 2007; Naccarato et al., 2010). Thus, this does not depict a story of independence nor a successful transition to adulthood.

Research findings from the 21st century indicate that many young adults need transition supports and economic resources well into middle adulthood. This is typically the responsibility of the biological family for non-fostered youth (Hamilton & Hamilton, 2003). Simultaneously, current and developing employment situations more often now require post-secondary education or advanced training; thus, job insecurity and career change are normative for those without such education or training (Naccarato et al., 2010). This again goes against the notion that making the transition to adulthood is a one-time event at 18 years of age that results in economic self-sufficiency and autonomous independent living. With the diversity evidenced in our 21st century demographics, the idea of a transition to independence as an adult at 18, 21, or even 25, is at best ambitious and at worst unachievable. Thus, the former expectation of what high school completion can provide is no longer justified, especially with the vulnerable population of youth in foster care.

As foster youth get closer to 18 years of age, they have the opportunity to decide whether or not to remain in foster care; or if they have left out-of-home care, they can decide to return. This decision has critical consequences for their immediate future financial stability, as well as being a key indicator of a young person's readiness for independence. Even at the age of 17, 29% of the foster youth participating in the NYTD survey (n = 4,523) had an affirmative response to one of the employment response options on the initial survey. Those response options were as follows: 1) full- or part-time employment; 2) paid or unpaid apprenticeship; 3) internship; or 4) other on-the-job training (USDHHS [Children's Bureau], 2014). By age 19, 51% of the survey respondents (n = 4,000) indicated that they had some employment-related experience. Of critical importance is the fact that 54% of youth in foster care at age 19 (n = 1,525), and 49% of youth not in care by age 19 (n = 2,459) had some employment-related experience. With further analysis, it is possible that this finding suggests that continuing in out-of-home care may have a relationship to having more access to employment opportunities for this population.

Background and Overview of American Youth Employment Programs

Scholarship that explores the origins of economic inequality reveals the systematized nature of poverty and wealth. Boix (2010) stated that ancient, pre-agricultural societies experienced relatively even distributions of wealth, but the advent of agriculture widened income disparities, and the subsequent creation of state institutions served to protect and perpetuate those disparities. This phenomenon persists today, as demonstrated by the disproportionately high rates of unemployment and poverty among certain populations in the United States, including foster youth and former foster youth (Naccarato et al., 2010; U.S. Department of Labor [Bureau of Labor Statistics], 2016a, 2016b, 2017). Studies have shown that periods of unemployment for youth often lead to greater difficulties in the job market during adulthood. These findings include the lower earnings and ongoing lower rates of employment; and that is particularly true for foster youth and former foster youth (Cruces, Ham, & Viollaz, 2012; Mroz & Savage, 2001; O'Sullivan, Mugglestone, & Allison, 2014; Schmillen & Umkehrer, 2013). Taken together, these findings illustrate a mechanism by which membership in a marginalized population such as foster youth or former foster youth, leads to ongoing economic marginalization, creating a self-perpetuating cycle.

Just as government and social institutions have the power to maintain economic inequality, so they also have the potential to diminish it. In the United States, there is a long history of government agencies and non-governmental organizations working to address these problems by influencing patterns of youth employment. Only in relatively recent years, though, have there been programmatic efforts to create employment opportunities specifically for foster youth (Dworsky & Havlicek, 2010). In recent history and up to the present day, the majority of employment programs available to foster youth in the United States have been designed to serve youth from low-income families, youth from low-income neighborhoods, and ethnic minority youth, including foster youth. These populations are often included in broader categories such as *disadvantaged* or *at-risk* youth (McWhirter, McWhirter, McWhirter, & McWhirter, 2013; Koball et al., 2011; Schonert-Reichl, 2000), and many youth employment programs use these terms to describe the populations they serve. Some of these programs are discussed here, and for reasons explained above, their target populations can be understood to include foster youth and former foster youth, even when the services may not be specifically targeted to foster youth.

Literature about early youth workforce development programs in the United States tended to refer to the youth they served as *disadvantaged youth* or simply *poor*, reflecting a focus on low-income family background as the primary factor of concern (Levitan, 1975; Rawlins, 1971). Until the 1930s, government interventions regarding youth employment consisted primarily of regulating and/or curtailing child labor (Trattner, 1970). The Great Depression prompted the institution of many new workforce development programs, including the well-known Civilian Conservation Corps (CCC), which initially employed men aged 18 to 25 years, and the Works Progress Administration (WPA), which included various employment programs for the same age group (Fernandez-Alcantara, 2012). These federal programs served hundreds of thousands of youth and focused on projects to improve infrastructure and government services, as well as placing youth in trades such as construction (Arnesen, 2007; Salmond, 1967).

The CCC and the WPA were decommissioned during World War II and it was not until the Lyndon Johnson era of the 1960s that new large-scale federal programs emerged to enhance employment opportunities for disadvantaged youth. Most notable among these was Job Corps, created by the Economic Opportunity Act of 1964 (P.L. 88-452), which was charged to improve the employability of youth and "rescue them from the cycle of poverty" by housing them in residential centers and providing them with intensive academic and vocational training (Levitan, 1975, p. 3). Job Corps is still in operation today, with 122 training centers around the United States, and is "the nation's largest and most comprehensive residential education and job training program for at-risk youth, ages 16 through 24" (U.S. Department of Labor, 2016, para. 1).

In the last three decades of the 20th century, the federal government repeatedly renewed and diversified funding for youth employment programs through a series of Congressional legislation, most recently the Workforce Investment Act (WIA; P.L. 105-220) of 1998 and its successor, the Workforce Innovation and Opportunity Act (WIOA; P.L. 113-128) of 2014. These laws provided for a variety of community-based youth employment programs such as the Youth Opportunity programs. Youth Opportunity programs were intended to deliver services in neighborhoods where at-risk youth live (U.S. Department of Labor [Employment and Training Administration], 2016). Federal funding has diminished or ended for many of these community-based programs, but fortunately, an increasing number of local governmental and non-governmental organizations, employing an ever-broadening array of innovative approaches to youth employment development, have stepped in to fill the gap (Fabian, 2007; Fernandez-Alcantara, 2012; Garcia-Iriarte, Balcazar, & Taylor-Ritzler, 2007; Juma Ventures, 2015a, 2015b).

Research on Youth Employment Programs

The growing emphasis on evidence-based practices in social service delivery means that youth employment providers have a vested interest in familiarizing themselves with research on youth employment interventions. Unfortunately, studies of programs that specifically target foster youth are hard to come by. However, some useful information on these programs can be found in outcome reports published by academic institutions and by the programs themselves. One example is a report on the Foster Youth Demonstration Project, funded by the U.S. Department of Labor, which created temporary employment and educational programs for foster youth in five states (Institute for Educational Leadership, 2008). Quantitatively, this report found that only 35% of program participants obtained employment during program participation, which may seem like a disappointing outcome. However, the program evaluation yielded valuable qualitative information on the importance of individual relationships between youth and program staff, suggesting that one-on-one services may be an important component of program success (Institute for Educational Leadership, 2008). The Community Assistance Programs (CAP) in Chicago provide job-readiness training and placement in subsidized employment for youth. A report about foster youth participation in CAP employment services between May 2007 and July 2009 stated that 46% of foster youth participants were placed in subsidized jobs. However, only 26% actually completed over an hour of work in the jobs in which they were placed (Dworsky & Havlicek, 2010). Again, it should be remembered that this information is not from controlled studies, but from outcome and evaluation reports.

There is a large body of available scientific research on Job Corps, going back several decades, but much of it has yielded inconsistent and inconclusive results. At least one government-funded study of Job Corps lacked a control group; others compared groups of students who successfully completed the program to control groups of youth who applied, but were not accepted into the program; or who started, but did not complete the program (LaLonde, 1995; Rawlins, 1971; Schochet, Burghardt, & McConnell, 2006, 2008). It seems unlikely that these control group participants constituted random samples of youth who were eligible for Job Corps, and additional bias probably arose from the fact that program administrators tended to admit youth who seemed more likely to get jobs after completing the program, as this would boost program outcomes (LaLonde, 1995). In spite of this history of ambiguity, some relatively recent and better-designed studies have found that Job Corps has increased youth's educational attainment and earnings for several years after program participation (Schochet et al., 2006, 2008). However, these researchers also found that, overall, Job Corps has not been cost-effective. Further, they found that enrollment in Job Corps did not lead to longer-term financial gains for the participant sample as a whole, but met these goals only for a subset of older students.

Unfortunately, studies of other employment-related interventions for youth have also found that the interventions failed to produce a long-term impact on the earnings of the youth who participated (McClanahan, Sipe, & Smith, 2004; Naccarato et al., 2010; Walker & Vilella-Velez, 1992). Some studies have focused on summer youth employment programs, which have long been popular in the

United States, and have found that the programs produce positive short-term results on earnings and other variables (McClanahan et al., 2004; Naccarato, Brophy, & LaClair, 2013; Walker & Vilella-Velez, 1992). For example, Naccarato et al. (2013) found that high-risk youth who spent more time engaged in the Summer Youth Employment Program in New York were slightly less likely to be rearrested than those who were less engaged. This highlights that there is a critical need for the development of more effective interventions (Naccarato et al., 2013). On a hopeful note, recent years have seen the inception of exciting and innovative new developments in the world of youth employment, many of which are in need of scientific study to help build an improved empirical evidence base.

Recent Promising Practices in Youth Employment

One approach that shows promise with youth is the Individual Placement and Support (IPS) model of supported employment (Ferguson, 2013). The IPS model, which was developed in the early 1990s at Dartmouth University, was designed for adults with mental illness, and focuses on rapid placement into competitive employment, which fits the preferences of the client (Drake, Bond, & Becker, 2012). The creators of IPS seemed to be intent from the beginning of their project to build a foundation for gathering evidence about their practices. To date, there have been at least 23 controlled studies demonstrating the effectiveness of IPS (Drake, Bond, Goldman, Hogan, & Karakus, 2016). However, the vast majority of these projects were studies of adults. A controlled study using IPS with homeless youth in Los Angeles is a promising start (Ferguson, 2013). This study shows a significant improvement in earnings among the experimental group in comparison to the control group. Again, however, this study focused primarily on short-term outcomes. More research on IPS and other individualized approaches to competitive employment of youth is needed; especially with regard to longer-term effects.

One of the fastest-growing types of youth employment programs is the social enterprise approach. In this context, an organization employs a *double bottom line* approach by attempting to generate self-sustaining revenue while addressing social issues. Innovative organizations are emerging in the United States and around the world to address youth unemployment through a combination of business acumen and commitment to social justice. The data from these programs suggest that incorporating a social mission often contributes to the success of a business, giving it an edge over *traditional* businesses (Wong, 2014). Unfortunately, despite the popularity of the social enterprise model, there is a dearth of available scientific research supporting its effectiveness with youth (VerWys, 2016). This is an important area of need for research in the near future.

In spite of the lack of available controlled studies exploring social enterprises for youth, a review of outcomes published by some organizations in the San Francisco Bay Area provides some very promising data. New Door Ventures was an early pioneer in the social enterprise field in the Bay Area, which began in 1981. New Door Ventures has grown into a thriving business, which today provides case management, job-readiness training, and paid internships to more than 300 youth every year (New Door Ventures, 2016). The program runs two social enterprises, a bicycle shop called Pedal Revolution and a screen printing business called Ashbury Images, which together generate $3 million in annual revenue; that is, 50% of New Door's annual expenses (New Door Ventures, 2016).

Another Bay Area organization, Juma Ventures, boasts similar outcomes. The organization began in 1993 with the purchase of a single Ben & Jerry's franchise ice cream shop in San Francisco, and today, the organization owns social enterprise businesses in sports arenas around the United States, again generating revenue equal to about 50% of their annual budget of $6 million (Juma Ventures, 2015a, 2015b). These numbers suggest that social enterprise may be a highly cost-effective intervention, provided that sufficient benefits can be documented for participating youth over time. Some of these youth social enterprise organizations incorporate other innovative components, which merit mentioning. For example, Juma Ventures provides extensive college-readiness and financial literacy training, and matches students' savings two-to-one, helping them to save significant amounts of money for their higher education (Juma Ventures, 2015b). Given the documented positive relationship between educational attainment and long-term earnings (Naccarato et al., 2010), Juma's model seems likely to lead to long-term improvements in self-sufficiency for its participants.

Potential Recommendations for Future Steps in Research to Inform Practitioners, Scholars, and Policy-Makers across Multiple Disciplines

The experiences of youth living in out-of-home care are specifically and qualitatively different from the experiences of youth living with their family. Further, children and youth who have lived in out-of-home care feel that difference very keenly. Each of these young people has been identified as requiring a change of living arrangements from their home to a government-sponsored and approved foster home. Because foster children are an identified, distinct, and therefore readily trackable group, there is a significant amount of research conducted regarding these young people. The available research documents that children and youth who have been in out-of-home care have more risk factors when they enter care, and as a result of their time in the foster care system, encounter additional risk factors.

Human capital theory suggests a policy goal of intervention so that upon leaving the foster care system, foster youth have accumulated the same level of human capital as their cohort in the general population. If successful, the theory goes, foster youth would then be as enabled as youth in the general population to independently obtain gainful employment, contribute to the economy, and earn wages.

The current policy to extend foster care beyond age 18 and related interventions to provide continuing support until age 21 for eligible foster youth, including supports for housing, health care, and schooling, are ripe for evaluation, utilizing human capital accumulation theory. As discussed above, a small number of studies have already been conducted, in an attempt to gauge the success and efficacy of continuing support for youth who would otherwise "age out" of the foster care system at age 18. Additional studies of the policy to continue to support and assist foster youth beyond age 18 using human capital accumulation theory are not only important, but appear to be critical to understanding how best to help foster youth utilize available resources in order to overcome the obstacles and barriers to healthy and productive adulthoods.

While providing additional assistance to foster youth who would otherwise *age out* of the system is a laudable and valuable policy, and will likely be demonstrated to result in greater capital accumulation, the success of this new policy and related interventions may be limited in the short term. This may be the practical outcome since, as analyzed under human capital and social capital theory, foster youth have reached 18 without best practice targeted interventions designed to increase social capital and human capital.

As practitioners, researchers, policy-makers, and funders move forward to implement policies and interventions to better assist and support foster youth to achieve healthy and productive adulthoods, we may do well to consider utilizing human capital and social capital theories to inform interventions to best enable foster youth to be prepared to attend and succeed in post-secondary education. Important moral and practical considerations moving forward are whether interventions will be designed to support each foster child to gain as much human capital as is possible for that child; or whether interventions should be and might be targeted to specific youth who are more likely to successfully complete an undergraduate degree and accumulate more human capital than in the previous scenario. In either case, long-term strategies to try to better the circumstances of foster youth, and longitudinal studies to test success and efficacy, are critical in our attempt to address and develop opportunities, resources, and strengths, and to mitigate any long-standing obstacles and barriers to healthy and productive adulthood.

Conclusion

Human capital has long held sway in economics. What is important today for foster youth is how to develop human capital in the new economy. Aging out and experiencing a positive transition into adulthood arguably was easier when low-skilled, manufacturing jobs dominated the economy. Not so now. Post-secondary education is a practical necessity, which raises the ante for foster youth and those who want and need to serve them. Thus, the population prioritized in this chapter must be served by a high school education that is technologically advanced. So, given the primacy of advanced education in the new economy, operationalized here as human capital accumulation, what are the consequences of continuing not to serve this population?

The objective of any intervention is to determine the positive effects within a short period of time. Intuitively, then, it would seem that if a youth was not focused predominantly upon their troubled past, and simultaneously was able to succeed at building a competitive education, they would be better equipped to be productive members of society. However, this would then require clearly stated programmatic goals, which focus upon labor productivity. The success of such an analysis would be benefited by the increased investigation by those in fields that do not typically address the issues of foster youth. Such diverse fields as economics, science, and engineering frequently develop similar models and methodologies of analysis within their own areas of interest; yet these models and methodologies can be designed to effectively measure human capital accumulation. Such cross-discipline approaches to examining the realities faced by foster youth could only help practitioners and researchers to bring the experiences of foster youth into mainstream consideration. From both social and economic perspectives, we would all be better off if we began to invest in the development of strategies to facilitate human capital accumulation in the areas of employment, education, health, economic capacity, and effective and supportive relationships.

Note

1   For-profit vocational training schools are currently losing their credibility (Hood, 2015a, 2015b).

References

Anda, R. F., Butchart, A., Felitti, V., & Brown, D. (2010). Building a framework of global surveillance of the public health implications of adverse childhood experiences. *American Journal of Preventive Medicine, 39*(1), 93–98.
Arnesen, E. (2007). *Encyclopedia of U.S. labor and working-class history.* New York, NY: Routledge.
Barrat, V. X., & Berliner, B. (2013). *The invisible achievement gap, Part 1: Education outcomes of students in foster care in California's public schools.* San Francisco: WestEd.
Barth, R. P. (1990). On their own: The experiences of youth after foster care. *Child and Adolescent Social Work, 7*(5), 419–440.
Becker, G. S. (1964). *Human capital.* Chicago: University of Chicago Press.
Becker, G. S. (1993). *Human capital: A theoretical and empirical analysis with special reference to education* (3rd ed.). Chicago: University of Chicago Press.
Blome, W.W. (1997). What happens to foster kids: Educational experiences of a random sample of foster care youth and a matched group of non-foster care youth. *Child and Adolescent Social Work Journal, 14*(1), 41–53.
Boix, C. (2010). Origins and persistence of economic inequality. *Annual Review of Political Science, 13*, 489–516.
Bruce, E. J., Naccarato, T., Hopson, L., & Morrelli, K. (2010). Providing a sound educational framework for foster youth: A proposed research agenda. *Journal of Public Child Welfare, 4*(2), 219–240.
Caspi, A., Wright, B. E., Moffitt, T., & Silva, P. (1998). Early failure in the labor market: Childhood and adolescent predictors in the transition to adulthood. *American Sociological Review, 63*(3), 424–451.
Christeson, W., Taggart, A. P., & Messner-Zidell, S. (2009). *Ready, willing, and unable to serve.* Washington, DC: Mission Readiness: Military Leaders for Kids. Retrieved from http://cdn.missionreadiness.org/NATEE1109.pdf

Coleman, J. S. (1990). *Foundations of social theory.* Cambridge, MA: Belknap Press of Harvard University Press.

Cook, R. (1994). Are we helping foster care youth prepare for their future? *Children and Youth Services Review, 16*(3–4), 213–229.

Corso, P. S., Edwards, V. J., Fang, X., & Mercy, J. A. (2008). Health related quality of life among adults who experienced maltreatment during childhood. *American Journal of Public Health, 98*(6), 1094–1100.

Courtney, M. E., & Barth, R. P. (1996). Pathways of older adolescents out of foster care: Implications for independent living services. *Social Work, 41*(1), 75–83.

Courtney, M. E., & Dworsky, A. (2006). Early outcomes for young adults transitioning from out-of-home care in the USA. *Child and Family Social Work, 11*, 209–219.

Courtney, M. E., Dworsky, A., Cusick, G., Havlicek, J., Perez, A., & Keller, T. (2007). *Midwest Evaluation of the Adult Functioning of Former Foster Youth: Outcomes at age 21.* Chicago: Chapin Hall at the University of Chicago.

Courtney, M. E., Dworsky, A., & Napolitano, L. (2013). *Providing foster care for young adults: Early implications of California's Fostering Connection Act.* Chicago: Chapin Hall at the University of Chicago.

Courtney, M. E., Dworsky, A., Ruth, G., Keller, T., Havlicek, J., & Bost, N. (2005). *Midwest Evaluation of the Adult Functioning of Former Foster Youth: Outcomes at age 19.* Chicago: Chapin Hall at the University of Chicago.

Courtney, M. E., Piliavin, I., Grogan-Kaylor, A., & Nesmith, A. (2001). Foster youth transitions to adulthood: A longitudinal view of youth leaving care. *Child Welfare, 6*, 685–717.

Courtney, M. E., Terao, S., & Bost, T. (2004). *Midwest Evaluation of the Adult Functioning of Former Foster Youth: Conditions of youth preparing to leave state care in Illinois.* Chicago: Chapin Hall Center for Children at the University of Chicago.

Cromer, D. (2007). Through no fault of their own: Reasserting a child's right to family connectedness in the child welfare system. *Family Law Quarterly, 41*(1), 181–195.

Cruces, G., Ham, A., & Viollaz, M. (2012). Scarring effects of youth unemployment and informality: Evidence from Argentina and Brazil [Monograph]. La Plata, Argentina: University of La Plata, Center for Distributive, Labor, and Social Studies.

Dodge, D. (2003, May). Human capital, early childhood development, and economic growth: An economist's perspective. Keynote address delivered at the Sparrow Lake Alliance's Annual Meeting. Retrieved from www.child-encyclopedia.com/importance-early-childhood-development/according-experts/human-capital-early-childhood-development.

Drake, R. E., Bond, G. R., & Becker, D. R. (2012). *Individual placement and support: An evidence-based approach to supported employment.* New York, NY: Oxford University Press.

Drake, R. E., Bond, G. R., Goldman, H. H., Hogan, M. E., & Karakus, M. (2016). Individual placement and support services boost employment for people with serious mental illnesses, but funding is lacking. *Health Affairs, 35*(6), 1098–1105.

Dworsky, A., & Havlicek, J. (2010). *An employment training program and job placement program for foster youth in Cook County, Illinois.* Chicago: Chapin Hall at the University of Chicago.

Fabian, E. S. (2007). Urban youth with disabilities: Factors affecting transition employment. *Rehabilitation Counseling Bulletin, 50*(3), 130–138.

Ferguson, K. M. (2013). Using the Social Enterprise Intervention (SEI) and Individual Placement and Support (IPS) models to improve employment and clinical outcomes of homeless youth with mental illness. *Social Work in Mental Health, 11*(5), 473–495.

Fernandez-Alcantara, A. L. (2012). *Vulnerable youth: Employment and job training programs* (CRS Report No. R40929). Washington, DC: Congressional Research Service.

Garcia-Iriarte, E., Balcazar, F., & Taylor-Ritzler, T. (2007). Analysis of case managers' support of youth with disabilities transitioning from school to work. *Journal of Vocational Rehabilitation, 26*, 129–140.

Hamilton, S. F., & Hamilton, M. A. (2003). School, work, and emerging adulthood. In J. J. Arnett & J. L. Tanner (Eds.), *Emerging adults in America: Coming of age in the 21st century* (pp. 257–277). Washington, DC: American Psychological Association.

Haskins, R., Wulczyn, F., & Webb, M. B. (2007). Using high quality research to improve child protection practice: An overview. In R. Haskin, F. Wulczyn, & M. B. Webb (Eds.), *Child protection: Using research to improve policy and practice* (pp. 1–33). Washington, DC: Brookings Institute Press.

Heckman, J. J. (1974). Effects of child-care programs on women's work effort. *The Journal of Political Economy, 82*(2, Part 2: Marriage, Family Human Capital, and Fertility), S136–S163.

Heckman, J. J. (2000). Policies to foster human capital. *Research in Economics, 54*(1), 3–56.

Hernandez, L., & Naccarato, T. (2010). Scholarship and supports available to foster care alumni: A study of 12 programs across the U.S. *Children and Youth Services Review, 32*(5), 758–766.

Hines, A. M., Merdinger, J., & Wyatt, P. (2005). Former foster youth attending college: Resilience and the transition to young adulthood. *American Journal of Orthopsychiatry, 75*(3), 381–394.

Hood, J. R. (2015a, October 20). Education Department tightens screws on ITT: The for-profit college faces stricter financial oversight. *Consumer Affairs*. Retrieved from www.consumeraffairs.com/for-profit-college-and-student-loan-news?page=2

Hood, J. R. (2015b, November 18). More Corinthian College students eligible for debt relief: Joint investigation by feds and California finds more evidence that placement rates were misrepresented. *Consumer Affairs*. Available at www.consumeraffairs.com/news/index/2015/11/

Hook, J. L., & Courtney, M. E. (2011). Employment outcomes of former foster youth as young adults: The importance of human, personal, and social capital. *Children and Youth Services Review, 33*(10), 1855–1865.

Institute for Educational Leadership. (2008). *Foster Youth Demonstration Project: Final evaluation report*. Retrieved from www.ncwd-youth.info/assets/background/casey_foster_care_full_report_july_2008.pdf

Julian, T., & Kominski, R. (2011). *Education and synthetic work-life earnings estimates*. American Community Survey Reports (ACS-14). Washington, DC: U.S. Census Bureau. Retrieved from www.census.gov/prod/2011pubs/acs-14.pdf

Juma Ventures. (2015a). *2015 Annual Report*. Retrieved from www.juma.org/2015-annual-report

Juma Ventures. (2015b). *Our mission & history*. Retrieved from www.juma.org/our-mission-history

Koball, H., Dion, R., Gothro, A., Bardos, M., Dworsky, A., Lansing, J., . . . Manning, A. E. (2011). *Synthesis of research and resources to support at-risk youth* (OPRE Report No. 2011-22). Washington, DC: Office of Planning, Research, and Evaluation, Administration for Children and Families, U.S. Department of Health & Human Services.

LaLonde, R. J. (1995). The promise of public sector-sponsored training programs. *Journal of Economic Perspectives, 9*(2), 149–168.

Levitan, S. A. (1975). Job Corps experience with manpower training. *Monthly Labor Review, 58*(10), 3–11.

Loury, G. C. (1981). Intergenerational transfers and the distribution of earnings. *Econometrica, 49*(4), 843–867.

McClanahan, W. S., Sipe, C. L., & Smith, T. J. (2004). *Enriching summer work: An evaluation of the Summer Career Exploration Program*. Philadelphia, PA: Public/Private Ventures.

McMillen, C., Auslander, W., Elze, D., White, T., & Thompson, R. (2003). Educational experiences and aspirations of older foster youth in foster care. *Child Welfare, 82*(4), 475–495.

McMillen, J. C., & Tucker, J. (1999). The status of older adolescents at exit from out-of-home care. *Child Welfare, 78*(3), 339–359.

McWhirter, J. J., McWhirter, B. T., McWhirter, E. H., & McWhirter, R. J. (2013). *At-risk youth: A comprehensive response*. Belmont, CA: Brooks/Cole.

Montgomery, P., Donkoh, C., & Underhill, K. (2006). Independent living programs for young people leaving the care system: The state of the evidence. *Children and Youth Services Review, 28*, 1435–1448.

Mroz, T., & Savage, T. (2001). *The long-term effects of youth unemployment* [Monograph]. Washington, DC: Employment Policies Institute.

Naccarato, T., Brophy, M., & Courtney, M. E. (2010). Employment outcomes of foster youth: The results of the Midwest Evaluation of the Adult Functioning of Foster Youth. *Children and Youth Services Review, 32*, 551–559.

Naccarato, T., Brophy, M., & Hernandez, L. (2008). The foster youth housing crisis: Literature, legislation and looking ahead. *St. John's Journal of Legal Commentary, 23*(2), 429–445.

Naccarato, T., Brophy, M., & LaClair, K. (2013). Summer engagement for at-risk youth: Preliminary outcomes from the New York State Workforce Development Study. *Child & Adolescent Social Work Journal, 30*(6), 519–533.

Naccarato, T., & DeLorenzo, E. (2008). Transitional youth services: Practice implications from a systematic review. *Child and Adolescent Social Work Journal, 25*(4), 287–308.

Naccarato, T., & Park, K. (2010). Educational goal advancement of foster youth and the Independent Living Skills program. *Journal of Public Child Welfare, 3*(4), 372–390.

New Door Ventures. (2016). *2016 impact report*. Retrieved from www.newdoor.org/wp-content/uploads/2017/03/New-Door-Impact-Report-2016-1.pdf

Nollan, K. A., & Downs, A. C. (Eds.). (1999). *Preparing youth for long-term success: Proceedings from the Casey Family program National Independent Living Forum*. Washington, DC: Child Welfare League of America Press.

Okpych, N. J., & Courtney, M. E. (2014). Does education pay for youth formerly in foster care? Comparison of employment outcomes with a national sample. *Children and Youth Services Review, 43*, 18–28.

Okpych, N. J., Courtney, M. E., & Charles, P. (2015). *Youth and caseworker perspectives on older adolescents in California foster care: Youths' education status and services*. Chicago: Chapin Hall at the University of Chicago.

Osgood, D. W., Foster, E. M., & Courtney, M. E. (2010). Vulnerable populations and the transition to adulthood. *Future of the Children, 20*(1), 209–229.

O'Sullivan, R., Mugglestone, K., & Allison, T. (2014). *In this together: The hidden cost of young adult unemployment.* Washington, DC: Young Invincibles.

Pecora, P. J., Kessler, R. C., O'Brien, K., White, C. R., Williams, J., Hiripi, E., ... Herrick, M. A. (2006). Educational and employment outcomes of adults formerly placed in foster care: Results from the Northwest Foster Care Alumni Study. *Children and Youth Services Review, 28,* 1459–1481.

P.L. 88-452: Economic Opportunity Act of 1964. (1964). Retrieved from www.gpo.gov/fdsys/pkg/STATUTE-78/pdf/STATUTE-78-Pg508.pdf

P.L. 99-272: Consolidated Omnibus Budget Reconciliation Act of 1985; Title XII – Section C: Independent Living Program. (1986). Retrieved from http://thomas.loc.gov/cgi-bin/bdquery/z?d099:HR03128:|TOM:/bss/d099query.html|

P.L. 105-220: Workforce Investment Act [WIA] of 1998. (1998). Retrieved from www.gpo.gov/fdsys/pkg/PLAW-105publ220/content-detail.html

P.L. 106-169: Foster Care Independence Act of 1999—Chafee Foster Care Independence Program [CFCIP]. (1999). Retrieved from www.gpo.gov/fdsys/pkg/PLAW-106publ169/html/PLAW-106publ169.htm

P.L. 107-133: Promoting Safe and Stable Families Amendments of 2001. (2002). Retrieved from www.congress.gov/107/plaws/publ133/PLAW-107publ133.pdf

P.L. 110-351: Fostering Connections to Success and Increasing Adoptions Act of 2008. (2008) . Retrieved from www.govtrack.us/congress/bills/110/hr6893

P.L. 113-128: Workforce Innovation and Opportunity Act [WIOA] of 2014. (2014). Available at www.congress.gov/bill/113th-congress/house-bill/803

Rawlins, V. L. (1971). Job Corps: The urban center as a training facility. *The Journal of Human Resources, 6*(2), 221–235.

Salmond, J. A. (1967). *The Civilian Conservation Corps, 1933–1942: A New Deal case study.* Durham, NC: Duke University Press.

Scannapieco, M., Schagrin, J., & Scannapieco, T. (1995). Independent living programs: Do they make a difference? *Child and Adolescent Social Work, 12*(5), 381–389.

Schmillen, A., & Umkehrer, M. (2013). *The scars of youth: Effects of early-career unemployment on future unemployment experience* (IAB Discussion Paper No. 201306). Nuremberg, Germany: Institute for Employment Research.

Schochet, P. Z., Burghardt, J., & McConnell, S. (2008). Does Job Corps work? Impact findings from the National Job Corps Study. *American Economic Review, 98*(5), 1864–1886.

Schochet, P. Z., Burghardt, J., & McConnell, S. (2006). *National Job Corps Study and longer-term follow-up study: Impact and benefit-cost findings using survey and summary earnings records data.* Princeton, NJ: Mathematica Policy Research, Inc.

Schonert-Reichl, K. A. (2000). *Children and youth at risk: Some conceptual considerations.* Vancouver: University of British Columbia.

Schultz, T. W. (1961). Investments in human capital. *American Economic Review, 51*(1), 1–17.

Stewart, C. J., Kum, H. C., Barth, R. P., & Duncan, D. F. (2014). Former foster youth: Employment outcomes up to age 30. *Children and Youth Services Review, 36,* 220–229.

Teachman, J. D., Paasch, K., & Carver, K. (1997). Social capital and the generation of human capital. *Social Forces, 75*(4), 1343–1359.

Trattner, W. I. (1970). *Crusade for the children: A history of the National Child Labor Committee and child labor reform in America.* Chicago: Quadrangle Books.

Trombley, W. (2003). *The rising price of higher education.* San José, CA: The National Center for Public Policy and Higher Education, Higher Education Policy Institute. Retrieved from www.highereducation.org/reports/affordability_supplement/affordability_1.shtml

U.S. Department of Health & Human Services. (1999). *Title IV-E independent living programs: A decade in review.* Washington, DC: U.S. Government Printing Office.

U.S. Department of Health & Human Services (Office of the Administration for Children and Families, Children's Bureau). (2014). *National Youth in Transition Database data brief #4: Comparing outcomes reported by young people at ages 17 and 19 in NYTD cohort 1.* Retrieved from www.acf.hhs.gov/sites/default/files/cb/nytd_data_brief_4.pdf

U.S. Department of Health & Human Services (Office of the Administration for Children and Families, Children's Bureau). (2016). *The AFCARS report. Preliminary FY 2015 estimates as of June 2016. No. 23.* Retrieved from www.acf.hhs.gov/sites/default/files/cb/afcarsreport23.pdf?

U.S. Department of Labor. (2016). *Job Corps.* Retrieved from http://www.dol.gov/general/topic/training/jobcorps

U.S. Department of Labor (Bureau of Labor Statistics). (2016a). *Unemployment rates by age, sex, and marital status, seasonally adjusted* (BLS Table A-10). Retrieved from www.bls.gov/web/empsit/cpseea10.htm

U.S. Department of Labor (Bureau of Labor Statistics). (2016b). *Unemployment rates by age, sex, and Hispanic or Latino ethnicity* (BLS Table E-16). Retrieved from www.bls.gov/web/empsit/cpsee_e16.htm

U.S. Department of Labor (Bureau of Labor Statistics). (2017). *Unemployment rate: 16 to 24 years* [BLS Data Viewer Series LNS14024887]. Retrieved from https://fred.stlouisfed.org/series/LNS14024887

U. S. Department of Labor (Employment and Training Administration). (2016). *Youth Opportunity Grants SGA*. Retrieved from www.doleta.gov/grants/sga/99-015sga.cfm

U.S. General Accounting Office. (1999). *Foster care: Effectiveness of independent living services unknown*. Retrieved from www.gao.gov/assets/230/228309.pdf

VerWys, R. J. (2016). *Social enterprise as an intervention for at risk youth: A grant proposal* (Master's thesis). California State University, Long Beach. Retrieved from https://csulb.edu/colleges/chhs/departments/social-work/documents/ePoster_VerWys.Robert_SocialEnterprise.pdf

Walker, G., & Vilella-Velez, F. (1992). *Anatomy of a demonstration: The Summer Training and Education (STEP) program from pilot through replication and postprogram*. Philadelphia, PA: Public/Private Ventures.

Weisbrod, B. A. (1962). Education and investment in human capital. *The Journal of Political Economy, 70*(5 Part 2), 106–123.

Westat, Inc. (1990). *A national evaluation of Title IV-E foster care independent living program for youth: Phase 1*. Washington, DC: Author.

Westat, Inc. (1991). *A national evaluation of Title IV-E foster care independent living program for youth: Phase 2 final report*. Washington, DC: Author.

Wilkinson, G. S. (1993). *Wide Range Achievement Test 3*. Hockessin, DE: Wide Range Inc.

Wong, K. (2014). Why social enterprise businesses are on the rise. *Leaders in Heels, December 2014*. Retrieved from http://leadersinheels.com/business/social-enterprise-businesses-rise/

Wulczyn, F. H., Barth, R. P., Yuan, Y. Y., Jones-Harden, B., & Landsverk, J. (2005). *Beyond common sense: Child welfare, child well-being, and the evidence for policy reform*. Somerset, NJ: Transaction Aldine.

Wulczyn, F. H., & Goerge, R. M. (1992). Foster care in New York and Illinois: The challenge of rapid change. *Social Service Review, 66*(2), 278–294.

Zetlin, A., & Weinberg, L. (2004). Understanding the plight of foster youth and improving their educational opportunities. *Child Abuse & Neglect, 28*(9), 917–923.

16

Access and Continuity of Transitional Living Services for Foster Youth

Mary Elizabeth Collins and Michelle Banks

Youth transitioning from foster care are a population that frequently faces great challenges, resulting in a contemporary social problem. Beginning in the mid-1980s, this problem has been acknowledged as requiring a policy response. Since that time there has been progress in developing policy supports and effective practices. Much more remains to be accomplished, however, in order to truly support youth as they make the transition from foster care into an independent adult life.

Societal understanding of the problem of youth leaving care has evolved over time as we have learned more, via research and practice, about the reality of this experience for young people (Courtney et al., 2011; Daining & DePanfilis, 2007; Pecora et al., 2006). Three developments, in particular, have influenced ways of thinking about the problems caused by lack of permanency attainment. First, there has been a shift in focus from "aging out" to "transition" from care (Collins, 2001). Aging out is abrupt and related directly to biological age. For example, historically, when youth turned 18, services and supports from the child welfare system were abruptly terminated, leaving youth on their own, typically with very little preparation (Avery & Freundlich, 2009). Transition is more normative, potentially more gradual, and not tied to a specific defined age or birthday. Recognition of the need for a more gradual transition from care has led to greater attention given to preparing youth for the transition and continuing supports after the age of 18. Further information on efforts to prepare and support youth during and after transition will be provided later in this chapter.

Second, there has been a movement from a nearly sole focus on independent living skills preparation to a more comprehensive approach tied to permanent relationships and concrete supports. Research evidence has identified the limitations of approaches focused primarily on instruction related to life skills. An early evaluation of independent living skills found a limited impact on key outcomes (Cook, 1994). A recent evaluation using a randomized design (U.S. Department of Health & Human Services [Administration for Children and Families], 2008) evaluated a 5-week life skills curriculum that involved 10 3-hour classes held twice a week in a community college setting. Competency skill areas included: education, employment, daily living skills, survival skills, choices and consequences, interpersonal/social skills, and computer/Internet skills. The evaluation found no significant impacts on outcomes related to education, employment, and housing, for example.

The inadequacy of an approach based on independent living skills training has contributed to a greater focus on developing permanent relationships and offering concrete supports related to housing, education, employment, and health care (Collins, 2004). This enhanced understanding is far more realistic, albeit difficult to implement and not yet well integrated in practice. A description of expanded supports will be provided later in this chapter. In regard to permanency, the field has distinguished between legal permanency and relational permanency. The Annie E. Casey Foundation (2012) identified legal permanency to mean that the law recognizes a child's relationship with a parenting adult. Relational permanence, on the other hand, recognizes many types of important long-term relationships that help a child or young person feel loved and connected. These relations can be with siblings, extended family, or family friends.

These critically important adults provide continuity in relationships and help youth in understanding their identity and sense of self (Samuels, 2009). Thus, existing family relationships and attachments, regardless of separation, often remain important to youth and can provide relational permanence (Frey, Cushing, Freundlich, & Brenner, 2007). A more explicit focus on facilitating and strengthening existing relationships in order to achieve a sense of relational permanence has expressed itself in increased attention related to the transitioning youth population (Cushing, Samuels, & Kerman, 2014; Greeson, 2013).

Third, there has been a recognition that the responsibility for the transition from care is not solely the responsibility of the child welfare system (Collins & Clay, 2009). There is an acknowledged need for other systems, such as education, housing, and health care, to be involved in supporting the transition and for community supports to be established. Efforts that are exclusively lodged within the child welfare system are less likely to offer the range and continuity of services that are needed for successful outcomes. Some of the efforts that involve the intersection of multiple systems will be described later in the chapter.

Key Theoretical Perspectives on Transition Out of Care

Early work on youth transition from care identified the lack of theory to guide policy and practice (Collins, 2001; Stein, 2006). While continuing further theoretical development is needed, there has been some theoretical progress that aids understanding and contributes to solutions. Best practice based on theoretical perspectives recognizes that the process of transition is often developmental, contextual, and macro-oriented.

The transition out of foster care is considered as a life transition toward independent adulthood. The newly conceptualized life stage of emerging adulthood, initially identified by Arnett (2000), captured the normative experiences of young adults which identified a more gradual movement to adulthood and widespread receipt of parental support. This perspective has been particularly helpful by providing a comparison to typical experiences of foster youth. The experiences of foster youth have often involved a sense of immediate adulthood when the state ends support and youth have little expectation of financial support from parents. This comparison with normative non-foster care experiences of achieving adulthood provided the justification for extending care and allowing youth who have left to return to care.

Integrated with life-stage models, theoretical perspectives frequently highlight attachment and relationship-based frameworks (Smith, 2011). The circumstances that bring youth into care (e.g., child abuse) and the separation from family members can affect important relationships, which has subsequent effects on relationships in later adolescent and adult stages. Risk and resilience theories (e.g., Masten, 2001) identify these disrupted or tenuous relationships as a risk factor for later development. Factors that promote resiliency, such as personal characteristics of self-regulatory skills and self-esteem (Buckner, Mezzacappa, & Beardslee, 2003) and sources of community support (Benzies & Mychasiuk, 2009) may offset the potential influence of these risk factors.

Additional theories have also been applied to youth leaving care. Collins (2015) identifies several theories that intersect at macro sociological and political levels. These include, for example, the role of young people as a political force in society (Faulkner, 2009) and the economic and social opportunities currently available for youth and young adults (Augsberger, Collins, Gecker, & Dougher, 2017). Successful transition to adulthood would certainly be enhanced in environments that provide robust educational and employment opportunities and that, overall, value young people as an important constituency in social life. Institutional forces—racism, classism, housing and job markets that constrain choices—are also powerful in influencing the life trajectory of young people in terms of achieving stability (Mortimer & Larson, 2002).

Some theoretical perspectives might also be appropriate for specific domains of risk. For example, because homelessness is a well-documented threat to this group, theories relevant to housing may be useful. In this regard, Collins and Curtis (2011) utilize the concept of the housing career as useful for tracing the ability of vulnerable young people to attain stable housing. A housing career approach takes account of the trajectory of housing settings, which can elucidate specific, influential turning points in a housing history that may be particularly amenable to intervention. Other risk domains might also benefit from analysis utilizing theories specific to the domain.

Current Child Welfare Policy Regarding Transition

Current child welfare policy regarding transition is guided by federal legislation. States, counties, and tribes, in turn, enact or revise legislation in accordance with federal legislation and issue or revise regulations for further implementation of legislation. The first formal federal policy specific to youth aging out of care was the Independent Living Initiative of 1986, an amendment to Title IV-E of the Social Security Act (1935), that allowed for federal funds to states to help adolescents in foster care, aged 16 years and older, to develop independent living skills (Consolidated Omnibus Budget Reconciliation Act of 1985). States could obtain federal funding according to a formula based on the percentage of children in the state who received federal foster care assistance. The services outlined in federal law included outreach programs for eligible youth, education and employment assistance, training in daily living skills, individual and group counseling, integration and coordination of services, and a written plan for transition to independent living for each participant. States were empowered to develop their own independent living programs and resources through flexible but limited dollars. Funding could not be used for housing assistance, however, which has always been an area of critical need for these youth. Additionally, services were limited to youth aged 16 and over whose foster care placements were reimbursed through Title IV-E. Youth in foster placements not reimbursed through Title IV-E were not eligible for the independent living services. This legislation emphasized youths' lack of skills as the critical problem limiting successful independence. Hence, the focus was primarily on the development of independent living skills (such as budgeting, obtaining a driver's license, opening bank accounts).

Two current federal child welfare policies drive state-level transition practice for youth leaving care at or beyond the age of 18. These policies are the Foster Care Independence Act (FCIA) of 1999 and the Fostering Connections to Success and Increasing Adoptions Act of 2008 (hereinafter, Fostering Connections Act). Additionally, the Adoption and Safe Families Act (ASFA) of 1997, although not specific to the transition from foster care, has an impact on the transition experience. The ASFA revised earlier legislation and emphasized improving child safety and further promoting permanency. Specific to permanency, the ASFA identified preferential options for those in foster care as: (1) safe reunification with parents or relatives; (2) adoption by relatives or another family; (3) permanent residence with relatives or another family serving as legal guardians; (4) youth connection to permanent resources via fictive kinship (considered part of their family though not related by blood or marriage) or customary adoption networks; and (5) youth safely placed in Another Planned Permanent Living Arrangement (APPLA) (Adoption and Safe Families Act of 1997). This last option has had particular implications for transitioning youth and will be discussed later. The term APPLA was created by the ASFA to replace the previous option of long-term foster care. It is considered a permanency option only when other options (e.g., reunification) have been ruled out.

The FCIA addressed several limitations of the earlier independent living policy. This legislation amended Title IV-E to provide states with more flexible funding in order to build capacity to provide services and establish a culture of practice in which youth are supported through their transition to functional independence in a way that is less tied to a specific age demarcation. This funding allowed child welfare agencies to provide services that assist youth to develop life skills, obtain employment and post-secondary education, and other tools to gain self-sufficiency. The FCIA established the Chafee Foster Care Independence Program (Foster Care Independence Act of 1999), which included: a $140 million-capped entitlement (requiring a 20 percent state match); an updated funding formula; expansion of eligibility—up to the age of 21 for those children who are likely to remain in foster care until the age of 18 and elimination of Title IV-E-funded restriction. Also, states could now use up to 30 percent of funds for housing assistance, defined in the legislation as room and board, for those youth aged between 18 and 21 who left foster care after they reached the age of 18. Use of funds to assist with housing was particularly beneficial given the risk of homelessness for the population. This housing assistance was available to those who stayed in care until their 18th birthday, thereby providing an incentive for the young person to stay connected to the system to receive this important benefit. States could also extend Medicaid health coverage, another critical concrete support, to foster youth (ages 18 to 21) who were in out-of-home placement on their 18th birthday. Other provisions focused on inclusion of young people in their case planning, funds for federal evaluation and training, and a requirement to develop a data collection system to track the independent living services and outcomes.

The purposes of the Chafee program (Foster Care Independence Act of 1999) were specified as: (1) to identify children who are expected to be in foster care to age 18 and help them make a transition to self-sufficiency; (2) to help these children receive the education, training, and services necessary to obtain employment; (3) to help them prepare for and enter post-secondary training and education institutions; (4) to provide them with personal and emotional support when aging out of foster care; and (5) to provide a range of services and support for former foster care recipients between the ages of 18 and 21 to further youth efforts to achieve self-sufficiency. The states, therefore, could use the funding for activities to achieve these purposes.

Chafee funding could be used to serve three eligible groups: (1) youth in foster care who are likely to remain in care until they are at least 18 years old; (2) former foster youth who left foster care when they were aged 18 or older; and (3) former foster youth who exited care for adoption or to live with a relative legal guardian when they were at least 16 years old. Eligibility for both groups of youth formerly in foster care extended until their 21st birthday. States had discretion in regard to the age limit for services up to age 21.

In concert with the focus on permanency established in the ASFA, the FCIA included a statement that establishing permanency for these youth should remain the priority. The FCIA, for example, explicitly stated that independent living services are not an alternative to adoption. A critical gap in regard to permanency, however, was that the legislation and its programs continued to make life skills training paramount in the utilization of funding and provided no specific focus on assisting youth to connect with family members or other adults who can provide permanency.

The Promoting Safe and Stable Families Amendments of 2001 added a new purpose to the Chafee Foster Care Independence Program; the amendments added support for post-secondary attainment through the Chafee Education and Training Voucher (ETV) program (Foster Care Independence Act of 1999). Prior to this, some states had developed a tuition waiver program for foster children in their states. The ETV program, a federal effort, provides resources to states to make available vouchers for post-secondary training and education to youth aging out of the foster care system, or to youth adopted from public foster care after the age of 16. States may allow youth to remain eligible for the voucher program until they attain 23 years of age as long as they are enrolled in a post-secondary education or training program and are making satisfactory progress toward completion of that program. The voucher is to be used for the cost of attendance at an institution of higher education as defined in the Higher Education Act of 1965, and can be up to $5,000 per year for each student. Funds can be used for post-secondary expenses such as tuition, room and board, books, transportation, and childcare. Financial assistance with childcare may be particularly important for the foster care population. Rates of pregnancy are higher for foster youth leaving care (ages 17 to 19) than for the general population (Dworsky & Courtney, 2010). Therefore, the ability of some female youth to attend higher education may be precluded without this childcare assistance.

The Fostering Connections Act, signed into law on October 7, 2008, included three provisions that affect older youth in foster care. First, youth 16 and older who were adopted or placed in a legal guardianship after the age of 16 can remain eligible for Chafee-funded independent living programs and ETV assistance. This eliminated a potential disincentive to adoption and guardianship. Second, young adults aged 18 to 21 can remain eligible for support under Title IV-E if the state chooses to continue to receive federal matching funds for licensed placements for young adults up to the age of 21. This can include supervised independent living settings for youth. The Title IV-E eligibility provision also allows states to continue to provide adoption subsidies and kinship guardianship subsidies on behalf of youth over the age of 16 until the youth is 19, 20, or 21 years old (depending on the state). Continued eligibility for Title IV-E reimbursement requires that the young adult be in school, or employed at least 80 hours a month, or participating in a program leading to employment readiness. Youth may remain eligible if they are unable to participate in any of these activities when they have a documented medical condition. The third provision of the FCA that affects transitioning youth is the requirement that caseworkers create a transition plan for youth at least 90 days before their 18th birthday (or other emancipation date). The plan should be individualized for each youth, involve the youth/young adult, and identify appropriate resources for housing, education, employment, health care, mentoring and other needed supports.

Under the Fostering Connections Act (2008), states are provided with Title IV-E reimbursement funding for fostering youth after the age of 18, and are provided with policy and practice directives for care prior to and at discharge. The Fostering Connections Act requires states submitting for Title IV-E reimbursement to provide transition and permanency planning for foster youth aged 16 and older. The success of these transition plans may involve or result in youth and young adults needing to access other critical systems in order to reach their personal goals and maintain their health, safety, and well-being. Some systems, discussed below, are housing, secondary and post-secondary education, and workforce investment. While navigating these systems can prove challenging for clients, social workers, and caregivers, knowing where the systems intersect and what policies are in place to serve the population can be critical to the successful execution of a transition plan.

Intersection of Transitional Living Services with Other Critical Systems

As noted, transition planning compliant with the Fostering Connections Act of 2008 must address a number of domains including housing, education, and employment. Below we pay specific attention to these areas.

Housing

Transition plans need only be as detailed as the young adult requests them to be, which could result in a plan that lacks depth and adequate services. Due to the multiple complex needs of foster youth, including mental health issues, trauma, and histories of unstable placement and sometimes running away, they need support to successfully connect with housing programs (Dworsky, Dillman, Dion, Coffee-Borden, & Rosenau, 2012). If young adults or those serving them are not identifying the need for adequate housing assistance during transition planning, the transition plan may prove ineffective. Homelessness is a very real threat for this population. Data from the National Youth in Transition Database (NYTD) show that nineteen percent of 19 year olds reported having been homeless at some point within the past 2 years (NYTD, 2014a).

Under the FCIA, states can elect to use up to 30 percent of funds on housing for youth discharged from care over the age of 18 until the age of 21. The FCIA also funds the ETV program which can assist post-secondary students from foster care with housing costs that are part of the cost of attendance at a college or vocational training program. When considering the ages and rates at which former foster youth are experiencing homelessness, the FCIA alone does not meet the demand and many youth are leaving care without adequate housing (Collins, 2015). Some additional federal programs to address housing needs for this population are explained below.

The Homeless Emergency Assistance and Rapid Transition to Housing Act (HEARTH) of 2009 funds the U.S. Department of Housing and Urban Development's (hereinafter, USDHUD) Continuum of Care Program. This program

> is designed to promote communitywide commitment to the goal of ending homelessness; provide funding for efforts by nonprofit providers, and State and local governments to quickly rehouse homeless individuals and families while minimizing the trauma and dislocation caused to homeless individuals, families, and communities by homelessness; promote access to and effect utilization of mainstream programs by homeless individuals and families; and optimize self-sufficiency among individuals and families experiencing homelessness.
>
> (USDHUD, 2017, p. 1)

In the program, youth have access to the Rapid Rehousing Model, in which the need to secure stable housing is a priority over other supportive resources such as employment or education programs; these can be provided after an individual is housed. In the Continuum of Care Model, the USDHUD defines youth as persons under the age of 25. The USDHUD strives to move youth toward permanent housing in short time frames, offers limited financial assistance, and case management and support services. Given that youth leaving foster care frequently are struggling with trauma and other mental health issues, the case management and youth-focused programming are a critical component of the program model for this population. The USDHUD has found promising programs utilizing this model, including the Valley Youth House in Pennsylvania which has a lesbian, gay, bisexual, transgender, or questioning/queer (LGBTQ) youth targeted program (USDHUD, 2015).

The USDHUD's Family Unification Program (FUP) was created by the Cranston-Gonzalez Affordable Housing Act of 1990. The FUP has a demonstration component for former foster youth who left care after the age of 16. Under Memoranda of Understanding between public housing and child welfare agencies, these youth may receive Housing Choice Vouchers. Housing Choice Vouchers are vouchers provided via a public housing agency to an individual or family, and can be used to secure private housing through a landlord in many different kinds of setting (apartment building, townhouse, single family home). Depending on the income of the family or individual utilizing the voucher, a portion of the rent is paid to the landlord by the public housing agency (USDHUD, 2016a).

The FUP vouchers are provided to two target populations. The first comprises families in which there is a risk of child welfare involvement or child placement out of the home mainly due to housing challenges. These vouchers have income considerations, but do not have a time limit. The second is young adults transitioning from foster care. The FUP vouchers for this second target population consider income and are limited to 36 months (USDHUD, 2016b). The FUP requires that vouchers for young adults be accompanied by support services. These support services are often funded by the FCIA. Additionally, FCIA funds can also be used for start-up costs such as utility installation, moving costs, and furniture (National Center for Housing and Child Welfare, 2013).

Some states utilize the FUP voucher to help a youth who is waiting for a non-FUP Housing Choice Voucher which does not have the same time limitation (Pergamit, McDaniel, & Hawkins,

2012). New York City includes former foster youth as a population granted priority access to Housing Choice Vouchers that are not time-limited. There are limited vouchers provided to states under the FUP Program; currently only 14 percent of FUP vouchers awarded nationally go to youth transitioning from foster care (Dion, Dworsky, Kauff, & Kleinman, 2014).

In some circumstances, youth with FUP vouchers may receive extensions to the time limit via Move to Work demonstration programs. In Move to Work, 39 public housing authorities are granted flexibility with USDHUD programs, such as FUP, to encourage innovation and greater cost-effectiveness. In Massachusetts, if youth from foster care utilizing FUP vouchers need more time with their voucher in order to complete an educational or vocational training program, they may apply to the Young Adult Transition to Success Program (YTTSP), funded by Move to Work (Commonwealth of Massachusetts Department of Housing and Community Development, 2016). If a youth needs an extension to their FUP voucher, the youth can be approved for YTTSP, which will allow them to stay in their apartment and pay toward their rent on a sliding scale until they complete their educational program or turn 23, whichever comes first. In this model, FUP and YTTSP voucher recipients must participate in life skills training and transition planning with an Adolescent Outreach Worker. The Outreach Worker is a transition specialist who works with the youth to develop goals and supports the youth in performing tasks to achieve these goals via weekly visits. The Outreach Worker service component is funded in Massachusetts by the FCIA (Massachusetts Department of Children and Families, n.d.).

Another source of housing-focused supports is the Family & Youth Services Bureau (2017) grant funds given directly to community service agencies via the Reconnecting Homeless Youth Act (RHYA) of 2008. These grants fund residential treatment for runaway and homeless youth and provide for programs serving homeless pregnant young adult women. Former foster care youth who need housing qualify for RHYA funds. A 2012 study of the role that the FCIA has in housing former foster youth pointed out that youth discharged from foster care are more likely to use RHYA programs than they are to access funding such as FCIA through the child welfare system (Pergamit et al., 2012). These funds and programs can be utilized together as youth who are in RHYA programs remain eligible for FCIA funding through to age 21 including the ETV program, which in some circumstances can be utilized until the age of 23. Youth may need the support and knowledge of caseworkers in either system in order to access the other. Collaboration among caseworkers may also be needed to maximize the benefits of both programs.

Secondary Education

The Fostering Connections Act also requires child welfare transition plans to address education. In addition, the legislation aims to promote educational stability for foster youth by protecting the rights of foster youth to remain in their own school districts even when they are placed in an out-of-district living situation. A major aspect of this service is providing transportation to students or reimbursement for transportation to caregivers who may transport students. Furthermore, when it is not in a child's best interest to remain in the same school, the Fostering Connections Act requires child welfare agencies to facilitate enrollment in a new school.

The Every Student Succeeds Act (ESSA) of 2015 is an education law and thus applies to schools. However, the ESSA addresses foster care students in a number of areas, including school stability provisions. The ESSA requires educational authorities to designate a point of contact for foster care students. In addition, whereas the Fostering Connections Act requires child welfare agencies to collaborate with education agencies, the ESSA requires collaboration of education agencies with child welfare. A successful collaboration requires both agencies to work together. A legal mandate that puts the responsibility of problem solving on one system over the other may compromise the spirit of collaboration. Thus, the ESSA seeks to provide a balance of responsibility within the two systems.

With reference to special education, the Individuals with Disabilities Education Act (IDEA) of 2004 impacts this population greatly, as studies show that 30 percent to 40 percent of foster youth receive special education services (van Wingerden, Emerson, & Ichikawa, 2002). Under the IDEA, students with disabilities are entitled to transition planning provided by the school district as part of their Individualized Education Program (IEP) (2007). The goal of the IDEA transition plan is to yield positive outcomes for a student after high school completion, based on the student's goals and strengths. In this effort, it is required that schools address academic preparation, community experience, development of vocational and independent living objectives, and, if applicable, a functional vocational evaluation. Many of these same domains are also required for foster youth via the Fostering Connections Act. Documentation of transition planning for eligible students through the IDEA begins at the age of 16 and is reviewed annually.

Transition plans that are compliant with both the Fostering Connections Act and the IDEA must be revisited and updated on a regular basis. Post-secondary schools must accommodate students with disabilities, including learning disabilities. An IEP that is updated through a student's last year of high school can prove useful to students who need to provide documentation of a disability to a college disabilities office in order to secure needed accommodations.

Post-Secondary Education

Foster care students benefit from post-secondary system programming that specifically targets them, as well as programs for the general student population who are economically or socially disadvantaged. We have already identified the ETV program above. This program, funded by the FCIA, provides vouchers to students who were in foster care when they reached the age of 18 as well as students who were placed in a guardianship arrangement with kin after the age of 16. The vouchers, which can grant students up to $5,000 annually, may be combined with federal and state financial aid packages, as well as FCIA funds and other resources. Students must apply for the voucher prior to the age of 21. If students are utilizing the voucher by the age of 21, the voucher can continue to be used until the age of 23.

The Higher Education Opportunity Act of 2008 includes specific language that encourages programming for foster youth and affords foster youth and former foster youth the ability to take advantage of support programs. The Act funds TRIO programs: the goal is to transition "disadvantaged" students, including students from foster care, from middle and high school into baccalaureate programs. The TRIO programs are so named because there were three original subprograms that fell under this umbrella—including Upward Bound, Talent Search, and Gear Up programs that rested in local school districts. Foster youth have access to these three programs and the other similar programs that have since been developed under TRIO. All of these programs provide academic and social support as well as economic and fiscal literacy services and other training for life skills development at the secondary and post-secondary level.

Workforce Investment

Although employment is an area that must be addressed as part of the Fostering Connections Act, foster youth struggle with unemployment and underemployment (Hook & Courtney, 2010). The Workforce Innovation and Opportunity Act (WIOA) of 2014 funds youth programming to help youth gain job training and other employment skills. Foster youth have emerged as a target population for youth-serving programs funded by the WIOA.

Job Corps is one of the oldest labor-funded youth programs dating back to 1964 (Job Corps, 2017). Now funded out of the WIOA, Job Corps currently exists in all 50 states. Foster youth aged 16 to 24 are a target population for Job Corps. All Job Corps programs provide on-campus housing, a critical need for transition-age youth who are without adequate education and/or employment skills to support stable housing.

The WIOA requires that state-level Workforce Investment Boards (WIBs) have the participation of youth-serving professionals to inform program development. The WIOA's Youth Activities Formula Grant program (U.S. Department of Labor, 2017) is provided to local agencies via WIBs and includes secondary educational support components, life skills development, seasonal work opportunities, and paid internships and job-shadowing opportunities. Participating youth must be between the ages of 14 and 24.

YouthBuild, a vocational training program focusing on civic engagement and construction skills, received its first federal grant funding through USDHUD (YouthBuild, 2014). In 2006, the funding was transferred to the U.S. Department of Labor where it currently rests. Community colleges, community-based agencies, and state agencies receive grants to combine job training with counseling and leadership development. Foster youth who are aging out of the foster care system are among the target populations for YouthBuild. In its *2014 Annual Report*, YouthBuild notes that since 2012, it has funded more than 190 programs in 31 different states (YouthBuild, 2014).

Summary: Intersection and Complications, Gaps, and Redundancies

Transition plans that rest within the child welfare system are no longer maintained or updated after a youth or young adult leaves the system. Transition services such as those that rest in the FCIA have limited resources that expire very early after the age of majority. Looking outside child welfare at programs that share the domains of the Fostering Connections Act transition plan is critical to serving youth and realizing the shared outcomes that cross these federally-supported youth-serving systems. On the one hand, it is helpful that other services systems, agencies, and programs are a part of assuring a successful transition. On the other hand, the increased complexity can result in substantial variation in state implementation of policies, differences across localities, and difficulties in coordination of services.

Interstate Variation and the National Landscape

Most of the information and knowledge related to youth leaving care has been generated at state and local levels. These studies identified some of the services that are provided for transition. For example, Collins and Ward (2011) reported on the services received by a sample of youth who had aged out (N=96) in Massachusetts. Services received after the age of 18 included: help accessing health care (62%), housing assistance (44%), assistance completing high school or gaining a GED (41%), employment services (33%), life skills training (28%), help reconnecting to family (21%), and "other" services (38%).

A critical information resource, the National Youth in Transition Database (NYTD), launched in 2010, has begun to produce some needed information to understand the national picture. The NYTD was authorized by federal legislation and collects data from state child welfare systems in two areas: youth receipt of independent living services and youth outcomes. The initial data from this effort have only recently become available. In Federal Fiscal Year 2013, states reported that 99,974 youth and young adults received at least one service to aid in the transition from foster care to adulthood (NYTD, 2014b). Additional analysis of the NYTD (Okpych, 2015) found that 50 percent of youth received at least one service. The most frequent service was secondary education (30%), followed by career preparation (26%), housing/home management (25%), health education/risk prevention (25%), budget/finances (23%), family/marriage (21%), education financial (18%), other financial (16%), post-secondary education (15%), employment/vocational (15%), supervised independent living (12%), mentoring (12%), and room/board financial (8%). Youth served in rural and non-metropolitan areas were the most likely to receive services and youth in large metropolitan areas were the least likely to receive services.

Additionally, the percentage of youth served was different across states. Okpych (2015) found that approximately one-fifth of states served 26 percent to 50 percent of eligible youth, and just over one-third of states served 51 percent to 75 percent of eligible youth. The estimates of service receipt found by Okpych were much lower than those of earlier studies. He suggested several possible reasons. First, his study examined only those services covered by the Chafee program (whereas other studies may include a wide range of services including those covered by the state). Second, other studies are often based on youth self-report whereas his uses state data collection systems. Third, the time period of his study is more constrained (at most, 2 years), whereas other studies may ask about services receipt during any time the youth was in care.

Observations from practice suggest two notable emerging trends in regard to states' approaches to transition services. First, among states there is an increasing macro approach to life skills training. More states are reporting using Chafee dollars to develop youth councils (Forenza & Happonen, 2015), as well as running youth leadership workshops and youth summits and conferences, developing foster child and normalcy bills of rights, and gathering youth for graduation and recognition events. Given the requirement of the youth voice in transition planning through the Fostering Connections Act, empowerment activities are instrumental in helping these youth become advocates for themselves as well as their communities. This is also consistent with increasing research efforts to insert more youth voice into our understanding of the transition experience (e.g., Cunningham & Diversi, 2012). It is important to consider, however, that traditional transition services are often perceived as designed for higher-achieving youth. Other transitioning youth may have greater service needs beyond those that are met by typical transition services.

Second, the field is moving away from life skills groups and classroom-based skills training and moving toward the use of specialized social workers, life coaches, or mentors to teach life skills (Collins, 2015; Greeson, 2013). This model centralizes services so that youth can work on developing life skills in a number of different areas (fiscal literacy, housing, healthy relationships) with the same transition specialist (e.g., in Massachusetts, Ohio, Washington, South Texas). Another way of centralizing services is to provide a physical space for youth to access multiple services. Examples of such physical spaces include Washington, DC's Child and Family Services Agency's Office of Youth Empowerment (OYE). This Office

> provides a host of programs and growth experiences for District teens and young adults in foster care. In partnership with social workers, foster caregivers, and the community, OYE's goals are to teach, train, and guide these young people—and ultimately to help each one begin to recognize and develop his/her unique potential.
>
> (Office of Youth Empowerment, 2017, p. 1)

The funding formula of the FCIA does not provide for all youth to have access to all services that exist. Thus, there can be variance from state to state in the amount of access youth have to transition specialists and transition services. Because in some states (e.g., California, Ohio, North Carolina), the FCIA programs are administered by county, there is variance within states regarding service model types and levels of access.

An additional area in which federal legislation regarding transition from care impacts transition services is through the mechanism of service plan goals. Legislation emphasizes certain service plan goals; this, in turn, influences practice within agencies and among workers. Specifically, in 1997, the Adoption and Safe Families Act (ASFA) created a way for states to terminate parental rights without an identified path to adoption. The language in the ASFA was restrictive around this action and required demonstration to the courts as to why neither adoption nor reunification were being pursued, as well as the identification of an appropriate and permanent living arrangement. As intended, this path would serve a youth who had the permanent support of an adult who could also provide for the young adult's needs so far as where he or she would live. However, the adult resource would not be a potential adoptive parent or legal guardian.

States assigned service plan goals such as "independent living" (New Hampshire) or "emancipation" (Kentucky) to youth who would turn 18 and the primary focus became skill building. As permanency legislation and the field's understanding of permanency in the lives of young adults evolved, "Permanency with Kin" (Massachusetts) and "Other or Alternative Planned Permanent Living Arrangement" (Colorado, Florida) replaced the independent living terminology. The language may have changed on family and youth service plans and permanency plans, but in service delivery plans, including Child and Family Service Reviews and FCIA state plans, the term independent living is still extensively utilized. It is unclear whether this change in language was followed by a significant change in practice. It can be difficult to measure one alternative plan versus another as to whether it was successful and/or permanent. If reunification is determined to no longer be a potential permanent option for a young person, the goal is changed. It is also unclear in the literature what effective permanency work looks like with a youth who has reached the age of 18 in care. The NYTD provides indicators of how some youth (those that could be engaged in the survey process) fare between the ages of 17 and 21. The survey, however, does not ask about service plan goals or permanency plans. Illustrative case examples of Tom and Lucy, below, provide further detail on the complex circumstances of some youth in regard to permanency.

> Tom and Lily have been friends their whole lives, even through Lily's battle with addiction. Tom has stepped in to help Lily over the years and has always been a friend and father figure to Lily's son, Jorge. When Lily's disease takes hold for an extended period of time, Tom is identified by the child welfare agency as a resource for Jorge. Tom engages with the child welfare system, but due to challenges from a divorce, he cannot commit to supporting Jorge financially, nor does he want to alienate Lily who is still on the periphery of Jorge's life. The child welfare agency may apply an APPLA service plan goal in this case, engaging Tom as a permanent resource for Jorge without pursuing adoption or guardianship.

In practice, however, there is the consensus that APPLA became a default goal for many transition-age youth and that when these goals are assigned to service plans for youth, permanency work stalls or ceases. These service plan goals continue to reflect a focus on skill development and post-secondary education attainment, rather than permanent familial stability in the life of the young adult.

> Lucy was an immigrant from South America who joined her mother a few years after her mother entered the United States illegally. Lucy came into care after a report of abuse was filed by Lucy's high school. Lucy's family network was very small and none of the family members had legal status, therefore they were unable or unwilling to work with the child welfare system including providing permanency via adoption for Lucy. At 16, Lucy was old enough to voice that she did not want to be adopted by her foster family. She stayed in foster care for 2 years before she moved out on her own. Lucy's social worker knew that she would need skills to be stable. She helped Lucy access job training, facilitated her immigration needs, and connected her with a housing agency which helped her obtain an apartment. The family work for Lucy, however, ceased. She and her mother declined any family therapy or mediation and Lucy had no committed adults in her life. Given that she had a job and an apartment, Lucy could be seen as a success story, but there was no permanency in her life. If the job was lost or the housing

> voucher expired, no safety net existed for Lucy. Even if she remained stable for several years and then faced economic, health, or other personal crisis in her early twenties, she was then too old to receive services from the child welfare agency. The living arrangement piece of the service plan goal was attained; however, the permanency piece remained unachieved. In this case, it is worthy to note that Lucy may have adults in her life who are caring and supportive, but in order to continue to have access to permanency, a social worker should be actively engaging these adults to help them understand Lucy's long-term needs and gain clarity about what they might be able to provide.

Conclusion

Knowledge, theory, policy, and practice have evolved since 1985. Understanding the problem has become more sophisticated and efforts to respond have as well. Multi-component and sustained efforts are needed to support these young people in the transition to a successful well-adjusted adulthood. Some of the examples discussed in this chapter identify the intersection of various policy domains at federal, state, and local levels, to provide a range of supports. This recognition of gaps, and efforts to close them, are needed to provide a sustained effort.

So where should we go from here in regard to policy and practice of access to and continuity of services? Furthermore, what advances in theory and research are needed that will add to the knowledge base?

An issue that is relevant to this field of practice is that it is difficult to tell when our interventions are successful. Unlike adoption, for example, in which the action of being adopted is considered a successful outcome, for youth transitioning from care, assessing outcomes is more complicated. Avoidance of negative outcomes (e.g., incarceration) is often used as a measure. Surely we want better outcomes than this for youth? Expectations for young people are high: stability, family connections, and career. It is very difficult, in the present, to know whether a young person is on a successful trajectory. Only in retrospect can we validly ascertain success.

Policy, program, and practice interventions are now delivered on a much more consistent basis compared to the early years of the field. Moreover, some consensus is developing in the field that more robust and prolonged interventions are needed. In the early days, we had little information to guide practice. It took several years of research to confirm that independent living skills training alone—the main intervention strategy—was ineffective at producing sustained, broad-based positive outcomes. This spurred attention to more promising approaches based on relationship-based strategies and concrete supports. While it is undeniable that relationships are a critical element of a successful transition and that permanence in relationships (not just legal permanence) is important, there remain challenges to policy and practice that support the development of positive relationships. Our understanding of how to construct relationships remains limited, particularly for this population who often have histories of trauma and attachment disruption. Further development and testing of interventions to bolster relationships should be a major focus of efforts.

In regard to concrete supports, policy developments such as the ETV (along with state assistance) and extensions of Medicaid through the FCIA and the Patient Protection and Affordable Care Act (2010) have led to progress in assisting youth to attend post-secondary education and access health care. Housing and employment remain more challenging; so many factors (such as housing supply and economic conditions) impact the ability of young people to secure housing and employment. Former foster youth are not the only young people struggling in these areas. Further efforts are needed, utilizing cross-system and multi-pronged solutions, in order to effectively tackle these problems.

Both access and continuity of transition services require further attention. Thus, the main policy recommendation is for increased flexibility in age limits, time limits, and use of funding. The policy resources identified in this chapter are sorely needed, but time limits and other rules of access frequently limit the amount of help to be provided. It is important that systems are not set up so that particular populations of vulnerable youth (e.g., foster youth, homeless youth, and justice-involved youth) compete with each other for opportunities in housing, education, and employment. Moreover, the variation in available services among states and localities remains problematic. As research evidence accumulates regarding the most effective strategies for assisting youth with transition, these policy and program interventions need to be transferred to other jurisdictions and eventually brought to scale at a national level.

Recommendations for research include a continued emphasis on evaluation and utilization of research designs that can advance the field. Access to services, supports, and opportunities continues to be a relevant issue. Many of the available resources are not fully known to the young people who are eligible and might benefit from them. Research that provides further understanding of which youth gain access and which do not addresses an important social justice question. Systems frequently operate with implicit biases that can result in disparities related to race, ethnicity, religion, sex, gender and gender identity, disability, and national origin. Greater understanding of these critical access issues is needed. Following from this, as well, is the need for further information regarding which services, supports, and opportunities are beneficial to different youth populations.

As a part of this research focus, increased efforts to include the youth voice in design and delivery of services are warranted. Models of research based on participatory action would be particularly relevant to understanding the circumstances of youth. Indeed, their input has long been neglected in terms of service decisions. Their participation in research as partners, rather than subjects, may lead to a better understanding of issues such as service access and would assist policymakers in designing the supports most likely to be used and result in program effectiveness.

Finally, professionals in the field should be recognized as strong advocates for these youth. Many practitioners are adept at case-oriented practice that involves securing access to education and other opportunities for the youth with whom they work. Practice should aim to increase the resources available to all youth. In regard to child welfare systems, specifically, practice should engage more youth-centric and young adult models of engagement and intervention. Child welfare systems have been focused primarily on child protection, and have been challenged to more effectively serve the older youth, transitioning, and young adult populations. New models of practice for transition-age youth are developing and should be tested, and replicated if proven effective.

References

Adoption and Safe Families Act of 1997, Pub. L. No. 105-89, 111 Stat. 2115. (1997). (Codified at 42 U.S.C.A. § 1305.)
Annie E. Casey Foundation. (2012). What is permanence? Blog post, February 5. Retrieved from www.aecf.org/blog/what-is-permanence/
Arnett, J. J. (2000). Emerging adulthood: A theory of development from the late teens through the twenties. *American Psychologist, 55*, 469–480.
Augsberger, A., Collins, M. E., Gecker, W., & Dougher, M. (2017). Youth civic engagement: Do youth councils reduce or reinforce social inequality? *Journal of Adolescent Research,* prepublished January 4, 2017. doi: 10.1177/0743558416684957
Avery, R. J., & Freundlich, M. (2009). You're all grown up now: Termination of foster care support at age 18. *Journal of Adolescence, 32*(2), 247–257.
Benzies, K., & Mychasiuk, R. (2009). Fostering family resiliency: A review of the key protective factors. *Child & Family Social Work, 14*, 103–114. doi:10.1111/j.1365-2206.2008.00586.x
Buckner, J. C., Mezzacappa, E., & Beardslee, W. R. (2003). Characteristics of resilient youths living in poverty: The role of self-regulatory processes. *Development and Psychopathology, 15*, 139–162.
Collins, M. E. (2001). Transition to adulthood for vulnerable youth: A review of research and implications for policy. *Social Service Review, 75*(2), 271–291.
Collins, M. E. (2004). Enhancing services to youths leaving foster care: Analysis of recent legislation and its potential impact. *Children and Youth Services Review, 26*, 1051–1065.

Collins, M. E. (2015). *Macro perspectives on youths aging out of foster care*. Washington, DC: NASW Press.

Collins, M. E., & Clay, C. M. (2009). Influencing policy for youth transitioning from care: Defining problems, crafting solutions, and assessing politics. *Children and Youth Services Review, 31*(7), 743–751.

Collins, M. E., & Curtis, M. (2011). Conceptualizing housing careers for vulnerable youths: Implications for policy. *American Journal of Orthopsychiatry, 81*(3), 390–400.

Collins, M. E., & Ward, R. L. (2011). Services and outcomes for transition-age foster care youth: Youths' perspectives. *Vulnerable Children and Youth Studies: An International Interdisciplinary Journal for Research, Policy and Care, 6*(2), 157–165.

Commonwealth of Massachusetts Department of Housing and Community Development. (2016). *Moving to Work Program annual plan for fiscal year 2017*. Boston: Author.

Consolidated Omnibus Budget Reconciliation Act of 1985, 100 Stat. 82. (1986).

Cook, R. (1994). Are we helping foster care youth prepare for their future? *Children and Youth Services Review, 16*, 213–229.

Courtney, M., Dworsky, A., Brown, A., Cary, C., Love, K., & Vorhies, V. (2011). *Midwest Evaluation of the Adult Functioning of Former Foster Youth: Outcomes at age 26*. Chicago: Chapin Hall at the University of Chicago.

Cranston-Gonzalez Affordable Housing Act, 42 U.S.C. § 12703. (1990).

Cunningham, M. J., & Diversi, M. (2012). Aging out: Youths' perspectives on foster care and the transition to independence. *Qualitative Social Work, 12*(5), 587–602.

Cushing, G., Samuels, G.M., & Kerman, B. (2014). Profiles of relational permanence at 22: Variability in parental supports and outcomes among young adults with foster care histories. *Children and Youth Services Review, 39*, 73–83.

Daining, C., & DePanfilis, D. (2007). Resilience of youth in transition from out-of-home care to adulthood. *Children and Youth Services Review, 29*, 1158–1178.

Dion, R., Dworsky, A., Kauff, J., & Kleinman, R. (2014). *Housing for youth aging out of foster care*. Washington, DC: U.S. Department of Housing and Urban Development.

Dworsky, A., & Courtney, M. E. (2010). The risk of teenage pregnancy among transitioning foster youth: Implications for extending state care beyond age 18. *Children and Youth Services Review, 32*, 1351–1356.

Dworsky, A., Dillman, K., Dion, M. R., Coffee-Borden, B., & Rosenau, M. (2012). *Housing for youth aging out of foster care: A review of the literature and program typology*. Washington, DC: Mathematica Policy Research.

Every Student Succeeds Act, 20 U.S.C. 6301. (2015).

Family & Youth Services Bureau. (2017). Retrieved from www.acf.hhs.gov/fysb

Faulkner, K. M. (2009). Presentation and representation: Youth participation in ongoing public decision-making projects. *Childhood, 16*(1), 89–104.

Forenza, B., & Happonen, R. G. A. (2015). Critical analysis of foster youth advisory boards in the United States. *Child & Youth Care Forum, 45*(1), 1–15.

Foster Care Independence Act, 42 U.S.C. § 1305, 113 Stat. 1822. (1999).

Fostering Connections to Success and Increasing Adoptions Act, 42 U.S.C. § 1305, 122 Stat. 3949. (2008).

Frey, L., Cushing, G., Freundlich, M., & Brenner, E. (2007). Achieving permanency for youth in foster care: Assessing and strengthening emotional security. *Child and Family Social Work, 13*, 218–226.

Greeson, J. K. P. (2013). Foster youth and the transition to adulthood: The theoretical and conceptual basis for natural mentoring. *Emerging Adulthood, 1*(1), 40–51.

Higher Education Act, 20 U.S.C. § 1001. (1965).

Higher Education Opportunity Act, 20 U.S.C. § 1001. (2008).

Homeless Emergency Assistance and Rapid Transition to Housing Act [HEARTH], 42 U.S.C. 11301. (2009).

Hook, J. L., & Courtney, M. (2010). *Employment of former foster youth as young adults: Evidence from the Midwest Study*. Chapin Hall Issue Brief. Retrieved from www.chapinhall.org/sites/default/files/publications/Midwest_IB3_Employment.pdf

Individuals with Disabilities Education Act, 20 U.S.C. § 1400. (2004).

Individualized Education Program (IEP). (2007). Definition. 20 U.S.C. 1414(d)(1)(A) and (d)(6).

Job Corps. (2017). *About Job Corps*. Retrieved from www.jobcorps.gov/page/citizens

Massachusetts Department of Children and Families. (n.d). *Chafee Foster Care Independence Program and Education and Training Voucher program*. Retrieved from www.mass.gov/eohhs/docs/dcf/chafee-and-etv-reports-2014.pdf

Masten, A.S. (2001). Ordinary magic: Resilience processes in development. *American Psychologist, 56*(3), 227–238.

Mortimer, J. T., & Larson, R. W. (2002). Macrostructural trends and the reshaping of adolescence. In J. T. Mortimer & R. W. Larson (Eds.), *The changing adolescent experience: Societal trends and the transition to adulthood* (pp. 1–17). New York, NY: Cambridge University Press.

National Center for Housing and Child Welfare. (2013). *HUD's Family Unification Program*. Retrieved from www.nchcw.org/uploads/7/5/3/3/7533556/fup_overview_june_2012.pdf

National Youth in Transition Database [NYTD]. (2014a). *Comparing outcomes reported by young people at ages 17 and 19 in NYTD cohort 1. Data brief #4*. Washington, DC: U.S. Department of Health & Human Services.

National Youth in Transition Database [NYTD]. (2014b). *Highlights from the National Youth in Transition Database, federal fiscal year 2013. Data brief #3*. Washington, DC: U.S. Department of Health & Human Services.

Office of Youth Empowerment. (2017). *Office of Youth Empowerment*. Retrieved from https://cfsa.dc.gov/page/office-youth-empowerment

Okpych, N. J. (2015). Receipt of independent living services among older youth in foster care: An analysis of national data from the U.S. *Children and Youth Services Review, 51*, 74–86.

Patient Protection and Affordable Care Act, 42 U.S.C. § 18001. (2010).

Pecora, P. J., Kessler, R. C., O'Brien, K., White, C. R., Williams, J., Hiripi, E., . . . Herrick, M.A. (2006). Educational and employment outcomes of adults formerly placed in foster care: Results from the Northwest Foster Care Alumni Study. *Children and Youth Services Review, 28*, 1459–1491.

Pergamit, M., McDaniel, M., & Hawkins, A. (2012). *Housing assistance for youth who have aged out of foster care: The role of the Chafee Foster Care Independence Program*. Washington, DC: Office of the Assistant Secretary for Planning and Evaluation.

Promoting Safe and Stable Families Amendments, 42 U.S.C. § 629, 115 Stat. 2413. (2001).

Reconnecting Homeless Youth Act [RHYA], 42 U.S.C. 5601. (2008).

Samuels, G. M. (2009). Ambiguous loss of home: The experience of familial (im)permanence among young adults with foster care backgrounds. *Children and Youth Services Review, 31*, 1229–1239.

Smith, W. B. (2011). *Youth leaving foster care: A developmental, relationship-based approach to practice*. New York, NY: Oxford University Press.

Social Security Act, Title IV-E, 42 U.S.C. § 1305. (1935).

Stein, M. (2006). Young people aging out of care: The poverty of theory. *Children and Youth Services Review, 28*, 422–434.

van Wingerden, C., Emerson, J., & Ichikawa, D. (2002, June). *Improving special education for children with disabilities in foster care*. Education Issue Brief. Seattle, WA: Casey Family Programs. Retrieved from www.gascore.com/documents/ImprovingSpecialEducationforChildren.pdf.

U.S. Department of Health & Human Services (Administration for Children and Families). (2008). *Evaluation of the life skills training program: Los Angeles County*. Washington, DC: USDHHS.

U.S. Department of Housing and Urban Development [USDHUD]. (2015). *Rapid rehousing for youth: Program profiles*. Retrieved from www.hudexchange.info/resources/documents/RRH-for-Youth-Valley-Youth-House-Program-Profile.pdf

U.S. Department of Housing and Urban Development [USDHUD]. (2016a). *Office of Housing Choice Vouchers*. Retrieved from https://portal.hud.gov/hudportal/HUD?src=/program_offices/public_indian_housing/programs/hcv/

U.S. Department of Housing and Urban Development [USDHUD]. (2016b). *Family Unification Program*. Retrieved from https://portal.hud.gov/hudportal/HUD?src=/program_offices/public_indian_housing/programs/hcv/family

U.S. Department of Housing and Urban Development [USDHUD]. (2017). *Continuum of Care Program*. Retrieved from https://portal.hud.gov/hudportal/HUD?src=/hudprograms/continuumofcare

U.S. Department of Labor. (2017). *WIOA Youth Formula Grants*. Retrieved from www.doleta.gov/Youth_services/wiaformula.cfm

Workforce Innovation and Opportunity Act, 29 U.S.C. § 3101. (2014).

YouthBuild USA, Inc. (2014). *YouthBuild USA Inc. 2014 annual report*. Retrieved from www.youthbuild.org/sites/default/files/YouthBuild%20USA%202014%20Annual%20Report_0.pdf

Part VI
Areas of Special Consideration in Foster Youth

17
Youth with Disabilities in Foster Care

Katharine Hill and Elizabeth Lightfoot

Youth with disabilities and their families are involved in the child welfare system at much higher rates than those without disabilities. Youth with disabilities are more likely to experience maltreatment, are more likely to be removed from their home because of maltreatment, and are more likely to be placed in institutional settings (Lightfoot, Hill, & LaLiberte, 2011; Slayter, 2016; Sullivan & Knutsen, 2000). Further, youth with disabilities and their families are often involved with multiple service systems simultaneously, which can be extraordinarily difficult to navigate (Hill, 2013; Hill, Lightfoot, & Kimball, 2010; Lightfoot, 2014). While the Americans with Disabilities Act of 1990 (ADA) requires that child welfare systems provide reasonable modifications to their services, services are often not modified (Lightfoot, LaLiberte, & Cho, 2017), and many working within the child welfare field are not trained on how to work with families that have a member with a disability. It is important for those working within child welfare to increase their knowledge of the unique needs of youth with disabilities and their families, disability services and supports, and policies in order to provide collaborative, integrated, and high-quality care. This chapter provides readers with an overview of the experiences of children and youth with disabilities and their family members with maltreatment, and their interactions with the child welfare system, and will discuss the intersections between the child welfare and disability services systems.

First, this chapter provides an overview on disability definitions and introduces readers to theories of disability. Next, the chapter discusses the latest prevalence data on child maltreatment, child welfare system involvement, and foster care involvement in relation to youth with disabilities. The chapter then moves into covering how youth with disabilities initially enter the child welfare system, the types of services they receive in that system, and how they enter foster care. This is followed by a discussion of how foster youth with disabilities typically leave foster care, including through adoption and transitioning to adulthood. As foster youth with disabilities are often involved in multiple systems, the chapter discusses various system interactions that youth with disabilities and their families face. The chapter concludes with a discussion of how child welfare workers could provide better services to youth with disabilities in foster care and their families.

What Is Disability?

The term "disability" is inherently broad and the definition of what constitutes a disability is influenced by a wide variety of factors. First, while conditions that cause impairments are universal, there are cultural variations in how these impairments are understood as a disability. For example, while a learning disability is a concept in the United States, it wasn't recognized as a disability until very recently in Japan (Kayama & Haight, 2013). Second, there have been numerous academic disciplines studying and defining disabilities over the years. These disciplines, including medicine, social work, rehabilitation sciences, sociology, psychology, public health, and education, all bring their unique perspectives to the understanding of disability. This unfortunately has led to many competing definitions of disability used by academics which make comparisons across studies difficult. Additionally, there are many competing definitions of disability in policies, which can complicate offering services and supports in an integrated and collaborative manner (Hill et al., 2010).

Finally, there are various competing world-views regarding disability, and much of the theory surrounding disability has focused on how to conceptually understand disability. Disability has historically been viewed via what is known as the "medical model." In the medical model, disability is understood as a problem or a deficit of an individual that must be addressed or treated by a professional. A professional working with a person with a disability either rehabilitated or treated an individual to an extent that he or she could function in society, or else the individual was sent to segregated institutions to live and/or spend their days. Much of our social work and child welfare system is based on this medical model orientation (Mackelprang & Salsgiver, 1997), with social service workers interacting with people with "problems" in order to fix these problems. Gilson and Depoy (2002) describe social workers as using a "diagnostic lens" when working with people with disabilities—viewing disability as an impairment that can first be identified or assessed, and then once it is identified, can be treated. There are a multitude of issues with the medical model, including its deficit focus, its neglect of environmental barriers, and its disregard of the capacities of individuals to assess their own issues and solutions.

While many social services still have a medical model world-view, there is another competing model, the social model of disability, which originated in England, but now is pervasive around the world (Oliver, 2013). Instead of viewing disability through a medical or diagnostic lens, the social model views disability through a socio-political lens, with a strong emphasis on the social construction or social creation of disability. The social model of disability views many of the problems associated with impairment as caused by an inaccessible and oppressive society, rather than by an individual or his or her impairment. Under the social model of disability, impairment is a neutral concept, being neither positive nor negative. Viewing disability through a social model lens brings attention to the barriers in society, such as inaccessible buildings, lack of accessible transportation, segregated schools, or lack of residential options, which are significant problems for people with disabilities and their families (Oliver, 2013). Viewing disability through a social model lens can lead social workers to focus on making accommodations for a person's disability, rather than trying to "fix" a person's disability. The social model encourages social workers to seek interventions in collaboration with a person with a disability, to recognize that a person with a disability is the best expert about their own needs, and to relate to a person with a disability as someone who might view their disability as a cultural identity, rather than as a barrier or medical diagnosis.

The social model of disability has been the dominant model used by disability studies researchers for nearly half a century, and its external emphasis has led scholars to focus on barriers that people with disabilities face, including social, administrative, cultural, and policy barriers (Watson, 2012). Researchers studying youth with disabilities in foster care who come from a disability studies background are more likely to use the social model to guide their research, with their emphasis on how youth and their families experience receiving unequal services in child welfare. This differs quite starkly from those who conceptualize disability as a "risk factor," which would align more with a medical model understanding of disability. It should be noted that the social model has not only been the dominant model that disability researchers used to shape their research and ideas about disability, but it also became the backbone of the successful international movement for establishing anti-discrimination policies for people with disabilities, including the United Nations Convention on the Rights of Persons with Disabilities (United Nations, 2006). Newer theories have been developed in an attempt to acknowledge the diversity among people with disabilities, and perhaps to address a neglect of the social model to consider the effects of impairment on individuals' lives, such as the social relational theory (Connors & Stalker, 2007) or critical disability studies (Campbell, 2008). However, these theories still point researchers to emphasize discrimination and oppression when studying disability or working with people with disabilities (Watson, 2012). This theoretical approach aligns quite well with the social work code of ethics.

Federal Definitions of Disabilities

While for many years, there was only anecdotal evidence that youth with disabilities were more likely to experience maltreatment and more likely to be involved in the child welfare system than youth without disabilities, researchers have more recently been building a body of evidence demonstrating that these earlier intuitions were indeed correct. Possible challenges to identifying children with disabilities who experience maltreatment include the wide variety of definitions of disabilities used in the social services field, and the lack of coordinated reporting efforts. The following narrative will discuss each of these in more detail.

As disability can be viewed from a variety of cultural perspectives, academic perspectives, and disability world-views, it is not surprising that there are many different definitions of disability in use. In fact, Adler and Hendershot (2000) found 43 different federal definitions of disability in the United States. States, counties, and agencies can also have their own definitions of disability. Definitions of disability can be based on diagnoses, types, and levels of impairment, functional limitations, receiving of assistance for completing tasks, receiving of disability benefits, self-identification, or general perceptions of disability. While the World Health Organization (2002) has developed a new biopsychosocial model of definitions that includes an intentional blending of the medical and social models of disabilities, this has not had much of an impact on definitions of disability used in policy in the United States.

The three main federal definitions that affect youth with disabilities in foster care come from the Americans with Disabilities Act of 1990 (ADA), the Individuals with Disabilities Education Act of 2004 (IDEA), and the Developmental Disabilities Assistance and Bill of Rights Act of 2000 (DD Act). (See boxed text below for a description of these policies.)

Federal Disabilities Policies that Affect Youth with Disabilities in Child Welfare

Americans with Disabilities Act of 1990 (ADA)

The ADA is a federal anti-discrimination law that guarantees civil rights protections and equal opportunity for individuals with disabilities in public accommodations, employment, transportation, state and local government services, and telecommunications. Title II of the ADA covers state and local government services. The ADA requires child welfare agencies to make reasonable modifications to its services to ensure that youth with disabilities can fully access any of its services.

Individuals with Disabilities Education Act of 2004 (IDEA)

The IDEA requires public schools to make available to all eligible children with disabilities a free appropriate public education in the least restrictive environment appropriate to an individual's needs.

> The IDEA mandates that schools collaboratively develop an Individualized Education Program (IEP) of special education and related services.
>
> ## *Developmental Disabilities Assistance and Bill of Rights Act of 2000 (DD Act)*
>
> The DD Act ensures that individuals with developmental disabilities and their families participate in the design of and have access to individualized services and supports that promote independence, productivity, and integration into all facets of community life through culturally competent programs authorized under the Act.

The broadest definition of disability comes from the ADA, which uses a functional definition of disability rather than a list of impairments. The ADA defines an individual with a disability as someone who "has a physical or mental impairment that substantially limits one or more of the major life activities, has a record of such impairment; or is regarded as having such impairment" (Americans with Disabilities Act, 1990, § 12102). The focus on limitations in activities of daily living (ADLs) is one of the broadest ways to cover disability, and this type of disability definition is most comparable across culture and contexts.

The second federal definition that affects youth with disabilities in foster care is the definition of disabilities used by the IDEA. The Individuals with Disabilities Education Act is the federal law that requires public schools to provide free and appropriate education to children and youth with disabilities. Unlike the ADA, the IDEA uses a definition that includes specific impairment type with the need for services. Thus, under the IDEA, a child is identified as having a disability if they have one of 13 impairment categories: autism, deaf-blindness, deafness, developmental delay, hearing impairment, mental retardation (the name will be changed to intellectual disabilities in future versions), multiple disabilities, orthopedic impairment, other health impairment, specific learning disability, speech or language impairment, traumatic brain injury, or visual impairment including blindness. In 2014, more than 6 million children received services through the IDEA, which represents 12.9% of all students aged between 3 and 21 (U.S. Department of Education, 2016, Chapter 2). In many cases, a youth with a disability is only identified as having a disability through the public school system. In other words, the youth will not be identified as having a disability in any other systems, such as child welfare.

The final federal definition that affects youth with disabilities is the federal definition of developmental disability defined by the Developmental Disabilities Assistance and Bill of Rights Act (DD Act). Many youth with disabilities also fall under the category of developmental disabilities. Developmental disabilities include youth with intellectual disabilities, cerebral palsy, autism spectrum disorder, fetal alcohol syndrome, genetic and chromosomal disorders such as Down syndrome, and some sensory disabilities. These youth can receive a variety of services through qualifying as having a developmental disability based on this federal definition. Under the DD Act, a developmental disability refers to a host of conditions that begin at birth or in childhood and cause a lifelong functional limitation. The specific definition of a developmental disability is:

> A severe, chronic disability of an individual that:
>
> (i) is attributable to a mental or physical impairment or a combination of mental and physical impairments;
> (ii) is manifested before the individual attains age 22;
> (iii) is likely to continue indefinitely;

(iv) results in a substantial functional limitation in 3 or more of the following areas of major life activity;

   a. self-care,
   b. receptive and expressive language,
   c. learning,
   d. mobility,
   e. self-direction,
   f. capacity for independent living,
   g. economic self-sufficiency; and

(v) reflects the individual's need for a combination and sequence of special, interdisciplinary or generic services, individualized supports, or other forms of assistance that are of lifelong or extended duration and are individually planned and coordinated.

(Developmental Disabilities Assistance and Bill of Rights Act of 2000, P.L. 106-402 §102)

While all three of these laws are important for protecting youth with disabilities against discrimination and providing services and support, their definitions of disability are so disparate that it is hard to track youth with disabilities when they move across systems. Thus, it has been extremely difficult to determine with precision how many youth with disabilities are in the child welfare system or in foster care.

The second main reason that our knowledge has been limited about maltreatment and child welfare involvement among youth with disabilities has been the lack of federal reporting requirements. Prior to the reauthorization of the Child Abuse Prevention and Treatment Act (CAPTA) in 2010, there was no federal requirement that state child welfare agencies had to report disability data about youth with disabilities. While some states did collect youth disability data, most did not (Shannon & Agorastou, 2006). Because there were no standard reporting requirements, most states that collected data depended on child welfare workers to determine these data with little standardization. Thus, state-level data were not comparable, and states showed wildly different prevalence rates (Bruhn, 2003). Complicating this was the fact that many child welfare workers did not receive adequate training in identifying children with disabilities and in identifying and connecting with disability-specific services and supports (AAP, 2001; Bonner, Crow, & Hensley, 1997; Bruhn, 2003; Lightfoot & LaLiberte, 2006; Shannon & Agorastou, 2006). The newer standardized CAPTA reporting requirements will most likely lead to much more comprehensive information, though they do not solve all of the data quality issues.

Prevalence of Maltreatment of Youth with Disabilities

Studies have found that children and youth with disabilities are over three times more likely to experience maltreatment than other children and youth (Sullivan & Knutson, 2000; Jones et al., 2012). Sullivan and Knutson (2000) conducted the most comprehensive (to date) child maltreatment epidemiological study examining children and youth with disabilities. In their study, they combined records from hospitals, law enforcement, schools, and foster care in Omaha, Nebraska, and found that children and youth with disabilities were 3.4 times more likely to experience maltreatment than children and youth without disabilities. These findings were confirmed in an international meta-analysis of 17 studies conducted by Jones and colleagues (2012), which found that children with disabilities were 3.68 times more likely to experience maltreatment than children without disabilities, only slightly higher than Sullivan and Knutson's findings. Youth with disabilities have greater risk levels for certain types of maltreatment. According to Jones et al.'s (2012) meta-analysis, youth with disabilities are 4.56 times more likely to experience neglect, 4.36 times more likely to experience emotional abuse, 3.56 times more likely to experience physical violence, and 2.88 times more likely to experience sexual violence than their peers without disabilities.

While it is clear that children with disabilities experience higher rates of maltreatment, current literature is inconclusive about the direction of the relationship. Most parents of children with disabilities do not maltreat their children, nor do they in any way contribute to their child's disability. However, some disabilities can be caused by maltreatment; for example, withholding nutrition or not allowing a child access to an adequate and safe living space can result in a developmental delay. In addition, some types of physical abuse can cause disabilities. For example, shaking an infant or severe physical abuse can also lead to developmental disabilities. Drug and alcohol use during pregnancy are also linked with disabilities in childhood. In their systematic review of the existing literature, Gilbert and colleagues (2009) found that children who have experienced maltreatment are more likely to have poor physical and mental health outcomes, including depression and post-traumatic stress disorder (PTSD). Most childhood disabilities are not caused by maltreatment, though, and people working with families who have a child with a disability must be careful not to make assumptions. It is possible that something which looks like abuse, such as bruising, might instead be related to a child's disability.

Children with disabilities are at higher risk for experiencing maltreatment in their lifetime (Jones et al., 2012; Sobsey, 2002; Sullivan & Knutsen, 2000). However, it might not be the disability itself causing the increased risk, but "rather, the broader society's response to disability, including discrimination, lack of supports and lack of opportunities, could increase the risk" (Lightfoot, 2014, p. 29). For example, Stoddard-Dare, DeRigne, Quinn, & Malett (2015) identified a higher prevalence of material hardship (i.e., an inability to pay bills, experiencing food insecurity, eligibility to access income-based public welfare programs) in families that include a child with a disability. Parenting a child with a disability can lead to financial strain for families, including demands or limits on parental employment (Earle & Heyman, 2012) and costs associated with limitations in insurance coverage and medical needs (Bringewatt & Gershoff, 2010; Stoddard-Dare et al., 2015). Additionally, the demands of caregiving may also have indirect impacts on the stability and emotional health of the family (Stoddard-Dare et al., 2015). All of these factors can lead to an increase in parental stress, which is associated with a higher risk of child maltreatment (Sobesy, 2002).

Prevalence of Child Welfare Involvement of Youth with Disabilities

While it is clear that children and youth with disabilities are more likely to experience maltreatment, their levels of involvement in the child welfare system are still very difficult to ascertain, even with the new CAPTA requirements. Prior to the CAPTA reporting requirement, the Westat organization, in collaboration with the National Center on Child Abuse and Neglect (NCCAN), conducted the first and only comprehensive national investigation of child welfare involvement of children and youth with disabilities. In their study, they found that about 14% of youth involved in the child welfare system had a disability (Crosse, Kaye, & Ratnofsky, 1992). This number is only slightly higher than recent data from the Children's Bureau, the agency within the U.S. Department of Health & Human Services (henceforth, USDHHS), Administration for Children and Families which collects the data reported from the states. The USDHHS (Children's Bureau) (2015) reported that 12.6% of children and youth with maltreatment confirmed by a child welfare agency were identified as having a disability in 2013. However, the USDHHS (Children's Bureau) data should be viewed with extreme caution as the states reported very different percentages of children and youth with disabilities. Nine of the states reported less than 1% of their children and youth as having a disability, while six states were identifying 30% or more of their children and youth as having a disability.

Although the national administrative data are somewhat suspect, we can begin to get an understanding of some of the demographic details of youth with disabilities involved in the child welfare system by looking at administrative data. Youth identified as having a disability are more likely to be involved in the child welfare system if they are males and white, compared to females and people from other races (Lightfoot et al., 2011). There have not been any further enquiries into why white youth with disabilities and male youth with disabilities are more likely to be involved with child welfare services. While younger children with disabilities are more likely to experience maltreatment, older children with disabilities are more likely to be involved in the child welfare system (Hill et al., 2010; Lightfoot et al., 2011). All of these demographic details could have a number of causes, ranging from the under- or over-identification of certain types of disabilities to the amount of time different groups spend in the child welfare system.

Youth with different types of disabilities also have different levels of involvement in the child welfare system. In the national USDHHS (Children's Bureau) data (2015), over half of the youth identified as having a disability have either a behavioral or an emotional disability. Many other studies have also found that children with behavioral or emotional disabilities are more likely to be involved in the child welfare system (Crosse et al., 1992; Jonson-Reid, Drake, Kim, Porterfield, & Han, 2004; Lightfoot et al., 2011). While children with intellectual or developmental disabilities make up a smaller percentage of the total number of youth with disabilities in child welfare, these youth also have a higher likelihood of child welfare involvement (Jones et al., 2012, Slayter & Springer, 2011). There are still very few studies of children with other types of disabilities involved in the child welfare system, including children with physical or sensory disabilities (Jones et al., 2012).

Prevalence of Youth with Disabilities in Foster Care

While federal administrative data show that 12.6% of youth with substantiated maltreatment by child welfare agencies have a disability, these same data show that 31.8% of youth in foster care have a disability (Slayter, 2016). While, as noted earlier, the federal administrative data still have quality issues, other studies have shown similar, though slightly lower percentages of youth with disabilities in foster care (Lightfoot et al., 2011). Also striking is that 40% of school-age (5–18) children in foster care have a disability (Slayter, 2016), and for those youth in foster care transitioning out, roughly 60% have a disability (Hill, 2010). Similar to youth with disabilities involved with child welfare services, foster youth with disabilities are slightly more likely to be male and white than youth without disabilities, and much more likely to be older than those without disabilities. These high rates of foster care involvement of youth with disabilities warrant much more attention in order to understand which processes lead to these disproportionate rates of involvement. Further, it also suggests that anyone whose work relates to foster care should be well versed in disability theory, disability issues, disability services, and disability supports.

Entry into Foster Care: Court Order and Voluntary Placements

While the majority of children with disabilities enter foster care through a court order due to a substantiated finding of child maltreatment, in some cases, children may enter the foster care system through a voluntary placement agreement (Friesen, Giliberti, Katz-Leavy, Osher, & Pullman, 2003; Hill, 2017; Slayter & Springer, 2011). While the use and regulation of voluntary foster care placements (sometimes referred to as voluntary placement agreements) vary among states, typically, they are intended to be short-term placements that families and child welfare providers enter into without court involvement (Hill, 2017). In these cases, child welfare agencies become legal custodians of the child until the court and medical providers determine that the child can be returned to the family home. For the duration of these voluntary agreements, the same state and federal programs that cover children who enter child welfare involuntarily become the custodians of the voluntarily-placed child's placement, care, and supervision. If a child is placed into state care, then foster care, Medicaid, and/or special education funds can be accessed to cover the costs of their care (Brennan & Lynch, 2008; National Alliance on Mental Illness—Minnesota, 2009). The parameters and regulations of voluntary placements vary from state to state; in some cases, relinquishing legal custody occurs at the same time; in others, parents retain legal custody, but give up physical custody in order to place their child in state care (Bringewatt & Gershoff, 2010; Friesen et al., 2003).

Children with certain types of disabilities are more likely to enter foster care through these voluntary placements. Children with intellectual disabilities, for example, have higher rates of voluntary placement agreements than children without intellectual disabilities (Slayter & Springer, 2011). The use of voluntary foster care placements is also commonly used to fill gaps in mental health services for children with significant mental health diagnoses, occurring in upwards of 25% of cases of families of children with mental health disabilities (Friesen et al., 2003; U.S. General Accounting Office, 2003). Systemic challenges, such as a lack of availability of necessary supports (including respite care, community-based services, and in-home care), and the financial demands to pay for the identified supports are all reasons why families may choose to relinquish a family member into a voluntary placement (Friesen et al., 2003; Nankervis, Rosewarne, & Vassos, 2011; U.S. General Accounting Office, 2003). While the placements are intended to be temporary, as are all foster placements, Hill (2017) found that children who are in voluntary foster care placements are in out-of-home placements for a longer period of time, over their lifetimes, than children who enter foster care through a court order. The use of these placements is not well-studied at this time, and is an area for further research.

Children and Youth with Disabilities in Foster Care

Children and youth with disabilities often have different experiences in foster care than children and youth without a disability diagnosis. For example, when children with disabilities are in foster care, they are less likely to be placed in kinship care placements—for example, with a grandmother or an aunt—and more likely to be placed in a foster care placement with strangers (Romney, Litrownik, Newton, & Lau, 2006; Rosenberg & Robinson, 2004). Children with disabilities are also more likely to be placed in congregate care settings, such as group homes or institutions, than in family foster care settings. Foster children with disabilities who are placed in family-style settings are more likely to be placed in a non-kinship placement (National Council on Disability, 2008; Slayter, 2016). There are multiple reasons why children with disabilities may be placed in these types of placement, ranging from their need for more complex care, to social expectations about where children with disabilities should or should not be placed, to lack of adequate community-based supports for families.

Children and youth with disabilities are also more likely to experience placement instability and disruptions than their peers without disabilities labels (Helton, 2011; Hill, 2012; Slayter & Springer, 2011; Slayter, 2016). Children with disabilities are more likely to be in foster care placements for longer periods of time than their peers without disabilities. They are also less likely to be reunified with their families of origin. Children with disabilities are also more likely to experience placement disruptions, meaning they are more likely to be moved from one placement setting to another over the course of their time in the foster care system. Thus, they often experience a higher number of unique foster care placements over the course of their time in the foster care system (Hill, 2012; Rosenberg & Robinson, 2004).

Placement instability for children with disabilities has been attributed to many causes, including the higher cost of care for these children, the greater demands on both foster and biological families, and a lack of appropriate supports for caregivers (Park & Ryan, 2009; Rosenberg & Robinson, 2004; Slayter & Springer, 2011). Children with intellectual disabilities and behavioral disabilities are particularly likely to experience a disrupted placement (Helton, 2011; Slayter & Springer, 2011).

Leaving Placement

Unfortunately, children and youth with disabilities are less likely to be reunified with their families of origin and are less likely to be adopted than their peers without disabilities (Hill, 2012; Humphrey,

Turnbull, A., & Turnbull, H., 2006; Romney et al., 2006; Slayter, 2016). Thus, there is an increased likelihood that a child with a disability who is placed in foster care will experience long-term foster care and ultimately age out of the system. Studies have identified that between 40% (Okpych, 2015) and 60% (Hill, 2012) of youth who are emancipating from foster care are identified as having at least one disability. Okpych (2015) found that youth with disabilities were more likely to access independent living services funded by the John H. Chafee Foster Care Independence Program, which is the federal program that provides grants to states to help current and former foster youth to achieve self-sufficiency. However, Okpych also found that there were differences in access among different diagnoses. For example, youth with hearing or visual impairments were more likely to receive more types of Chafee services than their peers without disabilities (Okpych, 2015). Youth with disabilities who emancipate are less likely to reunify with family members at emancipation—either a parent or other family member (Hill, 2012; Slayter, 2016). They are more likely to be transferred from foster care to the care of another state agency, such as a developmental disability service (Slayter, 2016). Despite these services, youth with disabilities who are emancipating from foster care are at risk for particularly poor adult outcomes. The research that has focused on the experiences of these youth has found that there are even lower rates of employment, educational attainment, and economic stability among youth with disabilities than among their peers without disabilities (Anctil, McCubbin, O'Brien, & Pecora, 2007; Anctil, McCubbin, O'Brien, Pecora, & Anderson-Harumi, 2007; Zetlin, 2006).

Adoption from Foster Care

While there are multiple studies which indicate that a child's disability diagnosis decreases their likelihood of adoption (Snowden, Leon, & Sieracki, 2008), there are many children and youth with disabilities who are placed with adoptive families. Once they are permanently placed with families, children with disabilities often continue to face challenges in adjustment to their new homes. Grotevant, Dunbard, Kohler, & Esau (2000) found that children and youth with at-risk histories often enter their adoptive families with multiple identified risk factors. Pre-adoptive risk factors, such as a history of maltreatment, a history of out-of-home placement, and prenatal drug or alcohol exposure may all manifest themselves in emotional or behavioral problems post-adoption (Wind, Brooks, & Barth, 2009). Foster parents of children and youth with disabilities have noted the positive relationship between the number of placements a child experiences and the difficulties she or he is likely to face, particularly in terms of behavioral and emotional adjustments (Brown, 2007; Wind et al., 2009). Thus, children and youth with an identified disability may also have experienced environmental or situational challenges that will negatively impact an adoptive family's adjustment to the child, as they are more likely to have experienced multiple placements (Schweiger & O'Brien, 2005; Wind et al., 2009).

Systems Interactions

Children and youth with disabilities who are in foster care are often also connected with other service systems, such as special education, disability services, or children's mental health services. Thus, there are many opportunities for collaboration and cross-system resource sharing and access for these young people. However, past research has identified challenges in providing integrated care for youth across systems (Bringewatt & Gershoff, 2010; Hill, 2013; Hill et al., 2010). Slayter (2016) discusses the differences in theoretical approaches to practice between child welfare and disability services, with child welfare typically taking a more time-limited and involuntary approach to services in comparison to disability services' lifetime approach. Other challenges to collaboration include limits on data sharing across different systems of care. For example, it is often difficult for privacy and/or bureaucratic reasons for child welfare agencies to share data with schools. In addition, there is a lack of knowledge about different areas of support offered by the various systems that affect children and youth with disabilities in foster care (Lightfoot, 2014; Hill, 2012; Slayter, 2016). For example, Geenen and Powers' (2007) study found that foster youth with disabilities generally have low rates of involvement in their Individualized Education Program (IEP) meetings. In addition, they often do not have family members, foster parents, or other advocates present at the meetings, and the IEPs themselves are generally of fairly low quality, with few goals listed in relation to independent living skills and postsecondary education. Other research has found that child welfare workers often do not consult a young person's IEP while working with youth with disabilities, or do not see it as a useful document in their own transition planning process with the young person (Hill et al., 2010). Different professionals, such as teachers, child welfare workers, and rehabilitation counselors, typically are all interested in improving a child's life, yet have different and sometimes conflicting methods. Further, a lack of knowledge on the breadth of policies and procedures that exist within all of these different systems of care can pose serious barriers to the successful provision of integrated, coordinated services (Noonan et al., 2012; Stone, D'Andrade, & Austin, 2007; Trout, Ortiz Lienemann, Reid, & Epstein, 2007). Thus, a greater emphasis on data-sharing and integrated services would help children and youth with disabilities succeed.

Improving Services for Youth with Disabilities in Foster Care

As roughly a third of youth in foster care are currently identified with some type of disability, it is important that child welfare workers have the appropriate knowledge and skills necessary to provide appropriate services and supports to this key client population. In addition, as people with disabilities often are involved with multiple systems, system collaboration is also important. Finally, for those working in the area of disabilities, whether as a disability case manager or a school social worker, knowledge on how to support youth with disabilities in the child welfare system is important.

Child Welfare Workforce Training

A key ingredient for improving services and supports for youth with disabilities in foster care is to ensure that those providing services to youth with disabilities and their families in child welfare are competent in providing services to people with disabilities. At the very least, child welfare workers should:

- understand the various models of disabilities and the key trends in disability services and supports;
- be aware of the increased rates of maltreatment, child welfare involvement, and foster care placement of children and youth with disabilities;
- have a firm understanding of the disability and child welfare policies that protect against discrimination of youth with disabilities in foster care and their families;
- be able to make appropriate disability modifications to services for foster youth and their families; and
- be able to help youth and their families access disability services and supports outside the child welfare system.

To help child welfare workers gain this type of competency, content on disabilities should be included in undergraduate and graduate social work programs, as well as during in-service training provided to new child welfare workers. Social workers could also gain disability knowledge through participation in continuing education and training. It is important for those working with foster youth with disabilities to be able to understand both the broad policy context of their work as well as the subtle biases that might affect their child welfare practice (e.g., "It will be hard to find an adoptive family for this older kid with a disability," or "College planning for this youth with a disability on my caseload isn't appropriate as he won't make it in college").

Increased Collaboration

While improving the disability competence of child welfare workers is certainly important, most child welfare workers will not become experts in disability issues. Thus, it is vital for child welfare workers to collaborate more effectively with those with disability expertise, such as disability service providers, mental health counselors, public health nurses, special education providers, and disability advocates. While informal collaborations are important, the more those collaborations can be formalized, the easier it will be to sustain them. Meaningful collaboration will include measures that allow service providers from different areas to share information; for example, for school social workers and children's mental health workers to be able to share detailed information about clients with foster care case managers. Another critical issue is a lack of understanding of services that are received or even possible for children and youth with disabilities through service providers outside the child welfare system (Hill et al., 2010). Additionally, increased collaboration will help to prevent duplicative or contradictory services and interventions, which will lead to better outcomes.

Another area for collaboration is increasing awareness of and advocacy for the needs of children and youth who are in foster care among professionals in schools and disability services. For example, children and youth who are in foster care are best served by making connections with caring adults, whether through permanent families or ongoing mentors or supports. Teachers, school social workers, and other disability service providers are well positioned to identify these relationships, due to their own work with students. They can all encourage adults to be involved. Additionally, there may be opportunities during regularly scheduled meetings— for example, an IEP meeting with a special education teacher and a school social worker—to talk with a child about permanency, planning for transition, or other issues that may arise for children and youth in foster care (Hill & Koester, 2015). For example, school social workers, during an IEP meeting, could ask a youth questions such as:

1. What is your current living situation? Is it stable?
2. Are you involved in the child welfare system? Have you ever been?
3. Do you have supportive adults in your life now? Who are they? Would you like them to be involved in some way in your transition planning?
4. What is your legal status (i.e., ward of state, etc.) and what is your permanency plan?
5. Are you involved in transition programs through any other sources (e.g., Education and Training Vouchers, Independent Living Plans)? If so, what are you working on? (Disability and Child Welfare Collaborative, 2013).

Knowing what questions to ask can help to identify resources and materials across systems, and create meaningful opportunities to improve communication, planning, and outcomes that may be very powerful.

Prevention

As families of children and youth with disabilities often report higher levels of stress, and as much of the stress they experience is related to a lack of adequate family supports, prevention should primarily focus on providing additional sources of support to families with a child or youth with a disability. This could include helping families to obtain respite care, tailored parenting training related to their child's specific disability needs, and helping parents to connect with other parents for informal support. Respite care is the provision of short-term, temporary breaks from caregiving, and has been found in repeated studies to reduce the family stress levels (Cowen & Reed, 2002; Hastings & Beck, 2004). Connecting families with formal respite care, or helping families work out informal respite care, can be an important step in preventing family stress from escalating to more harmful behaviors. Second, while child welfare organizations often mandate parental training for families who become involved in the system, and tailored, disability-specific training is indeed important in these cases, earlier parental training can help to prevent abuse or neglect among families of children with disabilities. Studies have found that parent-training classes for parents of children with disabilities reduce the number of negative parent–child interactions (McIntyre, 2008). Many disability organizations offer parental training and support groups, and these will likely be effective and relevant to families that have a child with a disability. Further, helping parents to connect with other parents who have a child with a disability can be an excellent source of support as well. Parents can find support groups in person or online. Parents who join support groups have found that such groups have helped them to learn parenting skills, gain a greater sense of agency in their daily activities, and develop important social supports (Law, King, S., Stewart, & King, G., 2002; Solomon, Pistrang & Barker, 2001). Finally, there is a need for systems change across the health and social service system to move away from the medical model of disability. Professionals do not help parents who have children and youth with disabilities by consistently considering their child with a disability as a problem that needs to be addressed. The less societal stigma there is attributed to disability, the less stress families would have.

Research and Model Development

The research data on the experiences of children and youth in the child welfare system would be well served by being more inclusive of the experiences of children and youth with disabilities in that system (Blakeslee et al., 2013; Hill, 2012; Lightfoot, 2014). As discussed by Blakeslee and colleagues (2013), barriers to including youth with disabilities in child welfare research include challenges in the identification of disability in existing data sets, obstacles related to confidentiality and legal consent for participation in research studies, and challenges in retention during longitudinal studies due to disruption and instability in the youth's foster care experiences. Other barriers to research may arise due to multi-system involvement. Additionally, in multiple previous studies, some children and youth with disabilities have been intentionally excluded from the sample, such as in the Midwest Evaluation of Adult Functioning of Former Foster Youth (Courtney & Hughes-Heuring, 2005) and the Northwest Foster Care Alumni Study (Pecora et al., 2005). Thus, there is a need for child welfare researchers to adopt strategies to intentionally recruit and retain children and youth with disabilities, their families, and the professionals who support them to participate in research studies (Blakeslee et al., 2013).

We call on researchers, policymakers, and programs to realign their understanding of disability as "the interplay of diverse human conditions with environmental barriers to full community inclusion" (Gilson & DePoy, 2002, p. 153), rather than solely a medical diagnosis or individual challenge (Oliver, 2013), as this could lead to a more inclusive and holistic approach to child welfare practice. Researchers, for example, could identify the common barriers to participation and inclusion of children and youth with disabilities in their work, and build on successful models to address these barriers. Previous work by Powers and colleagues (2012), and Geenen and colleagues (2012) both identify methods for successful inclusion in research of children and youth with disabilities who are in foster care. These methods include: comprehensive identification of eligible youth; systematic contact with and recruitment of possible study participants; developing and maintaining ongoing relationships with research participants; and using communication strategies that are favored by youth such as text messaging and social media contacts (Blakeslee et al., 2013). We encourage future researchers in child welfare to be similarly inclusive in their approaches, and to actively identify methods that incorporate into research and, ultimately, into policy and practice, the experiences of children and youth with disabilities. Including the voices of foster youth and their families in research and policy and program development will lead to more interventions that are more responsive to their needs and experiences.

Policy Changes

Federal legislation has called repeatedly for increased resource sharing among child-serving agencies. For example, the 2008 Fostering Connections to Success and Increasing Adoptions Act required schools and child welfare agencies to work together to improve academic outcomes for children and youth who are in foster care. Policy changes that continue to integrate services in a meaningful way are important. Additionally, policies that mandate collaboration and training across child welfare and disability systems could make a great impact. Increasing funding for services such as respite care, support groups, and tailored parenting training would help to prevent children and youth with disabilities from entering into foster care. If a child is placed in foster care, increasing disability-relevant supports for foster families, ensuring that foster placements are accessible for children and youth with disabilities, and working to integrate foster care with disability services would all be important policy interventions. Policies that promote adoption of and permanency for children and youth with disabilities, including ensuring access to disability-competent service providers on an ongoing basis for adoptive families and potential adoptive families, are very important. Finally, ensuring that all children and youth have access to adequate health care and mental health care, whether or not they are in the child welfare system, would be an important intervention.

Conclusion

Children and youth with disabilities represent a significant percentage of children who are in foster care, although reporting systems make arriving at exact numbers difficult. It is likely that many children and youth with disabilities who are in foster care are also receiving services from other systems, such as special education, children's mental health, or rehabilitation. However, providers in many of these systems work in isolation from each other, and often do not achieve a sufficient level of knowledge and awareness of the services available or of the challenges facing children and youth who fall into these multiple systems of care. There is an ongoing need to improve collaboration, resource sharing, and cross-training among and between the various systems of care that work with children and youth with disabilities. Child welfare workers need to become disability-competent, and disability service providers need to become child-welfare-competent. In addition, the foster care system should work to move away from a medical model of disability, and rather begin to approach children and youth with disabilities from a strengths-based perspective. There is much work to be done; however, policy changes such as the passage of the Fostering Connections to Success and Increasing Adoptions Act (2008) and the reauthorization of CAPTA (2010) have begun to lay the groundwork for these improvements. It is up to advocates and social workers to continue the charge.

References

Adler, M. C. & Hendershot, G. E. (2000). *Federal disability surveys in the United States: Lessons and challenges.* Proceedings of the Survey Research Methods Section, American Statistical Association. Available at: www.amstat.org/Sections/Srms/Proceedings/papers/2000_014.pdf

American Academy of Pediatrics [AAP] (Committee on Child Abuse and Neglect & Committee on Children with Disabilities). (2001). Assessment of maltreatment of children with disabilities. *Pediatrics, 108*(2), 508–512.

Americans with Disabilities Act of 1990, P.L. 101-336. (1990).
Anctil, T., McCubbin, L., O'Brien, K., & Pecora, P. (2007). An evaluation of recovery factors for foster care alumni with physical or psychiatric impairments: Predictors of psychological outcomes. *Children and Youth Services Review, 29*(8), 1021–1034.
Anctil, T., McCubbin, L., O'Brien, K., Pecora, P., & Anderson-Harumi, C. (2007). Predictors of adult quality of life for foster care alumni with physical and/or psychiatric disabilities. *Children and Youth Services Review, 29*(8), 1087–1100.
Blakeslee, J., Quest, A. D., Powers, J., Powers, L., Geenen, S., Nelson, M., ... members of the Research Consortium to Increase the Success of Youth in Foster Care. (2013). Reaching everyone: Promoting the inclusion of youth with disabilities in evaluating foster care outcomes. *Children and Youth Services Review, 35*, 1801–1808.
Bonner, B., Crow, S., & Hensley, L. (1997). State efforts to identify maltreated children with disabilities: A follow-up study. *Child Maltreatment, 2*(1), 52–60.
Brennan, E. & Lynch, F. (2008) Economic impact and supports. In J. Rozenweig & E. Brennan (Eds.), *Work, life, and the mental health system of care: A guide for professionals supporting families of children with emotional or behavioral disorders* (pp. 239–269). Baltimore, MD: Paul H Brooks Publishing.
Bringewatt, E. & Gershoff, E. (2010). Falling through the cracks: Gaps and barriers in the mental health system for America's disadvantaged children. *Children and Youth Services Review, 32*, 1291–1299.
Brown, J. (2007). Fostering children with disabilities: A concept map of parent needs. *Children and Youth Services Review, 2*, 1235–1248.
Bruhn, C. (2003). Children with disabilities: Abuse, neglect, and the child welfare system. *Journal of Aggression, Maltreatment, and Trauma, 8*(1/2), 173–203.
Campbell, F. (2008). Exploring internalized ableism using critical race theory. *Disability and Society, 23*, 151–162. doi: 10.1080/09687590701841190
Child Abuse Prevention and Treatment Reauthorization Act of 2010, P.L. 111-320. (2010).
Connors, C. & Stalker, K. (2007). Children's experience of disability: Pointers to a social model of childhood disability. *Disability and Society, 22*, 19–33.
Courtney, M. E. & Hughes-Heuring, D. (2005). The transition to adulthood for youth "aging out" of the foster care system. In D. W. Osgood, E. M. Foster & R. Gretchen (Eds.), *On your own without a net: The transition to adulthood for vulnerable populations* (pp. 27–32). Chicago: University of Chicago Press.
Cowen, P. & Reed, D. (2002). Effects of respite care for children with developmental disabilities: Evaluation of an intervention for at risk families. *Public Health Nursing, 19*(4), 272–283.
Crosse, S., Kaye, E., & Ratnofsky, A. (1992). *A report on the maltreatment of children with disabilities*. Washington, DC: Westat, Inc.
Developmental Disabilities Assistance and Bill of Rights Act of 2000, P.L. 106-402 § 102. (2000). Disability and Child Welfare Collaborative. (2013). *Questions to ask during IEP/transition planning meetings*. Retrieved from www.cascw.org/wp-content/uploads/2013/11/QuestionsToPromotePermanency_11_2016.pdf
Earle, A., & Heymann, J. (2012). The cost of caregiving: Wage loss among caregivers of elderly and disabled adults and children with special needs. *Community, Work & Family, 15*(3), 357–375.
Fostering Connections to Success and Increasing Adoptions Act of 2008, P.L. 110-351. (2008).
Friesen, B., Giliberti, M., Katz-Leavy, J., Osher, T., & Pullman, M. (2003). Research in the service of policy change: The "custody problem". *Journal of Emotional and Behavioral Disorders, 11*(1), 39–47.
Geenen, S. & Powers, L. (2007). "Tomorrow is another problem": The experiences of youth in foster care during their transition to adulthood. *Children and Youth Services Review, 29*(8), 1085–1101.
Geenen, S., Powers, L., Powers, J., Cunningham, M., McMahon, L., Nelson, M., ... other members of the Research Consortium to Increase the Success of Youth in Foster Care (2012). Experimental study of self-determination intervention for youth in foster care. *Career Development for Exceptional Individuals*. http://dx.doi.org/10.1177/2165143412455431
Gilbert, R., Widom, C., Browne, K., Fergusson, D., Webb, E., & Janson, S. (2009). Burden and consequences of child maltreatment in high-income countries. *The Lancet, 373*(9657), 68–81.
Gilson, S. & Depoy, E. (2002). Theoretical approaches to disability content in social work education. *Journal of Social Work Education, 38*(1), 153–165.
Grotevant, H., Dunbard, N., Kohler, J. K., & Esau, A. M. L. (2000). Adoptive identity: How contexts within and beyond the family shape developmental pathways. *Family Relations, 49*, 379–387
Hastings, P. & Beck, A. (2004). Practitioner review: Stress intervention for parents of children with intellectual disabilities. *Journal of Child Psychology and Psychiatry, 45*(8), 1338–1349.
Helton, J. (2011). Children with behavioral, non-behavioral, and multiple disabilities, and the risk of out-of-home placement disruption. *Child Abuse & Neglect, 35*, 956–964.

Hill, K. (2012). Permanency and placement for older youth with disabilities: An analysis of state administrative data. *Children and Youth Services Review, 34*(8), 1418–1424.

Hill, K. (2013). Special education experiences of older foster youth with disabilities: An analysis of state administrative data. *Journal of Public Child Welfare, 7,* 520–535.

Hill, K. (2017). Prevalence, experiences, and characteristics of children and youth who enter foster care through Voluntary Placement Agreements. *Children and Youth Services Review, 74,* 62–70.

Hill, K. & Koester, S. (2015). "All he needed was love": An examination of the impact of permanency on young adults' special education experiences. *Children and Schools.* doi: 10.1093/cs/cdv016

Hill, K., Lightfoot, E., & Kimball, E. (2010). Independent living services for youth with disabilities as they transition from foster care. *Child Welfare, 89*(6), 62–81.

Humphrey, K., Turnbull, A., & Turnbull, H. (2006). Impact of the Adoption and Safe Families Act on youth and their families: Perspectives of foster care providers, youth with emotional disorders, service providers, and judges. *Children and Youth Services Review, 28,* 113–132.

Individuals with Disabilities Education Act, 20 U.S.C. § 1400. (2004).

Jones, L., Bellis, M. A., Wood, S., Hughes, K., McCoy, E., Eckley, L., . . . Officer, A. (2012). Prevalence and risk of violence against children with disabilities: A systematic review and meta-analysis of observational studies. *The Lancet, 380*(9845), 899–907.

Jonson-Reid, M., Drake, B., Kim, J., Porterfield, S., & Han, L. (2004). A prospective analysis of the relationship between reported child maltreatment and special education eligibility among poor children. *Child Maltreatment, 9*(4), 382–394.

Kayama, M. & Haight, W. (2013). The experiences of Japanese elementary-school children living with "developmental disabilities": Navigating peer relationships. *Qualitative Social Work, 12*(5), 555–571.

Law, M., King, S., Stewart, D., & King, G. (2002). The perceived effects of parent-led support groups for parents of children with disabilities. *Physical and Occupational Therapy in Pediatrics, 21*(2–3), 29–48.

Lightfoot, E. (2014). Children and youth with disabilities in the child welfare system: An overview. *Child Welfare, 93*(2), 23–45.

Lightfoot, E., Hill, K., & LaLiberte, T. (2011). Prevalence of children with disabilities in the child welfare system. *Children and Youth Services Review, 33*(11), 2069–2075.

Lightfoot, E. & LaLiberte, T. (2006). Approaches to child protection case management for cases involving people with disabilities. *Child Abuse & Neglect, 30*(4), 381–391.

Lightfoot, E., LaLiberte, T., & Cho, M. (2017). A case record review of termination of parental rights cases involving parents with a disability. *Children and Youth Services Review, 79,* 399–407.

Mackelprang, R. W. & Salsgiver, R. O. (1997). *Disability: A diversity model approach in human service practice.* Pacific Grove, CA: Brooks/Cole.

McIntyre, L. (2008). Parent training for young children with developmental disabilities: Randomized controlled trial. *American Journal of Mental Retardation, 113*(5), 356–368.

Nankervis, K., Rosewarne, A., & Vassos, M. (2011). Why do families relinquish care? An investigation of the factors that lead to relinquishment into out-of-home respite care. *Journal of Intellectual Disability Research, 55*(4), 422–433.

National Alliance on Mental Illness—Minnesota. (2009). *Keeping families together: A guide for families to understand intensive treatment options for children with mental illnesses.* St. Paul, MN: Author.

National Council on Disability. (2008, February). *Youth with disabilities in the foster care system: Barriers to success and proposed policy solutions.* Washington, DC: Author.

Noonan, K., Matone, M., Zlotnik, S., Hernandez-Mekonnen, R., Watts, C., Rubin, D., & Mollen C. (2012). Cross-system barriers to educational success for children in foster care: The front line perspective. *Children and Youth Services Review, 34,* 403–408.

Okpych, N. J. (2015). Receipt of independent living services among older youth in foster care: An analysis of national data from the U.S. *Children and Youth Services Review, 51,* 74–86.

Oliver, M. (2013). The social model of disability: Thirty years on. *Disability & Society, 28,* 1024–1026.

Park, J. & Ryan, J. (2009). Placement and permanency outcomes for children in out-of-home care by prior inpatient mental health treatment. *Research on Social Work Practice, 19*(1), 42–51.

Pecora, P. J., Kessler, R. C., Williams, J., O'Brien, K., Downs, A. C., English, D., . . . Holmes, K. E. (2005). *Improving family foster care: Findings from the Northwest Foster Care Alumni Study.* Seattle, WA: Casey Family Programs.

Powers, L. E., Geenen, S., Powers, J., Satya, S., Turner, A., Dalton, L., . . . other members of the Research Consortium to Increase the Success of Youth in Foster Care (2012). My life: Effects of a longitudinal randomized study of self-determination enhancement on the transition outcomes of youth in foster care and special education. *Children and Youth Services Review, 34*(11), 2179–2187.

Romney, S., Litrownik, A., Newton, R., & Lau, A. (2006). The relationship between child disability and living arrangement in child welfare. *Child Welfare, 85*(6), 965–984.

Rosenberg, S. & Robinson, C. (2004). Out-of-home placement for young children with developmental and medical conditions. *Children and Youth Services Review, 26*(8), 711–723.

Schweiger, W., & O'Brien, M. (2005). Special needs adoption: An ecological systems approach. *Family Relations, 54*(4), 512–522.

Shannon, P. & Agorastou, M. (2006). Identifying children with developmental disabilities receiving child protection services: A national survey of child welfare administrators. *Families in Society, 87*(3), 351–357.

Slayter, E. (2016). Youth with disabilities in the United States child welfare system. *Children and Youth Services Review, 64*, 155–165.

Slayter, E. & Springer, C. (2011). Child welfare-involved youth with intellectual disabilities: Pathways into and placements in foster care. *Intellectual and Developmental Disabilities, 49*(1), 1–13.

Snowden, J., Leon, S.C., & Sieracki, J.H. (2008). Predictors of adoption out of foster care: A classification tree analysis. *Children and Youth Services Review, 30*, 1318–1327.

Sobsey, D. (2002). Exceptionality, education, and maltreatment. *Exceptionality, 10*(1), 29–46.

Solomon, M., Pistrang, N., & Barker, C. (2001), The benefits of mutual support groups for parents of children with disabilities. *American Journal of Community Psychology, 29*, 113–132. doi:10.1023/A:1005253514140

Stoddard-Dare, P., DeRigne, L., Quinn, L. M., & Mallett, C. (2015). Material hardship in families with children with health concerns: Implications for practice. *Children and Youth Services Review, 49*, 11–19.

Stone, S., D'Andrade, A., & Austin, M. (2007). Educational services for children in foster care: Common and contrasting perspectives of child welfare and education stakeholders. *Journal of Public Child Welfare, 1*(2), pp. 53–70,

Sullivan, P. & Knutson, J. (2000). Maltreatment and disabilities: A population-based epidemiological study. *Child Abuse & Neglect, 24*(100), 1257–1273.

Trout, A., Ortiz Lienemann, E., Reid, R., & Epstein, M. (2007). A review of non-medication interventions to improve academi performance of children and youth with ADHD. Remedial and Special Education, 28(4), 207–226.

United Nations. (2006). *Convention on the Rights of Persons with Disabilities*. Available at www.un.org/development/desa/disabilities/convention-on-the-rights-of-persons-with-disabilities.html

U.S. Department of Education (National Center for Education Statistics). (2016). *Digest of education statistics, 2015* (NCES 2016-014), Chapter 2.

U.S. Department of Health & Human Services (Administration for Children and Families, Children's Bureau). (2015). *Child maltreatment 2013*. Retrieved from www.acf.hhs.gov/programs/cb/research-data-technology/statistics-research/child-maltreatment

U.S. General Accounting Office. (2003). *Child welfare and juvenile justice: Federal agencies could play a stronger role in helping states reduce the number of children placed solely to obtain mental health services* (GAO Publication 03-397). Washington, DC: U.S. Government Printing Office.

Watson, N. (2012). Theorising the lives of disabled children: How can disability theory help? *Children & Society, 26*(3), 192–202.

Wind, L., Brooks, D., & Barth, R. (2007). Influences of risk history and adoption preparation on post-adoption services use in U.S. adoptions. *Family Relations, 56*(4), 378–389.

World Health Organization. (2002). *Toward a common language for functioning, disability and health: ICF*. Geneva: World Health Organization.

Zetlin, A. (2006). The experiences of foster children and youth in special education. *Journal of Intellectual and Developmental Disabilities, 31*(3), 161–165.

18

Racial and Ethnic Disproportionality in Foster Care

Samuel L. Myers, Jr., William J. Sabol, Man Xu, and Diana Vega Vega

Overview

This chapter examines the methodological issues in measuring disproportionality in foster care and out-of-home placement. We begin with some key definitions. This is followed by a concise review of the literature regarding racial and ethnic disparities along different stages of the child welfare system. Next, the chapter illustrates the concepts of disparities, disproportionalities, and discrimination with applications and original calculations using national data on child maltreatment cases, substantiations, and foster care placements. A concluding section discusses implications for practice and for professionals working in the field.

Definitions

A common misconception in the literature is that racial disparities and racial disproportionalities are the same. Or, put differently, there is the incorrect contention that whenever there is a racial disproportionality, there must also be a racial disparity (Myers, 2011). This confusion comes about partly from the fact that when there are only two racial groups, the statement is correct. However, when there are multiple groups, the statement can be incorrect (Ards, Myers, Malkis, with Sugre, & Zhou, 2003). Economists, moreover, object to the claim that disparities (and/or disproportionalities) mean discrimination (Heckman, 1998). Economists' objection to the claim that disparities measure discrimination arises from their focus on market equilibria (Darity & Mason, 1998). For example, in labor markets, there may be wage disparities between blacks and whites, but some portion of those disparities can be explained by measures of productivity, education, training, experience, or other relevant factors. It is the unexplained portion of the wage disparity that is considered to be discrimination (Oaxaca, 1973). A foster care placement disparity is defined as a difference in the placement rate between groups. A disparity ratio is the ratio of the placement rates, and when this ratio differs, there is a between-group disparity. A disproportionality exists when a given group's share of the foster care placement population differs from its representation among the base population, and in this case, the base population might be reported maltreatment cases. A group is disproportionately found among those in the foster care placement population if their share of foster care placements exceeds their share of reports (Hill, 2006; Fluke Harden, Jenkins, & Ruehrdanz, 2011).

Discrimination occurs when the disparity between two groups in foster care placement cannot be explained by relevant factors (Ards, Myers, Chung, Malkis, & Hagerty, 2003). Relevant factors might include the age of the child, the circumstances of the report, previous exposure to maltreatment, and whether the allegation is substantiated. The notion of discrimination advanced in the applied econometrics literature argues that one must account not only for differences in relevant explanatory factors, but also for differences in the effects that these explanatory factors have on the observed outcomes (Darity & Mason, 1998). What has become known as the Blinder–Oaxaca decomposition methodology attempts to distinguish between the differences in characteristics (endowment effects) and the differences in the effects that these characteristics have on the outcome (the treatment or coefficient effects). This entails estimating separate regressions for each group and computing the predicted values of the disadvantaged group under the condition in which it is treated the same as the advantaged group with the same characteristics. The difference between the equal treatment and the actual outcomes is a measure of the unexplained portion of the disparity and is a measure of discrimination (Blinder, 1973; Oaxaca, 1973; Oaxaca & Ransom, 1994).

In summary, disparities, disproportionalities, and discrimination measure different things and are not always present at the same time. There can be disparities when there is no disproportionality. These disparities can diminish once one controls for relevant factors. But, even then there remains the possibility that the disparities are due to both differences in characteristics and differences in treatment. Only the differences in treatment part of the disparity can be attributed to discrimination.

Racial Disproportionality in Foster Care

Much of what is known about racial disproportionality in foster care concerns black–white differences, although as we will see later in this chapter, there are significant differences in foster care placements among different communities of color. Following Myers (2011), we define disproportionality as the ratio of the percentage of persons of a certain race or ethnicity in a target population (e.g., children who are substantiated for maltreatment) to the percentage of persons of the same group in a reference (or base) population. For example, if black youth account for 40% of the youth entering foster care, but 15% of the youth population, the black disproportionality ratio for youth entering foster care would be 3.33. When we refer to disparities, we refer to differences in the race-specific rates of an outcome, such as out-of-home placements.

Commonly, disproportionality ratios are calculated for decision points in the child welfare system with respect to the entire youth population. These decision points include: report, investigation, substantiation, and out-of-home placement. When calculated with respect to the entire youth population, following Myers (2011), we define a disproportionality ratio as "unconditional." This unconditional disproportionality ratio is often described as the racial disproportionality index (RDI), where an RDI of 1 indicates a racial or ethnic minority group's equal representation in the target population and entire youth population (e.g., Child Welfare Information Gateway, 2016).

When taking into account the fact that only the youth who have progressed to a decision point in the child welfare system can proceed further, a disproportionality ratio can be calculated based upon a prior stage or decision point in the child welfare system. When calculated relative to a reference population in a decision point in the child welfare system, the disproportionality ratio is termed "conditional" (Myers, 2011). For example, in a simplified model of the child welfare system, key decision points include the decision to refer a case to child welfare, the outcome of the child welfare investigation (e.g., whether a case of maltreatment is substantiated), and the decision to place a youth out of home.

An unconditional disproportionality ratio for a stage of the child welfare system can be estimated as the product of a series of conditional disproportionality ratios. For example, in a simple system consisting of the decisions to refer, substantiate, and place, conditional disproportionality ratios can be calculated as: the ratio of the percentage of black youth referred to child welfare to the percentage of black youth population; the percentage of black youth whose cases were substantiated to the percentage of black youth who were referred; and the percentage of black youth placed out of home to the percentage of black youth in substantiated cases. As the product of the conditional disproportionality ratios, the unconditional disproportionality ratio could be decomposed into the stages or decision points in the process so that the sources of the disproportion could be identified.

Decline in Racial Disproportionality

Many studies have documented that black children are disproportionately represented in foster care relative to their representation in the general population. Depending upon the study sample or time period, the unconditional disproportionality ratio for black children in foster care varies considerably. Hill (2006), for example, estimated that black children were represented in foster care at 3.4 times their representation in the general population. Similarly, the cumulative risk of placement in foster care by the age of 18 at the national level is greater for black and Native American children than for white children. For the period from 2000 to 2011, Wildeman and Emanuel (2014) estimated that almost 12% of black children could expect to be placed in foster care as compared to less than 5% of white children.

Several categories of explanations for the disproportionality have been offered. As summarized by Fluke et al. (2011), these include: disparate needs of children and families of color and the effects of differential poverty; bias on the part of individual caseworkers; child welfare system factors such as resource constraints; and geographic context to include the availability of services and resources, as well as neighborhood social organization.

The research also points out that it is difficult to determine which specific factors at which specific levels have effects and to what degree. In addition, the role of federal and state policies in developing an appropriate balance between strengthening families while protecting children; local program administration efforts; community organization and resources; and individual and family factors are all presented as factors that contribute to racial disproportionality (Derezotes & Poertner, 2005).

Between 2000 and 2014, the racial disproportionality ratio for black children in foster care declined, while it increased for Native Americans (Figure 18.1). In 2014, the black racial disproportionality ratio was 1.8, down from higher than 2.5 in 2000 (Child Welfare Information Gateway, 2016). Summers (2015) notes the downward trend for black children and notes the importance of explaining this trend.

One factor contributing to the decline in the black disproportionality ratio in foster care is the decline in the number of black children in foster care (Fluke et al., 2011). Between 2000 and 2014, the number of black children in foster care declined by nearly 109,000 children, or 53% (from over 206,000 to fewer than 98,000) (see Table 18.1). The volume and rate of decline for black children was larger and faster than decreases for other race/ethnic groups. By comparison, the number of Asian/Native Hawaiians declined by 50%, but from a smaller base (of 5,600 in 2000), and the number of white children declined by 12%. By contrast, the number of Hispanic children increased by 16% over this period.[1]

As the decline in the number of black youth in foster care was faster than that of other racial groups, the share of black youth in foster care also declined. In 2000, for example, black youth accounted for 38% of the foster care population, but by 2014 they accounted for 24%. Over that same period, the black youth share of the general population declined only from about 15% to about 14%. As the decrease in the black youth share of foster care population was faster than the decrease in the black youth share of the general population, the black youth disproportionality ratio had to decline. This means that the black disproportionality in the foster care population declined.

The number of youth in foster care at a point in time is a function of the *number that enter foster care* during a period and *how long they stay*. Table 18.2 shows that between 2000 and 2014, the number

S. L. Myers, Jr. et al.

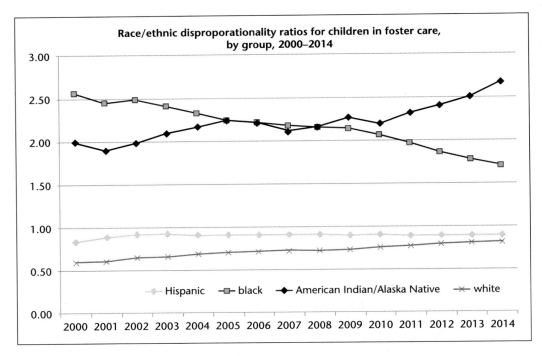

Figure 18.1 Change in the Measurement of Self-Reported Race

Source: Child Trends analysis of the Adoption and Foster Care Reporting System (AFCARS) (U.S. Department of Health & Human Services [Administration for Children and Families, Administration on Children, Youth and Families, Children's Bureau], 2000–2014).

Table 18.1 Change in the Number of Children in Foster Care, 2000–2014

Race group	Change 2000–2014		
	Number	Percent change	Contribution to total change
Hispanics	12,755	16.4%	−11.8%
American Indian Non-Hispanics	−869	−8.4%	0.8%
Asian or Native Hawaiian Non-Hispanics	−2,824	−50.2%	2.6%
Black Non-Hispanics	−108,695	−52.7%	100.1%
Multiple race Non-Hispanics	19,557	256.6%	−18.0%
White Non-Hispanics	−22,617	−11.5%	20.8%
Race unknown	−5,881	−31.6%	5.4%
Total	−108,574	−23.8%	100.0%

Source: Child Trends analysis of data from the Adoption and Foster Care Analysis and Reporting System (AFCARS), made available through the National Data Archive on Child Abuse and Neglect (U.S. Department of Health & Human Services [Administration for Children and Families, Administration on Children, Youth and Families, Children's Bureau], 2000–2014).

of youth *entering foster care* declined by 4% overall, and the number of black youth entering foster care declined much faster or by 28%. By 2014, black youth accounted for 22% of the youth entering foster care, down from 29% in 2000. Consequently, the decline in the share of black children entering foster care also contributed to the decline in the black youth in foster care disproportionality ratio.

Racial and Ethnic Disproportionality

Table 18.2 Change in the Number of Children Entering Foster Care, by Race and Hispanic Origin, 2000–2014

Race group	Change 2000–2014		
	Number	Percent change	Contribution to total change
Hispanics	16,039	39.9%	−145.0%
American Indian Non-Hispanics	−1,514	−20.3%	13.7%
Asian or Native Hawaiian Non-Hispanics	−2,043	−48.2%	18.5%
Black Non-Hispanics	−21,999	−27.7%	198.9%
Multiple race Non-Hispanics	11,302	224.4%	−102.2%
White Non-Hispanics	−9,761	−7.6%	88.3%
Race unknown	−3,084	−28.0%	27.9%
Total	**−11,060**	**−4.0%**	**100.0%**

Source: Child Trends analysis of data from the Adoption and Foster Care Analysis and Reporting System (AFCARS), made available through the National Data Archive on Child Abuse and Neglect (U.S. Department of Health & Human Services [Administration for Children and Families, Administration on Children, Youth and Families, Children's Bureau], 2000–2014).

We note that the number of Hispanic youth entering foster care increased by 40%, or by more than twice the rate of increase in the number of Hispanic youth in foster care.

There are indications that the length of stay in foster care for black youth also declined over time, but most of the decline occurred between 2000 and 2008, and since 2008, the length of stay has remained relatively constant. Black youth entering foster care in 2001, for example, could expect to stay about 2.6 years on average; by 2008, this had declined to 1.8 years and has remained constant since then. This estimate is based on our "stock-flow" estimate of expected length of stay, which is calculated as the ratio of the average population in foster care to the number of exits from foster care (Patterson & Preston, 2008). As Figure 18.1 shows, the black youth racial disproportionality ratio continued to decline beyond 2008. Given that the expected length of stay for black youth entering foster care remained constant from 2008 to 2014, factors other than length of stay contributed more to the decline in the black youth disproportionality ratio in foster care.

Changes in the share of youth of different race or ethnic groups in foster care provide important indicators of decision points to investigate in order to identify the factors that contributed to the changing proportions. For example, we need to know if there have been comparable declines in the racial composition of children referred, investigated, substantiated, and placed, and the extent to which changes in these distributions accounted for the change in the racial disproportionality. Further, if changes occurred at these key decision points, we also need to know the extent to which they may have been determined by a few or many geographical locations. If, for example, changes only in a few largely populated areas accounted for the decrease in the black disproportionality index, we would conclude that racial disproportionality was not declining in most places. To our knowledge, there has not been a systematic investigation of the decline.

Population-Based versus Decision-Point-Based Measures of Racial Disproportionality

Thus far we have reviewed unconditional disproportionality measures; that is, those based upon the general youth population as the reference group. By comparison, racial disproportionality measures can be developed based upon reference groups that reflect the subset of all youth who appear in a prior stage of the child welfare process, or at a prior decision point. With these conditional disproportionality measures, only the children whose cases have progressed through the child welfare system to the point at which an out-of-home placement decision is pending are included in the population base for calculating disproportionality measures. For foster care placement in a decision-points framework, only the youth in cases investigated and substantiated, or for whom a case has been opened, are considered as the reference population.

Racial disproportionality in foster care measures that are based upon comparisons to the general population have been critiqued on methodological grounds. Morton, Ocasio, and Simmel (2011) argue that unconditional disproportionality measures neglect to account for selection effects that occur as children are engaged by the child welfare system and move through various decision points. Only youth in families in which maltreatment is expected have investigations; only those youth or families involved in investigations can have a finding of substantiation or a case opening, and ultimately, entry into foster care. Using the general population as the denominator to measure racial disproportionality in the various stages of child welfare decision points creates a mismatch between child welfare practices and analytic methods. By using an unconditional measure, the critique continues, policy makers may make incorrect inferences about the decision points that give rise to racial disproportionality.

Conditional disproportionality ratios for black youth reported in the literature generally are closer to 1 (an indication of equality) than are unconditional disproportionality ratios. This is particularly the case for the investigation and substantiation stages of the child welfare system. For the decision to place a youth out of home, conditional upon substantiation or case opening, the studies generally find conditional racial disproportionality indexes of greater than 1, but smaller in value than the unconditional racial disproportionality measures for foster care placement.

For example, in its report on racial disproportionality in child welfare, the Children's Bureau presents both unconditional and conditional disproportionality ratios. The unconditional racial disproportionality index for black youth in foster care in 2014 was 1.8. By comparison, the conditional racial disproportionality index for black youth in foster care, based upon the proportion of black youth identified by Child Protective Services as victims, was 1.1, and the conditional RD1 for black youth entering foster care was less than 1, at 0.9 (Child Welfare Information Gateway, 2016).

Fluke et al. (2011) show a similar result using data from Colorado to measure three decisions made post referral to child welfare: investigation, open case, and removal from home. When using the general population to measure disproportionality, black youth were 2.3 times as likely to be referred to child welfare as white children, and between 2.2 and 2.6 times as likely as white children to have a case investigated, opened, or be removed from home. Conversely, taking into account the composition of youth in prior stages, black and white youth who had cases referred to child welfare were about equally likely to have cases investigated (the black-to-white ratio of case investigated conditional upon referral was 1.03). Of those who had cases investigated, black youth were slightly less likely than white youth to have cases opened (a ratio of 0.89). And, of those who had cases opened, black youth were 1.35 times as likely as white youth to be removed from home.

In their critique of methods used to describe the overrepresentation of black youth in the child welfare system, Morton et al. (2011) report a similar set of findings. Using the 2006 National Child Abuse and Neglect Data System (NCANDS) and U.S. Census Bureau data on population, and selecting the four states with the largest numbers of child maltreatment investigations (106 counties accounting for over 850,000 investigations), Morton and colleagues report reductions in disproportionality measures when moving from general population (or unconditional) measure to decision-point (or conditional) measures. Specifically, measuring racial disproportionality in investigations, substantiation, and foster care placements across the four states in the sample, they found racial general population (unconditional) disproportionality ratios in investigations and substantiation of between 1.8 and 2.6; and in foster care placements, the ratios ranged from 2.2 to 6. By comparison, by computing conditional disproportionality measures at each decision point and comparing the outcomes for black youth to white youth, they find that black youth were between

1.01 and 1.08 times as likely to have a case substantiated, and between 1.1 and 1.2 times as likely as white youth to enter into foster care.

The analyses of conditional disproportionality ratios suggest that post-investigation, the largest racial disproportionality ratios for black youth are in the decision to place black youth in foster care. For black youth nationally in foster care, the decision-point racial disproportionality ratios ranged from 1.1 to 1.35. For entry into foster care, black youth were between 0.9 and 1.2 times as likely to enter foster care as white youth. State-level studies using individual case-level data suggest that racial differences in the characteristics of cases, such as the presence of biological fathers, number of children in the household, and parental and household risk factors contribute to the racial disproportionality in out-of-home placement (Woodmass, Weisberg, Shlomi, Rockymore, & Wells, 2017).

Racial Disparities in Time Spent in Foster Care

Both unconditional and conditional racial disproportionality measures point out racial differences in time spent in foster care, based upon the difference between the racial disproportion in foster care admissions and youth in foster care. Fluke et al. (2011) document this with data from 2008. In that year, black youth made up 15% of the United States' child population, but represent 26% of children entering care and 31% of the foster care population; this yields racial disproportionality indexes of 1.6 for entering foster care and 2.1 for black youth in foster care. By comparison, white children accounted for 76% of the resident population and 44% and 40%, respectively, of those entering foster care and the foster care population. The increase in the black disproportion from entry to stock stems from longer time in foster care; the decrease observed for whites in these measures indicates less time in foster care.

Other research also confirms that time in foster care contributes to the overrepresentation of black youth in foster care. Rolock and Testa (2005) documented this in the state of Illinois, in which 3 years after entering out-of-home care, African American children living in Illinois are less likely to have exited the system to permanent homes, and more likely to stay in care than children of other races and ethnicities. In Texas, multivariate models of exit from kinship care show that both black and Hispanic children exited more slowly than did white children (Texas Health and Human Services Commission and Department of Family and Protective Services, 2006).

Compared to other children who need child welfare services, children with incarcerated parents have needs that are not easily met, and when placed in foster care, they may be less likely to achieve permanency through reunification. To the extent that a lower probability of reunification can contribute to foster care placements, Hayward and DePanfilis' (2007) study shows racial differences in reunification following parental incarceration. Using AFCARS data to predict reunification for children in foster care who had at least one incarcerated parent, they found that after controlling for child age, mental health, disability, family structure, and placement history, black parents had lower rates of reunification than parents of other race and ethnic groups.

Harris and Hackett (2008) report that African American and Native American children in King County (Washington) represented over half of the population in out-of-home care for stays longer than 4 years, and based on focus group interviews, conclude that racial inequity in service delivery and service availability contributed to the disproportionality. For families of color, the exclusion of fathers and other relatives from the process, and the perceptions that the court system was not fair, were identified as contributing to the disproportionality. Limited efforts by caseworkers to identify kin, particularly relatives residing out of state, was another issue perceived by families of color, and this was cited as contributing to the disproportionality in long-term out-of-home placements of minorities.

Stoltzfus (2005) suggests that a portion of the racial difference in the average stay in foster care (e.g., 24 months for white children as compared to more than 40 months for black children) may be attributed to the trend for African American children to spend more time in foster care with relatives. But kinship care differences alone did not account for all of the difference in the gap in time in foster care. Factors contributing to longer stays in foster care include a lower likelihood of reunification and adoption for black children as compared to their white counterparts as well as the larger proportion of black children in kinship or relative care (Barth, 2005; Bowman, Hofer, O'Rourke, & Read, 2009). The greater use of kinship care among black families has been described in several places as having both positive and potentially negative effects (e.g., Bowman et al., 2009; Foster, Hillemeier, & Bai, 2011). On the one hand, kinship care arrangements may be viewed by caseworkers as solutions (based upon cultural appropriateness and family ties) rather than temporary arrangements for African American children, thereby contributing to longer stays. On the other hand, children in kinship care generally receive less financial assistance and fewer support services. Efforts to find adoptive families that racially match the child can also contribute to lengthening time in foster care.

Racial disparities in service referrals and gaps for minority youth, especially differences in referrals to mental health services, contribute to racial disparities (Lovato-Hermann, Dellor, Tam, Curry, & Freisthler, 2017). The Children's Bureau identified gaps in culturally appropriate services, language differences, and states' difficulties in recruiting foster and adoptive parents who reflected the racial and ethnic diversity of children in need of out-of-home placement as contributing to racial disproportionality in placements (Child Welfare Information Gateway, 2011).

Racial differences in parental incarceration in the United States have negative consequences for children, including behavioral problems—such as increased physical aggression, externalizing, and internalizing (Wildeman, 2014)—that are correlated with foster care placement. Macro-social analysis by Edwards (2016) finds a relationship between the severity of criminal justice system punishments (e.g., the parental incarceration rate) and placement into foster care. Ross, Khashu, and Wamsley (2004) suggest that the direction of causality in the relationship between material incarceration and removal of a child goes from the removal to the mother's incarceration. In their study in New York City, they looked at the chronology of arrest, incarceration, and child placement to conclude that the vast majority (90%) of maternal incarcerations that overlapped with child placement started after the child placement, as did 85% of the arrests that led to those incarcerations. Child removal appeared to accelerate criminal activity among mothers, the majority of whom had prior drug convictions, and convictions for prostitution, petty theft, and crimes related to substance abuse, behaviors that could increase the risk of maltreatment and subsequent removal of children.

Other Factors Contributing to Racial Disproportionality in Placement

Studies using national datasets that aim to distinguish the effects of race from other significant contributing factors on the decision to place youth in foster care conditional upon substantiation show results that point to race effects. Summarizing an analysis of 2003 NCANDS data, Hill (2006) identifies a set of predictors of foster care placements that include: prior history of maltreatment, children younger than 4 years of age, and maltreatment type (in which children who were physically abused were more likely to be removed from the home than children who were sexually abused). Black children who were victims of maltreatment were 36% more likely to be placed in foster care than were white children. While the highest rates of out-of-home placement have been shown to be among infants under 1 year old, black infants were 3.4 times as likely as white children to be placed out of the home, according to analyses of the 2000 National Survey of Child and Adolescent Well-Being (NCSAW) data.

Knott and Donovan (2010) analyzed a sample of about 72,000 investigations of primary substantiated maltreatment in the 2005 NCANDS data to estimate the probability of placement and its association with racial identity. Controlling for child, caregiver, and household abuse characteristics, black children had a 44% higher odds of foster care placement as compared to white children. In a study using NSCAW data that examined the frequency and predictors of out-of-home placement in a 30-month follow-up period for a sample of children investigated for a report of maltreatment who remained in their homes following the initial child welfare report, Horwitz, Hurlburt, Cohen, Zhang, and Landsverk (2011) found that with few exceptions, the child and maltreatment report characteristics were unrelated to subsequent placement. Children initially reported with neglect as the most severe maltreatment type were more likely to be placed out of home than children for whom the most severe maltreatment type was identified as physical or sexual abuse; and while race was not significant after controlling for characteristics of cases, black children were almost twice as likely to be placed in the follow-up period.

In subnational studies, the effects of race on foster care placement are mixed. A statewide study in Texas, for example, did not find a significant direct effect of race on the decision to remove a child from home after controlling for variables such as family income, age of child, type of maltreatment, source of referral, and region of the state (Texas Health and Human Services Commission and Department of Family and Protective Services, 2006). Additional analyses of these data found an effect of race after controlling for the interaction between poverty and several risk measures (Rivaux et al., 2008). Graham, Dettlaff, Baumann, & Fluke (2015) examined more than 1,100 Child Protective Services caseworkers in Texas in 2007, matching their administrative records of cases and personnel records to survey responses. They found five factors to significantly influence case placement rates: primary among these were case factors such as the risk being assessed, a larger number of families with low income on a caseworker's caseload, and higher proportions of cases of Hispanic families on the caseload.

In a matched-pairs study in Minnesota, children of mothers with drug problems were more likely to be placed in out-of-home care if they were African American than if they were white (Wells, Merritt, & Weisberg, 2008a, 2008b). On the other hand, studies of placement decisions in Illinois (Harris, Tittle, & Poertner, 2005) found no effect of either the race of the child or the caregiver on the decision to place a child in out-of-home care or provide in-home services. And among families in Baltimore with substantiated child maltreatment, Zuravin and DePanfilis (1996) found that race had no significant effect on the decision to place a child in foster care.

Placement stability is cited as contributing to the racial disproportionality in foster care. Black youth in foster care also experience more frequent placement changes (Huebner, 2007; Zinn, DeCoursey, Goerge, & Courtney, 2006). In addition to the negative impact on children's development from frequent changes, multiple numbers of out-of-home placements of black youth can contribute to the racial disproportionality in placement decisions. Factors affecting placement instability also are related to the factors affecting placement. Applying a Blinder–Oaxaca statistical decomposition method (Blinder, 1973; Oaxaca, 1973) to the NSCAW data in order to distinguish between the average differences in characteristics (or endowments) of black and white children and the racial differences in the treatment of these characteristics (or return to the endowments), Foster et al. (2011) find that even after controlling for other factors, African American children have more out-of-home placements than white children. They also find that the predictors of placement instability differ between racial groups. For black children, older age, initial placement setting other than kinship care, and having more externalizing problems at the baseline measure were associated with greater placement instability. By comparison, among white children, only initial placement in foster care predicted placement instability. Finally, after decomposing the differences in endowments and returns to endowments, they find that they were unable to explain much of the racial gap in placement instability between black and white children, even with controls for child risks at baseline and family risk factors such as serious mental health problems, domestic violence experiences, difficulties paying for necessities, abuse and neglect history, and caregiver receipt of Temporary Assistance for Needy Families (TANF).

Foster et al. (2011) recommend the Blinder–Oaxaca decomposition method as a potentially useful tool for understanding racial differences in child welfare outcomes. The method requires estimating separate regressions for the groups under review in order to estimate the differences in treatments and returns to endowments. This represents an important difference from the common approach to measuring the effects of race on placement outcomes. Commonly, race enters into the analysis as an independent variable along with other variables in a regression framework. The effects of race are measured net of the effects of other variables, and a disparity is observed when the race variable is a statistically significant effect in the model. By including race among the variables in a model predicting placement outcomes, one can summarize the average effects of race, but not explain the racial disparity. The decomposition method explains the disparity in relation to endowments and treatments on the endowments.

Consistent with the Blinder–Oaxaca decomposition model of estimating race-specific equations to compare differences in treatments and characteristics of groups, Wulczyn and Lery study macro-level factors associated with racial disparities in foster care and aim to identify place-specific risks associated with the disparities (Wulczyn & Lery, 2007; Wulczyn, 2011). Focusing on racial disparities in foster care admissions as the dependent variable, they define the race-specific rates of admission into foster care as the number of admissions per resident population in a geographic area. For black youth, this is defined as the number of black youth admitted into foster care divided by the number of black youth in an area; for white youth or youth of other race or ethnic groups, the rate is defined in the same, race-specific manner.

Using county-level data for roughly 1,000 counties in states that contribute to the Multistate Foster Care Data Archive, Wulczyn and Lery found race-specific relationships. Focusing on black–white differences, they find that disparity in foster care admissions rates declined over time (between 2000 and 2005); this is consistent with the Children's Bureau reports on declining racial disproportionality for black youth (Child Welfare Information Gateway, 2016). The decline in disparity was largest in urban areas and among very young children. While the overall disparity declined, it increased for teenagers and moved from urban to non-urban counties, and among adolescents, disparity was greater in 2005 than in 2000. And, overall, black–white disparities persisted among young children, as black youth under 1 year at the time of admission were twice as likely to enter placement as white youth. Finally, placement rate disparities were greater in counties with a lower overall poverty rate, and conversely, were lower in areas with higher poverty rates and in counties with relatively fewer adults with more than a high school education. In a later study using Poisson event count models to analyze racial differences in placement rates, Wulczyn, Gibbons, Snowden, and Lery (2013) confirmed the finding that at the county ecological level, poverty is associated with a narrowing of the gap in black–white admissions into foster care, a finding that they explain by the fact that the relationship between poverty and placement rates depends on race.

Other area-based approaches also confirm the association between racial disparities in placement and geography. In their study of Shelby County, Tennessee, Lery and Wulczyn (2009) found an overall low rate of out-of-home placements, but a high African American to white disparity rate, as black children were 4.2 times more likely than white children to be placed in foster care between 2000 and 2006. For Cuyahoga County, Ohio, Crampton and Coulton (2008) use life table analysis to examine the prevalence of at least one foster care placement by age 10, finding that black youth in the county were expected to be placed at a rate that was four times that of white youth. Consistent with Wulczyn and Lery, the racial disparity in Cuyahoga County was greater for youth living in the suburban areas (lower poverty areas) than in Cleveland itself (higher poverty area). The suburban disparity in Cuyahoga County was on the order of 7 to 1 (for black versus white youth) as compared to about 2 to 1 in Cleveland.

Consistent with the main findings of this chapter, Kim, Chenot, and Juye (2011) examined racial and ethnic disparities in California's child welfare system, looking at substantiated allegations and entry into foster care between 2005 and 2008. Using latent growth curve models of the county-level trajectories of disparity index scores, they found racial disparities between black and white youth in substantiation and placement, but not between white and Hispanic youth. Higher levels of poverty and unemployment at the county level were associated with lower levels of disparity. Unemployment was associated with increasing rates of change in placement entry disparities between black and white children.

At the state level, Putnam-Hornstein, Needell, King, and Johnson-Motoyama (2013) examined child welfare outcomes for the cohort of children born in California in 2002, linking birth records to child protective services (CPS) records to identify children referred for maltreatment by the age of 5. Using a generalized linear model (GLM) to compute crude and adjusted racial and ethnic differences in risk of referral, substantiation, and entry into foster care, they found racial differences between black and white children in rates of contact with CPS. In the aggregate, black children were twice as likely as white children to be referred for maltreatment, to be substantiated as victims, and to enter foster care before the age of 5. But after controlling for socioeconomic and health factors that are correlated with CPS involvement, and adjusting for the racial differences in the distribution of these factors, they found that black children with low socioeconomic status (SES) had a lower risk of referral, substantiation, and entry into foster care than did their white counterparts.

Illustration from NCANDS

In this section, we provide original calculations on disproportionalities in foster care placement from data on persons who have come into contact with child protective services. First, we provide evidence that there are wide differences in measures of disproportionality in out-of-home placements across different racial and ethnic groups and over time. Then, we show that there is a statistically significant difference in foster care placement rates across groups and across time. The finding of racial disparities in placement rates, however, is not a finding that there is racial discrimination in foster care placement. We report on estimations using regression methodologies for measuring discrimination in foster care placement.

Evidence on Pathways to Foster Care across Groups and Time

Many naïve measures of disproportionality in foster care compare the percentage of children from a given group in the overall population to the percentage of children from that group in the foster care population. Figure 18.2 uses NCANDS Child File data from 2005 to make this point regarding putative overrepresentation of black children in the foster care system.

The National Child Abuse and Neglect Data System (NCANDS)[2] is a voluntary data collection system that gathers information from all 50 states, the District of Columbia, and Puerto Rico about reports of child abuse and neglect.[3] It shows that whereas 14.35% of the child population was black in 2005, 22.63% of the population placed into foster care from the cases of reported and substantiated child maltreatment were black. Thus, on the surface, it appears that black children were 1.5 times more likely to be placed into foster care as they are to be found in the child population. When one compares the black percentage of reports (22%) to the black percentage of foster care placements (22.63%), however, one notes that the two numbers are almost the same. When one compares the black percentage of substantiated cases (21.52%) to the black percentage of foster care placements (22.63%), one finds once again a disproportionality. In short, whether there is disproportionality depends on the relevant comparison along the pathway into and through the child protective services system.

Figure 18.3, similarly, provides the pathways to foster care placement among blacks for 2014. It shows a black share of the child population of 13.8%, a black share of reported and substantiated cases

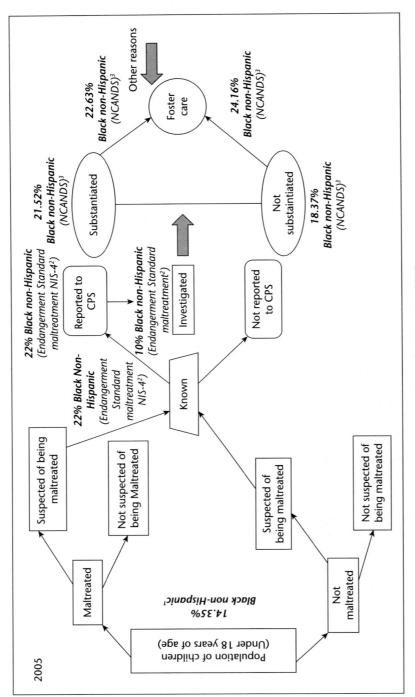

Figure 18.2 Flowchart from the Population of Foster Care, Black non-Hispanics, 2005

Notes:
1 U.S. Population Division, U.S. Census Bureau, Annie E. Casey Foundation.
2 Sedlak, A. J. & Basena, M. (2014).
3 U.S. Department of Health & Human Services (Administration for Children and Families, Administration on Children, Youth and Families, Children's Bureau). (2005).

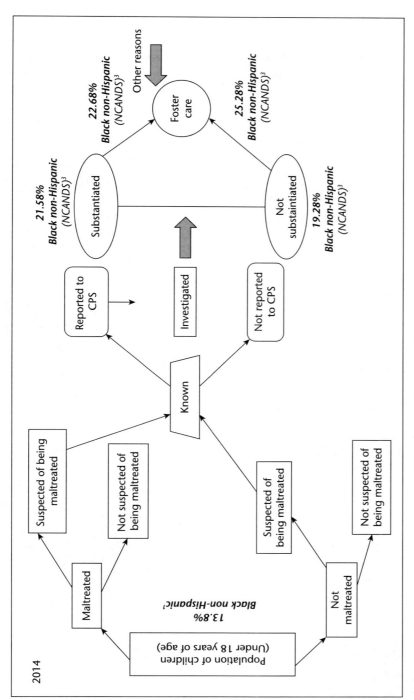

Figure 18.3 Flowchart from the Population of Foster Care, Black non-Hispanics, 2014

Notes:
1 Annual Estimates of the Resident Population by Sex, Age, Race, and Hispanic Origin for the United States and States: April 1, 2010 to July 1, 2014. Source: U.S. Census Bureau, Population Division. Release Date: June 2015.
2 Sedlak, A. J. & Basena, M. (2014).
3 U.S. Department of Health & Human Services (Administration for Children and Families, Administration on Children, Youth and Families, Children's Bureau). (2015).

of 21.58%, and a black share of foster care placements of 22.68%. The unconditional disproportionality ratio is 1.56, meaning that blacks are a little more than 1.5 times as likely to be found among those placed into foster care as they are to be found among the child population. The conditional disproportionality ratio is 1.05, meaning there is barely any difference between blacks' share of substantiated cases and blacks' share of foster care placements.

Figure 18.4 and Figure 18.5 show the pathways to foster care placement for American Indians and Alaskan Natives in 2005 and 2014. In 2005, American Indian and Alaskan Natives represented less than 1% of the child population, 1.41% of substantiated cases, and 2.17% of placements into foster care.

They were disproportionately represented among foster care placements whether the measure is conditional on substantiations or whether the measure is unconditional. In 2014, American Indians and Alaskan Natives represented .85% of the child population, 1.4% of substantiated cases, and 2.5% of foster care placements. Again, American Indians and Alaskan Natives were disproportionately placed into foster care, whether when compared to the child population or when compared to substantiations.

Figure 18.6 and Figure 18.7 report the corresponding findings for Asian, Native Hawaiian, and Pacific Islanders in 2005 and 2014. This group represented 4.04% of the child population in 2005, but 1.33% and 2.23% of substantiations and foster care placements, respectively. Asians, Native Hawaiians, and Pacific Islanders were disproportionately found among those placed into foster care relative to substantiations, but not relative to the child population. There was conditional disproportionality, but not unconditional disproportionality.

In 2014, Asians, Native Hawaiians, and Pacific Islanders accounted for 5.1% of the child population, 1.29% of substantiations, and 1.5% of foster care placements. Whereas there was no unconditional disproportionality, members of this group were 1.16 times as likely to be found among those placed into foster care as they were to be found among substantiated cases. Between 2005 and 2014, there was a decline in the conditional disproportionality ratio from 1.68 to 1.16.

Figure 18.8 and Figure 18.9 report the pathways to foster care placement for Hispanics in 2005 and 2014. In 2005, Hispanics represented 19.88% of the child population, 18.29% of substantiations, but 24.34% of foster care placements.

By 2014, Hispanics represented 24.8% of the child population, 24.31% of substantiations, and 27% of foster care placements. Thus, in both years, Hispanics were disproportionately found among those who had been placed into foster care, whether using the conditional or the unconditional measure of disproportionality.

Summary

The forgoing figures reveal that disproportionality in foster care placements differs among children of color. The figures show that the unconditional and conditional disproportionalities often diverge and yield different conclusions about whether there is an overrepresentation of a certain group among those placed into foster care. And, importantly, there are dynamics involved suggesting that a finding that is true in one year may not be true in another year.

Evidence on Racial and Ethnic Disparities in Foster Care Placement Rates

The previous section focused on disproportionalities. It is possible, however, for there to be a disparity but no disproportionality. The NCANDS data offer a unique window for examining racial and ethnic differences in foster care placement rates, either conditional on substantiations or based on all children who are reported for maltreatment (the base population for NCANDS).

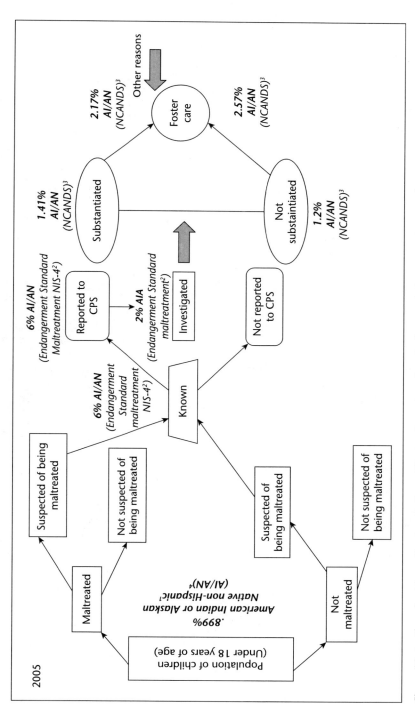

Figure 18.4 Flowchart from the Population of Foster Care, American Indian or Alaskan Native non-Hispanics (AI/AN), 2005

Notes:
1 U.S. Population Division, U.S. Census Bureau, Annie E. Casey Foundation.
2 Sedlak, A. J. & Basena, M. (2014).
3 U.S. Department of Health & Human Services (Administration for Children and Families, Administration on Children, Youth and Families, Children's Bureau). (2005).
4 Abbreviation used by the U.S. Census Bureau.

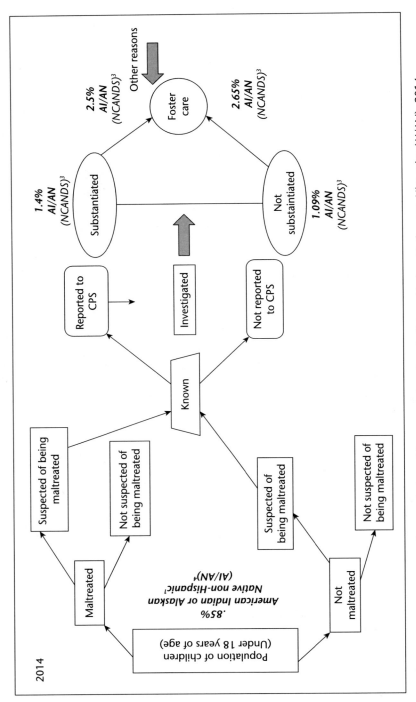

Figure 18.5 Flowchart from the population of foster care, American Indian or Alaskan Native non-Hispanics (AI/AN), 2014

Notes:
1 Annual Estimates of the Resident Population by Sex, Age, Race, and Hispanic Origin for the United States and States: April 1, 2010 to July 1, 2014. Source: U.S. Census Bureau, Population Division. Release Date: June 2015.
2 Sedlak, A. J. & Basena, M. (2014).
3 U.S. Department of Health & Human Services (Administration for Children and Families, Administration on Children, Youth and Families, Children's Bureau). (2015).
4 Abbreviation used by the U.S. Census Bureau.

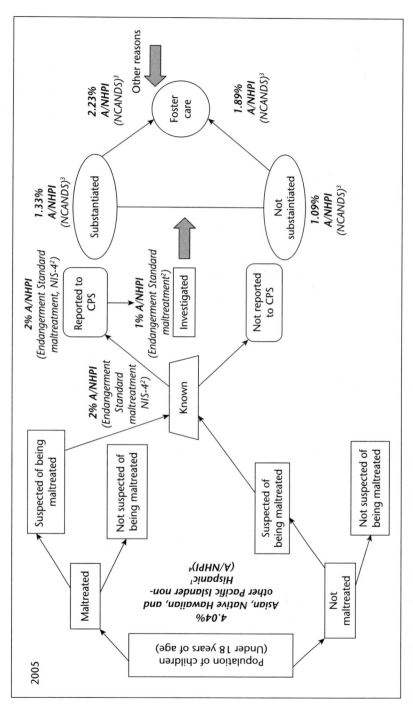

Figure 18.6 Flowchart from the population of foster care, Asian, Native Hawaiian, and other Pacific Islander non-Hispanics (A/NHPI), 2005

Notes:
1 U.S. Population Division, U.S. Census Bureau, Annie E. Casey Foundation.
2 Sedlak, A. J. & Basena, M. (2014).
3 U.S. Department of Health & Human Services (Administration for Children and Families, Administration on Children, Youth and Families, Children's Bureau). (2005).
4 Abbreviation used by the U.S. Census Bureau; 'A' added here to include Asians.

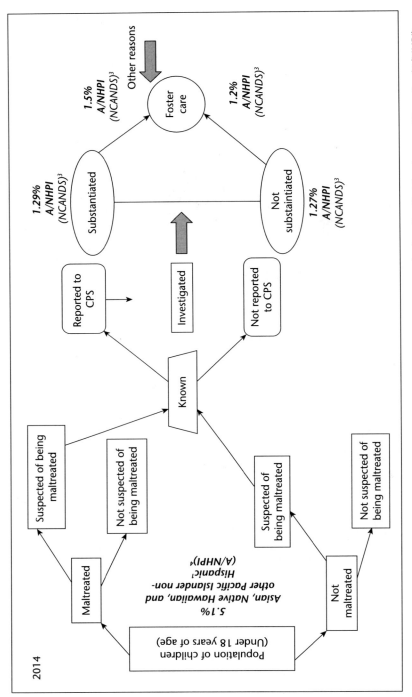

Figure 18.7 Flowchart from the population of foster care, Asian, Native Hawaiian, and other Pacific Islander non-Hispanics (A/NHPI), 2014

Notes:
1 Annual Estimates of the Resident Population by Sex, Age, Race, and Hispanic Origin for the United States and States: April 1, 2010 to July 1, 2014. Source: U.S. Census Bureau, Population Division. Release Date: June 2015.
2 Sedlak, A. J. & Basena, M. (2014).
3 U.S. Department of Health & Human Services (Administration for Children and Families, Administration on Children, Youth and Families, Children's Bureau). (2015).
4 Abbreviation used by the U.S. Census Bureau; 'A' added here to include Asians.

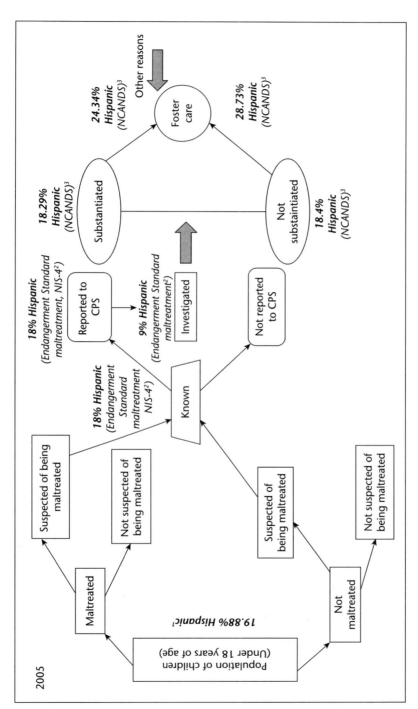

Figure 18.8 Flowchart from the Population of Foster Care, Hispanics, 2005

Notes:
1 U.S. Population Division, U.S. Census Bureau, Annie E. Casey Foundation.
2 Sedlak, A. J. & Basena, M. (2014).
3 U.S. Department of Health & Human Services (Administration for Children and Families, Administration on Children, Youth and Families, Children's Bureau). (2005).

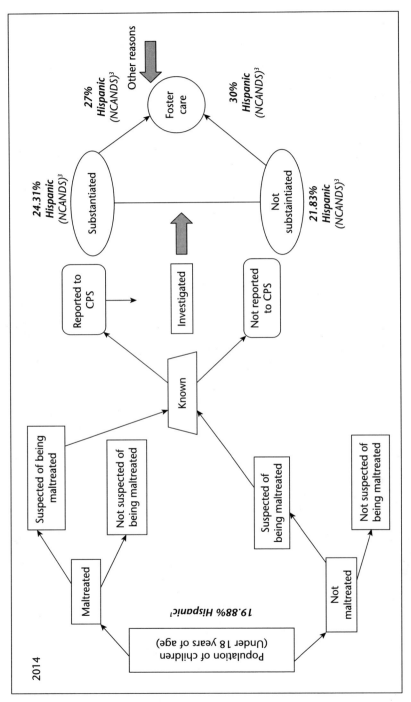

Figure 18.9 Flowchart from the Population of Foster Care, Hispanics, 2014

Notes:
1 Annual Estimates of the Resident Population by Sex, Age, Race, and Hispanic Origin for the United States and States: April 1, 2010 to July 1, 2014. Source: U.S. Census Bureau, Population Division. Release Date: June 2015.
2 Sedlak, A. J. & Basena, M. (2014).
3 U.S. Department of Health & Human Services (Administration for Children and Families, Administration on Children, Youth and Families, Children's Bureau). (2015).

Table 18.3 Means Difference Test on Unconditional Probability of Placement into Foster Care

	Mean (N)	Difference	T-score
Year of 2014			
White Non-Hispanics	0.10 (916,896)	/	/
Alaska Native or American Indian Non-Hispanics	0.19 (34,520)	−0.08	−39.757***
Asian/Hawaiian/Pacific Islander Non-Hispanics	0.15 (22,364)	−0.05	−19.982***
Black Non-Hispanics	0.11 (505,828)	−0.01	−17.725***
Hispanics	0.15 (442,914)	−0.05	−72.430***
Year of 2005			
White Non-Hispanics	0.11 (833,138)	/	/
Alaska Native or American Indian Non-Hispanics	0.31 (16,817)	−0.20	−39.757***
Asian/Hawaiian/Pacific Islander Non-Hispanics	0.28 (16,260)	−0.17	−48.186***
Black Non-Hispanics	0.13 (407,399)	−0.02	−29.358***
Hispanics	0.18 (302,538)	−0.07	−93.098***

Source: National Child Abuse and Neglect Data System (NCANDS) Child File, FFY 2005 and FFY 2014.

Notes:
1 White non-Hispanic children are the reference group.
2 * = p<0.10, ** = p<0.05, *** = p<0.01

Table 18.3 provides the results of a test of the hypothesis that the probability of placement into foster care differs between white non-Hispanics and minority children. The white non-Hispanic probability of foster care placement is lower than the black, Asian, American Indian or Hispanic probabilities. The disparity ranges from a low of 1 to 2 percentage points for African Americans in 2005 and 2014 to a high of 20 percentage points for American Indians and Alaskan Natives in 2005. Even the small disparity between blacks and whites is statistically significant.[4]

Table 18.4 provides the results of a test of the hypothesis that the conditional probability of placement, given substantiation, differs between white non-Hispanics and minority children. The conditional probability of placement into foster care, given substantiation, increased from 0.26 to 0.29 for whites between 2005 and 2014. It declined from 0.47 to 0.41 for American Indians and Alaskan Natives. It jumped from 0.26 to 0.40 for Asian/Pacific Islanders. It inched up from 0.28 to 0.29 for blacks, and declined from 0.35 to 0.34 for Hispanics. Between 2005 and 2014, the black–white disparity in foster care placement probabilities, conditional on substantiations, disappeared. For other groups, the disparities remained statistically significant and of non-trivial magnitude.

These results show that small disparities can be statistically significant and change over time. Moreover, the results show that disparities vary across racial and ethnic groups, even though whites generally have lower foster care placement rates than non-whites and Hispanics.

Table 18.4 Mean Difference Test on Probability of Placement into Foster Care Conditioning on Substantiated Case

	Mean (N)	Difference	T-score
Year of 2014			
White Non-Hispanics	0.29 (212,423)	/	/
Alaska Native or American Indian Non-Hispanics	0.41 (9,600)	−0.12	−23.304***
Asian/Hawaiian/Pacific Islander Non-Hispanics	0.40 (5,855)	−0.11	−16.718***
Black Non-Hispanics	0.29 (120,948)	−0.001	−0.632
Hispanics	0.34 (122,256)	−0.05	−31.755***
Year of 2005			
White Non-Hispanics	0.26 (236,942)	/	/
Alaska Native or American Indian Non-Hispanics	0.47 (6,686)	−0.22	−39.757***
Asian/Hawaiian/Pacific Islander Non-Hispanics	0.26 (6,731)	−0.02	−35.337***
Black Non-Hispanics	0.28 (120,087)	−0.02	−12.041***
Hispanics	0.35 (100,496)	−0.10	−55.552***

Source: National Child Abuse and Neglect Data System (NCANDS) Child File, FFY 2005 and FFY 2014.

Notes:
1 White non-Hispanic children are the reference group.
2 * = p<0.10, ** = p<0.05, *** = p<0.01.

Discrimination

Disparities do not necessarily mean that there is discrimination. Discrimination occurs when identically situated individuals from opposing groups are treated differently. One possible explanation for an observed disparity is discrimination. But there are other possible explanations as well. In this section, we present results from a regression methodology for testing for discrimination. The methodology, known as the Blinder–Oaxaca decomposition methodology, involves estimation of separate equations for the probability of foster care placement for each racial/ethnic group. Estimated coefficients in the probability model have the interpretation of being the change in the log odds ratio as a result of a change in the independent variables. Relevant variables in determining the probability of placement into foster care include characteristics of the child, characteristics of the alleged perpetrator, the nature of the maltreatment allegation, the reporter, and whether the allegation was substantiated. If these factors have the same impacts on the probability of foster care placement across groups, but the factors themselves differ between groups, then the disparity can be *explained*. If the underlying characteristics of children from different groups are exactly the same, but these characteristics have varying impacts on the probability of foster care placement, then the disparity is *unexplained*. Applied economists often refer to the unexplained portion of a disparity as "discrimination," or the portion of the disparity that is attributable to differential treatment of identically situated groups.

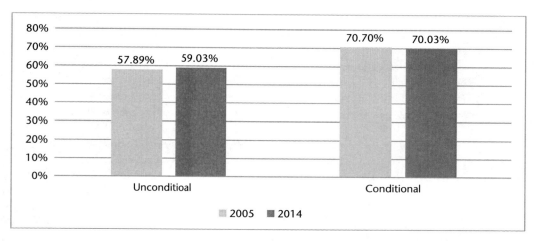

Figure 18.10 Unexplained Disparity in Foster Care Placement: White non-Hispanics versus American Indians/Alaskan Natives

Source: National Child Abuse and Neglect Data System (NCANDS) Child File, FFY 2005 and FFY 2014

Since the largest disparities in foster care placement are found between white non-Hispanics and American Indians/Alaskan Natives, we illustrate the regression methodology for these two groups. The full details of the analysis can be found at https://conservancy.umn.edu/handle/11299/189052. Suffice it to say, however, there are key factors that predict the probability of foster care placement. Figure 18.10 graphs the decomposition of the foster care placement disparity between white non-Hispanics and American Indians/Alaskan Natives for 2005 and 2014, conditional on a substantiation and unconditional.

Little of the disparity in foster care placement between white non-Hispanics and American Indians/Alaskan Natives can be explained by relevant characteristics of the child, the allegation, the reporter, or the type of maltreatment. The decomposition of the unconditional probabilities yields an unexplained percentage of 57.89% in 2005 and 59.03% in 2014. The decomposition of the probability of foster care placement, given a substantiation, yields a percent unexplained of 70.70% in 2005 and 70.03% in 2014. In the underlying regressions predicting the unconditional probability of foster care placement, the variable substantiated explains much of the variation within groups of the dependent variable.

Restricting the sample to just substantiated cases—producing a conditional probability of foster care placement—renders the disparity between white non-Hispanics and American Indians/Alaskan Natives largely unexplained. Put differently, comparable white non-Hispanic and American Indian/Alaskan Native children *whose alleged maltreatment has been substantiated* are treated differently. White non-Hispanic children are far less likely than identically situated American Indian/Alaskan Natives to be placed into foster care. From 59% to 70% of the disparity in foster care placements between white non-Hispanic children and American Indian/Alaskan Native children can be attributable to discrimination.

Implications for Practice

The key "take-away" from this chapter is that one must be extremely cautious in drawing conclusions about discrimination from evidence on disparities and disproportionalities. Conventional measures of disparities and disproportionalities do not control for relevant factors that might explain why there are disparities or disproportionalities. Relatedly, it is possible for there to be no disproportionality in foster care placement, but for there to be racial or ethnic disparities. These disparities, alone, do not tell us whether there is discrimination against specific racial or ethnic group members. Administrators and managers confronted with evidence of disparities in outcomes should conduct a thorough analysis of their databases to determine those instances where there is conflicting evidence about disparities versus disproportionalities along different decision points from entry to exit from the child welfare system. This will empower the decision makers to be able to target resources toward those transition points where there are the largest payoffs in reducing observed disparities or disproportionalities.

The simple explanation for why it is possible for there to be disparities, but no disproportionality, is that there are multiple racial/ethnic subgroups that have different experiences in and out of the child welfare system. Culturally appropriate services should recognize the considerable heterogeneity within each racial and ethnic group as well as the significant differences between groups.

Managers and administrators should consider conducting audits and detailed reviews of units that demonstrate large and persistent unexplained disparities. The regression methodology discussed in this chapter, however, is not an end. It does not provide uncontestable proof of discrimination. Rather, it is a starting point for selection of units for review and further examination. Notably, the regression methodology is subject to many limitations: omitted variable bias; selection bias; problems of unobservables and related model specification issues. But, the discrimination analysis is far superior to the simplistic reliance on measures of disparity or disproportionality to guide decision making. One of the worst consequences of inappropriate interpretation of disparities or disproportionalities as discrimination is to unfairly label caseworkers or child welfare employees as discriminators. Disparities and disproportionalities are not the same as discrimination. A key recommendation, then, is for managers and administrators to produce regular documentation on each of the measures outlined in this chapter so as to avoid the false conclusion that all of these measures capture the same qualitative concepts.

This chapter has surveyed the methodology and the techniques for measuring and detecting racial and ethnic disparities in out-of-home placement. The decision points from reports of child maltreatment to out-of-home placement produce differing racial and ethnic disparities. These disparities do not always result in disproportionate representation of specific racial or ethnic groups, nor do they necessarily prove discrimination. But, these disparities are a possible signal that there may be unequal treatment by race or ethnicity. Large and persistent disparities across all decision points, nonetheless, should raise alarms and justify more intensive analysis and review.

Notes

1. In this chapter, we adopt the convention used by the U.S. Census Bureau, referencing persons as "Hispanic or Latino" for persons of Cuban, Mexican, Puerto Rican, South or Central American, or other Spanish culture or origin regardless of race. Further, the use of the term "Hispanic" references "Hispanic or Latino." We use the terms "black" and "African American" interchangeably. We use the terms "Native American" and "American Indian/Alaskan Native" interchangeably. And, as noted in the tables, Native Hawaiians are included in the counts of Asian/Asian Pacific Islanders/Native Hawaiians.
2. For more information on NCANDS, see: www.acf.hhs.gov/cb/research-data-technology/reporting-systems/ncands
3. The number of cases for 2005 is 3,416,817. However, in 2005, the dataset does not include cases from North Dakota, Oregon, and Connecticut. There are 1,118 cases without the state information in 2005. For 2014 data, the number of cases is 3,731,303, which does not include the cases from North Carolina and Oklahoma. To perform the calculations in the figures, we used the child file, which is based on each child in each maltreatment case, so a child can appear multiple times in the annual dataset, and one case can refer to multiple children.
4. This finding arises from the large sample size, so caution should be exercised in interpreting small differences that are statistically significant.

References

Ards, S. D., Myers, Jr., S. L., Chung, C., Malkis, A., & Hagerty, B. (2003). Decomposing black–white differences in child maltreatment. *Child Maltreatment, 8*(2), 112–121.

Ards, S. D., Myers, Jr., S. L., Malkis, A., with the assistance of Sugre, E., & Zhou, L. (2003). Racial disproportionality in reported and substantiated child abuse and neglect: An examination of systematic bias. *Children and Youth Services Review, 25*(5–6), 375–392.

Barth, R. P. (2005). Child welfare and race: Models of disproportionality. In D. M. Derezotes, J. Poertner, & M. F. Testa (Eds.), *Race matters in child welfare: The overrepresentation of African American children in the system* (pp. 25–46). Washington, DC: CWLA Press.

Blinder, A. S. (1973). Wage discrimination: Reduced form and structural estimates. *The Journal of Human Resources, 8*(4), 436–455.

Bowman, A., Hofer, L., O'Rourke, C., & Read, L. (2009). *Racial disproportionality in Wisconsin's child welfare system.* Madison: Robert M. La Follette School of Public Affairs, University of Wisconsin, Madison.

Child Welfare Information Gateway. (2011). *Addressing racial disproportionality in child welfare.* Washington, DC: U.S. Department of Health & Human Services, Children's Bureau. Retrieved from www.childwelfare.gov/pubs/issue-briefs/racial-disproportionality/?hasBeenRedirected=1

Child Welfare Information Gateway. (2016). *Racial disproportionality and disparity in child welfare.* Washington, DC: U.S. Department of Health & Human Services, Children's Bureau. Retrieved from www.childwelfare.gov/pubPDFs/racial_disproportionality.pdf

Crampton, D., & Coulton, C. J. (2008). The benefits of life table analysis for describing disproportionality. *Child Welfare, 87*(2), 189–202.

Darity, Jr., W. A., & Mason, P. L. (1998). Evidence on discrimination in employment: Codes of color, codes of gender. *Journal of Economic Perspectives, 12*(2), 63–90.

Derezotes, D. M., & Poertner, J. (2005). Factors contributing to the overrepresentation of African American children in the child welfare system: What we know and don't know. In D. M. Derezotes, J. Poertner, & M. F. Testa (Eds.), *Race matters in child welfare: The overrepresentation of African American children in the system* (pp. 1–24). Washington, DC: CWLA Press.

Edwards, F. (2016). Saving children, controlling families: Punishment, redistribution, and child protection. *American Sociological Review, 81*(3), 575–595.

Fluke, J., Harden, B. J., Jenkins, M., & Ruehrdanz, A. (2011). A research synthesis on child welfare disproportionality and disparities. In *Disparities and Disproportionality in Child Welfare: Analysis of the Research* (pp. 1–93). Papers from a Research Symposium Convened by the Center for the Study of Social Policy and The Annie E. Casey Foundation on behalf of the Alliance for Racial Equity Child Welfare. Retrieved from www.cssp.org/publications/child-welfare/alliance/Disparities-and-Disproportionality-in-Child-Welfare_An-Analysis-of-the-Research-December-2011.pdf

Foster, E. M., Hillemeier, M. M., & Bai, Y. (2011). Explaining the disparity in placement instability among African American and white children in child welfare: A Blinder–Oaxaca decomposition. *Children and Youth Services Review, 33*(1), 118–125.

Graham, J. C., Dettlaff, A. J., Baumann, D. J., & Fluke, J. D. (2015). The decision making ecology of placing a child into foster care: A structural equation model. *Child Abuse & Neglect, 49*, 12–23.

Harris, G., Tittle, G., & Poertner, J. (2005). Factors that predict the decision to place a child into substitute care. In D. M. Derezotes, J. Poertner, & M. F. Testa (Eds.), *Race matters in child welfare: The overrepresentation of African American children in the system* (pp. 163–172). Washington, DC: CWLA Press.

Harris, M. S., & Hackett, W. (2008). Decision points in child welfare: An action research model to address disproportionality. *Children and Youth Services Review, 30*(2), 199–215.

Hayward, R. A., & DePanfilis, D. (2007). Foster children with an incarcerated parent: Predictors of reunification. *Children and Youth Services Review, 29*(10), 1320–1334.

Heckman, J. J. (1998). Detecting discrimination. *Journal of Economic Perspectives, 12*(2), 101–116.

Hill, R. B. (2006). *Synthesis of research on disproportionality in child welfare: An update.* Washington, DC: Casey–CSSP Alliance for Racial Equity in the Child Welfare System.

Horwitz, S. M., Hurlburt, M. S., Cohen, S. D., Zhang, J., & Landsverk, J. (2011). Predictors of placement for children who initially remained in their homes after an investigation for abuse or neglect. *Child Abuse & Neglect, 35*(3), 188–198. doi:10.1016/j.chiabu.2010.12.002

Huebner, R. (2007). *Descriptors, predictors, and outcomes of permanency stability.* Washington, DC: Presentation at the Casey–CWIA Outcomes Benchmarking Roundtable, March 1.

Kim, H., Chenot, D., & Juye, J. (2011). Racial/ethnic disparity in child welfare systems: A longitudinal study utilizing the Disparity Index (DI). *Children and Youth Services Review, 33*(7), 1234–1244.

Knott, T., & Donovan, K. (2010). Disproportionate representation of African-American children in foster care: Secondary analysis of the National Child Abuse and Neglect Data System, 2005. *Children and Youth Services Review, 32*(5), 679–684.

Lery, B., & Wulczyn, F. (2009). Racial disparity in admissions to foster care: A re-examination of county-level findings at a smaller spatial scale. Paper presented at the Presentation for the Alliance State Network Teleconference Series, Chapin Hall Center for Children at the University of Chicago.

Lovato-Hermann, K., Dellor, E., Tam, C. C., Curry, S., & Freisthler, B. (2017). Racial disparities in service referrals for families in the child welfare system. *Journal of Public Child Welfare, 11*(2), 133–149.

Morton, C. M., Ocasio, K., & Simmel, C. (2011). A critique of methods used to describe the overrepresentation of African Americans in the child welfare system. *Children and Youth Services Review, 33*(9), 1538–1542.

Myers, Jr., S. L. (2011). Response to a research synthesis on child welfare disproportionality and disparities. In *Disparities and Disproportionality in Child Welfare: Analysis of the Research* (pp. 107–112). Papers from a Research Symposium Convened by the Center for the Study of Social Policy and The Annie E. Casey Foundation on behalf of the Alliance for Racial Equity Child Welfare. Retrieved from www.cssp.org/publications/child-welfare/alliance/Disparities-and-Disproportionality-in-Child-Welfare_An-Analysis-of-the-Research-December-2011.pdf

Oaxaca, R. (1973). Male–female wage differentials in urban labor markets. *International Economic Review, 14*(3), 693–709.

Oaxaca, R. L., & Ransom, M. R. (1994). On discrimination and the decomposition of wage differentials. *Journal of Econometrica, 61*(1), 5–21.

Patterson, E. J., & Preston, S. H. (2008). Estimating mean length of stay in prison: Methods and applications. *Journal of Quantitative Criminology, 24*(1), 33–39.

Putnam-Hornstein, E., Needell, B., King, B., & Johnson-Motoyama, M. (2013). Racial and ethnic disparities: A population-based examination of risk factors for involvement with child protective services. *Child Abuse & Neglect, 37*(1), 33–46.

Rivaux, S., James, J., Wittenstrom, K., Baumann, D., Sheets, J., & Henry, J. (2008). The intersection of race, poverty, and risk: Understanding the decision to provide services to clients and to remove children. *Child Welfare, 87*(2), 151–168.

Rolock, N., & Testa, M. F. (2005). Indicated child abuse and neglect reports: Is the investigation process racially biased? In D. M. Derezotes, J. Poertner, & M. F. Testa (Eds.), *Race matters in child welfare: The overrepresentation of African American children in the system* (pp. 119–130). Washington, DC: CWLA Press.

Ross, T., Khashu, A., & Wamsley, M. (2004). *Hard data on hard times: An empirical analysis of maternal incarceration, foster care, and visitation*. New York: Vera Institute of Justice.

Sedlak, A. J., & Basena, M. (2014). *Online access to the Fourth National Incidence Study of Child Abuse and Neglect*. Rockville, MD: Westat.

Stoltzfus, E. (2005). *Race/ethnicity and child welfare*. Washington, DC: Congressional Research Services.

Summers, A. (2015). *Disproportionality rates for children of color in foster care, fiscal year 2013: Technical assistance bulletin*. Reno, NV: National Council of Juvenile and Family Court Judges.

Texas Health and Human Services Commission and Department of Family and Protective Services. (2006). *Disproportionality in child protective services: Statewide reform effort begins with examination of the problem*. Austin, TX: Author.

U.S. Department of Health & Human Services (Administration for Children and Families, Administration on Children, Youth and Families, Children's Bureau). (2005). *National Child Abuse and Neglect Data System (NCANDS) child file, FFY 2004; FFY 2005 [Datasets]*. From the National Data Archive on Child Abuse and Neglect website, available at www.ndacan.cornell.edu

U.S. Department of Health & Human Services (Administration for Children and Families, Administration on Children, Youth and Families, Children's Bureau). (2015). *National Child Abuse and Neglect Data System (NCANDS) child file, FFY 2014 [Dataset]*. From the National Data Archive on Child Abuse and Neglect website, available at www.ndacan.cornell.edu

U.S. Department of Health & Human Services (Administration for Children and Families, Administration on Children, Youth and Families, Children's Bureau). (2000–2014). *Child Trends analysis of data from the Adoption and Foster Care Analysis and Reporting System (AFCARS)*.

Wells, S. J., Merritt, L. M., & Weisberg, S. (2008a). *The impact of child welfare services on racial disparities in outcomes: Child welfare services for African American and Caucasian children in four Minnesota counties*. St. Paul: Minnesota Child Welfare African American Disparities Committee.

Wells, S. J., Merritt, L. M., & Weisberg, S. (2008b). *Qualitative analysis of racial disparities in child welfare*. St. Paul: Minnesota Child Welfare African American Disparities Committee.

Wildeman, C. (2014). How mass imprisonment has—and has not—shaped childhood inequality. *Communities and Banking*, Winter, 8–9.

Wildeman, C., & Emanuel, N. (2014). Cumulative risks of foster care placement by age 18 for US children, 2000–2011. *PloS ONE, 9*(3), e92785. https://doi.org/10.1371/journal.pone.0092785

Woodmass, K., Weisberg, S., Shlomi, H., Rockymore, M., & Wells, S. J. (2017). Examining the potential for racial disparity in out-of-home placement decisions: A quantitative matched-pair study. *Children and Youth Services Review, 75,* 96–109.

Wulczyn, F. (2011). Response to a research synthesis on child welfare disproportionality and disparities. In *Disparities and Disproportionality in Child Welfare: Analysis of the Research* (pp. 120–126). Papers from a Research Symposium Convened by the Center for the Study of Social Policy and The Annie E. Casey Foundation on behalf of the Alliance for Racial Equity Child Welfare. Retrieved from www.cssp.org/ publications/child-welfare/alliance/Disparities-and-Disproportionality-in-Child-Welfare_An-Analysis-of-the-Research-December-2011.pdf

Wulczyn, F., Gibbons, R., Snowden, L., & Lery, B. (2013). Poverty, social disadvantage, and the black/white placement gap. *Children and Youth Services Review, 35*(1), 65–74.

Wulczyn F., & Lery, B. (2007). *Racial disparity in foster care admissions.* Chicago: Chapin Hall Center for Children at the University of Chicago.

Zinn, A., DeCoursey, J., Goerge, R., & Courtney, M. (2006). *A study of placement stability in Illinois.* Chicago: Chapin Hall Center for Children at the University of Chicago.

Zuravin, S., & DePanfilis, D. (1996). *Child maltreatment recurrences among families served by child protective services, final report.* Baltimore: University of Maryland at Baltimore.

19

Commercial Sexual Exploitation and Sex Trafficking of Foster Children and Youth

Nadine M. Finigan-Carr and Amelia Rubenstein

Every day in the United States, children and adolescents become victims of commercial sexual exploitation and sex trafficking. Children and youth who have experienced maltreatment are more likely to be trafficked (U.S. Department of State, 2016). Although the consequences to victims are often serious and long-term, efforts to prevent, identify, and respond to this issue are hindered due to limited knowledge, support, and coordination. Related to this issue is the tendency for society to see commercially sexually exploited youth as delinquent, rather than as victims. Typically, child welfare services (CWS) research addresses the type of maltreatment, but the usual categories (i.e., physical abuse, neglect, sexual abuse, emotional abuse) are not mutually exclusive and sex trafficking is difficult to determine exactly. This chapter outlines the issues as they relate to the disproportionate involvement of youth who were maltreated as children as victims of commercial sexual exploitation and sex trafficking; and includes a framework for developing an effective child welfare response.

Commercial Sexual Exploitation of Children and Sex Trafficking

Commercial sexual exploitation of children (CSEC), also referred to as child sex trafficking or domestic minor sex trafficking, is a severe form of child maltreatment defined as any sexual acts performed by a minor under the age of 18 in exchange for anything of economic value (Albanese, 2007). These victims have been forced, coerced, or otherwise manipulated to perform sex acts, becoming engaged in prostitution, stripping, or pornography (Bounds, Julion, & Delaney, 2015; Estes & Weiner, 2002). Commercial sexual exploitation of children is one of the most destructive forms of child sexual abuse. Victims of CSEC have been found in pimp-controlled situations (street prostitution, pornography, etc.); trafficked in families and intimate partner relationships; recruited from networks of other runaway and homeless youth; in gang-related trafficking; and recruited within institutions and programs (e.g., by already trafficked youth in an after-school program) (U.S. Department of Health & Human Services [henceforth, USDHHS], 2013).

There are numerous risk factors for CSEC and child sex trafficking which include any set of experiences that may lead to increased emotional or physical vulnerability. These experiences include a history of neglect or abuse, homelessness, low self-esteem, poverty, and foster care placement. Youth of all gender identities, sexual orientations, and from a variety of racial, ethnic, and socioeconomic backgrounds are at risk for sex trafficking (Dank, 2011). These vulnerable youth may be lured into a sex trafficking situation using promises, psychological coercion, alcohol and/or substance use, threats, and violence. Females are more likely to be identified as trafficked, but males and transgender youth are also vulnerable (Boxill & Richardson, 2007; U.S. Department of State, 2016). Youth in foster care are characterized by their limited connections to family members and caring adults, exposure to sexual abuse, maltreatment, and other forms of violence, and limited skills to identify and access necessary resources (Finigan-Carr et al., 2015). This history of chronic trauma results in youth in the child welfare system being significantly more vulnerable to traffickers who manipulate a young person's unmet needs to coerce them into commercial sex.

Children who are victims of sex trafficking and/or CSEC are vulnerable to immediate harm while involved in the trade as well as suffering long-term damage, even after they have left the situation. Both those who are trafficking children as commodities and those who purchase the opportunities to use them, physically, mentally, and sexually, abuse these children and adolescents daily. There are immediate risks which include beatings, rape, and torture; as well as long-term damage in the form of potential substance addiction, sexually transmitted diseases including HIV/AIDS, and numerous mental illnesses such as depression and self-injurious behaviors (Barnitz, 2001). Children and adolescents in child welfare with experiences of interpersonal trauma and family instability are already a vulnerable population. Being trafficked exacerbates these vulnerabilities and can potentially have even more detrimental long-term effects.

Prevalence and Incidence of Trafficking in the United States

When most people hear the term "human trafficking," they think of foreign nationals smuggled into the United States. However, multiple cases of domestic human trafficking have been reported in all 50 states and the District of Columbia. From 2008 to 2010, 83% of confirmed sex trafficking incidents were of U.S. citizens with 40% of those being CSEC cases (Banks & Kyckelhahn, 2011). Between 244,000 and 325,000 American youth are considered at risk for sexual exploitation. The most recent population estimate of minor youth engaged in the commercial sex industry nationwide is between 4,457 and 20,994 youth (Swaner, Labriola, Rempel, Walker, & Spadafore, 2016). In the years between 2008 and 2012, the National Human Trafficking Resource Center received 5,982 reports of cases involving child sex trafficking, which is probably only a fraction of the number of youth actually trafficked (National Human Trafficking Resource Center, 2016). An exact estimate of the number of youth potentially involved in trafficking is difficult to generate due to both underreporting and the existence of well-organized underground trafficking networks. There are also issues with ensuring that those victims identified are not over-counted due to their having encountered multiple systems, such as health care, child welfare, juvenile justice, or victim services. These systems are limited in the ways that data on their clients can be shared with others.

As CSEC falls under the umbrella of sexual abuse, data on sexual abuse provide some information on the extent of the problem. According to the USDHHS (2016), in federal fiscal year 2014, there were more than 58,000 (8.3%) child abuse victims who were sexually abused. The definition of sexual abuse includes molestation, statutory rape, prostitution, pornography, incest, or other sexually exploitative activities. Unfortunately, these USDHHS data lack differentiation between the types of sexual abuse, which would be helpful to identify the prevalence and incidence of CSEC. It is important to note that child sexual abuse puts youth at risk for CSEC due to a complex interplay of factors, including involvement with the child welfare system (Bounds et al., 2015).

CSEC Risk Factors

Children and youth involved with the child welfare system due to abuse or neglect and placed in foster care or group homes are at high risk of being victims of human trafficking. This risk significantly increases their vulnerability to teen pregnancy, HIV/AIDS and other sexually transmitted diseases, depression and suicidal ideation. Often, the lack of stability in their living situation, physical distance from friends and family, and emotional vulnerability put them at risk for exploitation by traffickers who are actively seeking children and teens. While child welfare systems were not designed to specifically respond to victims of child trafficking, emerging evidence indicates that child welfare professionals are encountering children and youth who have been trafficked, due to this complex mix of vulnerabilities which also makes them targets of traffickers and pimps (Andretta, Woodland, Watkins, & Barnes, 2016; Bounds et al., 2015).

In a report by the California Child Welfare Council, it was found that anywhere from 50% to 80% of victims of commercial sexual exploitation, including child sex trafficking, are or were formally involved with child welfare (California Child Welfare Council, 2013). Other researchers have found that more than one-third of trafficked youth had previous child welfare involvement (Gibbs, Walters, Lutnick, Miller, & Kluckman, 2015). In Maryland, our research has found that the majority of youth identified as trafficked or suspected of being trafficked had previous involvement with the child welfare system in their lifetime (Finigan-Carr & Rubenstein, 2016). Despite these statistics, child welfare and juvenile services systems often do not recognize trafficking among their clients or do not consider it their responsibility to address trafficking (Gibbs et al., 2015). These examples indicate the contrary; child welfare professionals have a critical role in preventing, identifying, and protecting these youth.

Looking at this intersection of child welfare and child sex trafficking from a theoretical perspective, one should consider an ecological explanatory framework examining how behaviors, lifestyle, and environmental factors that promote contact with potential perpetrators may lead to re-victimization, in this case in the form of commercial sexual exploitation and/or sex trafficking (Grauerholz, 2000; Surratt, Kurtz, Chen, & Mooss, 2012). This framework would not only include Bronfenbrenner's Ecological Model (1992) as a conceptualization of the individual embedded in and influenced by multiple settings, but also Belsky's (1980) delineation of how personal history plays a part at the individual level in relation to the social-psychological phenomenon of child maltreatment.

In applying this ecological model to the problem of sex trafficking, the focus is on how factors at each level—individual/intrapersonal, relationship/interpersonal, institutional/societal and community—interact to contribute to an individual's vulnerability. This allows us to move beyond individualistic explanations of why sex trafficking occurs and consider the complex relationships between personal, interpersonal, and sociocultural factors which contribute to vulnerability for trafficking.

If child welfare involvement via child sexual abuse is seen as the first CSEC risk domain at the institutional/societal level of the ecological model, the second domain would include the constructs of poverty, mental illness, and substance abuse (U.S. Department of State, 2016) and their effects on both the individual/intrapersonal and interpersonal relationship levels. Only 16.9% of victims identified by professionals in one study were trafficked by a stranger (Cole & Sprang, 2015). Most of the others were trafficked by someone they knew (62.7%), with 45.8% of these traffickers being a parent or guardian (Cole & Sprang, 2015). Whether groomed by an unknown trafficker, a family member, or a "friend," many youth enter the commercial sex industry because they lack basic necessities—food, shelter, clothing—and do not have viable economic alternatives (Adamczyk, 2012; Dank, 2011). Relationships between trafficked youth and those who benefit from their labor are far more diverse and complex than simple coercion. Few CSEC victims are able to establish relationships with persons other than those responsible for victimizing them (Estes & Weiner, 2002).

Factors associated with prior victimization impair a survivor's ability to judge risky situations or people (Grauerholz, 2000); and increase the likelihood of mental disorder or substance use and abuse (Andretta et al., 2016). In many cases, this leads youth to enter into dangerous situations where they may encounter potential perpetrators of further abuse, such as traffickers. In addition, stigmatization and low self-esteem related to prior victimization (Finkelhor, 1987; Fong & Cardoso, 2010) can lead to associations with other stigmatized youth and the creation of deviant peer networks (e.g., runaways, gangs) (Finkelhor & Browne, 1985).

Commercial sexual exploitation of children occurs because youth are attempting to survive on their own; are escaping from difficult family situations; have a drug habit; or because they exist within the lowest socioeconomic strata in a system that is failing them (Marcus et al., 2012). Many youth without substance use prior to being trafficked become prone to substance use and abuse as a coping mechanism (Adamczyk, 2012; Pauli, 2014) or are forced to use substances as a means of coercion by their trafficker (Estes & Weiner, 2002). Some of these youth end up in situations where they need to rely on a deviant peer network for survival and may not have an identified trafficker per se. The more a youth relies on their deviant peer network for support and survival, the more embedded they become in that network, and the less likely they are to develop positive relationships outside this niche that could provide them with the social support and services that they need to leave CSEC situations (Pauli, 2014).

The third domain for CSEC risk operates at the individual/intrapersonal level. It is the state of being female, including transgender female (Varma, Gillespie, McCracken, & Greenbaum, 2015). Although CSEC victims can be from all genders, the majority of those identified are girls. All teenage girls are at risk for trafficking due to the struggles with the normal developmental task of being in adolescence. However, most exploited girls have survived chronic physical, emotional, and sexual trauma, as well as other forms of family dysfunction and loss (Fong & Cardoso, 2010; Grace, Starck, Potenza, Kenney, & Sheetz, 2012). In developing this theoretical framework, female victims have been placed at the center; however, it is likely that there are correlations and conclusions to be drawn related to male victims (Reid & Piquero, 2014).

While female youth of all races and ethnicities appear to be at similar risk, research is beginning to note that African American male youth are at heightened risk for CSEC (Reid & Piquero, 2014). Overall, the race and ethnicity of CSEC victims have been difficult to quantify due to the same issues that make it difficult to establish prevalence rates (e.g., misidentification, underreporting). When race has been reported in published studies, it varies depending on the geographic location of the sample population. As a result, there are studies which report predominantly Caucasian victims (Marcus et al., 2012; Salisbury, Dabney, & Russell, 2015), predominantly African American victims (Andretta et al., 2016; Twill, Green, & Traylor, 2010; Varma et al., 2015), and ethnically diverse victims (Dank, 2011; Gibbs et al., 2015). It is important to keep in mind that when determining whether racial and ethnic minority group children are disproportionately represented as CSEC victims, most agencies use national rather than local demographic patterns to determinine this statistic. For example, African Americans make up 13% of the national population, but in many cities, their percentage of the local population is much higher or lower than this national average. For example, African Americans make up 63% of the population of Baltimore, MD, but only 6% of the population of San Francisco, CA (U.S. Census Bureau, 2010). Therefore, any conclusions about particular racial or ethnic minorities' representation as CSEC victims should adjust for the prevalence of various racial and ethnic groups in the local, as opposed to the national, population. Despite the barriers to quantifying the race/ ethnicity of CSEC victims, it is known that minority youth, especially those from socioeconomically disadvantaged neighborhoods, are particularly vulnerable to sex trafficking and more likely to be arrested for the crime of prostitution (Estes & Weiner, 2002).

Child Welfare's Current Response

It is only in the past two decades that the United States has begun to formally address CSEC and child sex trafficking. In 2000, the Trafficking Victims Protection Act (TVPA) (P.L. 106-386) was the first federal law to define the crime of human trafficking, both labor and sex trafficking. It provided funding specifically to combat the trafficking of foreign women and children forced into the sex trade in the United States, with provisions specifically for cases of kidnapping, aggravated sexual abuse, or sex trafficking in children younger than 14. It also laid out the criteria of force, fraud, or coercion, except when the victims are under the age of 18. The Preventing Sex Trafficking and Strengthening Families Act (P.L. 113-183, 2014) and the Justice for Victims of Trafficking Act (JVTA) (P.L. 114-22, 2015) are recent legislation which specifically influence child welfare's response to CSEC and child sex trafficking. P.L. 113-183 requires that states identify, document, and determine services for trafficked youth and those at risk. It changes the reporting requirements for state child welfare agencies. Trafficked youth now are to be reported in the Adoption and Foster Care Analysis and Reporting System (AFCARS) and referred to law enforcement within 24 hours. The law also requires that child welfare staff report any youth missing from care to both law enforcement and the National Center for Missing & Exploited Children. The JVTA filled the funding gap for services to domestic victims that was created by the TVPA. The JVTA also expanded the definition of child abuse to include human trafficking and child pornography; amended the Child Abuse Prevention and Treatment Act (CAPTA) to require state child welfare agencies to investigate reports of child trafficking, identify victims, provide comprehensive services, and train workers; and included a requirement that states report the number of child sex trafficking victims to the U.S. Department of Health & Human Services. States had until September 2017 to begin this reporting requirement.

Concurrent to the federal legislation, many states began to amend and change their legislation in order to address the issue of human trafficking. In 2012, the Maryland Family Law (Article 5-701) was amended to add prostitution, pornographic photography, and human trafficking to the state's definition of sexual abuse. This meant that for the first time, child sex trafficking victims in Maryland could receive a child welfare response, rather than a juvenile delinquency response. Mandated reporters were now to report suspected cases of child sex trafficking to local CPS units, as they would for any other sexual abuse case. It also allowed the Department of Social Services to begin screening in, investigating, and responding to cases of reported child sex trafficking. Figure 19.1 shows the number of suspected child sex trafficking reports made to local child welfare agencies in the state child welfare administration's data system since this amendment went into effect. It is posited that the increase over the past few years is due to an increase in human trafficking awareness in Maryland following the implementation of this law.

Due to all of these changes to legislation at both federal and state levels, youth identified as trafficked are being reported more often to child welfare agencies. In addition, youth in child welfare

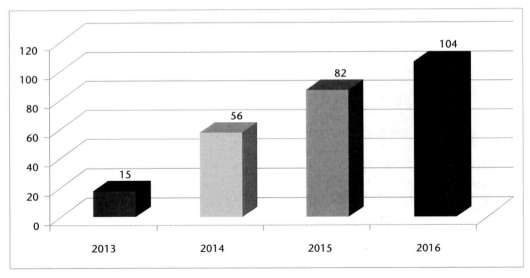

Figure 19.1 Number of Child Sex Trafficking Reports to Maryland CPS by Year (July-Dec of 2013 to 2016)

are at risk for being trafficked. As such, child welfare providers are expected to provide specialized services for trafficked youth, yet they tend to have limited training and resources provided to them for this purpose. To prepare for the implementation of P.L. 113-183, many states have been conducting focus groups and administering surveys to identify the level of awareness of child welfare professionals about CSEC and their readiness to intervene with at-risk or confirmed cases. As sex trafficking occurs in all geographic region types (urban, rural, suburban), professionals from different region types have been interviewed or surveyed. Professionals in non-urban settings have lower awareness, fewer training opportunities, and less experience in handling CSEC cases (Cole & Sprang, 2015). Additionally, most state infrastructure and victim services agencies are found in urban communities.

The chapter's authors have been working with Maryland's child welfare agency to conduct focus groups in preparation for the implementation of P.L. 113-183. From 2015 to 2016, five focus groups, with 10 to 12 child welfare professionals in each, were held in different geographical regions of the state similar to those noted in the extant literature (Finigan-Carr & Rubenstein, 2016). Participant responses supported the findings stated in the previous paragraph. One respondent in a suburban environment stated, "My frustration is child welfare workers haven't been trained, don't really understand complex issues, and why they [trafficked youth] really shouldn't go home." Another respondent in a semi-rural jurisdiction was even more specific:

> I've received no training in how to interview a child who's been a victim of human trafficking. We received sex abuse training for forensic interviewing, but a regular forensic interview would not work on a victim of human trafficking. So what I've done on my cases, like I've had to go and do my own research, because I've never been trained. And even when I'm paired up with a detective, the detective's like, I'm not trained either, and we're kind of like just winging it as we're going along.

It is evident that training for child welfare professionals specific to the needs of children who are victims of sex trafficking and CSEC is necessary.

Victim Identification

The Child Sex Trafficking Victims Initiative (CSTVI) in Maryland is one of nine projects funded by the Children's Bureau to build internal capacity for addressing the issue of human trafficking within the child welfare population. The authors are responsible for the implementation of this initiative, which has two main goals—training of child welfare professionals; and screening and identifying youth at risk for sex trafficking. A thorough examination of Maryland's child welfare system's administrative data, specifically the Child and Adolescent Needs and Strengths (CANS) assessment, is being utilized for victim identification. The CANS (Lyons, 1999) provides a comprehensive assessment of clinical and psychosocial factors which may impact treatment decisions and outcomes. This multipurpose tool is used by many states to support care planning and levels of care decision-making, and to allow for the monitoring of outcomes of services for system-involved children and youth.

The state of Maryland uses the CANS tool to collect data on youth involved in child welfare. The tool is divided into nine sections containing risk factors that youth may experience, as well as a Likert scale where zero (0) indicates a low level of risk and three (3) indicates a high level of risk (University of Maryland School of Social Work [henceforth, UMSSW], n.d.). The CSTVI reviewed existing research on human trafficking identification and screening tools (Administration of Children and Families, 2012; Covenant House New York, 2013; Vera Institute of Justice, 2014), as well as the use of CANS with trafficked youth. Based on this literature review, the CSTVI collaborated with UMSSW's Institute of Innovation and Implementation to establish CANS screening criteria from the indicators most valuable in identifying this population; among these were exploitation experiences, childhood trauma and abuse, family dynamics, runaway history, and substance abuse (UMSSW, n.d.).

To ensure that the screening criteria chosen were appropriate, the screening criteria were triangulated using CANS data for previously identified trafficked and exploited youth. These screening criteria were then piloted to establish thresholds for identification of youth at risk for sexual exploitation and trafficking.

At this point, the CSTVI has piloted two criteria in areas of the state where trafficked youth have previously been identified. These criteria can be used to screen both youth in out-of-home care and those receiving in-home services for trafficking risk, using data from the CANS assessments.

- *Criterion 1*: A youth is considered to be at risk for sex trafficking if they have a rating of "2" or greater on the CANS Runaway item, as well as a score of "2" or greater on any of the following items: Depression/Mood Disorder, Reckless Behavior, Sexual Abuse, Physical Abuse, Neglect, Substance Abuse, Delinquent Behavior, Judgement/Decision Making, and Sexual Development.
- *Criterion 2*: A youth is considered to be at risk of sex trafficking if they have a rating of "2" or greater on any of the following CANS items regardless of their score on other items: (1) Sexually Reactive Behavior; (2) Exploitation; or (3) Acculturation: Gender Identity.

Rating thresholds were determined after examination of both the literature and CANS data for youth confirmed to have been trafficking victims.

In August 2015, the screening criteria were piloted in two Maryland jurisdictions that have identified significant numbers of child sex trafficking victims. Eighty-seven suspected child sex trafficking cases were reported to Maryland's child protective services for these jurisdictions in 2015 (see Figure 19.1). Preliminary examination of CANS data indicates that more than double that number would have been captured under Criterion 1 in the urban jurisdiction alone (Table 19.1). These results indicate this to be a feasible process for identifying which youth in out-of-home and in-home care are at more pronounced risk of trafficking. Continued monitoring of the implementation of this screening protocol is warranted, including cross-checking against scores of known trafficked victims in order to minimize the potential of over-reporting the number of victims identified.

A complete screening process is being developed, including determination of how youth flagged by the CANS screening algorithm would be further assessed, who would conduct these secondary assessments, and how determination of confirmed, highly suspected, or at-risk cases are to be documented. Further investigation is also needed to determine appropriate services for those youth identified as trafficking victims and preventive care for those youth at high risk. These findings demonstrate how existing state administrative data can be used to identify those most at risk and develop interventions to prevent sex trafficking in this vulnerable population. By knowing how to identify and respond to those most at risk, professionals can reduce the number of victims and help to bring safety and healing to those traumatized by sex trafficking.

Case Management and Advocacy

Given what has been discussed about trafficking's consequences, it is evident that we need to respond in a coordinated and strategic manner in order to reduce the traumatic impacts of trafficking on

Table 19.1 CANS Screening for Two Jurisdictions in Maryland (July 1, 2014–June 30, 2015)

Geographic Location	Number of Assessments	Criterion 1	% of youth that met Criterion 1	Criterion 2	% of youth that met Criterion 2
Urban Area	1,875	168	8.96	141	7.52
Suburban Area	337	24	7.12	32	9.5

children and youth. Coordinated efforts should be both trauma-informed and victim-centered to avoid further stigmatization (Bounds et al., 2015; USDHHS, 2013). However, many states fail to treat sex-trafficked children as victims of trafficking. Instead, these states arrest and incarcerate them for crimes committed as a direct result of trafficking, such as prostitution or stripping (U.S. Department of State, 2016). Even when they are not charged with a crime directly, authorities place children in restrictive environments including lockdown residential facilities to protect them from their traffickers or to secure their testimony, which in most cases results in reduced trust of law enforcement and re-traumatization (U.S. Department of State, 2016). Victim-service advocates report that even when done with good intentions, this response creates barriers to care for victims as well as barriers to housing, future employment, and other essential needs for victims' recovery (Bounds et al., 2015).

The complexity of child sex trafficking cases combined with the significant vulnerabilities of many victims pre-dating the exploitation make the need for a coordinating role clear. There are varied terms for this role—case manager, advocate, coordinator—all used to describe the person for whom victim needs are the first priority. This chapter uses the terms case manager and case management here, recognizing that there will be different terms depending on the agency and setting.

For all human trafficking survivors, intensive case management can be an essential stabilizing service on which victims establish a foundation where basic needs are met, new goals conceived, and successful outcomes are achieved. All survivors of human trafficking can benefit; but for trafficked youth involved with large state systems like child welfare and/or juvenile justice, intensive case management is especially important. The case manager plays a critical role throughout the lifespan of a child sex trafficking case, both for the victim/survivor and other service providers and agencies involved in the case. In conceptualizing intensive case management for sex trafficking victims, it can be helpful to think about the four Cs: *Coordination, Consistency, Centered (victim), and CSEC-focused* (Office for Victims of Crime, n.d.).

Coordination

Lack of coordination of services and limited data sharing across systems were mentioned earlier in this chapter as barriers to determining the true prevalence of child sex trafficking cases in the United States. This limited coordination can also have an impact on treatment and case management for these highly complex cases. The case manager is expected to collaborate with multiple law enforcement, therapeutic, and criminal justice agencies that may be involved in a child trafficking case, alongside or on behalf of the victim. This is the primary service provided by the case manager and helps to prevent victims from becoming overwhelmed, de-prioritized, or re-traumatized, while they navigate the many large bureaucratic agencies and government systems. The case manager can help to alleviate anxiety for trafficked youth by assisting them in mapping out the various professionals involved in their case, the agencies those professionals represent, and the purpose of their involvement. The CSTVI project has developed a client map, which can be used by case managers to collect information for the team of people relevant to a specific child sex trafficking case (Figure 19.2). It is designed to help in keeping track of these professionals, and should be shared with the victim to help them understand the roles of everyone involved.

Imagine you are working with a child who was the victim of sex trafficking in your state. This youth is also a key witness in a criminal case against his trafficker. He is co-committed to the Department of Juvenile Services and the Department of Social Services. It is possible that there may be multiple attorneys representing your client in different roles (e.g., Child in Need of Assistance, delinquency case, immigration status), as well as a Victim's Rights attorney representing the interests of the youth in his role as the victim/witness in the criminal case against the trafficker (U.S. Department of Justice, 2015). Victims are not legally entitled to a Victim's Rights attorney, but some advocacy organizations or pro-bono networks will provide one if requested. Ensuring that the

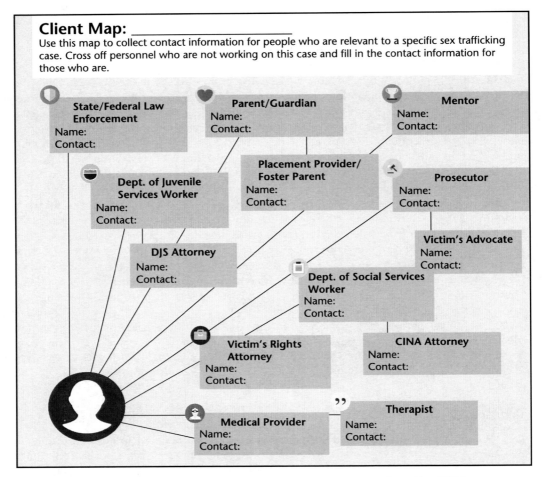

Figure 19.2 Case Management Client Map for Trafficking Victims Developed by CSTVI

Source: © CSTVI at University of Maryland-Baltimore School of Social Work, used with permission

survivor understands the role of each legal professional involved can help him to feel included and heard in the very important decisions being made about his life.

Some trafficking survivors may find it easier to have their case manager be responsible for managing communications across the systems involved and acting as a single point of contact. They may prefer to receive updates on the criminal case against their trafficker through their case manager, rather than hearing directly from prosecutors, witness coordinators, and law enforcement investigators. The case manager may need to work out ways for information sharing that prioritizes protecting the victim's privacy and confidentiality. Case managers can also help to ensure that timely answers are given to a victim's questions and prevent long periods of time when the victim hears nothing, thereby avoiding feelings of distrust.

Consistency

Establishing a hopeful and transformational relationship with the child survivor is crucial. In trafficking cases, the professional offering case management services helps the victim to rebuild trust, and positive feelings of self, and can offer a counter narrative to the one so often used by traffickers, that they are worthless, unloved, and a sexual object. The benefits from this rapport building occur slowly over time, while simultaneously more concrete resources are obtained through traditional case management provision (Office for Victims of Crime, n.d.). Because of the complexity of this role, ideally one individual is present and serving as case manager for the entirety of the case, from initial contact to long-term recovery. All efforts should be taken to prevent turnover, especially during the initial 6 to 12 months when the victim needs to establish trust in others.

Centered (Victim)

The standard for care in assisting victims of any type of crime is the *victim-centered approach* which describes the systematic focus on the needs and concerns of a victim in order to provide compassionate and sensitive delivery of services without judgement (Office for Victims of Crime, n.d.). Professionals serving as case managers or in similar roles with child trafficking cases utilize victim-centered approaches, where the victim's decision-making is supported, and their wishes, safety, and well-being take priority over all else. In trafficking cases, victims have often been marginalized long before the trafficking occurred, meaning that genuinely providing victim-centered care is paramount. Affirming a victim's desires and well-being is no small task for a case manager, particularly in representing the voice of a child in a room full of adults. In cases in which the trafficker is criminally charged, it is not at all unusual for the victim's desires and wishes to be very different from the outcomes desired by prosecutors or investigators. For youth in the child welfare system, whether because of their trafficking experience or experience prior to being trafficked, there are additional unique challenges inherent to the system itself. The needs of the agency at times may be counter to the needs of the trafficking victim. As mentioned above, this may mean that the victim is placed in a more restrictive environment or forced to testify against their wishes or when not psychologically ready.

Victim-centered care also requires that we use empowering language. This often starts with challenging the term "child prostitute," and using "victim/survivor of child sex trafficking or sexual exploitation" instead. For example, a case manager reads over a psychological evaluation submitted for dependency court which states, "[NAME of victim] entered into the prostitution lifestyle." While this may seem like a small point, she recognizes that if this youth had been sexually abused by a family member, the psychologist would never have described that maltreatment as "she entered into sexual abuse at age 12." Survivors of sex trafficking and their advocates frequently encounter this type of victim-blaming language in which the exploitation was made to seem like a choice, rather than a horrendous form of victimization.

Victim-centered care is also, at a bare minimum, trauma-informed, and ideally, is trauma-specific (Office for Victims of Crime, n.d.). The integration of a trauma-informed approach across all the different players on a survivor's case, and implementation in every interaction and context, are key to the victim's stabilization and engagement. This approach is one in which the survivor has positive and supportive interactions with the many professionals involved in their case and care, from the receptionist at social services to the state's attorney prosecuting the case against their trafficker. These trauma-informed interactions can reaffirm the message that the survivor is worthy, valued, strong, and respected. This trauma-informed approach includes the ability of first responders (advocates, law enforcement, and program staff) to utilize mental health first aid skills in evaluating and de-escalating crises (Aakre, Lucksted, & Browning-McNee, 2016).

CSEC-Focused

When treating child sexual abuse, public child welfare workers depend on licensed private therapists and providers who are knowledgeable in treating such abuse for mental health care (Farmer & Pollock, 2003). Sex trafficking victims often have therapeutic needs that differ from those of traditional sexual abuse clients; and, treatment modalities specific to these needs are still being developed. Mental health treatment for CSEC victims should be evidence-informed and based on best practices, including trauma-informed practice, as they have experienced multiple forms of trauma (Berliner & Kolko, 2016).

In addition to being trauma-informed, those working closely with the youth victim must have a detailed understanding of the specific traumas, and mental and physical injuries resulting from CSEC and sex trafficking. Among the most prominent mental health disorders seen among victims of human trafficking are post-traumatic stress disorder (PTSD), mood disorders, anxiety disorders, dissociative disorders, and substance-related disorders (Williamson, Dutch, & Clawson, 2010). One of the hallmarks of child sex trafficking cases which involve a male trafficker and younger cis-gendered female victims is the presence of trauma-bonding. Trauma-bonding describes the strong, emotional ties between two persons which develop from an abusive relationship where one of the persons is routinely the perpetrator of the abuse (Dutton & Painter, 1981). These relationships have power differentials at their core, leading to dysfunctional attachments and bonding issues. Due to the complexity of the trauma and the addition of attachment disorders via trauma-bonding, the treatment strategies required must be comprehensive and multi-dimensional and include an understanding of this power differential in order to achieve success (Adams, 1999).

Recommendations for Future Research and Practice

An ecological model has been posited to fully examine the factors which lead to CSEC at both micro and macro levels. Future research should delineate this model further and advance this theory in order to provide a framework for understanding this phenomenon, including both qualitative and quantitative methodology. It will be important not only to quantify the prevalence of victims and the scope of their needs, but also to provide qualitative data from victims themselves. These qualitative data should include the voices of foster youth victims and those who have worked with them. By embracing both quantitative and qualitative methodology, future research will be able to identify best practices for reaching victims and reintegrating them into society.

Children and youth who have been victims of child sex trafficking have serious immediate and long-term physical and mental health consequences. The provision of services to this vulnerable population requires a coordinated, multi-system approach with the collaboration of child protective services/child welfare, law enforcement (federal, state, and local), attorney general's offices, social workers, educators, physical and mental health providers, and victim services' agencies. Although the individual goals of each of these partners may vary, the ultimate goal should be to provide a safe environment for CSEC victims to recover and improve their overall well-being and long-term success.

Identification of CSEC victims along with the use of victim-centered language and a trauma-informed approach would improve the role of child welfare workers and agencies in addressing this issue. Services need to be established which include specialized housing and treatment programs. There is a need for tailored training courses for professionals who interact with CSEC victims across disciplines (health care, law enforcement, legal services, child welfare, education, etc.) along with the establishment of detailed multidisciplinary reporting data systems to identify CSEC victims, support their service needs, build awareness, and address legislative and regulatory gaps. The CSTVI in Maryland and similar nationwide initiatives currently in development in response to P.L. 113-183 are a start in how to create this coordinated, multidisciplinary approach.

Victims of CSEC have experienced a severe form of abuse, and assessment tools need to be able to reflect this trauma. Interventions and programs should include trauma-informed mental health services, with child welfare professionals collaborating with private agencies equipped to work with human trafficking victims. Treatment practices should allow victims to be empowered and to receive supportive and culturally appropriate treatments. The policies and practices of child welfare agencies need to determine if they can appropriately identify those at risk for CSEC, in order to provide preventive interventions, as well as to adequately assess the needs of those who have already been trafficked so as to identify the treatment best suited for the individual victim. Standard treatment referrals like those used for child sexual abuse may not always be appropriate. They need to work together with first responders and legal professionals to identify successful program components and adapt the practices that best fit their cultural context for the overall well-being of children and adolescents so that they can move from victim to survivor status.

As we continue to examine this issue, it is important to address the role of race and racism in creating this phenomenon. The intersection of race with other forms of subordination such as gender, class, and age has had a disproportionate impact on youth of color and their vulnerability to trafficking. This intersectionality leads to the persistence of the myth of the child prostitute as opposed to the child sex trafficking victim (Butler, 2015). In order to fully address the issues of CSEC in the United States, it is important to understand and address how racism helps to perpetuate the racial myths undermining the proper identification of minority youth as victims, leading to them being more likely to be arrested for the crime of prostitution (Butler, 2015; Estes & Weiner, 2002). Children of color, specifically African American children, are not only disproportionately represented in the child welfare system, but also more likely to be placed in out-of-home care (Child Welfare Information Gateway, 2016). This leads them to be at increased risk for trafficking, yet the extant literature is limited on how it quantifies race and ethnicity in discussing trafficking cases. Future research and practice should ensure that cultural competence is employed when intervening with CSEC victims.

Conclusion

This chapter sought to build awareness of the unique issues pertinent to sex trafficking and commercial sexual exploitation of children and youth. In doing so, it outlined the relationship between CSEC and child welfare, and provided a framework for examining the issue as well as a model for responding to victims in a trauma-informed and victim-centered manner. In order for child welfare to fulfill its mission to be the designated agency for protecting children as it pertains to human trafficking, support for these efforts will be needed at both the local and national levels. Local laws and policies as well as funding should all be aligned with the need to protect, identify, and respond to the needs of all CSEC victims. As social workers, there is a moral imperative for us to spearhead the work on this issue.

Acknowledgments

This work was partially supported by a grant from the Department of Health & Human Services, Administration for Children and Families, Children's Bureau, for the establishment of Maryland's Child Sex Trafficking Victims' Initiative (CSTVI).

References

Aakre, J. M., Lucksted, A., & Browning-McNee, L. A. (2016). Evaluation of Youth Mental Health First Aid USA: A program to assist young people in psychological distress. *Psychological Services, 13*(2), 121–126. doi:10.1037/ser0000063

Adamczyk, A. (2012). Review of the commercial sexual exploitation of children. *Journal of Youth and Adolescence, 41*(9), 1253–1255. doi:10.1007/s10964-012-9791-6

Adams, K. M. (1999). Sexual harassment as cycles of trauma reenactment and sexual compulsivity. *Sexual Addiction & Compulsivity, 6*(3), 177–193.

Administration of Children and Families. (2012). *Resources: Screening tools for victims of human trafficking.* Washington, DC: U.S. Department of Health & Human Services. Retrieved from www.acf.hhs.gov/sites/default/files/orr/screening_questions_to_assess_whether_a_person_is_a_trafficking_victim_0.pdf

Albanese, J. (2007). *Commercial sexual exploitation of children: What do we know and what do we do about it?* Washington, DC: U.S. Department of Justice, Office of Justice Programs. Retrieved from www.ncjrs.gov/pdffiles1/nij/215733.pdf

Andretta, J. R., Woodland, M. H., Watkins, K. M., & Barnes, M. E. (2016). Towards the discreet identification of commercial sexual exploitation of children (CSEC) victims and individualized interventions: Science to practice. *Psychology, Public Policy, and Law, 22*(3), 260–270. doi:10.1037/law0000087

Banks, D., & Kyckelhahn, T. (2011). *Characteristics of suspected human trafficking incidents, 2008–2010* (Special Report NCJ 233732). Washington, DC: Bureau of Justice Statistics. Retrieved from www.bjs.gov/content/pub/pdf/cshti0810.pdf

Barnitz, L. (2001). Effectively responding to the commercial sexual exploitation of children: A comprehensive approach to prevention, protection, and reintegration services. *Child Welfare: Journal of Policy, Practice, and Program, 80*(5), 597–610.

Belsky, J. (1980). Child maltreatment: An ecological integration. *American Psychologist, 35*(4), 320–335. http://dx.doi.org/10.1037/0003-066X.35.4.320

Berliner, L., & Kolko, D. J. (2016). Trauma informed care: A commentary and critique. *Child Maltreatment, 21*(2), 168–172.

Bounds, D., Julion, W. A., & Delaney, K. R. (2015). Commercial sexual exploitation of children and state child welfare systems. *Policy, Politics, & Nursing Practice, 16*(1–2), 17–26. doi:10.1177/1527154415583124

Boxill, N., & Richardson, D. (2007). Ending sex trafficking of children in Atlanta. *Affilia: Journal of Women & Social Work, 22*, 138–149.

Bronfenbrenner, U. (1992). Ecological systems theory. In R. Vasta (Ed.), *Six theories of development: Revised formulations and current issues* (pp. 187–249). London: Jessica Kingsley Publishers.

Butler, C. N. (2015). The racial roots of human trafficking. *UCLA Law Review, 62*(6), 1464–1514.

California Child Welfare Council. (2013). *Ending the commercial sexual exploitation of Children: A call for multi-system collaboration in California*. Sacramento, CA: Author. Retrieved from www.chhs.ca.gov/Child%20Welfare/Ending%20CSEC%20-%20A%20Call%20for%20Multi-System%20Collaboration%20in%20CA%20-%20February%202013.pdf

Child Abuse Prevention and Treatment Act [CAPTA], P.L. 93-247. (1974). Reauthorized in 2010, P.L. 111-320.

Child Welfare Information Gateway. (2016). *Racial disproportionality and disparity in child welfare*. Issue Brief. Retrieved from www.childwelfare.gov/pubPDFs/racial_disproportionality.pdf

Cole, J., & Sprang, G. (2015). Sex trafficking of minors in metropolitan, micropolitan, and rural communities. *Child Abuse & Neglect, 40*, 113–123. doi:10.1016/j.chiabu.2014.07.015

Covenant House New York. (2013). *Homelessness, survival sex and human trafficking: As experienced by the youth of Covenant House New York*. Retrieved from http://center.serve.org/nche/downloads/cov-hs-trafficking.pdf

Dank, M. (2011). *The commercial sexual exploitation of children*. El Paso, TX: LFB Scholarly Publishing LLC.

Dutton, D. G., & Painter, S. L. (1981). Traumatic bonding: The development of emotional attachments in battered women and other relationships of intermittent abuse. *Victimology: An International Journal, 1*(4), 139–155.

Estes, R., & Weiner, N. (2002). *The commercial sexual exploitation of children in the U.S., Canada, and Mexico.* Technical report. Philadelphia: University of Pennsylvania. Retrieved from http://abolitionistmom.org/wp-content/uploads/2014/05/Complete_CSEC_0estes-weiner.pdf

Farmer, E., & Pollock, S. (2003). Managing sexually abused and/or abusing children in substitute care. *Child & Family Social Work, 8*(2), 101–112. doi:10.1046/j.1365-2206.2003.00271.x

Finigan-Carr, N. M., Murray, K. W., O'Connor, J. M., Rushovich, B. R., Dixon, D. A., & Barth, R. P. (2015). Preventing rapid repeat pregnancy and promoting positive parenting among young mothers in foster care. *Social Work in Public Health, 30*(1), 1–17. doi:10.1080/19371918.2014.938388

Finigan-Carr, N., & Rubenstein, A. (2016). *It's not taken: Realities of domestic trafficking among foster youth*. Paper presented at the Healthy Teen Network Annual Meeting, Las Vegas, NV.

Finkelhor, D. (1987). The trauma of child sexual abuse: Two models. *Journal of Interpersonal Violence, 2*(4), 348–366.

Finkelhor, D., & Browne, A. (1985). The traumatic impact of child sexual abuse: A conceptualization. *American Journal of Orthopsychiatry, 55*(4), 530–541.

Fong, R., & Cardoso, J. B. (2010). Child human trafficking victims: Challenges for the child welfare system. *Evaluation and Program Planning, 33*(3), 311–316. doi:10.1016/j.evalprogplan.2009.06.018

Gibbs, D. A., Walters, J. L. H., Lutnick, A., Miller, S., & Kluckman, M. (2015). Services to domestic minor victims of sex trafficking: Opportunities for engagement and support. *Children and Youth Services Review, 54*, 1–7. doi:10.1016/j.childyouth.2015.04.003

Grace, L. G., Starck, M., Potenza, J., Kenney, P. A., & Sheetz, A. H. (2012). Commercial sexual exploitation of children and the school nurse. *The Journal of School Nursing, 28*(6), 410–417. doi:10.1177/1059840512448402

Grauerholz, L. (2000). An ecological approach to understanding sexual revictimization: Linking personal, interpersonal, and sociocultural factors and processes. *Child Maltreatment, 5*(1), 5–17.

Justice for Victims of Trafficking Act [JVTA], P.L. 114-22. (2015).

Lyons, J. (1999). *The CANS (Child and Adolescent Needs and Strengths) manual*. Chicago: Buddin Praed Foundation.

Marcus, A., Riggs, R., Horning, A., Rivera, S., Curtis, R., & Thompson, E. (2012). Is child to adult as victim is to criminal? Social policy and street-based sex work in the USA. *Sexuality Research & Social Policy: A Journal of the NSRC, 9*(2), 153–166. doi:10.1007/s13178-011-0070-1

National Human Trafficking Resource Center. (2016). Hotline statistics. Retrieved from https://traffickingresourcecenter.org/states

Office for Victims of Crime (Producer). (n.d.). *Human Trafficking Task Force e-guide*. Retrieved from www.ovcttac.gov/taskforceguide/eguide/

Pauli, C. (2014). Review of *The commercial sexual exploitation of children*. *Journal of Youth and Adolescence, 43*(11), 1949–1951. doi:10.1007/s10964-014-0191-y

Preventing Sex Trafficking and Strengthening Families Act, P.L. 113-183. (2014).

Reid, J. A., & Piquero, A. R. (2014). Age-graded risks for commercial sexual exploitation of male and female youth. *Journal of Interpersonal Violence, 29*(9), 1747–1777. doi:10.1177/0886260513511535

Salisbury, E. J., Dabney, J. D., & Russell, K. (2015). Diverting victims of commercial sexual exploitation from juvenile detention: Development of the InterCSECt screening protocol. *Journal of Interpersonal Violence, 30*(7), 1247–1276. doi:10.1177/0886260514539846

Surratt, H. L., Kurtz, S. P., Chen, M., & Mooss, A. (2012). HIV risk among female sex workers in Miami: The impact of violent victimization and untreated mental illness. *AIDS Care, 24*(5), 553–561. doi:10.1080/09540121.2011.630342

Swaner, R., Labriola, M., Rempel, M., Walker, A. R., & Spadafore, J. (2016). *Youth involvement in the sex trade: A national study*. New York, NY: Center for Court Innovation. Retrieved from www.courtinnovation.org/youthstudy

Trafficking Victims Protection Act [TVPA], P.L. 106-386. (2000).

Twill, S. E., Green, D. M., & Traylor, A. (2010). A descriptive study on sexually exploited children in residential treatment. *Child & Youth Care Forum, 39*(3), 187–199. doi:10.1007/s10566-010-9098-2

University of Maryland School of Social Work [UMSSW]. (n.d.). *The Child and Adolescent Needs and Strengths (CANS) assessment*. Retrieved from https://theinstitute.umaryland.edu/topics/sat/cans.cfm

U.S. Census Bureau. (2010). *QuickFacts*. Retrieved from www.census.gov/quickfacts/table/RHI125215/0667000,1077580,2430325,2436075,2401600,24510

U.S. Department of Health & Human Services [USDHHS]. (2013). *Guidance to states and services on addressing human trafficking of children and youth in the United States*. Washington, DC: Author. Retrieved from www.acf.hhs.gov/sites/default/files/cb/acyf_human_trafficking_guidance.pdf

U.S. Department of Health & Human Services [USDHHS]. (2016). *Child maltreatment 2014*. Retrieved from www.acf.hhs.gov/programs/cb/research-data-technology/statistics-research/child-maltreatment

U.S. Department of Justice. (2015). *The legal rights and needs of victims of human trafficking in the United States*. OVC Fact Sheet. Retrieved from https://ovc.ncjrs.gov/humantrafficking/Public_Awareness_Folder/Fact_Sheet/HT_Legal_Rights_Needs_fact_sheet-508.pdf

U.S. Department of State. (2016, June). *2016 trafficking in persons report*. Retrieved from www.state.gov/j/tip/rls/tiprpt/

Varma, S., Gillespie, S., McCracken, C., & Greenbaum, V. J. (2015). Characteristics of child commercial sexual exploitation and sex trafficking victims presenting for medical care in the United States. *Child Abuse & Neglect, 44*, 98–105. doi:10.1016/j.chiabu.2015.04.004

Vera Institute of Justice. (2014). *Screening for human trafficking: Guidelines for administering the Trafficking Victim Identification Tool (TVIT)*. Available atwww.vera.org/projects/improving-trafficking-victim-identification-study

Williamson, E., Dutch, N. M., & Clawson, H. J. (2010). *Evidence-based mental health treatment for victims of human trafficking*. Washington, DC: Office of the Assistant Secretary for Planning and Evaluation. Retrieved from https://aspe.hhs.gov/report/evidence-based-mental-health-treatment-victims-human-trafficking

20

Undocumented Immigrant Latin@ Youth and the U.S. Child Welfare System

Frank Anthony Rodriguez, Vivian J. Dorsett and John Jacob Rodriguez

The United States can be said to be a country that was established by immigrants and the children of immigrants. The growth of the country's population has resulted primarily from the children born in the United States to immigrants (Dawkins & Rodriguez, 2016; Hernandez, Denton, & McCartney, 2007). More recently, changes in immigration trends and patterns have considerably changed the demographic profile of America. Passel (2011) defines immigrant children as children under 18 years of age who are foreign-born or the U.S.-born children of immigrant parents. Foreign-born immigrants living in the United States have increased in recent years; a large proportion of this population consists of Latino and Latina children. Today's anti-immigrant sentiment and immigration policies affect the wellness of immigrant families and their U.S.-born children. As of July 2014, according to the annual report by the Adoption and Foster Care Analysis and Reporting System (AFCARS), Latinos represented 22% of the children in foster care (National Center for Child Welfare Excellence], 2015). Additionally, research established that children of Latino descent are younger when referred to the child welfare system, compared to non-Latino children (Garcia, Aisenberg, & Harachi, 2012).

In the United States, Latin@ children are the largest and fastest growing ethnic minority group (Dettlaff, 2015; Dettlaff & Johnson, 2011). Comparable to this growing population, the percentage of children in the U.S. welfare system has also increased (Dettlaff, 2015). In the 1990s, it was projected that 15 million immigrants would arrive in the United States, a 50% increase since the previous decade and more than 100% since the 1970s (Capps & Fortuny, 2006). According to Gryn and Larsen (2010), foreign-born immigrants represented 12.5% of the total U.S. population in 2009, and the estimated population of children of immigrants (defined as children with at least one foreign-born parent) more than doubled, from 8 million in 1990 to a surprising 16.4 million in 2007 (Fortuny, Capps, Simms, & Chaudry, 2009). There are more than 11 million undocumented immigrants in the United States (Passel & Cohn, 2016). According to Hidalgo (2013), there are "22 million noncitizens living in the U.S.": 11 million of those "have some form of immigration status" which legally allows them to stay in the United States (p. 37). In 2015, the Annie E. Casey Foundation, a leading organization in foster care and a premier source of data on children and families, conducted a project entitled Kids COUNT. It was discovered that in the United States, there are a little more than 16 million children living within an immigrant household: 90% of those children are U.S. citizens, and the largest populations are of Latino or Asian descent. Figures have also shown that nearly a quarter (25%) of all children in the United States have at least one foreign-born parent

(Fortuny et al., 2009). Children of Latin@ origin make up 56%, with 44% non-Latin@ white, Asian, or black (Fortuny & Chaudry, 2009).

In the United States, Latinos are the prevalent marginal ethnic group. Latinos/Hispanics are defined as individuals of Mexican, Cuban, Central American, Puerto Rican, and South American origin. As such, more than half of the immigrants in the United States come from Latin countries (U.S. Census Bureau, 2001). According to Lopez and Taylor (2010), the Latino population in the United States grew from 35.3 million in 2000 to more than 46.9 million in 2008. This is greater than the entire population of Canada. Immigrants (that is, foreign-born, not necessarily from Latin countries) or the children (U.S.-born) of immigrants in the United States are approximated at 70 million (Suárez-Orozco, C. & Suárez-Orozco, M., 2009).

The 14th Amendment of the U.S. Constitution is a written federal document specifying that any individual born within the United States is granted citizenship. More than 4 million children born in the United States as of 2009 had at least one parent who was undocumented (Passel & Taylor, 2010). Unfortunately, in today's America, the U.S. children of undocumented immigrants do not qualify to enjoy the benefits of citizenship or the feeling that they belong (Zayas, 2015). It was estimated that in 2011, there were a minimum of 5,000 Latino children in foster care due to parents either being detained or deported (Wessler, 2011). Unfortunately, regardless of the rapidly growing population of immigrants, the actual number of children with immigrant parents who are involved in the child welfare system is not known. According to Dettlaff and Earner (2012), governments at state and national levels do not collect data on this significant issue. Estimations have shown, however, that the number of Latino children in foster care due to deportation is increasing.

Furthermore, according to Haddal (2007), of the thousands of people apprehended crossing the U.S. border without proper documentation each year, approximately 80,000 were Latino children. Some of these children come with parents or guardians, but many were unaccompanied. Additionally, it was reported that Texas Governor, Greg Abbott, asked for additional help from the federal government for more agents and resources to help protect the border from an increase in undocumented and unaccompanied children at the U.S.–Mexican border (Rosenthal, 2015). Governor Abbott requested 250 additional Border Patrol agents, along with five supplementary aviation assets. Rosenthal (2015) discloses that Texas has 20,000 Border Patrol agents, with more than 3,000 in the Rio Grande Valley. The Texas Department of Public Safety (DPS) is seeking over $300 million additional subsidy, on top of a basic border-security budget of $750 million, to double the number of state troopers now posted along the border to 500, plus new equipment and technology including helicopters and airplanes (Ward, 2016). Texas DPS border security is the largest state-funded initiative in the United States, receiving roughly $2 billion in the previous 2 years (Ward, 2016). Nevertheless, state officials have criticized its ineffectiveness at preventing the flow of undocumented immigrants.

Although states such as Arizona and California also have an influx of Latino immigrants and immigrant Latino children, the states of California and Arizona have responded to this issue with opposite views and actions. The California Department of Social Services established the Latino Practice Advisory Committee, made of national and state specialists, to build the capability of county child welfare systems to simplify culturally responsive amenities (Dettlaff, 2015). Arizona, by contrast, has policies in place that unequivocally bar students who are undocumented from attending college with in-state tuition, no matter how long the undocumented student has lived in Arizona (Androff, Ayón, Becerra, & Gurrola, 2011).

Latino Immigrant Families

Almost 30% of the young children of immigrants live in families with one or more undocumented parent, and 81% of the young children of immigrants have a non-citizen parent (Capps, Fix, Ost,

Figure 20.1 Dr. Frank Anthony Rodriguez demonstrates how the U.S.–Mexico border wall is ineffective

Source: Photo by Hector Elizondo.

Note: Dr. Rodriguez spent the day riding his bicycle along the U.S.–Mexico border near Donna, Texas, looking at security improvements and speaking with different law enforcement agencies working along the U.S. border, July 3, 2017.

Reardon-Anderson, & Passel, 2004; Castañeda & Melo, 2014; Dye, 2005). Furthermore, Castañeda and Melo (2014), posited that the United States has approximately 2.3 million mixed-status families, containing a family member who is either a permanent legal resident, undocumented, or in legal limbo through an initiative such as Deferred Action for Childhood Arrivals (DACA) or having Temporary Protected Status (TPS) (Castañeda & Melo 2014; Passel, 2011). These Latino immigrant children now account for one-quarter of the United States' 75 million children (Passel, 2011). It is estimated that by 2050, these Latino children will make up one-third of more than 100 million children in the United States. These same projections indicate that non-Hispanic white children will decrease to 40%, while Latino children will increase to about 33% (Passel, 2011).

Approximately 4.5 million U.S.-born children have at least one undocumented parent, while an additional 1 million children are themselves undocumented (American Immigration Council, 2011; Capps, Castañeda, Chaudry, & Santos, 2007; Castañeda & Melo, 2014). According to Dettlaff (2015), the majority of Latin@ children are U.S.-born citizens, and more than half of the Latin@ children have at least one undocumented parent (Passel & Taylor, 2010). Furthermore, there are roughly 450,000 foreign-born children living in families as undocumented siblings of citizens (Passel, 2011). As indicated above, the fastest-growing child population in the United States comes from Latino families. Simultaneously, the proportion of Latino children in the child welfare system has increased (Dettlaff, 2015). Additionally, many of these Latino families who are forced to rely on welfare services are fearful of deportation, detention, and the removal of children from their care (Križ & Skivenes, 2012; Leyro, 2017).

Although Latinos are the fastest-growing population in the United States, Latino families continue to underutilize community and public services compared to U.S.-born citizens due to cultural differences in help-seeking behavior and language barriers (Ayón & Aisenberg, 2010; Finno-Velasquez, 2013). Latino families fear the child welfare system as they believe that the welfare system is an extension of the government and its sovereignty (Križ & Skivenes, 2012). In fact, studies have shown the link of immigration status with the underuse of a variety of community and public services by Latinos, due to ineligibility according to federal law and fear of detection (Capps et al., 2004; Lopez, Bergren, & Painter, 2008). Immigrant families are less likely to receive federal benefits and have health insurance (Detlaff & Rycraft, 2010). In order to meet the needs of Latino families, certain aspects of the facility provider, such as the ethnic match between the client and the provider, Spanish language proficiency, and demonstration of ethnic proficiency are vital (Ayón & Aisenberg, 2010; Finno-Velasquez, 2013; Gulbas & Zayas, 2017).

Latino Immigrant Risk Factors

Latino families and their U.S.-born children may possibly also have multifaceted immigration issues. It should be recognized that not all states in the United States offer welfare assistance to undocumented individuals. The federal level determines immigration status in the United States, but state-level practices and policies vary across time and place, determining immigrants' access to benefits and services in some states while constraining their access in other states (Philbin, Flake, Hatzenbuehler, & Hirsch, 2017). Restrictions on non-citizens to publicly funded services include income assistance, housing, and Medicaid; both local and state governments also vary in eligibility policies for such services (Finno-Velasquez, 2013). It should also be noted that undocumented Latino immigrants access services at lower rates than other immigrant groups (Finno-Velasquez, 2013; Ortega et al., 2007).

The immigration experience for undocumented youth in itself can be a life-threatening crisis. The initial act of leaving one's own country and entering the United States can be dangerous for undocumented immigrants, as well as for asylum seekers and refugees, with many immigrants experiencing violence, robbery, and sexual assault during the immigration process (Dawkins & Rodriguez, 2016; Gulbas & Zayas, 2017; Leyro, 2017; Rodriguez, 2013; Rodriguez & Dawkins, 2016). Immigration may result in children being separated from their parents and siblings for extended periods of time (Dawkins & Rodriguez, 2016; Garcia et al., 2012; Gulbas & Zayas, 2017; Leyro, 2017; Rodriguez, 2013; Rodriguez & Dawkins, 2016). Depression and anxiety are stressors associated with the initial stage of migration, while individuals who experience significant trauma during immigration may develop symptoms of post-traumatic stress disorder (Smart, J. F. & Smart, D. W., 1995; Weber, 2015). Many, if not most, undocumented immigrants have to deal with these stressors, but the worst of all stressors may be the levels of fear and poverty that children of immigrant families must endure. Immigrant families are twice as likely to have an income below the poverty level, with even working immigrant families remaining below the poverty line (Dettlaff & Earner, 2012; Dettlaff & Rycraft, 2010).

Exacerbating this, a quarter of these immigrant children have parents with no General Education Diploma (GED) or high school diploma, and over 60% of these children have a parent with limited English (Dettlaff & Earner, 2012). Children in immigrant families are considerably more likely to be uninsured, to be reported in fair or poor health, and are less likely to receive public benefits (Capps et. al., 2004; Dettlaff & Earner, 2012).

Because of the high chance of parental deportation, the number of immigrant youth who are U.S. citizens compared to the number of undocumented adults should be recognized as a risk factor for

Figure 20.2 Latin@ Families March Together on the Official 21st Anniversary of the Cesar E. Chavez March for Justice, March 25, 2017

Source: Photo by Dr. Frank A. Rodriguez.

Note: The March for Justice started at the west side of San Antonio, Texas, and ended at the Alamo. This is a yearly celebration of the life and legacy of an extraordinary human being and civil rights leader.

those youth experiencing mental health issues (Allen, Cisneros, & Tellez, 2015). As such, there is a need for child welfare service providers to understand the special needs of immigrant families (Chahine &Van Straaten, 2005; Dettlaff & Earner, 2012; Gulbas & Zayas, 2017; Pine & Drachman, 2005; Rodriguez & Dawkins, 2016). Moreover, the number of immigrant youth who are U.S. citizens *living with* undocumented adults should be recognized as a risk factor for those youth experiencing mental health issues (Allen et al., 2015; Gulbas & Zayas, 2017). Where possible, it is recommended that caseworkers dealing with Latino immigrant youth and their families participate in training programs focused on immigrant issues and cultural competency (Torrico, 2010), developing professional relationships with local U.S. immigration and citizenship services staff, as well as learning about all the available resources to assist Latino immigrant families and youth (Torrico, 2010). Given the diversity and increasing size of the Latino immigrant population in the United States, it is imperative to be mindful of cultural differences among the Latino population and be able to accurately respond to those differences (Dettlaff & Johnson, 2011).

Latino Immigrant Protective Factors

Communication issues between the caseworker and Latino families will cause the immigrant to not understand fully what is occurring and this may result in fear and a lack of trust among the Latino

Undocumented Immigrant Latin@ Youth

families (Gulbas & Zayas, 2017; Torrico, 2010). More research is needed in order to understand the Latino immigrant population in the child welfare system. It is important to identify practices that are successful in achieving positive outcomes for immigrant families and youth, both in the area of preventive services and with those who come to the attention of the child welfare system (Dettlaff & Earner, 2012).

It has been suggested that service providers also must consider how to utilize the unique positive attributes that immigrant families possess in order to formulate effective service plans which reduce the risk to children and ensure their well-being (Dettlaff & Earner, 2012; Dettlaff, Earner, & Phillips, 2009; Gulbas & Zayas, 2017). Learning to function in a new country can serve as a cause of stress for immigrant youth. To alleviate stress, research has shown that devotion to beliefs and cultural values is an important source of strength that allows immigrant youth to maintain cohesion and flexibility in an unfamiliar environment (Dettlaff & Johnson, 2011). Additional protective factors that may alleviate stress in immigrant families include extended family networks, strong parental supervision, social support from immigrant communities, and religious beliefs (Dettlaff & Johnson, 2011).

As an example, on July 2, 2017, from 2pm to 4pm, Acción de Gracia Immigration Assistance, a non-profit organization with 501(c)(3) status based in Weslaco, Texas, conducted a free immigration clinic to assist undocumented Latino families with legal help. Dr. Rodriguez (co-author of this chapter) attended this clinic. Their mission is to provide the Rio Grande Valley indigent community with low-cost immigration assistance, "know your rights" seminars, and advocate for civil rights issues (Giffin, 2017). Giffin (2017) states that if it were not for the volunteer staff, donors, and participants, it would not be possible to serve the citizens of the Rio Grande Valley by providing legal assistance to those who cannot afford it, or those that are not serviced through other organizations.

This organization was founded in 2017, and led by attorney Kenna S. Giffin. It was born out of the need for immigration assistance in the Latin@ community, and the anti-immigrant agenda being

Figure 20.3 Acción de Gracia Immigration Assistance, a non-profit organization with 501(c)(3) status based in Weslaco, Texas, conducted a free immigration clinic to assist undocumented Latino families, July 2, 2017.

Source: Photo by Dr. Frank A. Rodriguez.

set by U.S. government officials (Giffin, 2017). This non-profit organization assists in: citizenship, residency renewal, new/renewed DACA, power of attorney letters, public notary services, translations, and passport photos (Giffin, 2017). The aim of this organization is to keep families together, informed about new policies, and prepared in case of an altercation with officials. Coincidentally, one of the organizers of this clinic happened to be a participant in Dr. Rodriguez's (2013) dissertation research. The organizer's name will not be disclosed due to anonymity. Nevertheless, this undisclosed organizer revealed that individuals in need will fill out an intake form. Upon review of the intake form, volunteers may determine if the family or individual in need can be assisted. This is a great example of how members of the Latino immigrant community assist each another.

Juvenile Immigration Policy

The next sections of the chapter document immigration policy and reform as they relate to undocumented children (UC), special immigrant juvenile status (SIJS), and Undocumented, Undetected, and Unaccompanied (U3) Latino youth. An explanation of contemporary immigration laws, legal representation, and legal proceedings will be given to get a better understanding of the civil system as it pertains to undocumented children and their families. The results of these deportation proceedings can be traumatic and harmful, not only for the youth affected directly by parental removals, but also because these deportations can be devastating to entire communities. Current immigration policies attempt to keep families together when at all possible. However, not having well-defined federal policies or guidelines makes this reality almost impossible. Latino immigrant families who recently migrated to the United States are likely to be fearful of their interactions with the public welfare system. Social bond theory will be applied to explain the importance of family. Understanding the Latino family culture (Latino family paradox) is imperative for welfare personnel if they are to be successful with these Latino families. A comparison of Latin@ citizen versus non-citizen removals will attempt to determine variances in terms of abuse, after-care, and outcomes. Finally, recommendations will be made and future research topics will be described put forward, based on policy suggestions and research findings.

Social Bond Theory

Social control theories give an outlook on the reasons why families should be kept together and why there are negative outcomes for adults formerly in foster care, or foster care alumni. The social intervention of foster care can have unintended negative consequences as family, social, and cultural bonds are broken. The trauma of separation that a child endures can leave them with attachment, bonding, and relationship issues. Travis Hirschi's (2009) bonding elements—attachment, involvement, and commitment—are examples of individual needs for a common value system in society. If children in foster care are expected to become productive members of society through this social intervention, then the following bonds need to occur: attachment, involvement, and commitment. Attachment is "identification with peers or parents, including an emotional bond between the child and parent" (Dorsett, 2012, p. 29) and intimate communication with parents is important. Involvement includes time-consuming dedicated activities which provide structure for a child. These are norms and values learned by socialization, and lack of these could mean that a child will not be properly socialized for living in a social community (Bernard, 1987; Dorsett, 2012; Hirschi, 2009).

In *A Descriptive Analysis of Foster Care Transitional Service and Alumni Outcomes*, Dorsett (2012) claims that foster youth are not developing the healthy bonds and attachments which Hirschi and other social control theorists state are needed to allow youth to develop normal family and societal bonds. Regardless of the intent behind the intervention of child welfare to improve the lives of unaccompanied children and youth, these caregivers must be aware of the possible damage that can ensue when a child's family, social, and cultural bonds are broken. If every normal condition that surrounds the child is seemingly changed or disrupted, creating and placing them in an environment of normlessness and detachment, these children are in danger of low self-esteem and low self-control, and may succumb to attachment disorder. The only social norm that seems to follow the foster care child is constant change and disruption. According to Merton (1968) and Durkheim (1997), this disruption can lead to a state of anomie which can end in deviance, frustration, confusion, despair, and they simply stop trying.

Special Immigrant Juvenile Status (SIJS), and Undocumented, Unaccompanied, and Undetected (U3)

Immigration has been an important feature throughout the history of the United States. One-fifth of all school children in kindergarten through to high school are the children of immigrants, according to Fix and Passel (2003). While many of these children come with their families, others come alone, either of their own will, seeking jobs, protection, family reunification; or they are smuggled into the United States for sweatshop labor or sexual exploitation (National Juvenile Justice Network, 2006). The exact number of children and youth who attempt to enter the United States, however, remains unknown. Latino children crossing the border to the United States, without parents or guardians, is not a new phenomenon. Since 2012, the number of unaccompanied immigrant children has increased dramatically (Roth & Grace, 2015).

Among the approximately 1 million individuals who are apprehended each year while crossing the U.S. border, there are nearly 100,000 unaccompanied children (Roth & Grace, 2015). The most intriguing shift in the composition of undocumented children is that children from Mexico are now outnumbered by children from Central America (Roth & Grace, 2015). Customs and Border Protection (CBP) began tracking apprehensions by unaccompanied status in 2009; Mexican children represented 83% of all unaccompanied children. In 2014, apprehensions of Mexican children decreased to 23% (Roth & Grace, 2015). In contrast, Honduras had fewer than 1,000 unaccompanied children in 2009; in 2014, unaccompanied children from Honduras jumped more than 17-fold to represent 27% of unaccompanied children. Since the spike of unaccompanied children from Honduras in 2014, Central American migration has changed very little (Chishti & Hipsman, 2015). Violence by gangs continues to persist along with lack of economic opportunity and poverty in the Northern Triangle (El Salvador, Guatemala, and Honduras)—three of the five countries with the highest murder rates in the world (Chishti & Hipsman, 2015).

Another momentous change in the makeup of undocumented children is the shift in recent immigrant settlement patterns to "non-traditional" regions such as suburbs and the Southeast. Compared with destinations like Los Angeles, San Antonio, Houston, and San Francisco, Latino families from the Northern Triangle do not have as long a history of settlement in states such as Tennessee, North Carolina, Virginia, and Georgia (Roth & Grace, 2015).

Since 2003, unaccompanied minors who are subject to removal proceedings are under the care and custody of the Office of Refugee Resettlement (ORR), and are placed within the Division of Unaccompanied Children's Services (DUCS). These offices are under the authority of the Department of Health & Human Services (DHHS). While the ORR has existed since 1980, the creation of DUCS and DHHS are recent developments. Prior to 2003, all undocumented individuals subject to custody (both adults and children) came under the authority of the Department of Justice's Immigration and Naturalization Service (INS). When the Homeland Security Act of 2002 (HSA) created the Department of Homeland Security (DHS) and eliminated INS, it significantly reorganized the executive branch's immigration duties and lines of authority.

Unaccompanied immigrant minors, according to the Homeland Security Act (HSA) of the United States, are children who have no lawful immigration status in the United States, have not attained

Figure 20.4 Dr. Frank A. Rodriguez Joins a Group of Latin@ Youth Marching in the Official 21st Anniversary of the Cesar E. Chavez March for Justice, San Antonio, Texas, March 25, 2017

18 years of age, and with respect to whom (a) there is no parent or legal guardian in the United States, or (b) no parent or legal guardian in the United States is available to provide care and physical custody. These youth are usually forced to migrate to the United States due to natural disasters or war-like conditions, but there are instances where the youth are sent by their parents to assist them in living in a better environment.

The processing phase when the minor reaches U.S. soil can be traumatic in nature to a child left alone in a foreign land. Unaccompanied youth in the United States are first apprehended by the Department of Homeland Security and placed into a detention facility in the custody of the Office of Refugee Resettlement (ORR) (Aldarondo & Becker, 2011).

These youth are screened and forensic exams are conducted to determine if their age exceeds 18, which would disqualify them as a juvenile (Aldarondo & Becker, 2011). If the juvenile is determined to be under the age of 18, they remain in the custody of ORR which then seeks placement for them into an appropriate environment (Aldarondo & Becker, 2011). Those children are placed with a division of ORR called the Division of Unaccompanied Children's Services (DUCS); DUCS is a detention center in which all mental and physical health needs are met and tests are conducted within 90 days of placement there (Aldarondo & Becker, 2011). English as a second language as well as social skills and educational services are also provided (Aldarondo & Becker, 2011). These juveniles have an opportunity to become U.S. citizens only after obtaining a lawful permanent residency (LPR), and meeting certain criteria needed to apply for Special Immigrant Juvenile Status (SIJS).

Special Immigrant Juvenile Status (SIJS)

Immigration and placement in the child welfare system is complicated at best and contacting an immigration specialist or a state attorney for any questions is well advised. In 1990, the Special Immigrant Juvenile Status (SIJS) was created by the U.S. Congress to assist with immigration documents for youth under the age of 21 who are not married. Under SIJS, youth will be helped to obtain a lawful permanent residency (LPR). Obtaining SIJS status can aid a youth in becoming a citizen, achieving permanency, gaining benefits, or being adopted. This gives them a head start while still in care; the process to obtain citizenship can be a more complicated and lengthy process after the youth leaves the foster care system. Some states have options for extended foster care up to the age of 21, and staying in extended foster care gives unaccompanied youth more time to work on the SIJS, or LPR, status (Kemp Parker, 2014; Texas Department of Family Protective Services [henceforth, DFPS], 2016).

There are inconsistencies with immigration policy implementation when Special Immigrant Juvenile Status (SIJS) is considered. On behalf of the youth, caseworkers should contact the foreign consulate, and assist the child without documents to obtain SIJS. In many states, juvenile courts are confused or unaware and fail to encourage or inform undocumented youth who may be eligible to apply for SIJS (Križ & Skivenes, 2012). In fact, research by Garcia et al. (2012) revealed that child welfare caseworkers did not reference or were not aware of the Special Immigrant Juvenile Status (SIJS).

Undocumented, Unaccompanied, and Undetected (U3) Latino Youth

The exact number of children and youth who attempt to enter the United States remains unknown. It is further unknown how many of these children who have not been detected by immigration officials are living in the United States (Rodriguez, 2013; Rodriguez & Dawkins, 2016). A category of immigrants that has never been researched, according to Rodriguez (2013), are children who are Undocumented, Unaccompanied, and Undetected (U3). The term "U3" was coined by Rodriguez (2013). He interviewed youth who had not been detected by immigration officials (*Undetected*), arrived in the United States without parents or guardians (*Unaccompanied*), and are *Undocumented*. Research that is focused on the linkage between child welfare and Latino immigrant families is scarce, and even less studied when it comes to Latino U3 youth in the United States (Rodriguez, 2013; Rodriguez & Dawkins, 2016; Scott et al., 2014). Additional research found no results for the U3 category, suggesting that more research is needed on this population. This is a large enough population that policies and procedures should be in place to represent these children and youth who come to the attention of the child welfare system (Allen et al., 2015; Dawkins & Rodriguez, 2016; Dettlaff, 2015; Roth & Grace, 2015).

A qualitative research study conducted by Rodriguez (2013), entitled *Unaccompanied Latino Youth on the United States–Mexico Border* may be the only one of its kind. In this study, Rodriguez (2013) interviewed undocumented immigrant youth who cross the U.S.–Mexico border without parents or guardians and who have remained undetected. The influential years of childhood may be impacted by the experiences and perceptions constructed during the process of migration and the potential for, or actual occurrence of, deportation. Due to limited access to this surreptitious population, the following characteristics were relied on in selecting participants: being undetected; under the age of 21 when they first arrived in U.S. territory; unmarried when they first arrived in the United States; and with no adult supervision when crossing the U.S.–Mexican border.

The reason for choosing this particular sub-population of undetected immigrants was due to their potential eligibility to qualify for SIJS (Rodriguez, 2013). According to Byrne (2008), no child can be denied SIJS because of "age," as long as the petitioner was less than 21 years old at the time of application. This may have been the only time that these research participants could have the opportunity to lawfully apply once and for all for U.S. citizenship after living in the country for 5 years. Unfortunately, at the time of the interview with Rodriguez, many of the participants may have passed their 21st birthday (Rodriguez, 2013). It should be noted that youth who come from Mexico do not qualify for SIJS. As long as these youth remain in the United States with no immigration status, they may not obtain legal employment nor apply for college loans or other benefits, and they will remain susceptible to exploitation and victimization (Bronstein & Montgomery, 2011).

Through in-depth interviews with these youths, Rodriguez (2013) examined how legal status shapes the way these undocumented youth perceive their existence in the United States. Despite their undocumented status, minimal to no support from outside sources (e.g., parents, family, welfare), and multiple barriers, (e.g., language barrier, lack of health care, minimal education), these undocumented youths demonstrated high levels of resiliency by attempting to improve their lives while living on the U.S.–Mexico border (Rio Grande Valley of South Texas). Pseudonyms were used for anonymity. A few of the participants in Rodriguez's (2013) study described in this chapter are Bryan, Joey, and Victor.

At the age of 10, Bryan's grandmother took him to Guatemala City, Guatemala, and from there a "coyote" [trafficker] took him to Chiapas, Mexico. From Chiapas he headed to Vera Cruz, Mexico, and from Vera Cruz, that same coyote contacted another person to take him to Matamoros (border town), Tamaulipas, Mexico. A research question utilized in this study was: Tell me the last time you cried? Bryan replied by stating:

> I cried this past weekend. I realized that life is short and we need to live to the fullest. I realized that a lot of opportunities that I have been offered, I have had to turn down. I could not accept them because of my immigration status. I had to turn down many scholarships, the Coca Cola Scholarship, the Bill Gates Scholarship (my entire college [tuition and fees] was to be paid), Brown University offered me a scholarship too.

Bryan worked at a restaurant near his university in order to pay for his books and college tuitions. Bryan feared that he would not have money to pay his tuition or for books each semester. He also feared being deported at any time. The only medical help Bryan got was from his university clinic. As of 2014, Bryan had graduated from his university and for the time being, he was in good health.

Joey was back in the United States after being deported. This means that he had the experience of crossing the Rio Grande River twice. The deportation did not keep him away from his current home for too long. The first time that he trekked from Honduras, he was only 13 years old. He traveled from Honduras with four of his cousins. He paid a coyote $800 to get him to the United States. He did not have to look far to acquire a coyote—his own cousin was a human smuggler and charged him the $800 to get him to the United States the first time. Joey's actual experience in the United States differed from the expectation he had prior to coming there. "To be here undocumented is the worst part about being here. People would say that here you would earn money real easy. It is not that way." His experiences have impacted the person he has become. He said, "I am afraid to get deported again." He had become more cautious and suspicious of people. "Before, I was with my parents," continued Joey, "now I am alone. I have to pay for light, water, and rent." He said that life had changed little for the better for him and his cousins, since they arrived from Honduras.

Another research question utilized by Rodriguez (2013) was: What types of obstacles have the youths encountered in terms of education and work? The answer to this question falls under a broader theme of *unexpected suffering*. The unexpected suffering includes: a) a false perception that in the United States, *employment* would be plentiful, easier to obtain, and stable, with employers who would always treat them well; b) transportation difficulties (there was a common assumption that they would be able to walk to the places they needed to visit, as had been the case in their country of origin);

Table 20.1 Unexpected Suffering in the United States

Pseudonym	Employment	Transportation	Not accessing health care	Missing family	Persistent fear of deportation
Marvin**	X	X	X	X	X
Bryan	X			X	X
Cowboy	X	X		X	X
Morris*	X	X	X	X	X
Joey*	X	X		X	X
Bobby	X		X	X	X
Henry	X	X		X	X
Dynamo	X	X	X		X
Dan	X	X	X	X	X
Marco	X	X	X	X	
Christopher	X	X	X	X	X
Victor	X	X	X	X	X

Source: Rodriguez (2013).

Note: *Morris and Joey are brothers; **Marvin is the first cousin of Morris and Joey.

c) not being able to access health care (given their illegal status), and thus suffering through illnesses; d) missing family (these were, after all, rather young unaccompanied minors); and e) a persistent fear of detection and deportation (see Table 20.1).

Thus, as shown in Table 20.1 above, problems in accessing health care among the U3 population are detrimental to the lives of these youth.

The first time that Victor came to the United States, he was accompanied by his half-brother and brother-in-law who were captured by U.S. immigration officers. In a matter of days, he acquired a coyote and crossed the Rio Grande River again. This second time he crossed, he made it with his half-brother and a cousin who lived in Reynosa, Mexico, a U.S.–Mexico border town. Victor was now alone in the United States, and was eager to work in the cold weather, hot weather, every day of the week, in the fields and/or construction, whatever! Victor was one of two research participants who first entered the United States at the age of 19. He was also from Vera Cruz, Mexico, and had a 6th Grade education in Mexico. His father (by then deceased) was a medical doctor, and his mother was terminally ill in Mexico.

> My father was from Puebla and my mother is from Vera Cruz. My father was a doctor and he was a very good man. He passed away in 1988 and my mom was alone with four sons. She would sell things to try and make ends meet. Now I try to send my family a little money to help them out. My mom is now sick and she is alone. She has diabetes and is very skinny. My grandma is also ill.

Victor said that he wanted to be in the United States for work, but on the other hand, he would like to be in Mexico with his family. He said, "It is because I need to look for work to help out my family in Mexico. My only responsibility is to send them money, and I also have responsibilities here. I pay rent, light, water, and food, alone." He would like to go home one day.

> It is too dangerous to go because they [the coyotes] can kill you at any time. It has been not as bad as some people that are raped, are robbed, beaten, or drown in the river because they cannot swim. Others die on the train.

Victor thanked God that he had never become sick. "When I have pains I go to the store and buy pills for the pain or fever," he said. Victor has never gone to a doctor. He also stated that the only people he communicated well with were those who spoke Spanish. None of the U3 participants utilized the welfare system, as most were fearful of detection and others did not know of such opportunities (Rodriguez, 2013).

Legal Representation to Counsel

Based on research by Brabeck and Xu (2010), the stress of potential deportation of a parent directly affects the well-being of their children. Due to the traditional roles of the Latino family, the children are affected devastatingly when a parent is deported (Derby, 2012; Gulbas & Zayas, 2017). In the first 6 months of 2011, more than 46,000 mothers and fathers of children who were U.S. citizens were deported. When deportation is a possibility, these families should have representation before detection, as a precaution, and in all instances when a child may be taken away. Representation in child welfare is a must for the parents involved, as well as the children who are non-citizens, who should have the same legal representation as children who are citizens. If there is no clear case of abuse, neglect, or abandonment, child welfare agencies should not impose their own ethnocentric social standards upon the family when considering child removal. Prevention of the removal of Latino immigrant children from their families should be the key for caseworkers. Two thoughts on legal representation are: a parent has a constitutional right, a fundamental liberty to have custody and manage their child as stated in *Santosky v. Kramer* (where the state sought termination of parental rights on the statutory ground of "permanent neglect"); and the state has a burden to prove the parent unfit (Byrd, 2013). Furthermore, if a family or child becomes involved with the child welfare system, it is up to the court judge to mandate representation. A child has a right to legal representation prior to or while being placed in foster care.

Some states are more burdened than others with the responsibility of legal representation for these youth. The most southern U.S. states—California, Texas, and Florida—have the largest number of Latino and Hispanic immigrants and the largest numbers of children in child welfare. These states find themselves with the financial responsibility of the unaccompanied child population. State agencies have special programs and staff whose primary focus is working with and representing immigrant families and unaccompanied children. For example, the Texas Department of Family and Protective Services (DFPS) has immigration specialists who work alongside the department caseworker. The Florida Department of Children and Families has a refugee services department, and California immigration services are outsourced through Immigration Services Contractors.

A Miami lawyer utilized *Plyler v. Doe* (1982) when Florida was one of the first states to try to deny undocumented children rights by not allowing them into foster care, or permitting them to receive services. In Texas, the Supreme Court overturned a state statute denying funding for education to undocumented immigrant children, and at the same time struck down a municipal school district's attempt to charge undocumented immigrant youth an annual $1,000 tuition fee per student to compensate for the lack of state funding (*Plyler v. Doe*, 1982). Situations like this typically boil down to funding. The U.S. Supreme Court struck down state laws that were inconsistent with federal welfare provisions which denied individuals federal benefits.

Currently, the Texas child welfare system has a program in place to assist unaccompanied children. The DFPS has immigration specialists and caseworkers who are specifically trained to talk to parents, the child, and/or family members to get as much information as possible to complete Form 660, Basic Immigration Information. These specialists ask for copies of the child's birth record and any passport, visa, or other immigration document, and give notice to the foreign consul if required. And last, they assist with the application process for an eligible child or youth.

State and national representation should show a clear pattern of attempting to keep families together, maintaining the child/youth's cultural norms. There are national programs such as the

Immigrant Children's Legal and Service Partnership (ICLASP) which also assists with representation. Representation by ICLASP (Aldarondo & Becker, 2011) aims to:

1. provide legal counsel not afforded to UIMs (unaccompanied immigrant minors) by immigration law;
2. conduct language-specific and culturally appropriate assessments of children from diverse cultural backgrounds and with limited English proficiency;
3. provide UIMs with knowledge of the U.S. legal system and the immigration processes, because many such youth have little or no understanding of the system in which crucial decisions about their immigration status are being made;
4. harness expert knowledge of trauma resolution to better respond to the needs of children with histories of victimization and loss;
5. utilize expert knowledge of positive youth development strategies and programs to build and sustain UIMs' resilience and sense of hope while waiting through uncertainty for the resolution of their situation;
6. provide detention facility staff with education in child development and best practices for well-being promotion.

If the core set of needs described by ICLASP are met, it can minimize the trauma that can be caused by deportation.

Deportation and Trauma

The Child Welfare Information Gateway (2016, p. 1) states that when it comes to immigration and child welfare, these children experience trauma from "difficult immigration or refugee experiences, extended separation from parents, or a parent's detention/deportation" as well as "acculturation and language issues". Immigration can be a complicated process for unaccompanied children, causing fear and trauma. Along with fear of being deported, immigrant parents are afraid of being separated from their children (Detlaff & Rycraft, 2010; Gulbas & Zayas, 2017).

It is important that child welfare professionals provide immigrant families with the best procedures and resources to improve their lives. Deportations cause economic hardship, family separation, and emotional distress (Gulbas & Zayas, 2017; Leyro, 2017; Lugo, 2015). The Trump Administration has delivered two administrative orders that radically expand the intensity and scope of federal immigration enforcement efforts in the United States (Cervantes & Walker, 2017). The Department of Homeland Security arrested more than 40,000 individuals since President Trump signed these executive orders, a 40% increase, equated to the same period the previous year (Duara, 2017). One of these administrative orders turned 8 million people in the United States into priorities for deportation; by comparison, there were about 1.4 million people considered priorities for removal under President Obama (Duara, 2017). This policy change will have destructive consequences for children living in mixed-status families, many of whom are U.S. citizens, as well as unaccompanied children seeking protection (Cervantes & Walker, 2017). Families are separated and children are left without a parent or, in many cases, without both parents (Covarrubias & Hartman, 2015). These policies are detrimental to immigrant families, and at the same time, damaging to communities, not only by breaking up families, but also putting an overall economic burden on the U.S. welfare system.

An exploration done by the Immigrant Rights Clinic at New York University's School of Law (Covarrubias & Hartman, 2015) discovered that during 2005 and 2010, nearly 90% of processed cases in New York City were undocumented parents with U.S.-born children that resulted in deportation. The average cost of foster care for each child is estimated to be $26,000 annually (Derby, 2012). Children under the age of 5 whose parents are undocumented and processed for deportation are likely to be adopted; it is also unlikely that these children will ever reunite with their family (Covarrubias & Hartman, 2015). These Latino children face economic hardship and psychological trauma. The economic hardships faced when a parent is deported or detained can have an adverse effect on the youth (Brabeck, Lykes, & Hunter, 2014; Dawkins & Rodriguez, 2016; Gulbas & Zayas, 2017).

Parents and caregivers who work with children from other cultures and/or countries should be aware that the children may have healing which needs to take place due to past trauma. The term "trauma-informed care" is sweeping across the United States in child welfare. This is a much-needed paradigm shift for the betterment of children and the child welfare community. One such research-based program, titled Trust-Based Relational Intervention (TBRI) in Fort Worth, Texas, and offered at the Karyn Purvis Institute of Child Development, teaches the child welfare community intervention modality and how to connect with children who have been abused, neglected, and/or traumatized. These TBRI-trained practitioners who include members of the child welfare community, educators, medical personnel, and more, are located all over the United States, utilizing techniques, principles, and practices to assist the physical and emotional needs of adopted and fostered children (Purvis, Cross, & Pennings, 2009). Additionally, child welfare state agencies and child placement agencies are adding required training for staff and foster and adoptive parents. Prior to this paradigm shift in child welfare, a child who "acted out" after being separated from family was often diagnosed and prescribed psychotropic medication to control their outbursts or negative behavior. However, trauma training indicates that children who are not protected and nurtured at an early age have connectors in the upper brain that do not fully develop. Traumatized children's behavior might be destructive to the untrained eye and these children are more likely to respond with the "fight or flight" mechanism, and battle with not knowing how to trust or bond, being insecure. So, nurturing and understanding, not medications or solitude, are what these children need, and the needs of children traumatized by deportation and immigration issues deserve the same trauma-informed community serving them (Maxwell, 2007; Purvis et al., 2009).

Parental deportation causes increased emotional and behavioral distress among children, including sleep problems, depression, anxiety, and poor grades (Baum, Jones, & Barry, 2010; Brabeck & Xu 2010; Derby, 2012; Gulbas & Zayas, 2017). After going through the deportation of a parent or parents, children become fearful themselves. Latino children of deported parents are affected with emotional and mental health problems as a result of the loss (Allen et al., 2015; Gulbas & Zayas, 2017). For example, young children who are not yet able to understand all aspects of how the immigration system works become distrustful of the law themselves. Failure to maintain the family unit can cause the youth to experience problems in accessing and maintaining appropriate health care needs (Allen et al., 2015). Children begin to lose focus in school and even to miss days. These children are under an excessive amount of stress, and find it difficult to concentrate on school work. It is already established that children of deported immigrants experience behavioral changes (Koball et al., 2015). Some become depressed and others become extremely angry. They might have thoughts such as, "Why is this happening to me?" and so they act out. Some children, uncharacteristically, fight with other students, or with teachers, in class (Koball et al. 2015). Many students even stop going to school completely to tend to their siblings; college students drop out because they can't afford tuition due to the financial situation at home (Koball et al., 2015).

Fear of deportation is a common theme among Latino immigrants in general. This fear not only impacts the lives of Latino children and their families, but the fear of deportation has implications for entire communities. A study conducted by Leyro (2017) explored the role of deportation and its effects on the process of integration. Through in-depth interviews with 33 participants, Leyro revealed how vulnerability to deportation impacted immigrants' lives. The fear of deportation produced psychological and emotional distress, which created barriers to integration into American life. "The effect of deportability on immigrants' lives is of interest on the level of both individual integration and community cohesion" (2017, p. iv).

The child welfare community that services this population should be aware of this and be trained in ways to minimize trauma. The TBRI program (discussed above) began by teaching and training parents how to care for "Children from Hard Places" a term coined by Dr. Karyn Purvis, TBRI co-founder. From the program's inception, there was a focus on assisting parents who had adopted and/or fostered children of a different race, ethnicity, and culture, and whose children were dealing with past trauma. This program has expanded to teach and train state child welfare agency staff, as well as the child welfare community across the world. Children placed in out-of-home care deal with loss and trauma and the cognitive effects of their suffering can hinder their growth. These children need special understanding and care. Caregivers should be aware that abuse, neglect, abandonment, the experience of being refugees, and even natural disasters can embed memories of endured hardships and trauma that last a lifetime (Maxwell, 2007). Trauma training helps to better equip child welfare staff, and adoptive and foster families, as they come from a different culture and often do not understand the needs and behaviors of these children (Carr, 2009; Mares & Jureidini, 2004; Perez, 2001).

Prevention, Kinship, and Reunification

It is common knowledge in child welfare and protective services that states have the right to protect the children. However, families have a right to stay together and children have a constitutional right not to be taken away from their family unless the parents fail the "parental fitness standards" of the middle- to upper-class echelon of American society. State agencies must be careful not to have systematic biases toward immigrants and the undocumented population which could separate families. In an article in the *Journal of Child and Adolescent Psychiatric Nursing*, Raphel (2012, p. 106) warns that "increased enforcement of immigration laws has led to separating more children from their parents who await disposition or deportation". The Adoption Assistance and Child Welfare Act of 1980 (AACWA) was enacted with the goal of keeping families together and aims to achieve permanency or a permanent living situation for the child. Although there are no well-defined federal policies or guidelines, the goal is to have families reunited by immigration and child welfare (Hidalgo, 2013).

Another issue with immigrant families is the fear of collaborating with state agencies due to language barriers. Even with the aforementioned representation rights, undocumented families are fearful of child welfare agencies, which face barriers such as lack of understanding of Latino families, and minimal multi-language and multi-cultural skills which can result in communication failures (Ayón, Aisenberg, & Cimino, 2013; Byrd, 2013; Hidalgo, 2013; Scott et al., 2014). This is problematic because language barriers can hinder communications between caseworkers and clients, which may lead to inaccurate assessments of problems and needs (Finno-Velasquez, 2013). It has been documented that 90% of immigrant parents speak Spanish at home, though only 50% have a Spanish-speaking caseworker assigned (Finno-Velasquez, 2013). The child welfare workforce, including social workers, tends to be white and non-Latino (Child Welfare Information Gateway, 2016).

Understanding Latino Families

It is important for welfare caseworkers to know the Latino family value system in order to have the trust and full cooperation of individuals who may need public assistance. Welfare workers need to become more culturally adaptive in assisting Latino families and children (Detlaff & Rycraft, 2010). Understanding how to address Latinos begins with understanding the diversity in Latino and Hispanic cultures (National Center for Child Welfare Excellence, 2015). Cultural differences as well as their country of origin and religious backgrounds are factors in successful engagement with Latino families (National Center for Child Welfare Excellence, 2015). Knowledge of the Latino family system can assist caseworkers when facing cultural differences.

The Latino family value system can be divided into four sections which explain their cultural reasoning: *familismo*, *personalismo*, *simpatia*, and *respeto* (Ayón & Aisenberg, 2010; Guilamo-Ramos, Dittus, Jaccard, Johannson, & Acosta, 2007). In the context of relations with child welfare, the first two are the most important. *Familismo* is the manner in which the Latinos value the family as a unit by placing an emphasis on the total well-being of the unit (Guilamo-Ramos et al., 2007). The *familismo*, family unity, should be a priority if at all possible so children can maintain their cultural and religious values and norms (Ayón et al., 2013). A good example of this was implemented as early as 2005 in New York when collaboration between immigrant advocacy groups and child welfare overcame barriers for the betterment of these families. Active discussion among the multidisciplinary group of child welfare workers and immigrant families has identified numerous impediments such as rights to benefits, language barriers, fear of government officials, deportation, etc. (Chahine & Van Straaten, 2005). A modest but influential outcome in this situation was the development of the Language Identification Card (LIC), which helped child welfare staff in recognizing the home's primary language. The LIC card was kept by families and utilized when necessary.

Personalismo is the importance placed on the ability to work with others as well as a personal importance placed on relationships (Ayón & Aisenberg, 2010). Thus, trust may be the best description for *personalismo*. *Personalismo* also factors into areas of trust between social workers and Latino families. Latinos view unannounced visits from social workers as a lack of trust and this causes a breach in their relationship (Ayón & Aisenberg, 2010). *Personalismo* can be established by making frequent visits to the home, as the frequency allows a relationship to be built up (Ayón & Aisenberg, 2010). Familiarity or being acknowledged by the welfare employee are basic elements in establishing *personalismo* with the family (Ayón & Aisenberg, 2010). Respectfulness (*respeto*) to the family and the household maintains a level of trust, and this helps to increase the interaction between the welfare system and Latin@ families. Latino immigrant families who recently migrated to the United States are likely to be fearful of their interactions with the public welfare system, as their documentation status may be questioned and deportation may take place (Ayón, Aisenberg, & Erera, 2010).

Removal of Children: Latin@ Citizens versus Non-Citizens

Research indicates that Latino children are removed at higher rates, and this creates overrepresentation of Latino children in the child welfare system across states (Dorsett, 2012; Pecora et al., 2010; Scott et. al., 2014). A preventive measure and alternative to removing children from families is called kinship care, when children can be placed in the informal or formal care of family relatives (Child Welfare Information Gateway, 2016). Keeping families together is a priority and studies suggest that kinship placements are better for children than state placements. A recent article, titled "Kinship care and undocumented Latino children in the Texas foster care system: Navigating the child welfare–immigration crossroads," suggests that "kinship placements are better able to facilitate a child's continued connections with biological parents and siblings, provide more emotional stability and support than non-relative caregivers" (Scott et al., 2014, pp. 55–56). The article goes further, stating that "Latino children are more likely to be placed in out-of-home care and, once in foster care, stay for longer periods of time than non-Hispanic white children" (Scott et al., 2014, p. 56). And last, "child welfare workers may be failing to look across international boundaries to find 'appropriate' kinship placements" (Scott et al., 2014, p. 66).

The *Texas Foster Care Alumni Study Technical Report* (Roller-White et al., 2012) found that a larger proportion of Latino youth with legal immigration status were placed in kinship care (30.17%), compared to undocumented Latino youth (15.84%). Some studies conclude with contradictory results in regard to legal and undocumented Latino youth. In one study, Latino youth with legal immigration status were more likely to come to the attention of child welfare agencies due to "active drug and alcohol use in the home" (Scott et al., 2014, p. 63). While another study conducted by Landale, Hardie, Oropesa, and Hillemeier (2015), using data on 2,535 children, which investigated how immigrant parents shape the behavioral functioning of the children, declared that children of undocumented Mexican migrants had significantly higher risks of externalizing and internalizing behavior problems than their counterparts with naturalized citizen or documented mothers (Landale et al., 2015). Although these studies mentioned several possibilities as to why immigration status may affect kinship placement, the possibility that staff or child welfare biases may be the reasoning for child placement, as U.S. history has indicated, was not mentioned. Thus, one can conclude that child welfare agencies attempt to terminate the parental rights of detained or deported parents at a higher rate than those of Latino citizens.

There is, however, a case recorded where a deported father was able to come back to the United States to obtain custody of his children. Byrd (2013) shared the story of Felipe Montes who illegally entered the United States, married a U.S. citizen, and started a family. State agencies had investigated the family and Felipe was deported back to Mexico for law violations, leaving his pregnant wife and two children. The mother, now single, and mentally ill, struggled to care for her children and child welfare removed the children. Officials refused to send the children to live with their father in Mexico, deeming his home unfit for small children. But after the story gained national attention, resulting in a public petition, and a lengthy legal battle, the children were allowed to live with the father in Mexico for a "trial placement." This was a fortunate and rare story, but an example of how kinship placement can be used beyond international borders (Byrd, 2013). This could be a precedent for future cases, attempting to keep U.S.-born children with undocumented biological family. The Adoption and Safe Families Act (ASFA) of 1997 states that it is a requirement of jurisdiction to make efforts to promote family reunification. However, states can begin proceedings to terminate parental rights if a child stays in foster care for 15 of the previous 22 months (Child Welfare Information Gateway, 2016).

Abuse, After Care, and Outcomes

Child welfare has been plagued with reported issues of abuse and neglect of children within the child welfare system. Studies have indicated that children in the child welfare system are often over-medicated, malnourished, under-educated, separated from siblings, and even die while in state custody (Barth & Blackwell, 1998; Douglas & Poletti, 2016; Pecora et al., 2005; Pecora et al., 2010; Roller-White et al., 2012). This issue can be exacerbated for unaccompanied children when biological family connections are broken and not maintained, especially if family members are deported. The immediate family and extended family are an important component for Latino juveniles in child welfare cases (Dettlaff & Johnson, 2011). Furthermore, Latino children can lose their cultural identity when placed into foster care. Monolingual youth are often placed with non-bilingual foster parents (Garcia et al., 2012). The failure to place them into a bilingual home causes them to lose their ability to speak their native language. Even those who can be placed into a bilingual setting require the placement to be long term to ensure that the native culture is not lost (Garcia et al., 2012).

Latino and undocumented children face the same bleak future as documented children in foster care. If a child stays in custody until they age or emancipate out of care, they are looking at a bleak immediate future and a struggle to live as adults. Reports indicate that large percentages of young adults from foster care are homeless, incarcerated, on social assistance, experience early pregnancies, and are under-educated; only approximately 50% of children from care graduate from high school and lower percentages graduate with a 4-year college degree (Courtney, Piliavin, Grogan-Kaylor, & Nesmith, 2001; Courtney, Terao, & Bost, 2004; Dorsett, 2012; Pecora et al., 2005; Pecora et al., 2010; Roller-White et al., 2012). The book *What Works in Family Foster Care* indicates that Latino children are overrepresented in foster care, and "children that did not know their mother or father while growing up were less likely to complete high school" (Pecora et al., 2010, p. 221). These authors go on to suggest that foster parents should be aware that their role in a foster child's life is to ensure stability and enhance birth family relationships. Last, they encourage children in care to develop lifelong connections (Pecora et al., 2010). There is no better lifelong connection than to know your nuclear and extended biological family. Although child welfare is mandated to give children their lifelong paperwork such as birth certificates, legal papers, social security, etc., agencies are not mandated to assist a youth in reconnecting with family after they leave care.

There are limited resources for youth who age out of the foster care system. Most financial and physical assistance ends at age 18, or possibly 21 years old, depending on the individual state. Some states pay for continuing education and health insurance, but again availability differs per state, and does not cross state lines. Although gaining citizenship while in care assists unaccompanied children, it will not prepare them to live on their own after child welfare benefits are over. If reunification never takes place for a child, at a minimum, maintaining a relationship with their family while they are in care can assist them in their future, preserving family and cultural bonds.

In 2005, Casey Family Programs put out the Northwest study which surveyed and interviewed young adults formerly in foster care, terming this population "foster care alumni" (Pecora et al., 2005). Foster care alumni authors in the book, *Flux*, discuss issues discovered while and after transitioning from care. Issues dealt with include the biological family, support systems, intimacy, even a chapter titled, "Who Am I Now?" The book is loaded with stories of insecurity and loneliness (Ecke & Foster Care Alumni of America, 2010). Thus recently, a social movement began to improve child welfare and to bring awareness to society by those formerly in foster care by discussing the issues that children from foster care endure and will face as adults. This book will assist the U3 population as well as the American documented foster care population aging out of foster care.

Recommendations and Future Research

Several recommendations have been made throughout this chapter, ranging from cultural and trauma training for the child welfare community, seeking citizenship for U3 youth, allowing kinship care for children, reunification of families, and seeking nuclear and extended family across international borders. Keeping biological families together should be prioritized if the environment is safe for the child. Federal government and child welfare agencies should work together to make sure that every avenue for keeping the family unit together is explored. However, if separation is imminent, then the closest and safest biological family reunification situation should be sought. Separation and the dysfunction of foster care can lead families and children into a state of despair and hopelessness. The results and the negative outcomes of children from foster care, or foster care alumni, have indicated that the intention of child welfare to improve the lives of children and families does not always work (Roller-White et al., 2012).

A national descriptive analysis conducted by Dorsett in 2012 on the outcomes of youth from foster care indicated that no specific research was conducted on children involved in immigration and child welfare, with minimal research on Hispanic and/or Latin@ children in child welfare. This research discusses the census and child welfare figures which present the Latin@ population as the second largest race/ethnicity at 16% in the U.S. census, and the third largest race/ethnicity of children in foster care at 21%. Current numbers and population statistics remain the same, indicating an overrepresentation of Hispanic/Latin@ children in the child welfare system. Dorsett (2012) suggested that research on Hispanic and Latin@ children in child welfare was minimal, and her content analysis found that only 22 of 48 articles on transitional service and alumni outcomes written between 2003 and 2011 focused on the Hispanic and Latin@ populations. Therefore, more research specific to the immigration and child welfare relationship should be conducted as well as specific research on Hispanic/Latin@ children in the child welfare system.

Conclusion and Final Remarks

For the purpose of this chapter, the term "undocumented" was utilized to refer to immigrants residing in the United States with no legal permanent residency or without citizenship. Efforts were made to avoid the terms "alien" or "illegal" that underpin a destructive and criminalization frame. Immigration policies in the United States should be made less punitive, allowing millions of undocumented individuals in America to come out of the shadows. The disclosure on immigration must be shifted away from a criminalization edifice. This is imperative for the improvement of the U.S. immigration system and welfare system and to fulfill its aims. Progressive and political correctness in the United States no longer mentions African Americans with the "N" word; the same goes for undocumented immigrants—we must not refer to them with treacherous labels. Harmful underpinnings of this type are popular among politicians, the media, and individuals who may not know the difference between the criminal justice system and the civil justice system in the United States. It may take 50 or even 100 years for some to realize that it is wrong to denote others, even undocumented individuals, as "illegals."

A misconception regarding mixed-status families is that U.S.-born children cannot "anchor" parents by providing either protection from deportation or automatic citizenship. Even for individuals

Figure 20.5 Unknown Woman Holds Up a Sign during the Official 21st Anniversary of the Cesar E. Chavez March for Justice, March 25, 2017

Source: Photo by Dr. Frank A. Rodriguez.

who are lawfully in the United States, mixed families are repeatedly mediated by this conversational construction (Castañeda & Melo, 2014).

Since the Latin@ population will continue to grow, the United States should respect the immigration and child welfare relationship and take the necessary steps for responsibility and legal representation. The authors believe it is in the best interest of immigration and child welfare professionals to be informed, educated, and trained to work with these populations and their families for the best interest of the children and the Latin@ communities.

Acknowledgments

Dr. Vivian J. Dorsett would like to acknowledge all the foster care alumni who work immensely hard to improve the child welfare system for those still in care. She would also like to thank her three sons, Zach, Malachi, and Jonathon, for their endless love and patience.

Dr. Frank Anthony Rodriguez would like to acknowledge all the people who crossed borders to make a better life for themselves and their families. Immigrants are the foundation of this nation. Also, Dr. Rodriguez would like to acknowledge his grandfather who is now 93 years old. Don Erasmo Alvarado, Sr., thank you for crossing borders multiple times to have a better life and future for our familia.

References

Adoption Assistance and Child Welfare Act [AACWA] of 1980, P.L. 96-272. (1980).
Adoption and Safe Families Act [ASFA] of 1997, P.L. 105-89. (1997).
Aldarondo, E., & Becker, R. (2011). Promoting the well-being of unaccompanied immigrant minors. In L. Buki & L. Piedra (Eds.), *Creating infrastructures for Latino mental health* (pp. 195–214). New York, NY: Springer.
Allen, B., Cisneros, E., & Tellez, A. (2015). The children left behind: The impact of parental deportation on mental health. *Journal of Child and Family Studies, 24*(2), 386–392.
American Immigration Council. (2011, March 22). *The unauthorized population today: Number holds steady at 11 million, three-fifths have been here more than a decade.* Immigration Policy Center. Retrieved from www.immigrationpolicy.org/just-facts/unauthorized-population-today
Androff, D. K., Ayón, C., Becerra, D., & Gurrola, M. (2011). US immigration policy and immigrant children's well-being: The impact of policy shifts. *Journal of Sociology and Social Welfare, 38*, 77–98.
Annie E. Casey Foundation. (2015, January 30). More children in immigrant families. Blog post. Retrieved from www.aecf.org/blog/more-children-in-immigrant-families/
Ayón, C., & Aisenberg, E. (2010). Negotiating cultural values and expectations within the public child welfare system: A look at familismo and personalismo. *Child and Family Social Work, 15*, 335–344. doi:10.1111/j.1365-2206.2010.00682
Ayón, C., Aisenberg, E., & Cimino, A. (2013). Latino families in the nexus of child welfare, welfare reform, and immigration policies: Is kinship care a lost opportunity? *Social Work, 58*(1), 91–94. doi:10.1093/sw/sws014
Ayón, C., Aisenberg, E., & Erera, P. (2010). Learning how to dance with the Public Child Welfare System: Mexican parents' efforts to exercise their voice. *Journal of Public Child Welfare, 4*, 263–286. doi:10.1080/15548732.2010.496077
Barth, R. P., & Blackwell, D. L. (1998). Death rates among California's foster care and former foster care populations. *Children and Youth Services Review, 20*(7), 577–604. https://doi.org/10.1016/S0190-7409(98)00027-9
Baum, J., Jones, R., & Barry, C. (2010). *In the child's best interest? The consequences of losing a lawful immigrant parent to deportation.* Retrieved from the University of California Davis Law School website at www.law.ucdavis.edu/news/images/childsbestinterest.pdf
Bernard, T. J. (1987). Structure and control: Reconsidering Hirschi's concept of commitment. *Justice Quarterly, 4*(3), 409–424. doi:10.1080/07418828700089421
Brabeck, K., Lykes, M., & Hunter, C. (2014). The psychosocial impact of detention and deportation on U.S. migrant children and families. *American Journal of Orthopsychiatry, 84*(5), 496–505. doi.org/10.1037/ort0000011
Brabeck, K., & Xu, Q. (2010). The impact of detention and deportation on Latino immigrant children and families: A quantitative exploration. *Hispanic Journal of Behavioral Sciences, 32*(3), 341–361. https://doi.org/10.1177/0739986310374053

Bronstein, I., & Montgomery, P. (2011). Psychological distress in refugee children: A systematic review. *Clinical Child and Family Psychology Review, 14*, 44–56. doi:10.1007/s10567-010-0081-0

Byrd, S. (2013). Learning from the past: Why termination of a non-citizen parent's rights should not be based on the child's best interest. *University of Miami Law Review, 68*(1), 323–352.

Byrne, O. (2008) *Unaccompanied children in the United States: A literature review*. New York, NY: Vera Institute of Justice. Retrieved from www.f2f.ca.gov/res/pdf/UnaccompaniedChildren-US.pdf

Capps, R., Castañeda, R. M., Chaudry, A., & Santos, R. (2007). *Paying the price: The impact of immigration raids on America's children*. Washington, DC: Urban Institute.and National Council of La Raza. Retrieved from www.urban.org/UploadedPDF/411566_immigration_raids.pdf

Capps, R., Fix, M., Ost, J., Reardon-Anderson, J., & Passel, J. S. (2004). *The health and well being of young children of immigrants,* Washington, DC: Urban Institute. Retrieved from www.urban.org/UploadedPDF/311139_ChildrenImmigrants.pdf

Capps, R., & Fortuny, K. (2006). *Immigration and child and family policy*. Washington, DC: Urban Institute.

Carr, B. A. (2009). Incorporating a "best interests of the child" approach into immigration law and procedure. *Yale Human Rights & Development Law Journal, 12*(1), Article 3.

Castañeda, H., & Melo, M. A. (2014). Health care access for Latino mixed-status families: Barriers, strategies, and implications for reform. *American Behavioral Scientist, 58*(14), 1891–1909. doi:10.1177/0002764214550290

Cervantes, W., & Walker, C. (2017). *Five reasons Trump's immigration orders harm children*. Retrieved from www.clasp.org/resources-and-publications/publication-1/Five-Reasons-Immigration-Enforcement-Orders-Harm-Children.pdf

Chahine, Z., & Van Straaten, J. (2005). Serving immigrant families and children in New York City's child welfare system. *Child Welfare, 84*(5), 713–723.

Child Welfare Information Gateway. (2016, September). *Immigration and child welfare* [Issue Brief, April 2015]. Retrieved from www.childwelfare.gov/pubPDFs/immigration.pdf

Chishti, M., & Hipsman, F. (2015). The child and family migration surge of summer 2014: A short-lived crisis with a lasting impact. *Journal of International Affairs, 68*(2), 95.

Courtney, M. E., Piliavin, I., Grogan-Kaylor, A., & Nesmith, A. (2001). Foster youth transitions to adulthood: A longitudinal view of youth leaving care. *Child Welfare, 80*(6), 685–717.

Courtney, M. E., Terao, S., & Bost, N. (2004). *Midwest Evaluation of the Adult Functioning of Former Foster Youth: Conditions of youth preparing to leave state care*. Chicago: Chapin Hall Center for Children at the University of Chicago.

Covarrubias, N., & Hartman, A. (2015). *Information packet: Deportation and child welfare in mixed status families with unauthorized parents and citizen children*. National Center for Child Welfare Excellence. Retrieved from www.nccwe.org/downloads/info-packs/HartmanCovarrubias.pdf

Dawkins, M., & Rodriguez, F. (2016). Undocumented and unaccompanied Latino youth who are exposed to violence are more likely to turn to crime to overcome disadvantage. LSE US Centre *USApp–American Politics and Policy Blog*. Retrieved from http://bit.ly/24UlxKW

Derby, J. (2012). The burden of deportation on children in Mexican immigrant families. *Journal of Marriage and Family, 74*, 829–845. doi:10.1111/j.1741-3737.2012.00989

Dettlaff, A. J. (2015, January). Emerging strategies to address the needs of Latino children in the child welfare system: Innovations and advances in California. In *Society for Social Work and Research 19th Annual Conference: The Social and Behavioral Importance of Increased Longevity*. Fairfax, VA: SSWR.

Dettlaff, A., & Earner, I. (2012). Children of immigrants in the child welfare system: Characteristics, risk, and maltreatment. *Families in Society: The Journal of Contemporary Social Services, 93*(4), 295–303. https://doi.org/10.1606/1044-3894.4240

Dettlaff, A. J., Earner, I., & Phillips, S. D. (2009). Latino children of immigrants in the child welfare system: Prevalence, characteristics, and risk. *Children and Youth Services Review, 31*, 775–783. doi:10.1016/j.childyouth.2009.02.004

Dettlaff, A., & Johnson, M. (2011). Child maltreatment dynamics among immigrant and U.S. born Latino children: Findings from the National Survey of Child and Adolescent Well-Being (NSCAW). *Children and Youth Services Review, 33*, 936–944.

Dettlaff, A., & Rycraft, J. (2010). Adapting systems of care for child welfare practice with immigrant Latino children and families. *Evaluation and Program Planning, 33*, 303–310. doi:10.1016/j.evalprogplan.2009.07.003

Douglas, K., & Poletti, A. (2016). Introduction. In K. Douglas with R. Kobo (Eds.), *Life narratives and youth culture* (pp. 3–32). London: Palgrave Macmillan.

Dorsett, V. J. (2012). *A descriptive analysis of foster care transitional service and alumni outcomes* (Doctoral dissertation). Texas A&M University System.

Duara, N. (2017, May 17). Arrests on civil immigration charges go up 38% in the first 100 days since Trump's executive order. *Los Angeles Times*. Retrieved from www.latimes.com/nation/la-na-ice-deport-trump-20170517-story.html

Durkheim, E. (1997). *The division of labor in society*. New York, NY: The Free Press.

Dye, J. L. (2005, December). *Fertility of American women: June 2004* (Current Population Reports P20-555). Washington, DC: U.S. Census Bureau. Retrieved from www.census.gov/prod/2005pubs/p20-555.pdf

Ecke, L., & Foster Care Alumni of America. (2010). *Flux*. Alexandria, VA: Foster Care Alumni of America.

Finno-Velasquez, M. (2013). The relationship between parent immigration status and concrete support service use among Latinos in child welfare: Findings using the National Survey of Child and Adolescent Well-Being (NSCAW II). *Children and Youth Services Review, 35*(12), 2118–2127.

Fix, M., & Passel, J. S. (2003). *U.S. immigration: Trends and implications for schools*. Washington, DC: Urban Institute.

Fortuny, K., Capps, R., Simms, M., & Chaudry, A. (2009). *Children of immigrants: National and state characteristics*. Washington, DC: Urban Institute. Retrieved from www.urban.org/publications/411939.html

Fortuny, K., & Chaudry, A. (2009). *Children of immigrants: Immigration trends*. Washington, DC: Urban Institute. Retrieved from www.urban.org/publications/901292.html

Garcia, A., Aisenberg, E., & Harachi, T. (2012). Pathways to service equalities among Latinos in the child welfare system. *Children and Youth Services Review, 34*, 1060–1071. doi:10.1016/j.childyouth.2012.02.011

Giffin, K. S. (2017). *Acción de Gracia immigration assistance. Resisting by assisting future citizens*. Retrieved from http://accionimmigration.org/

Gryn, T. A., & Larsen, L. J. (2010). *Nativity status and citizenship in the United States: 2009*. American Community Survey Briefs. Washington, DC: U.S. Census Bureau.

Guilamo-Ramos, V., Dittus, P., Jaccard, J., Johannson, M. B., & Acosta, N. (2007). Parenting practices among Dominican and Puerto Rican mothers. *Social Work, 52*(1), 17–30.

Gulbas, L. E., & Zayas, L. H. (2017). Exploring the effects of US immigration enforcement on the well-being of citizen children in Mexican immigrant families. *RSF: The Russell Sage Foundation Journal of the Social Sciences, 3*(4), 53–69.

Haddal, C. C. (2007). *Unaccompanied alien children: Policies and issues (RL33896)*. Washington, DC: Congressional Research Service.

Hernandez, D., Denton, N., & McCartney, S. (2007). *Family circumstances of children in immigrant families: Looking to the future of America*. New York, NY: Guilford Press.

Hidalgo, R. (2013). Crossroads: The intersection of immigrant enforcement and the child welfare system. *Juvenile & Family Court Journal, 64*(4), 35–44. doi:10.1111/jfcj.12010

Hirschi, T. (2009). *Causes of delinquency*. New Brunswick, NJ: Transaction Publishers.

Homeland Security Act of 2002, P.L. 107-296. 107th Congress, 2nd session. (2002).

Kemp Parker, P. (2014). ICWA and SIJS: Complicated acronyms, difficult issues. *40th Annual Advanced Family Law Course*, Chapter 15, August 4–7, 2014.

Koball, H., Capps, R., Perreira, K., Campetella, A., Hooker, S., Pedroza, J. M., & Huerta, S. (2015). *Health and social service needs of US-citizen children with detained or deported immigrant parents*. Washington, DC: Urban Institute and Migration Policy Institute.

Križ, K., & Skivenes, M. (2012). How child welfare workers perceive their work with undocumented families: An explorative study of challenges and coping strategies. *Children and Youth Services Review, 34*(4), 790–797.

Landale, N. S., Hardie, J. H., Oropesa, R. S., & Hillemeier, M. M. (2015). Behavioral functioning among Mexican-origin children: Does parental legal status matter? *Journal of Health and Social Behavior, 56*(1), 2–18. https://doi.org/10.1177/0022146514567896

Leyro, S. P. (2017). *The fear factor: Exploring the impact of the vulnerability to deportation on immigrants' lives*. New York: CUNY Academic Works.

Lopez, C., Bergren, M. D., & Painter, S. G. (2008). Latino disparities in child mental health services. *Journal of Child and Adolescent Psychiatric Nursing, 21*(3), 137–145.

Lopez, M. H., & Taylor, P. (2010). *Latinos and the 2010 Census: The foreign born are more positive*. Washington, DC: Pew Hispanic Center. Retrieved from www.pewhispanic.org/files/reports/121.pdf

Lugo, B. M. (2015). *God, children and country: An in-depth study of the condition of immigrant illegality through the experiences of Mexican domestic workers in Dallas, Texas* (Doctoral dissertation). University of Texas at Austin.

Mares, S., & Jureidini, J. (2004). Psychiatric assessment of children and families in immigration detention: Clinical, administrative and ethical issues. *Australian and New Zealand Journal of Public Health, 28*(6), 520–526. doi:10.1111/j.1467-842X.2004.tb00041

Maxwell, L. F. (2007). Purvis, Karyn Brand & others. The connected child: Bring hope and healing to your adoptive family. *Library Journal, 132*(6), 113.

Merton, R. K. (1968). *Social theory and the social structure*. New York, NY: The Free Press.

National Center for Child Welfare Excellence. (2015, May). *Information packet: Latino youth and the foster care system*. Retrieved from www.nccwe.org/downloads/info-packs/Salcedo.pdf

National Juvenile Justice Network. (2006). *Undocumented immigrant youth: Guide for advocates and service providers*. Policy Brief No. 2, Building Bridges to Benefit Youth series. National Collaboration for Youth & National Juvenile Justice Network.

Ortega, A. N., Fang, H., Perez, V. H., Rizzo, J. A., Carter-Pokras, O., Wallace, S. P., & Gelberg, L. (2007). Health care access, use of services, and experiences among undocumented Mexicans and other Latinos. *Archives of Internal Medicine, 167*(21), 2354–2360.

Passel, J. S. (2011). Demography of immigrant youth: Past, present, and future. *The Future of Children, 21*(1), 19–41. Available at www.jstor.org/stable/41229010

Passel, J., & Cohn, D. (2016, September 20). *Overall number of U.S. unauthorized immigrants holds steady since 2009*. Pew Research Center: Hispanic Trends. Retrieved from www.pewhispanic.org/2016/09/20/overall-number-of-u-s-unauthorized-immigrants-holds-steady-since-2009/

Passel, J., & Taylor, P. (2010). *Hispanic trends*. Pew Research Center. Retrieved from www.pewhispanic.org/2010/08/11/unauthorized-immigrants-and-their-us-born-children/

Pecora, P. J., Kessler, J. W., O'Brien, K., Downs, A. C., English, D., White, J., & Holmes, K. (2005). *Improving family foster care: Findings from the Northwest Foster Care Alumni Study*. Available at www.casey.org /resources/

Pecora, P. J., Kessler, J. W., Williams, J., Downs, A. C., English, D. J., White, J., & O'Brien, K. (2010). *What works in family foster care? Key components of success from the Northwest Foster Care Alumni Study*. New York, NY & Oxford: Oxford University Press.

Perez, R. M. (2001). When immigration is trauma: Guidelines for the individual and familyclinician. *American Journal of Orthopsychiatry, 71*(2), 153–170. http://dx.doi.org/10.1037/0002-9432.71.2.153

Philbin, M. M., Flake, M., Hatzenbuehler, M. L., & Hirsch, J. S. (2017). State-level immigration and immigrant-focused policies as drivers of Latino health disparities in the UnitedStates. *Social Science & Medicine*. doi: 10.1016/j.socscimed.2017.04.007

Pine, B. A., & Drachman, D. (2005). Effective child welfare practice with immigrant and refugee children and their families. *Child Welfare, 84*(5), 537–562. Retrieved from http://cssr.berkeley.edu/cwscmsreports/LatinoPracticeAdvisory/Effective%20Child%20Welfare%20Practice%20with%20Immigrant%20and%20Refugee%20Children%20and%20Their%20Families.pdf

Plyler v. Doe. (1982). 457 U.S. 202, 102 S.Ct. 2382, 72 L.Ed.2d 786.

Purvis, K. B., Cross, D. R., & Pennings, J. S. (2009). Trust-Based Relational Intervention: Interactive principles for adopted children with special social-emotional needs. *Journal of Humanistic Counseling Education and Development, 48*, 3–22.

Raphel, S. (2012). Latest on child welfare systems and continued call for White House Conference on Children. *Journal of Child and Adolescent Psychiatric Nursing, 25*(2), 105–107. doi:10.1111/j.1744-6171.2012.00327.x

Rodriguez, F. A. (2013). *Unaccompanied Latino youth on the United States–Mexico border: A qualitative study* (Unpublished doctoral dissertation). Prairie View A&M University, Prairie View, TX.

Rodriguez, F. A., & Dawkins, M. (2016). Undocumented Latino youth: Migration experiences and the challenges of integrating into American society. *Journal of International Migration & Integration, 18*(2), 419–438. doi:10.1007/s12134-016-0484-y

Roller-White, C., O'Brien, K., Pecora, P. J., Kessler, R. C., Sampson, N., & Hwang, I. (2012). *Texas Foster Care Alumni Study technical report: Outcomes at age 23 and 24*. Retrieved from www.casey.org/media/StateFosterCare_TX_fr.pdf

Rosenthal, B. M. (2015, September 30). Abbott urges feds to boost border security after uptick in crossings. Retrieved from www.chron.com/news/politics/texas/article/Abbott-urges-feds-to-boost-border-security-after-6540468.php

Roth, B. J., & Grace, B. L. (2015). Falling through the cracks: The paradox of post-release services for unaccompanied child migrants. *Children and Youth Services Review, 58*, 244–252. http://doi.org/10.1016/j.childyouth.2015.10.007

Santosky v. Kramer (1982). 455 U.S. at 747, 102 S.Ct. 1388.

Scott, J., Faulkner, M., Cardoso, J. B., & Burstain, J. (2014). Kinship care and undocumented Latino children in the Texas foster care system: Navigating the child welfare–immigration crossroads. *Child Welfare, 93*(4), 53–69.

Smart, J. F., & Smart, D. W. (1995). Acculturative stress of hispanics: Loss and challenge. *Journal of Counseling and Development, 73*(4), 390.

Suárez-Orozco, C., & Suárez-Orozco, M. (2009). Educating Latino immigrant students in the twenty-first century: Principles for the Obama Administration. *Harvard Educational Review, 79*(2), 327–340. http://dx.doi.org/10.17763/haer.79.2.231151762p82213u

Texas Department of Family Protective Services. (2016, September). Questions and procedures for working with foreign born children in foster care—March 2013 [Form 2013]. Retrieved from www.dfps.state.tx.us/Search/default.asp?q=immigration+form+2013

Torrico, R. (2010, June). Meeting the needs of immigrant children and youth in child welfare. *Children, Youth & Families Practice Update*. Washington, DC: NASW. Retrieved from www.socialworkers.org/assets/secured/documents/practice/clinical/wkf-misc-45510.childrenpu.pdf

U.S. Census Bureau. (2001). *The foreign-born population in the United States: March 2000*. Retrieved from www.census.gov/prod/2000pubs/p20-534.pdf

Ward, M. (2016, August). Texas DPS seeks border-security budget hike increase to $1 billion. *Houston Chronicle*. Retrieved from www.chron.com/news/politics/texas/article/DPS-seeks-border-security-budget-hike-increase-to-9190661.php

Weber, C. (2015). Living in the shadows or government dependents: Immigrants and welfare in the United States. *Comparative Advantage, Stanford Undergraduate Economics Journal*, 3(1), 4–20.

Wessler, S. (2011). *Shattered families: The perilous intersection of immigration enforcement and the child welfare system*. Aiken, SC: Applied Research Center.

Zayas, L. H. (2015). *Forgotten citizens: Deportation, children, and the making of American exiles and orphans*. Oxford: Oxford University Press.

21
Sexual and Gender Expansive Youth in Foster Care

Nicholas Forge and Robin Hartinger-Saunders

Introduction and Background

> As a Nation, we have a duty to empower each child so they have the same sense of promise and possibility as any other young person—no matter who they are, where they come from, or what their circumstances are.
>
> (Barack Obama, Proclamation No. 9432, 81 F.R. 26663, 2016)

While in office, President Obama made several Presidential Proclamations for National Foster Care Month. In his statements, the President called for the United States to provide coordinated and competent services to youth in foster care and to the families who provide them with a home. His Presidential Proclamations have emphasized the rights of all children and youth in foster care, including those who identify as sexual and gender expansive,[1] underscoring the need to provide all children with the "chance to dream and grow in a loving, permanent home" (Obama, 2015, para. 3). President Obama is the first standing President to specifically include sexual and gender expansive youth in his proclamations. His acknowledgment of sexual and gender expansive youth is a positive indicator that the rights and well-being of these youth are being included in discussions at the highest level of policy making.

Despite the President's Proclamations, youth placed in foster care continue to face negative labeling, or stigmatization, by peer groups, educational systems, partner agencies, communities, and even from within the child welfare system itself. For example, youth in foster care are frequently labeled (i.e., foster kid, abused, neglected, delinquent) and treated differently based on their foster care status. Often, people make assumptions about youth in foster care (i.e., they are troubled), making it difficult for foster youth to establish an identity beyond the labels. Child-welfare-involved lesbian, gay, bisexual, transgender, and questioning and/or queer (LGBTQ) youth experience an additional intersecting layer of stigma based on their sexual orientation and/or gender identity. Too often, LGBTQ youth enter a foster care system that is ill-equipped to competently meet their needs, subjecting them to further prejudice, bias, and discrimination (Human Rights Campaign, n.d.), leading to short- and long-term negative outcomes.

Young people enter foster care at varying ages and stages of development, and their sexual orientation, gender identity or gender expressions may not have developed or be openly expressed. Identifying as LGBTQ can vary widely, and how and when youth choose to identify is highly diverse and can change over time. *If* and *when* young people choose to disclose, or to "come out," is related to a number of factors, including whether they perceive their environment as safe and identity affirming (Heatherington & Lavner, 2008; Higa et al., 2014). All children removed from their caregivers and placed into foster care have the right to a safe, loving, and affirming foster care placement (Child Welfare Information Gateway, 2013), and this includes those who have formed or are questioning an identity that is sexual and gender expansive or LGBTQ.

Until recently, limited attention has been given to the experiences of sexual and gender expansive young people in the child welfare system (McCormick, Schmidt, & Terrazas, 2016). The general lack of knowledge about sexual and gender expansive youth contributes to the perpetuation of negative stereotypes related to both groups. When organizations serving children and youth fail to address the knowledge gaps, negative attitudes and beliefs, and discriminatory practices of administrators, supervisors, employees, foster and adoptive parents, and those of partner agencies, sexual and gender expansive youth in foster care remain vulnerable and at an increased risk of further victimization. It is a harsh reality that the very system created to protect children and youth all too often knowingly and unknowingly contributes to their re-traumatization. The goals of the chapter are to give voice to the presence of sexual and gender expansive youth in the foster care system. In doing so, we will explore terminology and ways in which these young people choose to identify themselves, and place their experience in the foster care system within a developmental context. Additionally, we highlight the experiences that some young people encounter, and introduce best practices, policies, and resources that caregivers can use when caring for, and advocating on behalf of, those in care.

Sexual and Gender Expansive Youth

Historically, the term "homosexuality" was included as a psychiatric diagnosis in the *Diagnostic and Statistical Manual of Mental Disorders (DSM)*, which pathologized homosexuality. Theories of pathology deemed homosexuality to be a "defect" or "morally bad," attributing its origin (cause) to either an internal defect or an external pathogenic agent (Drescher, 2015). The field of psychiatry largely ignored the growing body of sex research contradicting early theories of homosexuality up until the early 1970s (Lewes, 1990). Gay activists were instrumental in gaining the attention of the American Psychiatric Association (APA), which resulted in the removal by 1973 of homosexuality as a diagnosis from the *DSM-II* and all subsequent editions (Bayer, 1981), no longer classifying homosexuality as a "disorder."

The recognition of transgender persons gained attention around the middle of the last century, when disparities between a person's anatomical sex and their gender identification began to be studied. This incongruence was identified as psychopathological by the APA and was included with the named diagnosis of Gender Identity Disorder in the *DSM-III* in 1980 (APA, 1980, p. 261). Currently, the APA uses the term "gender dysphoria" when diagnosing individuals who experience "a marked incongruence between one's experienced/expressed gender and their assigned gender" (2013a, p. 215). This new term is significant as being a recognition that not all individuals who are transgender or gender expansive should be diagnosed with gender dysphoria; the distinction being that gender dysphoria is marked by clinically significant distress (APA, 2013b). Given that it is recognized that gender is a non-binary (i.e., male/female) construct, the APA revision reduces the stigmatization of transgender and gender expansive individuals.

Defining Sexual and Gender Expansive Youth

Until recently, the phrase *sexual and gender minority* was used as a broad classification to include those who may not identify with the acronym LGBTQ (lesbian, gay, bisexual, transgender, or questioning and/or queer) (Steever, Francis, Gordon, & Lee, 2014). The term *sexual minority* was used to refer to a non-heterosexual identity including lesbian, gay, bisexual, and questioning and/or queer youth

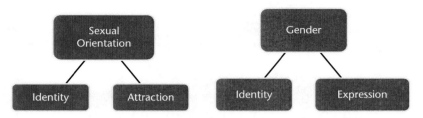

Figure 21.1 Dimensions of Sexual Orientation and Gender Identity

(LGBQ). *Gender minority* referred to a non-cisgender person, including those who identify as transgender or gender expansive (see Table 21.1). The term *cisgender* signifies an individual whose gender identity corresponds with their biological sex at birth. However, the language and terminology that we use to define and ascribe identity to people is an important component in their empowerment and affirmation. When individuals are labeled as a "minority" or "non-conforming," there is an assertion that such an identity is in opposition to those in the "majority" or those who do "conform." Thus, we choose to use the term *sexual and gender expansive*, as it is viewed as being normalizing and inclusive of all identities, no matter where they identify on the broad spectrum of sexual orientation or gender identity (Price, Wheeler, Shelton, & Maury, 2016).

Both sexual and gender identity are multidimensional (see Figure 21.1). *Sexual orientation* is the emotional and physical attraction felt toward another individual and is comprised of sexual identity and sexual attraction. *Sexual identity* refers to whether an individual considers themselves to be straight, gay, lesbian, bisexual, or questioning and/or queer. *Sexual attraction* refers to whether an individual is romantically attracted to males, females, or transgender individuals. *Gender identity* refers to how an individual describes their gender, which may or may not be the same as the sex they were assigned at birth; whereas *gender expression* is the outward demonstration of masculine or feminine characteristics and behaviors.

There are numerous terms used as self-identifiers by members of the sexual and gender expansive community. Arguably, the most commonly used terms are lesbian, gay, bisexual, transgender, and

Table 21.1 Definition of Terms Related to Sexual Orientation and Gender Identity

Term	Definition	Common Terms Used by LGBTQ/Sexual and Gender Expansive Youth to Describe Themselves
Sexual Orientation	The romantic and sexual attraction that one has toward another individual.	Lesbian, gay, bisexual, queer, pansexual, same gender loving
Gender Identity	The self-concept (internal perception) that one has about being female, male, both or neither.	Masculine, feminine, butch, fem
Gender Expression	The external display of one's gender through factors such as demeanor, dress, social behavior, etc.	Gender presentation
Transgender	An umbrella term used to describe individuals who do not identify with the sex they were assigned at birth. There are many ways in which transgender individuals identify their gender.	Gender expansive, gender queer, bigendered, gender variant, gender non-conforming
Cisgender	Refers to people whose sex is congruent with their gender identity.	Cis

questioning and/or queer (LGBTQ). While the often-used acronym LGBTQ denotes a collective identity, it is critical for those working with sexual and gender expansive youth to recognize that each letter represents a unique identity, experience, and needs. Additionally, within each unique identity, there are individuals who have unique life experiences; for example, not all women who identify as bisexual have the same experiences.

Developmental Perspectives on Sexual and Gender Identity

Sexual Identity Formation

Sexual identity is formed at varying developmental stages of life. It is often fluid, and not necessarily connected to or mutually exclusive from gender identity. There are few developmental theories of sexual identity formation, but those that do exist generally fall into two categories. The first is the *stage model*, where an individual goes through linear stages, meeting certain markers (see the Homosexual Identity Model; Cass, 1979). The second is the non-linear, *life span approach*, where sexual identity is seen as fluid, and certain identity processes could be independent of one another (see the Life Span Development Approach; D'Augelli, 1994) and take into account social context. Identifying oneself as lesbian, gay, or bisexual (LGB) is the most personally significant developmental milestone (Savin-Williams & Cohen, 2007). Increasingly, youth are self-identifying as LGB at earlier ages, often by the age of 15 (Savin-Williams & Cohen, 2007). Despite the continued stigmatization of LGBTQ identity in society, advances in technology have provided much-needed avenues for information, social networks, and support for youth. Many LGBTQ youth turn to the internet to access information that may be otherwise unavailable to them. Additionally, online communities for youth provide an opportunity to connect and access peer support, while still providing a sense of anonymity if so desired. Such resources and support may assist youth with understanding and formulating their identity, may promote better well-being, and may allow youth to accept and publicly express their identity (GLSEN, CiPHR, & CCRC, 2013). It is important to note that initial feelings of same-sex attraction may not necessarily result in an LGB identity, as sexual attraction is commonly accepted to be fluid and may vary depending upon situations and time. It is not uncommon for individuals to feel temporarily attracted to members of the same, or opposite, gender identity, or have an attraction or sexual feelings for a specific person, regardless of orientation/gender. Furthermore, youth may identify as LGB without having had a sexual experience. It is also possible for youth to not identify as LGB, yet experience same-sex attractions and engage in sexual behavior with the same sex.

For those youth who do identify as lesbian, gay, or bisexual, the public disclosure of their sexual identity can be immediate or it may be delayed for many years. Research indicates that the average time between self-identification and public disclosure can range from 1 to 2 years for males and even less for females (Savin-Williams & Ream, 2007). During this period, LGB youth can experience increased sexual identity distress as they struggle with the decision to come out. This distress is attributed to both personal and environmental factors and has negative outcomes, such as significant mental health problems, especially among older youth (Wright & Perry, 2006). Although there are individual factors (e.g., self-esteem, trauma history) that influence whether a youth will come out, it is imperative that child welfare systems address negative environmental factors by creating safe, affirming environments in which foster youth feel empowered to make the choice to disclose when they are ready (see Table 21.4.).

Gender Identity Formation

Gender identity is typically formed by 2 years old, when young children identify as either a boy or a girl (Stieglitz, 2010), and by the age of 3, they typically begin to refer to one another using gendered pronouns (i.e., him or her) (Grossman & D'Augelli, 2007). Society enforces prescribed norms for gender identity. Those children who do not identify with, or exhibit, norms associated with their prescribed gender are said to be "gender non-conforming" (Steever et al., 2014, p. 653) or the more normalizing term, "gender expansive" (Price et al., 2016). It is important to note, however, that this does not necessarily mean that a child is in fact transgender, as many children exhibit gender expansive behaviors before claiming a cisgender identity.

Exploring gender identity is a part of the developmental process and should be accepted by caregivers (i.e., parents, foster parents) as normative behavior (Grossman & D'Augelli, 2007; Mallon & DeCrescenzo, 2006). Not doing so can have significant negative outcomes (Mallon & DeCrescenzo, 2006) such as depression or anxiety, and can even result in suicide (Grossman & D'Augelli, 2007). There is a distinct lack of theoretical models which address the formation of gender identity for transgender individuals. Lev (2004) articulated a stage model comprised of six stages of development (see the Transgender Emergence Model) that highlight the experience of the individual, but also include considerations for a professional counselor at each stage. While studies of identity development have largely focused on adults, findings have indicated that transgender individuals balance a desire for their authentic gender with such things as having resources (or not), their level of personal support and coping skills, and the consequences of their transition (social acceptance) (Levitt & Ippolito, 2014). These factors may or may not have an impact on transgender and gender expansive youth, and can largely depend upon their desire, support, and ability to undergo gender-affirming therapies that include medical (e.g., hormone therapy) and surgical procedures (e.g., masculinizing chest surgery) (see Deutsch, 2016).

The research on transgender identity development has led best practices for this population. For example, the Child Welfare League of America recommends that caregivers (i.e., parents, foster parents, kinship parents) allow children to express themselves in a way that is consistent with their gender identity. This includes gender expression in terms of clothing choices, as well as names and preferred gender pronouns (Fostering Transitions, 2012). It should be noted that gender identity development has traditionally focused on Western, Eurocentric notions and concepts of gender, such as binary genders (male/female) and gender-specific roles (breadwinner/homemaker). Other cultures are known to identify and construct both gender identity and sexual orientation differently (Brown, 1997). For example, in some Native American cultures, a "two spirit" identity describes people who manifest both masculine and feminine spiritual qualities (Faiman-Silva, 2011, p. 11). Foster youth who do not identify with Western, Eurocentric culture or values may express their gender in ways that might be considered as non-conforming by child welfare workers or foster parents, and should be allowed to do so without being prescribed a label or diagnosis that is not representative of their true selves.

There is increased societal attention to support gender expansive children and youth in their self-identified gender. Normalizing the experiences of gender expansive youth is essential to their healthy development. Rejecting a culture of binary gender identity in the child welfare system is critical to the safety of transgender youth in foster care. Additionally, it is important for workers and caregivers to understand that the identification of gender expansive behavior does not necessarily mean that the child desires to undergo gender-affirming therapies. Such therapies are available, and can include puberty-blocking agents, cross-gender hormones, and surgical treatments (Steever et al., 2014). Although not every state in the United States has codified its legal duty to provide medically necessary care to those in guardianship (Turner, 2009), litigation has resulted in at least one state child welfare agency being ordered to pay for gender confirmation treatment and surgery (Lesbian and Gay Law Association of Greater New York, 2014; NYC Administration for Children's Services, 2010). While such treatments and therapies are costly, if the child demonstrates distress related to their gender, or a desire to affirm their gender through medical or psychological therapies, workers and caregivers should advocate to access them as medically necessary care. Failure to do so can contribute to the proximal physical and psychological anguish that many gender expansive youth face, which is intensified by effects of distal rejection, discrimination, and victimization (Turner, 2009).

Unique Issues and Experiences of Sexual and Gender Expansive Youth

There are more similarities that unite sexual and gender expansive youth with their heterosexual and cisgender counterparts than there are differences, as sexual orientation and gender, although important, are not the only aspects that comprise an individual's identity. Despite this, unique issues and experiences do exist and it is important to acknowledge and address them. These range from individual-level factors such as health, mental health, and well-being to environmental-level factors including acceptance, support, and safety. It is important to note the lack of research available concerning the experiences of sexual and gender expansive youth in foster care. Therefore, unless specifically indicated, we report on the experiences of sexual and gender expansive youth in general.

Sexual and gender expansive youth experience various disparities when compared to their heterosexual, cisgender counterparts. They experience higher rates of rejection, abuse, and victimization from their families of origin (Liu & Mustanski, 2012; Marshal et al., 2011; Wilson & Kastanis, 2015). Since education has a significant impact on the lives of children and youth, the experience of students in school is often a focus of research and reports. In their comprehensive study of high school students, the Centers for Disease Control (CDC) reported that lesbian, gay, and bisexual students experienced sexual and physical dating violence at a rate of more than twice that of heterosexual students (Kann et al., 2016). They also had been forced to have sexual intercourse by their peers at a rate three times that of heterosexual students. The National School Climate Survey of LGBT youth reported that 38% of youth felt unsafe in school, 55% were verbally harassed, 23% were physically harassed (e.g., pushed, shoved, etc.), and 11% were physically assaulted (e.g., punched, kicked, or assaulted with a weapon) because of their gender expression (Kosciw, Greytak, Palmer, & Boesen, 2014).

Educational staff, curriculum, and school environment have an impact on the well-being and success of sexual and gender expansive students. While at school, lesbian, gay, and bisexual youth are approximately twice as likely to be bullied (Kann et al., 2016), which has been shown to result in lower self-esteem, weaker grades, and increased absences (Birkett, Russell, & Corliss, 2014; Goodenow, Szalacha, & Westheimer, 2006; Kosciw, Palmer, Kull, & Greytak, 2013; Kosciw et al., 2014). The visibility of different types of adults (e.g., teachers, principals, social workers) who are viewed as supportive by sexual and gender expansive students has a positive effect on how engaged they are with their school and learning (Seelman, Forge, Walls, & Bridges, 2015). However, the willingness and ability of adults to act on behalf of LGBTQ students are imperative; one national study found that 62% of sexual and gender expansive students who reported being bullied or victimized at school found that no action was taken on their behalf (Kosciw et al., 2014). Schools with positive representations of LGBTQ culture in the curriculum have been shown to have fewer incidences of victimization and greater academic success for LGBTQ students (Kosciw et al., 2013). Additional support structures (e.g., clubs, organizations, and groups) are important for creating a safe, affirming environment for LGBTQ students. Many schools have Gay–Straight Alliances (GSAs), student-run clubs that provide safe spaces for students to meet and provide support for one another related to sexual and gender minority identity. Such clubs can assist with gender expression and identity disclosure (Heck, Lindquist, Stewart, Brennan, & Cochran, 2013; Walls, Wisneski, & Kane, 2013) and have also been shown to have a positive effect on students' self-esteem (Toomey, Ryan, Diaz, & Russell, 2011).

Although lesbian and bisexual girls are less likely to conform to media portrayals of "ideal" female body images (Berlan, 2010), young gay and bisexual males are at greater risk for poor body perceptions and subsequent unhealthy methods of weight control (Blashill, 2010) such as diuretic and laxative use, vomiting, fasting, binging, and purging. Lesbian, gay, and bisexual youth are more likely to report binge eating from early to late adolescence (Austin et al., 2009). Bisexual and lesbian females are more likely to report binge eating; however, only bisexual females are more likely to report purging. Bisexual and gay males are more likely to report both binge eating and purging compared to heterosexual males (Austin et al., 2009). Gender expansive young people may also experience negative perceptions of their bodies. In one study of transgender youth, 70% of participants responded with feelings of dissatisfaction with their bodies, which the authors articulated into three contexts: gender dissociation (a disconnect with an undesired body feature); dissatisfaction with body size; and the intersection of gender dissociation and dissatisfaction with body size (McGuire, Doty, Catalpa, & Ola, 2016). Such dissatisfaction places transgender youth and young people at increased risk for disordered eating; however, therapeutic treatments for gender dysphoria are successful at increasing body satisfaction and improving body image (Jones, Haycraft, Murjan, & Arcelus, 2016).

Experiences of homophobia, transphobia, and stress associated with sexual and gender identity are significant threats to the mental health of youth (Steever et al., 2014). Lesbian, gay, and bisexual youth report low levels of social support and high rates of depression (Marshal et al., 2011), and feelings of sadness or hopelessness that were greater than twice the rate of their heterosexual, cisgender counterparts (Kann et al., 2016). They are also at increased risk for self-harm and suicidal ideation (Liu & Mustanski, 2012; Marshal et al., 2011), with one study reporting that lesbian, gay, and bisexual youth were four times more likely to attempt suicide (Kann et al., 2016). Transgender youth face a similar trend in reports of mental health. Research shows that when compared to cisgender youth, transgender youth are at two to three times greater risk for depression, anxiety, suicidal ideation and attempts, and self-harm (Reisner et al., 2015).

Sexual and gender expansive youth also tend to start using illicit substances at a younger age when compared to their heterosexual counterparts (Steever et al., 2014). When examining only sexual orientation, lesbian, gay, and bisexual youth are two to five times more likely to use substances such as hallucinogens, ecstasy, heroin, and methamphetamines (Kann et al., 2016) and more likely to use increased quantities of cigarettes and alcohol (Schauer, Berg, & Bryant, 2013) compared to heterosexual youth. Substance use among transgender youth has also been reported at higher rates when compared to cisgender youth; one study reported that 69% of transgender female youth, aged 16 to 24, had recently used substances, and that those youth with PTSD or experience of gender-related discrimination had increased odds of substance use (Rowe, Santos, McFarland & Wilson, 2015).

Sexual and Gender Expansive Youth in the Child Welfare System

Until recently, LGBTQ youth in foster care have faced a "disavowal of their existence," largely driven by cultural and religious bias (Mallon, 1998, p. 7). Although many LGBTQ youth come into foster care through traditional routes (i.e., reports of child maltreatment by their biological parents or caregivers), they also enter the child welfare system under circumstances uniquely attributed to their sexual orientation or gender identity, including harassment, rejection, and alienation by parents, caregivers, and other family members. Referrals for child welfare services for LGBTQ youth may initially seem unrelated to their sexual and gender expansive identity; however, further investigation reveals that maltreatment is primarily in response to the youth's sexual orientation or gender identity (Mallon, 2011). Approximately 30% of sexual and gender expansive youth in foster care reported experiencing violence after revealing their identity to their family members (Laver & Khoury, 2008). Studies suggest that LGBTQ youth are 1.2 times more likely to be physically abused and 3.8 times more likely to experience sexual abuse at the hands of a parent or caregiver than their heterosexual peers (Friedman et al., 2011).

The primary data repository for tracking children and youth involved with the state and tribal child welfare system in the United States is the Adoption and Foster Care Analysis and Reporting System (AFCARS) (Children's Bureau, 2015), managed by the Children's Bureau of the Administration for Children and Families. Historically, the AFCARS system has not collected case-level data related to the sexual orientation or gender expansive identity of children and youth in the foster care system and/or of those who have been adopted. This limits current research designs by the need to rely on retrospective reports of sexual and gender expansive youth once they have exited the child welfare system (e.g., homeless populations) and restricts the applicability of study findings. However, after several years of steadfast advocacy efforts, states will be required to report on the sexual orientation of (1) youth in foster care, (2) foster parents, and (3) adoptive parents and guardians, using the AFCARS system (Kelly, 2017). Although gender expansive identity was not included in the revisions of the data tracking system, nonetheless, this is substantial progress and will provide much-needed visibility that can be used to advocate further to address the needs of sexual expansive youth.

Data on LGBTQ foster youth are lacking in several overlapping areas including health, mental health, criminal justice, and education (Martin, Down, & Erney, 2016). Efforts to obtain data related to sexual and gender identity must be conducted through an ethical lens across systems (Martin et al., 2016). Various professions have an established Code of Ethics (e.g., National Association of Social Workers [NASW], American Psychological Association [APA], National Association of Case Management [NACM], and American Case Management Association [ACMA]) prohibiting discrimination based on an individual's sexual or gender minority status. Professionals are further required to maintain the confidentiality of all clients. Therefore, releasing personal information to biological parents, foster parents, adoptive parents, congregate care providers, or other professionals who work with LGBTQ youth without consent is a violation of their confidentiality.

Current Overview of Child Welfare Policies and Protections

There are federal and state constitutional and statutory rights afforded to every child placed in state custody, regardless of their sexual orientation or gender identity (see Table 21.2). All youth placed in the child welfare system have a legally enforceable, basic right to safety when they are removed from their homes and placed into the care and custody of state child welfare agencies. However, many LGBTQ youth regularly have their rights violated by the very systems put in place to protect them (Estrada & Marksamer, 2006). On the federal level, the 1st Amendment (Freedom of Speech), 14th Amendment—Due Process protections (Right to Safety), and the 14th Amendment—Equal Protections laws are what have been applied to protect LGBTQ youth from discrimination. However, there are no federal laws or policies in place that specifically address the discrimination of LGBTQ youth in foster care. Under the 14th Amendment—Due Process protections, youth placed in out-of-home care have the right to be protected against threats to their physical, mental, and emotional well-being, the right to services to prevent harm, and the right to be monitored and supervised in out-of-home placements (Estrada & Marksamer, 2006).

Currently, only 14 U.S. states have foster care non-discrimination laws or policies in place that are inclusive of both sexual orientation and gender identity. Seven additional states have implemented foster care non-discrimination laws or policies, yet they are only inclusive of sexual orientation and not gender identity (Human Rights Campaign, n.d.) (see Table 21.3).

Unfortunately, misinformation, common misconceptions about, and prejudice against the LGBTQ community continue to interfere with the application of rights to and treatment of LGBTQ youth in care. Accordingly, LGBTQ youth have successfully sued state child welfare and juvenile justice agencies for violating their basic right to safety while in their care and custody (Estrada & Marksamer, 2006).

Negative Experiences of Youth in Foster Care

Sexual and gender expansive youth have a lot in common with heterosexual, cisgender foster youth, including strained relationships with their parents and/or caregivers, and histories of trauma. However,

Table 21.2 Federal and State Constitutional and Statutory Rights of Youth in Foster Care: Basic Right to Safety

Basic Right	Application	Responsibility of States	Common Violations of Rights against LGBTQ Youth in Care
Right to protection of physical, mental, and emotional well-being	14th Amendment: Due Process protections	Placing agencies have the obligation to protect children from physical, sexual, and emotional abuse and neglect by foster parents, kinship care providers, child welfare workers, congregate care staff, and other individuals that provide care.	When LGBTQ youth are not protected from disapproval, harassment, isolation, and rejection from caretakers including foster parents, kinship care providers, child welfare workers, congregate care staff, and other individuals that provide care.
Right to services to prevent harm	14th Amendment: Due Process protections	Placing agencies have the obligation to provide professional medical and mental health services to children to address trauma and prevent further psychological harm.	When LGBTQ youth are exposed to unethical religious or therapeutic practices intending to involuntarily change a youth's sexual or gender identity, including condemned "conversion therapies," or if they are denied access to necessary services to assist them in identifying community and peer resources.
Right to monitoring and supervision	14th Amendment: Equal Protections	Placing agencies have the obligation to ensure that children placed in out-of-home placements are afforded regular supervision and oversight to ensure a child's safety.	When the safety of LGBTQ youth in their placement, in school, and in the neighborhood, is not regularly assessed by placing agencies, foster parents, kinship providers, congregate care staff, and other caregivers; when safety concerns are identified and not immediately addressed.

Table 21.3 States with Foster Care Non-Discrimination Laws or Policies: Inclusivity

Sexual Orientation and Gender Identity	Sexual Orientation Only
Washington, Oregon, California, Colorado, New Mexico, Texas, Iowa, Ohio, New York, Maine, Rhode Island, Connecticut, New Jersey, District of Columbia	Wisconsin, Missouri, Louisiana, Virginia, Maryland, New Hampshire, Delaware

Source: Human Rights Campaign (n.d.).

they also have distinct experiences related to their sexual and gender identity including: exposure to unsafe and inconsistent living environments; placement in more restrictive environments; chronically severed ties with their parents/caregivers; peer victimization within their placement environment (Elze, 2014); and rejection or isolation by child welfare staff and foster parents (Child Welfare Information Gateway, 2013).

Despite the disproportionate and large numbers of sexual and gender expansive youth who are in foster care, up to 20% in one study (Wilson, Cooper, Kastanis, & Nezhad, 2014), their experiences are all too often negative. With the varied pathways of these youth into the child welfare system that include abuse and neglect, the reality is that they are often met by a system that is neither competent nor equipped to address their needs, and further subjects them to bias, discrimination, isolation, and neglect from the very caregivers and system meant to protect them (Mallon, 1998; Mallon & Woronoff, 2006; McCormick et al., 2016; Woronoff, Estrada, & Sommer, 2006).

The bias and discrimination that sexual and gender expansive youth face while in care are frequently intensified due to the intersection of identities to which they belong; many youth in care who identify as LGBTQ are also youth of color, and/or have disabilities, and mental health challenges, presenting further barriers for permanence (Human Rights Campaign, n.d.; Wilson et al., 2014). Youth who identify as LGBTQ are less likely to achieve permanence (by reunification or adoption) than other youth, with transgender youth having the most difficult time achieving permanency (Fostering Transitions, 2012). There is a distinct lack of acceptance and affirmation of the identities of sexual and gender expansive youth who are in foster care (Woronoff et al., 2006; Wilber, Reyes, & Marksamer, 2006a). Additionally, youth who "come out" while in care have experienced negative changes in how they are treated by caregivers after they have done so (Mallon, 2011). Many sexual and gender expansive youth experience bullying, harassment, and isolation from their peers, caseworkers, and foster parents (Mallon, 2011; Wilson et al., 2014; Woronoff et al., 2006).

Child welfare professionals and foster families should be aware of the possibility that LGBTQ youth in foster care may have already experienced significant trauma because of their identity, making it imperative that youth experience affirming environments to avoid re-traumatization. There are potentially severe, damaging, and long-lasting ramifications for youth in foster care who are mistreated and un-affirmed. Youth who are not affirmed in their identity are at risk for experiencing identity distress. Research shows that youth who have a negative image of themselves because of their sexual identity are more likely to report significant mental health problems (Wright & Perry, 2006). It is imperative that families and professionals do not frame any psychological distress experienced by youth as being directly caused by their identity, nor conclude that their identity should be changed. What should be understood, however, is that the stigma, rejection, discrimination, and victimization that many sexual and gender expansive youth experience can contribute to negative mental health outcomes (Wright & Perry, 2006). Attempts by "professionals" and spiritual leaders to convert youth who identify as LGBTQ (often known as reparative or conversion therapy) have been reported. However, such "therapies" are known to have serious psychologically damaging effects (Adelson & AACAP CQI, 2012; McCormick et al., 2016; Woronoff et al., 2006). A large number of youth-serving professional organizations have released statements that condemn such attempts to convert the sexual orientation and gender expansive identity of LGBTQ youth. These include the American Medical Association (Davis et al., 1996), the American Psychiatric Association (2000), the American Psychological Association (Anton, 2010), the Child Welfare League of America (2015), and the National Association of Social Workers (2015).

Creating Safe and Supporting Environments in Out-of-Home Placements

Education and Training within the Child Welfare System

In general, the child welfare system continues to experience high staff turnover, contributing to a chronic shortage of competent staff and caregivers, including foster parents (Wilber, Reyes, & Marksamer, 2006b). Furthermore, there is a shortage of foster parents willing to provide care to LGBTQ youth (Mallon, 2011). Those LGBTQ youth who remain in care have been reported to have a higher number of foster care placements and are more likely to be placed in a group home (Wilson & Kastanis, 2015). Sexual and gender expansive youth are therefore at a greater risk for placement disruptions (Administration for Children and Families, 2011; Wilson et al., 2014) when foster parents are not accepting of the youth's sexual and/or gender identity once it is revealed. In a recent study, an alarming 20% of lesbian, gay, and bisexual youth were moved from their first foster care placements at the request of their foster family or caregiver, because of their sexual orientation, as compared to 9% of heterosexual youth (Martin et al., 2016).

The education and training of child welfare administrators, caseworkers, foster/adoptive parents, congregate care providers, and community partners (i.e., mental health, criminal justice, health care, substance abuse, educational systems, etc.) are critical to creating a safe, supportive, affirming environment for LGBTQ youth in out-of-home placements. In a recent study, McCormick et al. (2016) found that foster family acceptance plays a critical role in creating a safe, affirming, and inclusive environment for LGBTQ youth. Foster parents are less inclined to exhibit rejecting behaviors when they are educated about the negative consequences it has on LGBTQ youth in their care (McCormick et al., 2016).

Ensuring LGBTQ Competency of Partner Agencies

State-run child welfare systems often work in partnership with private agencies when providing care. Many of these privately-run agencies are faith-based providers, which have provided important and much-needed services, motivated by their religious doctrine. Regardless of motivation, all child welfare agencies have a legal obligation to ensure the safety of all children and youth in their care and custody. This includes any organizations which uphold ideology that contradicts the acceptance and affirmation of the diverse identities of sexual and gender expansive youth. All youth in care have the right to be provided with care that is free from discrimination and indoctrination (Fostering Transitions, 2012). Therefore, child welfare professionals must remain diligent about maintaining regular contact with partner agencies to assess the safety of youth, and to examine the institutional culture to make sure that it is reflective of an affirming, safe environment for LGBTQ youth. Historically, identifying an adequate number of foster homes willing to provide an accepting and affirming environment to LGBTQ youth has been challenging (Mallon, 2011; Wilber et al., 2006a). In response to this shortage, child welfare agencies routinely place LGBTQ youth in more restrictive environments such as group homes and other congregate care settings (Woronoff et al., 2006), despite the fact that the placement is an inappropriate level of care. One survey of youth revealed that LGBTQ youth were seven times more likely to be placed in group homes than their heterosexual, cisgender counterparts (Irvine & Canfield, 2016). The placement of LGBTQ youth in these environments is usually non-therapeutic and often initiated to ensure their personal safety (Elze, 2014), but it often has deleterious effects. Such placements can further stigmatize youth, exposing them to potential harassment and victimization, and can reduce the likelihood of permanency (Elze, 2014; Fostering Transitions, 2012).

Best Practices: Ensuring Successful Transitions to Permanence

The process of establishing, maintaining, and achieving permanency for youth in foster care can be difficult (McCormick et al., 2016). Youth identified as sexual and gender expansive often make the decision to leave care and spend time on the streets because they feel safer there than they did in care (Ream & Forge, 2014). One study reported that 56% of LGBTQ foster youth spent time on the streets for this reason (Feinstein, Greenblatt, Hass, Kohn, & Rana, 2001). Consequently, homeless LGBTQ youth often resort to "survival crimes" such as drug sales, sex work, theft, and other criminal activities to pay for housing and food, placing them at an increased risk of entry into the juvenile justice system (Irvine & Canfield, 2016).

As Mallon (2011) points out, family support and engagement are usually a salient starting point when working with families whose children are in care; however, this has not been the case for

LGBTQ youth. Often, child welfare caseworkers do not consider the fluidity of initial feelings and perceptions experienced by parents when their child discloses their sexual orientation and/or gender identity; therefore, they often dismiss the possibility of reuniting older LGBTQ youth with their families (Ryan, Huebner, Diaz & Sanchez, 2009). The lack of involvement by parents or other supportive adults in the lives of LGBTQ youth is a substantial barrier to permanence and leads to the overrepresentation of LGBTQ youth in the "aging out" population (McCormick et al., 2016). When the decision is made to no longer involve the parents and/or caregivers in permanency planning (i.e., the youth cannot safely return home), child welfare professionals must be steadfast in identifying positive adult role models to support sexual and gender expansive youth, or they risk becoming homeless or involved in the juvenile justice system once they exit care. In a recent study, almost 30% of youth experiencing homelessness in a large metropolitan city reported histories of foster care, and 19% reported some child welfare system involvement other than foster care (Wright et al., 2016). Once a foster youth becomes homeless, their risk of substance abuse, risky sexual behavior, victimization, and contact with the criminal justice system as an adult increases (Bender, Yang, Ferguson, & Thompson, 2015; Dworsky, Napolitano, & Courtney, 2013; Fowler, Toro, & Miles, 2009). This can further add to trauma already experienced both prior to entering, and while in, the child welfare system. Sexual and gender expansive youth, who have been in foster care, fare worse than their heterosexual, cisgender peers when they experience homelessness. One recent study found that LGBTQ youth were homeless for longer periods, were more likely to be trafficked, experienced higher rates of victimization, and were more likely to report using substances while they were homeless (Forge, Hartinger-Saunders, Wright, & Ruel, 2018).

Changing our Approach: A Paradigm Shift

The LGBTQ population is gaining visibility, as evidenced by the legalization of same-sex marriages on June 26, 2015, and by the marked increase of dialogues surrounding transgender rights. However, a significant amount of work is necessary to transform the child welfare service delivery system to ensure that universal legal rights are established and protected so that sexual and gender expansive youth reside in safe, affirming environments free from discrimination, rejection, and violence. This can be viewed as a two-sided argument. On the one hand, we should not require youth to "out" themselves to family court judges, attorneys, child welfare staff, foster parents, etc., to ensure a safe placement that is accepting of LGBTQ youth. On the other hand, agency staff are left to make placement decisions without this information, subsequently placing youth at risk of further victimization.

There is a growing body of literature that supports the presence of a disproportionate number of sexual and gender expansive youth in the child welfare system. Considering this, child welfare staff, foster parents, adoptive parents, and contracted service providers should approach every child as if they identify as sexual and gender expansive. Doing so would require a system-wide paradigm shift away from a heterosexist view of sexual orientation and a binary perspective of gender (e.g., male or female). Recognizing that gender is not exclusively determined by an assigned sex at birth, but determined by a youth's sense of identity and expression (Substance Abuse and Mental Health Services Administration, 2012) opens the door to more inclusive policies and best practice models for working with sexual and gender expansive youth and their families. To establish a child welfare system which values all youth, regardless of sexual orientation or gender identity and expression, requires a zero-tolerance stance against explicit and implicit discrimination of sexual and gender expansive youth.

The continued education of all people who come into contact with youth in foster care is vitally important; the body of evidence, best practices, and culture are in no way static. This requires a shift from the often-used notion that one can be "culturally competent" in issues that relate to youth who identify as sexual and gender expansive. Such a belief implies that competence is attainable as an endpoint, which is in opposition to the continual changes expressed above. The shift, therefore, is toward a system where child welfare staff, foster parents, group home staff, etc., practice "cultural humility"

(Hook, Davis, Owen, Worthington, & Utsey, 2013, p. 354). Within the context of the child welfare system, demonstrating cultural humility involves the adoption of a stance that is focused on the child, rather than on the self, with the demonstration of respect, and cognizance that the adult is not superior in their own cultural background and experience (Tervalon & Murrey-Garcia, 1998). In addition, a commitment to lifelong learning is demonstrated, rather than a belief that one can achieve competence as an end-point (Tervalon & Murrey-Garcia, 1998). Therefore, a shift toward cultural humility is a necessary step in the direction of reducing and eliminating the behavioral and organizational factors that contribute to negative health and mental health outcomes for this population.

Best Practices

There are a number of best practice strategies that agencies can employ to create an affirming and safe environment for sexual and gender expansive youth in out-of-home placements. Of particular note is the Model Standards Project, the first comprehensive effort to develop practice standards, based on the unique needs of LGBTQ youth, to improve services and subsequent outcomes (Wilber et al., 2006a). The Model Standards Project put forth the following best practice standards: (1) create an inclusive organizational culture; (2) recruit and support competent caregivers and staff; (3) promote healthy adolescent development; (4) respect the privacy and confidentiality of LGBTQ youth; (5) provide appropriate placements; and (6) provide sensitive support services (Wilber et al., 2006a). The initiative was implemented in three counties in California, where informational sessions and training courses were conducted for child welfare workers and community partners in an effort to bring effective and long-lasting improvements in the experiences of LGBTQ youth in the child welfare system (California Family to Family Initiative, 2007). Since its introduction in 2002, the Model Standards Project has collaborated with various child-welfare-serving organizations, including the Child Welfare League of America, the nation's oldest and largest, to create and disseminate best practice guidelines (Wilber et al., 2006b).

Policy Advocacy

For the sake of all youth in foster care, practice, research, and policy discussions must continue to center upon the development and implementation of best practices to promote the safety, permanence, and well-being of sexual and gender expansive youth through competent service provision aimed to reduce the cumulative effects of being in foster care and identifying as LGBTQ. Lambda Legal continues to be a leader in advocating for policies that protect the fundamental rights of LGBTQ children and youth in the child welfare system. Policy advocacy has been a critical step toward moving the public child welfare system forward in their mission of promoting well-being and permanence. On January 13, 2017, the Administration on Children, Youth and Families finalized changes within the AFCARS data collection system. This was the first change to the AFCARS data collection system since 1993. The Final Rule was an effort to regulate and enhance data collection on children in foster care. The section most relevant to this chapter is the major provision mandating state and tribal child welfare agencies to collect data on the sexual orientation of the child, legal guardian, foster, and adoptive parents (Administration for Children and Families, 2017). Up until this ruling, state and tribal child welfare agencies did not collect any data on the sexual orientation of children in foster care. Although the new data collection mandates do not include gender expansive identity, it is certainly a step in the right direction.

Addressing Needs

Advocating on behalf of LGBTQ youth in the foster care system is essential, as currently, they do not have a voice. They face unique risks in foster care specifically related to their sexual orientation,

Table 21.4 Practice Tips for Working with Sexual and Gender Minority Youth

- Acknowledge that LGBTQ young people are in foster care.
- Reflect upon personal beliefs and attitudes about LGBTQ people.
- Treat LGBTQ clients with the same dignity and respect as you do all children in care.
- Have the same expectations of LGBTQ clients as you do of all children in care.
- Be aware of the language you use at all times to ensure that you do not offend or hurt LGBTQ youth.
- Do not perpetuate the stereotypes about LGBTQ people. Make a conscious decision to reject stereotypes.
- Create a positive physical environment that welcomes and affirms LGBTQ youth.
- Work closely with parents/caregivers around the child returning home. Do not assume that they can't return home.
- Learn how to respond when an LGBTQ youth "comes out." Your reaction is critical to an affirming environment.
- Agencies should be strategic and purposeful in creating safe, affirming placements for LGBTQ youth.
- Be prepared to work effectively with transgender youth by educating yourself about their unique challenges.
- Become familiar with resources available to young LGBTQ people in the community so you can connect them with these.
- Provide support and resources to others in the young person's life to help build and strengthen support systems.
- Ensure that LGBTQ young people receive developmentally appropriate sexual health services.
- Advocate for supportive, competent care for LGBTQ youth involved with the child welfare system.
- Examine the organizational cultures of partner agencies around LGBTQ youth to ensure their safety.
- Examine the organizational competency and practices when serving LGBTQ youth to ensure best practices.
- Know that your acceptance and/or rejection directly affects the health and well-being of LGBTQ youth in care.
- Respect the privacy and confidentiality of LGBTQ youth in care at all times.
- Know the dangers and increased risks for LGBTQ youth involved in the child welfare system.
- Acknowledge that there is more to an individual than sexual orientation and gender identity.

Source: Adapted from Fostering Transitions (2012).

gender identity and expression, and it is the responsibility of child welfare organizations charged with the care and custody of sexual and gender expansive youth to minimize those risks (Child Welfare Information Gateway, 2013) and keep them safe.

Mallon (1998) conducted in-depth interviews with lesbian and gay adolescents in the U.S. and Canadian child welfare systems, the results of which remain applicable to frame efforts in addressing needs. The experiences of the interviewed youth were organized around three central themes: searching for a good fit within the family system, searching for a good fit in an out-of-home care setting, and escaping a bad fit. A "good fit" for the youth was comprised of three overall features; (1) safety; (2) an environment that enables a youth to safely incorporate their identity into all facets of life; and (3) the ability to engage and interact with others who affirm and nurture that identity (Mallon, 1998, pp. 119–120).

National policies need to be developed and implemented to ensure that explicit non-discrimination protections are afforded to sexual and gender expansive youth in foster care across every state in the United States. Relying on the interpretation of the 14th Amendment—Equal Protections and the 14th Amendment—Due Process protections places youth at risk. Advocacy efforts should focus on the Administration for Children and Families (ACF) taking the necessary steps for federally funded, state and tribal child welfare organizations to collect information on sexual orientation and gender identity and expression to further highlight the existence and needs of this vulnerable population.

Protecting the confidentiality of sexual and gender expansive youth will be paramount to keeping youth safe, and this needs to be considered well in advance of collecting these data. However, collecting sexual orientation and gender identity and expression data will benefit sexual and gender expansive youth. It will help to quantify the number of sexual and gender expansive youth within the foster care population so that child welfare organizations can plan more effectively for their needs.

In addition to identifying sexual and gender expansive youth among the foster care population, state administrators, front-line staff, foster parents, adoptive parents, and all contracted agencies and staff must be competent to work with sexual and gender expansive youth. This involves a critical self-inventory of one's current values and beliefs about sexual and gender expansive youth, as well as a commitment to learn about the issues that LGBTQ-identified youth face. Being competent also requires the acquisition of new knowledge and the demonstration of best practice skills to keep sexual and gender expansive youth safe (Wilber et al., 2006b). Changing the heteronormative and binary gender culture of child welfare organizations will be a critical first step in reducing the likelihood of sexual and gender expansive youth being exposed to discriminatory, unsafe, unaffirming environments within the system developed to protect them from harm.

Additionally, child welfare organizations need to identify, track, and designate LGBTQ affirming foster parents and homes. This information will allow organizations to: (1) identify the current number of LGBTQ-competent foster care placements available; and (2) compare the number of placements with the number of sexual and gender expansive youth needing such placements. This will help to identify gaps in resources so that recruitment efforts for LGBTQ-competent foster care placements can be increased. Such efforts have been conducted in some states, including New York City, where advertising campaigns to recruit LGBTQ foster families conducted by the Administration for Children's Services sought to find welcoming homes for children in care (Gay, 2013).

Myriad resources exist at the national, state, and local levels to support sexual and gender expansive youth, child welfare professionals, and foster parents (see Appendix). Collaborations between child welfare organizations and community partners that provide services and support for sexual and gender expansive youth should be sought and nurtured. For example, there are LGBTQ community centers, youth groups, and Gay–Straight Alliances (GSAs) within educational settings that can provide opportunities and resources to assist and affirm youth who are involved with the child welfare system. Such organizations can also be meaningful collaborators for child welfare providers, not only in resource provision, but also in shifting the culture of the child welfare system from one of tolerance, at best, to one that reflects values of acceptance and competence in affirming the identities of all youth in foster care.

While contemporary society and culture have made significant progress in affirming the lives of sexual and gender expansive/LGBTQ people in the United States, many continue to face stigmatization, discrimination, and victimization because of their identity. Each year, LGBTQ children and youth continue to be placed in out-of-home care due to abuse and neglect. However, they are all too often met with a system that struggles to provide safe and affirming care. Within the child welfare system, LGBTQ youth are challenged to cope with prior trauma while realizing and incorporating their identity into their lived experiences. To successfully accomplish this, they rely on caseworkers and foster parents to create a safe space for them to heal and further develop their sense of self. While efforts exist within the realm of child welfare to address their unique needs and provide a supportive and affirming environment, much more is needed to address the disproportionality and disparities that LGBTQ youth in the child welfare system face. On a national level, the progress made has included Presidential Proclamations for National Foster Care Month (Obama, 2015, 2016) which are inclusive of sexual and gender expansive youth, and official, system-wide acknowledgment from AFCARS that LGBTQ youth exist in the system. However, this may be overshadowed by the continuing reports of youth who have run away from the very system that was designed to provide them with care. We are challenged to advocate for affirming and protective policies, and to ensure that they are faithfully enacted, so that youth in care achieve their desired goal for permanency and well-being. Future research should include the voices of sexual and gender expansive youth currently in the foster care system. Presently, research has relied heavily on retrospective, purposive samples of LGBTQ youth who report prior child welfare system involvement. Understanding their experiences within the child welfare system as they occur can move research and practice forward by opening up useful dialogue around various targets for systemic change. All who participate in the child welfare system, from family court judges to foster parents to caseworkers, must equip themselves with effective tools to address the needs of sexual and gender expansive youth, and indeed all youth, using a lens of cultural humility, truly acting in the best interest of the child.

Note

1   Throughout this chapter, the terms, "sexual and gender expansive" and "lesbian, gay, bisexual, transgender, and questioning and/or queer (LGBTQ)" are used interchangeably. For an in-depth explanation of each, refer to the section, "Defining Sexual and Gender Expansive Youth."

References

Adelson, S. L., & American Academy of Child and Adolescent Psychiatry [AACAP] Committee on Quality Issues [CQI]. (2012). Practice parameter on gay, lesbian, or bisexual sexual orientation, gender nonconformity, and gender discordance in children and adolescents. *Journal of the American Academy of Child and Adolescent Psychiatry, 51*(9), 957–974. http://dx.doi.org/10.1016/j.jaac.2012.07.004

Administration for Children and Families. (2011). *Information memorandum: Lesbian, gay, bisexual, transgender and questioning youth in foster care.* Washington, DC: U.S. Department of Health & Human Services. Retrieved from www.acf.hhs.gov/sites/default/files/cb/im1103.pdf

Administration for Children and Families. (2017, January). *Adoption and Foster Care Analysis and Reporting System: A rule by the Children and Families Administration on 12/14/2016.* 81 FR 90524. Retrieved from www.federalregister.gov/documents/2016/12/14/2016-29366/adoption-and-foster-care-analysis-and-reporting-system

American Psychiatric Association [APA]. (1980). *Diagnostic and statistical manual of mental disorders* (3rd ed.). Washington, DC: Author.

American Psychiatric Association [APA]. (2000). Position statement on therapies focused on attempts to change sexual orientation (reparative or conversion therapies). *American Journal of Psychiatry, 157*(10), 1719–1721.

American Psychiatric Association [APA]. (2013a). *Diagnostic and statistical manual of mental disorders* (5th ed.). Washington, DC: Author.

American Psychiatric Association. (2013b). *Gender dysphoria factsheet.* Washington, DC: Author. Available at www.dsm5.org/documents/gender%20dysphoria%20fact%20sheet.pdf

Anton, B. S. (2010). Proceedings of the American Psychological Association for the legislative year 2009: Minutes of the annual meeting of the Council of Representatives and minutes of the meetings of the Board of Directors. *American Psychologist, 65*, 385–475. doi:10.1037/0003-066X.63.5.360

Austin, S. B., Ziyadeh, N. J., Corliss, H. L., Rosario, M., Wypij, D., Haines, J., . . . Field, A. E. (2009). Sexual orientation disparities in purging and binge eating from early to late adolescence. *The Journal of Adolescent Health: Official Publication of the Society for Adolescent Medicine, 45*(3), 238–245. doi:10.1016/j.jadohealth.2009.02.001

Bayer, R. (1981). *Homosexuality and American psychiatry: The politics of diagnosis.* Princeton, NJ: Princeton University Press.

Bender, K., Yang, J., Ferguson, K., & Thompson, S. (2015). Experiences and needs of homeless youth with a history of foster care. *Children and Youth Services Review, 55*, 222–231. doi:10.1016/j.childyouth.2015.06.007

Berlan, E. D. (2010). Sexual orientation and bullying among adolescence in the Growing Up Today Study. *Journal of Adolescent Health, 46*(4), 366–371. doi:10.1016/j.jadohealth.2009.10.015

Birkett, M., Russell, S. T., & Corliss, H. (2014). Sexual-orientation disparities in school: The mediational role of indicators of victimization in achievement and truancy because of feeling unsafe. *American Journal of Public Health, 104*(6), 1124–1128. doi:10.2105/AJPH.2013.301785

Blashill, A. J. (2010). Elements of male body image: Predictions of depression, eating pathology and social sensitivity among gay men. *Body Image, 7*(4), 310–316. doi:10.1016/j.bodyim.2010.07.006

Brown, L. B. (1997). Women and men, not-men and not-women, lesbians and gays: American Indian gender style alternatives. In L. B. Brown (Ed.), *Two spirit people: American Indian lesbian women and gay men* (pp. 5–20). New York, NY: Harrington Park Press.

California Family to Family Initiative. (2007, September). *Highlights from the Model Standards Project.* Retrieved from www.f2f.ca.gov/res/ModelStandardsProjectHighlightsSept07.pdf

Cass, V. C. (1979). Homosexual identity formation: A theoretical model. *Journal of Homosexuality, 4,* 219–235.

Children's Bureau. (2015, July). *The AFCARS report. Preliminary FY 2014 estimates as of July 2015. No. 22.* Washington, DC: U.S. Department of Health & Human Services. Retrieved from www.acf.hhs.gov/sites/default/files/cb/afcarsreport22.pdf

Child Welfare Information Gateway. (2013). *Supporting your LGBTQ youth: A guide for foster parents.* Factsheet for Families. Washington, DC: U.S. Department of Health & Human Services, Children's Bureau. Retrieved from www.childwelfare.gov/pubPDFs/LGBTQyouth.pdf

Child Welfare League of America. (2015). *Position statement on parenting of children by lesbian, gay, bisexual, and transgender adults.* Retrieved from www.cwla.org/wp-content/uploads/2016/01/PositionStatementOnParentingOfChildrenbyLGBT.pdf

D'Augelli, A. R. (1994). Identity development and sexual orientation: Toward a model of lesbian, gay, and bisexual development. In E. J. Trickett, R. J. Watts, & D. Birman (Eds.), *Human diversity: Perspectives on people in context.* San Francisco: Jossey-Bass.

Davis, R. M., Genel, M., Howe, J. P., Karlan, M. S., Kennedy, W. R., Numann, P. J., . . . O'Neill, J. F. (1996). Health care needs of gay men and lesbians in the United States. *Journal of the American Medical Association, 275*(17), 1354–1359. doi:10.1001/jama.1996.03530410068036

Deutsch, M. E. (2016). *Guidelines for the primary and gender-affirming care of transgender and gender nonbinary people* (2nd ed.). San Francisco: Center of Excellence for Transgender Health.

Drescher, J. (2015). Out of DSM: Depathologizing homosexuality. *Behavioral Sciences, 5*(4), 565–575. doi:10.3390/bs5040565

Dworsky, A., Napolitano, L., & Courtney, M. (2013). Homelessness during the transition from foster care to adulthood. *American Journal of Public Health, 103*(S2), S318–S323. doi:10.2105/AJPH.2013.301455

Elze, D. (2014). LGBTQ youth and their families. In G. P. Mallon & P. McCartt Hess (Eds.), *Child welfare for the 21st century: A handbook of practices, policies and programs* (2nd ed.; pp. 158–178). New York City, NY: Columbia University Press.

Estrada, R., & Marksamer, J. (2006). The legal rights of LGBT youth in state custody: What child welfare and juvenile justice professionals need to know. *Child Welfare, 85*(2), 171–194.

Faiman-Silva, S. (2011). Anthropologists and two spirit people: Building bridges and sharing knowledge. *Anthropology Faculty Publications, 23,* 1–21. Retrieved from http://vc.bridgew.edu/anthro_fac/23

Feinstein, R., Greenblatt, A., Hass, L., Kohn, S., & Rana, J. (2001). *Justice for all? A report on lesbian, gay, bisexual, and transgendered youth in the New York juvenile justice system.* New York, NY: Lesbian and Gay Project of the Urban Justice Center.

Forge, N., Hartinger-Saunders, R., Wright, E., & Ruel, E. (2018). Out of the system and onto the streets: LGBTQ-identified youth experiencing homelessness with past child welfare system involvement. *Child Welfare.*

Fostering Transitions. (2012). *Getting down to basics: Tools to support LGBTQ youth in care.* New York, NY: Child Welfare League of America and Lambda Legal.

Fowler, P. J., Toro, P. A., & Miles, B. W. (2009). Pathways to and from homelessness and associated psychosocial outcomes among adolescents leaving the foster care system. *American Journal of Public Health, 99*(8), 1453–1458.

Friedman, M. S., Marshal, M. P., Guadamuz, T. E., Chongyi, W., Wong, C. F., Saewyc, E., & Stall, R. (2011). A meta-analysis of disparities in childhood sexual abuse, parental physical abuse, and peer victimization among sexual minority and sexual nonminority individuals. *American Journal of Public Health, 101*(8), 1481–1494. doi:10.2105/AJPH.2009.190009

Gay, M. (2013, June 2). City to diversify foster system. *The Wall Street Journal.* Retrieved from www.wsj.com/articles/SB10001424127887324563004578521604208702758

GLSEN, CiPHR, & CCRC. (2013). *Out online: The experiences of lesbian, gay, bisexual and transgender youth on the internet.* New York, NY: GLSEN.

Goodenow, C., Szalacha, L., & Westheimer, K. (2006). School support groups, other school factors, and the safety of sexual minority adolescents. *Psychology in the Schools, 43*(5), 573–589. doi:10.1002/pits.20173

Grossman, A. H., & D'Augelli, A. R. (2007). Transgender youth and life-threatening behaviors. *Suicide and Life-Threatening Behavior, 37,* 527–537. doi:10.1521/suli.2007.37.5.527

Heatherington, L., & Lavner, J. A. (2008). Coming to terms with coming out: Review and recommendations for family systems-focused research. *Journal of Family Psychology, 22*(3), 329–343. doi:10.1037/0893-3200.22.3.329

Heck, N. C., Lindquist, L. M., Stewart, B. T., Brennan, C., & Cochran, B. N. (2013). To join or not to join: Gay–straight student alliances and the high school experiences of lesbian, gay, bisexual, and transgender youths. *Journal of Gay & Lesbian Social Services, 25*(1), 77–101. doi:10.1080/10538720.2012.751764

Higa, D., Hoppe, M. J., Lindhorst, T., Mincer, S., Beadnell, B., Morrison, D. M., . . . Mountz, S. (2014). Negative and positive factors associated with the well-being of lesbian, gay, bisexual, transgender, queer, and questioning (LGBTQ) youth. *Youth and Society, 46*(5), 663–687. doi:10.1177/0044118X12449630

Hook, J. N., Davis, D. E., Owen, J., Worthington, E. L. Jr., & Utsey, S. O. (2013). Cultural humility: Measuring openness to culturally diverse clients. *Journal of Counseling Psychology, 60*(3), 353–366. doi:10.1037/a0038582

Human Rights Campaign. (n.d.). *LGBTQ youth in the foster care system*. Retrieved from http://hrc-assets.s3-website-us-east-1.amazonaws.com//files/assets/resources/HRC-YouthFosterCare-IssueBrief-FINAL.pdf

Irvine, A., & Canfield, A. (2016). The overrepresentation of lesbian, gay, bisexual, questioning, gender nonconforming and transgender youth within the child welfare to juvenile justice crossover population. *Journal on Gender, Social Policy, and the Law, 24*(2), 243–261.

Jones, B. A., Haycraft, E., Murjan, S., & Arcelus, J. (2016). Body dissatisfaction and disordered eating in trans people: A systematic review of the literature. *International Review of Psychiatry, 28*(1), 81–94. doi:10.3109/09540261.2015.1089217

Kann, L., Olsen, E. O., McManus, T., Harris, W. A., Shanklin, S. L., Flint, K. H., . . . Zaza, S. (2016, Summer). Sexual identity, sex of sexual contacts, and health-related behaviors among students in grades 9–12—United States and selected sites, 2015. *MMWR Surveillance Summaries, 65*(SS-9), 1–202.

Kelly, J. (2017, January 13). New AFCARS data collection: What to know. *The Chronicle of Social Change*. Retrieved from https://chronicleofsocialchange.org/subscriber-content/new-afcars-collection-know/23970

Kosciw, J. G., Greytak, E. A., Palmer, M. J., & Boesen, M. J. (2014). *The 2013 National School Climate Survey: The experiences of lesbian, gay, bisexual, and transgender youth in our nation's schools*. New York, NY: GLSEN. Retrieved from www.glsen.org/sites/default/files/2013%20National%20School%20Climate%20Survey%20Full%20Report_0.pdf

Kosciw, J. G., Palmer, N. A., Kull, R. M., & Greytak, E. A. (2013). The effect of negative school climate on academic outcomes for LGBT youth and the role of in-school supports. *Journal of School Violence, 12*(1), 45–63. doi:10.1080/15388220.2012.732546

Laver, M., & Khoury, A. (2008). *Opening doors for LGBTQ youth in foster care: A guide for lawyers and judges*. Washington, DC: American Bar Association.

Lesbian and Gay Law Association of Greater New York. (2014, April). NY judge orders city to pay for transgender youth's surgery. *Lesbian/Gay Law Notes, 4*, 139–141. Retrieved from http://le-gal.org/ny-judge-orders-city-pay-transgender-youths-surgery/

Lev, A. I. (2004). *Transgender emergence: Therapeutic guidelines for working with gender-variant people and their families*. New York, NY: Routledge.

Levitt, H. M., & Ippolito, M. R. (2014). Being transgender: The experience of transgender identity development. *Journal of Homosexuality, 61*(12), 1727–1758. doi:10.1080/00918369.2014.951262

Lewes, K. (1990). The psychoanalytic theory of male homosexuality. *American Journal of Psychiatry, 147*, 518–519. doi:10.1176/ajp.147.4.518

Liu, R. T., & Mustanksi, B. (2012). Suicidal ideation and self-harm in lesbian, gay, bisexual, and transgender youth. *American Journal of Preventive Medicine, 42*(3), 221–228. doi:10.1016/j.amepre.2011.10.023

Mallon, G. P. (1998). *We don't exactly get the welcome wagon: The experiences of gay and lesbian adolescents in child welfare systems*. New York, NY: Columbia University Press.

Mallon, G. P. (2011). Permanency for LGBTQ youth. *Protecting Children, 26*(1), 49–57.

Mallon, G. P., & DeCrescenzo, T. (2006). Transgender children and youth: A child welfare practice perspective. *Child Welfare, 85*(2), 215–241.

Mallon, G. P., & Woronoff, R. (2006). Busting out of the child welfare closet: Lesbian, gay, bisexual, and transgender affirming approaches to child welfare. *Child Welfare, 85*(2), 115–122.

Marshal, M. P., Dietz, L. J., Friedman, M. S., Stall, R., Smith, H. A., McGinley, J., . . . Brent, D. A. (2011). Suicidality and depression disparities between sexual minority and heterosexual youth: A meta-analytic review. *Journal of Adolescent Health, 49*, 115–123. doi:10.1016/j.jadohealth.2011.02.005

Martin, M., Down, L., & Erney, R. (2016). *Out of the shadows: Supporting LGBTQ youth in child welfare through cross-system collaboration*. Washington, DC: Center for the Study of Social Policy.

McCormick, A., Schmidt, K., & Terrazas, S. (2016). LGBTQ youth in the child welfare system: An overview of research, practice, and policy. *Journal of Public Child Welfare, 11*(1), 1–13. doi:10.1080/15548732.2016.1221368

McGuire, J. K., Doty, J. L., Catalpa, J. M., & Ola, C. (2016). Body image in transgender youth people: Findings from a qualitative, community based study. *Body Image, 18*, 96–107. doi:10.1016/j.bodyim.2016.06.004

National Association of Social Workers. (2015, May). *Sexual orientation change efforts (SOCE) and conversion therapy with lesbians, gay men, bisexuals, and transgender persons*. Washington, DC: Author.

NYC Administration for Children's Services. (2010). *ACS non-medicaid reimbursable policy guidance for trans-related health care*. New York, NY: Administration for Children's Services. Memorandum. Retrieved from www1.nyc.gov/assets/acs/pdf/lgbtq/NMR_Guidance_for_Trans_Related_Healthcare.pdf

Obama, B. (2015). Proclamation No. 9263, 80 F.R. 25575.

Obama, B. (2016). Proclamation No. 9432, 81 F.R. 26663.

Price, C., Wheeler, C., Shelton, J., & Maury, M. (Eds.). (2016). *At the intersections: A collaborative report on LGBTQ youth homelessness*. New York, NY: True Colors Fund and the National LGBTQ Task Force.

Ream, G., & Forge, N. (2014). Homeless LGBTQ youth in New York City: Insights from the field. *Child Welfare, 93*(2), 7–22.

Reisner, S. L., Vetters, R., Leclerc, M., Zaslow, S., Wolfrum, S., Shumer, D., & Mimiaga, M. J. (2015). Mental health of transgender youth in care at an adolescent urban community health center: A matched retrospective cohort study. *Journal of Adolescent Health, 56*(3), 274–279. doi:10.1016/j.jadohealth.2014.10.264

Rowe, C., Santos, G. M., McFarland, W., & Wilson, E. C. (2015). Prevalence and correlates of substance use among trans*female youth ages 16–24 years in the San Francisco Bay Area. *Drug and Alcohol Dependence, 147*, 160–166. doi:10.1016/j.drugalcdep.2014.11.023

Ryan, C., Huebner, D., Diaz, R. M., & Sanchez, J. (2009). Family rejection as a predictor of negative health outcomes in white and Latino lesbian, gay, and bisexual young adults. *Pediatrics, 23*(1), 346–352. doi:10.1542/peds.2007-3524

Savin-Williams, R. C., & Cohen, K. M. (Eds.). (2007). *The lives of lesbians, gays, and bisexuals: Children to adults*. Fort Worth, TX: Harcourt Brace College Publishing.

Savin-Williams, R. C., & Ream. G. L. (2007). Prevalence and stability of sexual orientation components during adolescence and young adulthood. *Archives of Sexual Behavior, 36*(3), 385–394. doi:10.1007/s10508-006-9088-5

Schauer, G. L., Berg, C. J., & Bryant, L. O. (2013). Sex differences in psychosocial correlates of concurrent substance use among heterosexual, homosexual and bisexual college students. *American Journal of Drug and Alcohol Abuse, 39*(4), 252–258. doi:10.3109/00952990.2013.796962

Seelman, K. L., Forge, N., Walls, N. E., & Bridges, K. (2015). School engagement among LGBTQ high school students: The roles of safe adults and gay–straight alliance characteristics. *Children and Youth Services Review, 57*, 19–29. doi:10.1016/j.childyouth.2015.07.021

Steever, J., Francis, J., Gordon, L. P., & Lee, J. (2014). Sexual minority youth. *Primary Care: Clinics in Office Practice, 41*, 651–669. doi:10.1016/j.pop.2014.05.012

Stieglitz, K. A. (2010). Development, risk, and resilience of transgender youth. *Journal of the Association of Nurses in AIDS Care, 21*(3), 192–206. doi:10.1016/j.jana.2009.08.004

Substance Abuse and Mental Health Services Administration. (2012). *Top health issues for LGBT populations information & resource kit*. HHS Publication No. (SMA) 12-4684. Rockville, MD: Author.

Tervalon, M., & Murray-Garcia, J. (1998). Cultural humility versus cultural competence: A critical distinction in defining physician training outcomes in multicultural education. *Journal of Health Care for the Poor and Underserved, 9*, 117–125.

Toomey, R. B., Ryan, C., Diaz, R. M., & Russell, S. T. (2011). High school gay–straight alliances (GSAs) and young adult well-being: An examination of GSA presence, participation, and perceived effectiveness. *Applied Developmental Science, 15*(4), 175–185. doi:10.1080/10888691.2011.607378

Turner, J. L. (2009). From the inside out: Calling on states to provide medically necessary care to transgender youth in foster care. *Family Court Review, 47*(3), 552–569. doi:10.1111/j.1744-1617.2009.01273.x

Walls, N. E., Wisneski, H., & Kane, S. B. (2013). School climate, individual support, or both? Gay–straight alliances and the mental health of sexual minority youth. *School Social Work Journal, 37*, 88–111.

Wilber, S., Reyes, C., & Marksamer, J. (2006b). *CWLA best practice guidelines*. Washington, DC: CWLA Press.

Wilber, S., Reyes, C., & Marksamer, J. (2006a). The Model Standards Project: Creating inclusive systems for LGBT youth in out-of-home care. *Child Welfare, 85*(2), 133–149.

Wilson, B. D. M., Cooper, K., Kastanis, A., & Nezhad, S. (2014). *Sexual and gender minority youth in foster care: Assessing disproportionality and disparities in Los Angeles*. Los Angeles: The Williams Institute, UCLA School of Law.

Wilson, B. D. M., & Kastanis, A. A. (2015). Sexual and gender minority disproportionality and disparities in child welfare: A population-based study. *Children and Youth Services Review, 58*, 11–17. doi:10.1016/j.childyouth.2015.08.016

Woronoff, R., Estrada, R., & Sommer, S. (2006). *Out of the margins: A report on regional listening forums highlighting the experiences of lesbian, gay, bisexual, transgender, and questioning youth in care*. Washington, DC: Child Welfare League of America and Lambda Legal.

Wright, E. R., & Perry, B. L. (2006). Sexual identity distress, social support, and the health of gay, lesbian, and bisexual youth. *Journal of Homosexuality, 51*(1), 81–110.

Wright, E., Ruel, E., Justice Fuoco, M., Trouteaud, A., Sanchez, T., LaBoy, A., . . . Hartinger-Saunders, R. (2016). *Atlanta youth count! Homeless youth count and needs assessment. Final report*. Atlanta: Georgia State University. Retrieved from http://atlantayouthcount.weebly.com/uploads/7/9/0/5/79053356/aycna_final_report_may_2016_final.pdf

Appendix

National, State and Local Resources Related to Sexual and Gender Expansive Youth

ALLIANCES

Name	Information	Website
Child Welfare League of America (CWLA)	Provides child welfare support and resources	www.cwla.org
Gay, Lesbian and Straight Education Network (GLSEN)	Advocacy for safer schools	www.glsen.org
Gay–Straight Alliance (GSA) Network	Advocating safer schools and communities for LGBT youth	www.gsanetwork.org
GLBT National Help Center	Provides local and national resources including support groups, hotlines, and health	http://bit.ly/2sEYx5P
Human Rights Campaign (HRC)	Provides a guide for child welfare providers in caring for LGBTQ children and youth	www.hrc.org http://bit.ly/2r74rKU
Lambda Legal	Out of Home Care project: creates resources available to LGBTQ youth, and professionals who work with LGBTQ youth in out-of-home (foster) care settings	www.lambdalegal.org
National Center for Lesbian Rights (NCLR)	Legal advocacy for LGBT equality Document: *The Legal rights of lesbian, gay, bisexual, and transgender youth in the child welfare system*	www.nclrights.org
Parents, Families, Friends, and Allies of Lesbian and Gays (PFLAG)	Various chapters domestically and internationally	www.pflag.org
Safer Schools Coalition	Resources, training and other information for LGBTQ youth and education	http://bit.ly/2s5O2eP

ORGANIZATIONS FOR FOSTER PARENTS

Name	Information	Website
Advocates for Youth	LGBTQ Issues Info for Parents	http://bit.ly/2sUzL0M
Child Welfare Information Gateway	Guide for foster parents caring for LGBTQ youth	www.childwelfare.gov
Lambda Legal	Know Your Rights: Youth	www.lambdalegal.org
National Foster Parent Association (NFPA)	An organization created by the Child Welfare League of America, NFPA supports foster caregivers with resources, local and national services, and education and training	www.nfpaonline.org
Parents, Families, Friends, and Allies of Lesbians and Gays (PFLAG)	Assists in locating community resources to support care for LGBT youth	www.pflag.org

TRAINING, WEBINARS and VIDEOS

Name	What they Do	Additional Information	Website	Contact
Child Welfare Information Gateway	Search available training and other needs of foster caregivers according to state	National Foster Care & Adoption Directory Search	www.childwelfare.org	Access and search directory at: http://bit.ly/1oAxHU1
Family Acceptance Project	Provides specific training to meet the needs of the requested organization/entity	LGBT youth and out-of-home care/foster care	http://bit.ly/2rCuugl	Contact: fap@sfsu.edu
The Trevor Project: Trevor Ally Training; Trevor CARE Training	Suicide prevention training for individuals working with LGBT youth	LGBT youth in academic grades 6–12	http://bit.ly/1cpnJMB	Contact: 1866-488-7386
American Bar Association (ABA): Opening Doors/LGBTQ Youth in Foster Care	Training on the legal aspects and supports for improved outcomes of LGBTQ youth in foster care		http://bit.ly/1fn1FYn	Opening Doors Project 1050 Connecticut Avenue, NW Suite 400 Washington, DC 20036
Human Rights Campaign: All Children—All Families (ACAF)	Provides training, resources, and tools in promoting cultural competency of child welfare agencies	Three-part training program	www.hrc.org/acaf	

Name	What they Do	Additional Information	Website	Contact
Lambda Legal partnership with National Association of Social Workers (NASW)	Locate Master Trainers or access curriculum for child welfare services for LGBT youth in foster care		www.lambdalegal.org	Contact: 212-809-8585
Family Acceptance Project: Family Video Series		Diverse/Different families and how they support their LGBT youth	http://bit.ly/2r3Cqss	

RELEVANT WEBSITES

Name	Information and Website
Affirmation: Gay and Lesbian Mormons	Supporting the relationships between LGBT Mormons and their family and friends www.affirmation.org
GLBT National Help Center	Resources and support for the LGBT community www.glbthotline.org
Health Professionals Advancing LGBT Equality	Health professionals ensuring the quality of LGBT persons' health www.glma.org
Matthew's Place	A website created by and for LGBT youth with resources including health, spiritual, and faith communities, GSAs and centers www.matthewsplace.com
National Juvenile Defender Center (NJDC)	Works to ensure fair legal treatment of juveniles www.njdc.info
National Association of LGBT Community Centers (Center Link)	National and community resources www.lgbtcenters.org
National Center for Cultural Competence at Georgetown University	Practice Brief: *Helping families support their lesbian, gay, bisexual, and transgender (LGBT) children* http://bit.ly/1HG1G8u
National Center for Lesbian Rights (NCLR)	Legal advocacy for LGBT equality www.nclrights.org
Centers for Disease Control and Prevention (CDC)	A resource for LGBT youth, CDC Youth Resources http://bit.ly/2rX2apF

Part VII
Social Policy and Institutional Support

22

Fostering "Belonging-ness"
The Role of Private Foster Care Agencies with Foster Parents and Youth

Marlo A. Perry and Mary E. Rauktis

Introduction

Child welfare has historically been a public entity, with funding streams coming through the federal and state governments. While collaboration with private organizations is common, the public child welfare agencies are primarily responsible for investigating reports of child maltreatment, assessing family needs, and, if necessary, providing out-of-home care for children (Child Welfare Information Gateway, 2012). Private agencies have more typically provided other supportive services, such as parenting classes, mental health services, or substance abuse treatment (Child Welfare Information Gateway, 2012). However, in recent years, there has been a movement toward privatizing some or all child welfare services.

Proponents of privatization claim that contracting out child welfare services to private agencies will allow for more efficient and more cost-effective services that result in better outcomes (Courtney, 2000). However, research comparing privatization to previous public administration has been difficult, and the research that has been done has shown equivocal findings. When looking at outcomes, studies looking at permanence showed no clear advantage between private and public entities, while studies examining child safety showed a decline after privatization (Steen & Smith, 2012). Mixed findings were also reported by stakeholder groups when interviewed following privatization. Perceptions of foster care providers, service providers, and judges were that privatization negatively impacted access to mental health services and aftercare services and resulted in a lack of appropriate placements for children and youth (Humphrey, Turnbull, A. P., & Turnbull, H. R., 2006). However, some respondents felt that privatization made family preservation services more accessible (Humphrey et al., 2006).

Privatization allows for new opportunities for collaboration across public and private child welfare agencies. Several factors have been noted as helping to facilitate successful collaboration. These include good communication between the two entities, a shared vision, clear expectations about roles, a mutual belief in the importance of teamwork, and consistent meetings (Lewandowski & GlenMaye, 2002; Spath, Werrbach, & Pine, 2008). Barriers to collaboration include different views about how to work with families, system changes and staff turnover, lack of communication between parties, and lack of agency and/or family involvement in the decision-making process (e.g., the development of the child's case plan; Lewandowski & GlenMaye, 2002; Spath et al., 2008). Friesen (2001) surveyed foster parents who were part of community-based teams as a result of privatization, and many respondents expressed the view that they wanted their children's unique strengths and needs to be more of a focus of these collaborative team meetings. Additionally, they stated that they wanted to be more active participants in the decisions that were made at these meetings, and not just a nominal member of the team (Friesen, 2001).

There is little research on how foster parents feel about privatization, but Friesen's (2001) study suggests that foster parents were more satisfied after privatization than before. Specifically, they reported being more satisfied with training, and they felt that the children in their care received more attention from agency workers than they did previously. However, their feelings about involvement in planning and satisfaction with timeliness of communication were more equivocal. Foster parents in another study (Steen & Smith, 2011) were relatively ambivalent about privatization itself; they were more concerned with the competence and responsiveness of the workers at the private agency. Additionally, their feelings about training, involvement in decisions regarding their foster child, and their relationship with the foster care worker were strongly related to their satisfaction with the private agency (Steen & Smith, 2011).

Foster care agencies, whether private or public, are charged with recruiting, hiring, training, and monitoring foster parents. Additionally, they are responsible for helping to facilitate the relationship between a youth, his or her biological parent(s), and the foster parent(s). Private and public agencies work with both foster parents (a non-relative who cares for the child) and kinship parents (a family member—e.g., a grandmother or uncle—who cares for the child). However, some kinship arrangements are informal in nature, which means that there is no involvement or oversight by the public agency. Thus, although private agencies may work more frequently with kinship parents, the present chapter focuses solely on foster parents. An overview of the research on recruitment, retention, compensation, and training of foster parents follows.

Recruitment

Recruitment of high-quality, committed foster parents is crucial for foster care agencies. The most recent data show just over 415,000 children in foster care, with nearly half in non-relative foster family homes (Child Welfare Information Gateway, 2016). Foster families are particularly difficult to find for older youth and youth with special behavioral, emotional, and/or physical needs. This is especially concerning given that estimates suggest that 25% to 33% of children in care exhibit intellectual disabilities, developmental delays, physical disabilities, and/or health problems; if emotional and behavioral challenges were also included, these rates would be even higher (Orme, Cherry, & Krcek, 2013). Further, approximately 40% of youth in care are between the ages of 11 and 20 (Tao, Ward, O'Brien, DiLorenzo, & Kelly, 2012). In an effort to combat these challenges, the U.S. Department of Health & Human Services, Administration for Children and Families, Children's Bureau awarded 22 cooperative agreements to jurisdictions between 2008 and 2013, with the focus of these 5-year projects being diligent recruitment of foster families (National Resource Center for Diligent Recruitment, n.d.).

The Parent for Every Child initiative (PFEC; Feldman, Price, & Ruppel, 2016), a project resulting from one of these cooperative agreements, is a promising practice focused on matching youth with special needs who had been living in group care settings with caring, committed adults. The goal is to improve permanency outcomes for these youth, including both legal and relational permanence (Feldman et al., 2016). Legal permanence includes both adoption and legal guardianship, while relational permanence refers to a "lifelong connection to a caring adult, without legal certification" (Feldman et al., 2016, p. 27). The initiative focuses on individualized, diligent recruitment strategies, including: "family search and engagement, Adoption Chronicles videos, internet photo listings, targeted recruitment, adoption panels and exchanges, and general recruitment efforts" (p. 27). Findings from a randomized controlled study of PFEC showed that child-welfare-involved youth in the intervention group (n=88) had statistically higher numbers of permanent relationships than their counterparts in the control group (n=89); however, the groups were comparable when looking at legal permanence outcomes (Feldman et al., 2016). While legal adoptions didn't necessarily increase with these efforts, the importance of relational permanence cannot be overstated, particularly for older youth and youth with special needs (Feldman et al., 2016; Samuels, 2008).

Successful recruitment of foster parents is facilitated by messaging and branding, targeted recruitment, child-specific recruitment, and utilizing current foster parents as recruiters (Casey Family Programs, 2014). Positive messaging is crucial, particularly since foster care often has negative connotations. Additionally, successful messaging will include clear expectations of foster parents (e.g., setting a clear tone about the role of foster parents and their relationship with birth families) and will emphasize that foster parents are professionals who are an integral part of a child's team (Casey Family Programs, 2014). Some research has shown that intrinsic motivators are crucial to successful recruitment. For example, capitalizing on individuals' desires to help children may be beneficial, provided that the message also clearly communicates goals around partnership, permanency, and (potentially) reunification (Casey Family Programs, 2014; MacGregor, Rodger, Cummings, & Leschied, 2006; Marcenko, Brennan, & Lyons, 2009; Rodger, Cummings, & Leschied, 2006). Targeted recruitment may take different forms, including utilizing faith-based communities to reach potential foster parents, focusing on specific geographic locations, and/or developing multi-stage recruitment plans instead of one-time events (Casey Family Programs, 2014). Child-specific recruitment may look analogous to PFEC (discussed above) or a similar program, where the target child is involved in their own permanency planning. For example, a child might help to create a presentation that helps to tell his/her unique story that can then be used at a recruitment event (National Resource Center for Diligent Recruitment, n.d.). Finally, some research has shown that current foster parents serve as better recruiters for new foster parents than do agency professionals, in part because potential foster parents feel that current foster parents are more expert in what fostering realistically entails (Casey Family Programs, 2014; Rodger et al., 2006; Sullivan, Collins-Camargo, & Murphy, 2014). Barriers to recruitment may include fears and misconceptions about children in care and the fostering process (e.g., worries about mental health problems), concerns about the licensing process, and financial concerns (e.g., low compensation rates) (Sullivan et al., 2014).

Retention

Once foster parents are recruited, the difficulty for agencies is often then how to keep them. Fostering brings with it many challenges, including navigating new relationships with children, birth families, and agencies, as well as parenting a child who probably has a trauma history, attachment issues, and/or emotional and behavioral difficulties. There are few data on the turnover of foster parents, but estimates are reported to be between 30% and 50% in some agencies (Gibbs & Wildfire, 2007; Rhodes, Orme, & Buehler, 2001), with a median length of service between 8 and 14 months (Gibbs & Wildfire, 2007).

Negative interactions with agency staff have been one of the most commonly cited reasons why foster parents discontinue fostering (Gibbs & Wildfire, 2007). Foster parents frequently feel that they are treated disrespectfully by agency staff, or that communication from agency staff is faulty, nonexistent, or lagging (Gibbs & Wildfire, 2007; MacGregor et al., 2006; Rhodes et al., 2001). Relatedly, foster parents want to be viewed as part of their foster child's team and have their viewpoints and experiences respected and validated by team members; however, they often feel that this is not the case (MacGregor et al., 2006). When efforts are made by the foster care agency to engage and communicate with foster parents respectfully and treat them as an integral part of the team, foster parents are more likely to continue fostering (Daniel, 2011; MacGregor et al., 2006).

Another important factor in the retention of foster parents is training. This includes education about trauma and emotional/behavioral challenges that children in the foster care system may exhibit, preparation for dealing with loss, training in how to interact effectively and appropriately with birth families, as well as more specific training about what fostering entails (Buehler, Cox, & Cuddeback, 2003; Denby & Rindfleisch, 1996; Gibbs & Wildfire, 2007; Rhodes et al., 2001; Vanderfaeilllie, Van Holen, De Maeyer, Gypen, & Belenger, 2015). In addition to training, foster parents also voice a need for ongoing support, whether it be more regular support from agency staff (Daniel, 2011) or from peer mentors (MacGregor et al., 2006). When foster parents are able to make a more informed decision about what fostering entails, they are more likely to stay on as foster parents.

Compensation

While low reimbursement has been cited by some as a barrier to the recruitment and retention of foster parents, little research has been done in this area. The most frequently cited study on this topic is by Chamberlain, Moreland, and Reid (1992), where foster parents were randomly assigned to one of three groups: extra support and training plus an increased payment; an increased payment only; and foster care as usual. They found that foster parents who received both the additional stipend and the additional support were least likely to discontinue fostering (9.6% dropout rate), followed by the stipend-only group (14.3%), and then the foster-care-as-usual group (25.9%) (Chamberlain et al., 1992). Even the foster-care-as-usual group had a significantly lower dropout rate than the state average; the authors hypothesized that just providing foster parents with a little bit of special attention (e.g., being part of a research study focused on foster care) served as a motivation booster (Chamberlain et al., 1992). Results clearly indicated, however, that foster parents in the study were not motivated by compensation alone—it was the increased compensation combined with extra support that seemed to contribute to their longevity, which echoes findings about retention above.

An important issue related to compensation is the professionalization of foster care. There is debate among researchers, policy makers, and foster parents themselves as to whether or not the provision of foster care should be viewed as a job—and paid as such—or if it is simply an act of altruism and an extension of family life (Kirton, 2001; Wilson & Evetts, 2006). While the limited research on the topic of compensation supports the Chamberlain et al. findings above—that it isn't typically the primary motivator for fostering—there still seems to be some ambiguity about the role of fostering itself and what, if any, payment should accompany it. Much of the inquiry with foster parents on this topic has taken place in the UK, and findings are equivocal at best. Some foster parents report that they would take on this role regardless of compensation; others state that given the challenges that often accompany fostering and the skills necessary to successfully deal with those challenges, it is only fair that they be compensated (Kirton, 2001; Wilson & Evetts, 2006). However, as will be noted in the qualitative study findings at the end of this chapter, youth are often keenly aware that their caregivers are financially compensated and frequently feel that their only function in the family is that of conduit to a paycheck, or as described by a foster youth in one qualitative study, the foster parent is "getting paid to pretend to like her" (Storer et al., 2014, p. 113). Thus, there is a fine line between recognizing the role of a foster parent and the skill level and commitment it requires to fulfill that role well, and making the youth feel like s/he is a job.

Promising Practices in Training of Foster Families

While training has been identified as an important factor in the retention of foster parents, there is little to no regulation over what kind of training they should receive. Federal policy, in the form of the Foster Care Independence Act of 1999 (H.R. 3443), dictates that before a child is placed with foster parents, the latter need to be prepared with knowledge and skills in order to appropriately meet the needs of the child; further, this support should continue, as necessary, after the child is placed with them (Dorsey et al., 2008; Grimm, 2003). However, states are given considerable leeway in how they implement this mandate. Almost all states require some sort of training as part of the licensing process for foster parents, with the required number of hours ranging from 4 to 30 (Dorsey et al., 2008; Grimm, 2003). Furthermore, in order for foster parents to maintain licensure, additional in-service training is required, with state requirements ranging from 6 to 20 hours annually (Dorsey et al., 2008).

There are two training curricula that are most widely used to fulfill this training requirement: (1) *Model Approach to Partnerships in Parenting/Group Preparation and Selection of Foster and/or Adoptive Families (MAPP/GPS)* and (2) *Foster Parent Resource for Information, Development, and Education (PRIDE)*. The MAPP/GPS training was developed in the mid-1980s and revised in the mid-1990s by the Child Welfare Institute; PRIDE was originally developed in 1993 and was revised in 2003 by the Child Welfare League of America. The overarching goal of both is to help new/potential foster parents to develop the basic knowledge and skills in order to successfully foster (e.g., knowledge about the foster care system, how to deal with challenging child behaviors; Christenson & McMurtry, 2007; Dorsey et al., 2008; Puddy & Jackson, 2003). Despite wide use of these curricula, little research has been conducted to assess their effectiveness. Further, the research that has been done has shown minimal to no impact on foster parent knowledge and skills (see Dorsey et al., 2008; Puddy & Jackson, 2003). Instead, both curricula seem to be more geared toward helping individuals make an informed decision about whether or not to foster, as well as the policies and procedures associated with being a foster parent (Dorsey et al., 2008; Puddy & Jackson, 2003).

Buehler, Rhodes, Orme, and Cuddeback (2006) reviewed existing literature on foster parent training programs and developed a list of 12 training domains, which include competencies such as "promoting social and emotional development, managing ambiguity and loss for the foster child, and managing the demands of fostering on personal and familial well-being" (p. 523). Many of these topics echo what foster parents have voiced as training needs. While there is no existing training curriculum that necessarily covers all of the competencies that Buehler and colleagues describe, there is a slowly growing body of literature on evidence-based practices (EBPs) in foster parent training.

A promising practice in foster parent training is the Keeping Foster and Kin Parents Supported and Trained (KEEP) program. This program is comprised of 16 weeks of training, supervision, and support in behavior-management methods using non-punitive discipline methods (Chamberlain, Price, Reid, & Landsverk, 2008; Price et al., 2008). Youth assigned to KEEP were found to be more likely to exit care for a positive reason, such as a return to home, kinship care, or adoption. The causal mechanisms were thought to be that participation in KEEP increased foster parent competencies in managing behavior problems, which in turn contributed to the likelihood of the youth making the transition back to their birth parents, a relative, or being adopted.

Trauma-Focused Cognitive Behavioral Therapy (TF-CBT) is an EBP that includes specific trauma treatment components as well as a parenting component (Cohen, Mannarino, & Deblinger, 2006; Dorsey & Deblinger, 2012). It is a short-term intervention (12 to 25 sessions) targeting children and youth from ages 3 to 21 who have had significant emotional or behavioral difficulties related to one or more traumatic life events (see Cohen et al., 2006; Dorsey, Briggs, & Woods, 2011 for more details). Trauma-Focused Cognitive Behavioral Therapy has been found to be effective in reducing trauma symptoms, placement changes, and runaway attempts for youth in foster care (Dorsey et al., 2011; Dorsey et al., 2014). However, studies have also found implementation challenges, including high attrition rates and difficulty engaging foster parents in the intervention (Weiner, Schneider, & Lyons, 2009). Dorsey et al. (2014) examined the impact of supplementing TF-CBT with evidence-based engagement strategies such as a pre-treatment telephone call and a discussion of potential barriers to treatment. The youth who were receiving the TF-CBT plus supplement were more likely to remain in care. However, if there was a disruption in placement, it remained difficult to engage the new foster parents.

Although individual agencies cannot change the larger child welfare system, there are opportunities for agencies to play a positive role. One strategy is recruiting and hiring foster parents who have positive attitudes toward therapeutic interventions. Behavioral-based interviewing may help to identify foster parents who can most easily be engaged in EBPs; criteria for performance evaluation could include willingness to access such interventions. The private agency supervisors of foster parents can also advocate for the competency of the foster parent and the value of the EBP. Coaching and reinforcing EBP parental interventions and helping to identify and remove concrete barriers (e.g., childcare or transportation) to EBP participation fall within this domain.

Asking Youth about their Experiences in Foster Care: A Qualitative Exploration

This chapter so far has focused on describing system, agency, and parent perspectives on foster care practice models. However, youth voice about out-of-home care is critical, yet frequently absent in the research (Rauktis, Fusco, Cahalane, Bennett, & Reinhart, 2011). The goals of foster care are to provide a safe, permanent, and nurturing environment for children and youth and to support the youth's development into early adulthood. Successful youth development depends on committed adults who are involved in a youth's life, which may not readily occur for youth growing up in foster care. As this chapter is focused on the role that agencies play in providing youth with quality foster care, it was important to answer the question: "According to foster youth, what is the role of foster care parents in supporting successful youth development?"

The data used in answering this question were collected as part of a measurement development study of youth perception of out-of-home placements (Rauktis et al., 2011). These data were re-analyzed for this chapter, with a particular focus on youth's experiences with and perceptions of foster parents, and using the lens of three theoretical constructs—emerging adulthood theory, therapeutic alliance, and capital development—all of which are thought to be critical to successful youth development. These theories have been identified by other researchers as being important to understanding the experiences of youth transitioning from foster care to independence (Schelbe, 2013), as well as the promotion of emotional and behavioral well-being (Southerland, Mustillo, Farmer, Stambaugh, & Murray, 2009). Foster parents are the individuals who have the best opportunity to support successful development for young adults, and youth voice about foster parent behaviors and characteristics is needed.

Theoretical Perspectives

Some of the reasons youth give for exiting child welfare services when they could remain until the age of 21 are frustration and a desire for change in their life circumstances (McCoy, McMillen & Spitznagel, 2008). Geenen and Powers (2007) found that child-welfare-involved youth transitioning into adulthood reported frustration that they had little self-determination and did not feel that they were heard or respected, which also contributed to their leaving care. Goodkind, Schelbe, and Shook (2011) found that one of the reasons youth left care was due to a desire for autonomy and independence from system constraints. However, the youth equated "adulthood" with "independence," a finding also observed by Samuels and Pryce (2008), who found that young adults who had once been in the child welfare system espoused an attitude of survivalist self-reliance in order to be independent. Both groups of researchers propose that by confusing independence with adulthood, the youth were negating the importance of supportive relationships that could help them in their transition to adulthood (Goodkind et al., 2001). Moreover, a reluctance to be emotionally engaged, most likely a form of protection from further harm, seemed to result in limited connections to potentially helpful individuals and communities. Goodkind and colleagues suggest that a goal for youth should be "connected autonomy" (2001, p. 1047) as they transition. The chapter authors propose that in furthering this idea of connected autonomy for older youth in foster care, several models could provide an overarching theoretical framework for a practice model.

The first is the theory of emerging adulthood (Arnett, 2000; Arnett & Taber, 1994). This theory posits that the transition from adolescence to adulthood is an extended process that is not achieved at a set time point, like an 18th birthday, graduation from college, or aging out of care. Instead, the years from 18 to 25 are seen as a period of exploration and gradual progress toward independence; this is a time when family and friends support the young adult as s/he continues to develop cognitively, emotionally, and behaviorally (Arnett & Taber, 1994).

A second important theoretical construct is therapeutic alliance. Commonly used in the psycho-therapy literature, therapeutic alliance is considered to be an essential element in achieving positive therapeutic outcomes (see Martin, Garske, & Davis [2000] for a meta-analysis). In research specific to foster and residential care, therapeutic alliance has been defined in terms of a positive emotional bond, mutual agreement on tasks and goals, and perceived sense of openness and truthfulness between the youth and the helping professional (Manso, Rauktis, & Boyd, 2008). Although the majority of research has focused on alliances between adults and therapists, there is a small but growing body of research on alliance between helping adults and youth in residential and foster care (Manso et al., 2008; Rauktis, Andrade, Doucette, McDonough & Reinhart, 2005; Southerland et al., 2009). In describing their positive alliance with helping adults in residential care, youth identified a connection to the adult, based on intrapersonal characteristics of the adult, as well as the behaviors of the adult and how they interacted with the youth (Manso et al., 2008). A positive therapeutic relationship between a parent figure and a youth has also been found to be associated with better emotional and behavioral functioning for the youth (Southerland et al., 2009).

The final theoretical construct is that of capital development, which has typically been conceptualized as economic, social, and cultural (Bourdieu, 1986). Economic capital refers to assets and money, whereas social capital is about social connections and networks. Cultural capital is an understanding of social norms and the ability to practice socially desirable skills; it is developed through parenting, educational systems, and by functioning in everyday situations (Bourdieu, 1986). All are thought to be important, but Schelbe (2013) believes that a related fourth type, human capital, is particularly critical for youth aging out of foster care. Human capital is a form of cultural capital, perceived to be a person's skill level, which is related to education and employment, social skills, and opportunities afforded by class and race. Helping youth to develop cultural capital was found to be a missing component in many transitional and residential programs for adolescents aging out of foster and residential care (Schelbe, 2013). Living in a group home or foster home may not necessarily translate to the development of these kinds of independent living skills. Foster youth also have limited economic capital (Schelbe, 2013) and don't have access to a parent's economic capital when they experience financial problems. Lacking capital and without the extended support often given to "typical" young adults, foster youth struggle when leaving foster care (Schelbe, 2013). Ways in which foster parents can help youth to develop these different forms of social capital should be further explored.

Data Collection and Analysis

Young adults were recruited to participate in the focus groups if they were aged 18 or older, were currently in or had exited from child welfare services in the past 5 years, and had experienced at least one out-of-home placement of any type during their time in care. Recruitment for the study was done through the Independent Living Coordinators located in six regions of Pennsylvania (West, Southwest, Northwest, Central, Southeast, and Northeast). Six focus groups were then conducted over a period of 4 months in 2010. Each group was facilitated by a researcher and co-facilitated by a student who was also a foster care alumnus. The groups typically lasted 90 minutes and were held in a variety of settings, including community centers, residential provider agencies, and a county human services office. At the end of the focus group, participants completed a short demographic survey and received a $25 Target gift card for their participation in the group and for completing the survey. The study was approved by both the University of Pittsburgh Institutional Review Board and Casey Family Programs Institutional Review Board. The average size of the group was kept small (six participants) to allow for extended discussion of each question. Ten questions were asked; three pertained to the type and characteristics of the placements, while the remaining questions asked about various aspects of their experiences in care, particularly as they related to restrictiveness. Although the intent of the study was to define restrictiveness, the discussion produced a "thick" description of different placement types and relationships with foster parents and caseworkers. The focus groups were digitally recorded and professionally transcribed.

Thematic Analysis was used as the primary qualitative analytic method (Braun & Clarke, 2006). Thematic Analysis is a flexible and straightforward method of analysis that allows the analyst to take an essentialist or realist approach, reporting experiences and the reality of the participants. In this analysis, we were interested in hearing what youth identify as the characteristics and behaviors of foster parents that support successful development of young adults, using the theoretical frameworks of emerging adulthood, therapeutic alliance, and capital development. As a result, this analysis focused on reviewing the transcripts in order to answer the following sub-questions. First, when youth talk about a positive experience in foster care, what are the characteristics that they describe the foster parent(s) as having, and what are the behaviors that the parents demonstrate? Second, what do youth view as indicators that the foster parent is committed to them and to their development? Third, what do foster parents do in order to help the youth develop the personal and social capital that will help them to navigate aging out of the child welfare system into independent living, and do they offer ongoing support?

Participants

A total of 40 young adults, with an age range of 18 to 20, participated in the focus groups. The participants were primarily female (64%) and African American (62%). A sizable percentage were still living in a foster care home (47%), with smaller percentages living independently (22%), in supervised independent living (13%), or with birth or former foster families (13%), and the remaining 5% living in shelters, on the couches of friends, or on the street. A little over one-third of the participants (39%) had been in care four years or less, suggesting that they came into care as an adolescent, while 42% had been in care nine to 15 years. The participants had experienced a range of living environments, from living with relatives, to short stays in shelter or respite homes, kinship foster care, therapeutic foster care, non-kin foster care, supervised independent living, small group homes, residential treatment centers, wilderness camps, jails, and homeless shelters. The majority of participants had multiple placement moves and, as a result, had experienced a variety of placement types, with all of them having had at least one stay in foster care.

Topic 1

When youth talk about a positive experience in foster care, what are the characteristics that they describe the foster parent(s) as having and what are the behaviors that the parents demonstrate?

Much of the discussion across all of the groups was focused on negative characteristics of foster parents, which made it difficult for those who had positive experiences to talk about what makes a parent and a placement "good." However, with persistent probing from the facilitators, the youth did provide information about positive experiences with foster parents, and they were able to identify specific behaviors and characteristics of foster parents that relate to youth development. The positive characteristics and behaviors that emerged from the discussions were identified and then organized into themes.

Theme 1.1: Foster Parents "Naming" them as Son or Daughter—"Oh, This Is my Son."

When talking about good foster care placements, one indicator of a good foster parent was when they referred to the foster child as "son" or "daughter" in public, instead of introducing them as a "foster child." This is an outward symbol of an emotional connection as illustrated by this exchange between several youth in one group:

E: When you are not treated like an outsider, when they call you "son" in public . . .

T: Yep, my foster parents do that. "That's my daughter," and they are White.

C: Another thing, though, is like, say, when you're out with your foster parent and say like their friend or something, I know . . . my foster mom did this *all* the time . . . "Oh, this is *my son*! She's parading me around saying this is my son, you know like, check out *my son* . . . When they have that relationship to call you their son or daughter in front of somebody they know or they're introducing you to kind like, just makes you feel good like, this *is* like my mom, this *is* like my dad, like I'm part of their family.

F: Yeah, the one foster family I was at, when me and my sisters were all together, she would go . . . like she went to church and when she got out, she would go, "Did you meet my girls yet? They're my girls."

This was mutual behavior, in that the youth begin to name the foster parent as "Mom" or "Dad".

C: Yeah, my foster mom was like that. She's like my mom.

R: Like I actually call them mom, sister, dad and uncle . . . .like, it's just family.

F: I'm in foster care now and like I have a mom . . . it's not something I wanted, I never you know wanted a family or nothing, but you know, I got it and it's good.

In some cases, the foster family became their family when they aged out of care.

P: I had a friend who was in foster care and he stayed. He loved his foster mom and it came to a point he was out of DHS but he still goes there. Still goes there for Thanksgiving. That's his family. He's like, "This is my family," I'm not in foster care anymore and she still calls him "my son, this is my son."

Being "named" as one of the family was felt to create a sense of normalcy and belonging.

F: Most of the foster families I went to that were genuine foster parents, they didn't really like the term "Oh, these are my foster kids" or something like that. They wanted to make it as comfortable and as family-oriented, normal as possible. The good ones that I've had, I always had that sense of home, and that sense of, you know, belonging-ness.

However, belonging to a family and being "named" as a child of the foster family did not mean that they gave up dreams of being with their birth families. While youth wanted to be part of the new family, to be named as a child of the foster parent, and may call a foster parent "Mom" or "Dad," they still wanted to be with their birth families. Several of them spoke of this apparent paradox:

C: I definitely wanted to be back with my mom and my brother . . . that feeling, felt so strong, when I was younger, that I wanted it back so bad, but I never could get it back . . . when your real family is not really there for you, it hurts. But you just continue to dream like, she's

> gonna' be there anyway, or we're gonna' get back together, but that was mine. I wanted definitely to be back with my family.
>
> F: It was really hard for me ... I would never change anything because I know that, like, my mom, my mom's problem was drugs, so when she was sober and she was clean, she was a good mother, she was there, she did what she had to do. But then, when she was back on it ... I know that I would not grow up with the skills and knowledge that I have today but like, I just wish I could have grown up there.

Theme 1.2: Demonstrating Consistency across All the Youth in the Home

Being part of a family means that you are treated the same as all the other youth in the home, and that distinctions are not made between the foster children and the biological children of the foster parent:

> T: What tells me when a foster parent loves you is when you do something and they reprimand you, and their actual kids does it and they reprimand their kid too. They don't just get on you. You get the same consequences as they do their own kid. They raise you like their own child. I think that's love because in some foster homes they reprimand you and their kid will turn around do the same thing, but not reprimand their kid.

This consistency, fairness, and non-exclusion extended to clothes, shoes, and food, which were outward signs of being included in the family.

> E: The thing that touched my heart, my grandparents [foster parents] would go shopping at Foot Locker, big name brand stores. We never would go to Gabriel Brothers [discount store]. There are some foster parents, you know, their kids get the hippest clothes and you get hand me downs.

Theme 1.3: Race Was Not Important

Race was mentioned as a factor by youth in three of the six groups, in that having a foster parent of the same race or a different race was not a factor in being in a good foster home or building a good relationship with a foster parent. How they were treated by the parent seemed to be more important than sharing racial or cultural similarities. One youth noted how her foster father would be sure to say (and even argue with people) that she was his daughter, even though she was of another race. Interestingly, another youth identified that having a White foster parent was an asset in creating cultural capital:

> E: She taught me the little things that people really catch on to and she was telling me as a White woman. Because the higher ups are predominately White and she was teaching me as a White woman.

This could be considered a form of "bridging social capital," when youth are fostered by parents who make it a point to make the code of privilege clear.

Topic 2

What do youth view as indicators that the foster parent is committed to them and to their development?

Theme 2.1: Motivation for Fostering Is Not Primarily Monetary

All of the groups discussed how foster parents need to commit to the youth and the relationship, and not to the paycheck. In some groups, there was a lot of discussion about how people only did it for the money, how foster parents took the youth's money and used it for gambling or for their own uses rather than for food, clothes, and shoes for the youth, and didn't parent them although they were being paid to do so. Youth were also troubled by parents who made the fact that they were being paid obvious to the youth and reduced them to a "paycheck":

> T: [W]hy waste your time going to classes and paying money for doing this and that just to say "I'm a foster parent." You don't even get enjoyment, hope, or a feeling out of it. I mean, I don't understand. How could you get any type of enjoyment or peace if that's what your motive was, because of a paycheck coming in?
>
> P: My foster mom used to say, "They don't pay me enough for this." Every time I did something, she'd say, "They don't pay me enough for this," so you're here for the paycheck.
>
> H: Half the foster parents that's in there don't even work. You all's income is the foster care agency money ... and that's how they look at it. They look at it as a check. She's here because that's a check.

Youth believed that foster parenting should be more than a job, but the reality is that foster parents are compensated for their role. There were some examples of how foster parents can balance this paradox of being a "paid parent," so that it became clear to the youth that their relationship was not about the paycheck:

> A: Like, when she got that check in the mail for me, she put it right on the table, was like, "Now what do you need?" She was straight up ... it would still be her check but she would ask me, "Y'all doing something with school lately? You need some new shoes?" ... every week she gave me, I think I got $30 ... she told me when it was time for me to graduate, that whatever I had in my bank account she would double it.

Theme 2.2: They Make a Commitment and Make Good on it

Unfortunately, the youth had many examples of a lack of commitment to share with us, with many of the stories focusing on being asked to leave with no explanation, or losing the foster family when they aged out of care. The youth in the groups admitted that they were not easy to parent, because of their anger, disruptive behaviors, running away, and/or difficulty in forming attachments. However, they felt that it was the responsibility of the foster parent to understand and manage behaviors, and to persist in the relationship even when it was difficult.

> T: Work with the child. So many foster parents give up on kids so easy. The kids are going to have issues. Let's all just get over it. The kids are not coming to your house as angels.
>
> B: A home is a place where you know you can come back to no matter what you did, no matter what has happened, they'll always want you back.

Having a committed foster parent meant that the parent made the commitment up-front:

> C: [S]o it wasn't the whole transition to the new house, it was just the fact of not knowin' how long you're goin' to stay there. Now my foster mom that I live with now, she was the only foster parent to tell me that this would be my last placement. And I didn't think she was

telling the truth. I thought I was probably goin' to go back to my mom in my senior year or something. But it turned out to be my last placement. Her sayin' that, kinda' like, you know. It made me feel good kind of thing.

They also felt that commitment to the youth was demonstrated when the relationship continued even when the compensation ended:

> E: I wasn't kicked out, but when I was discharged from care when I was 18, and before [name] won her case [legal case allowing the youth to remain in care], they told me I would be out of care, but my grandmother [foster parent] chose to keep me regardless of getting that stipend. She loves me regardless of the money. I was thinking to myself, "How many foster children experience this?"
> S: I'm going to be going to college. And my first thoughts were, "Where am I going to go at Christmas, where am I going to go on vacation?" She's like, "You're coming back."
> A: [A]nd then she was still there for me like while I was in treatment all that. Like, she went beyond the call of duty of a foster mom. I'm in treatment now, so like they're not getting a check for me . . . but yet she was still coming up, still kept watch.

Topic 3

What do foster parents do in order to help the youth to develop the capital that will help them navigate aging out of the child welfare system into independent living and young adulthood?

Theme 3.1: Teach "Values" and Life Skills

Values are not the same as "rules," which are about what you can and cannot do and the consequences. Values are about how to live one's life or cultural capital. Several youth mentioned this as important to their development.

> J: My foster mom, she taught me the values that I have. She wouldn't pay attention to me until I said "Ma'am." It helps me to this day to always remember my manners. She basically laid the foundation. Since she passed away, it was for other people to build on. So my second foster family taught me how to become more of a man, I guess you could say, and helped me to realize that life isn't just a game. It's serious also. So they helped me to see things from a man's perspective and stop being such a kid. My third foster parent let me see what freedom is, not to abuse it and how basically to be on my own.

The youth also identified that it was important that foster parents help them with practical skills such as budgeting, managing money, establishing a credit history, cooking, learning how to rent an apartment, and drive. These skills help to develop human, economic, and cultural capital for youth, which help them make the transition into independence.

> C: She's helping me with my credit score. My credit's like, amazing. I have a credit card that I do not have in my possession. She uses it to buy gas and then pays it off so it looks like I'm paying the bill. She helped . . . put me on her car insurance.

Some skills were more subtle, such as when one youth describes how her foster parent taught her how to understand what wasn't being said in social and business situations.

A: She taught me how to learn a snaky landlord when you see one. She taught me to how to read between the lines . . . She taught me how to really read stuff, even if people don't say things.

Despite complaining about it, most of the youth viewed chores and helping around the house as positive and as part of their life skills preparation:

B: My foster dad, he like, I had chores and he always told me, "I'm not doing this for me, I'm doing this for you and for your tomorrow."
R: My foster mom teaches me to do things . . . I know how to cook . . . budget my money. I got my first job ever as a waitress and I already knew how to do half the stuff, 'cause she taught me how to remember things . . . A lot of the stuff she prepared me for.
L: I think that a foster mom or dad was like that, like basically being a regular mom, teaching you life skills, like a girl and a mom . . . I think, put me in the kitchen, teach me how to cook, don't keep screaming at me, show that you care.

Discussion

The degree to which youth are positively connected to others, exposed to regulating forces, and encouraged to develop autonomy will facilitate healthy adult development (Barber & Olsen 1997). Connection is a consistent and positive emotional bond with significant adults, and regulation is having fair and consistent limits and expectations. This is what the youth in the study have identified as "good foster parenting"—being "named" as part of the family, having fair and equal expectations for all the youth in the family, consistency in the relationship that is not perceived as a business transaction, and being prepared to live independently. They may wish to remain part of the family even when they age out of care.

However, foster parenting is not "typical" parenting. It differs in critical ways, primarily because it is conducted within a larger system of child welfare and the legal systems. Birth parents and extended families may remain in the picture, if not in terms of physical presence, in the memories of the youth. Foster parents are employees of an agency and they must follow agency policies, as well as public child welfare agency policies. They are trained, supervised, and paid—unlike a birth parent. Finally, the youth themselves may have emotional and behavioral challenges. They may act in ways that challenge and exhaust even the most committed of foster parents. The behavioral health problems, if left untreated, may mean that managing acute behaviors takes precedence over developing life skills such as driving, vocational skills, part-time employment, and/or community involvement. Consistency and fairness across all the foster and biological youth in the family may be difficult when one youth may not be allowed the same level of independence or privilege due to safety or legal concerns.

However, youth testimony suggests that good foster parents "parent" like typical parents, even though the circumstances in which they parent are far from typical. They transcend the system and individual circumstances, and try to put into place the important aspects of parenting: creating a sense of family, emotional connection and alliance; they demonstrate fairness, consistency, and transparency. They have an eye on the future and prepare the youth for what they will need to be successfully independent. They continue some aspects of support when the youth ages out of care, offering a home during college semester breaks, providing a holiday dinner, or acting as a sounding board. A longitudinal ethnographic study of youth who have aged out of care found that just because a youth has accomplished a goal and life is going smoothly for her/him, it does not mean that support is not needed now or will not be needed in the future (Schelbe, 2013). "Success" was found to be fluid, with a swift downturn often occurring after a youth experienced an event like losing a job, leaving school, or ending a relationship. Schelbe (2013) found that youths' lives could fall apart rapidly; she attributed this swift descent to a lack of ongoing support and resources that families would typically provide during periods of economic and emotional stress.

Conclusions

As public child welfare agencies move toward privatizing some or all of their services, it becomes more important to look at the role of private child welfare agencies with both foster parents and foster youth. The recruitment and retention of high-quality foster parents are dependent on several factors. Appealing to intrinsic motivators of potential foster parents seems to be most effective, as long as there is a clear understanding of roles and expectations (i.e., parents don't feel like they are "rescuing" a child or "giving" them a family when the child already has a family of his or her own) (Casey Family Programs, 2014; MacGregor et al., 2006; Marcenko et al., 2009; Rodger et al., 2006). Utilizing current foster parents to help recruit potential foster parents is also effective, in that parents are more likely to see them as peers and trust their assessment of what fostering entails (Casey Family Programs, 2014; Rodger et al., 2006; Sullivan et al., 2014). Retention relies heavily on support, communication, and mutual respect between foster parents and agency workers. The research clearly shows that foster parents often feel disrespected by the agencies for whom they work; they want to be seen as an integral part of the child's team, and want their voices to be heard (Denby, Rindfleisch, & Bean, 1999; Gibbs & Wildfire, 2007; MacGregor et al., 2006). While compensation is important, it is typically not the primary reason that parents start or continue to foster (Chamberlain et al., 1992; Kirton, 2001; Wilson & Evetts, 2006).

Training is also crucial, both for new and continuing foster parents. Commonly used existing curricula may help individuals decide whether or not fostering is for them; however, these are not sufficient for foster parents to do their jobs well. Foster parents need more in-depth training on how to deal with challenging emotional/behavioral challenges in youth, how to deal with loss (their own as well as that of the youth in their care), and managing the multiple demands that fostering places on self and family life (Buehler et al., 2003; Denby & Rindfleisch, 1996; Gibbs & Wildfire, 2007; Rhodes et al., 2001; Vanderfaeilllie et al., 2015). Promising practices in training for foster parents include involving foster parents in therapeutic interventions with the youth in their care, and learning more specialized techniques to manage challenging behaviors. It is important to note that both of these practices incorporate foster parents as a vital part of the treatment team; this could be an additional reason for their success.

A significant challenge that emerged from both the literature as well as the qualitative study presented here is that foster parents need to traverse a fine line—while they want (and deserve to be) treated as professionals (and compensation may be part of this), foster youth are frequently all too aware of their position in the foster family, and are wary and resentful of being perceived as a "job." Additionally, although they often want to be viewed and treated as a true family member, they may also continue to yearn for relationships with their "real" families. Similar to all youth, they wish to be independent, yet they want and need continued support from families. Foster parenting is neither simple nor intuitive. Those who hire and train foster parents must recognize the ambiguities in their roles as parents to foster children and employees of an agency which is under contract to a larger public system of child welfare. As part of ongoing training or coaching, foster parents need assistance in managing ambiguity, conflict, and contradiction in order to provide consistent and nurturing care. This "in-between" space of foster parenting can be very difficult. However, the findings from the youth study suggest that parents can move into the space of being parents, as evidenced by "naming" the youth as part of the family, and by making a commitment to the youth. Recognizing this process as well as the contradiction in feelings and roles should be part of foster parent training; it needs to be recognized, validated, and understood by the agency workers who have relationships with the youth and foster parents.

The theoretical lens of emerging adulthood supports the notion that independence does not equal lack of connection, and that interdependence into adulthood is normative. A positive working relationship with foster parents or therapists has been associated with better outcomes for clients (Martin et al., 2000). Schelbe's (2013) research highlights how the lack of social and economic capital can result in a rapid downward trajectory for youth after they leave care. The results from the present study suggest that a fruitful area for further research would be to explore how foster parents can help youth to be connected to them, the family, and the community, yet at the same time, be self-determining. The research should also include how systems must change in order to support youth voice, autonomy, and self-determination. The child welfare system was created to care for children (Goodkind et al., 2011), but youth and young adults do not have the same dependency needs as children. As youth age in care, recognizing the need for connection, interdependence, autonomy, self-determination, and voice will be critical if we are to move to training and practice models supporting youth development.

Acknowledgments

The qualitative study described in this chapter was supported in part by Casey Family Programs and the University of Pittsburgh School of Social Work, Research Development Fund.

References

Arnett, J. J. (2000). Emerging adulthood: A theory of development from the late teens through the twenties. *American Psychologist, 55*, 469–480. Available at http://psycnet.apa.org/doi/10.1037/0003-066X.55.5.469

Arnett, J. J. & Taber, S. (1994). Adolescence terminable and interminable: When does adolescence end? *Journal of Youth and Adolescence, 23*, 517–537.

Barber, B. K. & Olsen, J. A. (1997). Socialization in context: Connection, regulation, and autonomy in the family, school and neighborhood, and with peers. *Journal of Adolescent Research, 12*, 287–315.

Bourdieu, P. (1986). The forms of capital. In I. Szeman & T. Kaposy (Eds.), *Cultural theory* (pp. 81–94). Chichester, UK: Wiley–Blackwell.

Braun, V. & Clarke, V. (2006). Using thematic analysis in psychology. *Qualitative Research in Psychology, 3*, 77–101.

Buehler, C., Cox, M. E., & Cuddeback, G. (2003). Foster parents' perceptions of factors that promote or inhibit successful fostering. *Qualitative Social Work, 21*, 61–83. https://doi.org/10.1177/1473325003002001281

Buehler, C., Rhodes, K. W., Orme, J. G., & Cuddeback, G. (2006). The potential for successful family foster care: Conceptualizing competency domains for foster parents. *Child Welfare, 85*, 523–558.

Casey Family Programs. (2014, December). *Effective practices in foster parent recruitment, infrastructure, and retention.* Seattle, WA: Author.

Chamberlain, P., Moreland, S., & Reid, K. (1992). Enhanced services and stipends for foster parents: Effects on retention rates and outcomes for children. *Child Welfare, 71*, 387–401.

Chamberlain, P., Price, J. M., Reid, J. B., & Landsverk, J. (2008). Cascading implementation of a foster and kinship parent intervention. *Child Welfare, 87*, 27–48.

Child Welfare Information Gateway. (2012). *What is child welfare? A guide for educators.* Washington, DC: U.S. Department of Health & Human Services, Children's Bureau.

Child Welfare Information Gateway. (2016). *Foster care statistics 2014.* Washington, DC: U.S. Department of Health & Human Services, Children's Bureau.

Christenson, B. & McMurtry, J. (2007). A comparative evaluation of preservice training of kinship and nonkinship foster/adoptive families. *Child Welfare, 86*, 125–140.

Cohen, J. A., Mannarino, A. P., & Deblinger, E. (2006). *Treating trauma and traumatic grief in children and adolescents.* New York: Guilford Press.

Courtney, M. E. (2000). Managed care and child welfare services: What are the issues? *Children and Youth Services Review, 22*, 87–91. https://doi.org/10.1016/S0190-7409(00)00067-0

Daniel, E. (2011). Gentle iron will: Foster parents' perspectives. *Children and Youth Services Review, 33*, 910–917. https://doi.org/10.1016/j.childyouth.2010.12.009

Denby, R. & Rindfleisch, N. (1996). African Americans' foster parenting experiences: Research findings and implications for policy and practice. *Children and Youth Services Review, 18*, 523–551. https://doi.org/10.1016/0190-7409(96)00021-7

Denby, R., Rindfleisch, N., & Bean, G. (1999). Predictors of foster parents' satisfaction and intent to continue to foster. *Child Abuse & Neglect, 23*, 287–303. https://doi.org/10.1016/S0145-2134(98)00126-4

Dorsey, S., Briggs, E. C., & Woods, B. A. (2011). Cognitive behavioral treatment for posttraumatic stress disorder in children and adolescents. *Child and Adolescent Psychiatric Clinics of North America, 20*, 255–269. https://doi.org/10.1016/j.chc.2011.01.006

Dorsey, S. & Deblinger, E. (2012). Children in foster care. In J. A. Cohen, A. P. Mannarino, & E. Deblinger (Eds.), *Trauma-focused CBT for children and adolescents: Treatment applications* (pp. 49–72). New York: Guilford Press.

Dorsey, S., Farmer, E. M. Z., Barth, R. P., Greene, K., Reid, J., & Landsverk, J. (2008). Current status and evidence base of training for foster and treatment foster parents. *Children and Youth Services Review, 30*, 1403–1416. https://doi.org/10.1016/j.childyouth.2008.04.008

Dorsey, S., Pullmann, M. D., Berliner, L., Koschmann, E., McKay, M., & Deblinger, E. (2014). Engaging foster parents in treatment: A randomized trial of supplementing trauma-focused cognitive behavioral therapy with evidence-based engagement strategies. *Child Abuse & Neglect, 38*, 1508–1520. https://doi.org/10.1016/j.chiabu.2014.03.020

Feldman, S. W., Price, K. M., & Ruppel, J. (2016). Not too late: Effects of a diligent recruiting program for hard to place youth. *Children and Youth Services Review, 65*, 26–31. https://doi.org/10.1016/j.childyouth.2016.03.008

Foster Care Independence Act of 1999 (H.R. 3443), P.L. 106-169. (1999).

Friesen, L. D. (2001). Privatized child welfare services: Foster parents' perspectives. *Child Welfare, 80*, 309–324.

Geenen, S. & Powers, L. E. (2007). "Tomorrow is another problem": The experiences of youth in foster care during their transition to adulthood. *Children and Youth Services Review, 29*, 1085–1101.

Gibbs, D. & Wildfire, J. (2007). Length of service for foster parents: Using administrative data to understand retention. *Children and Youth Services Review, 29*, 588–599. https://doi.org/10.1016/j.childyouth.2006.11.002

Goodkind, S., Schelbe, L., & Shook, J. (2011). Why youth leave care: Understandings of adulthood and transition success and challenges among youth aging out of care. *Children and Youth Services Review, 33*, 1039–1048. https://doi.org/10.1016/j.childyouth.2011.01.010

Grimm, B. (2003). Child and family services reviews: Part II in a series. Foster parent training: What the CFS reviews do and don't tell us. *Journal of the National Center on Youth Law, XXIV*(1).

Humphrey, K. R., Turnbull, A. P., & Turnbull, H. R. III. (2006). Perspectives of foster-care providers, service providers, and judges regarding privatized foster-care services. *Journal of Disability Policy Studies, 17*, 2–17. https://doi.org/10.1177/10442073060170010101

Kirton, D. (2001). Love and money: Payment, motivation and the fostering task. *Child and Family Social Work, 6*, 199–208. doi:10.1046/j.1365-2206.2001.00208.x

Lewandowski, C. A. & GlenMaye, L. F. (2002). Teams in child welfare settings: Interprofessional and collaborative processes. *Families in Society, 83*, 245–256. https://doi.org/10.1606/1044-3894.25

MacGregor, T. E., Rodger, S., Cummings, A. L., & Leschied, A. W. (2006). The needs of foster parents: A qualitative study of motivation, support, and retention. *Qualitative Social Work, 5*, 351–368. https://doi.org/10.1177/1473325006067365

Manso, A., Rauktis, M. E., & Boyd, A. S. (2008). Youth expectations about therapeutic alliance in a residential setting. *Residential Treatment for Children and Youth, 25*, 55–72. http://dx.doi.org/10.1080/08865710802209826

Marcenko, M. O., Brennan, K. D., & Lyons, S. J. (2009). *Foster parent recruitment and retention: Developing resource families for Washington State's children in care*. Seattle, WA: Partners for Our Children.

Martin, D. J., Garske, J. P., & Davis, K. (2000). The relation of therapeutic alliance with outcomes and other variables: A meta-analytic review. *Journal of Consulting and Clinical Psychology, 68*(3), 438–450. Available at http://psycnet.apa.org/doi/10.1037/0022-006X.68.3.438

McCoy, H., McMillen, J. C., & Spitznagel, E. L. (2008). Older youth leaving the foster care system: Who, what, when, where and why? *Children and Youth Services Review, 30*, 735–745. https://doi.org/10.1016/j.childyouth.2007.12.003

National Resource Center for Diligent Recruitment. (n.d.). *Diligent recruitment grantees*. Retrieved September 26, 2016, from http://nrcdr.org/diligent-recruitment/dr-grantees

Orme, J. G., Cherry, D. J., & Krcek, T. E. (2013). Who is willing to foster children with disabilities? *Journal of Public Child Welfare, 7*, 566–585. http://dx.doi.org/10.1080/15548732.2013.843494

Price, J. M., Chamberlain, P., Landsverk, J., Reid, J. B., Leve, L., & Laurent, H. (2008). Effects of a foster parent training intervention on placement changes of children in foster care. *Child Maltreatment, 13*, 64–75. https://doi.org/10.1177/1077559507310612

Puddy, R. W. & Jackson, Y. (2003). The development of parenting skills in foster parent training. *Children and Youth Services Review, 25*, 987–1013. https://doi.org/10.1016/S0190-7409(03)00106-3

Rauktis, M. E., Andrade, A. R., Doucette, A., McDonough, L., & Reinhart, S. (2005). Treatment foster care and relationships: Understanding the role of therapeutic alliance between youth and treatment parent. *International Journal of Child and Family Welfare, 4*, 146–163.

Rauktis, M. E., Fusco, R. A., Cahalane, H., Bennett, I. K., & Reinhart, S. M. (2011). "Try to make it seem like we're regular kids": Youth perceptions of restrictiveness in out-of-home care. *Children and Youth Services Review, 33*, 1224–1233. https://doi.org/10.1016/j.childyouth.2011.02.012

Rhodes, K. W., Orme, J. G., & Buehler, C. (2001). A comparison of family foster parents who quit, consider quitting, and plan to continue fostering. *Social Service Review, 75*, 84–114.

Rodger, S., Cummings, A., & Leschied, A. W. (2006). Who is caring for our most vulnerable children? The motivation to foster in child welfare. *Child Abuse & Neglect, 30*, 1129–1142. https://doi.org/10.1016/j.chiabu.2006.04.005

Samuels, G. M. (2008). *A reason, a season, or a lifetime: Relational permanence among young adults with foster care backgrounds*. Chicago: Chapin Hall Center for Children at the University of Chicago.

Samuels, G. M. & Pryce, J. M. (2008). "What doesn't kill you makes you stronger": Survivalist self-reliance as resilience and risk among young adults aging out of foster care. *Children and Youth Services Review, 30*, 1198–1210. https://doi.org/10.1016/j.childyouth.2008.03.005

Schelbe, L. (2013). *"Some type of way": An ethnography of youth aging out of the child welfare system* (Doctoral dissertation). University of Pittsburgh. Retrieved August 7, 2016, from http://d-scholarship.pitt.edu/id/eprint/19159

Southerland, D. G., Mustillo, S. A., Farmer, E. M., Stambaugh, L. F., & Murray, M. (2009). What's the relationship got to do with it? Understanding the therapeutic relationship in therapeutic foster care. *Child and Adolescent Social Work, 26*, 49–63. doi:10.1007/s10560-008-0159-4

Spath, R., Werrbach, G. B., & Pine, B. A. (2008). Sharing the baton, not passing it: Collaboration between public and private child welfare agencies to reunify families. *Journal of Community Practice, 16*, 481–507. http://dx.doi.org/10.1080/10705420802473766

Steen, J. A. & Smith, K. S. (2011). Foster parent perspectives of privatization policy and the privatized system. *Children and Youth Services Review, 33*, 1483–1488. https://doi.org/10.1016/j.childyouth.2011.03.007

Steen, J. A. & Smith, S. (2012). An organizational view of privatization: Is the private foster care agency superior to the public foster care agency? *Children and Youth Services Review, 34*, 851–858. https://doi.org/10.1016/j.childyouth.2012.01.016

Storer, H. L., Barkan, S. E., Stenhouse, L. L., Eichenlaub, C., Mallilin, A., & Haggerty, K. P. (2014). In search of connection: The foster youth and caregiver relationship. *Children and Youth Services Review, 42*, 110–117.

Sullivan, D. J., Collins-Camargo, C., & Murphy, A. L. (2014). Identifying barriers to permanency: The recruitment, selection, and training of resource parents. *Child & Youth Services, 35*, 365–389. https://doi.org/10.1080/0145935X.2014.973488

Tao, K. W., Ward, K. J., O'Brien, K., DiLorenzo, P., & Kelly, S. (2012). Improving permanency: Caseworker perspectives of older youth in another planned permanent living arrangement. *Child and Adolescent Social Work Journal, 30*, 217–235.

Vanderfaeilllie, J., Van Holen, F., De Maeyer, S., Gypen, L., & Belenger, L. (2015). Support needs and satisfaction in foster care: Differences between foster mothers and foster fathers. *Journal of Child and Family Studies, 25*, 1515–1524.

Weiner, D. A., Schneider, A., & Lyons, J. S. (2009). Evidence-based treatments for trauma among culturally diverse foster care youth: Treatment retention and outcomes. *Children and Youth Services Review, 31*, 1199–1205. https://doi.org/10.1016/j.childyouth.2009.08.013

Wilson, K. & Evetts, J. (2006). The professionalisation of foster care. *Adoption & Fostering, 30*, 39–47. https://doi.org/10.1177/030857590603000106

23

Continuous Quality Improvement (CQI) in Child Welfare Agencies

Jane Burstain, Brock Boudreau, and Jesse Booher

What Is Continuous Quality Improvement?

Since the advent of manufacturing, the private sector has always focused on improving efficiency as a way to increase profits through increasing quantity. The quality of the product was important as well, but the original focus was on achieving a minimum standard enforced through an extensive inspection process, which usually occurred after the product had been produced. After World War II, however, the focus on quality shifted. As Japan's manufacturing sector started rebuilding, they embraced the ideas of Dr. William Deming, an American statistician. The main thesis of Deming (1950) is to reduce costs not just by having more efficient processes, but by focusing those processes on producing quality. Deming posits that by improving the quality of what is produced, there will be fewer errors, which will translate into less reworking and less waste of manpower and resources which will in turn reduce costs (Crosby, 1984). Improved quality will not only increase profits in the short term, but will improve customer satisfaction, and thereby increase market share, ensuring an organization's long-term viability (Kruger, 2001).

This shift in defining quality work did not begin in earnest in the United States until the late 1980s when the automobile industry started employing the Deming technique (Kruger, 2001). Since then, the focus on quality improvement has expanded beyond manufacturing and is employed in some form in virtually every private industry. Over time, the quality improvement principles have evolved and developed into what is now often referred to as Continuous Quality Improvement (CQI).

The theoretical framework and conceptual model for CQI is essentially a data-driven process that enables organizations to improve their overall performance on an ongoing basis. It is based on a systematic approach commonly known as the Plan-Do-Check-Act (PDCA) cycle (Deming, 1950; Masaaki, 1986; Shewhart, 1939). The PDCA cycle contains four stages:

1. the Plan stage where the problem that is causing the poor quality is defined;
2. the Do stage where the solution to correct the problem is implemented;
3. the Check stage where the results of the solution are evaluated;
4. the Act stage where the results are interpreted and the process returns to the Plan stage, whereby the solution is adjusted to further improve quality or replaced with a new solution if the results did not improve quality.

CQI in Child Welfare Agencies

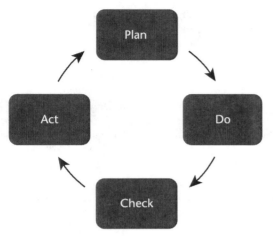

Figure 23.1 The Plan-Do-Check-Act Cycle

Note: This figure illustrates the continuous nature and stage sequence of quality improvement.

The terms Quality Assurance (QA) and CQI are sometimes used interchangeably. For our purposes, however, they are substantively different. There are common elements. Both have Check and Act phases. For QA, however, the Check and Act phases are a retrospective process that identifies and corrects defects after they have occurred, and the process essentially ends once a minimum target or threshold is met. For CQI, the Check and Act phases are part of a larger, proactive process that never ends as it continually seeks to eliminate defects before they occur.

Translating the CQI Framework and Model to Child Welfare

The concept of quality has been a formal part of child welfare since 1994 when amendments to the Social Security Act (SSA) authorized the Children's Bureau to ensure that state plans were in substantial conformity with the SSA's requirements. With this authorization, the Children's Bureau (Public Welfare, 2002) adopted regulations that require states to have systems in place to "regularly assess the quality of services under the Child and Family Services Plan and assure that there will be measures to address identified problems" (p. 7). In addition to these requirements, Title IV-E of the SSA (Social Security Act, 1994) requires agencies to monitor and conduct periodic evaluations of foster care activities and to implement standards to ensure that children in foster care are provided with quality services that protect their safety and health.

To enforce these requirements, the Children's Bureau conducts periodic Child and Family Services Reviews (CFSR). The first round of CFSR started in 2001 and found that 31 states had quality improvement systems that met basic requirements (Children's Bureau, 2012). By the second round of CFSR, which started in 2007, the number of qualifying states had increased to 40.

Through Round 1 and Round 2 of CFSR, however, the Children's Bureau (2012) found that the quality improvement systems which states had adopted were primarily traditional QA. The systems involved a retrospective inspection of casework through case reviews which focused on correcting defects after they had already occurred. Moreover, the systems were often dismantled after a state met whatever goals and targets had been established in their program improvement plan (PIP).

As a result of these findings, in preparation for the third round of CFSR, in 2012, the Children's Bureau provided guidance to the states on anticipated changes in standards for complying with federal requirements around quality. In the guidance, the Children's Bureau encouraged states to move from QA to CQI. In doing so, the Children's Bureau defined CQI as: "[T]he complete process of identifying, describing, and analyzing strengths and problems and then testing, implementing, learning from and revising solutions. It relies on an organizational culture that is proactive and supports continuous learning" (2012, p. 2).

The Children's Bureau (2012) further identified five essential components of a fully functioning CQI system in child welfare. These elements can be grouped into two concepts. The first concept is an infrastructure and process for creating and disseminating high-quality quantitative and qualitative data on how the child welfare system is functioning, which includes (1) quality data collection; (2) a method for conducting ongoing case reviews; and (3) a process for the analysis and dissemination of quality data on all performance measures. The second concept is an infrastructure and process to ensure that stakeholders, agency leadership, and other decision-makers proactively and strategically use data to make systemic improvements. This includes (1) an administrative structure to oversee effective CQI system functioning; and (2) a process for providing feedback to stakeholders and decision-makers and, as needed, adjusting state programs and processes.

In addition to CQI for a child welfare system overall, the federal government has recognized that CQI is particularly important on disproportionality issues. All the CFSR rounds have included an evaluation of the state's effort to recruit and retain foster and adoptive parents who reflect the racial and ethnic diversity of the state's foster care population (Child Welfare Information Gateway, 2016). Round 3 of the CFSR is still underway, but in CFSR Round 2, only 19 states received a positive rating in this area (Child Welfare Information Gateway, 2016).

The State of CQI Implementation in Child Welfare Agencies Nationwide

Using information from the National Child Welfare Resource Center for Organizational Improvement's (henceforth, NRCOI) database (n.d.), we examined the state of CQI implementation for 26 public state child welfare agencies in 2012. We grouped CQI implementation for the 26 states as of 2012 into one of three categories.

The first category is focused almost exclusively on compliance with CFSR as defined by:

1. an infrastructure for creating and disseminating data focused almost exclusively on meeting the requirements of CFSR;
2. dedicated quality improvement staff spending most of their time conducting CFSR-mandated case reviews with no specialized training in CQI principles or data analysis and analytics;
3. no formalized process or established infrastructure to ensure that stakeholders, agency leadership, and other decision-makers proactively and strategically use data to make systemic improvements.

The second category, which goes beyond CFSR, but is still not fully functioning CQI, is defined by:

1. an infrastructure for creating and disseminating data that extends beyond meeting CFSR requirements and includes other parts of the system outside the CFSR;
2. multiple teams generating data and conducting case reviews, with at least one other team focused on other compliance with policy or mandates outside CFSR, but their work is not well coordinated or integrated, and they have no specialized training in CQI principles or data analysis and analytics;
3. either no, or only a limited, formalized process or established infrastructure to ensure that stakeholders, agency leadership, and other decision-makers proactively and strategically use data to make systemic improvements.

The third category is fully-functioning CQI as evidenced by:

1. expanded infrastructure for creating and disseminating high-quality quantitative and qualitative data on how the whole child welfare system is functioning;
2. multiple teams generating data and conducting case reviews, and their work is standardized and coordinated;

3. a team with specialized training in CQI whose sole responsibility is to take information from case reviews and integrate it with other data to regularly review system functioning, identify systemic strengths and areas needing improvement, and work with stakeholders, agency leadership, and other decision-makers to continuously, proactively, and strategically make systemic improvements.

Based on the definitions above (NRCOI, n.d.), of the 26 states reviewed in 2012, five states fell into Category 1, 20 states (including Texas) fell into Category 2, and one state (Kentucky) fell into Category 3.

As of 2012, quality improvement efforts in Category 1 states were concentrated on improving performance, included both quantitative and qualitative data, and could include dedicated staff. The efforts, however, were focused almost exclusively on compliance with CFSR, the staff had no specialized training in CQI or data analysis, and there was no established infrastructure for stakeholders and agency leadership to proactively and strategically use data to improve the system. For example, one state in this category described its quality improvement efforts as conducted by a dedicated team who conducted CFSR case reviews and disseminated reports on CFSR data measures. This team, however, had no specialized CQI or data analysis training. The CFSR case review process did include a self-assessment completed by the individual counties to help them make necessary practice change, but this state had no dedicated staff to help county leadership use the information to craft actionable plans or follow up on implementation. Another state in Category 1 was even more restricted in that they reported that most of their quality improvement efforts were directed to meeting the CFSR performance improvement plan (PIP) for data collection.

The vast majority of the reviewed states fell into Category 2. These states were similar to Category 1 states, except that they had expanded their quality improvement efforts beyond simple compliance with CFSR. They also may have made some efforts at making necessary improvements, but the efforts were not well coordinated or structured. For example, one state's quality improvement team focused their case reviews not only on areas covered by the CFSR, but on processes related to areas such as ongoing monitoring and assessments, safety and permanency assessments, permanency panels, voluntary agency reviews, and child fatality work (NRCOI, n.d.). This team also helped local areas to develop individualized CFSR PIPs based on the results of the case reviews. The team, however, did not address systemic issues outside the scope of the case reviews, had no specialized CQI or data analysis training, and was still inextricably linked with the CFSR. This state also had various committees dedicated to making changes to improve quality, but there was not a coordinated system to track and follow up on their work. Finally, while some coordination existed to disseminate information, there was no formal system for integrating the results of all the case reviews, quantitative data, and information on systemic issues into a more holistic view of system functioning.

Other Category 2 states had dedicated quality-improvement staff utilize data from qualitative reviews beyond the CFSR as well as quantitative data from their case management systems to improve performance and items related to CFSR. These states had staff dedicated to quality improvement; however, these staff also performed other functions. In one state, the leader of the regional quality improvement teams was expected to perform other unspecified functions within the regions. In another state, quality improvement staff were expected to respond to reports of abuse/neglect and complete other casework when field caseloads became too high. Additionally, these states did not generally have an established infrastructure for integrating and disseminating all of the available data and information.

The common themes among Category 2 states were multiple qualitative reviews, incorporating quantitative data into the QA process, and mechanisms for reviewing some systemic issues. However, quality improvement teams in these states still spent most of their time conducting case reviews, and there was generally no system which coordinated the integration and dissemination of all available data or for supporting stakeholders and agency leadership to proactively and strategically use the data to improve the system.

As of 2012, only Kentucky had developed a fully-functioning CQI system. In the NRCOI interview, Kentucky outlined a unique structure for CQI efforts. Kentucky had a clear structure for agency-wide CQI efforts, from state office down to local jurisdictions; and clear expectations, missions, and objectives around agency-wide CQI efforts. Quality improvement efforts went well beyond the CFSR. Efforts included all parts of the child welfare system such as intake and investigation, ongoing assessment, case planning, out-of-home care, and fostering and adoption. Efforts also included work beyond case reviews such as program evaluation, data collection, and the use of multiple sources of quantitative data, including data from critical incident reports regarding incidents, accidents, and other safety concerns involving staff, customers, and other stakeholders. For example, when the CQI Specialists began their work in 2000, only three reports were available to regional leadership. By 2012, more than 100 data reports were regularly disseminated weekly, monthly, quarterly, and yearly.

Kentucky separated the task of doing QA case reviews from the work of CQI. Staff doing CQI work integrated the information from the reviews with data from other sources to help leadership strategically and proactively make necessary system changes. They also tracked progress on identified issues and followed up to support implementation. Staff doing the CQI received specialized training, including principles of CQI, manipulation of data, spreadsheet work, technical skills, and best practice in data analysis.

Based on the NRCOI report, as of 2012, most states had expanded quality improvement efforts beyond CFSR activities. Only one state, however, had really implemented a CQI process by moving quality improvement into broader operational practice, separating quality improvement staff from case-reviewing activities, and developing a more coordinated system for data integration, dissemination, planning, and follow-up.

Texas as a Case Study[1]

Child Welfare in Texas

Texas has a state-run child welfare system with a centralized case-management computer system known as the Information Management Protecting Adults and Children in *Texas* (IMPACT), in which caseworkers document case-related information and activities. The Child Protective Services (CPS) division within the Texas Department of Family and Protective Services (DFPS) is responsible for investigating all reports of child abuse or neglect and providing any ongoing services needed to mitigate the risk of future abuse or neglect. In 2015, the agency received 274,448 reports of child abuse or neglect (Texas Department of Family and Protective Services, 2016). The agency provided in-home services (known as Family Based Safety Services [FBSS]) to 85,215 children and had 47,348 children who were in state custody (known as Conservatorship [CVS]) at some point during the year (Texas Department of Family and Protective Services, 2016). In 2015, the agency had more than 9,200 CPS staff and spent over $1.3 billion a year on CPS, not including the cost of health insurance, for children in state custody (Texas Department of Family and Protective Services, 2016).

Texas is split into different geographic areas and the investigation of abuse or neglect and provision of services to families in each area is administered by a regional director (RD). As of 2017, Texas had a total of 11 RDs; they report to the Director of Field who reports to the Associate Commissioner for CPS who reports to the DFPS Commissioner. There are also various divisions centralized at the state office in Austin that are responsible for managing state-wide policy, practice, contracts, and quality efforts.

The Texas Child Welfare Quality System in 2012

In 2012, the agency's quality improvement system fell squarely within Category 2— QA that expanded beyond the CFSR. The agency had an extensive infrastructure for creating high-quality data on system functioning that included the following teams:

1. a dedicated Accountability team that reviewed a random sample of FBSS and CVS cases, along with their corresponding investigations, to ensure conformity and alignment with federal requirements on safety, permanency, and well-being, and conducted structured and ad hoc case reviews on general practice issues;
2. a dedicated Investigations case review team that reviewed a random sample of closed investigations for compliance with state policy;
3. a team of Child Safety Specialists (CSSs) that reviewed certain investigations before closure to ensure that child safety issues had been addressed;
4. an Analytics and Evaluation (Analytics) team that conducted formal program evaluations, including in-depth statistical analyses;
5. a centralized Management, Reporting and Statistics (MRS) division that created a wide range of quantitative data reports produced monthly, and sometimes even weekly or daily.

Texas also had an established process for disseminating information and data. The Accountability team and the Investigations case review team generated monthly or quarterly reports that aggregated patterns and trends from the reviews, and the reports were sent to the state office and regional leadership. The Accountability team and CSSs also did individual case debriefings with staff over the cases they reviewed. Analytics created reports from its work that were provided to leadership and to external stakeholders such as the Legislature. In total, in 2012, Texas had more than 150 specialized staff dedicated to creating and disseminating data and information about system functioning.

In 2012, however, the process for using the data and information was largely a QA format. The reports and feedback provided from the case reviews focused primarily on retrospectively identifying and correcting errors in past casework and judgment. Moreover, there was no established process for integrating information from the various case reviews and MRS-created reports into a more holistic systemic view. Although the various teams reported through the state office in Austin, they were housed in different state office divisions and their work was only loosely coordinated. In addition to the lack of structured coordination among the various QA efforts, in 2012, the agency had the ironic problem of having too much data with hundreds of different reports available. For the timeliness of investigations alone, there were more than 30 different reports. As a result of the overabundance of data, outside CFSR standards, there was no consistency across the state, or even within the regions, as to how to measure progress or outcomes for children and families.

Finally, there was no established process for leadership and stakeholders to strategically use the wide array of reports and information to make proactive and meaningful change. Accountability team members were certified in DAPIM (Define, Assess, Plan, Interpret, and Monitor) facilitation, and facilitated meetings with management to identify root causes and develop plans. Use of the DAPIM process, however, was voluntary, and it was left to each individual region to decide how and when to use it. When DAPIM was used, there was no established process for following up on implementation of plans developed in the DAPIM sessions.

The Evolution of the Texas Child Welfare Quality System from QA to CQI

To better coordinate and support use of the data that were already being created and disseminated, in 2012, the agency created a new position: Director of Systems Improvement. The job of the

Director was to coordinate all the various data-related efforts and to help CPS leadership proactively and strategically use data to make systemic improvements. The Director who was hired had experience working in the child welfare system and with the Legislature on child welfare policy and legislation, and in conducting research and data analysis on child welfare issues.

One of the first tasks for the new Systems Improvement division was to help the agency to create a standardized dashboard of quantitative metrics for safety, permanency, and well-being for each stage of service: investigations, FBSS, and CVS. After reviewing all the available reports in the DFPS data warehouse, the metrics used in Round 2 of the CFSR, and input from both state office and field staff, leadership narrowed it down to 32 key metrics, including seven measures for investigations, six measures for FBSS, seven measures for children while in state custody, six measures of outcomes for children exiting state custody, and six measures of key decision points in investigations, FBSS, and CVS, broken out by race and ethnicity.

It is important to note that while the measures on the dashboard tracked the general areas targeted in the CFSR, CPS did not adopt the exact Round 2 CFSR measures themselves. The purpose of the CFSR measures is to create a standardized way to compare and evaluate child welfare systems across all states, and those measures change with each round. The purpose of the CPS dashboard was to create a standardized way for Texas to compare and evaluate its child welfare system across different geographic areas and over time. As a result, CPS chose metrics and methodologies for its internal dashboard that reflected the nuances and actual operation of the Texas child welfare system. Recognizing the need to be able to respond to the Children's Bureau, however, CPS continued to have a separate report with the Round 2 CFSR measures.

After working with leadership to finalize the measures and methodologies for the CPS dashboard, the Systems Improvement division worked with the MRS division to create a usable report format that would be available at the state, region, and business unit level. The Systems Improvement division then provided training to all regional and state office leadership on the dashboard, so that management at all levels understood the functioning of their individual part of the system as well as how their work fitted into the broader CPS mission.

Embedding CQI as Part of Ongoing Operations

After creating a standardized dashboard of measures for use across CPS, the next step was to continue embedding CQI as part of ongoing operations. Part of that work involved helping agency leadership to strategically and proactively use data to make necessary systemic improvements.

Historically, when the agency undertook a review of certain processes or practices, the solution for improvement often consisted of considering potential policy changes and additional training programs. Having a dedicated Systems Improvement division allowed the agency to expand such reviews to include the use of data for a better understanding of the root causes and to develop a wider array of potential solutions. One example is a recent review of a particular type of placement. For this review, the Systems Improvement division was able to coordinate work across several different divisions for a more comprehensive review. The review included not only a quantitative analysis examining characteristics of children, outcomes, and circumstances in this particular placement compared to other placement types, but also a qualitative analysis through a structured review of a sample of cases, surveys of caregivers, and focus groups with families.

In less than 2 months, the Systems Improvement division coordinated the gathering of the quantitative and qualitative information, and analyzed and integrated all of it into a comprehensive overview of the placement process and its outcomes, and then made recommendations for improvement. Based on the review, the agency created a caregiver assessment tool to improve upfront assessments of the placements. It also piloted a special team to work with the caregivers to make sure they had the support they needed. Finally, CPS created a process to review cases before closure to ensure that plans were in place for the caregiver to safely meet the child's needs, and to follow up with the caregiver after case closure to provide any additional support that was needed. After implementing these changes, the Systems Improvement division tracks and monitors the placement process and its outcomes while supporting leadership in making additional improvements to ensure child safety.

Using Existing Staff to Expand Continuous Quality Improvement

To expand the scope of CQI and further embed it into ongoing operations, the agency integrated the CPS Analytics and Evaluation team (Analytics) into the Systems Improvement division. Analytics had been part of the agency in some form for more than 30 years. The Analytics team manager had a PhD in Educational Psychology with experience in multivariate statistics and evaluation design, but had no direct experience of working in the CPS system. The other team members were similarly strong quantitatively, with advanced degrees, but also had no direct CPS experience. Staff in the regions and other state office divisions were the exact opposite; most had extensive field experience from working in the CPS system, but very few had quantitative and analytics training or experience. As a result, it was often difficult for the Analytics team to communicate the results of the work they were doing in a format that was understandable and usable by state office and regional leadership and staff.

After becoming part of Systems Improvement, Analytics refocused its work. It hired staff who had both direct experience working in the CPS system and some basic data analysis skills to complement the staff already on the team with strong analytics skills, but little direct CPS experience. Analytics also changed the way it communicated about the work it did. Instead of producing technical, research reports, when the team did an analysis, the key results and recommendations were highlighted in a one-page executive summary in understandable language.

Another part of the refocus was the timing as to when Analytics got involved. Analytics still conducted program evaluations. Instead of being asked to do an evaluation after the initiative had already been fully implemented, however, Analytics team members are now part of the initial work in developing the initiative or program change. With this shift, Analytics is able to help the state office division responsible for the initiative to identify upfront what they are trying to accomplish, and how success will be measured. Analytics is also able to help structure the initiative roll-out so that they can do a process evaluation during implementation and identify necessary changes almost in real time.

The involvement of Analytics in the recent roll-out of differential response, known in Texas as Alternative Response (AR), is a good example of the refocused work. In AR, lower-priority investigations involving older children are investigated through a separate process. Although both a traditional investigation and AR assess child safety and future risk of abuse or neglect, AR takes a more collaborative approach, and there is neither a formal finding about whether abuse or neglect occurred nor a designated perpetrator. Instead, the focus is on understanding family dynamics and circumstances and engaging the family in needed services, usually through the community, as soon as possible. Texas started the staged AR roll-out in November 2014. As of 2016, AR had been rolled out to three regions around the state with another four regions scheduled for roll-out in 2017.

Analytics supported the design and implementation of AR from the outset. Analytics helped CPS leadership and the AR project manager to identify the intended outcomes for AR and how success would be measured. Analytics researched work in other states and the academic literature for what was known about the AR practice approach and synthesized the findings to help inform the AR model. To ensure that AR staff were properly trained in the new model, Analytics developed pre- and post-training tests to assess learning, and supported CPS in winning two grants to fund an outside entity to develop the specific curriculum and administer the training.

To evaluate the AR roll-out, Analytics designed dashboards to monitor the performance of the AR stage as it was implemented across the state. These dashboards provide a high-level assessment of how many cases went to AR, their duration, the percentage of cases progressed to other stages of service, and any recidivism. Analytics also developed, deployed, and analyzed family and staff surveys to assess stakeholder satisfaction and practice fidelity to the AR approach. An evaluation of outcomes over the first 18 months of implementation found that families going through AR were more satisfied with CPS, were less likely to need FBSS or CVS services, and had lower recidivism versus a comparable group of families going through a traditional investigation. The evaluation also identified some necessary process changes that the AR team was able to incorporate into the subsequent roll-out areas.

Their work on AR is just one example of how Analytics has become embedded in the work that CPS does. Analytics is now involved with virtually every major CPS program change and initiative. They help to set the strategic framework, do a process evaluation as the change is implemented, help to identify needed adjustments in real time as the change is rolled out, and do an outcome evaluation to ensure that the change is having the intended effect.

Embedding CQI in Regional Operations

By 2015, although the CQI system in the agency was more fully developed at the state level, there was less support for CQI in the regions. Texas is the second largest state in the United States with an area of 268,820 square miles. Not only is it large, but the population, communities, and circumstances are very different around the state. As a result, the systemic needs and issues were different for each different region.

In 2015, the Texas Legislature funded 12 positions to create a Regional Systems Improvement team, as part of the Systems Improvement division. The team had a manager and 11 Regional System Improvement (RSI) specialists. The manager was housed in the state office in Austin and reported to the Director of Systems Improvement, but the specialists were housed in the regions. Each Regional Director (RD) was assigned an RSI, with the largest region (Dallas/Fort Worth) being assigned two RSIs. To promote cross-regional collaboration and exchange of best practices, the RSIs were grouped into three different teams based on the geographic areas they were covering.

The RSI division has been up and running since January 2016. Since that time it has supported regional management in using data more strategically. For example, when a county within a particular region experienced an increase in staff leaving and rising caseloads, regional leadership wanted to use staff from other areas within the region to assist that county. Using data, the RSIs were able to quickly identify exactly how many cases leadership could divert to other counties, and which units within the other counties were best positioned to absorb the additional work.

Another example involves using qualitative data from a structured case review of high-risk in-home cases. In a particular region, the RSIs determined that there was a pattern of follow-up that was needed on two different critical safety items. The RSIs facilitated a strategy and root-cause meeting with leadership, and identified that the issues were not occurring in the in-home case, but actually began in the investigation before the case was transferred. The RSIs worked with regional leadership to develop a process to ensure that these issues would be addressed before the case was transferred to in-home services. Within 2 months of implementation, there was a 50% improvement in addressing one of the items and a 14% improvement in the other.

In addition to work on issues within each region, the RSIs have helped regional leadership to develop a CQI infrastructure across all regions. For 2017, the RSIs supported regional leadership in developing an annual regional business plan. The RSIs analyzed and aggregated data and information from existing data warehouse reports and case reviews. Using that information, each RD met with their regional leadership to identify areas to target for improvement in the upcoming year. From that meeting, each region developed a plan that starts with each RD's strategic vision for their region, and provides a roadmap for what they will focus on in the upcoming year, including quarterly and annual targets to monitor progress. The RSIs have helped each RD to set up quarterly systems improvement meetings for each program area within their region, during which progress on the annual business plan is discussed and action plans developed to address any obstacles impeding progress toward the business plan goals.

Lessons Learned and Recommendations for States Moving from QA to CQI

As discussed above, since 2012, Texas has made significant progress toward moving from QA to a more fully-functioning CQI system. The following are some lessons learned and recommendations for other states that are attempting to make the same move.

Centralize the Coordination of CQI Efforts

There is no right or wrong CQI structure. Every state is different and has to adapt and create something that works within their particular system. However, at a minimum, all CQI work should be centrally coordinated. The individual managing the coordination needs to have a clear understanding about what CQI is and how it is different from QA. Ideally, they will have some type of direct child welfare experience along with education and training in analytics, data analysis, and qualitative and quantitative research methodology. They need to understand where the agency currently falls along the CQI continuum, and have a clear vision about how to move the agency to a full CQI implementation.

Continuous Quality Improvement work can be categorized into three different functions:

1. creating quantitative reports by pulling data from the state or county case-management system and creating qualitative reports from case reviews;
2. analyzing and integrating data and information into a usable format for leadership that highlights areas of strength and identifies areas needing improvement;
3. supporting leadership in using data and information to prioritize areas to target, track and monitor progress, and make any adjustments needed.

In Texas, all CPS CQI work is coordinated through the Systems Improvement division. The MRS division creates quantitative reports for all of DFPS, not just CPS. As a result, they report through the DFPS Operations division. Their work in creating CPS reports, however, is coordinated through the Systems Improvement division which directs the substance, format, and methodology for all CPS reports that the MRS creates with input from staff and leadership. With respect to qualitative reports from case reviews, the actual reviews themselves are conducted through various case-review teams that report through different divisions within the agency. The Systems Improvement division, however, creates standardized, structured case-review tools for use by all the case-review teams (except for the CFSR case reviews which use the federally mandated form), and analyzes and aggregates patterns and trends from the reviews. Further, the Systems Improvement division conducts process and outcome evaluations for major program changes and initiatives. Analyzing and integrating all of that data and information, the Systems Improvement division works with the state office and regional leadership to strategically and proactively use that data to craft actionable plans and follow up on implementation.

Communicating Around Data

One of the biggest barriers to effectively implementing CQI is the communication gap between those who create and understand the data and those who have to act on it. The CQI staff must focus their reports and communications on key elements that decision-makers need to know, in language that audiences without extensive data expertise can understand. In reports, however, it is important to be transparent about the methodology used to come to the conclusions and any limitations or assumptions that were made. Those details can be put in an appendix so that they are available if needed, but do not require the decision-maker to wade through pages of technical details to get to the key points. In presentations, effective visual presentation of data is also important. Each chart or graph should have only one or two points, and the conclusion drawn from the graph or chart should be readily apparent. The headline or title of the graph or chart should also be explanatory, not just descriptive, so that the words reinforce the point of the picture.

Promoting a Balanced and Effective CQI Team

For CQI to be effective, CQI staff must have both a deep understanding of the system they are evaluating and a deep understanding of quantitative and qualitative methodologies for gathering and analyzing data and information. It can be difficult to find individuals who have both. Most are either strong on the program side or strong on the quantitative or research methodology side. As a result, when building a CQI team, it is important to have a mix and to create a culture where the CQI team members can learn from and support each other.

A critical factor in the success of CQI is establishing a partnership between CQI staff and leadership. Child welfare agencies are some of the most complex, high-stakes operations in the world. Leadership has to respond to competing external and internal priorities and pressures as well as attend to the day-to-day activities of running the agency. Amidst all of this, the job of CQI staff is to help leadership to focus on the most critical components of the system and strategically allocate the agency's limited resources to those changes that will have the greatest impact on outcomes. In doing so, it is important for CQI staff to remember that CQI exists solely to make the job easier for direct delivery staff who are doing the real work of helping children and families. The CQI staff may spend most of their time working with leadership, but direct delivery staff and the families they serve are the real clients, and all work should be organized and directed around their needs.

Include the Input of Children, Youth, and Families in the CQI Effort

In doing CQI, the input of the children, youth, and families that the agency serves is critical for identifying potential problems and crafting actionable improvement plans. As discussed above, in its CQI work, the agency solicits feedback from caregivers and families, which is used to help craft policies and practices to meet their needs more effectively. CPS is incorporating similar feedback from youth into its ongoing work of improving services that help youth to make the transition to living independently. The agency has an annual youth conference and uses that opportunity to solicit feedback from youth on issues affecting them, such as barriers to completing preparation for adult living services and participating in social and school events. CPS also employs several former foster youth as youth specialists to provide insight and input into issues, policy, and practice affecting youth.

Conclusion

Child welfare agencies have only recently begun implementing robust CQI processes, and there is little research on CQI's application in the field of child welfare to guide their efforts. As of 2012, most states, including Texas, had relatively robust systems for doing case reviews and creating quantitative reports. These states, however, lacked a coordinated system for integrating all the different reports and information. There also was no infrastructure to focus leadership on the most critical components of the system and strategically allocate limited resources. Since then, the Texas agency has moved toward a more fully-functioning CQI system, identified lessons learned, and made recommendations that other child welfare agencies can use as they make their own transition.

Note

1 Unless otherwise noted, all years refer to the Texas fiscal year which runs from September 1 to August 31.

References

Children's Bureau. (2012). *Continuous Quality Improvement in Title IV-B and IV-E programs* (ACYF-CB-IM-12-07). Washington, DC: Administration on Children, Youth and Families.

Child Welfare Information Gateway. (2016, November). *Racial disproportionality and disparity in child welfare*. Issue Brief. Washington, DC: U.S. Department of Health & Human Services, Children's Bureau. Retrieved April 6, 2017, from www.childwelfare.gov/pubPDFs/racial_disproportionality.pdf

Crosby, P. B. (1984). *Quality without tears*. New York: McGraw-Hill.

Deming, W. E. (1950). *Elementary principles of the statistical control of quality: A series of lectures*. Tokyo: Nippon Kagaku Gijutsu Renmei.

Kruger, V. (2001). Main schools of TQM: "The big five." *The TQM Magazine, 13*(3), 146–155.

Masaaki, I. (1986). *Kaizen: The key to Japan's competitive success*. New York: McGraw-Hill.

National Child Welfare Resource Center for Organizational Improvement [NRCOI]. (n.d.). *CQI descriptions by state*. Retrieved September 14, 2017, from http://muskie.usm.maine.edu/helpkids/CQIproj/cqistate.htm

Public Welfare. (2002). *Code of federal regulations, 45 § 1357*. Washington, DC: U.S. Government Printing Office.

Shewhart, W. A. (1939). *Statistical method from the viewpoint of quality control*. W. E. Deming (Ed.). New York: Dover.

Social Security Act [SSA] Amendment of 1994, Pub. L. 103-432. H.R. 5252: 103rd Congress: Social Security Act Amendments of 1994. (1994). Retrieved April 6, 2017 from www.govtrack.us/congress/bills/103/hr5252

Texas Department of Family and Protective Services. (2016). *2015 Annual report and data book*. Retrieved December 4, 2017, from www.dfps.state.tx.us/About_DFPS/Annual_Report/

24

Foster Care and Juvenile Justice Systems
Crossover and Integration of Services

Melissa Jonson-Reid, Allison Dunnigan, and Joseph Ryan

While debate exists as to the relative contribution of pre-disposing factors prior to foster care and experiences during it, little debate exists as to the common participation of youth in both the child welfare and juvenile justice systems. The incidence of youth being involved in both systems is common enough, in fact, that such youth have recently earned their own label, "crossover youth" (Dannerbeck & Yan, 2011; Herz, Ryan, & Bilchik, 2010). Crossover youth are of concern for several reasons. First, by definition, they are a high-cost group due to their involvement in at least two (and often more) publicly funded service systems. Such service systems include, but are not limited to, Medicaid, special education, and mental health. Second, the risks of longer-term negative outcomes for youth in foster care, even without the added burden of engaging in delinquent behaviors, are often high (Pecora et al., 2006; Taussig, Clyman, & Landsverk, 2001). Cusick, Goerge, and Bell (2009) classify four crossover pathways: (1) a youth with a current child protection case (involved with child welfare) commits a delinquent offense—also called dually involved; (2) a youth with a past child welfare history later commits a delinquent offense; (3) a youth who commits a delinquent offense is then reported to child protection; and (4) a youth exits juvenile justice confinement and is placed into child welfare foster care due to lack of family options.

The focus of this book is on foster youth, their challenges, strengths, and voices, and this chapter synthesizes what we know about crossover youth, since being "crossover" represents an important challenge both for the youth themselves and the systems that serve them. Cusick and colleagues (2009) describe four different potential patterns, but not all are equally common. To illustrate this, data were drawn from a longitudinal study of youth first reported for maltreatment from birth through to the age of 11, who were 17 years old at the end of the study (unpublished data: see Jonson-Reid, Drake, & Kohl [2009] for a description of methods). Almost 23% of the youth in this sample who never received services after a report of alleged abuse or neglect had at least one juvenile delinquency petition. The vast majority (about 99%) of these youth (i.e., the 23%) were reported for suffering alleged maltreatment prior to their first contact with the juvenile justice system.

A greater proportion (over 40%) of the youth who entered foster care had involvement with the juvenile justice system, and were more likely to have begun in the juvenile justice system than reported children who never entered care (about one-third had a delinquency petition prior to entering foster care).

Different patterns of crossover may suggest differing systemic problems. Youth who cross over from child welfare to juvenile justice in many ways represent the limitation of the child welfare system's ability to adequately promote youth well-being as per the required element in the Child and Family Services Reviews (Jonson-Reid & Drake, 2016; Leone & Weinberg, 2010). Permanence, another goal of child welfare, is also often unmet for these youth (Herz et al., 2010). Youth who are first involved with juvenile justice prior to their involvement with child welfare may represent the latter system's inability to detect and address abuse and neglect earlier in the lives of these youth.

This chapter will review what is known about the path that youth take from foster care to juvenile justice involvement, as well as the path from juvenile justice to foster care, and the ongoing relationship between the two. We will also explore the broader needs of this population that result in the simultaneous involvement with additional allied systems such as mental health services. We review emerging evidence-based and evidence-informed practices to prevent delinquent behaviors or to intervene to improve outcomes after crossover has occurred. Policy solutions and means of evaluation, including the increasing use of big data, will also be discussed.

Definition and System Issues

Before discussing what is known about crossover youth, it is important to highlight a few policy, system, and definitional issues that may confound our understanding of this process. As the entire volume is focused on foster youth, we do not take time here to discuss the foster care system in great detail. It is, however, important to note that older studies (samples drawn prior to 1980) include youth who entered care prior to the permanency policies set in place in the early 1980s which made it less common to go into care, and emphasized reunification within 18 months. While more recent policy shifts have shortened the permanency timeline for returning home (Adoptions and Safe Families Act, 1997), these changes were not as dramatic as those in the 1980s. These changes are reflected in the differences in foster care rates between more recent studies and the older studies. Only about 5% of maltreated youth (Rivaux et al., 2008) enter the foster care system after their first report today, with a placement rate of about 25% over time (Jonson-Reid, unpublished data). In comparison, 85% of the children entered care following a court-substantiated case of maltreatment in the late 1960s and early 1970s in Widom's seminal study (1991).

While a youth in foster care can commit a delinquent offense while in care and transition directly to the juvenile justice system, most youth return to their biological family or live with relatives fairly quickly after placement. Such youth may cross over after leaving foster care. Finally, not all youth who enter care do so because of youth abuse and neglect, even though they may have had a report filed. Some youth enter foster care for reasons of parental death or incarceration, and these youths have been found to have differing exit patterns from other youth in care (Shaw, Bright, & Sharpe, 2015). Youth may also enter care due to serious developmental or behavioral disabilities as "voluntary placements," but less is known about their trajectories (Križ, Free, & Kuehl, 2016). These youths may also become involved in the juvenile justice system, but fall outside the traditional conceptualization of a crossover youth as someone who has experienced maltreatment. It is unclear how many studies of crossover youth include youth who entered foster care for reasons other than maltreatment, which confounds our understanding of the potential role of placement as compared to pre-existing behavioral issues.

Crossover youth research is limited to youth who become officially involved with the juvenile justice system, but the level of justice system involvement varies across studies. Youth involvement may end at an arrest or citation, or may progress to the filing of a juvenile court petition. Some court petitions result in intervention like community probation or detention, but many do not (Jonson-Reid, 2011). Dispositions for juvenile court petitions that do result in intervention include a wide array of services and placements, from in-home probation to incarceration in juvenile correction facilities. Studies of crossover youth cut across all of these levels of system involvement, making generalizations more challenging.

Who "Crosses Over"? Prevalence and Characteristics

While the overlap of participation in the foster care and juvenile justice systems is well established, the exact prevalence and the contribution of modifiable risk and protective factors are less clear. Studies vary in regard to their sampling, correspondence with major policy shifts, and differences in measures available.

Early Studies

Prior to 2000, the study of crossover youth was limited to two studies of youth in care who entered care in the later 1960s to early 1970s (Widom, 1991) or the late 1970s through to about 1981 (Runyan & Gould, 1985). In the Widom (1991) study, youth who entered care after a substantiated maltreatment report prior to the age of 12 stayed for an average of about 5 years, and the prevalence of later juvenile arrest was about 15%. Runyan and Gould (1985) studied youth who entered foster care after the age of 7 and were in foster care for at least 3 years; they found that 11% of these youth had later court adjudications for delinquent offenses. Neither study found a significant difference between youth in foster care and the comparison groups in the rate of juvenile arrest (Widom, 1991) or conviction (Runyan & Gould, 1985). Both studies did, however, find that placement instability while in care increased the risk of delinquency. As mentioned previously, entry into foster care was more common, as were longer lengths of stay in care, prior to the policy changes in the 1980s and 1990s.

Later Studies (Post Permanency Policy Changes)

The remaining review of studies published after 2000 is divided according to level of juvenile justice system involvement and timing and direction of the crossover.

Juvenile Court Petitions

A few studies have looked at juvenile court petitions as an outcome following foster care. Most studied youth to age 17. Ryan and Testa (2005) investigated the risk of delinquency for maltreated youth (at least one substantiated complaint) in Cook County, Illinois, from birth. The comparison group was comprised of youth who were also reported, but remained at home. About 16% of youth with foster care histories had a delinquency petition, compared to 7% of those who remained in the home. The risk of delinquency was higher for youth who were older at the time of their first substantiated allegation of maltreatment. Another study using Illinois data divided cases according to whether the youth remained in the home after a first report after the age of 7, were placed into care with a strong rationale for placement, or were placed into care without a strong rationale (Doyle, 2007). A higher risk of delinquency petitions was found for youth in care, but primarily limited to those in the borderline group (i.e., placed without a strong rationale).

Using Missouri data, a third study examined the risk of a juvenile court petition for both status and delinquent offenses for youth with a first report of maltreatment between the ages of 6 and 11 (Bright & Jonson-Reid, 2008). The study had additional controls for involvement in other systems (income maintenance and special education), as well as community poverty, and 7% of the sample was placed into foster care. Female youth who entered foster care had an almost three times higher risk of status offense petitions than those who remained at home, but there was no association between foster care entry and delinquency for males or females. A more recent study, also in Missouri, used propensity score matching to compare youth who were reunified following care to those who received intensive in-home services, but were not placed out of the home. Among youth whose first placement occurred after the age of 4, youth who entered care were between 38% and 45% more likely to have a delinquency petition, controlling for known mental health diagnoses and special education eligibility (Lee & Jonson-Reid, under review). A final study using a retrospective case control design in South Carolina compared youth with delinquency histories with those without, and found that youth with foster care histories were about 35% more likely to be among those with delinquency histories (Barrett, Katsiyannis, Zhang, & Zhang, 2013).

Juvenile Incarceration

Two studies have focused on the risk of incarceration in youth corrections as an outcome. A California study found that receipt of any child welfare (foster care combined with in-home services) following a maltreatment report at age 7 or later was not associated with entry into juvenile corrections compared to those without services overall, but there was a small reduction of risk for Black or Latino youth who received these services (Jonson-Reid & Barth, 2000a). A Missouri study found that about 4% of youth who entered foster care after the age of 5 later entered juvenile corrections. The rate was somewhat higher among youth who received in-home services, but then entered care (4.8%) and between 2% and 3% for those who were not served or received in-home services only (Jonson-Reid, 2002). White youth placed in care were at greater risk of later entering juvenile corrections, but this was not true for non-White youth. Additionally, when controlling for any record of mental health treatment, the researchers found little difference between youth in foster care due to maltreatment and those receiving in-home services. However, using those same controls, youth who entered foster care for reasons other than maltreatment were found to be at nearly three times higher risk of entering juvenile corrections than those who received in-home services.

Transition from Child Welfare Foster Care to Juvenile Justice Foster Care

One study examined youth who exited child welfare foster care and then entered probation-supervised foster care. Less than 7% of the youth exiting child welfare foster care re-entered care supervised by probation. Similar to other studies, placement instability and multiple spells in child welfare foster care were associated with a higher risk of crossover (Jonson-Reid & Barth, 2003).

Transition from Juvenile Justice to Child Welfare Foster Care

Less is known about the transition from juvenile justice to child welfare. A study of youth aged 12 to 17 in Los Angeles County, California, looked at youth who were arrested for the first time in 2008 (n = 5,061). Arrested youth with a child welfare history and females were more likely to be placed out of the home (Tam, Abrams, Freisthler, & Ryan, 2016). While research on sexual minority youth is just emerging, one national study suggested that these youths are overrepresented among crossover youth, and that this association may reflect an increased tendency to place these youths into foster care following juvenile justice system involvement (Child Welfare League of America & Lambda Legal, 2006; Irvine & Canfield, 2015).

What Do we Know? Summarizing Prevalence and Characteristics of Crossover Youth

Prevalence

Relatively few crossover studies provide the data necessary to estimate prevalence. At the arrest or petition level, the prevalence of crossover across known studies was between 11% and 50% (Halemba,

Siegel, Lord, & Zawacki, 2004; Lee & Jonson-Reid, under review; Runyan & Gould, 1985; Ryan & Testa, 2005; Widom, 1991). Differences in time period, sample composition, and outcome measure make comparison difficult. Studies looking at juvenile corrections or out-of-home placement through probation range in prevalence from 4% to 7% (Jonson-Reid, 2002; Jonson-Reid & Barth, 2003).

It is even less clear what the rate of crossing over in the other direction may be. In a recent study of approximately 52,000 formally processed juvenile offenders in Michigan, 56% had at least one prior Child Protective Services (CPS) investigation, 26% had at least one CPS investigation subsequent to their delinquency petition, 9% had at least one prior foster care placement, and 3% had at least one foster care placement subsequent to their delinquency petition (Ryan & Moore, unpublished data).

Demographic Factors

The import of demographic characteristics varies across studies. In all studies that examined gender, males were at the greatest risk of crossover to juvenile justice. The association of crossover and race is unclear. Some studies found differences in prevalence by race, with youth of color having higher rates of crossover overall (Jonson-Reid & Barth, 2000b; Ryan & Testa, 2005), with some of this difference explained by an interaction with gender in two studies (Bright & Jonson-Reid, 2008; Jonson-Reid & Barth, 2000b). Another study controlling for cross-sector services and limited to youth who were reunified found no difference by race (Lee & Jonson-Reid, under review). Only two studies had sufficient percentages of youth who were not White or Black to examine crossover for other groups, and only a single study has addressed sexual minority youth.

Generally, youth who were reported for suffering maltreatment or who entered the foster care system at a later age were at an increased risk of delinquency (Randall, 2015). Only three studies included children younger than the age of 5 at placement, and the variation in sample time period and controls makes conclusions difficult (Lee & Jonson-Reid, under review; Ryan & Testa, 2005; Widom, 1991).

Other Factors

One consistent finding across studies is the association of placement instability with a higher risk of delinquency (Jonson-Reid & Barth, 2003; Lee & Jonson-Reid, under review; Runyan & Gould, 1985; Ryan & Testa, 2005; Widom, 1991). It remains unclear how much of this risk is associated with difficulties in finding good placement matches, administrative changes, or unaddressed behavioral health problems that underlie placement disruptions and justice system contact. In two California studies, youth in congregate care settings (i.e., group homes) or kinship care homes had an increased risk of delinquency compared to youth in non-relative family foster care settings (Ryan, Hong, Herz, & Hernandez, 2010; Ryan, Marshall, Herz, & Hernandez, 2008). Another study found attachment to foster parents to be protective for African American males in care (Ryan, Testa, & Zhai, 2008).

Mental health problems, often measured according to the presence of diagnoses, have been found to be associated with a greater risk of crossover, though this has only been captured in a few studies (Herz et al., 2010). A recent dissertation suggested that the prevalence of mental health disorder may vary by whether youth are dually involved, or had closed child welfare cases and then became involved in the juvenile justice system (Giallella, 2015). One study suggested an increased risk for youth having contact with child welfare who had histories of family or community poverty, controlling for behavioral health problems served through special education (Bright & Jonson-Reid, 2008). However, many gaps remain regarding the importance of school, community, and other family factors. These gaps complicate attempts at conceptual and theoretical explanations for crossover.

Theoretical Conceptions about Why Crossover Occurs

One explanation for crossover revolves around the well-accepted association between maltreatment and delinquency, due to the fact that the majority of crossover youth have had this dual history. Even within this literature, there remains much debate about the mechanisms and relative contribution of maltreatment type or accumulation of victimization events (Jonson-Reid & Bright, 2015; Jonson-Reid, Kohl, & Drake, 2012). The research on multiple forms of trauma (polyvictimization) is largely limited to cross-sectional examinations of detained youth, single gender samples, or samples using self-report delinquency (Cyr et al., 2012; Dierkhising et al., 2013; Ford, Elhai, Conner, & Frueh, 2010; Ford, Grasso, Hawke, & Chapman, 2013; Marsiglio, Chronister, Gibson, & Leve, 2014). Although some studies found higher rates of polyvictimization among child welfare- or justice-involved samples (Bright & Jonson-Reid, 2015; Dannerbeck & Yan, 2011; Dierkhising et al., 2013) than in community samples (Finkelhor, Shattuck, Turner, Ormrod, & Hamby, 2011; Ford et al., 2010), others found lower rates (Ford et al., 2013). Some posit that chronic trauma leads to over- or under-reaction to other later events in life. These reactions in turn impact school success, and poor school performance is associated with increased likelihood of delinquent behaviors (Ford et al., 2010). To the extent that foster youth have these experiences and negative behavioral impacts, the various theories and paths connecting maltreatment to offending behavior may apply (Jonson-Reid & Bright, 2015).

There are many theories of delinquency, such as social disorganization, learned behavior, strain theory, and others, that may also be relevant, but have yet to be adequately explored for this population. One exception is a study that examined the relevance of social control theory among African American males in foster care (Ryan, Testa, et al., 2008). Findings supported the importance of attachment to certain social institutions and significant adults (e.g., foster care providers) in reducing the risk of delinquency.

As alluded to above, foster care itself might play a role in accentuating or decreasing the risk of delinquency, depending on the results of the placement experience. Attachment theory is both relevant to the influence of maltreatment and trauma on delinquency as well as to foster care itself, due to the changes in caregivers and significant others over time (Hoeve et al., 2012). To the extent that foster care produces trauma related to separation and/or instability in care, risk of delinquent outcomes might increase (e.g., Jonson-Reid & Barth, 2000b; Ryan et al., 2010; Ryan & Testa, 2005; Taussig & Clyman, 2011). However, few studies have attempted to tease out the relative contribution of simply experiencing actual placement into foster care by controlling for other prior experiences (Berger, Bruch, Johnson, James, & Rubin, 2009).

Although the qualitative literature on the experiences of youth in foster care is relatively limited, the following quotations (from Unrau, Seita, & Putney, 2008) on placement instability do suggest a role for instability in foster care heightening the risk of crossover: "Constantly changing school. I think my education suffered . . . Having no close friends because you knew you would be moving again" (p. 1260).

> [I]t made it real difficult to trust people . . . I have become more guarded cause I get so scared to lose somebody. It takes me a long time to drop my guard . . . As soon as they are nice to me, I automatically think they want something. I become really defensive. It made it difficult for me to become attached . . . Eventually I became an angry, angry person who could not trust anybody.
>
> (Unrau et al., 2008, p. 1261)

There could be decreased risk of delinquency associated with foster care if child safety is increased, or if effective services are provided to individual youth and their families (Jonson-Reid, 2004;

Widom, 1991). While the advances in policy related to permanency and reunification are helping to produce shorter stays in care (Jonson-Reid, 2003), shorter stays may also pose challenges to leveraging existing services (Ayón, 2009: Mekonnen, Noonan, & Rubin, 2009). For example, Multidimensional Treatment Foster Care is a well-known evidence-based model, but it typically requires a placement lasting between 6 and 9 months (Henggeler & Sheidow, 2012). Much work remains to be done to put forth a framework that acknowledges the potential contributions of several theories relevant to a youth's prior context as well as what happens once he or she is placed in care.

What Happens Once Crossover Occurs?

Relatively little information exists about how the child welfare and juvenile justice systems manage and process crossover youth or what happens to these youths in the long term.

Management of Crossover Youth

Chuang and Wells (2010) used data from the National Study of Child and Adolescent Well-Being (NSCAW) to examine the system trajectories for dually involved youth (i.e., those involved in any child welfare and juvenile justice systems) who also needed behavioral health care (n = 178). This study explored whether service delivery, interagency communication, and outcomes of youth differed based on which agency was responsible for the youth. Child welfare agencies retained case management control for 36% of youth, juvenile justice agencies assumed accountability for 42%, and the remainder were under joint control. Youth supervised solely by the child welfare system were more likely to receive mental health and substance abuse services compared to those under joint control. The time order of the development of the behavioral health problems relative to child welfare involvement was unclear.

Outcomes

Most of the studies of outcomes of crossover youth focus on re-offending. These studies indicate that crossover youth are more likely to recidivate as compared to juvenile offenders without child welfare involvement (Halemba et al., 2004; Herz et al., 2010; Huang & Ryan, 2014). In a Washington State study, Ryan, Williams, and Courtney (2013) reported that compared to youth with only delinquency records, crossover youth (past child welfare case, but open case in juvenile justice) and dually involved youth (open cases in both systems) reported higher levels of physical violence in the home, more school behavior problems, more mental health issues, fewer pro-social friends, and other significant barriers to positive functioning. Furthermore, dually involved youth had a significantly higher risk of re-offending than either crossover or delinquency-only youth. Another study of delinquent youth in a large urban county also found that crossover youth had more risk and fewer protective factors, and that this was associated with recidivism (Lee & Villagrana, 2015). A Florida study of youth placed in juvenile justice residential settings did not find a direct impact of self-reported adverse childhood experiences (ACES) on re-offending. Youth reporting high numbers of ACES, however, were more likely to have histories of child welfare involvement, which in turn was associated with higher rates of recidivism. The impact of crossover or dual involvement was found to vary by race and gender. Dual involvement was a risk factor for White youth and female Hispanic youth, but not for other groups (Baglivio et al., 2016).

A few studies suggest that crossover youth experience other untoward outcomes. A large Los Angeles study found that over 30% of dually involved youth experienced at least one additional episode of maltreatment (Huang, Ryan, & Herz, 2012). A study of young adult perpetration of intimate partner violence found that risk associated with prior maltreatment history (not specific to foster care) was partially mediated by an additional record of violent juvenile delinquency (Millett, Kohl, Jonson-Reid, Drake, & Petra, 2013). A study of youth emancipating from child welfare foster care only, juvenile justice probation only, or both, found higher rates of correctional system, public assistance, and inpatient or outpatient health services involvement for the crossover group (Culhane et al., 2011). A recent dissertation (Baetz, 2015) using follow-up data from an older crossover study (i.e., Widom, 1991) used interview data at age 29 to compare outcomes for crossover youth (n = 180), maltreatment only youth (n = 480), juvenile justice only (n = 91), and youth without system involvement (n = 496). The study found poorer outcomes for crossover youth related to education, employment, and re-offending, but not for mental health disorders.

What Is Known about the Participation of "Crossover Youth" in Other Systems?

Crossover youth are often also engaged in many other systems and services beyond child welfare and juvenile justice. In Dannerbeck and Yan's study (2011), about 37% of crossover youth had known histories of mental health treatment, and 34% had diagnosed learning disorders in education. In a study of youth corrections involvement following foster care in a Midwest state, Jonson-Reid (2002) found that approximately 6% of the youth in foster care had histories of mental health treatment which was associated with nearly double the risk of crossover. In a latent class analysis of system involvement and offending behavior (Bright & Jonson-Reid, 2015), all three classes of persistent offenders (urban/recurrent poverty/multi-problem; suburban/recurrent maltreatment/multi-problem; and city/recurrent maltreatment/multi-problem) had records of multiple system contacts, though the combination varied (e.g., family income maintenance, mental health, health care for sexually transmitted diseases [STDs], status offenses). Only one of four low-offense groups had both recurrent maltreatment and multiple system contacts, and this group was primarily female.

Simultaneous involvement with multiple service systems is not problematic if in fact an individual youth presents co-occurring problems and requires a range of services. Ideally, service systems would intervene early so that problems do not become more complicated over time. Figure 24.1 shows that there is often ample time to mount a preventive intervention (dark grey) between a first child welfare system entry and a first delinquency petition (lightest shading; unpublished data: see Jonson-Reid et al. [2009] for methods).

While this gives us hope, it becomes very important to be able to select the most efficacious means of intervention. Relatively little work exists to inform intervention choices for this population,

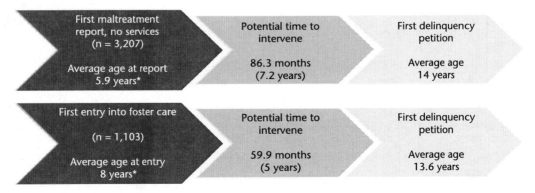

Figure 24.1 Age and Potential Time to Intervene Prior to Crossover

Note: *On average, youth who did not cross over had their first child welfare contact 6 months to 1 year earlier.

although promising evidence-based approaches do exist that target aforementioned risk factors for crossover.

The State of the Evidence for Best Practices in Prevention and Intervention

There are a host of intervention efforts that target youth maltreatment or delinquency in the hope of decreasing system involvement. For example, there are newer mandates to collaborate with health care (Jaudes, Champagne, Harden, Masterson, & Bilaver, 2012) and move toward trauma-informed systems (Ko et al., 2008) that may hold promise for addressing the risk factors faced by youth in care. As yet, outcome data for such approaches are not available. There are also examples of specific programs designed to support the placements and educational outcomes for youth in care (e.g., Pecora et al., 2006; Taussig & Clyman, 2011). Again, however, much remains unknown regarding the ability of these programs to prevent crossover per se.

One exception to the lack of information specific to crossover youth is the Crossover Youth Practice Model (CYPM), developed by the Center for Juvenile Justice Reform at Georgetown University. The CYPM represents a multi-system, collaborative approach to identifying crossover youth early, assessing needs, developing treatment plans, and conducting case management. The CYPM is currently being used in 96 counties across 21 states (Center for Juvenile Justice Reform, n.d.). A multi-county evaluation of CYPM was conducted in Minnesota after the first 4 years (Haight, Bidwell, Choi, & Cho, 2016; Haight, Bidwell, Marshall, & Khatiwoda, 2014). The researchers found that practitioners appreciated the collaborative approach and felt they were better able to provide needed services to youth and their families as a result (Haight et al., 2014). The following quotation captures the perceived impact according to the service providers:

> I have a kid in lock-up right now who wants to meet me. And, I called (juvenile probation officer) yesterday saying, "Let's go out and meet this kid together . . ." And, we are at every court hearing together. Even if it's just my stuff, I will invite him and he will do . . . likewise. . . . And, we're consulting together at meetings about our kids . . . and trying to do joint recommendations and we always sit together up front so the judge can address us both and I think it's made it a much more unified process than in the past.
>
> (Haight et al., 2014, p. 94)

The Minnesota study also investigated recidivism of crossover youth who received CYPM, in comparison to crossover youth who did not receive CYPM, and found a significant reduction of risk for the group receiving CYPM (Haight et al., 2014). Another study in a single Midwestern county reported similar results (Haight et al., 2016). While the initial findings are promising, further evaluation is needed to support widespread adoption of this model.

Gallegos and White (2013) also advocate for multi-system collaboration and suggest that this collaboration be used to leverage the following services (see Table 24.1) that address individual needs in the academic and social domains.

The literature is also quite clear on the high rates of substance abuse among crossover youth and their mental health needs. Researchers stress the importance of attending to these issues early in the life of a case to improve long-term outcomes (Herz & Ryan, 2008). An example from Hedges' (2012, pp. 319–321) case study illustrates this point:

> Arizona first took custody of Kasey when she was four years old and suffered a burn as result of neglect. The youth were abused in their first foster home and returned a year later to their substance addicted mother. The family moved around and a series of sexual assault instances followed. Kasey began drinking when she was nine. After being shifted between relatives she returned by herself to Tucson when she was 14, got expelled from school for sexual behavior and

Table 24.1 Program Recommendations to Prevent Crossover and Improve Outcomes

Academic or Social Need	Service
Early intervention	Attachment and Biobehavioral Catch-up (ABC): parenting program using videotaping and parent coaches to provide immediate and individualized feedback to improve nurturing and behavioral and regulatory capabilities
Literacy	Success Maker: reading and math intervention program targeting youth in Grades K–8 (Grade 8 being just prior to peak offending years) that is continuously adaptive to meet the individual needs of high-risk youth
Mentoring	Twelve Together: 1-year peer support and mentoring program for Grades 6–12
Positive school discipline	Restorative Justice: aimed at repairing the harm caused by crime rather than solely punishing the offender
Behavioral intervention	Multidimensional Treatment Foster Care: program specifically designed for youth in foster care and their family of origin and foster family. Specialized programs target youth aged 3–17.

re-entered CPS in a group home. She began using a variety of other drugs and running away from placement. Finally, it was a juvenile judge that detained her after an arrest at about age 16 that resulted in her first comprehensive assessment and treatment plan.

While there are many things that could have been done to improve stability in this case, it is hard to escape the conclusion that a treatment plan for substance abuse early on might have offset some of the later problems and her eventual entry into juvenile justice.

In addition to the programs mentioned by Gallegos and White (2013), evidence is slowly accumulating regarding interventions that may positively impact mental health outcomes for youth in care (Taussig & Culhane, 2010). Cognitive Behavioral Therapy, for example, is reported to be efficacious for substance-abuse treatment among adolescents (Waldron & Turner, 2008). Another group-based trauma-informed program, Structured Psychotherapy for Adolescents Responding to Chronic Stress (SPARCS) has been implemented with youth in foster care and has shown promise in several small studies (National Child Traumatic Stress Network, 2008), though further research is needed to support widespread adoption.

Finally, given the number of studies which conclude that foster care placement instability increases the risk of delinquency, efforts to minimize placement disruptions may well be preventive. There is at least one evidence-based model for reducing placement moves, Keeping Foster and Kin Parents Supported and Trained (KEEP), that has been extensively researched (Price et al., 2008). Multidimensional Treatment Foster Care has also been shown to reduce placement instability (Lynch, Dickerson, Saldana, & Fisher, 2014). While not focused on placement change per se, there are some other promising practices that engage foster parents in treatment for youth behavioral or substance-abuse problems (e.g., Haggerty, Barkan, Skinner, Packard, & Cole, 2016) that may also diminish placement moves. Currently, however, there are a wide range of practices aimed at improving placement instability across states, few of which appear to include promising or evidence-based approaches or the evaluation of novel approaches (Blakey et al., 2012).

The State of the Evidence for Best Practices in Policy

In theory, several of the policy changes that have been made to enhance connection to services or improve permanency within and upon exiting foster care should decrease the likelihood of crossing over. As mentioned previously, federal policy since the 1980s has sought to increase permanency, both in terms of movement while in foster care and successful, permanent exits. Federal and state incentives exist to increase the use of kinship placements and de-emphasize use of congregate care (Adoption and Safe Families Act, 1997). Hypothetically, if successful in reducing instability, such efforts should reduce the risk for crossover. In practice, however, it is difficult to find research to validate this connection.

Dual-Status Programming

There are increasing references to dual-status programs and courts that move beyond the call for collaboration to actual simultaneous assessment of crossover youth needs (Coleman, 2015; Rogers, 2014). In theory, these approaches, sometimes called "one family/one judge," provide an opportunity for a holistic assessment and intervention. A 2005 national survey indicated that many states had some variant of this approach, but that there was a tremendous range from dual assessment processes only to true dual service plans (Petro, 2005). While such systems do have accountability structures proposed or in place, outcome information could not be located as yet.

Policies that May Mitigate Risk

The multiple needs of youth, and especially youth placed into care, are well documented, prompting calls for improved access to and quality of health and mental health care (Pecora, 2010). The 2008 Fostering Connections to Success and Increasing Adoptions Act requires states to develop an ongoing system of oversight and coordination of health care services for foster youth to ensure continuity of care and better access. In particular, the Medical Home model has been endorsed by the Patient Protection and Affordable Care Act (2010) and the Health Care and Education Reconciliation Act (2010). Several resources are available that provide guidelines for the implementation of various forms of medical home (Szilagyi et al., 2015). Studies thus far have focused on the success of screening for health and developmental outcomes, so the actual impact of this model on the health and functioning of youth is unclear. Further placement instability and exits from care may confound the ability to provide treatment following assessment (Mekonnen et al., 2009). Of course, the success of such models is also dependent on caseworkers or other adult caregivers of youth in care. In at least one medical home program, only about half of the youth who were entering care had caseworkers who followed through to make appointments for their medical and mental health screening exams (Plax, Jonson-Reid, Kaushik, & Nishi, 2016).

The recognition of trauma and the role it plays in child development has led to an emerging consensus among national organizations (National Council of Juvenile and Family Court Judges, n.d.; National Child Traumatic Stress Network, n.d.; Substance Abuse and Mental Health Services Administration, 2015) recommending the creation of trauma-informed court systems to improve youth outcomes. This same call has been made for the child welfare system, and some states, such as Illinois, have been early adopters of such an approach. Thus far, there is little research on how trauma-informed systems influence outcomes (Ko et al., 2008; Pilnik & Kendall, 2012; Taylor, Steinber, & Wilson, 2006).

A variety of policy initiatives have focused on the needs of older youth transitioning from care, including most specifically the Foster Care Independence Act (1999), which established the John H. Chafee Foster Care Independence Program that provides supportive services and housing. Additional monies for education and training were provided in the Promoting Safe and Stable Families Amendments of 2001. To the extent that the services are of sufficient quality and quantity, these programs should impact the economic and stability factors that may increase the risk of engaging in criminal behavior. Additionally, states have the flexibility to extend time in care or allow youth to re-enter care until a certain age. At least one study found that allowing youth to remain in care longer (past the age of 18) was associated with decreased crossover to juvenile justice (Courtney & Dworsky, 2006). Many youth, however, do not choose to remain in care despite that option due to misperceptions of the policy, lack of investment from caseworkers, frustration with remaining in the system, and misconceptions about independence as an adult (Goodkind, Schelbe, & Shook, 2011).

Gaps in the Knowledge Base

As illustrated by the review of the current literature, despite significant concern, much remains unknown about the modifiable risk and protective factors, as well as best practices for prevention at the policy or program level, for youth who cross over from child welfare to the juvenile justice system. We know even less about the group of young people whose first contact is with juvenile justice and then are placed in foster care. Another gap in our understanding concerns the longer-term trajectories of various types of crossover populations beyond re-offenders. Other outcomes like education, employment, family formation, and health are also important in understanding both negative and resilient trajectories. Such trajectories may open windows onto additional opportunities to improve outcomes for crossover youth. Finally, there remain significant gaps in our understanding of crossover for certain racial and ethnic groups as well as sexual minority youth.

Intervention

Evidence-based approaches to addressing trauma and other behavioral health needs do exist, as well as promising practices to address placement stability (see earlier review). It is not clear how often these approaches are being used or if they impact the risk of crossover. Studies are needed that follow youth over time and take into account various services and interventions at the earliest point of child welfare contact to help us to understand which approaches are most effective.

Policy and System Issues

The need to make evidence-based programs available for vulnerable youth seems clear, but the best location of these services remains unknown. In Illinois, a statewide effort to train a number of agencies that provide services for youth in trauma-informed care to deliver interventions like SPARCS is currently underway (Illinois Collaboration on Youth, 2016). Gallegos and White (2013) advocate for service delivery in school settings. In Texas, both health and behavioral health needs of youth are coordinated through the specialized STAR Health program (Texas Department of Family and Protective Services, n.d.). It is not clear whether one form of service delivery is superior to another, and it may be that different models work for different regions. This is an empirical question that requires research and evaluation.

Similarly, several relevant policy initiatives exist at the regional, state, and federal levels that seek either to address crossover specifically, or related needs for behavioral health, transitional services, and permanency among youth in foster care. Few appear to have been rigorously evaluated in terms of youth well-being or delinquency outcomes. In areas with access to linked, multi-year administrative data, it may be possible to look at the implementation of some of these prior efforts and to examine whether they appear associated with changes in intermediate outcomes (e.g., access to care or stability) as well as decreases in the proportion of crossover youth. Going forward, the creation of university and state data linkage centers (e.g., the University of Michigan's Child and Adolescent Data Lab) may make policy evaluations more feasible. It may be possible to analyze administrative data across policy change time periods to attempt to understand whether there were changes in foster care experiences or outcomes associated with various policy approaches. Of course, any such effort needs to be accompanied by a thorough assessment of how a policy is being implemented in a given region.

Conclusion

The prevalence and consequences of youth crossing over between child welfare and juvenile justice systems make it imperative that we make a concerted effort to prevent the onset of delinquency and minimize the lingering effects of justice involvement. Increasing attention is being paid to this population, and there seem to be several promising approaches at the practice and policy levels that may demonstrate success. Currently, the replication of promising practices is outpacing the necessary body of evidence. We hope that the knowledge base catches up with those adopting and implementing new models for crossover youth. Additionally, we hope that researchers will be inspired to address the many critical questions that remain unanswered.

Acknowledgments

Unpublished data included in the present chapter were based on data from a study funded by the National Institute of Mental Health (R01MH061733). Points of view and opinions expressed in this chapter do not necessarily reflect those of the funding agency.

References

Adoption and Safe Families Act of 1997, Pub. L. No. 105-89, 111 Stat. 2115 (codified as amended in scattered sections of 42 U.S.C.). (1997).

Ayón, C. (2009). Shorter time-lines, yet higher hurdles: Mexican families' access to child welfare mandated services. *Children and Youth Services Review, 31*(6), 609–616.

Baetz, C. L. (2015). *A long-term follow-up of crossover youth: Young adult outcomes for maltreated youth in the juvenile justice system* (Doctoral dissertation). City University of New York. Retrieved from http://academicworks.cuny.edu/gc_etds/847

Baglivio, M. T., Wolff, K. T., Piquero, A. R., Bilchik, S., Jackowski, K., Greenwald, M. A., & Epps, N. (2016). Maltreatment, child welfare, and recidivism in a sample of deep-end crossover youth. *Journal of Youth and Adolescence, 45*(4), 625–654.

Barrett, D. E., Katsiyannis, A., Zhang, D., & Zhang, D. (2013). Delinquency and recidivism: A multicohort, matched-control study of the role of early adverse experiences, mental health problems, and disabilities. *Journal of Emotional and Behavioral Disorders, 22*(1), 3–15.

Berger, L. M., Bruch, S. K., Johnson, E. I., James, S., & Rubin, D. (2009). Estimating the "impact" of out-of-home placement on youth well-being: Approaching the problem of selection bias. *Child Development, 80*, 1856–1876.

Blakey, J. M., Leathers, S. J., Lawler, M., Washington, T., Natschke, C., Strand, T., & Walton, Q. (2012). A review of how states are addressing placement stability. *Children and Youth Services Review, 34*(2), 369–378.

Bright, C., & Jonson-Reid, M. (2015). Multiple service system involvement and later offending behavior: Implications for prevention and early intervention. *American Journal of Public Health, 105*(7), 1358–1364.

Bright, C. L., & Jonson-Reid, M. (2008). Onset of juvenile court involvement: Exploring gender-specific associations with maltreatment and poverty. *Children and Youth Services Review, 30*(8), 914–927.

Center for Juvenile Justice Reform. (n.d.). Retrieved from http://cjjr.georgetown.edu/

Child Welfare League of America & Lambda Legal. (2006). *Out of the margins: A report on regional listening forums highlighting the experiences of lesbian, gay, bisexual, transgender, and questioning youth in care.* Washington, DC: Author.

Chuang, E., & Wells, R. (2010). The role of inter-agency collaboration in facilitating receipt of behavioral health services for youth involved with child welfare and juvenile justice. *Children and Youth Services Review, 32*, 1814–1822.

Coleman, S. (2015). Crossover court: An integration of child welfare and juvenile justice, and the next step in the reformation of the juvenile system in Texas. *The Scholar: St. Mary's Law Review on Race and Social Justice, 17*, 375.

Courtney, M. E., & Dworsky, A. (2006). Early outcomes for young adults transitioning from out-of-home care in the USA. *Child & Family Social Work, 11*(3), 209–219.

Culhane, D. P., Byrne, T., Metraux, S., Moreno, M., Toros, H., & Stevens, M. (2011). *Young adult outcomes of youth exiting dependent or delinquent care in Los Angeles County* (Unpublished paper). Retrieved from http://works.bepress.com/dennis_culhane/113/

Cusick, G. R., Goerge, R. M., & Bell, K. C. (2009). *From corrections to community: The juvenile reentry experience as characterized by multiple systems involvement*. Chicago: Chapin Hall at the University of Chicago.

Cyr, K., Chamberland, C., Lessard, G., Clement, M., Weimmers, J., Collin-Vezina, D., . . . Damant, D. (2012). Polyvictimization in a child welfare sample of children and youth. *Psychology of Violence, 2*, 385–400.

Dannerbeck, A., & Yan, J. (2011). Missouri's crossover youth: Examining the relationship between their maltreatment history and their risk of violence. *OJJDP Journal of Juvenile Justice, 1*, 78–97.

Dierkhising, C. B., Ko, S. J., Woods-Jaeger, B., Briggs, E. C., Lee, R., & Pynoos, R. S. (2013). Trauma histories among justice-involved youth: Findings from the National Child Traumatic Stress Network. *European Journal of Psychotraumatology, 4*, 10.

Doyle, J. J. (2007). Child protection and youth outcomes: Measuring the effects of foster care. *American Economic Review, 97(5)*, 1583–1610.

Finkelhor, D., Shattuck, A., Turner, H. A., Ormrod, R., & Hamby, S. L. (2011). Polyvictimization in developmental context. *Journal of Child & Adolescent Trauma, 4*(4), 291–300.

Ford, J., Elhai, J., Conner, D., & Frueh, B. C. (2010). Poly-victimization and risk of posttraumatic, depressive, and substance abuse disorders and involvement in delinquency in a national sample of adolescents. *Journal of Adolescent Health, 46*, 545–552.

Ford, J., Grasso, D., Hawke, J., & Chapman, J. (2013). Poly-victimization among juvenile justice-involved youths. *Child Abuse & Neglect, 37*, 788–800.

Foster Care Independence Act, 42 U.S.C. § 1305. (1999).

Fostering Connections to Success and Increasing Adoptions Act (H.R. 6893). (2008). Retrieved from www.congress.gov/bill/110th-congress/house-bill/6893

Gallegos, A. H., & White, C. R. (2013). Preventing the school–justice connection for youth in foster care. *Family Court Review, 51*(3), 460–468.

Giallella, C. E. (2015). *Are crossover youth a distinct group? Comparing the mental health and substance use needs of crossover youth and delinquent-only youth* (Unpublished doctoral dissertation). Drexel University, Philadelphia, PA.

Goodkind, S., Schelbe, L. A., & Shook, J. J. (2011). Why youth leave care: Understandings of adulthood and transition successes and challenges among youth aging out of child welfare. *Children and Youth Services Review, 33*(6), 1039–1048.

Haggerty, K. P., Barkan, S. E., Skinner, M. L., Packard, W. B., & Cole, J. J. (2016). Feasibility of Connecting, a substance-abuse prevention program for foster teens and their caregivers. *Journal of the Society for Social Work and Research, 7*(4), 639–659.

Haight, W., Bidwell, L., Choi, W. S., & Cho, M. (2016). An evaluation of the Crossover Youth Practice Model (CYPM): Recidivism outcomes for maltreated youth involved in the juvenile justice system. *Children and Youth Services Review, 65*, 78–85.

Haight, W. L., Bidwell, L. N., Marshall, J. M., & Khatiwoda, P. (2014). Implementing the Crossover Youth Practice Model in diverse contexts: Child welfare and juvenile justice professionals' experiences of multisystem collaborations. *Children and Youth Services Review, 39*, 91–100.

Halemba, G., Siegel, G., Lord, R. D., & Zawacki, S. (2004). *Arizona dual jurisdiction study: Final report*. Pittsburg, PA: National Center for Juvenile Justice.

Health Care and Education Reconciliation Act, 42 U.S.C. § 1305. (2010).

Hedges, K. (2012). Teens in the grey zone: The structural violence of substance-using youth being raised in the system. *Human Organization, 71*(3), 317–325.

Henggeler, S. W., & Sheidow, A. J. (2012). Empirically supported family-based treatments for conduct disorder and delinquency in adolescents. *Journal of Marital and Family Therapy, 38*(1), 30–58.

Herz, D. C., & Ryan, J. P. (2008, September). Exploring the characteristics and outcomes of 241.1 youth crossing over from dependency to delinquency in Los Angeles County. *Center for Families, Youth & the Courts Research Update*, 1–13.

Herz, D. C., Ryan, J. P., & Bilchik, S. (2010). Challenges facing crossover youth: An examination of juvenile justice decision-making and recidivism. *Family Court Review, 48*(2), 305–321.

Hoeve, M., Stams, G. J. J., van der Put, C. E., Dubas, J. S., van der Laan, P. H., & Gerris, J. R. (2012). A meta-analysis of attachment to parents and delinquency. *Journal of Abnormal Child Psychology, 40*(5), 771–785.

Huang, H., & Ryan, J. P. (2014). The location of placement and juvenile delinquency: Do neighborhoods matter in child welfare? *Children and Youth Services Review, 44*, 33–45

Huang, H., Ryan, J. P., & Herz, D. C. (2012). The journey of dually-involved youth: The description and prediction of rereporting and recidivism. *Children and Youth Services Review, 34*(1), 254–260.

Illinois Collaboration on Youth. (2016). *Trauma-informed youth services*. Retrieved from www.icoyouth.org/trauma-informed-care

Irvine, A., & Canfield, A. (2015). Overrepresentation of lesbian, gay, bisexual, questioning, gender nonconforming and transgender youth within the child welfare to juvenile justice crossover population. *American University Journal of Gender, Social Policy & the Law, 24*, 243–261.

Jaudes, P. K., Champagne, V., Harden, A., Masterson, J., & Bilaver, L. (2012). Expanded medical home model works for youth in foster care. *Child Welfare, 91*(1), 9–33.

Jonson-Reid, M. (2002). Exploring the relationship between child welfare intervention and juvenile corrections involvement. *American Journal of Orthopsychiatry, 72*(4), 559–576.

Jonson-Reid, M. (2003). Foster care and future risk of maltreatment. *Children and Youth Services Review, 25*(4), 271–294.

Jonson-Reid, M. (2004). Child welfare services and delinquency: The need to know more. *Child Welfare, 83*(2), 157–173.

Jonson-Reid, M. (2011). Disentangling system contact and services: A key pathway to evidence-based youth's policy. *Children and Youth Services Review, 33*, 598–604.

Jonson-Reid, M., & Barth, R. P. (2000a). From maltreatment report to juvenile incarceration: The role of child welfare services. *Child Abuse & Neglect, 24*(4), 505–520.

Jonson-Reid, M., & Barth, R. P. (2000b). From placement to prison: The path to adolescent incarceration from child welfare supervised foster or group care. *Children and Youth Services Review, 22*(7), 493–516.

Jonson-Reid, M., & Barth, R. P. (2003). Probation foster care as an outcome for youth exiting child welfare foster care. *Social Work, 48*(3), 348–361.

Jonson-Reid, M., & Bright, C. (2015). Youth maltreatment: An environmental pathogen? In M. Delisi & M. Vaughn (Eds.), *Handbook of biosocial criminology*. Abingdon, UK: Routledge.

Jonson-Reid, M., & Drake, B. (2016). Child well-being: Where is it in our data systems? *Journal of Public Child Welfare, 10*(4), 457–465.

Jonson-Reid, M., Drake, B., & Kohl, P. (2009). Is the overrepresentation of the poor in child welfare due to bias or need? *Children and Youth Services Review, 31*(3), 422–427.

Jonson-Reid, M., Kohl, P. L., & Drake, B. (2012). Child and adult outcomes of chronic child maltreatment. *Pediatrics, 129*(5), 839–845.

Ko, S., Ford, J., Kassam-Adams, N, Berkowitz, S., Wilson, C., Wong, M., ... Layne, C. (2008). Creating trauma-informed systems: Child welfare, education, first responders, health care, juvenile justice. *Professional Psychology Research & Practice, 39*, 396–404.

Križ, K., Free, J., & Kuehl, G. (2016). How youth are removed from home in the United States. In K. Burns, T. Poso, & M. Skiveness (Eds.), *Child welfare removals by the state: A cross-country analysis of decision-making systems* (pp. 197–222). New York: Oxford University Press.

Lee, S., & Jonson-Reid, M. (under review). *Untangling the association between foster care placement and later juvenile delinquency*. Washington University.

Lee, S. Y., & Villagrana, M. (2015). Differences in risk and protective factors between crossover and non-crossover youth in juvenile justice. *Children and Youth Services Review, 58*, 18–27.

Leone, P. E., & Weinberg, L. A. (2010, May). Addressing the unmet educational needs of children and youth in the juvenile justice and child welfare systems. Paper presented at a symposium, May 7, Washington, DC, Georgetown University, Center for Juvenile Justice Reform.

Lynch, F. L., Dickerson, J. F., Saldana, L., & Fisher, P. A. (2014). Incremental net benefit of early intervention for preschool-aged youth with emotional and behavioral problems in foster care. *Children and Youth Services Review, 36*, 213–219.

Marsiglio, M. C., Chronister, K. M., Gibson, B., & Leve, L. D. (2014). Examining the link between traumatic events and delinquency among juvenile delinquent girls: A longitudinal study. *Journal of Child & Adolescent Trauma, 7*(4), 217–225.

Mekonnen, R., Noonan, K., & Rubin, D. (2009). Achieving better health care outcomes for youth in foster care. *Pediatric Clinics of North America, 56*(2), 405–415.

Millett, L., Kohl, P., Jonson-Reid, M., Drake, B., & Petra, M. (2013). Youth maltreatment victimization and subsequent perpetration of young adult intimate partner violence: An exploration of mediating factors. *Child Maltreatment, 18*, 71–84.

National Child Traumatic Stress Network. (n.d.). *Creating trauma-informed systems*. Retrieved from www.nctsnet.org/resources/topics/creating-trauma-informed-systems

National Child Traumatic Stress Network. (2008, August). *SPARCS: Structured Psychotherapy for Adolescents Responding to Chronic Stress*. Retrieved from www.nctsnet.org/nctsn_assets/pdfs/promising_practices/SPARCS_General.pdf

National Council of Juvenile and Family Court Judges. (n.d.). *Trauma informed system of care*. Retrieved from www.ncjfcj.org/our-work/trauma-informed-system-care

Patient Protection and Affordable Care Act, 42 U.S.C. § 18001. (2010).

Pecora, P. (2010). Why current and former recipients of foster care need high quality mental health services. *Administration and Policy in Mental Health and Mental Health Services Research, 37*(1), 185–190.

Pecora, P. J., Kessler, R. C., O'Brien, K., White, C. R., Williams, J., Hiripi, E., . . . Herrick, M. A. (2006). Educational and employment outcomes of adults formerly placed in foster care: Results from the Northwest Foster Care Alumni Study. *Children and Youth Services Review, 28*(12), 1459–1481.

Petro, J. (2005). *Juvenile justice and child welfare agencies: Collaborating to serve dual jurisdiction youth survey report*. Washington, DC: Research and Evaluation Division, Child Welfare League of America. Retrieved from https://pdfs.semanticscholar.org/2b9d/34520e90ca360d94cecf24140b5b323fd0ca.pdf

Pilnik, L., & Kendall, J. (2012). *Identifying polyvictimization and trauma among court involved children and youth: A checklist and resource guide for attorneys and other court-appointed advocates*. Bethesda, MD: Safe Start Center, Office of Juvenile Justice and Delinquency Prevention, Office of Justice Programs, U.S. Department of Justice.

Plax, K., Jonson-Reid, M., Kaushik, G., & Nishi, E. (2016). *Final evaluation summary for COACH*. Washington University: School of Medicine, The SPOT.

Price, J. M., Chamberlain, P., Landsverk, J., Reid, J. B., Leve, L. D., & Laurent, H. (2008). Effects of a foster parent training intervention on placement changes of youth in foster care. *Child Maltreatment, 13*(1), 64–75.

Promoting Safe and Stable Families Amendments of 2001, Title IV-B, Subpart 2, Social Security Act, 42 U.S.C. §§ 629–629g. (2002).

Randall, K. G. (2015). *Crossover youth: Person-centered approaches to understanding youth involved in the child welfare and juvenile justice systems* (Doctoral dissertation). University of Connecticut. Retrieved from http://digitalcommons.uconn.edu/dissertations/742

Rivaux, S. L., James, J., Wittenstrom, K., Baumann, D., Sheets, J., & Henry, J. (2008). The intersection of race, poverty and risk: Understanding the decision to provide services to clients and to remove youth. *Child Welfare, 87*(2), 151–168.

Rogers, J. K. (2014). It's a kid with a chance: Reconciling California's delinquency and dependency courts under dual status programs. *Los Angeles Public Interest Law Journal, 35*. Retrieved from https://ssrn.com/abstract=2887610

Runyan, D. K., & Gould, C. L. (1985). Foster care for youth maltreatment: Impact on delinquent behavior. *Pediatrics, 75*(3), 562–568.

Ryan, J. P., Hong, J. S., Herz, D., & Hernandez, P. M. (2010). Kinship foster care and the risk of juvenile delinquency. *Children and Youth Services Review, 32*(12), 1823–1830.

Ryan, J. P., Marshall, J. M., Herz, D., & Hernandez, P. M. (2008). Juvenile delinquency in child welfare: Investigating group home effects. *Children and Youth Services Review, 30*, 1088–1099.

Ryan, J. P., & Testa, M. F. (2005). Child maltreatment and juvenile delinquency: Investigating the role of placement and placement instability. *Children and Youth Services Review, 27*(3), 227–249.

Ryan, J. P., Testa, M. F., & Zhai, F. (2008). African American males in foster care and the risk of delinquency: The value of social bonds and permanence. *Child Welfare, 87*(1), 115–140.

Ryan, J. P., Williams, A. B., & Courtney, M. E. (2013). Adolescent neglect, juvenile delinquency and the risk of recidivism. *Journal of Child and Adolescence, 42*(3), 454–465.

Shaw, T. V., Bright, C. L., & Sharpe, T. L. (2015). Child welfare outcomes for youth in care as a result of parental death or parental incarceration. *Child Abuse & Neglect, 42*, 112–120.

Substance Abuse and Mental Health Services Administration. (2015, August 14). *Trauma-informed approach and trauma specific interventions*. Retrieved from www.samhsa.gov/nctic/trauma-interventions

Szilagyi, M. A., Rosen, D. S., Rubin, D., Zlotnik, S., Harmon, D., Jaudes, P., . . . Williams, P. G. (2015). Health care issues for youth and adolescents in foster care and kinship care. *Pediatrics, 136*(4), e1142–e1166.

Tam, C. C., Abrams, L. S., Freisthler, B., & Ryan, J. P. (2016). Juvenile justice sentencing: Do gender and child welfare involvement matter? *Children and Youth Services Review, 64*, 60–65.

Taussig, H. N., & Clyman, R. B. (2011). The relationship between time spent living with kin and adolescent functioning in youth with a history of out-of-home placement. *Child Abuse & Neglect, 35*(1), 78–86.

Taussig, H. N., Clyman, R. B., & Landsverk, J. (2001). Youth who return home from foster care: A 6-year prospective study of behavioral health outcomes in adolescence. *Pediatrics, 108*(1), e10.

Taussig, H., & Culhane, S. (2010). Impact of a mentoring and skills group program on mental health outcomes for maltreated youth in foster care. *Archives of Pediatrics & Adolescent Medicine, 164*(8), 739–746.

Taylor, S., Steinber, A., & Wilson, C. (2006). *The child welfare trauma referral tool*. San Diego, CA: Chadwick Center for Youth and Families, Rady Children's Hospital.

Texas Department of Family and Protective Services. (n.d.). *STAR Health: A guide to medical services at CPS*. Retrieved from www.dfps.state.tx.us/Child_Protection/Medical_Services/guide-star.asp

Unrau, Y. A., Seita, J. R., & Putney, K. S. (2008). Former foster youth remember multiple placement moves: A journey of loss and hope. *Children and Youth Services Review, 30*(11), 1256–1266.

Waldron, H. B., & Turner, C. W. (2008). Evidence-based psychosocial treatments for adolescent substance abuse. *Journal of Clinical Child & Adolescent Psychology, 37*(1), 238–261.

Widom, C. S. (1991). The role of placement experiences in mediating the criminal consequences of early childhood. *American Journal of Orthopsychiatry, 61*(2), 195–209.

25

Permanent and Formal Connections

Mentors, Community Services, and Connectedness

Preston A. Britner and Ciara M. Collins

Youth who have been placed in foster care or other out-of-home placements, such as residential facilities or group homes, may lack the permanent, stable, and supportive relationships that most youth enjoy. This may be true for the tens of thousands of youth who "age out" of the child welfare system in the United States each year. During adolescence and emerging adulthood, all youth encounter critical decisions around education, careers, relationships, and other life circumstances. Youth with child welfare histories frequently face this developmental transition perceiving less family-based support than their general population peers (Duke, Farruggia, & Germo, 2017; Farruggia, Greenberger, Chen, & Heckhausen, 2006). Given this potential deficit in familial adult support and guidance for transitioning foster youth, mentoring and other supportive programs have been identified as possible means for promoting non-parental supports and connections.

In this chapter, we will describe theoretical models (i.e., attachment, social support, resilience, Positive Youth Development, and mentoring) that have been or could be used to understand the formal connections for foster youth, and then review literature on types of programs and their effectiveness in promoting such important connections. We will conclude with some key next steps for the field.

Theoretical Models

In this section, we briefly review some theoretical models of relevance to the process of developing relationships and connections for youth in care. These models seem useful as frameworks for guiding mentoring and other supportive programs that might promote supports and connections for youth in foster care, as well as raising some potential areas of concern to consider when working with this vulnerable population.

Attachment

Human attachment theory (Bowlby, 1969/1982) is one of the most widely utilized frameworks to understand the nature and influence of close relationships across the lifespan. The theory links the qualities of social interaction and caregiving behaviors within close social relationships to internal representations, also referred to as working models, of relationships, and to a variety of behavioral outcomes. Youth with histories of separations from caregivers and exposure to trauma are more likely to develop insecure attachments, characterized by concerns about the consistency of caregivers' warmth or support; or even disorganized attachment relationships, characterized by even greater unpredictability and fear for their own safety, and linked to a host of negative behavioral outcomes (Britner, Randall, & Ahrens, 2014; Dozier & Rutter, 2008). The consequences of early experiences on relationship style have also been shown to persist into adulthood with adult romantic relationships and caregiving relationships (Thompson, 2008).

Attachment theory has specific implications for mentoring relationships among youth in foster care. As these youth establish relationships with mentors, early life disruptions and/or perceived rejections in parental relationships may influence working models and shape how relationships with teachers, mentors, coaches, and other key adults are viewed (Britner et al., 2014). For example, given their interpersonal histories of abuse or neglect and experiences of removals from parents and home, youth in foster care may perceive rejection in mentoring relationships in response to seemingly minor actions or events (e.g., a missed meeting; a neutral comment interpreted as a negative one) that would be unlikely to affect other youth (Rhodes, 2002). A history of experiencing rejection may also complicate the initial relationship building; mentors of youth in foster care might encounter more anger or resistance on the part of the youth. Attachment theory may be useful for the conceptualization and measurement of mentoring processes, relationship disruption, youth's perceptions of rejection, and youth's long-term development of views of connections with important others (Britner et al., 2014).

Social Support

Social support is the utilization of relationships to increase positive outcomes or to buffer negative outcomes. Social support can be broadly defined as "verbal and non-verbal information or advice, tangible aid, or action that is proffered by social intimates or inferred by their presence and has beneficial emotional or behavioral effects on the recipients" (Gottlieb, 1983, p. 28). More specifically, House and Kahn (1985) defined social support as encompassing support along four dimensions: 1) emotional, 2) instrumental, 3) informational, and 4) appraisal. Emotional support includes expressions of empathy, love, trust, and caring; for example, when a trusted other uses active listening, validation, and reflecting back to show interest in and concern for what is being shared. Instrumental support involves tangible aid and resources, usually in instances in which someone provides money, housing, or time to help someone else. Informational support consists of providing advice and information, such as giving someone the phone number for a doctor's office or providing advice about one's own experience with a certain situation. Appraisal support is affirming and constructive feedback used for self-evaluation and is helpful when trying to encourage someone about her or his strengths or positive qualities.

Many theories and models have been used to explain social support. A few of the most influential have been social control theory (Hirschi, 1969), Bronfenbrenner's (1986) bioecological model, social convoy theory (Kahn & Antonucci, 1980), developmental contextualism (Lerner, 1995), risk/protective factors framework (Bogenschneider, 1996), Schofield's (2002) biopsychosocial model, and attachment theory (discussed previously in this chapter; Bowlby, 1969/1982). Although many theories and models describe social support, there are common elements among them. First, social support is viewed as transactional/bidirectional, meaning that support is given to one another by both people in a relationship instead of unidirectionally, flowing from one person to another (Armstrong, Birnie-Lefcovitch, & Ungar, 2005). Second, relationships with others and the environment act as buffers against the development of psychological (e.g., anxiety, irritability, depression, lack of focus) or physical symptoms (e.g., fatigue, body aches, pains), primarily in individuals who are under stress. Social support theories, in general, suggest that the development of these symptoms can be lessened if a strong social support network exists (Cohen & McKay, 1984). Last, membership in multiple social support networks is viewed as a protective factor that aids in the prevention of negative physical and mental health outcomes. This is similar to the second point, but emphasizes the importance of multiple support networks so that failure of any one network to provide support is balanced by the existence of other networks (Perry, 2006).

Social support theories can provide an excellent framework for understanding the well-being of adolescents in foster care and those aging out of the system; however, the application of social support theories in programming for and studying foster youth has been inconsistent and mediocre. The systematic and rigorous use of social support theories would help to inform how foster youth make connections, whom they connect with, and how this influences their well-being. Additionally, social support theories provide a context for the many systems that foster youth are a part of, such as foster families, biological families, and the child welfare system. Social support theories emphasize contextual factors, social networking, and types of support that are important in understanding the permanent and formal connections foster youth make in adolescence and young adulthood.

One area in the realm of social support that shows promise in its application to foster youth is the social network perspective. This perspective adds to the concept of social support by looking at how various people in one individual's network communicate with each other and work together to help the individual (Blakeslee, 2012). Blakeslee (2012) suggests that looking at these interconnections might show differences in the level of transition support that foster youth receive when aging out of care, helping us to understand some of the nuances that are still unexplained in the social support literature. Further, she suggests that an ideal foster youth network might have both personal and service network members connected to each other by collaborative interaction over time. Additionally, by using this perspective, researchers would be better able to measure these relationships and systematically account for the role of social service workers and other formal supports in support provision during the transition out of care (Blakeslee, 2012).

Resilience

Resilience is a broad term that has an elusive definition. Bundick, Yeager, King, and Damon (2010) emphasize that in order to determine whether resilience has occurred, there must be a history of threats to an individual's equilibrium, or adequate level of functioning, and the utilization of a stored capacity of skills needed to respond effectively to that threat, which results in at least a return to equilibrium in the wake of adversity. This means that once a person experiences a threat or adverse situation, there is often a dip in functioning that, with the appropriate set of skills, can be overcome to return to the initial level of functioning or a better one. Other definitions have included similar concepts that revolve around the ability to succeed despite adversity or negative circumstances (Gartland, Bond, Olsson, Buzwell, & Sawyer, 2011; Quisenberry & Foltz, 2013). The current literature views resilience as both a personal characteristic, as well as the process of an individual utilizing personal characteristics and environmental resources (Gartland et al., 2011; Ungar, 2004). Masten (2001) wrote, "Most of the resilience investigators of the past decade have assumed that resilience arises from many dynamic interactions within and between organism and environment, but the systematic study of such patterns and pathways is in the nascent stage" (p. 233). In the two decades after Masten's (2001) critique, there has been some progress in the area of studying resiliency, but there is still much more work that needs to be done.

Resilience is a relevant theory and framework for foster youth, given the amount of trauma and adverse childhood experiences that usually precede placement in the child welfare system. As specifically applied to youth who have recently aged out of the foster care system, Jones (2012) found that resilience included: 1) maintaining connection to the adult world through a job or education, 2) having stable housing, 3) avoiding substance abuse, 4) not being in the criminal justice system, 5) having optimism about the future, and 6) preparedness for independent living. In looking for factors that contribute to resilience, he found that higher resilience was associated with: 1) being older at the time of exiting care, 2) feeling close to a greater number of people, and 3) higher competence on independent living skills; while lower resilience was associated with returning to live with biological family members (Jones, 2012). Additionally, Strolin-Goltzman, Woodhouse, Suter, and Werrbach (2016) found that student engagement, especially student–teacher relationships, increased educational resilience among foster youth, which led to a greater likelihood of students enrolling or intending to enroll in higher education.

Positive Youth Development

Positive Youth Development (PYD) and resilience research go hand in hand, and yet represent two somewhat different perspectives. Positive Youth Development uses developmental assets as a way to identify both internal attributes and external resources for children and youth, instead of focusing on risks or negative attributes that might lead children to be at risk or delinquent. The asset-building component of PYD is the underpinning for resilience (Edwards, Mumford, & Serra-Roldan, 2007). According to Masten and Coatsworth (1998), resilience is derived from: 1) within-child factors (e.g., cognitive abilities, emotion and behavioral regulation, and positive affect/temperament), 2) within-home factors (e.g., secure attachment to parent), and 3) outside-home factors (e.g., school environments). Edwards and colleagues (2007) further suggest that the developmental assets that resilient children demonstrate come from corresponding categories of personal, social-emotional, and environmental domains. These developmental assets serve as protective factors that are aligned with the three sources of resiliency mentioned previously. Therefore, PYD and developmental assets are seen as a primary prevention method for engendering resilience characteristics in all children before intervention is necessary.

Positive Youth Development is a newer branch of research compared with resilience and social support and has therefore not been applied to foster youth extensively. However, longitudinal research identifying developmental assets in foster youth might be useful in explaining why some foster youth appear more resilient than others during and after aging out of care. Those who have argued for PYD's application to the foster care system state that foster youth need more skill-building opportunities, and that social workers should use the PYD framework to assist foster youth in their transition out of care (Scannapieco, Connell-Carrick, & Painter, 2007). Certainly, a better understanding of the assets with which youth enter and leave care would help to inform more efficient and effective services for foster youth. However, more research is needed as to whether the external assets required for resilience according to PYD theory, such as consistent support, empowerment, and appropriate boundaries and expectations, exist for those foster youth who have experienced abuse, and especially, multiple foster placements.

Mentoring

The most widely cited model of youth mentoring is Rhodes's (2002) pathways of mentoring influence model, which suggests that there is a crucial step to mentoring in which mentor and youth protégé form an emotional bond, not dissimilar to an attachment–caregiving bond. Only then can the mentor influence the youth's developmental outcomes by enhancing social and cognitive skills through dialogue, teaching, and an array of interactions, and serve as a role model and advocate for the youth. Positive mentoring relationships can foster social and emotional development by challenging the youths' views of themselves in relationships, by providing a compensatory experience that revises internal working models and generalizes to other relationships, by helping youth to regulate their emotions, and by alleviating relationship stress (Rhodes, 2002).

Applying this model to youth in foster care, experiences of trauma or disrupted relationships with caregivers early in life and resultant maladaptive approaches to relationships later in life (Dozier &

Rutter, 2008) may make it more difficult for foster youth to form a social bond with a mentor. Relationship duration, a moderator of mentoring impact proposed by Rhodes (2002), may be influenced by out-of-home placement in that placement changes may truncate even high-quality mentoring relationships and thus decrease their impact. In sum, youth in foster care, as a population, are highlighted by this theoretical model as having characteristics and experiences that likely make it more difficult for mentoring relationships or programs to achieve positive effects on youth (Britner et al., 2014).

Despite these concerns, Rhodes's (2002) model also points toward the potential for certain processes that could facilitate the positive effects of mentoring. It could be that in the absence of family connections and consistent external support (i.e., due to multiple foster placements), the life circumstances of these youth are often such that the introduction of a mentor may represent a notably more salient and potentially positive influential source of change in the youth's social resources and self-esteem than is the case for most other youth.

Whereas Rhodes's (2002) model is the most popular, other researchers have proposed ideas to explicate how mentoring works. For example, Parra, DuBois, Neville, Pugh-Lilly, and Povinelli (2002) presented a structural model in which mentoring, and particularly the development of a significant bond, widens the youth's social support networks, which in turn bolsters self-esteem. Keller's (2005) systemic conceptual model emphasizes the interdependent network of relationships established between mentor, child, parent/guardian, and caseworkers, all of which develop within various formal systems. The importance of these multiple relationships—and issues like communication from mentor to foster parent about a youth's behaviors or progress—leads nicely into a discussion of the types of program that exist to help support youth in care.

Program Types

Attempts to build meaningful and sustained non-parental relationships and connections for youth in or aging out of care could occur in many types of intervention or program. Although they are not mutually exclusive, we have organized the review of program types as: child welfare-specific programs; mentoring programs; community-based programs; and educational/vocational programs. Of course, these interventions have a variety of intended outcomes, in addition to the outcome focus of this chapter—the development of permanent connections for foster youth.

Program Type I: Child Welfare-Specific Programs

One major type of program sponsored by child welfare agencies is the Independent Living Program (ILP). In 1986, Congress allotted funds to help states with independent living initiatives for foster youth (Consolidated Omnibus Budget Reconciliation Act of 1985, P.L. 99-272). Independent Living Programs were created to help current and former foster youth with skills related to becoming self-sufficient before or while aging out of care. These ILPs often help youth with employment, housing, physical and mental health, substance abuse, and provide a mentoring relationship and/or connection to adults. However, more than a decade after the creation of ILPs, there was little improvement in outcomes among youth aging out of care, which resulted in Congress passing the Foster Care Independence Act of 1999 (P.L. 106-169). This Act created the John H. Chafee Foster Care Independence Program (CFCIP), which provides health care coverage to former foster children until age 21, and doubled the funding for ILPs that covered mentoring, life skills, housing, and college tuition assistance. More recently, the Fostering Connections to Success and Increasing Adoptions Act of 2008 (P.L. 110-351) gives states the ability to extend Title IV-E foster care to the age of 21 and requires states to have a transition planning process in place for youth leaving care. However, despite these policy gains, very little is known about the effectiveness of ILPs, largely due to a lack of studies with rigorous methodological quality (Greeson, Garcia, Kim, & Courtney, 2015).

The first randomized controlled trial (RCT) of an ILP measured the effectiveness of the program on social support utilization in foster youth (Greeson et al., 2015). The program used a relationship-based model that paired each foster youth with an outreach worker who helped youth with individualized goals, as well as identifying social support networks (Greeson et al., 2015). The study found that the program did not have an impact on foster youth's social support utilization as compared to foster youth who were not in the program, and in fact, social support significantly decreased across 2 years (Greeson et al., 2015). Similarly, Singer, Berzin, and Hokanson (2013) found that foster youth expected formal supports to provide for emotional, instrumental, and appraisal needs. However, this was found to be at the expense of informal supports (Greeson et al., 2015; Singer et al., 2013). These findings suggest that reliance on formal social supports might lead foster youth to decrease engagement with informal social supports.

The Midwest Evaluation of the Adult Functioning of Former Foster Youth (Midwest Study; Courtney & Dworsky, 2006) also yielded mixed findings regarding social support. The Midwest Study was a longitudinal study of foster youth aging out of care and transitioning to adulthood in Illinois, Iowa, and Wisconsin (Courtney & Dworsky, 2006). The Midwest Study interviewed youth at five time points on a broad range of topics related to their experiences in foster care and since aging out or leaving care (Courtney, Dworsky, Brown, Love, & Vorhies, 2011). Since the passage of the Foster Care Independence Act of 1999 (P.L. 106-169), states which had increased the age at which foster youth could remain in the system allowed foster youth to sign themselves out of care at 18 if they chose. Therefore, in this study, youth who aged out and youth who chose to leave care are considered commensurate.

The Midwest Study found no significant differences in levels of social support on a self-report measure between youth who chose to or were allowed to remain in foster care after their 18th birthday, and youth who chose to leave care or were forced out of care. However, there were differences in the type and extent to which youth still in care utilized formal supports compared with their peers who were not in care. Youth still in care were more likely to have health insurance and be enrolled in a 2- or 4-year college, which increased their access to and use of health and mental health services, and independent living services, as well as reducing the likelihood of pregnancy, and decreasing the risk of economic hardship or criminal justice involvement (Courtney & Dworsky, 2006). This suggests that remaining in care with formal supports had a positive impact on a wide array of outcomes, but not necessarily an impact on perceived social support. Therefore, studies that just use a self-report measure of social support might not be adequately capturing the benefits that foster youth receive from formal supports while in care.

Permanent connections were a primary theme that came up in focus groups with foster youth, foster parents, and caseworkers involved with a PAL (Preparation for Adult Living) program (Scannapieco et al., 2007). Every youth stated that a relationship with a support person or network was needed upon exiting care. The researchers concluded that caseworkers and foster parents have a role in helping foster youth to plan thoughtfully and seek out permanent connections, whether formal or informal, and caseworkers should invite supportive adults to meetings to encourage adults to participate in the youth's life (Scannapieco et al., 2007).

Program Type II: Mentoring Programs

Since 2002, unsuccessful attempts have been made to establish and support state-wide mentoring programs through a Foster Care Mentoring Act in the U.S. Congress. Nonetheless, there is an array of formal mentoring and informal mentoring programs that occur with youth in care. In some programs, mentoring is offered only after the child is in a stable placement. Other programs will combat foster care drift, an all-too-common series of removals and/or returns to the family, by assigning a mentor or supporting a natural mentor in an attempt to present a rare constant in a youth's life. As outlined in the theoretical models section on mentoring, programs for youth seek to minimize an array of risk factors and to maximize multiple protective factors. For a detailed review of all outcomes of naturally occurring and formal mentoring for youth in care, please see Britner et al. (2014). In this section, we draw upon Britner et al. (2014), but retain a focus on the specific outcome of building stable connections for foster youth.

Naturally Occurring Mentors for Foster Youth

Natural mentors are adults such as coaches, teachers, youth workers, or extended family who serve as role models for youth (Greeson & Bowen, 2008). Although there is evidence that the presence of a natural mentor is associated with a variety of positive outcomes for youth in foster care, until recently, there has not been much research on how these relationships function or on which aspects are particularly effective. For example, researchers used qualitative interviews to determine the mentoring relationship qualities and forms of support offered that matter most to these youth as they transitioned out of foster care (Munson, Smalling, Spencer, Scott, & Tracy, 2010). The study was comprised of youth (19 years old) (N=189) who reported having a natural mentor. Certain qualities of the mentors themselves were mentioned in many of the interviews; mentors were reported to be approachable, easy to be with, and understanding. Additionally, some youth emphasized the similarities between themselves and their mentors (e.g., enjoying the same activities, being close in age) as factors that enhanced the relationship. In looking at qualities of the relationships, consistency and longevity were reported to be significant factors. Often, the mentoring relationship was one of the most stable and longest lasting in the youth's life. Other important relationship qualities were authenticity, respect, trust, and empathy, the latter two of which are key qualities in the Rhodes (2002) model discussed in the previous section. Finally, support received from the mentors included advice, emotional support, tangible support (e.g. money, transportation), instrumental support, and helping to hold the youth accountable.

These findings are consistent with those of another study addressing the quality and important aspects of mentoring relationships. Greeson and Bowen (2008) conducted interviews with seven female foster youths of color and focused on their relationships with natural mentors. The age range of this small sample was 13 to 20 (mean = 16.3 years), so this study included some younger foster youth. Several themes emerged from the data. In general, the relationship characteristics reported as most important were trust, love, and caring, and being like the relationship between parent and child, reinforcing the theoretical importance of attachment or acceptance. The youth also gave examples of the support they received from their mentor, including availability to talk, giving advice, sharing their point of view, and providing needed material items. Additionally, the youth discussed how their mentors helped them to make positive changes such as bettering academic performance or improving relationships with others in their lives.

Greeson, Usher, and Grinstein-Weiss (2010) analyzed the National Longitudinal Study of Adolescent to Adult Health (Add Health) to compare how the presence of natural mentors might be associated with increased assets available to foster and non-foster youth. The authors point out that natural mentors may be particularly important as role models for youth in foster care who might not have biological family members to serve in this capacity. They found that the presence of a natural mentor was associated with greater likelihood for foster youth of having a bank account. Additionally, the presence of a natural mentor who took on a parental role was associated with increased earnings expectations.

Ahrens and colleagues (2011) conducted qualitative interviews with 23 former foster youth (ages 18 to 25). Although they found that natural mentor relationships were varied in their nature, duration, and impact, many of the themes that characterized the best relationships (e.g., being caring, respectful, and authentic) mirrored the findings of other studies cited above. Consistent with our summary of attachment theory, some young adults in the study described having difficulties forming and/or maintaining a bond with non-parental adults, and they related these difficulties to prior (difficult) experiences with caregivers and/or other adults. Some described mentors who were able to overcome initial rejection and/or fear of emotional risk on the part of the youth. Other youth reported being more open to mentoring during times of vulnerability, such as transitions out of foster care, suggesting that timing is an important factor in the initiation of mentoring relationships.

Hirsch, Mickus, and Boerger (2002) note difficulties in recruiting formal mentors in many communities and suggest that recruitment of informal mentors within afterschool and community center programs may be more viable for a variety of youth at risk. Greeson et al. (2010) concur and propose that the gradual building of the relationship is less pressure-filled than what might occur in a formal mentoring program; furthermore, relationships with natural mentors may be more likely to be maintained over time because youth and mentor already share a social network. Ahrens et al. (2011) speculate that professionals associated with the child welfare system may be particularly strong natural mentors for this population, in that they are likely to understand these youths' unique challenges.

Duke et al. (2017) interviewed 99 young adults who had recently emancipated from foster care about the very important non-parental adults in their lives. Interestingly, 40% of those relationships came from pre-existing familial networks and 78% of these natural mentoring relationships had formed before or during adolescence. In other words, many youth in care and aging out of care do see themselves as having non-parental support persons, even if those adults are not routinely identified or recognized by child welfare systems as mentors.

Formal Mentors

In contrast to informal mentoring, formal mentoring occurs in programs that intentionally recruit mentors and mentees, match them, and monitor the relationship and mentee outcomes (Rhodes, 2002). Some mentoring programs are specifically tailored to working with foster youth, but there is little research on the effectiveness of these programs in terms of long-term stable supports. One factor that might increase the success of a mentor match is the mentor having similar experiences to those of youth in foster care. In a study of a campus-based learning program for transitioning foster youth, Kirk and Day (2011) reported the inclusion of a positive, peer-based mentoring model between the participating youth and the program counselors. Participating youth were aged 15 to 19 and were either currently in foster care or had previous involvement in the child welfare system. Undergraduate students served as counselors in the program; most were foster care alumni. Focus group discussions with youth suggest that of the many positive role models in the program, those with the greatest impact were those who had been through the foster care system themselves. Consistent with attachment theory, the youth participants felt that they could easily identify with, trust, and build relationships with those who had shared similar experiences to themselves.

Some comprehensive mentoring programs serve foster youth, although they are not specifically designed to do so. Within larger studies of such comprehensive programs, there are some examples of mentoring research that directly address youth in foster care. Using the Public/Private Ventures impact study of urban Big Brothers Big Sisters programs, Rhodes, Haight, and Briggs (1999) studied 90 mentored foster youth (78 in kinship care, 12 in non-relative care) in comparison to (a) non-foster youth with mentors and (b) foster youth without mentors. At the 18-month follow-up, mentored foster youth were more likely to demonstrate improved social skills and comfort/trust interacting with others, based on parental (i.e., biological or foster parent, depending on placement at the point of follow-up) reports, in comparison to (mentored) non-foster youth. There was evidence of improvements in self-esteem and prosocial support from friends (e.g., "Would your friends agree to do you a favor if you asked?") for mentored foster youth, whereas declines on these outcomes were apparent for foster youth without mentors. This study is useful because of its longitudinal, experimental design. Findings are limited, however, by the small sample size, limited range of outcomes evaluated, and also by a lack of information regarding the maltreatment and placement histories of foster youth.

Program Type III: Community-Based Programs

Community-based programs include programs aimed at increasing positive outcomes for foster youth that are not run or evaluated by child welfare agencies. The Under One Sky summer camp for older youth in foster care is an example of a community-based program that was created according to a Positive Youth Development (PYD) framework and evaluated by an independent research team (Howse, Diehl, & Trivette, 2010). The aim of the camp was to increase developmental assets and the likelihood of adoption. In order to understand the receptivity of youth to adoption, camp staff were encouraged to create a space for informal conversations about youth perspectives on adoption. Camp staff then worked with social workers to match youth who were open to adoption with adoptive families (Howse et al., 2010). Developmental assets are "positive relationships, opportunities, skills, and values that help young people grow up healthy" (Scales & Leffert, 1999, p. 1) and are categorized into internal and external assets. Internal assets include positive values, positive identity, and social competencies, while external assets include support, empowerment, and clear boundaries and expectations (Howse et al., 2010). They found that internal assets increased over time and that youth who had been adopted reported a higher level of internal assets than youth who had not been adopted; however, these findings did not extend to external assets.

Similarly, Osterling and Hines (2006) found that the community-based Advocates to Successful Transition to Independence program for older foster youth aging out of care was successful in training adult advocates to help the youth learn how to access resources and assistance. Youth (N=52) routinely described advocates as being very supportive in qualitative interviews, and they reported strong connections with their advocates. Advocates helped with a variety of tasks such as "obtaining a job, opening a bank account, saving money, completing tax forms and completing their education" (p. 249). However, youth were more likely to report acquiring social skills than independent living skills from the program.

Program Type IV: Educational/Vocational Programs

There is often a gap between students' aspirations (i.e., the desire to pursue higher education) and expectations (i.e., the belief that one is actually capable of doing so and that it will one day happen) (Reynolds & Pemberton, 2001), and this gap may be even larger among foster youth. Whereas higher education has the potential to improve their future earnings and mediate the effects of traumatic childhood experiences, many youth in care do not perceive that they have a mentor for the college experience. Having such a mentor was a key predictor of intention to persist past the first semester of college in a study of 237 college students who were not in foster care (Baier, Markman, & Pernice-Duca, 2016). College attendance rates among foster youth are as low as 20%, whereas only about 5% of foster youth will actually complete a Bachelor's degree; this is compared with 60% attendance and 20% completion among their non-foster peers (Wolanin, 2005).

Congress established the Education and Training Voucher (ETV) program in 2001 as part of the John H. Chafee Foster Care Independence Program (P.L. 106-169) to help combat barriers to post-secondary education. The ETV program provides additional federal funding to states to disburse to foster youth to assist with tuition, room and board, or other education-related costs. However, the impact of the ETV program on the pursuit of post-secondary education is unknown and the program does not help foster youth with any non-financial needs during the transition and completion of their education (Dworsky & Pérez, 2010).

An alternative approach that began in the late 1990s is to have campus support programs that provide financial, academic, social/emotional, and logistical support. These campus support programs are usually financed in part by private funding and are also not well researched. So far, one exploratory study has evaluated program components and student experiences of campus support programs in California and Washington (Dworsky & Pérez, 2010). These programs were aimed at supporting foster youth while in college and were either based at specific colleges or were centralized and helped youth at multiple colleges. Using a social support framework, instrumental and informational support came up again and again as the areas of greatest need. Students indicated that these programs were most helpful with: financial aid, housing (both during the academic year and during breaks), living expenses, leadership development, graduate school advising, and career counseling (Dworsky & Pérez, 2010). Housing during academic breaks is often overlooked, but represents a major barrier for foster youth to attend school full-time. Many universities/colleges do not provide housing and most financial aid does not cover housing during breaks, which puts foster youth who have aged out of the system, and have no permanent home, at a disadvantage. The study found that foster youth had unmet needs in the area of informational support, such as understanding the new work load and different environment of college. Emotionally, students stated that the campus support programs helped with their feelings of loneliness, but they would have appreciated more events to socialize with other participants and more one-on-one support from staff. The majority of students also remarked on the usefulness of staff mentors and appreciated the "sense of family" in the campus support programs (Dworsky & Pérez, 2010, p. 261). One criticism of campus-based support programs is that they do not help youth get into or make the transition to college, and therefore cannot affect the number of foster youth applying to and attending college, only the number completing college.

One short-term summer camp program in Michigan was created to support foster youth aging out of the system with the transition from high school to college (Kirk & Day, 2011; also reviewed above under mentoring). Although the theory behind the program was not described in detail, focus groups completed with foster youth after the program indicated that the greatest perceived benefit was information learned about campus life and scholarships for college, suggesting an increase in informational support (Kirk & Day, 2011). Other benefits of the program perceived by youth included help with taking responsibility for one's own actions, feeling an enhanced sense of self, feeling more competent, and feeling more optimistic about the future. The authors claimed that the mentoring component of the program increased social support for the youth, which contributed to an increase in resilience; however, additional research is needed to corroborate these findings.

Several studies have gathered information from former foster youth who successfully enrolled in or completed college to determine factors that led to their success (Hass & Graydon, 2009; Hines, Merdinger, & Wyatt, 2005; Mendis, 2015). The former foster youth in these studies displayed a clear sense of self-efficacy and motivation that led them to pursue higher education. In responding to questions regarding their capabilities, the majority responded positively (Hass & Graydon, 2009). Mendis (2015) described a subset of students who showed initiative in working toward attending college despite a lack of resources and social support. Even though they may not have had a supportive adult in their lives, these individuals were likely to seek out assistance from professionals when they needed help (Mendis, 2015). Although these studies begin to shed light on what might distinguish resilient youth in care, especially in terms of educational attainment, little is known about the nature or processes of the mentoring or other formal connections that may be at work.

Social support is a significant factor in the promotion of academic self-efficacy. Kirk, Lewis, Nilsen, and Colvin (2011) found that while parental support was predictive of academic aspirations and expectations, foster youth were rated lower in terms of this support than their non-foster peers. Many foster youth experience a lack of social support that may impede their academic success (Britner et al., 2014). Geenen and Powers (2007) conducted a qualitative study of foster youth, parents, and professionals, gathering their thoughts and suggestions based on their experiences with youth transitioning into adulthood. Foster parents and professionals emphasized the importance of caring relationships to provide youth with stability and support. However, many foster youth spoke of feeling isolated, noting that they did not have any stable or supportive relationships in their lives (Geenen & Powers, 2007).

Day, Riebschleger, Dworsky, Damashek, and Fogarty (2012) reported the results of a foster youth forum on barriers to educational success. High-school- and college-age youth (N=43) reported the importance of stable, caring relationships with adults both in and out of the school setting. Teachers who were attentive to their personal problems and needs helped them to succeed academically, while guardians had the opportunity to encourage and monitor school attendance and homework completion. Youth who did not have such adults in their lives were not motivated to put effort into their academic studies or recognize the importance of education (Day et al., 2012).

In one study of former foster youth, many participants cited the support from figures in school and community settings as being a positive influence on their success (Hass & Graydon, 2009). The former foster youth said that they felt the teachers treated them well in school, and that they had someone, often a teacher or mentor, to whom they could turn in times of need. Although supportive relationships are vital for successful outcomes for foster youth, these relationships do not exist for all youth in or aging out of the foster care system. Thus, programs that facilitate natural mentoring or promote formal mentoring must be expanded and studied. Interventions to promote educational outcomes for youth in care need to consider relationships with mentors or other long-term connections as an important outcome, in and of itself, and as a facilitator for educational outcomes.

Example of an Academic-Based Summer Program for Foster Youth

The University of Connecticut (UConn) First Star Academy (First Star Academy, n.d.) is a program that aims to improve college attendance and completion among foster youth. Since 2013, the program has recruited adolescents in foster care to spend a month on the UConn campus in the summer, during which they form peer and mentoring relationships and participate in academic programming. In each summer (i.e., after 9th, 10th, and 11th Grade), students can earn up to three college credits, taking core classes such as English, math, and science. They are also provided with programming on study skills and college preparation, in addition to other life and social skills, such as interpersonal communication, emotion regulation, and mindfulness practices. First Star also runs sessions once a month on Saturdays throughout the school year to allow for continuing support. The focus of the program is on academic achievement (i.e., high school graduation, college matriculation, and success), and preliminary outcomes have been excellent, to date.

Ongoing evaluation of the program (by the authors of this chapter) also involves looking at students' perceived social support, self-efficacy, and locus of control, as well as outcome measures of Positive Youth Development and academic achievement. Locus of control refers to the extent to which people believe they have control over their lives. An internal locus of control indicates a greater belief in one's agency, while an external locus of control indicates a greater belief in chance and the inability to change things in one's life (Rotter, 1966). Students' reviews of the program, and qualitative responses related to their meaning-making, sense of identity, and presence of risk and protective factors, are also used to determine the program's impact on youth in a holistic way. The contribution of youth voices in the process of evaluating the program helps to develop effective interventions that increase positive outcomes. As linked to this chapter, one future area of inquiry for the program will be to understand how students' relationships with program teachers, counselors, resident assistants, and peers persist (or do not) over time as the students pursue higher education, enter the workforce, and exit the child welfare system.

Next Steps

There is a limited research base on the frequency, quality, duration, and effectiveness of stable relationships and connections for youth in foster care and those aging out of care. With few exceptions, most of the research reviewed consisted of rich qualitative data from small, selected samples or limited investigations of the impact of having a mentor within larger quantitative studies. Additionally, this chapter illustrates the wide number of theoretical models that have been or could be applied to foster youth in and aging out of the child welfare system, yet the application of theory and rigorous methodology have been lacking. Part of the reason for this is the lack of clarity within constructs, especially ones like social support and resilience, which have many different theoretical and operational definitions that make it difficult to compare within—much less across—constructs. Subsequently, trying to use multiple constructs to understand the experience of foster youth becomes convoluted.

Another important factor to consider when studying foster youth is that many avenues for assessing foster youth are based on the mainstream society's view of normal (Ungar, 2004). For example, the predominant discourse on resilience outcomes is led by White, middle- and upper-class professional men, who are often far removed demographically from the subjects being studied (Ungar, 2004). The "objective" assessment of development and predetermination of what is acceptable for individuals who comprise the cultural minority that is foster youth limit the possibilities available to youth from the start. Constructs that do not take into account youth's own definitions of success and resilience set interventions up to fail before they are even implemented (Ungar, 2004).

Future longitudinal research should take into account the heterogeneity among youth who have experienced foster placements by testing for differences across such potential moderators as: type and severity of abuse or neglect; duration, type, number, and quality of foster placements (all of which vary widely); and natural and informal mentoring versus formal interventions. Youth in foster care are also disproportionately represented in other special populations (e.g., juvenile offenders, those with mental health needs, or at educational risk), so there is a need for greater integration of services in order to eliminate "support overload" or redundant or conflicting messages from multiple adult authority figures (e.g., social workers, caregivers, parents, foster parents, mentors). We must also study the overlapping protocols and samples within larger child welfare systems in order to begin to disentangle risks, services, and outcomes related to promoting non-parental connections for youth in care and those transitioning out of care (Britner et al., 2014; Keller, Cusick, & Courtney, 2007). More intentional and large-scale research is needed to gain a better understanding of what foster youth need in their transition to adulthood and out of care. However, findings also need to be disseminated to policy makers so that 1) laws are informed by developmental research on the supports foster youth need to make the transition to adulthood; and 2) funding and resources are allocated accordingly.

References

Ahrens, K. R., Garrison, M., Spencer, R., DuBois, D. L., Lozano, P., & Richardson, L. P. (2011). Qualitative exploration of the adult mentoring relationships in the lives of former youth in foster care. *Children and Youth Services Review, 33*, 1012–1023. doi: 10.1016/j.childyouth.2011.01.006

Armstrong, M. I., Birnie-Lefcovitch, S., & Ungar, M. T. (2005). Pathways between social support, family well being, quality of parenting, and child resilience: What we know. *Journal of Child and Family Studies, 14*, 269–281. doi: 10.1007/s10826-005-5054-4

Baier, S. T., Markman, B. S., & Pernice-Duca, F. M. (2016). Intent to persist in college freshmen: The role of self-efficacy and mentorship. *Journal of College Student Development, 75*, 614–619. doi: 10.1353/csd.2016.0056

Blakeslee, J. (2012). Expanding the scope of research with transition-age foster youth: Applications of the social network perspective. *Child & Family Social Work, 17*, 326–336. doi: 10.1111/j.1365-2206.2011.00787.x

Bogenschneider, K. (1996). An ecological risk/protective theory for building prevention programs, policies, and community capacity to support youth. *Family Relations, 45*, 127–138. doi: 10.2307/585283

Bowlby, J. (1969/1982). *Attachment and loss: Vol. 1. Attachment.* New York: Basic Books.

Britner, P. A., Randall, K. G., & Ahrens, K. R. (2014). Youth in foster care. In D. DuBois & M. Karcher (Eds.), *Handbook of youth mentoring* (2nd ed.; pp. 341–354). Thousand Oaks, CA: Sage.

Bronfenbrenner, U. (1986). Ecology of the family as a context for human development: Research perspectives. *Developmental Psychology, 22*, 723–742. doi: 10.1037/0012-1649.22.6.723

Bundick, M. J., Yeager, D. S., King, P. E., & Damon, W. (2010). Thriving across the life span. In R. M. Lerner & W. F. Overton (Eds.), *The handbook of life-span development* (pp. 882–923). Hoboken, NJ: John Wiley & Sons, Inc.

Cohen, S., & McKay, G. (1984). Social support, stress and the buffering hypothesis: A theoretical analysis. In A. Baum, S. E. Taylor, & J. E. Singer (Eds.), *Handbook of psychology and health* (pp. 253–267). Hillsdale, NJ: Lawrence Erlbaum Associates, Inc.

Consolidated Omnibus Budget Reconciliation Act of 1985, P.L. 99-272, 100 Stat. 82. (1986).

Courtney, M. E., & Dworsky, A. (2006). Early outcomes for young adults transitioning from out-of-home care in the USA. *Child & Family Social Work, 11*, 209–219. doi: 10.1111/j.1365-2206.2006.00433.x

Courtney, M. E., Dworsky, A., Brown, A., Love, K., & Vorhies, V. (2011). *Midwest Evaluation of the Adult Functioning of Former Foster Youth: Outcomes at age 26*. Chicago: Chapin Hall at the University of Chicago.

Day, A., Riebschleger, J., Dworsky, A., Damashek, A., & Fogarty, K. (2012). Maximizing educational opportunities for youth aging out of foster care by engaging youth voices in a partnership for social change. *Children and Youth Services Review, 34*, 1007–1014. doi: 10.1016/j.childyouth.2012.02.001

Dozier, M., & Rutter, M. (2008). Challenges to the development of attachment relationships faced by young children in foster and adoptive care. In J. Cassidy & P. R. Shaver (Eds.), *Handbook of attachment: Theory, research, and clinical applications* (2nd ed.; pp. 698–717). New York: Guilford.

Duke, T., Farruggia, S. P., & Germo, G. R. (2017). "I don't know where I would be right now if it wasn't for them": Emancipated foster care youth and their important non-parental adults. *Children and Youth Services Review, 76*, 65–73. doi: 10.1016/j.childyouth.2017.02.015

Dworsky, A., & Pérez, A. (2010). Helping former foster youth graduate from college through campus support programs. *Children and Youth Services Review, 32*, 255–263. doi: 10.1016/j.childyouth.2009.09.004

Edwards, O. W., Mumford, V. E., & Serra-Roldan, R. (2007). A Positive Youth Development model for students considered at-risk. *School Psychology International, 28*, 29–45. doi: 10.1177/0143034307075673

Farruggia, S. P., Greenberger, E., Chen, C., & Heckhausen, J. (2006). Perceived social environment and adolescents' well-being and adjustment: Comparing a foster care sample with a matched sample. *Journal of Youth and Adolescence, 35*, 349–358. doi: 10.1007/s10964-006-9029-6

First Star Academy. (n.d.). *First Star Academy*. Retrieved from http://cap.uconn.edu/hsi/fsa/

Foster Care Independence Act of 1999, P.L. 106-169, 113 Stat. 1882. (1999).

Fostering Connections to Success and Increasing Adoptions Act of 2008, P.L. 110-351, 122 Stat. 3949. (2008).

Gartland, D., Bond, L., Olsson, C. A., Buzwell, S., & Sawyer, S. M. (2011). Development of a multi-dimensional measure of resilience in adolescents: The Adolescent Resilience Questionnaire. *BMC Medical Research Methodology, 11*, 134. doi: 10.1186/1471-2288-11-134

Geenen, S., & Powers, L. E. (2007). "Tomorrow is another problem": The experiences of youth in foster care during their transition into adulthood. *Children and Youth Services Review, 29*, 1085–1101. doi: 10.1016/j.childyouth.2007.04.008

Gottlieb, B. H. (1983). Social support as a focus for integrative research in psychology. *American Psychologist, 38*, 278–287. doi: 10.1037/0003-066X.38.3.278

Greeson, J. K. P., & Bowen, N. K. (2008). "She holds my hand": The experiences of foster youth with their natural mentors. *Children and Youth Services Review, 30*, 1178–1188. doi: 10.1016/j.childyouth.2008.03.003

Greeson, J. K. P., Garcia, A. R., Kim, M., & Courtney, M. E. (2015). Foster youth and social support: The first RCT of Independent Living Services. *Research on Social Work Practice, 25*, 349–357. doi: 10.1177/1049731514534900

Greeson, J. K. P., Usher, L., & Grinstein-Weiss, M. (2010). One adult who is crazy about you: Can natural mentoring relationships increase assets among young adults with and without foster care experience? *Children and Youth Services Review, 32*, 565–577. doi: 10.1016/j.childyouth.2009.12.003

Hass, M., & Graydon, K. (2009). Sources of resiliency among successful foster youth. *Children and Youth Services Review, 31*, 457–463. doi: 10.1016/j.childyouth.2008.10.001

Hines, A. M., Merdinger, J., & Wyatt, P. (2005). Former foster youth attending college: Resilience and the transition to young adulthood. *American Journal of Orthopsychiatry, 75*, 381–394. doi: 10.1037/0002-9432.75.3.381

Hirsch, B. J., Mickus, M., & Boerger, R. (2002). Ties to influential adults among Black and White adolescents: Culture, social class, and family networks. *American Journal of Community Psychology, 30*, 289–303. doi: 10.1023/A:1014689129369

Hirschi, T. (1969). *Causes of delinquency.* Berkeley, CA: University of California Press.
House, J. S., & Kahn, R. L. (1985). Measures and concepts of social support. In S. Cohen & S. L. Syme (Eds.), *Social support and health* (pp. 83–108). San Francisco: Academic Press.
Howse, R. B., Diehl, D. C., & Trivette, C. M. (2010). An asset-based approach to facilitating Positive Youth Development and adoption. *Child Welfare, 89*, 101–116.
John H. Chafee Foster Care Independence Program of 2001, P.L. 106-169, 113 Stat. 1882 (1999).
Jones, L. (2012). Measuring resiliency and its predictors in recently discharged foster youth. *Child & Adolescent Social Work Journal, 29*, 515–533. doi: 10.1007/s10560-012-0275-z
Kahn, R. L., & Antonucci, T. C. (1980). Convoys over the life course: Attachment roles and social support. In P. Baltes & O. Brim (Eds.), *Life span development and behavior* (Vol. 3, pp. 253–286). San Diego, CA: Academic Press.
Keller, T. E. (2005). A systemic model of the youth mentoring intervention. *The Journal of Primary Prevention, 26*, 169–188. doi: 10.1007/s10935-005-1850-2
Keller, T. E., Cusick, G. R., & Courtney, M. E. (2007). Approaching the transition to adulthood: Distinctive profiles of adolescents aging out of the child welfare system. *Social Service Review, 81*, 453–484. doi: 10.1086/519536
Kirk, C. M., Lewis, R. K., Nilsen, C., & Colvin, D. Q. (2011). Foster care and college: The educational aspirations and expectations of youth in the foster care system. *Youth & Society, 45*, 307–323. doi: 10.1177/0044118X11417734
Kirk, R., & Day, A. (2011). Increasing college access for youth aging out of foster care: Evaluation of a summer camp program for foster youth transitioning from high school to college. *Children and Youth Services Review, 33*, 1173–1180. doi: 10.1016/j.childyouth.2011.02.018
Lerner, R. (1995). *America's youth in crisis: Challenges and options for programs and policies.* Thousand Oaks, CA: Sage Publications, Inc.
Masten, A. S. (2001). Ordinary magic: Resilience processes in development. *American Psychologist, 56*, 227–238. doi: 10.1037/0003-066X.56.3.227
Masten, A. S., & Coatsworth, J. D. (1998). Development of competence in favorable and unfavorable environments: Lessons from research on successful children. *American Psychologist, 53*, 205–220. doi: 10.1037/0003-066X.53.2.205
Mendis, K. (2015). One size does not fit all: The educational needs of children in out-of-home care. *Adoption & Fostering, 39*, 135–144. doi: 10.1177/0308575915588721
Munson, M. R., Smalling, S. E., Spencer, R., Scott, L. D. Jr., & Tracy, E. M. (2010). A steady presence in the midst of change: Non-kin natural mentors in the lives of older youth exiting foster care. *Children and Youth Services Review, 32*, 527–535. doi: 10.1016/j.childyouth.2009.11.005
Osterling, K. L., & Hines, A. M. (2006). Mentoring adolescent foster youth: Promoting resilience during developmental transitions. *Child and Family Social Work, 11*, 242–253. doi: 10.1111/j.1365-2206.2006.00427.x
Parra, G. R., DuBois, D. L., Neville, H. A., Pugh-Lilly, A. O., & Povinelli, N. (2002). Mentoring relationships for youth: Investigation of a process-oriented model. *Journal of Community Psychology, 30*, 367–388. doi: 10.1002/jcop.10016
Perry, B. L. (2006). Understanding social network disruption: The case of youth in foster care. *Social Problems, 53*, 371–391. doi: 10.1525/sp.2006.53.3.371
Quisenberry, C. M., & Foltz, R. (2013). Resilient youth in residential care. *Residential Treatment for Children & Youth, 30*, 280–293. doi: 10.1080/0886571X.2013.852448
Reynolds, J. R., & Pemberton, J. (2001). Rising college expectations among youth in the United States: A comparison of the 1979 and 1997 NLSY. *The Journal of Human Resources, 36*, 703–726. doi: 10.2307/3069639
Rhodes, J. E. (2002). *Stand by me: The risks and rewards of mentoring today's youth.* Cambridge, MA: Harvard University Press.
Rhodes, J. E., Haight, W. L., & Briggs, E. C. (1999). The influence of mentoring on the peer relationships of foster youth in relative and nonrelative care. *Journal of Research on Adolescence, 9*, 185–201.
Rotter, J. B. (1966). Generalized expectancies for internal versus external control of reinforcement. *Psychological Monographs: General and Applied, 80*, 1–28. doi: 10.1037/h0092976
Scales, P. C., & Leffert, N. (1999). *Developmental assets: A synthesis of the scientific research on adolescent development.* Minneapolis, MN: Search Institute.
Scannapieco, M., Connell-Carrick, K., & Painter, K. (2007). In their own words: Challenges facing youth aging out of foster care. *Child & Adolescent Social Work Journal, 24*, 423–435. doi: 10.1007/s10560-007-0093-x
Schofield, G. (2002). The significance of a secure base: A psychosocial model of long-term foster care. *Child & Family Social Work, 7*, 259–272. doi: 10.1046/j.1365-2206.2002.00254.x

Singer, E. R., Berzin, S. C., & Hokanson, K. (2013). Voices of former foster youth: Supportive relationships in the transition to adulthood. *Children and Youth Services Review, 35*, 2110–2117. doi: 10.1016/j.childyouth.2013.10.019

Strolin-Goltzman, J., Woodhouse, V., Suter, J., & Werrbach, M. (2016). A mixed method study on educational well-being and resilience among youth in foster care. *Children and Youth Services Review, 70*, 30–36. doi: 10.1016/j.childyouth.2016.08.014

Thompson, R. A. (2008). Early attachment and later development: Familiar questions, new answers. In J. Cassidy & P. R. Shaver (Eds.), *Handbook of attachment: Theory, research, and clinical applications* (2nd ed.; pp. 348–365). New York: Guilford.

Ungar, M. (2004). *Nurturing hidden resilience in troubled youth.* Toronto, ON: University of Toronto Press, Scholarly Publishing Division.

Wolanin, T. R. (2005). *Higher education opportunities for foster youth: A primer for policy makers.* Washington, DC: Institute for Higher Education Policy.

Index

Abbott, Greg 377
Abrams, L. S. 181
abuse: amygdala 46; conceptual model 103–104; health and developmental problems 118–119; in placements 86; responses to 102, 108, 108–109; and sexual risk behaviors 137; suicide and self-harm 112; trauma-bonding 372; USDHHS 363 *see also* child maltreatment; polyvictimization; sexual abuse
academic achievement 156, 210
academic foundation 290
academic self-efficacy 482
access to care services 309–310
Acción de Gracia Immigration Assistance 381–382
accountability expectations 6
accrediting bodies 13
Achenbach, T. 65
achievement 121
activities of daily living (ADLs) 322
Adam Walsh Child Protection and Safety Act (2006) 21
Add Health *see* National Longitudinal Study of Adolescent to Adult Health (Add Health)
Adler, M. C. 321
Administration for Children and Families (ACF) 139, 147, 263, 414 *see also* Children's Bureau
administration of foster care 127, 184
Administration on Children, Youth and Families 413
administrative orders 389
Adolescent Outreach Workers 307
adolescents: changing world 77; childbearing 140, 142; and childhood 63; contraception 136; health of boys compared to girls 122; parental assistance 285; parenting skills 141; sexual activity 136; substance use 159, 160; terminating parents' legal rights 84–85
adopted caregivers 65
adopted children 196
adopted family relationships 194–197
adoption: children and youths with disabilities 327; complexity of emotions 202; dissolution 195; exit from care 68; family relationships 194–197, 201–202; Latino children 389–390; numbers waiting for 174; special needs 194–195; youth feelings awaiting for 260
Adoption and Foster Care Analysis and Reporting System (AFCARS): adopted children 194–195; changes to data 147, 413; emancipated youth 284; foster care children 284, 285; Latinos in care 376; report (2015) 174; report (2016) 78; sexual orientation/gender expansive data 407–408; trafficked youth 366
Adoption and Safe Families Act 1997 (ASFA) 7, 24, 25, 61, 70, 133, 303, 310–311, 393
Adoption Assistance and Child Welfare Act of 1980 (AACWA) 7, 23–24, 57, 61, 391
Adoptions and Safe Families Act (1997) 457
adult functioning 290
adulthood: challenges in 176; health outcomes 123; and independence 432
Adverse Childhood Experiences (ACEs) 67, 155, 462
adversities 63, 67, 194
Advocates to Successful Transition to Independence program 481
Affleck, B. 11
African-Americans: children in out-of-home care 341; criminal justice system 247; employment 245; FFY 245–246; foster care 8; job-seeking 246; risk for CSEC 365; social control theory 461 *see also* black youth
African American to white disparity rate 344
age entering foster care 8
agency staff 268, 429
age out of care: EFY 227; emancipation 179; high school 82; importance of non-parent adults 173; intervention approaches 183; multiple risk factors 285; not ready as independent young adults 77–78; reaction of foster family 437–438; relationships with biological families 89; resources 394; sibling relationships 201; study 309; termination of care 301 *see also* exiting care; transitioning out of care
aggressive problem behaviors 63
Ahrens, K. R. 183, 479, 480
Aid to Families with Dependent Children (AFDC) 119, 124
Ainsworth, Mary Salter 20

Index

Ake, G. S. 194
Alameda County (CA) 145
Alanis, E. 202
Alaskan Natives (AN) 26–27, 348, *349–350*, 357
alcohol 156–159, 324 *see also* substance use
Alessandrini, E. A. 125
"alien," use of term 395
Alink, L. R. 44
allostasis 42
allostatic load 42
alternative homes *see* out-of-home placements
Alternative Response (AR, Texas) 451–452
ambiguous loss 198–199
American Academy of Pediatrics (AAP) 119, 125–128, 160
American Indians (AI) 6, 26–27, 348, *349–350*, 357
American Psychiatric Association (APA) 402
American Psychological Association (APA) 103
American Public Human Services Association (APHSA) 145
Americans with Disabilities Act of 1990 (ADA) 319, 321, 322
amphetamines 157
amygdala 45, 46
anger management 83
Annie E. Casey Foundation 145, 302, 376
Another Planned Permanent Living Arrangement (APPLA) 24, 25, 303, 311
anti-discrimination policies 321
appraisal support 181, 474
area-based approaches 344
Arizona 377, 464–465
Arnett, J. J. 226, 302, 433
Ashbury Images 294
Asians 337, 348, *351–352*
Asok, A. 49
assessments 101–114; challenges 111–112; evaluating outcomes/programs 113; expense 111–112; methods 109–110; strategy for 108–109; time constraints 111; treatment recommendations 112; youth and adult raters 111
asset accumulation 249–250
asthma 120, 122–123
a-theoretical approaches to research 149
Atlas.ti 7 software 81
at-risk youth 292
attachment: difficulties 193, 197, 202; disorders 193–194; impairments 193, 194; relational permanence 302, 428; risk of delinquency 461; social bond theory 382
Attachment and Biobehavioral Catch-Up (ABC) 44–45, 49–50, *465*
attachment theory 20–21, 191, 473–474
attention deficit hyperactivity disorder (ADHD) 46
attorneys 369–370
Attride-Stirling, J. 81
Auslander, W. F. 157
autonomy 432

Babor, T. F. 163
Bachelor of Arts (BA) 242
Bachelor of Science (BS) 242
bad foster parents 200
Baltimore 58, 118, 343
bank accounts 250
Bank, S. P. 191
Barnett, D. 60
Barney, M. 9
barriers: to care 125–127; to educational success 483; long-lasting relationships 184; to research 330; sexual and reproductive health 142–143; social model of disability 320; substance use services 163
Barth, R. P. 88
basal cortisol 44
basic life skills 271
Becker, G. S. 282
behavioral intervention *465*
behavioral problems: dysregulated cortisol rhythms 44; and early sexual intercourse 135; and emotional problems 8; LONGSCAN study 65; Mexican migrants 393; prefrontal cortex 46; sexual risk behaviors 137
behavioral regulation 47, 211
Bell, K. C. 456
Beltran, A. 22
Ben & Jerry's franchise ice cream shop 294
Bergh, Henry 5
Berkowitz, G. 124
Bernard, K. 49
Berrick, J. D. 24, 181, 193, 194
Berzin, S. C. 478
Best Health Status groups 122, 123
Bexar County study (Texas) 80–81
Bible 4
bidirectional crosstalk 49
Biehal, N. 106
Big Brothers Big Sisters programs 176, 480
Bilaver, L. A. 119, 120, 128–129
bilingual homes 393
Bioecological System Theory *261*
biological families: amygdala 46; children's reactions 196; complex relationships with 89; visiting children in foster care 191–192; youth perspective 198
biological parents: children in foster care visiting 192; interviews 60; over-reporting misbehavior 109; separation anxiety 106; social stigma of adoption 195–196; substance use 120
biological sensitivity to context model 42
biopsychosocial model of definitions of disabilities (WHO) 321
biopsychosocial model of definitions (WHO) 321
birth control 141
birth rates 139, 140–141
bisexual males 406–407
black children: decline in foster care 337–339; foster care placement 342–345

489

Index

Black, J. 192
black–white differences, race-specific relationships 344
black youth: conditional disproportionality ratios 340; pathways to foster care placement 345–348; reunification 26; time spent in foster care 339, 341; unconditional disproportionality ratios 340 *see also* African-Americans
Blakeslee, J. 330, 475
Blakeslee, J. E. 260
Blankenhorn, D. *261*, 263
Blinder–Oaxaca decomposition methodology 336, 343–344, 356
Bloom, Sandra 7
blunted diurnal rhythm of cortisol 43–44
board leadership 13
body perceptions 406–407
Boerger, R. 480
Boix, C. 291–292
bonding elements 382
Border Patrol agents 377
border security 377
Bourdieu, P. 433
Bowen, N. K. 183, 479
Bowlby, John 20, 191, 193, 473–474
Boyce, W. T. 42
Brabeck, K. 388
Brace, Charles Loring 4
Braciszewski, J. M. 159–160, 163
brain structure and function 45–47
Braxton. C. 10
Brief Child and Family Phone Interview (BCFPI) 32
brief interventions (BIs) 160, 163
Brief Screening Instrument for Adolescent Tobacco, Alcohol, and Drug Use (BSTAD) 162
Briere, J. 110
Briggs, E. C. 480
Bright, C. L. 458
broad-band rating scales 102, 110
Bronfenbrenner, U. 117, 202–203, 258–259, 270
Bruce, J. 43
Bruck, M. 105
Brunsink, A. M. 173
Bryan (undocumented immigrant youth) 386
Bucharest Early Intervention Project 42, 47
Buchi, K. F. 120
Buehler, C. 243, 244, 250, 431
bullying 406
Bundick, M. J. 475
business start-ups 249
Byrd, S. 393
Byrne, O. 385

California: campus support programs 216–217, 482; Chafee grants 252; disparities in welfare system 344–345; financial responsibility for unaccompanied children 388; health service use 124; Hispanic immigrants 388; Immigration Services Contractors 388; Latino immigrants 377, 388; *non-minor dependents* 286; physical health care services 126; PTC (2010) 144; teenage birth rates 139; transitional housing program 244, 252
California Child Welfare Council 364
California Department of Social Services 377
California Foster Youth Pregnancy Prevention Institute 145, 146
California Youth Transitions to Adulthood Study (CalYOUTH Study) 133–134, 138–139, 140–141, 143, 286
campus support programs 216–217, 480, 482
Canada 196
capital, and employment 246–247
capital development (Bourdieu) 433
cardiovascular disease 44
caregiver characteristics (FTF interviews) 60
caregiver involvement 112–113, 212–213, 214, 215
caregiver ratings 109
caregivers: children expressing gender identity 405; mistrustful of 8; and sexual and reproductive health 143; under-utilized 23; working with other cultures 390; workshops 215
caregiving environments 42
caring adults 329
Carpenter, S. 123
case management client map (CSTVI) *370*
caseworkers 23, 86, 380–381
Casey alumni data 245
Casey Family Foundation 247
Casey Family Programs 157, 253, 394, 433
Casey Field Office Mental Health Study 157
Casey Young Adult Survey 244
Cashel, M. L. 110
Caspi, A. 288
Castañeda, H. 378
Ceci, S. J. 105
Center for Juvenile Justice Reform (Georgetown University) 464
Center of the Developing Child (Harvard University) 197
Centers for Disease Control (CDC) 71, 406
Central America 383
central paradox (Miller and Stiver) 180
Cesar E. Chavez March for Justice (2017) *380*, *384*
Chafee funding 252, 304, 310 *see also* Foster Care Independence Act 1999 (FCIA/Chafee Legislation)
Chafee, John H. 6
Chamberlain, P. 29, 44, 430
Champagne, V. 120, 128–129
Chapin Hall (University of Chicago) 175
Chase, S. K. 163
CHECK (Comprehensive Health Evaluations for Cincinnati's Kids) Foster Care Center 129
Chenot, D. 344–345
Chicago 58, 118; Community Assistance Programs (CAP) 293

"child," definition 178
Child Abuse & Neglect (journal) 62
Child Abuse Prevention and Treatment Act 1974 (CAPTA) 6, 57, 128, 323
Child and Adolescent Data Lab (University of Michigan) 467
Child and Adolescent Functional Assessment Scale (CAFAS) 32
Child and Adolescent Needs and Strengths (CANS) 105, 162, 367, 368
Child and Adolescent Policy Research Institute (UTSA) 263
Child and Family Services Agency (Washington, DC) 310
Child and Family Services Reviews (CFSR) 311, 445–448, 450, 457
Child Behavior Checklist (CBCL) 65
child characteristics (FTF interviews) 60
Child Health and Illness Profile–Adolescent Edition (CHIP–AE) 121
childhood adversities 49, 63
childhood trauma 140
child maltreatment: long-term effects 79; removal from the home 193; research 59; sex education curricula 142; and sexual risk behaviors 137; and teenage births 141 *see also* abuse
child maltreatment epidemiological study (Sullivan and Knutson) 323
child protection legislation 5–6
Child Protective Services (CPS) 58, 62–63, 102, 345
Child Protective Services (CPS, DFPS Texas) 63, 448, 450–451, 452, 454
children: attachment styles 193; exiting care 65; immigrant households 376–377; stress of parental deportation 388, 390; unaccompanied immigrant minors 383–384; undocumented parents 377
children and youth with disabilities 319–331; adoption 327; anti-discrimination policies 321; barriers to inclusion 330; and caring adults 329; children in welfare system 324–325; definitions 319–320; experiences in foster care 326; federal definitions 321–323; in foster care 325; foster placements 331; IEP meetings 329; improving services 328–331; leaving placement 326–327; maltreatment 323–324; "medical model" 320; specific training 330; stress 329; systems interactions 327–328 *see also* disadvantaged youth
"Children from Hard Places" (Purvis) 391
children in foster care: changes in number *338*; changes in number by race group *339*; closeness experiential activity 201; cortisol reactivity 43; ethnic and racial backgrounds 27; Latin@ 376; of parents who were in foster care 142; visiting biological family 192
children of prisoners 178, 341, 342
Children's Bureau: adoption dissolution 195; AFCARS 407–408; CFSR 445; children in foster care 3; culturally appropriate services 342; defining CQI 445–446; disabled in welfare system 324; disproportionality ratios 340; racial disproportionality 344; recruiting foster parents 428; statistical information 174; substance use screening 161 *see also* Administration for Children and Families (ACF)
child sex trafficking 364, 366–367 *see also* commercial sexual exploitation of children (CSEC)
Child Sex Trafficking Victims Initiative (CSTVI, Maryland) 367–368, 369, *370*
child sexual abuse: CSEC 362; rate of disclosure 105
Child Sexual Behavior Inventory (CSBI) 110
child welfare agencies: children of youth in foster care 142; disability-specific training 330; LGBTQ affirming foster parents 415; privatization 427–428, 440; resource sharing 331; responses to CSEC 366; substance use screening 165; Texas 448; training for human trafficking 367; wage files 243
Child Welfare Information Gateway (CWIG) 5, 20, 192, 195, 389
Child Welfare League of America 405, 413, 431
child welfare policies: LGBTQ youth 408, *409*; transition to adulthood 303–305
child welfare-specific programs 477–478 *see also* Independent Living Programs (ILP)
child welfare system: education and training 410–411; racial disproportionality 340; transition from juvenile justice 459
child welfare workers: and federal policies 173–174; not consulting IEPs 328; sexual and reproductive health 143; training for foster youth with disabilities 328–329; turnover and establishing permanency 184, 268
chlamydia infections 138
chores 439
Chow W. Y. 31
chronic health conditions 119–121
chronic psychological stress 48–49
chronic trauma, reaction to events in life 461
chronosystem 259–260, *261*, 275
Chuang, E. 462
Cicchetti, D. 60
Cincinnati Children's Hospital 129
Circles of Support 271, 274
citizenship 377
Civilian Conservation Corps (CCC) 292
CLASP 25
Cleveland 344
clinical interviewing 110
Clyman, R. 123
coaches *see* mentoring
Coatsworth, J. D. 161, 164, 476
cocaine 157
Code of Ethics 408
cognitive assessments 101
Cognitive Behavioral Therapy 465
cognitive control 46

Index

cognitive development 42
cohabitation 262
Cohen, N. A. 14
Cohen, S. D. 343
Coleman, J. S. 289
collaboration across agencies 165, 265
college education: ETV grants 286; performance 214; raising incomes 287; transition to adulthood 283
Collins, M. E. 6, 302, 303, 309
Colorado 311, 340
Colvin, D. Q. 482
"coming out" 410
commercial sexual exploitation of children (CSEC) 362–373; ecological model 372; identification of victims 372; individual/intrapersonal level 365; race and racism 373; reasons 365; risk factors 362–365; sexual abuse data 363; victim-centered approaches 371; victims involved in child welfare 364 *see also* sex trafficking
communication: between care providers 126; caseworker and Latino families 380–381; caseworkers and foster parents 23; and coordinating services 129; CQI 453–454
Community Assistance Programs (CAP, Chicago) 293
community-based programs 160, 293, 481
community partners 415
community support 483
co-morbidity 102
compensation 430
complex trauma 106, 193, 194
comprehensive mentoring programs 480–481
Computerized Intervention Authoring Software (CIAS) 163
conceptualizing stability 71
conceptual model of impact of abuse (Spaccarelli) 103–104
concurrent planning 24
conditional disproportionality ratios 336–337, 340, 341
conditional probability of placement 355, *356*
condoms 134, 136, 141
confidentiality 159, 415
congregate care settings 326, 460
"connected autonomy" (Goodkind) 432 *see also* transition to adulthood
connection in relationships 180, 439
Connell-Carrick, K. 260
consents for medical care 126, 160
consistency 370–371, 436
Consolidated Omnibus Budget Reconciliation Act 1985 (COBRA) 177, 285, 303, 477
constituent leadership 12
constitutional rights 408, *409*
Continuous Quality Improvement (CQI) 444–455; balanced and effective team 454; categories 446–448; communications 453–454; coordination 453; definition 445–446; embedding in ongoing operations 450–451; expanding scope 451–452; functions 453; PDCA cycle 444–445; regional operations 452–453
Continuum of Care Program (USDHUD) 306
contraception 141
contracting out 427–428
conversion therapies 410
Cook, A. 193, 194
Cook County (Illinois) 458
coordination of services 126, 129, 369–370
core developmental processes 180
corporate parenting 227
cortisol 42–45, 211
couch surfing 262, 270 *see also* homelessness
Coulton, C. J. 344
Council of Europe 192
Council of Family and Child Caring Agencies 118, 124
Council on Foster Care, Adoption, and Kinship Care (COFCAKC) 127
Courtney, M. E. 138, 176, 227, 242, 243, 244, 246, 247, 249, 252, 253, 262, 284, 288, 291, 462, 478
court orders 325–326
coyotes (traffickers) 386
CRAFFT screening tool 162
Crampton, D. 344
Cranston-Gonzalez Affordable Housing Act (1990) 306
crisis housing 270 *see also* homelessness
critical disability studies 321
critical self-inventory 415
Cromer, K. D. 66
crossover pathways 456
crossover youth: age and time to intervene *463*; best practices in policy 465–467; child welfare/juvenile justice 456–457; demographic factors 460; early studies 458; evidence-based approaches 467; explanations for 461–462; management 462; mental health problems 460, 463; multiple service systems 463; outcomes 462–463; prevalence 459–460; recommendations to prevent *465*; re-offending 462 *see also* juvenile justice; risk of delinquency
Crossover Youth Practice Model (CYPM) 464
Cuddeback, G. 431
cultural capital 433
cultural competence 113–114, 412
cultural humility 14, 413
cultural identity 393
culturally appropriate services 342
current drinking 156
Curry, S. R. 181
Curtis, M. 303
Cusick, G. R. 456
Customs and Border Protection (CBP) 383
Cuyahoga County (Ohio) 344
cytokines 48

Damashek, A. 483
Damon, M. 11
Damon, W. 475
D'Andrade, A. 24
Dannerbeck, A. 463
DAPIM (Define, Assess, Plan, Interpret, and Monitor) 449
Dasgupta, D. 145
data reduction procedures 66
data sharing 265
data "triangulation" 264
Davis, I. 66
Day, A. 10, 480, 483
deaths 8
decision-making processes 27–28, 182
decision-point-based measures 339–341
Deferred Action for Childhood Arrivals (DACA) 378
deficits in regulatory systems 210–211
delinquency 135, 461, 464 *see also* risk of delinquency
Deming, William 444
dental health 120
Denver Developmental Quotient 196
DePanfilis, D. 341, 343
Department of Health & Human Services (DHHS) 383
Department of Homeland Security (DHS) 383, 384, 389
Department of Justice 383
depathologizing information 111
deportations 379, 382, 388–391, 390, 393
Depoy, E. 320
depression 324
Descriptive Analysis of Foster Care Transitional Service and Alumni Outcomes (Dorsett) 382, 394
DeSena, A. D. 30
detention facilities for minors 384
Dettlaff, A. 377
developmental approaches 118, 160
developmental assets 476, 481
developmental disabilities 322–323, 457
Developmental Disabilities Assistance and Bill of Rights Act 2000 (DD Act) 322–323
developmental environment 275
developmental pathways 137, 140
developmental timing 42
deviant peer networks 365
Diagnostic and Statistical Manual of Mental Disorders (DSM) 162, 402
Diagnostic Interview Schedule for Children and Young Adults (DISC) 60, 67
DiClemente, C. C. 163
Diehl, D. C. 182
differential susceptibility model 42
dimensions of health 121
disadvantaged youth 249, 292 *see also* children and youth with disabilities
discipline procedures 65–66

discomfort 121
disconnections in relationships 180
discrimination 335–336, 356–358, 408
disorders 121
disparities 335, 356, 357–358
disparity ratio 335
disproportionality in foster care 345
disproportionality ratios 336
diurnal cortisol rhythms 43, 44, 211
Division of Unaccompanied Children's Services (DUCS) 383, 384
domestic minor sex trafficking *see* commercial sexual exploitation of children (CSEC)
Donovan, K. 342
Doris Duke Charitable Foundation (DDCF) 60
Dorsett, V. J. 382, 394
double bottom line approach 294
Dozier, M. 49
drugs *see* substance use
dually involved youth 462
dual-status programs 466
DuBois, D. L. 183, 184, 477
Duke, T. 480
DuMont, K. A. 197
Durkheim, E. 383
Dworsky, A. 138, 145, 216, 242, 244, 245, 246, 248, 249, 262, 478, 483
dysregulated cortisol rhythms 44
Dziegielewski, S. 196

early academic skills 210
early adversities 63, 211, 212
early childhood education (ECE) 211–212
early institutional care 42
early intervention *465*
early literacy and numeracy 210
early pregnancies *see* pregnancies
Earner, I. 377
earnings 227, *228–241*, 242–245
Echols, D. 9, 10
Ecke, L. 394
Ecological-Developmental Theory 59–60
ecological model *261*, 276, 364–365, 372
Ecological Model (Blankenhorn) *261*, 263
Ecological System Theory (Bronfenbrenner) 117, 202–203, 258–259, 270
economic and social opportunities 283, 302–303
economic capital 286–289, 433
economic hardships 250
economic inequality 291–292
Economic Opportunity Act (1964) 292
economic self-sufficiency 291
economic stress 250
economic well-being 142, 244
education: child welfare system 410–411; and "cultural humility" 412; deficits 225; held back in a grade 212; and housing 269; human capital 287; stability 307

Index

educational achievement 262–263, 282–283
educational attainment 215, 288
educational outcomes 208; buffering effects 214–215; factors contributing to 209–215; future directions 217; high school completion rates 290; interventions to improve 215–217; long-term outcomes 214–215; poor outcomes 78, 176, 275
educational programs 481–483
educational success 208, 483
educational trajectories *209*, 217
Education Amendments (1972), Title IX 12
Education and Training Voucher (ETV): education-related costs 269; and the FCIA 306; post-secondary education 178, 304, 308, 481; states allocating funding 214; support for job training 263; transitioning foster youth support 286 *see also* Foster Care Independence Act 1999 (FCIA/Chafee Legislation)
education trajectories 289–291
Edwards, F. 342
Edwards, O. W. 476
electroencephalograms (EEG) 46
eligible youth 310
Ellis, B. J. 42
Elze, D. E. 88
emancipated foster youth (EFY): cash on leaving care 249; college completion rates 242; definition 227; earning degrees 242; employment rates 242, 243–244; financial and transportation problems 253; income 244; public benefit programs 248
emancipation: case plan goal 84; definition 174–175, 227; discharging from care 284; ILP services 179; service plan goals 311; state support 226
Emanuel, N. 337
emergency rooms (ER) 124–125
emergency shelters 29–30, 270
emerging adulthood 226, 251, 433, 441, 473
emotional disturbance 212
emotional regulation 79, 83
emotional resources 10
emotional self-regulation 211
emotional support 181, 285, 474
emotional understanding 210
employment: and capital 246–247; challenges 312; and earnings 227, 242–245; human capital 288; and incarceration 247; studies *228–241*; training 252, 283
employment instability 251
employment opportunities 269, 271
employment outcomes 250–253, 291
employment programs 291–294
employment trajectories 291
empowering language 371
entry into foster care 8, 118, 325–326
environmental stressors 42, 50 *see also* maltreatment; poverty
Epstein, H. R. 22
ethnicity *see* race and ethnicity

Eurocentric notions of gender 405
Evaluation of Adolescent Pregnancy Prevention Approaches (PPA) 144
event-related potentials (ERPs) 46
Every Student Succeeds Act 2015 (ESSA) 307
evidence-based approaches to trauma 467
evidence-based assessments 103
evidence-based interventions 162, 163
evidence-based practices (EBPs) 431
evidence-based programs 143–144, 149, 158, 467
evidence-based treatments 112
evolutionary-developmental theories 42
Ewart, S. 242
exiting care: before emancipation 227; for employment 251; reasons for leaving 432; statistical information 260; tangible resources 253; terminating support 226; theoretical frameworks 179–182 *see also* age out of care; transitioning out of care
Exodus (22:22) 4
exosystems of foster youth 60, 259, *261*, 272–273, 274 *see also* ecological model
extending foster care 77–78, 251, 286, 295, 466–467
external assets 481
Externalizing Behavior Problems 65
externalizing behaviors 197

face-to-face (FTF) interviews 59, 60
faith-based child welfare agencies 143
families: children with disabilities 326–327, 329–330; keeping together 392, 394; motivated 107; relational permanence 302; reunification 24, 192, 244, 326–327; right to stay together 391; support and engagement 411–412
families of color 341
familismo 392
Family & Youth Services Bureau 307
family-centered approach to permanency placement 29
family foster care placements 28
family planning 82–83, 143 *see also* pregnancy prevention; sex education
family privilege 7
Family Unification Program (FUP) 268, 306–307
Family Welfare Research Group (FWRG) 144
Fan, M. 183
Fanshel, David 58
fatherhood 140
Faver, C. A. 202
fear of abandonment 196
fear of deportation 390 *see also* deportations
Federal law 42 U.S.C. § 671 (a)(20) 21
federal legislation 5–8, 177–178, 303 *see also* named Acts
federal support 259
Feldman, S. W. 428
Felitti, V. J. 194

female Hispanic youth 462
females: CSEC victims 365; effect of group homes 31; EFY pregnancies 247; employment and earnings 246; foster care 8; status offense petitions 458; trichomonas infections 138
Fergus, S. 197
Feudtner, C. 125
Fields, E. S. 196
"fight or flight" mechanism 390
final analytic models 63
financial independence 226
financial literacy training 253
financial problems 253
financial support 23, 285
1st Amendment (Freedom of Speech) 408
First Star Academy (UConn) 483
Fisher, P. A. 43, 44
Five Cs (PYD) 80
Fix, M. 383
Flaherty, E. G. 63
flanker tasks 47
Florida 311, 388
Florida Department of Children and Families 388
Fluke, J. 337, 340, 341
Flux (Ecke & Foster Care Alumni of America) 394
focus groups: Bexar County and West Texas 81–91; CSEC 367; experiences in foster care 433–438; housing research 264; LONGSCAN 60, 67; PAL program 478; role models 480
Fogarty, K. 483
Foli, K. J. 196
Folman, R. D. 10–11, 15
Food Stamps 247
Forbes, H. 196
foreign-born immigrants 376 *see also* undocumented immigrants
Form 660 (Basic Immigration Information, DFPS) 388
formal mentoring 183, 480–481 *see also* mentoring
former foster youth (FFY): definition 227; economic stress 250; education 176, 262–263; employment and earnings 227, 242–245, 250; homelessness 269; housing stability 262–263; public benefits 244; research interviews 91; school and community support 483; studies *228–241*; subgroups 253; substance use 158–159; transition to adulthood 226; vocational outcomes 176; vulnerable groups 253
foster-adopt homes 28
foster care: definition 20; entry into 325–326; experiences in 326, 432–440; extending beyond 18 years 77–78, 251, 286, 295, 466–467; by gender and race 8; goals of permanency and adoption 194–195; historical need 3–4; improving 10–14; length of stay 284–285, 341–342; navigating new relationships 193; numbers in care 3; quality of homes 14; reasons for 8; short term effects 67; youth experience 190 *see also* out-of-home placements
foster care alumni: leadership 11; recommendations 15; voices 8–10
Foster Care Alumni of America 394
foster-care-as-usual group 430
"foster care drift" 23
Foster Care Independence Act 1999 (FCIA/Chafee Legislation): background 6–7; ETV program 306; fiscal allocation 286; foster parent training 430–431; funding 252, 304, 310; housing funds 306; ILP reforms 177, 304, 466, 477; Midwest Study 175; NYTD data 139, 247; and state-level transition practice 303; state to state variations 310, 311; transition services 309 *see also* Education and Training Voucher (ETV); John H. Chafee Foster Care Independence Program (CFCIP)
Foster Care Mental Health study (FCMH) 58–59, 64
foster care non-discrimination laws 408
Foster Care Passport Program (Washington State) 216
foster care placements: abuse and neglect 190; disparities 335, 357; disproportionalities 345, 348; predictors 342; types 27–32; youth in foster care 260
foster care satisfaction 10
foster-care-specific clinics 129
Foster, E. M. 343–344
foster families: consistency across all the youth 436; multiple children 194; placement with siblings 26; race 436; relationships 192–194; and sexual and gender expansive youth 411
Fostering Connections to Success and Increasing Adoptions Act 2008 (Fostering Connections Act/FCSIAA): academic outcomes 331; child welfare legislation 61; educational stability 216, 307; education and training 78; federal funding 30; foster youth before the Act 226; health care services 128, 466; kinship and guardianship 178; notifying relatives 25, 29; older youth in foster care 290–291, 305; self-sufficiency 248; sibling relationships 201; state-level transition practice 303; Title IV-E eligibility to 21st birthday 146, 477; Title IV-E federal guardianship payments 25–26; transition from care 286; transition planning 184, 305, 308, 309 *see also* Title IV-E (Social Security Act 1935)
foster parent licensing 192–193
Foster Parent Resource for Information, Development, and Education (PRIDE) 431
foster parents: abuse by 225; adversity or trauma history 194; ambiguities in role 440; attachment difficulties 194, 260; attitude to paycheck 430, 437; background checks 21; commitment to foster youths 436–438; communication with caseworkers 23; *good* and *bad* 199–200; as a "jail" 268; as "Mom" or "Dad" 435; placement problems 86; reasons to stop fostering 23;

495

Index

recruitment 22–23, 428–429; retention 23, 429–430, 440; and sexual and gender expansive youth 410–411; sexual and reproductive health 143, 145–146; teaching values/practical skills 438–439; training 160, 429–432, 440; treatment of youth in care 112–113

foster youth: being "named" as one of the family 435–436; deciding to remain in care 291; favorable outcomes 79; FCSIAA 305; health outcomes 122; leaving with no explanation 437; "paycheck" for foster parents 437; perceptions of biological families 198; perceptions of foster parents 198–201; race and foster parents 436; research 79; risk of poor outcomes 78; satisfaction with placement 199; and siblings 200–201; stigma of being "bad" 87; unstable and uncaring world 10; vulnerable population 263

Foster Youth Demonstration Project 293
Foster Youth Life Investment Partners 269
4-year college 283
14th Amendment (Due Process protections) 408, 414
14th Amendment (Equal Protections laws) 377, 408
Frame, L. 24
frequent alcohol use 156
Freundlich, M. 30
Friedrich, W. N. 110
Friesen, L. D. 428
Fuentes-Pelaez, N. 198
functional magnetic resonance imaging (fMRI) 45–46
funders of foster care agencies 13
FUP vouchers 306–307

Gallaudet University 12
Gallegos, A. H. 464, 465, 467
Gardner, H. 201
gay males 406–407
Gay–Straight Alliances (GSAs) 406
Gear Up program 308
Geenen, S. 328, 330, 432, 482–483
gender: final analytic models 63; foster care satisfaction 10; identity and expression 412; income differences 246; predictors of substance use 157
gender-affirming therapies 405–406
"gender dysphoria" (APA) 402
gender expansive identity 405, 407–408
gender expression 403
gender identity 403, 404–406, 407
Gender Identity Disorder (*DSM-III*) 402
gender minorities 403
"gender non-conforming" (Steever) 405
General Education Development (GED) 81
General Education Diploma (GED) 283
General Equivalency Diploma (GED) 242
generalized linear model (GLM) 345
General Social Survey (GSS) 244
Georgetown University 464

Gerry, Elbridge 5
Gibbons, R. 344
Gibbs, A. 202
Gibbs, D. 23
Giffin, Kenna S. 381–382
Gilbert, R. 324
Gilson, S. 320
glucocorticoid receptors 45
Goerge, R. M. 244, 245, 246, 456
gonorrhea infections 138
good foster parents 199, 435, 439
Goodkind, S. 432
Good Will Hunting (Damon & Affleck) 11
Gould, C. L. 458
government 292
grandparents 25, 29
Great Depression 292
Greeson, J. K. P. 173, 183, 185, 479, 480
Grey, I. K. 265
Grinstein-Weiss, M. 479
Grounded Theory 81
group homes 31
Growth Mixture Modeling 67–68
Gryn, T. A. 376
guardianship-focused programs 178

Hackett, W. 341
Haddal, C. C. 377
Hadley, T. 125
Haight, W. L. 192, 464, 480
Halfon, N. 124, 126
hallucinogens 157
Harden, A. 128–129
Hardie, J. H. 393
harmful behaviors 262
Harris, M. S. 245–246, 341
Harvard University 197
Hasbargen, K. 14
Hawaii 145
Hayward, R. A. 341
hazard analysis 248
Head Start 212
health care: coordinating 128; and education 208; financing 126; overweight/obese 123; recommendations 129–130; records 114, 125–126, 129; stable housing 271; youth in foster care 118–122, 127
Health Care and Education Reconciliation Act (2010) 466
"Health Passport" (medical file) 129
health service use 123–124, 124
health status 122–123
Healthy Foster Care America 128
Hebdon, M. 196
Heckman, J. J. 282, 287
Hedges, K. 464
Hegar, R. L. 200
Hendershot, G. E. 321

Hersen, M. 113
Hidalgo, R. 376
higher education 304–305, 482
Higher Education Opportunity Act (2008) 308
high-risk children: ECE 212; shorter telomeres 49
high school completion by a traditional diploma (HSD) 242
high school completion rates 242, 290
high school graduates: earnings 242, 287; economic opportunities 283; employment 291; and youth in foster care 214
Hillemeier, M. M. 393
Hill, R. B. 337, 342
Hines, A. M. 481
Hirsch, B. J. 480
Hirschi, Travis 382
Hispanics: definition 377; in foster care 8, 337, 339; income as FFY 245; overweight/obese 122; pathways to foster care placement 348, *353–354*; research 394–395
HIV-risk behaviors 136
Hokanson, K. 478
Hollingsworth, L. D. 195
home-based settings 28
Homeland Security Act of 2002 (HSA) 383
Homeless Emergency Assistance and Rapid Transition to Housing Act 2009 (HEARTH) 306
homelessness: crisis housing 270; economic outcomes 79; and family instability 88; LGBTQ youth 411–412; NYTD data 306; occasional 262; prenatal infections 49; rates of 176, 273; risk factors 270 *see also* housing
homeownership rates 249–250
home studies 21–22
homophobia 407
"homosexuality" (DSM) 402
Honduras 383
honeymoon stage of adoption 196
Hook, J. L. 246, 247, 284, 288
Horwitz, S. M. 343
households 226
housing: challenges 312; collaborations 275; crises after transitioning 269; exosystem 274–275; foster youth 87–89; and harmful behaviors 262; risk factors *266–267*, 270; transitioning from care 268–269, 305–307 *see also* homelessness; stable housing
housing assistance 303, 304
housing career approach 303
Housing Choice Vouchers 269, 306
Housing for youth aging out of foster care (USDHUD, 2014) 262
housing modes 269–270, 275–276
housing outcomes 260–262
Howse, R. B. 182
human capital 245, 286–289, 296, 433
human capital accumulation 282, 287

human capital theory 295
human trafficking 363, 367–368 *see also* sex trafficking
Hurlbut, M. S. 343
hyporesponsive periods 43
hypothalamic pituitary adrenal axis (HPA axis) 41, 42–45, 211

Iglehart, A. P. 252
iHeLP (Interactive Healthy Lifestyle Preparation) 163, 164
"illegal," use of term 395
Illinois: Department of Children and Family Services 145; knowledge of contraception 141; Midwest Study 286; provider models 127–128; race and foster care 341, 343; risk of delinquency 458; sexual health and pregnancy prevention training 145–146; trauma-informed care 467
immigrant children: definition 376; parental education 379; population 376; screening for 384 *see also* undocumented children (UC)
Immigrant Children's Legal and Service Partnership (ICLASP) 389
Immigrant Rights Clinic (New York University) 389
immigrants: collaborating with state agencies 391; language barriers 391; settlement patterns 383; stress 381; unique positive attributes 381 *see also* undocumented immigrants
Immigration and Naturalization Service (INS, Department of Justice) 383
immigration trends 376
immune system 47–50
impairments 320 *see also* children and youth with disabilities
improving foster care 10–14
inadequate clinical conceptualization 108
incarceration: and employment 247; of parents 178, 341, 342
income 244–246
independence 432
independent living 78, 262, 268, 274, 301, 303
Independent Living Coordinators (PA) 433
Independent Living Initiative (1986) 303
"independent living" (New Hampshire) 311
Independent Living Programs (ILPs): background 177, 282; effectiveness 285–286, 477–478; logistic regression study 288–289; services to older youth 179; states developing their own 303; transition to independent living 284 *see also* John H. Chafee Foster Care Independence Program (CFCIP)
Independent Living Services (ILS) 245, 251–253, 262
Indian Child Welfare Act 1978 (ICWA) 6, 26–27
Individual Development Accounts (Casey Family Programs) 253
Individual Placement and Support (IPS) 294
Individualized Education Program (IEP) 308, 328

Index

Individuals with Disabilities Education Act 2004 (IDEA) 308, 321–322
informal respite care 330
informational support 181, 474, 482
information dissemination 449
information integration tools 105
Information Management Protecting Adults and Children in *Texas* (IMPACT) 448
inhibitory control 210–211
insecure attachment 191
instability of placements 66–67, 143
Institute of Medicine (IOM) 58, 61
Institutional forces 303
Institutional Review Board (IRB, UTSA) 263
institutional/societal level of ecological model 364
instrumental support 181, 474 *see also* social support
integrating services 331
intellectual disabilities 326
interagency alliances 165
Interethnic Placement Act (1996) 27
internal assets 481
internalizing behaviors 44, 46, 200
internal working models 193
intervention modality 390
interventions: aging out of care 183–186; educational outcomes 215–217; immune dysfunction 49; maltreatment and delinquency 464
Iowa Blueprint for Forever Families 2011 184
Iowa Department of Human Services 184

Jaffe, C. J. 196
James, S. 135
jargon 108
Jaudes, P. K. 120, 122, 128–129
Jee, S. H. 119
Jha, M. 196
job coaching 253
Job Corps 283, 292, 293, 308–309
job maintenance skills 252
Joey (undocumented immigrant youth) 386
John H. Chafee Foster Care Independence Program (CFCIP) 139, 177, 304, 327, 466, 477, 481 *see also* Foster Care Independence Act 1999 (FCIA/Chafee Legislation); Independent Living Programs (ILPs)
Johnson, H. 244, 250
Johnson, K. 196
Johnson-Motoyama, M. 345
Johnson, P. R. 198, 199
Johnstone, J. 202
Jones, L. 323
Jones, L. P. 199, 475–476
Jonson-Reid, M. 88, 458, 463
Joseph (Bexar County study, Texas) 84–85
Joseph, R. M. 14
Juma Ventures 294–295
Justice for Victims of Trafficking Act 2015 (JVTA) 366

juvenile court petitions 458–459
juvenile immigration policy 382
juvenile incarceration 459
juvenile justice 456–468, 459 *see also* crossover youth
Juye, J. 344–345

Kahn, M. D. 191
Karyn Purvis Institute of Child Development 390
Kasey (crossover youth) 464–465
Kavaler, F. 118
Keeping Foster and Kin Parents Supported and Trained (KEEP) 431, 465
Keller, T. E. 184, 477
Kelly, S. M. 162
Kentucky 311, 448
Kessler, L. 242
Khashu, A. 342
Kids COUNT (Annie E. Casey Foundation) 376
Kim, H. 344–345
kindergartens 383
King, B. 345
King County (Washington) 341
King Jordan, I. 12
King, P. E. 475
kinship care: black families 342; children in care 3; contact with biological parents 198; foster care placement 29; health outcomes 123; Maryland 14; preference for 24–25; risk of delinquency 460; and state placements 392 *see also* relative foster care
kinship-focused programs 178
kinship placements 179, 393
Kirk, C. M. 482
Kirk, R. 480
KITS Program 215
Klee, L. 124, 126
Knight, J. R. 162
Knott, T. 342
Knutson, J. 323
Kohlenberg, E. 157
Kools, S. 121, 122, 123
Kosanovich, A. 14

labor market outcomes 142
Lambda Legal 413
Landale, N. S. 393
Landsverk, J. 343
Langford, C. P. H. 181
language barriers 391
lapses in preventative care 120
Larsen, L. J. 376
latent modeling 62
Latin@ (Latinos/Latinas) 376–396; communication issues 380–381; cultural identity in care 393; definition 377; deportation 390; ethnic minority group 376–377, 394; immigrant families 377–379; immigrant protective factors 380–382; immigrant

risk factors 379–380; population 376, 377, 394; removal rates 392; undocumented parents 378; use of public services 379 *see also* undocumented immigrants
Latino family value system 391–392
Latino Practice Advisory Committee (California Department of Social Services) 377
lawful permanent residency (LPR) 384, 385
laws 4–5
lawsuits 14
learning problems 46 *see also* educational outcomes
least restrictive environments 20, 31
Leathers, S. J. 26, 200, 245
leaving care *see* age out of foster care; exiting care; transitioning out of care
Lee, B. 27, 31
Lee, C. 181
Lee, J. 246
legal permanency 179, 302, 428
legal representation 388–389
Legal Representation to Counsel 388–389
legislation 12–13
length of stay in foster care: black youth 339; health status 122; overweight/obese 123
Lenz-Rashid, S. 245, 247
Lerner, R. M. 80
Lery, B. 344
lesbian, gay, bisexual, transgender, or questioning/queer (LGBTQ) youth: acronym as a collective identity 404; addressing needs 413–416; barrier to permanence 410; binge eating 406–407; bullied at school 406; Code of Ethics 408; competency of partner agencies 411; competent foster care placements 415; Continuum of Care Model 306; cultural and religious bias 407; employment and earnings 246; family support and engagement 411–412; foster care non-discrimination laws 408; homelessness 412; identifying as 401–402; interviews 414; leaving care 411; legal permanency 179; mental health 407; over-represented in foster care 148–149; self-identifying 404; sex education curricula 142; trauma of identity 410; violation of rights 408 *see also* sexual and gender expansive youth
Leslie, L. K. 118
Levy, S. 162
Lewis, R. K. 482
Leyro, S. P. 11–12, 390
Liang, B. 184
licensed kinship care 25
licensing foster homes 21–22
life coaches 310
life course perspectives 69
"life event narratives" 60
lifelong connections 393
lifelong relationships 173–174, 394
life skills preparation 438–439
life span approaches 404

life-stage models 302
Lim, E. 196
literacy 210, *465*
Litrownik, A. J. 66, 67
Littner, N. 192
local housing programs' policies 264–265
Localio, A. R. 125
local resources *421–423*
locus of control 483
Lofquist, W. 182
logistic regression study 288–289
London, K. 105
longer-term prospective quantitative analyses 66
longitudinal prospective studies 71
Longitudinal Studies of Child Abuse and Neglect (LONGSCAN) Consortium 57–71; characterizing maltreatment 62–63; common measurement protocols 59; findings 68–69; multi-site studies 58–59; peer-reviewed studies 61–62; socioemotional problems 64–65
long-term care 24
Lopez, M. H. 377
Los Angeles 294
Loury, G. C. 289
low-cost immigration assistance 381
low-incomes 211, 243
low incomes *see* poverty
low minority populations 26
Lozano, P. 183
Lyons, J. S. 112

Macgill, S. 26
Macomber, J. 243, 244–245, 251
macrosystem of foster youth 259, *261*, 274–275 *see also* ecological model
Maheu, F. S. 46
Making Proud Choices! program 145
males: criminal justice system 247; disabled in welfare system 324–325; in foster care 8; getting a partner pregnant 140; gonorrhea and chlamydia infections 138; placement in group home 31
Mallon, G. P. 411–412, 414
maltreatment: co-morbidity 102; early academic skills 210; exposure to 62–63; intervention 464; negative impact 64; prefrontal cortex 45; risk of delinquency 458–460, 461; violent juvenile delinquency 462–463; youth with disabilities 323–324 *see also* environmental stressors
Maltreatment by Life Events interactions 63
Maltreatment Classification System (Barnett, Manly, and Cicchetti) 60
Management, Reporting and Statistics (MRS) reports 449, 453
managing money 252
Manly, J. T. 60
MAPP/GPS training 431
March, C. 195
marijuana 156–157

Index

Maryland: CSTVI 367–368; kinship care 14; PTC (2010) 144; teenage birth rates 139; trafficking 364, 366–367
Maryland Family Law (2012) 366
Massachusetts: aged out youths study 309; FUP vouchers 307; "Permanency with Kin" service plan goals 311
Massachusetts Department of Housing and Community Development, Move to Work (2016) 307
Masten, A. S. 476
Masterson, J. 128–129
matched-pairs study 343
material hardships study 250
maternal prenatal health 48
McCormick, A. 411
McKinney-Vento Homeless Education Assistance Improvements Act (1987) 216
McLain, K. B. 194
McMillen, J. C. 183
McWey, L. M. 198
means-tested benefits 248
measures 111–112
Medicaid 124, 126
medical history/records 114, 125–126, 129
medical home model 127–129, 466
medical model 320 see also children and youth with disabilities
medical professionals 129
Melo, M. A. 378
Memoranda of Understanding (FUP) 306
Mendis, K. 482
mental health problems: and adoptive parents 196; crossover youth 460, 463; earnings 245; lesbian, gay, and bisexual youth 407; and sexual risk behaviors 137
mental health providers 103
"mental status exam" 105
mentoring: empowering 183–184; and family connections 176; formal mentoring 480–481; and job coaching 253; natural mentors 479–480; permanent connections 186; preventing crossover 465; relationship qualities 479; Rhodes' pathways model 476–477; teaching life skills 310; transition process 185, 271
mentoring programs 178, 478–479
Merton, R. K. 383
mesosystem of foster youth 259, 260–262, 272, 274
Mettrick, J. E. 31
Meuchel, J. M. 196
Mexican migrants 383, 386, 393
Meyer, G. J. 110
Miall, C. E. 195
Michigan 482
Michigan Council on Developmental Disabilities 13
Michigan Mental Health Code (1974) 13
Mickus, M. 480

microsystem of foster youth 258–259, *261*, 274 see also ecological model
microsystems (FTF interviews) 60
Midwest Evaluation of the Adult Functioning of Former Foster Youth (Midwest Study): birth control information 141; birth rates 139; caring non-parent adults 183; criminal justice system 247; EFY employment 242–243; excluding disabled 330; homeownership rates 249; housing instability 260–262; human capital 287; Illinois 286; longitudinal study of former foster youth 175–176; low-income jobs 243–244; material hardships 250; means-tested benefits 248; mental health problems 245; and the NYTD 246–247; predictors of substance use 157; pregnancy rates 138, 139; repeat pregnancy rates 138; school changes 159; sexual behavior 133–134; social support 478; STIs 143
Mignon, S. 5
Milan, S. E. 193
military service 283
Miller, J. B. 179–180
Miller, W. R. 160, 163
minimum housing requirements 22
minimum-wage workers 251
Minnesota 145, 343, 464
Minnesota Multiphasic Personality Inventory (MMPI) 110
"minor parents" 147
misdiagnosis 106
Missouri 138, 140, 458–459
mistrustful of caregivers 8
mixed-status families 378, 395–396
mobile students 212, 213, 216
Model Approach to Partnerships in Parenting/Group Preparation and Selection of Foster and/or Adoptive Families (MAPP/GPS) 431
Model Intervention for Youth/Young Adults with Child Welfare Involvement At-Risk of Homelessness (ACF) 263
Model Standards Project 413
modes of housing 269–270
Moffitt, T. 288
Monitoring the Future (MTF) 156
monolingual youths 393
Montes, Felipe 393
Moore, R. S. 159–160
Moreland, S. 430
Morton, C. M. 340
Moses, J. O. 66
mothers: and child relationships 193; drugs problems 343
motivation 265
Motivational Interviewing (Miller & Rollnick) 160, 163
Move to Work demonstration programs 306–307
Mueller, S. C. 46
Mullis, A. 198

multidimensional measures 110
Multidimensional Treatment Foster Care for Preschoolers (MTFC-P) 44, 47, 49–50
Multidimensional Treatment Foster Care (MTFC) 145, 462, 465
Multiethnic Placement Act 1994 (MEPA) 7, 27
Multiethnic Placement Act as Amended by the Interethnic Provisions (MEPA-IEP) 27
multilevel regression modeling 63
multiple children 194
multiple forms of trauma *see* polyvictimization
multiple placement changes 213
multiple placements 184
multiple service systems 463
Multi-Site Evaluation of Foster Youth Programs 252
Multistate Foster Care Data Archive 344
multi-system collaboration 464
multivariate models of exit from kinship care 341
Munson, M. R. 183
Murray, K. J. 194
mutuality in relationships 180
Myers, Jr., S. L. 336

Naccarato, T. 245, 252, 253
Napolitano, L. 253, 262
national administrative data 324–325
National Campaign to Prevent Teen and Unplanned Pregnancy 145
National Center for Health Statistics (NCHS) 136
National Center for Missing & Exploited Children 366
National Center on Child Abuse and Neglect (NCCAN) 57, 61, 324
National Child Abuse and Neglect Data System (NCANDS) 340, 342, 345–348
National Child Welfare Resource Center for Organizational Improvement (NRCOI) 446, 448
National Comorbidity Survey–Adolescent (NCS–A) 157
National Foster Care Month 401, 415
National Human Trafficking Resource Center 363
National Institute of Drug Abuse (NIDA) 60, 67
National Institute on Alcohol Abuse and Alcoholism (NIAAA) 162
National Institute on Drug Abuse 156
National Longitudinal Study of Adolescent to Adult Health (Add Health): economic hardships 250; and EFY employment/earnings 243; homeownership rate 249; ideal comparison group 175; median yearly income 244; natural mentors 479; pregnancy rates 138; STI rates 138; waves of data 134
National Longitudinal Survey of Youth 243
National Look at the Use of Congregate Care in Child Welfare (USDHHS) 80
National Research Council (NRC) 58, 61
national resources *421–423*
National School Climate Survey of LGBT youth 406

National Survey of Child and Adolescent Well-Being (NSCAW): chronic conditions 119, 120; cohorts I and II in study 134–136; crossover youth 462; ER data 125; funding 61; out-of-home placement study 342–343; pregnancy rates 138; sexual risk behaviors 148
National Survey of Families and Households (1988) 243
National Survey of Family Growth (NSFG) 136
National Survey on Drug Use and Health (NSDUH) 156–157
National Youth in Transition Database (NYTD) 139, 140, 246–247, 290, 306, 309–310
Native Americans 337, 341, *349–350*, 405
Native Hawaiians 337, 348, *351–352*
natural immunity 48
natural mentoring 173, 183, 185, 479–480
Nebraska 323
Needell, B. 345
needs 105, 265, *266–267*
neglect, and sexual risk behaviors 137
Neil, E. 202
nervous system 48
networks 180–181
neurobiological development 41–51; early institutional care 42; effects of interventions 50; and foster care 41, 50; individual differences 50; nervous and immune system 48; stress 42
Nevada 249
Neville, H. A. 477
New directions in child abuse and neglect research (IOM/NRC) 61
New Door Ventures 294
New Hampshire 311
New Jersey 128
Newton, R. R. 66
New York Children's Aid Society 4
New York City: health problems in foster care 118; homeless children 4; LGBTQ studies 246; maternal incarcerations and child placement 342; Summer Youth Employment Program 294; undocumented parents with U.S.-born children 389
New York state 124
New York University 389
New Zealand 202
Nilsen, C. 482
Noam, G. 184
non-bilingual foster parents 393
non-cisgender people 403
non-citizens 379
non-discrimination protections 414
non-FUP Housing Choice Vouchers 306–307
non-heterosexual identities 402–403
non-Hispanic Whites 245
non-marijuana drug use 157
non-marital childbearing 177 *see also* pregnancies
non-parental relationships 173, 176, 477 *see also* mentoring

Index

non-relative foster homes 3
non-traditional life-course change 260
non-White youth 179, 459
Norbeck, J. S. 121
normative experiences 302
normed measures 111–112
North Carolina 58, 145
Northern Triangle 383
Northwest Foster Care Alumni Study 175, 242, 330, 394
numeracy 210

Oakes, E. J. 30
Obama, Barack 389, 401, 415
obesity *see* overweight/obese
observations of programs 264–265
Ocasio, K. 340
Office of Adolescent Health 143, 144
Office of Refugee Resettlement (ORR) 383, 384
Office of Youth Empowerment (OYE) 310
Office on Child Abuse and Neglect (OCAN) 61
Oklahoma 144
Okpych, N. J. 291, 310, 327
Omaha (Nebraska) 323
Ondersma, S. J. 163
"one family/one judge" approaches 466
opioids/heroin 157
Orme, J. G. 431
Oropesa, R. S. 393
Orphan Train Movement 4, 5
Oshiro, M. 275
Osterling, K. L. 481
"Other or Alternative Planned Permanent Living Arrangement" (Colorado, Florida) 311
outcome data 247
outcome measures 6
outcomes for youth exiting care 175–176
out-of-home care 3, 135, 290
out-of-home caregivers 21
out-of-home placements 3, 26, 46, 410–411 *see also* foster care
over-reporting misbehavior 109
overweight/obese 44, 120–121, 122, 123

Pacific Islanders 348, *351–352*
Painter, K. 260
PAL (Preparation for Adult Living) program 478
paradigm shifts 14, 15
"parental fitness standards" 391
parental loans 249
parental rights *see* terminating parental rights
parental support 482
parental training 330
parent–child attachment 191
Parent for Every Child initiative (PFEC) 428–429
parenthood in foster care 140, 141–142
parenting programs 192

parenting skills 141
Parent Mutual Aid Organizations 192
parents: children with disabilities 324, 330; deporting 379, 390; immigrant children 379; incarceration 178, 341, 342; interviews 64; sexual activity 141; and sexual risk behaviors 137; support for young adults 285; "trauma-informed care" 390
Parra, G. R. 477
Passel, J. S. 376, 383
pathways of mentoring influence model (Rhodes) 476–477
pathways to foster care placement 345–348
Patient Protection and Affordable Care Act (2010) 466
Paul, S. M. 121
Payne, J. L. 196
Pecora, P. J. 242, 290, 393–394
Pedal Revolution 294
peer connections 262 *see also* independent living
peer-like relationships 191
peer social capital 270
Pérez, A. 216
Perez, B. F. 262, 269
Pergamit, M. 244, 250
permanency: and child welfare worker turnover 184; concurrent planning 23–24; crossover youth 456–457; definition 23; family-centered approaches 29; goal of child welfare 23, 190; LGBTQ youth 410; older youths 25; special needs youth 428; transgender youth 410
"Permanency with Kin" (Massachusetts) 311
permanent connections 176, 179, 271, 274, 478
permanent placements 65, 70
permanent relationships 174–175, 301–302
persistent offenders 463 *see also* crossover youth
personal capital 288
personalismo 392
"personal responsibility" 7
Personal Responsibility and Work Opportunity Reconciliation Act (1996) 24–25
person of color 11
phone services 250
physical development 44
physical examinations 129
physical health 117–130; chronic health conditions 119; moderators of 122–123; poor outcomes 117–118; transition to adulthood 176; youth self-report studies 121–122
physiological stress regulatory systems 211
Pilowsky, D. J. 157
Pinderhughes, E. E. 193
placement considerations 24–27
placement disparity 335
placement disruptions 410–411
placement instability: attachment difficulties 193; children with disabilities 326; disrupting education and social relationships 263; mitigating risk 466;

negative outcomes 61; risk of delinquency 458, 460, 461–462
placements: age of the youth 25; amygdala activation 46; decision-making 27; frequent changes 225; LGBTQ youth 411, 412; and maternal incarcerations 342; moderators of health status 122; non-Hispanics and minority children 355; physical safety 192–193; predictors of resilience 197; problems with 86–87; race and culture 26; with relatives 24–25; with siblings 25–26; traumatic impact 104
placement stability 44, 343
placement types 122–123, 175
Plan-Do-Check-Act (PDCA) cycle 444–445
Plyler v. Doe (1982) 388
policies to mitigate risk 466–467
policy advocacy 413
policy recommendations 147–148
policy statements 127
politicians 249
Pollak, S. D. 46
polyvictimization 105–106, 120–121, 461 *see also* abuse
poor diagnostic skills 108
poor educational outcomes 209–210
Poor Health Status groups 122
poor outcomes of foster care 78
population-based racial disproportionality measures 339–341
Portland State University 260
positive messaging 429
positive parenting 192
positive relationships 176
positive school discipline *465*
positive self-image 21
Positive Youth Development (PYD) 80, 182, 184, 287, 476, 481
post-adoption depression 196
post-high-school training 216–217
post-secondary education 308
post-traumatic stress disorder (PTSD) 8, 109–110, 164, 324
post-traumatic stress (PTS) symptoms 102–103, 112
poverty 79, 142, 344 *see also* environmental stressors; low incomes
Povinelli, N. 477
Powers, L. E. 328, 330, 432, 482–483
POWER Through Choices (PTC 2010) 144–145
pre-academic deficits 210
predictors of foster care placements 342
predictors of homelessness 262
predictors of resilience 197–198
predictors of sexual risk behaviors 136–137
predictors of substance use 157–158
prefrontal cortex 45–46
pregnancies: consequences for adolescents 141–142; drug and alcohol use during 324; early parenthood 141–142; factors contributing to 140–141; female EFY 247; in foster care 138–142; as the norm 140; PTC 2010 curriculum 145; state-level data 146–147
pregnancy prevention 143–148 *see also* family planning; sex education
prekindergarten readiness for school 210–212
prenatal infections 48, 49
Preparation for Adult Living program (PAL, Texas) 88, 263, 264–265, 271–272, 274
preschool-aged children 118, 210
Presidential Proclamations 401, 415
preventative care 120, 129–130
Preventing Sex Trafficking and Strengthening Families Act (2014) 27–28, 146, 366
Preyde, M. 32
Price, C. 405
Price, K. M. 428
prior victimization 364–365
private agencies 411
privatization 427–428, 440
Prochaska, J. O. 163
Proclamation No. 9432, 81 F.R. 26663 (2016) 401
Proctor, L.J. 66, 67
professionalization of foster care 430
pro-inflammatory cytokines 48
Promoting Safe and Stable Families Amendments 2001 (PSSFA) 61, 178, 214, 286, 304, 466
promoting well-being 69–70
prosocial behaviors 210
protective factors: housing experiences 270; needs/risks 265, *266–267*; substance use 161
provider models 127–128
Pryce, J. M. 432
psychiatric assessments 129
psycho-educational parenting programs 192
psychological disorders 44
psychological distress 225, 410
psycho-social interventions 70
psychosocial stress 44
psychosocial well-being 208
public assistance: benefits 247–249; FFY in Wisconsin 244; non-citizens 379; research *228–241*; teenage parenthood 142
public schools 322
public transportation 253, 268
Pugh-Lilly, A. O. 477
Purvis, Karyn 391
Putnam-Hornstein, E. 345

Quality Assurance (QA) 445, 453
quality-improvement staff 447
quality of care 13–14, 21
Quinn, P. 15
Qur'an 4

race and ethnicity: children in care 27, *339*; CSEC victims 365, 373; disproportionality ratios *338*; foster care placement 26, 343; foster care satisfaction 10; health problems in adults 122;

Index

and income 245–246; predictors of substance use 157; pregnancy rates 138; protocols for entering care 26
racial differences: average stay in foster care 341–342; child welfare outcomes 344–345; parental incarceration 342
racial disparities 335
racial disproportionality 335–358; area-based approaches 344; decline 337–339; definition 336–337; measures 339–341; placement 342–345; population-based/decision-point measures 339–341; time in foster care 341–342
racial disproportionality index (RDI) 336
randomized controlled trials (RCT) 478
Raphel, S. 391
Rapid Rehousing Model 306
Readiness Ruler question 163–164
recent alcohol use 156 *see also* substance use
recipients, decision-making processes 182
Reconnecting Homeless Youth Act 2008 (RHYA) 307
reconnections in relationships 180
records and reports: evaluating 107–108; medical history 114, 125–126, 129; transferring between schools 216
recruitment of foster parents 22–23, 428–429
re-entering care 466–467
referral questions 108
Regional System Improvement teams (RSI, Texas) 452–453
regulatory systems 210–211
rehabilitation counselors 328
Reid, J. B. 29
Reid, K. 430
Reilly, T. 123, 249
Relational–Cultural Theory (RCT) 179–180, 184, 186
relational permanence 302, 428
relationships: authenticity and mutuality 180; maladaptive approaches to 476–477; preserving with family 179
relative foster care 25, 61, 65–66 *see also* kinship care
reliability 105, 197
religiously affiliated child welfare agencies 143
removal from the home 199
re-offending 462 *see also* crossover youth
reparative therapies 410
repeat pregnancy rates 138
research: employment and earnings *228–241*; and model development 330–331; youth health 117–118
residential treatment centers (RTCs) 31–32, 270
resilience 121, 201, 202, 265, 302, 475–476
resilience theory 197–198
Resource Parent Curriculum 194
resources: decision-making processes 182; sharing 331; youth as 182

respeto 392
respite care 30, 330
Restorative Justice *465*
retention of foster parents 23, 429–430, 440
reunification 24, 192, 244, 326–327
Rhode Island 145
Rhodes, J. E. 184, 476, 477, 480
Rhodes, K. W. 431
Richardson, L. P. 183
Richardson, S. M. 201
Riebschleger, J. 483
Rio Grande Valley indigent community 381
risk and resilience theories 302
risk of delinquency: and foster care 461–462; maltreatment 458; placement instability 458, 460, 461–462 *see also* crossover youth; delinquency
risky sexual behaviors 134, 135, 137 *see also* Sexually Transmitted Infections (STIs)
Robbins, N. R. 121
Rodriguez, Frank Anthony *378*, 381, 382, *384*, 385
Roesch, S. 67
Roller-White, C. 392
Rollnick, S. 160, 163
Rolock, N. 195, 341
Romanelli, L. H. 162
romantic relationships 83–84
Romney, Mitt 249
Romo, H. D. 262, 269
Rosen, J. B. 49
Rosenthal, J. A. 200
Ross, T. 342
Roth, T. L. 49
Rubin, D. M. 125
Runyan, D. K. 458
Ruppel, J. 428
Russell, J. 26
Russian children 202
Ryan, J. P. 458, 462

Salazar, A. 244, 250
Salvation Army emergency shelters 270
same-sex attraction 404
Samuels, G. M. 199, 432
San Diego 118
San Diego LONGSCAN Foster Care Study 57, 58–59, 60, 65, 67–68
San Francisco 246, 294
Santosky v. Kramer (1982) 388
satisfaction with health 121
savings accounts 253
Scannapieco, M. 260
Schelbe, L. 432, 433, 441
Schneider, A. 112
Schneiderman, J. U. 122, 123
school adjustment 79, 212–213
school attendance 216–217
school-based sex education programs 142

school mobility 159, 213–214, 216
school readiness 210, 215
schools: drop-out rates 78; sexual and gender expansive youth 406; support from 483
Schultz, T. W. 282
Schuster, C. R. 163
Scott, J. 392
screening: CANS 162; meaning of term 104; substance use 159, 163, 165; symptoms of abusive/traumatic events 104–105
Screening, Brief Intervention, and Referral to Treatment (SBIRT) 163
Screening to Brief Intervention (S2BI) 162
secondary education 216–217, 307–308
Secondary School Completion and Dropouts in Texas Public Schools for 2012–13 (Texas Education Agency) 81
secure attachment 191
Seita, John R. 3, 7, 11
self-determination 432
self-identification 404 *see also* sexual identity
self-reliance 89
self-reporting maltreatment 62
self-reporting studies 121–122
self-sufficiency: asset accumulation 249–250; ecological system theory 270; public benefits 247–249; school-to-work transition 227; staying in care 251 *see also* transition to adulthood
semi-structured interviews 110
sensitive caregiving 49
separation anxiety 106
separation issues 106
service plan goals 310–311
service providers 128, 381
sex education 82, 140–141, 142 *see also* family planning; pregnancy prevention
sex trafficking 363, 369–370 *see also* commercial sexual exploitation of children (CSEC); human trafficking
sexual abuse 105, 123, 136, 363 *see also* abuse
sexual activity 136, 141
sexual and gender expansive youth 401–423; acceptance and affirmation of identities 410; best practice strategies 413; bias and discrimination 410; confidentiality 415; critical self-inventory of values and beliefs 415; defining 402–404; and foster family acceptance 411; heterosexual and cisgender similarities 406; LGBTQ as a collective identity 404; national, state and local resources *421–423*; negative experiences 408–410; non-discrimination protections 414; placement disruptions 410–411; rejection, abuse, and victimization 406; schools 406; self-identifiers 403–404; sexual and physical dating violence 406; substance use 407; universal legal rights 412 *see also* lesbian, gay, bisexual, transgender, or questioning/queer (LGBTQ) youth
sexual and gender minority youth 402, *414*

sexual and reproductive health 133–150; access to care services 143; care services 148; data collection 148–149; policy context 146–147; talking with foster youth 145–146; training 149; youth voice 149
sexual attraction 403, 404
sexual exploitation 363
sexual identity 403–404, 407
sexual intercourse 134, 136, 140–141
sexualized behaviors 105, 110 *see also* sexual abuse
Sexually Transmitted Infections (STIs) 133, 134, 138, 143, 148
sexual minorities 402–403
sexual orientation 403, 410, 412
sexual risk behaviors 133–140
sexual risk reduction programs 143–146, 149
sexual risk reduction strategies 147–148
Shea, N. 275
Shelby County (Tennessee) 344
shelters 29–30
Shlonsky, A. 193, 194
Shook, J. 432
short-term care 30
Shuman, D. W. 105
siblings 25–26, 191, 200–201
Silva, P. 288
Silverthorn, N. 184
Simmel, C. 340
simpatia 392
Singer, E. R. 478
skill deficits 208
Skriner, L. C. 67
Slayter, E. 327
smoking 162
Snowden, L. 344
social assistance 285
social bond theory 382–383
"social buffering" 49
social capital 247, 283–284, 288, 289, 433
Social Capital Theory 180–181
social control theory 382, 461
social creation of disability 320
Social-Development Theory 59
social enterprise approach 294
social institutions 292
social model of disability 320
social network perspectives 475
Social Network Theory 180–181
social relational theory 321
Social Security Act (1935) 20 *see also* Title IV-E (Social Security Act 1935)
Social Security Act Amendments 1994 (SSA) 445
social services 129, 271
social skills 210
social support 181, 197, 478, 482
social support theories 180–181, 474–475
social well-being 271
social work education 160

Index

social work practice *174*, 320
socioemotional development 44, 64–65, 67–68
South Carolina 245, 459
South, S. C. 196
Spaccarelli, S. 103–104
special education 212, 308
special immigrant juvenile status (SIJS) 382–386
specialized education 286
specialized settings 29–31
specialized social workers 310
special needs 194–195, 428
specific immunity 48
Spencer, R. 184
stability 71
stability study 66
Stable Adopted groups 68
stable employment 251
stable housing 260–263, 270, 271–273, 306 *see also* housing
stable living situation 65
stable placement trajectories 66
Stable Relative/Non-relative groups 68
Stable Reunified groups 68
staff "burnout" 268
staff turnover 184, 268
stage models 404
standard interpretations of T scores 113
standardization 103
standardized assessments 113
STAR Health program (Texas) 467
state agencies 391
state-level data 146–147
state-level transition practice 303
state resources *421–423*
states: independent living programs 303; transition services 310; unaccompanied children 388; varying standards 22
state support, and emancipation 226
statutory rights 408, *409*
staying in care 251
staying with acquaintances 262
Steele, J. S. 120
Steever, J. 405
Stephan, S. H. 31
stigmatization 87, 159, 364–365
stimulants 157
Stiver, I. P. 180
Stoltzfus, E. 341–342
Stout, R. L. 159–160
"straw man" argument 103
strength-based perspectives 80
strengths 105
stress: immigrants 381; immune dysfunction 48–49; neurobiology 42; potential deportation of a parent 388
Stressful Life Events Screening Questionnaire 194
Strolin-Goltzman, J. 476
Structural Ecosystems Theory (SET) 161, 164–165
structural model of mentoring 477
structural violence/marginalization 180
structured clinical interviews 110
Structured Psychotherapy for Adolescents Responding to Chronic Stress (SPARCS) 465, 467
student engagement 476
studying foster youth 484
subnational studies 343
Substance Abuse and Mental Health Services Administration (SAMHSA) 156
substance dependence 157
substance misuse 157–158, 159
substance use 155–166; and academic achievement 156; adult caregivers 64; amplified risks 160; brief interventions (BIs) 160, 163; and disabilities 324; lifetime data 157–158; during pregnancy 324; research 165; screening and assessment 159–160, 161–162, 165; sexual and gender expansive youth 407; theoretical approach 160–161; and trafficked youth 365; training in recognizing and addressing 160; transgender youth 407; treatment 159; *vulnerability* for 155–156
substance use disorders (SUDs) 157, 158, 162
substance use services 159, 163
suburban disparities 344
"success" 439
Success Maker *465*
suicidal ideation 63
suicidal thoughts 109
suicide risks 183
Sullivan, K. M. 194
Sullivan, P. 323
summer camp program (Michigan) 482
Summer Youth Employment Program (New York) 294
support-based parenting programs 192
supportive placements 30–31
supportive relationships 137, 141, 174
support services 214
survival 270
survivalist self-reliance 432
Suter, J. 476
Sutherland, E. 8–9, 10
Svikis, D. S. 163
Swire, M. R. 118
symptomatology 104
systemic challenges 326
systemic conceptual model (Keller) 477
Systems Improvement division (Texas) 449–450, 451, 452, 453
systems interactions 327–328
systems theory 203
Szapocznik, J. 161, 164

Taber, S. 433
Talent Search program 308
tangible resources 253 *see also* exiting care

Index

targeted recruitment 429
Tata, L. 192
Taylor, P. 377
teachers 328, 329
teaching life skills 310
Teachman, J. D. 289
technology 114, 286–287
technology-based assessments 166
teenage births 139, 141
teenage mothers 142
teenage parents 141–142
teenage pregnancy rates 141, 145
telomeres 49
temporary accommodation 262
Temporary Assistance for Needy Families (TANF) 247, 248–249
temporary placement of youth 20
Temporary Protected Status (TPS) 378
terminating parental rights 24, 84–85, 201–202, 310
terms, meaning 104–105
Testa, M. F. 245, 341, 458
Texas: border security 377; child welfare case study 448–453; child welfare system 448–453; coordination of services 128; Director of Systems Improvement 449–450; Education and Training Voucher (ETV) 274; former foster youth homelessness 269; Latino and Hispanic immigrants 388; multivariate models of exit from kinship care 341; outcomes 260, 275; PAL program 263; regional operations 452–453; STAR Health program 467; subnational studies 343; Systems Improvement division 449–450, 451, 452, 453; unaccompanied children 388
Texas Aftercare Room and Board Assistance Program 269
Texas Department of Child Protective Services 274
Texas Department of Family and Protective Services (DFPS) 260, 264–265, 388, 448
Texas Department of Public Safety (DPS) 377
Texas Education Agency 81
Texas Foster Care Alumni Study Technical Report (Roller-White) 392
Texas Transitional Living Allowance 269
Thematic Analysis 434
Thematic Network Analysis (Attride-Stirling) 81
theoretical frameworks 179–182, 302–303
Theory of Change 272, *273*
therapeutic alliance 433
"therapeutic foster care placements" 28–29
Thompson, A. E. 173
Thompson, R. 63
Thompson, R. G. 157
Thompson, R. W. 27, 31
time constraints 111
time in foster care 259–260, 341–342
Title IV-E (Social Security Act 1935): eligibility provision 305; eligibility to 21st birthday 146, 477; evaluations of foster care activities 445;

FCIA amending for flexible funding 304; federal guardianship payments 25–26; federal reimbursement for EFY 251; independent living skills 303 *see also* Fostering Connections to Success and Increasing Adoptions Act 2008 (Fostering Connections Act/FCSIAA)
Title IX (Education Amendments 1972) 12
tobacco use 162
Tobit analysis 287
Total Behavior Problems 65
traditional foster care 190
trafficked youth 364, 365, 366–367
trafficking case management 370
Trafficking Victims Protection Act (TVPA) 365–366
training: child welfare system 410–411; CSEC cases 367; evidence-based assessments 103; foster parents 429–430, 430–432, 440; older youth in foster care 263; sexual and reproductive health 149
trajectory groups 66
Trammell, R. 4
transactional models 104
transgender individuals 402, 405
transgender youth 407, 410
transient nature of foster care 120, 125
transition-age foster youth 284
transitional foster placements 30–31
transitional housing 270, 275
transitional housing programs (California) 244, 252
transitional services 251, 301–313
transitioning out of care: and "aging out" 301; assessing outcomes 312; campus-based learning program 480; child welfare policies 303–305; federal legislation 303; housing crises 269; key recommendations 281; multiple risk factors 285; service needs 310; theoretical perspectives 302–303 *see also* age out of care; exiting care
transition planning: Adolescent Outreach Worker 307; housing 305–307; positive youth development framework 184; youth voice 310
transition services 309, 310, 312–313
transitions to permanence 411–416
transition to adulthood: child welfare policies 303–305; "disadvantaged" students 308; disruptive by lack of support 284; extended process 433; gradual movement 77, 302; gradual process 77; military service 283; negatively anticipated 285; negative outcomes 176; state responsibility 226–227; support to middle adulthood 291; unstable housing 264; vocational programs 283 *see also* self-sufficiency
transphobia 407
transportation 253, 307
Transtheoretical Model (Prochaska & DiClemente) 163–164
trauma: CSEC victims 372–373; foster care 8, 10; instability studies 66; predictors of health status 123; and resilience 475–476; separation 382; and socioemotional development 64–68

507

Index

trauma-bonding 372
Trauma-Focused Cognitive Behavioral Therapy (TF-CBT) 431
"trauma-informed care" 390
trauma-informed court systems 466
trauma-informed parenting 194
trauma-informed programs 465
trauma perspective of caregivers 7
Trauma Symptom Checklist for Children (TSCC) 102, 110, 112
trauma symptoms: internalizing behaviors 200; relationships with foster parent 200
traumatic events: "fight or flight" mechanism 390; identifying symptoms 104
Traumatic Symptom Checklist for Young Children (TSCYC) 102, 110, 112
Treatment Foster Care Oregon (TFCO) 145
treatment foster care placements 28–29
"triangulation" of data sources 264
trichomonas 138
TRIO programs 308
Trivette, C. M. 182
Trump, Donald 249, 389
Trust-Based Relational Intervention (TBRI, Fort Worth, Texas) 390, 391
tuition waiver programs 82, 304
Twelve Together mentoring 465
"two spirit" identity 405

U3 youth 394
unaccompanied immigrant minors 383–384, 388
Unaccompanied Latino Youth on the United States–Mexico Border (Rodriguez) 385
unconditional disproportionality ratios 336, 340, 341
unconditional probability of placement into foster care 355
Under One Sky summer camp 481
Understanding Child Abuse and Neglect (NRC) 58
under-utilized caregivers 23
undocumented children (UC) 382, 383, 393–394 *see also* immigrant children
undocumented immigrants 376–396; meaning of term 395; population in U.S. 376 *see also* immigrants; Latin@ (Latinos/Latinas)
undocumented parents: Latin@ children 378; with U.S.-born children 378, 389
undocumented siblings 378
Undocumented, Undetected, and Unaccompanied (U3) Latino youth 382, 383–384, 385–388
undocumented youth 379, 385–386
unemployment 243, 292
unexpected suffering 387
unidimensional measures 109–110
United Kingdom 196
United Nations Convention on the Rights of Persons with Disabilities 321
universal legal rights 412

universities: courses on assessment 103; data linkage centers 467; transition to adulthood 283
University of California (Berkeley) 144
University of Chicago 175
University of Connecticut (UConn) 483
University of Michigan 467
University of Pittsburgh Institutional Review Board 434
University of Texas at San Antonio (UTSA) 263
unplanned pregnancies 133
Unrau, Y. 10
unstable housing 258, 263, 264
Unstable Placement Groups 68
unstable placement trajectories 66–67
Upward Bound program 308
U.S.-born children of undocumented parents 378, 389
U.S. Census Bureau data 340
U.S. Constitution: 1st Amendment (Freedom of Speech) 408; 14th Amendment (Due Process protections) 408, 414; 14th Amendment (Equal Protections laws) 377, 408
U.S. Department of Health & Human Services (USDHHS) 61, 77, 80, 174–175, 260, 263, 324–325, 363, 428 *see also* Administration for Children and Families (ACF); Children's Bureau
U.S. Department of Housing and Urban Development (USDHUD) 262, 306
U.S. Department of Labor 309
U.S. General Accounting Office 285–286
Usher, L. 479
U.S.–Mexico border 377, *378*, 385–386
Utah 127–128
utility bills 250

validity 105
Valley Youth House (Pennsylvania) 306
Vaughn, M. G. 157
veneer of self-reliance 180
Vermont 127–128
victim-centered approaches 371, 372
victim identification 367–368
victimization 364–365
Victim's Rights attorneys 369–370
Victor (undocumented immigrant youth) 387–388
Villodas, M. T. 62, 66
violent juvenile delinquency 463
vocational outcomes 176
vocational programs 283, 481–483
voluntary placements 325–326, 457
volunteer staff 381
Von Waldner, C. A. 31
Voss, R. 198
vulnerable groups 253, 263

wage disparities 335
Wamsley, M. 342
Ward, R. L. 309

warm relationships 200–201
Washington, DC 310
Washington State 124, 216–217, 462, 482
Watson, D. 9, 15
web-based platforms for assessment 114
Webb, M. 9
Weinberg, L. A. 275
Weiner, D. A. 112
Weisbrod, B. A. 287
well-being of adolescents in foster care 475
well-developed pre-academic skills 210
Wells, R. 462
Werrbach, M. 476
Westat, Inc. 290, 324
West Texas study 80–81
What Works in Family Foster Care (Pecora) 393–394
Wheeler, Etta 5
White alumni 245, 245–246
White, C. R. 159, 464, 465, 467
White foster youth: dual involvement 462; in foster care 8; foster care placement 342–343, 357; juvenile incarceration 459; legal permanency 179; reunited with families 26
White, K. R. 195
Wide Range Achievement Test (WRAT) 287–288
Widom, C. S. 458
Wildeman, C. 337
Wildfire, J. 23
Williams, A. B. 462
Williams, J. 242
Wilson, Fanny 5
Wilson, Mary Ellen 5
Wilson, Tom 5
Wisconsin 244, 248
"wise" interventions 71
Wojciak, A. S. 200–201
Woodhouse, V. 476
Workforce Innovation and Opportunity Act 2014 (WIOA) 283, 293, 308–309
workforce investment 308
Workforce Investment Act 1998 (WIA) 252, 283, 292
Workforce Investment Boards (WIBs) 309
Workman, C. 192
work opportunities 252
workshops for caregivers 215
Works Progress Administration (WPA) 292

World Health Organization (WHO) 321
Worst Health Status groups 122, 123
Wright, B. E. 288
writs of habeas corpus 5
Wulczyn, F. 344
Wu, L. T. 157

Xu, Q. 388

Yan, J. 463
Yates, T. M. 201, 265
Yeager, D. S. 475
Yoken, C. 198
young adults: bonding with non-parental adults 480; political force in society 302–303; substance use in care 158; support under Title IV-E 305; transition supports 291
Young Adult Transition to Success Program (YTTSP) 307
youth: defining 306; numbers in care 22, 338
YouthBuild 309
youth councils 310
youth development 117, 182
youth disability data 323
Youth initiated mentoring (YIM) 185–186
youth of color: over-represented in foster care 148–149; placement 26; sex education curricula 142; vulnerability to trafficking 373
Youth Opportunity Passports (Casey Family Programs) 253
youth perspectives/voices 77–91; biological families 198; foster care alumni 8–10; foster families 198–199; insecurity 260; listening to 71, 80, 90, 202; out-of-home care 432; removal from birth parents 260; sexual and reproductive health 149; transition planning 310; uncertain about foster care 198; unwanted while awaiting adoption 260
Youth Risk Behavior Surveillance System (YRBSS) 135
youth with disabilities *see* children and youth with disabilities

Zhang, J. 343
Zimmerman, M. A. 197
Zinn, A. 252
Zuravin, S. 343

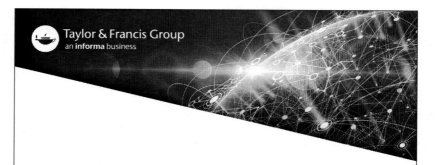